Human-centred Systems

Springer
London
Berlin
Heidelberg
New York
Barcelona
Budapest
Hong Kong
Milan
Paris
Santa Clara
Singapore
Tokyo

Karamjit S. Gill (Ed.)

Information Society

New Media, Ethics and Postmodernism

Springer

Karamjit S. Gill, BA (Hons), MA, MSc, DPhil
Director, SEAKE Centre, Department of Library and Information Studies, University of Brighton, Falmer, Brighton BN1 9PU, UK

ISBN-13:978-3-540-76036-8 e-ISBN-13:978-1-4471-3249-3
DOI: 10.1007/978-1-4471-3249-3

British Library Cataloguing in Publication Data
Information society : new media, ethics and postmodernism.
- (Human-centred systems)
1.Human-computer interaction 2.System design
I.Gill, Karamjit S.
004.2

Library of Congress Cataloging-in-Publication Data
A catalog record for this book is available from the Library of Congress

Softcover reprint of the hardcover 1st edition 1996

Typesetting: Camera ready by editor
Printed and bound at the Athenæum Press Ltd., Gateshead, Tyne and Wear
34/3830-543210 Printed on acid-free paper

Preface

Human-centredness: A Challenge to Post-industrial Europe?

The key power in industrial society has been linked to the possession of capital and factory. In the "information society" it could be rather different. If one accepts that that the key power in the information society will be linked not so much to the ownership of information but to human creativity nourished by that information, the productive force of today and tomorrow, could be more and more the human brain.

Making use of one's intelligence is always accompanied by positive emotion, which in turn further activates the intelligence. But, unfortunately, under present conditions workers of all levels live in fear, anxiety and stress rather than desire and motivation. The question of "basic human ecology" (quality of life) is, therefore, a major strategic factor. It is precisely the opposite to the mechanisms of exclusion that currently dominate our society: exclusion of young people through joblessness - but also exclusion through technology, as with the helplessness of older people or the poorly educated confronted with ticket dispensing machines or other automats.

This is not idle theorizing, it corresponds to concrete facts. It is, for example, how some observers interpret the crisis at IBM. Because its programs were less 'human-friendly', it was shaken to its foundations by Apple and Microsoft - though it seems since to have learnt its lesson.

In order to make full use of human intellectual capacities, the "intelligence society" is going to have to adapt machines to people. This presupposes deep and important changes in our vision of the human and society. This implies, among others, changes of epistemology in the way we reconcile unity and diversity. Some speak of change of paradigm. It should be researched further along these lines.

The social vision and the initiative of Karamjit S. Gill is thus well focused and forward looking. We will have to look for new economic frameworks and new (post-) industrial strategies for tomorrow's Europe along these lines.

Bruxelles, 19 December 1995

Marc Luyckx
Commission Européenne
Cellule de Prospective

Contents

Contributors

Peter van den Besselaar
Department of Social Science Informatics SW1, University of Amsterdam
Roeterstaat 15, NL - 1018, Amsterdam, The Netherlands

Michael T. Black
CSC Index, London W1X 1RB, UK

Chris W. Boyne
Department of Computing, Faculty of Information Technology
University of Brighton, Brighton BN2 4GJ, UK

John Clay
School of Education, University of Brighton, Falmer, Brighton BN1 9PU, UK

Mike Cole
Faculty of Education, Sport and Leisure, University of Brighton
Falmer, Brighton BN1 9PU, UK

Mike Cooley
International Research Institute in Human Centred Systems (IRIHCS) &
Technology Innovation Associates, Slough, UK
95 Sussex Place, Slough, Berkshire SL1 1NN, UK

Janet Cooper
British Library for Development Studies, Institute of Development Studies
University of Sussex, Falmer, Brighton BN1 9RE, UK

Fatima Portela Cysne
(Federal University of Ceará - Brazil)
Department of Library and Information Studies, University of Brighton
Falmer, Brighton BN1 9PU, UK

Peter Day
Department of Library and Information Studies, University of Brighton
Falmer, Brighton BN1 9PU, UK

Karamjit S. Gill
SEAKE Centre, Department of Library and Information Studies
University of Brighton, Falmer, Brighton BN1 9PU, UK

Barbara Gorayska
Department of Computer Science, City University of Hong Kong
Tat Chee Avenue, Kowloon, Hong Kong

Dave Hill
Chichester Institute of Higher Education, Bognor Regis, UK

Arild Jansen
Department of Informatics, Finnmark College, Follums vei, 9500 Alta, Norway

Matthew Jones
Judge Institute of Management, Cambridge University, Cambridge, UK

Fernando Leal
University of Guadalajara
Paseo de los Robles 4169-7 45110 Guadalajara, Jal. Mexico

Paul Levy
CENTRIM, University of Brighton, Falmer, Brighton, UK

Inger Lytje
Department of Communication, Aalborg University
Langagervej 8, DK-9220 Aalborg Ø, Denmark

Graham McFee
The Chelsea School, University of Brighton
1 Denton Road, Eastbourne, Sussex, UK

Jacob L. Mey
Department of Linguistics, Odense and Northwestern Universities
55 Campusvej, DK-5230 Odense M, Denmark

Teresa Mom
PVK - Management Consultants
Middenweg 203, NL-1098 AN Amsterdam, The Netherlands

Luis Montaño Hirose
Department of Economics, Universidad Autonoma Metropolitana-Iztapalapa
Av. Purisima y Michoacan s/n, Col. Vicentina, C.P.09340. Mexico, D.F.

Robert C. Muller
H-IT & The International Research Institute of Human Centred Systems
1 East Street, Osney Island, Oxford OX2 2AU, UK

Patricia Shipley
Stress Research & Control Centre, Department of Organizational Psychology
Birkbeck College (University of London), Malet Street, London SW1E 7HX, UK

Peter Squires
Social Policy, Department of Community Studies
University of Brighton, Falmer, Brighton, UK

Jeff Taylor
Department of Library and Information Studies, University of Brighton
Falmer, Brighton BN1 9PU, UK

Jim Thorpe
(The Open University)
17 Belton Road, Bristol BS5 0SJ, UK

Tom Whiston
Science Policy Research Unit (SPRU)
University of Sussex, Falmer, Brighton BN1 9RF, UK

Summaries

Chapter 1. Knowledge and the Post-industrial Society

Karamjit S Gill

The hallmark of the post-industrial society is the accelerating pace and the multi-dimensional nature of information and communication technologies and their penetration in all facets of societies globally. While there is an increasing belief in the notions of knowledge society, common economic spaces and diverse cultural spaces, the dilemmas of exclusion and inclusion; identity and integration; valorisation and homogenisation; and vulnerability and sustainability, are becoming more and more intractable. One of the paradoxes of the post-industrial society is that while knowledge is seen as the new social and economic resource, new technologies demand increasing exclusion of both the knowledge and the participation of the majority of world population (and even nations) from the processes of social and economic development. This exclusion undermines the diversity of social and cultural contexts of knowledge bases and linguistic diversities of interaction, and thereby limit the very potential of new technology for the transfer of knowledge and models of experiences between and across cultures.

The paper discusses some of the dilemmas and paradoxes arising from the convergence of information, communication and media technologies and consequent shifts in the relationships between knowledge, culture and technology arising from the ethos of the 'social market'. The discussion draws upon the debates on human-centred systems, post-capitalist society and European programmes on information society and technology and cohesion. It is argued that we need a new vision of social and economic cohesion in which *diversity drives evolution, and evolution generates diversity*. In this vision, diversity is described not only in terms of the diversity of products, production processes, organisational forms, and customer characteristics but also in terms of local processes of innovation, education and learning, organisation of change processes, and social diffusion of science and technology. Knowledge networking, based on the complementarity of the technological interface and the cultural interface, is proposed as a human-centred (socio-technological) framework for knowledge transfer and sustainability of the local-global nexus of development. The proposal of knowledge networking is rooted in the notions of the symbiosis between human and machine as well as the symbiosis between the 'tacit' (local) knowledge and the 'objective' (global) knowledge. This perspective of knowledge transfer reflects a belief in the much wider diffusion of knowledge between societies for mutual benefit. The discussion accepts the argument that whereas the notion of technology transfer has been central to the development of industrial society, knowledge transfer in the wider sense has become a cornerstone of co-development in the post-industrial society.

Chapter 2. Media and the Cultural Condition: Language & Education

Inger Lytje

The paper discusses the educational challenges that the transformation of Western societies into post-industrial societies causes. First, the educational challenges that arise from change in the social structures, caused by media and information technology, is analysed and discussed. Second the cultural conditions of education and training is analyzed and third the conditions caused by re-thinking the notion of knowledge and language is discussed in relation to training and education. Finally, the media education 'humanistisk informatik' is presented briefly.

Chapter 3. Knowledge Transfer and Sustainable Development: Towards the furtherance of a global Communication System

Tom Whiston

Education and training is for a purpose. In global terms one of the prime purposes must be to reduce the gap between the world's rich and poor. This is critical if a global sustainable environment is to ensue. That in turn implies one of the main aims should be improvement of the circumstances determining,*'technology and knowledge transfer'*. With that transfer comes the ability of *all* societies to respond, both in local appropriate ways and through better, more efficient international collaboration, to the enormous globally interactive challenges which face the world now and increasingly in the future.

Now, an enormous literature exists relating to Technology Transfer. It is not our intention to review that literature here. Rather our aim is to discuss some issues of *global* importance relevant to the transfer of 'knowledge'. Subsequently we will attempt to relate the more specific (and tangible) area of technology transfer to the much wider concept of knowledge transfer. We must also recognise that to talk of 'knowledge' as if it is a codified, 'once and for all', concept is highly misleading. That idea must be dismissed at once. Knowledge is open ended, developing, self creative. Equally some knowledge can become 'obsolescent', or at least superseded by more contemporary gains. Thus to talk of knowledge as if it is a static, stationary concept is not only wrong, but can also lead to counterproductive or less than optimal activity or policies, especially in relation to education.

Chapter 4. The Keyboard Blues : Modern Technology and the Rights and Risks of People at Work

Patricia Shipley

Health and safety at work is a moral imperative, but the debates emphasise only the economic and legal sides. Autonomy and freedom in work process control enhances the power that responsibly-minded workers may need to protect their health. Drawing on case material from working with VDUs and other forms of modern technology, it is shown, on the other hand, that loss of control over their immediate work processes can be stressful and potentially harmful to them. It is suggested that unquestioned divisive and dualistic practices at workplaces are a potent and unnecessary reason for this problem.

Chapter 5. Ethics is Fragile, Goodness is Not

Fernando Leal

This paper first illustrates what kind of ethical issues arise from the new information, communication and automation technology. It then argues that we may embrace the popular idea that technology is ethically neutral or even ambivalent without having to close our eyes to those issues, and in fact that the ethical neutrality of technology makes them all the more urgent. Finally, it suggests that the widely ignored fact of normal responsible behaviour offers a new and fruitful starting point for any future thinking about such issues.

Chapter 6. Organisational Spaces and Intelligent Machines: A metaphorical approach to Ethics

Luis Montaño Hirose

This paper tackles the main changes that have taken place in the mechanical worldview -of simple, self-regulating and intelligent machines- and studies their repercussions at the ethical and organisational level. These views of machines agree with the scientific, human-relations and postmodern proposals in organisation theory, in that they are in fact reflections on human nature which depend on metaphorical devices within which the machine metaphor is central.

Chapter 7. Information System Design: Human Centred Approaches

Jim Thorpe

Distinguishing marks of Human Centred system designers are to be found more in the range of concerns brought to the activity of information system design than in a predilection for particular techniques of software engineering. If not partnered by an account of the themes central to the Human Centred tradition, notably the social context in which IT artefacts exist, the cultural and personal realities of people using technology or subject to its pervasive activity, and an acknowledgement of the forms taken by knowledge as a social phenomenon, Human Centred design could be dismissed as simple pragmatism.

The Human Centred designer may exclude methods of design which are unable to match the richness of the information environment of which the proposed artefacts are to be a part; other methods will be judged according to their value in supporting human judgement: the methods themselves will not dominate. On occasions certain methods of system development may be particularly compatible with insights into knowledge, communication, and organisations promoted by the Human Centred tradition. This point will be expanded below with reference to making judgements and to the social nature of the information environment.

The Human Centred design tradition emphasises the context in which IT is to be used. The functioning of organisations and how people interact with one another and with machines are considered a proper concern of the system developer. Hence the term 'information environment' is favoured, more effectively to highlight that space in which humans and machines touch one another than if information systems and the situation of their use were spoken of as if no profound interplay existed between them. This profundity is ignored when people constituting the information environment are referred to simply as 'users'.

Human Centred perspectives counter the prevailing bias towards an over-strong belief in rationality and the dominant metaphor of the machine, which encourage IT designers to reduce design issues too slickly to ones of simple functionality. We speak of 'the social machinery' and may be misled into believing that society is a machine. The undoubted value in the past of the Enlightenment faith in rationality to free us from the dogma of tradition released a force which empowered the Industrial Age and its successor the Information Age, but the power of the rational to remove uncertainty, and likewise the value of doing so, was exaggerated. Now overarching rationality is attacked by critiques from a variety of often opposing camps. In particular we see the rise of the post-modern critique with its view of the world as multi-faceted rather than governed by a single rationality. There are here, we believe, lessons for us as designers.

Chapter 8. Technological Change, Social Innovation and Employment

Peter van den Besselaar and Teresa Mom

Policy statements about the future of the European welfare state and about the emerging European information society emphasise that, apart from technological innovation, there is an urgent need to support social innovation. Social innovation is generally defined in terms of the adaptation of society to the needs of a globalising economy and to the development and diffusion of the so called 'information superhighway'. This notion of social innovation focuses on more market and less government regulation, for liberalisation of markets and for flexibilisation of the labour market. Perceived in this way, social innovation is not any more based on political values and decision making, but it is reduced to the mere adaptation of social institutions to the one and only possible development left for society: a market
dominated information society.

This paper argues that this view of social innovation is seriously flawed. It is argues that the future is open, and that very different types of information societies are possible. Therefore, there is a need for various visions of the future, and for a conscious decision
making within the political arena about the developments we want to bring about, and about the developments we want to prevent from occurring. It emphasises that in the recent past no fundamental differences existed between the various developed countries on this issue. The concept of the 'post-industrial society' does not cover one type of society, but various types of societies, that did differ in important respects. More specifically, underlying the growing share of service employment, post-industrial societies do have very different employment structures. Also the role of unpaid work is different in the different post-industrial societies. These differences are strongly related to political (i.e., normative) choices that were made during the processes of building the various 'welfare states'. This indicates that, despite some general tendencies, political choices do matter. The same holds true, in our view, for the information society. Although the role of information, knowledge and communication, and the related technologies, will increase everywhere, there is no one best way of organising the information society. Therefore, we need alternative designs for the institutional make up of the information society, based on equality, inclusion of all, social security, and cultural diversity. The dominant political (and technocratic) paradigm of more technology, more market, more flexibility, and, consequently, less equality, has to be read as it is: only one possible view of the future.

Chapter 9. Empowerment and Enslavement: Business Process Reengineering and the Transformation of Work

Matthew Jones

Business Process Reengineering (BPR) is currently attracting immense interest in the management field as a means of achieving dramatic improvements in organisational productivity. It is widely seen as providing the blueprint for the future development of organisations in developed capitalist economies. Many of its features may be seen as similar to other influential models of organisational change such as the network organisation or the horizontal organisation.

One of the main elements of BPR is the promotion of a fundamental transformation of organisational work which is presented as inexorable, novel and emancipatory. A critical analysis of the literature, however, indicates that each of these claims may be questioned. BPR may be seen as part of a broader discourse of social transformation with particular disciplinary effects. Despite the protestations of some of its main proponents, many of its features may be seen as being based on well-established approaches to work organisation. The emancipatory character of BPR may be seen to be based on an impoverished model of organisational power relationships. The implications of the influence of the BPR model of organisations for the nature of the 'Information Society' are discussed.

Chapter 10. The Role of Creativity in Post-Industrial Society: Exploring the Implications of Non-Conventional Technologies for Work and Management Organisation.

Paul Levy

Competitive industrial markets demand state of the art use of new emerging technologies and manufacturing processes. To use new technologies effectively the dimension of human responsibility has to be explored and properly managed. Work has been carried out at CENTRIM in the area of the human implications associated with the management of conventional technologies. However, non-conventional technologies and their associated organisational problems pose new challenges for the technology managers of the future. In this paper the problems of acquiring new knowledge of the worker and integration of technology and work and management processes is discussed drawing on comparative case data from the UK and Slovenia. Issues of creativity and motivation are stressed as being key factors in realising maximum human potential. The paper presents a tool for analysing the 'non-conventional' organisational design required to support exploitation of non-conventional technologies. This tool - the *'creativity matrix'* examines the differing levels of creativity present in organisations and acts as a catalyst to organisational re-design. Environmental and organisational conditions of Factory 2000 are analysed in order to facilitate best practice exploitation of new non-conventional technologies, particularly the flexibility required to cope with increasing rates of market turbulence.

Chapter 11. The Global Information Society and Rural Economies

Arild Jansen

What does the development towards the 'post-industrial' society mean to rural areas? Will it imply an increase in information and knowledge based jobs locally, and stimulate an indigenous development? Or will it just lead to a new form of a branch plant, 'fordist' economy, characterized by a high level of external control and a narrow range of technical skill?

This chapter reports some findings from a study of the diffusion of information technology in rural areas in Norway. It shows that this diffusion leads to a stronger integration of the local industries into the national economy through the development of vertical linkages, and to an increased import of services into the region. However, we also see substantial improvements of the quality and availability of private and public services, and that the competence and skills have increased in many sectors of the economy.

During the years to come, we expect to see dramatic changes in the telematic infrastructure and their use, both technically, organisationally and economically. From the present experiences with IT diffusion, the question is discussed: is it likely that initiatives like 'a national information infrastructure' will serve the interests of rural societies, or will we see more of a branch plant economy?

Chapter 12. Information Society and Community

Peter Day

This chapter focuses on the issue of social exclusion from the developing information infrastructure. It discusses the need for guaranteed public spaces as a means of addressing the problems of social exclusion, and proposes a model of tripartite collaboration as a way of creating these public spaces on the 'infostructure'. The chapter argues that urgent consideration must be given to the social implications of information communication technology (ICT) and their relationship to the broader information society debate. It discusses European Union and UK government approaches to the development of the information infrastructure, and how this development is often interpreted as being the sole information society issue. It examines deficiencies of the techno-economic approach to the information society, and suggests universal participation as an alternative to the current paradigm. Community networks and community telecentres are used as exemplars of this alternative.

Chapter 13. Technology Transfer and Development

Fatima Portela Cysne

The transfer of technology and information systems and information as input and output of technological development are discussed. It is proposed that information services and information providers should play a key role in technology transfer for development. Information services and systems are analysed as an important element of the debate on technology transfer and development through the mechanisms of science parks. A research project of technology transfer for Brazil is used as an example to illustrate the discussion.

Chapter 14. Information, Knowledge and Empowerment

Janet Cooper

This paper is concerned with the role of information as it relates to development in the rural areas of the least developed countries, principally those of sub-Saharan Africa. It points out that the lack of or misleading information has been a major contributory factor in the failure of development projects, indicating the need for dialogue between development personnel and beneficiaries and the importance of involving rural people at every stage of the development process.

It argues that the principal objective of rural development is the empowerment of ordinary people to identify and take action to alleviate the conditions which affect their lives. Without this rural people will continue to be dependent on the aid of donor agencies; for development to become sustainable they must be enabled to become self-reliant and to take control of their own development. The discusses emphasises that the information worker has a vital role to play in ensuring that the information needs of both development personnel and rural people are accurately identified and that appropriate measures are taken to supply timely and relevant information in support of development.

Chapter 15. Participative Citizenry in the Information Age: The role of science and technology towards democratic education in a multicultural society

John Clay

The teaching and learning of science and technology have to be considered carefully if we are to avoid the systematic disenfranchising of many children and young people. Science has to be viewed as a cultural construct with a clear social dimension. The history of `modern science', its philosophical underpinnings and its applications need to be critically examined. The very nature of science has to be explored and questioned.

In this paper I will argue that the aims of science and technology in schools have little to do with empowering future citizens to become scientifically literate but concerns itself primarily with producing a reified work force. This is partly because the prevailing orthodoxy as to what constitutes a valid scientific and technological education for the compulsory school years has continued to foster the notion that there is a single and unproblematic way of doing and knowing. The curriculum thus offered continues to produce outcomes that do little to empower learners but instead separates and pigeonholes people either as 'experts' or 'non-experts'. Instead this paper argues for a scientifically and technologically literate and participative citizenry for the next century.

Chapter 16. New Media and Cultural Representation

Jeff Taylor

The debate on postmodernism in this paper is concerned with the tension between global cultural hegemony and local distinctiveness; opportunities for cross-cultural community communication and dangers of cultural homogenisation for consumerism; conflicting new media potentials for both fragmentation and synthesis, for incoherence and holism; reality versus authenticity, 'truth' versus revisionism; the appropriateness of image-driven and experiential media in cultural representation; and broadly, the rhetoric versus the reality of the new media. This discussion is contextualised within a critical postmodern perspective on culture, heritage and the new media, and within a framework that situates and identifies the new media itself as postmodern artefact. The discussion reinforces and raises several issues concerning the representation of culture and heritage through new electronic media, with reference to current examples found on CD-ROM, in museums and on the World Wide Web. These issues concern cultural identity and the role of story versus game; the collision between traditional narrative and new media interactivity, between linearity, multilinearity and non-linearity; and the changing roles of authorship and readership.

Chapter 17. Consensus and Authenticity in Representation: Simulation as Participative Theatre

Michael T. Black

Representation was invented as an issue during the 17th century in response to specific developments in the technology of simulation. It remains an issue of central importance today in the design of information systems and approaches to artificial intelligence. Our cultural legacy of thought about representation is enormous but as inhibiting as it is productive. The challenge to designers of representative technology is to reshape this legacy by enlarging the politics rather than the technics of simulation.

Chapter 18. Cognitive Technology

Barbara Gorayska and Jacob L. Mey

A new programme of research is emerging, called Cognitive Technology (CT). Its main foci of interest are: (a) the role which 'informational artifacts' play in the construction of the human mental world, and (b) the role which this constructed ('fabricated') world must be assigned in the development of new 'informational artifacts'. While 'classical' HCI focuses mainly either on the engineering aspects of information technology, or draws attention to the strictly human problems involved in that technology, in CT we aim at integrating these two trends. Doing that, we emphasize the total world aspect of HCI (and not, say, exclusively such aspects as those gathered under metaphors like 'tool', 'black box', 'machine', etc.). Furthermore, this world is considered not only as something on which humans operate, but something humans work in and with. In particular, we want to stress the aspect of the (computerized) world as a purveyor of guidance, by virtue of its structuredness, rather than as a collector of mere data. CT is presented as sui generis: it has its own direction of enquiry which cannot be reduced to any of the current practices of building Ecological Systems, Cognitive Ergonomics or Cognitive Engineering.

Chapter 19. Electronic Mail, IT Productivity and Workplace Culture

C. W. Boyne

Electronic mail is becoming widespread as an aid to organizational efficiency, but the belief that it increases productivity rests on questionable foundations. Organizations have failed to specify how electronic mail systems are supposed to be used, and the way the technology functions also helps to prevent efficient usage. Electronic mail is, however, a significant phenomenon. From the organization's standpoint, it indicates a tendency, or at least a desire, to become in some sense a democratic, participatory institution. More significantly, perhaps, it fosters a more convivial and complete (if less productive) attitude to work from the employee's standpoint. Unless the way organizations use electronic mail alters, it may come to play an important part in shaping the culture of work in the future.

Chapter 20. Deadly Technology in the Post-Industrial Society: A case study of firearms and firearms control

Peter Squires

The invention of the firearm played a vital role in the establishment of modern nation states. In turn, the process of industrialisation reinforced the growing power of these states by equipping their enlarged armies with the firepower to subdue the world. The power of the West was to rest for many years upon the relative monopolisation of access to weapons.

In the post-industrial world, this relative monopoly has been broken, both within the developed nation states themselves, and across the wider world. A dangerous new situation has been created and the gun is causing a new kind of havoc. This article begins with a review of the origins of a debate in the Britain and America about rights, citizenship and access to firearms. It then proceeds to bring these debates up to date with an examination of the problems resulting in these two societies from widespread access to guns, concluding with a review of the seemingly inadequate methods of gun control currently adopted to reverse the dangerous new culture of the gun.

Chapter 21. 'Resistance Postmodernism': Emancipatory Politics for a New Era or Academic Chic for a Defeatist Intelligentsia?

Mike Cole and Dave Hill

In this paper, we attempt an evaluation of what has been described as 'postmodernism or resistance'. We conclude that, while there are clear differences in intention and in emphasis between it and what has described as 'postmodernism of reaction', the 'two postmodernisms' have too much in common to be thought of as separate discourses. It is more accurate, we suggest, to think of a continuum, with 'postmodernism of reaction' at one end and 'postmodernism of resistance' at the other. While one end of the continuum is peopled by reactionaries, engrossed in 'games of despair', the other is composed of defeatist ex-socialists, engaged in a rhetoric of left posturing.

Next, we refer to some key problems with postmodernism per se. Contra the postmodern rejection of the metanarrative, a Marxist analysis, we argue, still has most purchase in explaining economic, political, social and cultural changes and developments in capitalist societies. While recognising the value of some salient features in some aspects of the 'postmodernism of resistance' end of the continuum, we argue that postmodernism analyses, in general, marginalise and/or neglect the determining effects of the relations of production. In particular, we suggest that postmodernism, albeit unwittingly, serves to disempower the oppressed, by denying the notion of 'emancipation in a general sense'.

We argue that recent major processes of restructuring, underpinned by market-led strategies, are in line with the current requirements of capitalist states. This is either denied, ignored or underplayed, or else the changes are designated merely as 'postmodern', in the discourse of postmodernism. In rejecting the determining effects of capital, or in neutralizing capitalism itself, postmodernism, we argue, serves to uphold the Radical Right in their two nation hegemonic project. Ideologically, this project involves the privileging of individualism and greed. Economically, it entails a privatisation programme, incorporating the creation of a hierarchy of provision in the 'public' services.

Chapter 22. Postmodernism, Dance and Post-Industrial Society

Graham McFee

The paper explores the meaning of the expression "post-industrial society" and points out that it is not a society whose industry has shut down, but one where industrial activity is no longer needed! It seeks an explanation of Freud's hopes for technology as a solution for human suffering, and explores the relation of the arts to such a society: in particular, whether arts might fill some of the civilising role identified by Freud? The discussion centres around Freud's 'centrality of reason' and a human being's relation to others. For Freud, in order to ensure a civilisation with a (justified) future what was needed was 'a real change in the relation of human beings to possessions', and what Freud called "the dictatorship of reason". The discussion uses post-modern dance for exploring the role of arts in post-modern society and concerns itself questions such as: (i) what we can understand and (ii) what concepts are mobilised in doing so (plus how we came by or learned them). It argues that judgements of dance in a post-industrial society are not necessarily subjective, they involve objectivity. But it is crucial to understand that a commitment to objectivity here does not require that there be 'one right answer', only one acceptable judgement of a particular dance. Second, objectivity does not require a check-list, or set of criteria being employed. In other words objectivity can involve a number of acceptable accounts. This perspective of dance within the post-industrial society enables us to reflect on the relationship between the subjective and the objective and between rationality and irrationality.

Chapter 23: Creativity Constellation for Innovation and Cooperation

Robert C. Muller

"Where my heart lies, let my brain lie also."
Robert Browning

The paper explores the creative thinking process and throws a light on creativity enhancement. From the perspective of possible creativity enhancement both the characteristics of creativity and the creative thinking process are discussed, together with an analysis of the process and its common factors. Constraints on innovation (as a special type of creativity), innovation management and the acceptance of change are discussed; creativity between cooperating individuals is also examined. Some possible computer-based tools to enhance creativity, including innovation, are discussed. A framework of facilities to help promote and support the use of creativity enhancement techniques and tools (SOLI) is proposed. The paper is the result of a study undertaken by the author into creativity, innovation and cooperation.

Introduction

Information Technology and the Culture of the Post-industrial Society is about a critical exploration and ethical reflection on the potential, limitations and implications of the growing convergence of information and media technologies as envisioned by current debates on post-industrial society, information society, and postmodernism. While there is an increasing belief in the notions of the information society and the emergence of common economic spaces and diverse cultural spaces, the societal dilemmas of exclusion and empowerment, identity and integration, diversity and homogenisation, social vulnerability, and economic sustainability, are becoming more and more intractable. The book examines these issues within a wider perspective of an interdependent world of work and learning. It covers three themes: Culture and Technology; Information Society; and the Information Society and the Postmodernism debate.

The theme of Culture and Technology brings together key topics of knowledge and society, knowledge and development, media and language, technology and ethics, and human centredness. It examines some of the dilemmas and paradoxes arising from the convergence of information, communication and media technologies and consequent shifts in the relationships between knowledge, culture and technology arising from the ethos of the 'social market'. Technology and knowledge transfer in this shift are seen as the key determining factors of the ability of *all* societies to respond, both in local appropriate ways and through better, more efficient international collaboration, to the enormous globally interactive challenges which face the world now and increasingly in the future. This focus of transfer recognises a much wider concept of knowledge, a dynamic relationship of interdependency between the 'objective' and the 'tacit' dimensions of knowledge: an open- ended, developing, self creative transfer. It emphasises that to talk of knowledge as if it is a static, stationary concept is not only limiting, but can also lead to counter-productive or less than optimal activity or policies of development.

It is argued that educational challenges of the knowledge society that arise from change in the social structures are caused by media and information technology, and require re-thinking the notion of knowledge and language for developing humanistic traditions of learning and training. The discussion on technology and ethics critically examines the ethical neutrality of technology and the prevailing belief that technology is ethically neutral or even ambivalent. The notion of 'goodness' broadens the ethical debate and suggests that the widely ignored fact of normal responsible behaviour offers a new and fruitful starting point for any future thinking about ethical issues of technology and ethics. In this perspective, it is argued that autonomy and freedom in work-process-control enhances the power and responsibly minded of workers in the purposeful use and evaluation of modern technology, and suggests that unquestioned divisive and dualistic *(ethical)* practices at workplaces are a potent and unnecessary reason for problems of stress arising from the loss of control over their immediate work processes.

The theme of Information Society examines the relationship between information technology, social innovation, empowerment and creativity, participation and economic regeneration, and information transfer at the work place and within learning environments. Technology transfer and information transfer are seen from developmental perspectives rather than from traditional technical perspectives. The discussion on information society focuses on the regeneration of community networks and rural development within the European context, and argues for alternative designs for the institutional make-up of the information society, based on equality, inclusion, social security, and cultural diversity. The dominant political (and technocratic) paradigm of more technology, more market, more flexibility, and, consequently, less equality, has to be read as only one possible view of the future. Technological innovations can also be seen in terms of a fundamental transformation of organisational work and a key factor for creativity and motivation in realising maximum human potential. Innovations should not just be presented as inexorable, novel and emancipatory; but they should also be seen as part of a broader discourse of social transformation with particular disciplinary effects.

The theme of the Information Society: the postmodernism debate situates the multimedia trends in wider social, cultural and political contexts. Multimedia as a post-modern artifact and an instrument of social shaping raises issues of cultural representation, cognitive communication, power, identity and control. Inherent in this notion of the artifact are the conflicting abilities of synthesis and fragmentation, and a growing tendency of seeing "history, politics, memories, even subjectivity, our senses of identity" as "representations in narrative form, signifiers chained together in temporal, spatial, and causal sequence". A further post-modern tendency towards fragmentation and incoherence leads to a confusion of post-modern artifact as an egalitarian tool. This theme examines some of these post-modern trends. It argues that our cultural legacy of thought about representation is enormous but as inhibiting as it is productive. The challenge to designers of representative technology is to reshape this legacy by enlarging the politics rather than the technics of simulation. The discussion on representation is complemented by a discussion on post-modern dance as a cultural form, exploring the role of arts in post-modern society and the overlapping relationships between continuity and discontinuity. It is argued that judgements of dance in a post-industrial society are not necessarily subjective, they involve objectivity. A commitment to objectivity does not either mean a commitment to 'one right answer', only one acceptable judgement of a particular dance, or technical criteria for evaluation. Post-modern dance bridging the gap of continuity and discontinuity enables us to reflect on the relationship between the subjective and the objective and between rationality and irrationality. Seeing the multimedia artifact from a perspective of cognitive technology, the debate from representation shifts to the world of human computer relations. This world is considered not only as something on which humans operate, but something humans work in and with. In particular, it stresses the aspect of the (computerized) world as a purveyor of guidance, by virtue of its structuredness, rather than as a collector of mere data. Cognitive technology is presented as sui generis: it has its own direction of enquiry which cannot be reduced to any of the current practices of building Ecological Systems, Cognitive Ergonomics or Cognitive Engineering.

The discussion on postmodernism moves onto a wider socio-political arena embodied in two perspectives of postmodernism: 'postmodernism of resistance' and 'postmodernism of reaction'. It is suggested that while there are clear differences in intention and in emphasis between these 'two postmodernisms', they have too much in common to be thought of as separate discourses. It is suggested that it more accurate to think of a continuum, with 'postmodernism of reaction' at one end and 'postmodernism of resistance' at the other. While recognising the value of some salient features in some aspects of the 'postmodernism of resistance' end of the continuum, it is argued that the analyses of postmodernism, in general, marginalise and/or neglect the determining effects of the relations of production, and thereby, albeit unwittingly, serve to disempower the oppressed, by denying the notion of 'emancipation in a general sense'. The theme then examines postmodernism from a perspective of an historical relationship between firearms and the monopoly of power and control, and the implications of this relationship to the citizen rights and citizenship in the USA and Britain.

Finally the discussion concludes with a post-modern reflection on creativity, innovation and cooperation. Creativity constellations are proposed as a way forward to create a network of creativity centres which are inclusive, enabling, developmental, and participative. SOLI, a framework of creativity constellations, illustrates the creation of interdependent networks of human machine relations to promote creativity, knowledge transfer, facilitating and promoting innovation and cooperation. Here a vision of new forms of work, living and learning creatively, begins to emerge, and we again re-enter the world of realities through debates on information society, ethics, technology and postmodernism.

The present volume adds to the growing literature that approaches post-industrial society from social and cultural perspectives, such as *Human machine symbiosis* (Gill, Springer-Verlag, 1996), *Post-capitalist society* (Drucker, 1994), *Spaces of identity: global media, electronic landscapes and cultural boundaries* (Morley and Robins, Routledge, 1995), *Cult of information* (Roszak, 1988), *Preparing for the twenty - first century* (Kennedy, P., Vintage Books, 1990), *Information technology and changes in organizational work.* (Orlikowski, Chapman & Hall, 1996). *Democracy and technology* (Sclove, Guilford Press, 1995), *Knowledge frontiers* (Faulkner & Senker, Clarenden Press, 1994), *Science, technology and society* (Webster, Macmillan, 1991). *The mode of information. poststructuralism and social context* (Poster, Polity Press, 1990), *Person-centred ergonomics: a Brantonian view of human factors* (Oborne, et al. Taylor & Francis, 1993). *Border Crossing* (Giroux, Routledge, 1992); *Postmodern semiotics* (Gottdiener, Blackwell, 1995).

This volume brings together three critical debates of the post-industrial society on culture and technology, information society and postmodernism. The interdisciplinary focus of the contributions makes this book accessible to students, researchers and practitioners from a variety of disciplines such as information and communication systems, arts and multi-media, education, computer science, social sciences, humanities, science and technology policy, design studies, and business studies. The aim is to provide theoretical and methodological underpinnings for the analysis and design of information, communication and multimedia technologies. The book should also be of interest to researchers and practitioners who are concerned with wider policy, social, cultural, philosophical and ethical issues of information society. Contributions in this volume emphasise multidisciplinary perspectives and reflect the diversity of fields and experiences of the contributors.

This book is based on the proceedings of the international conference on New Visions of the Post-industrial Society, which was held at the University of Brighton in July 1994. The volume includes contributions based on the papers presented at the conference, as well as a number of invited contributions. The conference and this volume have their origins in the debate on 'The Changing Society, the New Technologies', initiated by the European Commission in the White Paper on Growth, Competitiveness, Employment (CEC, Brussels, Luxembourg, 1993). This volume is part of the research into human centred systems and social innovation undertaken by the SEAKE Centre, Department of Library and Information Studies at the University of Brighton. I owe special gratitude to Mark Luyckx (Cellule de Prospective, CEC), Alain Stekke (DGXIII, CEC) and Mike Cooley (IRIHCS) for their support of the SEAKE Centre's work into human centred systems and social cohesion; Peter Enser, Gordon Bull, and Maggie Deacon of University of Brighton for their support of the New Visions conference, and Ajit Gill for her moral support for completion of this volume. I give special thanks Hilary Webb and Tania Funston for their help in organising the New Visions conference; Jan Fielding for organising the material for this book; Satinder Gill, Tola Dabiri, Glyn Hughes and Rajinder Gill for their help in preparing the manuscript for the book, and Beverley Ford and Rosie Kemp of Springer-Verlag, London for bringing out this volume. Above all I thank the authors for their contribution to this volume.

Karamjit S Gill
Brighton
January, 1996

Visions and Problems of the Post-Industrial Society

Invited Lecture

Mike Cooley
President, International Research Institute in Human Centred Systems (IRIHCS)
Chairman Technology Innovation Associates, Slough, UK

For me the year 2001 connotates not just the end of the 20th Century and the beginning of the 21st century but rather the end of the most extraordinary millennium in human history. Within that millennium we have seen the decline of feudalism, the growth of capitalism the weakening of religion as a leading edge in society. But above everything else we have seen the emergence of Cartesian science and related to that a causal explanation of everything.

We should reflect on the double edge nature of this process. The delinquent genius of our species has produced on the one hand the beauty that is Venice and on the other the hideousness that is Chernobyl, the caring therapy of Renkins X-rays and the application of that science to the destruction of Hiroshima. Through our science we now appear to be the first generation of the only species that has within its power to destroy itself and the planet as we know it. This is an awesome responsibility for which I believe we are ill equipped socially, culturally and intellectually.

The last decades of this century have been characterised by a frantic and exponential rate of technological change. Our speed of communication has gone up by ten to the power of seven, travel ten to the power of three, data handling by ten to the power of six, the speed at which we deplete our resources by ten to the power of four, and weapon power by ten to the power of seven, a hurricane of change. This is going to mean that the organisations in which we work will have to think of themselves in future as earning and learning organisations, institutions in which there will be cascades of information facilitated in many ways by the technology.

But we do need to look at the double edge nature of all of this. In the last hundred years we have learned to fly, we have killed 40 million people in one year in one war, called Jackson Pollack a great artist and we have played golf on the moon. Clearly we see ourselves to be a upwardly mobile species. But there is this incredible contradiction built into the development to this kind of technology. A key issue for me is firstly to try and see in historical perspective where we are in all of this process.

If you think of the whole life of the universe as being 46 years then we have had as a species some definition of ourselves for a mere 4 hours. Our agriculture we discovered one hour ago and our industrial revolution which is doing such incredible damage to the environment and to ourselves as a species, I would suggest, has only been about for one minute on this time scale.

It is only our species' arrogance to believe that we are infinite. As we approach the 21st Century, we do really need to reflect on our place in nature and our relationship with nature and the other species around us. A discernible feature of this development is that we have gradually begun to waste one of the most precious assets that any society can have, which is the skill, ingenuity, creativity and imagination of its people. Probably no other asset is so outrageously wasted world-wide. This even applies to the biggest corporations in the world. They do not understand that they place their own future in jeopardy. Recently there was a heading on the front of Time Magazine which asked and I quote, "can America still compete?" and the article pointed out that in America we tend to treat our people as a cost and a liability, whereas our major competitors treat them as an asset whose skill should be ever enhanced. When General Motors sought to compete with Toyota it went thorough typical hi-tech fix: front end vision systems on its robotics devices and quasi-expert systems on the shop floor. It is a matter of fact that they spent so much on the technology that they could have actually bought Toyota with the same amount, but they still could not complete with it because they had not got the human organisational aspects right. That is partly because of a tradition of Taylorism. Taylor once said that "in my system the workman is to know precisely what he is to do and how he is to do it, and any improvement he makes to the instruction he is given is disastrous to its success."

It is widely emphasised that the very existence of our societies and companies will depend on the ability to mobilise every ounce of intelligence. I think we have to question what is meant in this context by intelligence. On the one hand we have been developing these extraordinary technologies but at the same time we ourselves are becoming more like machines. There is a convergence of the two different capabilities which is a symbiosis of human capability and machine capability. It is extraordinary in all of this how we underestimate the human mind. In the English language if we want to point out that something is absurdly simple you say it is as easy as crossing a road. As an aerospace technologist I have been ever impressed by peoples ability to cross a road. They go to the edge of the road, look up and down in both directions, they work out the rate of change of the image of oncoming vehicle , from that they call up massive memory bank to know if it is mini or a bus. From that they compute the velocity of each one separately, in the meantime they are working out the width of the road , their own acceleration, the peak velocity of the system, and they cross the road. This astonishing capability of humans is trivial as compared to the diagnostic capability of a nurse, and the teaching capability of the teacher.

So we seem determined for some reason to underestimate this extraordinary human capability in our culture and in the way we design machines. The human mind and brain are of course extraordinary, some would say pieces of equipment, but I don't like to refer to them in those terms. The human memory which has an understanding of size and shape, of language, of solutions, of non-solutions, of problems embedded in the brain in something like 10,000 million nerve cells. There are something like 10 million, million connections and pathways between them. If we were to count each of those connections in one second and go one, two three, four...........I would like you to guess how long it would take to count all the connections in the human mind.

Just reflect for a moment what it might be. Depending on your experience it would be between 3 and 30 million years! Now you imagine if some great research institute produced a new computing device with something like these capabilities. People would rush from all over the world to stand there in awe at the great device. Cherniak (1) suggests that the massively complex battle management software of the SDI(Star Wars) with its 10,000,000 lines of code is perhaps one hundredth of the estimated size of the mind's program. I think a deep problematic, as we approach the 21st Century and post-industrial society, is to understand why it is that we are so obsessed with the artificial and so disrespectful of the natural. In particular systems designers in my view should set out to design systems to celebrate and enhance human skill and ingenuity rather than to objectivise. There is also virtue in reality.

The tendency has been that when we design a system, we look at the technology required, we then decide what sort of organisational form will be necessary to use the technology, and at the end we then gradually admit that there are these people around and they are often referred to as a problem, "The People Problem". What we have been suggesting is that a much richer way is to reverse the whole process, start from the people to the organisational form, and from the organisational form to the technology. If one does what I suggest then we end up with a system that is much richer, is more humane and is far more useful.

We tried to explain some of these in a paper called "European Community Competitiveness in the 21st Century: the Integration of Work, Culture and Technology."(2) The system designers view of the world is of course a nice rigid, hierarchical structure a box with everybody in their own little place. It is a rule based system. I always find it extraordinary that management and others talk about the need to run companies and presumably all universities, on rule based systems. The first thing any active trade unionist knows is the way to stop anything in its tracks is to work to rule. It is all the things we do outside the rules that keep everything going. Now why don't we be honest with each other and face reality. We all know that what goes on is that people cut corners, break the rules, bend the rules, have informal networks, chat to each other, and that is how things happen. We need to have the courage to say in organisations that what is required is what I now refer to as "successful disobedience". The awful thing about modern organisations is that they have been run on a management by objectives basis, using the technology to provide a ridged framework rather than finding means by which we have a human machine symbiosis in which we can link these two different capabilities in a way which could be helpful.

What we are witnessing is a kind of turning point historically in which we have got to decide where it is we are going. There is no doubt that Taylor's division of labour gave rise to increased productivity and wealth. That increased productivity and wealth gave rise to education and leisure pursuits. This of course is laudable. But as a result of that, industrial work lost its attractiveness to those who had these higher expectations, so there was a growing lack of skilled workers. The traditional response has been to automate further with increased centralisation. That in turn leads to a lack of creativity and competence within these sectors and ultimately to a lack of competitiveness. What we are suggesting is to look at a new human machine interaction which will lay the basis for innovation and flexibility.

So these are the issues which I think we have to take very seriously as we approach the 21st Century. Because every job of any kind is now affected by this technology, not only is it a question of the jobs being changed but in many cases the jobs being totally destroyed. Even in the most successful economy in Europe, and I still hold it to be the German economy, there is a widespread fears about growing unemployment. I think it beholds all of us to seriously address the issue of unemployment. There are about 20 million people out of work in the EC, the official figures puts it at 18.2 million. The figure grows daily. It is not the case that unemployment is going to go away. There are three kinds of people who believe it will go away of its own accord, the economist, the fool and the politicians, and frequently the three are embodied in the one person.

In fact we are changing the organic composition of capital, we are making processes capital and energy intensive rather than labour intensive. We actually introduce what is known as labour saving devices and are then surprised that we are putting large numbers of people out of work. Indeed the more we invest in certain sectors of industry the greater it will be the number of people we put out of work. It is no longer true that the only people out of work will be unqualified manual workers. But what is certainly true is that all sectors of the community are now being affected by these tremendous changes.

The economic context in which these new technologies are being introduced is unlikely to mean that their potential advantages will be widely diffused through society. The economic policies which drive the introduction of these technologies render companies and organisations efficient at the micro level but often disastrously inefficient at the macro level of the nation state. Thus whilst it is being pointed out that information technologies greatly increase productivity, we should not forget that there are twenty million people unemployed in the EU member states who are denied the right to be productive at all!

In some member states such as Britain, the average working week in many sectors of industry is now actually longer that it was at the end of the war with related stress and anxieties widely reported. There have already been legal cases for compensation for "industrial damage" arising from overwork and stress and large amounts have been paid. The politicians tell us that there is no work for the unemployed. This I regard as an insult to my intelligence. Are they really saying that our hospitals are so well staffed and equipped, our public transport systems so well maintained, safe and ecologically desirable or the care for the elderly so good that there is no work? We could be using the new technologies in exciting ways to provide hosts of new jobs in newly developed social markets.

There are now massive demographic changes across Europe. New technologies could provide communication systems and special equipment and facilities which would allow the elderly to retain their dignity and independence much later into their lives. Exciting new possibilities would exist with multi media techniques if properly applied to the so-called cultural industries. Remote diagnostic techniques could enhance the work of general medical practitioners in more remote and isolated areas across Europe and the world more widely.

At work itself, we could set up "learning and earning organisation" in which technologies would be used to render the commercial and industrial sectors educationally dynamic. They could use software such as my own "curiosity generators" to provoke people into "transcendence". The sensitive and creative use of distance working could enhance life in rural areas and link the centre and the periphery in an entirely new fashion. Even in the urban conurbations, distance working could reduce the stress and environment damage of large number battling their way into inner cities each day. Local support organisation could be set up such as tele village halls which could in part overcome the danger of "cocoonism" which has been identified by some sociologists.

The new communication technologies would also support the shifts from economy of scope and on to economy of networking. Within such systems virtual companies could be set up which links SMEs and even individuals across national boundaries and allow these small groups to undertake projects which previously would only have been possible for larger organisations. Communication technologies would also facilitate the development of distributed manufacturing systems in regional economies so as to overcome the terrible environmental damage and wastage of energy involved in the mass production of products in one concentrated area with long distribution lines across the whole of the EU countries.

New technology could also be used to optimise energy consumption in individual homes and offices and graphically demonstrate energy utilisation as a means of consciousness raising. If local communities and countries are to succeed in accomplishing their transition to sustainable energy systems as part of a progression towards post fossil fuel economies, computer programmes and graphical outputs could render such options more visible. It is spurious and dishonest to talk of democratic societies if we do nor develop systems which facilitate the involvement of our citizens in such processes. In Denmark, there are already good examples of how this might me done in the field of energy policy.

Such thoughts relate to the potential of science and technology. However, the gap between that potential and the reality is a growing chasm. Probably at no time in human history have so many citizens felt alienated from and threatened by the societies they are producing, In our cities during the day, children choke in their fume filled canopies whilst at night citizens are fearful of walking the streets. In rural areas we are turning the countryside into a junkie incapable of producing without its next chemical fix. The chemical input is now so great that the milk from a mother's breast is so polluted that it would be illegal to sell it in a bottle according to the EU's own rules. Meantime we destroy the flora and fauna around us on such a scale as to threaten the very basis of bio diversity itself.

Likewise cultural and linguistic diversity is increasingly threatened as the notion of "the one best way" is driven by all pervasive technocratic assumptions. And so, without concern, we glibly talk about the manipulation of data , the exploitation of resources and the control of nature. Perhaps as we approach the 21st Century we should , in the light of current experience, examine the assumptions built into our science and technology and seek to build upon its positive feature whilst minimising its negative multiplier affects.

The forms of science and technology which are now giving rise to fundamental concerns have arisen primarily in those cultures which at the time were Jewish and Christian and put the human being in domination over the rest of nature. This results in an obsession with control, predictability of processes, disregard for nature except as a 'utility' and a tendency to treat the planet as inert material. Gradually those values have been consolidated to a notion of science in which we can only regard a device, a development or a process as 'scientific' if it displays the three predominant characteristics of the natural sciences: predictability, repeatability and mathematical quantifiability. By definition these preclude intuition, subjective judgement and tacit knowledge. Furthermore, with the tradition we only accept a causal explanation and within such an explanation the human being is perceived to be as machine.

Howard Rosenbrock, in his seminal work "Machines with a Purpose" (3) has described an alternative explanation based on purpose. This has partly arisen out of his work on Human Centred Systems and raises profound questions which I urge all of you to address. Many papers at this conference address the concept of human centredness in a wide range of contexts and are to be greatly welcomed. Karamjit Gill in organising this conference and the journals and books which have laid the basis for it, has made a huge contribution to our understanding of these questions.

Viewed historically, technologies tend to render human beings passive and systems active. We confer life on machines and diminish ourselves. We see a convergence of the human and the machine. Humans become more like machines and machines become more like humans. In the Human Centred System it is not this convergence which is advocated but rather a symbiosis which builds on the different strengths of the human being and the machine.

There are now those who suggest that the world is becoming so complex that human beings are incapable of coping with it. Therefore we must increasingly develop machines to act on our behalf. It is part a form of technological narcissism.

We initially developed machines that can 'walk' such as the great clock mechanisms and automata. Alongside this, drawings, representations and descriptions of humans began to perceive us as machines. then we proceeded to produce machines that 'feed'. Related to this are our obsessions about diets, calorific value etc. Finally, we are now producing machines that 'think' and in consequence human beings are regarded as mere thinking machines. A computer scientist referred to the human mind as "just a computer built by amateurs". Furthermore, hard AI protagonists in the United States recently said "Human beings will have to accept their true place in the evolutionary hierarchy - animals, human beings and intelligent machines."

If we continue to design IT systems as we now do, then this could well turn into a self fulfilling wish. The emergent design concept of Human Centred Systems shows a constructive alternative well worthy of further investigation.

Human progress has been largely based on devising means arising from the question "Can we do it?". Our science and technology has now reached a level in fields of artificial intelligence and genetic engineering that instead of a frantic linear drive forward we should pause at events of this kind to consider the questions "Should we do it?" and "What are the constructive alternatives of doing it?".

This conference raises many of these questions in a stimulating and challenging fashion. I am sure the conference itself and the proceedings which will subsequently be published, will provide a rich context in which some of the matters can be considered.

I wish the conference well and leave you with the thought that we should provide systems which function as tools for human purposes rather that as machines which objectivise and subordinate human capabilities. In all our endeavours we should seek to enhance human imagination and creativity. The narrow reductionist, rationalist "scientific" tradition is far too shallow and arid a soil in which to transplant the roots of our humanity.

Post Industrial Society will require those capable of taking a sensitive holistic view in which we seek to combine the perspective of a historian, the imagination of a poet, the ignition of the spark of the imagination and the creative energy and excitement which it propagates.

As the poet Seamus Heaney pointed out: "The most difficult thing is the generation of excitement That is why poets are so panic stricken. They are afraid that the unexpected accidental kick start that sends poems into action will desert them."

I am confident that this conference will generate controversy and excitement and 'kickstart' many constructive ideas into action.

Notes

1. For an excellent overview of Human Centred Systems research in Europe see Gill K. S. *Summary of Human Centred Systems Research in Europe*. SEAKE Centre, Department of Library and Information Studies, Faculty of Information Technology, University of Brighton, August 1990.
2. The topics covered in this opening address are discussed in greater detail and with extensive reference material, In Cooley M J E. *Architect or Bee? The Human Price of Technology*. The Hogarth Press, Chatto & Windus, London 1987. Available only from TIA, 95 Sussex Place, Slough, SL1 INN, at £9.50 inc p&p. Details are also available from TIA of the various foreign language editions of this 180 page book including Japanese, Irish and Swedish.

References

Cherniak, Undebuggability and Cognitive Science, *Communications of the ACM*; 1988:V 31.4

Cooley, M (1989). *European Competitiveness in the 21st century*. FAST, EC, June 1989

Rosenbrock H. H. *Machines with a Purpose*. Oxford University Press 1990.

Section I
Culture and Technology

Chapter 1

Knowledge and the Post-industrial Society

Karamjit S Gill

The hallmark of the post-industrial society is the accelerating pace and the multi-dimensional nature of information and communication technologies and their penetration in all facets of societies globally. While there is an increasing belief in the notions of knowledge society, common economic spaces and diverse cultural spaces, the dilemmas of exclusion and inclusion; identity and integration; valorisation and homogenisation; and vulnerability and sustainability, are becoming more and more intractable. One of the paradoxes the post-industrial society is that while knowledge is seen as the new social and economic resource, new technologies demand increasing exclusion of both the knowledge and the participation of the majority of world population (and even nations) from the processes of social and economic development. This exclusion undermines the diversity of social and cultural contexts of knowledge bases and linguistic diversities of interaction, and thereby limit the very potential of new technology for the transfer of knowledge and models of experiences between and across cultures.

The paper discusses some of the dilemmas and paradoxes arising from the convergence of information, communication and media technologies and consequent shifts in the relationships between knowledge, culture and technology arising from the ethos of the 'social market'. The discussion draws upon the debates on human-centred systems, post-capitalist society and European programmes on information society and technology and cohesion. It is argued that we need a new vision of social and economic cohesion in which *diversity drives evolution, and evolution generates diversity*. In this vision, diversity is described not only in terms of the diversity of products, production processes, organisational forms, and customer characteristics but also in terms of local processes of innovation, education and learning, organisation of change processes, and social diffusion of science and technology. Knowledge networking, based on the complementarity of the technological interface and the cultural interface, is proposed as a human-centred (socio-technological) framework for knowledge transfer and sustainability of the local-global nexus of development. The proposal of knowledge networking is rooted in the notions of the symbiosis between human and machine as well as the symbiosis between the 'tacit' (local) knowledge and the 'objective' (global) knowledge. This perspective of knowledge transfer reflects a belief in the much wider diffusion of knowledge between societies for mutual benefit. The discussion accepts the argument that whereas the notion of technology transfer has been central to the development of industrial society, knowledge transfer in the wider sense has become a cornerstone of co-development in the post-industrial society.

Towards a Post-industrial Knowledge Trajectory

The current debate on the information society builds upon the convergence of information, communication and media technologies and shifts the discussion on knowledge, culture and technology in a fundamental way. Various established notions of the human condition, such as those of knowledge and power, work and living, identity and cultural space, products and process, are being increasingly challenged, redefined and refined. The distinction between working, living and learning is being blurred; individual and community identities which until now have been rooted in physical locations and local cultures, are being seen as part of global economic and cultural spaces. This blurring of distinctions and globalisation of identities are some of the issues which provide a catalyst for discussion here on information society.

There are two main strands of information society. The dominant strand focuses on the information and communication infrastructures and the market philosophy, and the other emphasises the continuity of technological and social innovation building upon the symbiosis between the human and the machine. This second strand sees technology as more than a matter of technical innovation, as neutral, objectified and separated from the social and cultural contexts. Rather, it sees technology as an integral part of social and industrial innovations, and thereby as supporting and facilitating the transfer, exchange and sharing of knowledges, cultures, skills and models of experiences between and across cultural, regional and national boundaries. This chapter is concerned with some of the issues raised above, in particular the relationship between technology and knowledge transfer. The discussion builds upon the debates on human-centred systems, post-capitalist society, knowledge and development, technology and cohesion, and spaces of identity (Gill, 1990, 1994; Drucker, 1994; Whiston, 1992; Cohendet & Llerena, 1994; Morley and Robins, 1995).

In his book on *Post-Capitalist society*, Drucker (1993) provides an enlightened managerial framework for a knowledge trajectory of the information society. He argues that with the dawn of the 1990s, we have entered the age of the *Knowledge Society* in which the knowledge economy replaces the production economy and knowledge becomes a new economic resource. In other words the 'means of production' are no longer capital, natural resources, or 'labor', but knowledge. The application of knowledge to 'productivity' and 'innovation' creates new social groups in the knowledge society: 'knowledge workers', 'knowledge professionals' and 'knowledge executives'. Knowledge workers own tools of knowledge. The new economic challenge is about productivity of knowledge work and of the knowledge worker (ibid.: 7).

His discussion on the evolving nature of the meaning of knowledge over centuries signifies the place of knowledge as a crucial determinant in the evolution of societal innovations. Each shift in the meaning of knowledge has coincided with a new innovation, be it an industrial, technological, organisational or social one. This is illustrated in the change in the meaning of knowledge from knowledge as *'being'* and *skill* during the pre-industrial era to knowledge as *technology* during the industrial revolution (1750-1880), to knowledge as *'production resource'* during the Productivity Revolution (1880-1945), and to knowledge as *'organisational resource'* during the Management Revolution (1945-1990). Drucker argues that we have come a long way from knowledge as being a 'private good' to knowledge as being a social and economic 'resource'. During the Industrial revolution, the application of technology to production changed the meaning of knowledge from *'skill'* to *'technology'*. The productivity revolution coincided with the emergence of Taylorism, and knowledge was now applied to work, and skill became a production resource. The rise of management science established the management revolution within which knowledge is being applied to knowledge itself (ibid. 17-18; 30-31). As the new Century dawns upon us, we enter into the new knowledge society revolution, in which social networks and cultural knowledge bases support the world of network economies, social innovation networks and networks of co-development (ibid.: 38-42).

Drucker cites the *Encyclopédie* (Denis Diderot and Jean d" Alembert) as the most significant book of the Enlightenment period, which brought together in organised and systematic form the knowledge of all crafts (ibid.: 25). The significance of this social innovation was a fundamental shift in the meaning of the technologist from being a craftsman to being an 'information specialist'. Even a non-apprentice could learn to be 'technologist'. For example, the articles about craft were not written by craftsmen but by 'information specialists', including Voltaire and Rousseau. The *Encyclopédie* project made two significant contributions: i) a systematic analysis and purposeful application of knowledge leads to effective results in the material universe - in tools, processes and products, and ii) the shift from *craft* to *information* enables the generalisation of results, and thereby the transfer of knowledge across social and professional boundaries (ibid.: 25-26). By separating the skill (experiential knowledge) from information (objective knowledge), the enlightenment project laid the foundation for the productivity and management revolution and for the current information society revolution.

The management revolution can be regarded as a natural continuation of Taylorism. Since the mid-1940s, knowledge applied to knowledge itself gave rise to the management revolution which still dominates today. Drucker argues that the change in the meaning of knowledge over the last two centuries has transformed society and economy. Formal knowledge is now seen as both the key personal resource and economic resource, replacing the traditional key resources of land (natural resources), capital and labour. In its new meaning, knowledge is seen as the only meaningful resource, a social and economic utility, and a resource for systematic innovation, while traditional resources are seen as constraints. Knowledge as the key resource rather than as a resource defines the post-capitalist society. "It changes, fundamentally, the structure of society. It creates new social dynamics. It creates new economic dynamics. It creates new politics" (ibid.: 41).

It is this hold of formal knowledge over the tacit dimension of knowledge which is at the centre of the paradox of the information society. Whilst information technology has the potential of production, reproduction, and dissemination of a variety of knowledges, it can only do so by objectifying all knowledge in propositional forms, thereby excluding the tacit dimension which is the very form which gives it the meaning. This exclusion undermines the diversity of social and cultural contexts of knowledge bases and linguistic diversities of interaction. This leads to defining information in terms of the quantity of it transfer and its processing speed; defining the potential of information society mainly in terms of technical infrastructures; and defining the equality of access in terms of the determinants of standardisation and generalisation. Inspite of the potential of sharing information and knowledge across social and cultural boundaries, the underlying notions of the '*one best way*' are likely to cause the exclusion of those knowledge bases of communities and societies which do not fit into the predetermined notions of information and information society.

The challenge facing the information society thus is to reintegrate diversity of knowledge bases into the present *Encyclopédie* project of the information society. One way forward is to develop knowledge networking for co-development, building upon the notion of 'valorisation of diversity'. The notion of co-development here refers to the equitability and harmony between local and global social systems. The notion of 'valorisation' here refers to common/global knowledge networks which build upon the commonalities of local knowledge bases while sustaining the local diversities. Both these notions are rooted in the idea of the symbiosis between human and the machine; between technology and knowledge, and in this particular case a symbiosis between the 'objective' knowledge and the 'tacit' dimension of knowledge. This symbiosis recognises the essential contribution of the 'objective' knowledge as a global resource for knowledge transfer and development, while emphasising the centrality of the 'tacit' dimension for transfoming the global knowledge to the local environment, thereby facilitating sustainable development.

A Paradox of Knowledge Trajectory

In our technological culture, the scientific view of knowledge dominates in the area of skill and knowledge transfer. This view assumes a homogeneous understanding of reality and the world as systems of norms and agreements. Information and communication technologies (ICTs) are merely another technical medium of transfer, a sort of one-way transmission, separating language and knowledge from their context and thereby widening the gulf between knowledge and peoples' experiences. Here skill is separated from practice, and language from experience. This separation inculcates isolation of the individual from the group and the social context. Paraphrasing Toulmin (1991), it is now generally accepted that manufacturing organisations must adapt to the skills needs defined by the technical capacity of, for example, computer aided design, robotics, vision systems, and decision support systems. However, technical skills made possible by microelectronics calls for, at the same time, organisational responses that rest on the understanding that goes far beyond technical ingenuity, it demands competence and reflective action and adaptive capability.

Sällström (1991) emphasises that only those who reflect on their experiences develop competence - ability to deal with new situations similar to those they have already experienced. An unreflecting, purely habitual action does not transcend what has once been learnt. Knowledge requires inner reflection, a 'dialogue with things'. It is through reflection of experiences, through rhythmic exchanges between participation and distance, between action and reflection, that knowledge grows. The growth of knowledge, in all its various shades and forms, is a process that requires an inner life of its own, its own breathing rate. It can never be a uniform linear progression. Nor it can be fed with a series of technical data and technical skills. Dialogue as a mediation of knowledge is the concept that expresses the dynamics of language, skill and knowledge: the dynamics of the objective and the tacit dimensions. Simple faith in the information and communication technologies to transfer knowledge and skill misses the essential condition of the context (e.g. language and cultural space) and human mediation (e.g. skill and tacit knowledge) in making sense and purposeful usability of knowledge and its transfer from one culture to another.

Hilton (1991) uses the Pygmalion myth (based upon the English play, Pygmalion by George Bernard Shaw) to illustrate the limitation of the technical notion of knowledge and skill transfer even within the same culture. Knowledge transfer here is constained by the dynamics of language, skill, and knowledge. In the play, Professor Higgins, a natural language expert, bets his friend Colonel Pickering to transform Eliza Doolittle from a 'cockney' to a 'duchess' in six months. The transfomation here deals not just with language in the technical sense, but also with the comlexity of human characteristics such as "Eliza's appearance, her manners, her speech and her thoughts." The transformation also takes note of the English Society, in which class is determined less by appearance than by accent and linguistic practice, and Eliza's success is therefore significantly more dependent upon her voice than her face (ibid.: 61). Higgins succeeds in making Eliza look like a duchess to an extent that all London society is inflamed by Eliza's success. The essential point of the play is that although Higgins succeeds in making "Eliza sound like a duchess, but what she actually says (her thoughts) remain unchanged: she still thinks and swears like a cockney, but in perfect aristocratic tones" (ibid.: 61). She may be able to cope wih learnt situtions, but is unable to cope with unforeseen social situations - a new cultural environment; she does not know how to respond in polite way when she is ruffled, so she swears. In other words, her learning is quite distinct from her understanding. She has learnt the skill and acquired knowledge deposited by the expert, Professor Higgins, but she has not attained competence to use the skill and knowledge in unforeseen situations. Competence and expertise are, by implication, always dynamic and tacit. Eliza may have absorbed the static knowledge but not the tacit dimension of the knowledge environment.

The Eliza myth illustrates a paradox of the skill and knowledge transfer in the post-industrial society. On the one hand information and communication technologies (ICTs) are seen to offer technological resources for the transfer of knowledge, skill and experiences between and across regions, nations and cultures, and on the other hand it requires transforming knowledge and skill into technical formats to satisfy the technical condition of transfer. In the Eliza sense, the transfer includes only the static form of knowledge, and excludes the tacit dimension, and hence the social and cultural contexts of both the sender and the receiver, and the expert and the learner. In this perspective the learners find themselves in the Eliza situation; they acquire new skills and knowledge which they may not be able to practice competently in their new environments and they may also be unable to use these new skills purposefully in their old environments. Learners and experts of static knowledge thus become situated in the technological culture, the 'third' culture - the culture of the artificial. The exclusion of the tacit dimension raises issues such as: i) how to transfer the context and culture of knowledge and skill from the host environment to the new environment into which it is being transferred; ii) how to cope with the 'Baconian' notion of the "contract of error" with the error, uncertainty, ambiguity, and loss of knowledge which is natural part of the transfer process itself (ibid.:62); iii) how to reskill the learner in acquiring new skills while being able to remain located in the personal environment and becoming situated in both the 'third' environments. The issue of reskilling is to do with the competence, the learner may lose some aspects of the old skill but may retain the core competencies, thus enabling the learner to relearn old skill and cope with the old environment. Hilton sees reskilling as analogous to the actor who learns a new role, a new skill to perform the new role, and after playing the role is able to go back to the old role or to another new role without being deskilled. The actor has acquired competence and tacit knowledge of the acting environment which provide a foundation to learn skill and perform roles. In a technical sense the actor learns the facts and rules of the new role and presents them to the audience. In reality, however, the performance is much more complex, below the subtext of the actor's role lies in a vast tacit dimension of the role, the likeness of character (the actor is playing), what the character would do in various situations. While the actor convinces the audience of the role he is playing, he does not allow his own identity collapse into that of his role's, but rather maintains an objectifying, defamiliarizing distance (ibid.: 60-63).

Just as the actor combines dialogue with technology as a medium for communication and transfer, so we need to build a new dialogical medium for knowledge transfer, a new 'cultural interface' based on the notion of human and machine symbiosis. It is proposed that such a cultural interface uses human mediation for the transmission of the tacit dimension of knowledge while using ICTs for the transfer of the objective dimension. This perspective of knowledge transfer, however, requires a deep understanding of the notion of dialogue. The understanding of the concept of dialogue as a medium of transformation can be gained from the domains of theatre and drama. In theatre dialogue occurs where roles meet; it sets them in motion, leading to unexpected results. It turns the scene into a place where firm positions and sharp contours cannot be maintained. In dialogue differences can appear and be played off against one another, both within the individual and between people, and it sets all their various voices and contradictions in motion. In true dialogue, order and disorder are two sides of the same system; together they serve renewal and growth in society. Dialogue thus requires a certain measure of scepticism: disagreement is not simply reconcilable with dialogue - it is one of the conditions. Here dialogue emphasises reciprocity and mutual dependence. It is this mutuality which fulfils the sufficient condition for purposeful knowledge transfer, facilitating co-development through the exchange and sharing of knowledges and cultures.

It is suggested here that ICTs can be shaped to satisfy the necessary condition of transfer, i.e. building a technological interface which enables the transfer of the 'static' knowledge. Cultural interface encompassing human mediation and human information networks can be created to satisfy the sufficient condition of transfer in the sense that it facilitates the transfer of the 'tacit' dimension of knowledge and its absorption in the new environment. *The complementarity of the technological interface and the cultural interface, satisfying both the necessary and sufficient conditions of transfer, can therefore be said to provide a human-centred (socio-technological) framework for knowledge transfer.*

A move towards this developmental notion of knowledge transfer, meeting the sufficient condition, has to cross not only the barrier of the scientific notion of knowledge but also the professional barrier of knowledge and expertise which is rooted in the traditional university education and research. Cook (1992) points out that the social exclusion of the majority from the places of learning is mirrored in an attitude towards knowledge, that it is "exclusive, esoteric and property of the elite" (ibid.: 236). This image of knowledge is mirrored in the cult of the professional, expert, and the specialist. The social exclusion also ensures the scarcity of knowledge, producing an image of knowledge as something that is difficult to access and is the preserve of the elite. Inspite of the increasing opportunities for university education, knowledge is increasingly being regarded as a scarce commodity produced by the elite professionals and marketed to the majority at a competitive cost. Social knowledge on the other hand is rooted in the social and cultural practices of society. It is cellular in character: a multiplicity of overlapping expertise, experiences, practices, norms and diversities, at one point it may be exemplified by the knowledge of the nurse, at another by the skill of the artisan, at another by the practice of a community group, and yet at another point by the forms of working and learning organisations. Cook suggests that the exclusive forms of knowledge, formalised and objectified, are appropriated from the social knowledge. During the process of the transfer of social knowledge to the scientific or 'pure' knowledge, the social value of knowledge is subtracted from it, and scientific or 'objective' value added to it. This 'objective' knowledge is technical in nature, is measured in terms of its performance value, and is valued in terms of their scarcity and exclusiveness, making it almost marginal for social purposes. He further notes that this notion of 'pure' knowledge separating the 'disinterested' or 'objective' form the social and practical, has in modern times been shaped by the technical rationality rooted into the university culture. Experiential Knowledge and practical skills embodied in social and working life activities are perceived to be at lower levels of the hierarchy as compared to the 'pure' knowledge. The university affirms this hierarchy of knowledge by sustaining existing and creating new "alliances between power and knowledge", as well as "through its capacity of exclusion of certain types of knowledge and certain types of people" (ibid.: 240).

This notion of exclusion of knowledge and people from traditional university culture is increasingly being reflected in form of a *new paradox* of the post-industrial society: While policy makers increasingly claim that the changing nature of work and work life in the advanced industrialised countries requires a highly educated and multi-skilled work force and argue for new innovations of life long learning, the short-term ethos and cost-effective criteria of the 'social market' lead either to the exclusion of the majority from higher education, or to the marketing of education as a product, again excluding those who cannot afford it. It seems that 'exclusion' has taken another form, but the notions of 'scarcity' and 'exclusiveness' of knowledge still hold as firmly as ever. What is new to this paradox is that 'scientific' rationality of exclusion is being replaced by the rationality of the 'social market'. The 'exclusion' is now being determined by the 'short-term' ethos of the social market, and the degree of exclusion is determined by the criteria of cost effectiveness rather than the traditional criteria of 'pure' knowledge, as if the 'new exclusion' were more transparent and therefore more democratic. Whiston notes that the consequences of this exclusion are that society may not fully benefit from the long-term horizons of educational input to the dissemination and absorption of knowledge into a culture, while at the same time creating another 'mismatch problem' between the short-term perspective of the political process and the long-term fundamental social needs. The danger is that the social market agenda of OECD countries may lead to the legitimation of this agenda and its predominance at a global level, thereby separating the educational processes from the development process for the developing countries, irrespective of the fact that they are at a different historical phase of social and economic development than the OECD countries.

There seem to be a perceived wisdom that ICTs can be shaped to overcome the limitations of the short-termism of the social market by including the majority of citizens within the information society networks such as the internet, superhighways, and telematics (see for example, Bangemann 1994). This perceived wisdom, based on the faith in technological infrastructures and cheapness of information transmission, fails to grasp the essential condition of knowledge transfer, that the diffusion of mass information can only contribute to sustainable development if societies possess the educational and learning infrastructures which support the dissemination and absorption of knowledge. ICTs may have the potential for minimising the knowledge and technology transfer barriers through the formation of mutually beneficial information and knowledge networks. However this developmental role of ICTs is very much linked to the educational resources, skills and expertise of both the donor and the recipient. For example Whiston (1992) emphasises that the idea of a sustainable information society requires complementary relationships between the formal learning infrastructures and mass media. In the case of knowledge transfer between the industrialised countries and developing countries, the balance of these relations will however depend upon the ownership and intent. This requires a considerable 'value change' on the part of both the developing countries and the developed countries. For example a mass media dedicated to the spread of a 'social market' and economic competitiveness may enforce a view point which may be alien to the needs and aspirations of peoples and societies in many developing countries. Whiston further notes that children reared on Western television (or cinema) may acquire a viewpoint that reinforces an earlier era that may become obsolescent - or have become obsolescent. This may lead to unforeseeable consequences. Personal choice and individual choice may be hallmarks of democracy, "yet there remains an haunting suspicion that the reality of effects, the aggregate influence of this wider media is not all that one would wish. . .". (ibid.: p63).

It is important to note that international trends of knowledge networking has always been to improve the comparative advantage of the advanced industrialised nations, and the globalisation of communications and information networking developments is no different. It continues to develop along contemporary trajectories. Whiston argues that this network dualism in terms of both intra and inter-characteristics will not bridge the gap between the technological centre and the periphery, and is thereby likely to compromise global sustainability. Some of the major characteristics of the old trajectory have been the knowledge barrier, the technology transfer barrier and trade barrier which have led to inappropriate developments, increasing inequality and poverty, and environmental problems. The danger is that once again poor nations may not be able to develop human resources and thereby remain excluded from this new technological potential. Whiston emphasises the centrality of education for development and quotes a recent World Bank Report (1991) which commences its section entitled "investing in People" with a quotation from K'han-Tzu (551A79 BC) which states:

> "If you plan for a year, plant a seed. If for ten years, plant a tree. If for a hundred years teach the people. When you sow a seed once, you will reap a single harvest. When you teach the people, you will reap a hundred harvests" (ibid.: 27).

The significance of this message has until now been reflected by the move towards universal education and major scientific and technological strides which have been made especially by the OECD countries. However, we now see a growing gap between resource allocation for education and the increasingly recognised need a more educated, flexible and highly skilled populace and work force. ICTs in the form of the Telematics programme of the EU provide a model for developing new forms of networks of education and training to fill the developmental gap. It is important to recognise that the EU network programmes on education and training subscribe to the notions of 'social-market' ethics, which means that "the time delay effects of educational input into society are such that often long-term consequences reach far beyond the more limited time horizons of those with political-tenure" (ibid.: 31). This 'mismatch' between the long-term horizons of societal benefits of the education process and the short-term horizon of political and commercial benefits of resource allocation illustrates the limitations of the social market ethos and the dilemma of the global competitivity. If this 'mismatch' can be overcome through the shaping of the Telematics programme for long-term education and training in the EU, it could also provide a model for long-term process of co-development between the EU and developing countries. The EU with its collaborative research and education network programmes for Latin America, Asia, Eastern Europe and Africa is already building a long term basis for sustainable development. These network collaborations can act only as a catalyst for bridging the gap between technological innovations and their diffusion in the wider society. The ICTs and media technologies have the potential to enhance and speed up the process of knowledge and technology transfer and thereby shorten the time span between scientific development and its diffusion in the wider society. Multimedia technologies offer a potential for informal education and learning; they are a tool for overcoming the barriers of formal education and the mismatch of the production of knowledge and its diffusion, and open new learning and training horizons for those who may otherwise be excluded from the system of formal education.

Information Society - some glimpses and challenges

The dominant image of the global information society presents it as a borderless world, dominated by the technological paradigm and economic competitivity. The other image presents it as an interdependent world consisting of technological gaps and economic disparities. The former image promotes universality, technological solutions, and a global market, whilst the latter promotes the 'valorisation' of diversity, social innovation and economic cohesion.

The Borderless World
Kennedy (1993) gives a stimulating insight into the global technological and human dilemmas, and some of the issues on the borderless world and the media society are summarised below. He notes that the idea that we are entering into an era in which there are only global technologies and economies, global products and industries, must be bewildering to the vast majority of citizens whose life sustainability, hopes, fears and aspirations, and even survival all depend upon their own national social, economic and political structures and cultural foundations. While the logic of the 'global technology and economy' may be eminently plausible for global competitivity, it must also be complemented by the logic of codevelopment rooted in the diversity of social and cultural innovations. Otherwise, the consequences are that local communities and in some cases nations are increasingly ceding control of their social and economic destiny. Indeed, the real 'logic' of the borderless world is that nobody is in control - except the 'global technology', the 'new sovereign'.

Borderless Knowledge Structures
In the industrialised world, new patterns of knowledge structures and a new borderless professional class are emerging. Shaped by media and supported by communication technologies, a new breed of knowledge professionals such as communication consultants, lawyers, biotechnology engineers, economics editors, software designers, and strategic planners, have become 'added value' professionals, serving the interests and demands of the global market. Unlike the local school teacher, the nurse, local planner, blue collar worker or the local shopkeeper, their 'added value' is no longer linked to a regional or even a national economy. We are again seeing the emergence of knowledge professionals who are serving the needs of the global market outside the social and cultural bases of societies, and beyond the social and economic horizons of ordinary citizens, communities and even nations. If this trend of the all embracing globalisation of technology and knowledge continues to exclude the majority of citizens and communities, there is a danger of increasing social, cultural and political instability. This demands a new symbiosis between technological innovations, educational systems and social structures to attain sustainability of the local-global nexus while enabling individual creativity and social innovation. This requires the creation of new forms of cultural interfaces for supporting global harmony and cultural diversity (Gill, 1994, 95).

Re-inventing another dominant global reference system
Petrella (1991) notes the dangers of placing an increasing emphasis on a 'homogenised technocratic world' which does not recognise the diversity of cultures and regions. He argues that the challenge of the information society is to harness information and communication technologies for creating a borderless world. The harnessing of ICTs to

create a borderless world may be a noble aim but the dominant electronic village model of internets, virtual reality and cyborgs tends to create an illusion of local identity and global harmony through technical slogans such as 'network delivery', 'inter-connectivity', 'integration', 'personal space and global integration'. For example, if one situates local identity within cyberspace, one is taking it out of the social space and, in effect, shifting the purpose of local identity from a social process to a mechanism of technology transfer. Social progress is no longer about creating social structures and social knowledge bases but about coping with life cycles of technology. It freezes social learning and fails to recognise the diversity of the present and the uncertainty of the future. It reduces the complex social process of social innovation into a series of independently measurable technological products which may be organised into various permutations to suit the consumer needs of the day. This notion of 'technological determinism' limits the vision of the present and freezes the future in terms of the past, thus seeking respectability of the 'predetermined learning' in the name of the natural phenomenon of human destiny.

The Cyborg Future?
The recent electronic shaping of industrial cultures gives us a glimpse into the rise of 'electronic functionality' as the 21st Century's tool of governance. Artificial intelligence recasts human relations from the social to the symbolic; information technology defines social and economic wealth in terms of units of information and thereby categorises societies into information poor and information rich; the cyborgs offer a boundariless world where the individual has no social or cultural roots; communication technologies offer the globe as a market of individual opportunities; virtual reality offers virtual tools for redesigning the human itself with no ethical constraints and no obligations.

Can we shape the electronic revolution to support social innovation and create new forms of working, living and learning? Or is the era of electronic cottages, teleshoping, distance learning, remote working, virtual design, remote manufacture, virtual planning and electronic management once again going to cause a separation between the private and public, the individual and the community, technology and society, and in this process exclude the majority of citizens and, in some cases, whole nations from social and economic progress.

At a global level, the debate on the information society identifies the gaps of economic and social development between information rich and information poor societies, and leads to the idea of the equality of access to information in order to narrow this gap. This idea of equality centres around the access to technology and information which is controlled by its producers. It ignores the reality that the majority of citizens are unlikely to have access to technology, and that those who may have this access are unlikely to share knowledge and information on an equitable basis. The idea of the equality of information exchange may be true of academia and industry, but it certainly excludes ordinary citizens from its equality equation.

The Paradox of the Media society

The homily of the 'information revolution' goes like this: the world is becoming smaller and interaction between people of diverse cultures and nations is increasing; global networks will link every citizen of the globe, sharing virtual space, knowledge, and cultures; the globe is becoming one big family sharing the same popular culture, same media and technological language. Two scenarios are presented as an outcome of this global communication: i) a potential for hostility and conflict; and ii) a potential source of co-operation and harmony in the world. In both cases, it is suggested that the Western System (popular culture, linguistic, economic, industrial, and political) has become the only dominant reference system for all global developments, thanks to the ICT revolution (Huntingdon, Samuel P., *The Clash of Civilisations?*, in Foreign Affairs, vol. 72, nr Summer 1993, pp 22-49). It is interesting to note that both of these scenarios are based on the assumption that since technology is Western and so is the industrial culture, the only way forward is either a 'homogenised technocratic world' or a world of ethnic/religious tribalism. So it follows that the developmental model for a prosperous and harmonious world is the global technocratic model based on the Western techno-centric model. Hence the new challenge for the technocratic elite is to harness ICTs to achieve this universal cultural goal.

Just like the global market place, the homily of the global network talks about access to every citizen of the world to the vast global information and knowledge base. Development in this vision of globalisation is seen in terms of the very Western concept of individual choice - the individual has the choice of sharing cultures and pooling resources, and creating a system of democratic participation. In this democratic system the public can always exercise its free choice in the market-place, just like it can choose not to own a satellite dish, rent a tv cable link car or own a computer. But even in this utopian scenario of choice, for those who can make a choice to link into the computer network, the reality is that the network keeps running merrily along without any public interference, so the only choice you have is whether or not to remove yourself entirely from the system. By the time we get to notice what is happening, we have already become so encircled by these technologies that it is profoundly difficult to see outside them or to remember that it was once another way. Here lies a dilemma of the global network: there are only two choices, either you get connected to the network or you remain excluded from the information society and the future itself. If you are already connected to the network, then the only choice available to you is to remain connected at any price, otherwise join the world of the 'excluded'. In this narrow world view of the global information society, the danger is that 'development' may be seen in terms of 'being connected' rather than seeing information and communication technologies (ICTs) as potential resources for co-development.

But the problem is more complex than merely linking and de-linking from the network. Global networks create artificial environments, in which we becomes uprooted from our own contexts, become part of the virtual space, floating unconnected, adrift, living in our own virtual reality and utterly dependent on network technology for sustenance, survival and knowledge. Just like processed food is reaching us from far away places, the knowledge we may have is indirect, processed, mediated, digested for us through television and other mass media. Our lives are increasingly being spent totally in a process of interacting with our own creations, the products of our own minds. We live inside them, we relate to them, we use them, we become them. *We co-evolve with them* (Jerry Mander, 1994).

Creating a New Culture of the Artificial?

Are we creating a new culture of the artificial in which the traditional issue of human-machine interaction, usability, human-machine symbiosis, and the cybernetic feedback have become part of the technological history. In this culture of the global artificial, we are all cognitive beings. Human identity, values, and beauty reside in the representation of the cognitive product and its interpretation to suit the cognitive space.

The increasing penetration of new technology raises ethical and moral issues which cannot just be treated in terms of technological efficiency and market forces. Issues such as commercial patentability of a micro-organism and Intellectual Property Rights (IPR), medically assisted procreation (i.e. gene transplants or gene manipulation), genetic code identification, and electronic networking, disturb the very social, cultural, moral and ethical balance which sustains humans and societies (STOA, *Bioethics in Europe*, Science and Technology Options, European Parliament, Luxembourg, 1992). Although these issues are fundamentally social and moral, they are presented and implemented in technological terms and the criteria for judgement is dominated by economic and cost consideration. Technologists also tend to influence public opinion and decision makers in favour of adopting technological solutions to social and economic problems by arguing the case for technological revolutions as the source of human well-being and prosperity." Technology will do" is the slogan which suits both the technologist and the producer of technology.

The Dream of the Post-Industrial Society

Toulmin (1991) places the debate on the dream of the post-industrial society within the wider debate on the shaping of science and technology in the Western tradition. The shaping of science and technology, he emphasises, is rooted in the basic themes of 'the dream of the exact language', 'one best way' and the 'sameness of science'. Through its 'dream of the exact language', the 'ideal of certainty', and 'rational method', the artificial machine expounds the dream of the 'symbolic man', replacing the 'natural, by the artificial'. Does the charm of the *artificial* lie in its *characteristica universallis* eluding to the supposed liberation of the individual from the realities, complexities and uncertainties of diversity?, Toulmin asks. Does this charm lie in its outlining the contours of 'secular technological culture' and transcending the national, cultural, linguistic and religious boundaries? (ibid.: 36). Or is the 'technological dream' about the celebration of the dream of the separation of the individual and the community, private and public, reason and the emotion, function and the social, work and living, technology and society? Or is it about redefining and redirecting societal issues and the social agenda in terms of the culture of 'sameness' and the science of the 'one best way'?

Whereas in the past technology had a much longer time scale of innovation than the human life cycle, societies had a much longer period to disseminate, experiment, reflect and absorb technological innovations. As the human life span has increased, the life cycle of technological innovations has shortened to the extent that a serious mismatch has emerged between technological innovation and societies. This mismatch between the human and machine cycles puts societies, especially of the developing world into difficult dilemmas. Until the arrival of the internet and 'virtual' networks, the world built upon the culture of Walt Disney's Donald Duck which gave us Coca Cola, the Denim Jean and the IBM, at least had a physical reality; societies could still make choices, interpret and reflect upon them, absorb and sometimes reinvent them in their own socio-economic contexts. Now that the physical is being turned into the 'virtual', the confusion between the 'Donald Duck' culture and the 'virtual reality' blurs further the scientifically objective. This confusion of objectivity, in losing the capacity to distinguish between the physical object and the virtual object, between the seeing and 'seeing as', between the sensuality and the sensory, first creates an allusion of the sameness, may that be language, culture, knowledge, economics, history or politics, and then creates a 'virtual reality' to substantiate the new universal culture.

The illusion of the technological dream

Salvation, people are told, lies in technology. Competitive technological innovation in global markets imposes itself as the only effective regulator of the logic of dynamic of the fight for survival (Kennedy: 77). The novelty of recent microelectronics technology lies in the nature and the way in which it has penetrated the main pillars of human society, and the way our knowledge of the world and our actions are being shaped by it. The new technology has influenced the design and production of goods (automation, AI); the way we manage animals, plants and human bodies (drugs, genetic engineering etc.); the way we interact and communicate (computer networks, multimedia); and the way we express our individual and collective creativity (virtual reality, imaging, computer animation). (The Social and Economic Impact of New Technology, Society and Technology Towards the Future, 2 volumes, FAST (EC), 1991). The glorification of the Information and Communication technologies (ICTs) is glamorised in terms of hyper-definitions such as "information society", "paperless society", "information economy", informediation society", "information technology paradigm", "information is power", "information poor and information rich societies". But the reality of the "information society" is that a huge explosion and globalisation of financial and business services have taken place, and market forces have been seen as the main vehicle for social and economic transformation. ICTs have also contributed to the redesigning of firms and countries' industrial cultures, leading to the crisis of employment, social, welfare and educational services. It has also led to an increasing concentration of the access of information decision making and control of power, resulting in the further marginalization and exclusion of the majority of citizens in many industrialised countries. This however, has not the slightest impact on the ever bulging army of techno-utopias and technology fixes invading and dominating the global scene.

In its naive form, the electronic superhighway creates an illusion of local identity and global space through the use of technical slogans such as 'network delivery', 'inter-connectivity', 'integration', 'personal space and global integration'. It shifts the purpose of local identity from a social process to a mechanism of technology transfer. Social innovation is no longer about creating social structures and social knowledge bases but about coping with life cycles of technology. This view of social innovation abandons any illusion of the future and life after tomorrow. The electronic network can only handle predetermined inputs (the past) and is incapable of producing outputs which fit into the uncertain future. The danger of this suspension of the future and building the present in the image of the past is to deny humans of their future and their creativity, imagination, aspiration, consciousness, ideology and self development. This freezing of social learning is rooted in the inability of the scientific 'reductionism' and the biological 'determinism' to recognise diversity of the present and the uncertainty of the future. It reduces complex social process of social innovation into a series of independently measurable technological products which may be organised into various permutations to suit the consumer needs of the day. This notion of 'determinism' limits the vision of the present and the freezes the future in terms of the past, thus seeking respectability of the 'predetermined learning' in the name of the natural phenomenon of human destiny.

Overcoming the Culture of Exclusion

'Internet' or 'superhighways' as an embodiment of the global information society creates in its own orthodoxy of exclusion. Holderness (1994) comments that the net paradoxically offers both an egalitarian and voluntarist culture, and the culture to join a self-defined elite. *Exclusivity* is important. (Mike Holderness, Perspective, *The Times Higher*, April 22, 1994). This exclusivity may appear to be paradoxical, but it is no more paradoxical than the exclusivity rooted in the mechanistic world view of scientific rationality. Advanced technological societies, let alone the developing world, are enmeshed into the mechanistic paradigm of development. This paradigm is expressed in terms of two powerful notions of exclusion: the notion of 'productive functionality' and 'the ideology of efficiency'. The view of 'productive functionality' has been shaped by two powerful industrial processes, the mechanisation of industry and the bureaucratisation of organisations, both of which are rooted in the mechanistic world view. This world view enshrines the notions of 'one best way' of action, 'the one, the only way' of thinking, and 'the one best solution'. The notions of the 'one best way' form the basis of the methodologies of 'exclusion'. While this functional world view has led to increasing production and consumption and new possibilities of autonomy, especially in the industrial world, its has also led to an increasing alienation of individuals and communities from enhancing their potential and affecting change. Citizens, communities, and societies which are unable to contribute to industrial productivity are excluded from consultation and participation in decision making processes. This is now evidenced throughout the European Community which is struggling with problems of social and economic exclusion arising out of increasing unemployment, brittleness of welfare services, and increasing social and racial tensions. Although the problems of exclusion are prominently recognised in the Fourth Framework of the European Community (199-98), the ideological strait-jacket of the 'one best way' is still being used for excluding the design and use of science and technology which does not fit into the mechanistic criteria of quantitative measurement such as regularity, precision, speed, efficiency, and thereby excludes people and societies which do not fit into the ideology of 'productive functionality', in other the words the ideology of global market

Those individuals and communities who are not 'productive' have become mere observers to the technological and bureaucratic innovations. The 'productive functionality' redefines the nature and purpose of work, from 'social utility' to 'economic disutility'. In this view of 'productive functionality' human work and social provision are regarded just any part of the industrial production, obeying the rules of production and consumption. What happens when, as we are now witnessing, the level and quality of industrial production cannot be sustained and industrial decline leads to social pessimism? Does this mean that neither human work nor social provision can any longer be sustained even at the present levels? Has not the very existence of the social and cultural systems already become dependent on the sustainability of the technological systems?

Recent technological innovations in the form of electronic networking, virtual reality and cyborgs give us a glimpse of the electronic shaping of bureaucratic innovation. In the name of 'productive efficiency', we may already be witnessing the rise of 'electronic functionality', as the 21st Century tool of governance. In the realm of the innovations of new technology, artificial intelligence recasts human relations from the social to the symbolic; information technology defines social and economic wealth in terms of units of information and thereby categorises societies into information poor and information rich; the cyborgs offer a boundariless world where individual has no social or cultural roots; global networks regard the globe as a market of individual opportunities; virtual reality offers virtual tools for redesigning the human itself with no ethical constraints and no obligations. 'Electronic Fordism' in the form of computer networks, for example electronic mail, is bridging the gap between the technological and management of change innovations. We are in the era of electronic cottages, information transfer, distance learning, remote working, virtual design, remote manufacture, virtual planning and electronic management (Gill 1993, Haraway 1990, Petrella 1991).

The danger is that in the virtual world of illusion (of reality), work and living may no longer be regarded as social, cultural or even economic concepts, they may well be just regarded as electronic concepts, totally explicit, symbolic, certain, quantifiable and measurable. There may no longer be any no room for intuition, creativity, uncertainty, error, initiative. The danger of an electronic world view is that neither the governance nor the governed would be left with the capacities and capabilities of dealing with the complex and diverse social, cultural, political and economic issues arising out of the industrial decline and the breaking down of the civic, social and cultural boundaries of industrial societies. The cost of the ideology of 'efficiency' may be very high. It is time to reflect on social and human cost of the ideology of 'productive functionality' which has far too long shaped the technological and bureaucratic innovations, and seek alternative concept of 'social utility' as the guiding principle for social innovations.

Bonding without Frontiers?

Morley and Robins (1995) discuss the role of information and communication technologies in shaping new communications landscapes and creating a global space of information flows, a symbolic language and cultural boundaries. The globalisation of communications space and localisation of the cultural identity raises a new tension between globalism and localism, in which local cultures and identities are seen as "an inflexion of global culture that favours diversity, plurality and discontinuity" (ibid.: 2). They note this tension in the European project of 'Europe without frontiers' which encompasses the notions of 'unity in diversity', solidarity, and common destiny, and at the same time gives rise to "cultural regionalism and small nationalisms (Basques, Scots, Bretons and so on)" (ibid.: 3). Europe is experiencing a process of economic and social transformation which is weakening older institutions and structures. The geography of Europe - economic, political and cultural - is being refashioned in the context of even more apparent global-local nexus. On the one hand this nexus offers a "great scope and potential for elaborating new forms of bonding: new sense of community, new attachments and allegiances and new identities". The challenge is how to harness information, communication and media technologies which support this vision of the global-local nexus while facilitating dialogue between "communities of common interest and communities of difference" (ibid.: 5).

What we are beginning to see is a much more fundamental process of transformation, in which the entertainment and information business are converging with the communications industry. The aim of the superhighway is on the one hand to push the process of standardisation to the limit, and on the other, to move us beyond the era of mass media into that of personalised media and individual choice (ibid.: 14). However, personalised media and individual choice will be dictated by the market, through delivering 'personalised' and 'individualised' services to specialised and 'niche' markets while pushing the frontiers of cultural and linguistic 'homogenisation' through marketing the culture of the 'global village'. While global networks push towards greater standardisation and homogenisation, there are contrary forces at work which challenge the imperative of globalisation, as exemplified by the "resurgent interest in regionalism in Europe, appealing to the kind of situated meaning and emotional belonging that appear to have been eroded by the logic of globalisation. This new regionalism puts value on the diversity and difference of identities in Europe, and seeks to sustain and conserve the variety of cultural heritage, regional and national" (ibid.:.17). The European Community's debates on European identity and citizenship reflect the dilemmas of the global-local nexus. New alliances of local and regional identities mark a preference for a particularistic sense of community. The notion of 'unity through diversity' holds up 'rich pluralism' of regional traditions, languages, dialects and cultures as the basis of a more meaningful experience of the community. It is also seen as a European project working against the tide of homogenisation which threatens the very idea of European culture. The dilemma of globalisation for Europe is how the transition from the past project of 'universalism' to a new sense of 'European particularism(s) can be achieved without the danger of finding a refuge in a European "fortress identity and a superstate mentality". Here the language of the European Community's 1992 project on 'integration' , such as cohesion, community, unity, integration and security illustrates a possibility of a "new European order defined by a clear sense of its own coherence, and integrity" as a counter to the global world order. Thus if globalisation exposes a powerful region like Europe to a crisis of cultural identity and citizenship, how can developing regions of Asia, Africa and Latin America flourish in a new world order?

Wittrock (1992) considers the dilemmas of the transition from the modern industrial cultures of Europe to the present era of 'extended modernity'. He points out that "prominent institutions of the organised modernity, be they the system of political parties, of interest organisations, and even nation states - is loosening. Thus individuals may experience a sense of disembededness, of disenchantment with those institutions that have appeared as the major carriers of social trust for a century or more" (ibid.: 136). This loosening process is part of the restructuring of institutions in the wake of the microelectronics and communications revolution. Whereas in the past, the collaboration of the universities, firms and the state was more imbued with national concerns. They were more closely tied together on the national level, but their activities are now becoming more transnational and global. The role of universities is shifting from education and research to high quality training institutions, building skills, competencies and knowledge that are deemed to be of strategic importance to economic and societal performance. The other two elements of modernity, the modern corporation and the modern nation state, are also caught up in the globalisation trap. Both of them are losing their own natural advantages and spatial niches and have to seek links at regional and global levels to find an appropriate place in the global economy. This search for global competencies and knowledge by universities, and a competitive place by corporation and nations states in the global market may very well serve the purpose of technological and economic competitivity, but "it leaves open the crucial questions of the nature of political order and cultural identity in the period of extended modernity" (ibid.: 137). These questions are now even more crucial as the very notion of the nation state as consisting of a relatively homogeneous people has become incompatible with the aspirations, needs and interests of large groups from different cultures, linguistic diversities, and "minority communities". The fundamental questions of individual identity and cultural diversity go far beyond the global issues of technological and economic competitivity, they are at the very heart of social sustainability itself. The problem is that globalisation like virtual reality may further widen the gap between the social realities and virtual economies. The challenge of development is how to achieve compatibility between the sustainability of societies and global nature of science and technology.

Just like other technologies, information and communication technologies can play a part in social and economic innovations. ICTs can be shaped to serve not only professional and scientific functions but also to build knowledge networks, combining the capacity of ICTs and the capabilities of human information networks. The issue here is not just that ICTs It is, however, important to recognise that new directions in interntaional networking for codevelopment, an internationalisation of fraternity, a feeling of communality, and an international kinship, in the spirit of 'valorisation of diversity'. However, the more marketable commodity knowledge becomes, the more 'intellectual property rights' intrude upon scientific endeavour, the more development is seen as blind of diversity and difference, the more rapidly that fraternity breaks down.

Diversity in the Common Cultural Space

The emerging world of information networks and networks of economies is presented as representatives of the post-industrial world and as an alternative to Fordism. In this post-Fordist world, 'flexible specialisation', is manifest in new forms of decentralised production and niche markets in which economies of scope replace economies of scale and workers acquire skills of flexibility, adaptability and regain a new sense of autonomy. The network model of 'Third Italy' (Emilio Romgna region of Italy) is offered as an exemplar of regional economy based on the decentralised networks of small artisan based companies using new computing technologies (Mitter, 1992.: 10). Here the local-global nexus is seen very much a continuum of the post-Fordist era of decentralisation of production, flexible specialisation, and the emergence of economies of scope, such as the centre-periphery interdependence between dominant companies linked to the small and medium size companies in contractor/subcontractor relationships. information and communication technologies are seen to map onto the networks of economies , facilitating the exchange transfer, sharing and dissemination of knowledge, skill and expertise. The logic of flexible specialisation and customer based standardisation is extended by communication technologies to the social and cultural spaces as part of the drive towards globalisation of economies. For example, the television channel and the Cable News Network (CNN) "exploit local difference and particularity. Cultural products are assembled all over the world and turned into commodities for a 'cosmopolitan' marketplace: world music and tourism; ethnic arts, fashion and cousine; third world writing and cinema" (Morley & Robins, op. cit: 113). This move towards both economies of scale and economies of scope illustrates the power and scope of the global media industries to determine not only the future shape of cultural spaces but also the shape of the local-global nexus of economies. On one hand these economies of scale ignore the difference and otherness of local and regional cultures, and on the other hand the economies of scope give recognition to the diversity of cultures and otherness through the production of cultural products. The dilemma here is that diversity and otherness become just another form of representation, and ultimately become a visual representation forming a part of the 'virtual reality', thereby ignoring social, economic and political realities of peoples who are excluded and marginalised.

Morley and Robins note that these visions of post-Fordism perceive the transformation of the centralised space into new forms of decentralisation and dissemination. What we are moving towards, they argue, is a fundamentally delocalised world order articulated around a small number of "concentrated centres for the production of knowledge and storage of information as well as centres for the emission of images and information" (Castells, 1983 qouted by ibid: 29). The consequences, Castells believes, is "the formation of a new historical relationship between space and society" (Castells, 1983 qouted by ibid: 29). In this new space global centred corporations such as Sony and Microsoft, and global communication empires such as those of Murdoch or Bertelsmann, produce products on the global assembly lines aimed at world markets. The core thesis of the global assembly line is the externalisation of risks and exploitation of local and regional cultural resources (ibid.: 33). In this sense there is no contradiction between the localisation of production and its dissemination at a global level: a new form of local-global nexus based on the plurality of cultures at the local level and its valorisation at the global level. This view of local-global nexus allows for the distribution of the local cultures as an integral component of the dynamic global cultural network. It seems that this new era of culture is seen as another form of information flow within the global communication and media networks. This emerging symbiosis between the local plurality and global integration may prove to be a sustainable model for 'unity in diversity'.

This local-global nexus is at the heart of the 'European Home' project, building a common knowledge and skill base linking universities, SMEs, cities, and regions under the EU programmes such as Socrates and Leonardo. The larger vision of the European project is about the creation of a common economic and cultural space based on "common cultural roots as well as social and economic realities" (Commission of the European Communities, 1983:3). The emphasis is on "maintaining and promoting the cultural identity of Europe", of "improving mutual knowledge among our peoples and increasing their consciousness of the life and destiny they have in common" (Commission of the European Communities, 1988:3, 11) (ibid.: 35). The focus on cultural and economic spaces in the European project illustrates an increasing awareness of the place of diversity and its valorisation as against the forces of homogenisation and standardisation being brought out by the convergence of information, communication and media technologies. While emphasising the local and regional identities of Europe and at the same time supporting global communication and media industries, the European project seeks a symbiosis between the local and the global both within the European as well as in the global contexts. Here the individual is both a part of the local and the global, being situated within a particular social and cultural space, while identifying with virtual social and cultural spaces mediated by the ICTs and media technologies. This symbiosis recognises that local identity remains mediated by the shared social and cultural spaces, while global identity is mediated by the communication and media technologies. At a certain level, this relationship between the local and global identities is a continuum of the symbiotic relationship of the subjective and the objective, with the subjective remaining rooted in the human domain and the objective becoming increasingly embedded in the technological domain. The difference, however, is that while the objective has until now been mediated by human experience, the virtual is only mediated by technology. If virtual reality is about blurring of the subjective and the objective, then it is also about the blurring the local and global. The issue here is not of the valorisation of diversity of local identities but the globalisation of a particular local/regional identity through control of the communication and media technologies. It is in this context that the debate on the information society, involving an integrated vision of culture, technology and economy, is dominated by the issues of ownership and control of the infrastructure on the one hand and the creation of European cultural and economic spaces on the other hand. Morley and Robins note the 'interrelationship between the economy, technology and culture (CEC, 1987: 3) and raise a question: "Can the new communications media really be so unproblematically and starightforwardly instrumental in promoting a cohesive and coherent Europe for the twenty-first century?" (ibid.: 77). The paradox of this technology and cultural cohesion is that it promotes borderless communication and media technologies in the name of common cultural space, while at the same time defending national and regional boundaries in the name of diversity. This European paradox is what will shape the reality of information society in Europe. Communication and media infrastructures cannot in themselves be either determinants or mediators of common economic and cultural spaces, they are just one of many social and technological determinants which vary from society to society and culture to culture. The infrastructure may be global but its applications and impacts can only be determined by the local human condition. The local and regional determinants include unemployment, poverty, exclusion and inequality. This is in addition to culture, language, and social and economic factors. Replacing human infrastructures of social welfare, health, education, and training by information technology may expand and speed up information flows and create virtual spaces of global cultures, it is unlikely to solve any deep social, economic or political problems.

Diversity and Cohesion: a framework for technology shaping

The process of social and economic cohesion of Europe illustrates the dilemmas and opportunities of diversity (*AI & Society*, vol 8.2, 1995). For example the process of economic integration raises issues of integrating diversified patterns of innovation in the national and regional economies, while supporting regional innovation based on increasing regional diversity. We need a new vision of social and economic cohesion in which *diversity drives evolution, and evolution generates diversity*. In this vision, diversity is described not only in terms of the diversity of products, production processes, organisational forms, and customer characteristics but also in terms of local processes of innovation, education and learning, organisation of change processes, and social diffusion of science and technology.

Cohendet and Lierena's discussion on 'cohesion' (1994) broadens the debate on the 'European Home' within a broader framework of EU policies on technology and cohesion. They note that European cohesion policy is led by the belief that technological policies must contribute to the achievement of a greater cohesion throughout the EC. The increasing focus on cohesion emphasises that the lack of economic integration hinders the proper functioning and deteriorates the performances of European markets. It is argued that there is still a high degree of dispersion of technological development and significant differences of growth and productivity among European countries. It is however recognised that such differences relate interactively to their complexity of social, institutional, and regulatory conditions. Given that the global aim of the EU is economic competitivity, the question is how the concept of cohesion fits into this global aim, and how it can be used to minimise the social and economic disparities between regions, and how cohesion can provide a basis for the integration of all innovative and creative efforts, while maintaining a certain diversity.

Cohesion in this wider global perspective deals with both integration and diversity, in the sense of 'valorisation of diversity', in other words making the most of the commonalities while respecting the differences. Any discussion on cohesion meets two extreme attitudes towards diversity. On the one hand, diversity is generally identified as an obstacle to exploiting economies of scale. This view focuses on a reduction of disparities and argues for the implementation of the best practice model of production at the European level. On the other hand, diversity is said to present a central component of a 'resource pool', which stimulates innovation, creativity, and thereby supports the economy of scope and sustainable competitivity. This view argues for the valorisation of diversity as a guarantee to compete and to survive in the presence of uncertainty.

These two attitudes towards diversity pose a policy dilemma for the EU, for example what role should diversity play in social cohesion, economic development and technological change?, and what are the sources of diversity and what mechanisms can be used to generate or reduce diversity, and in what ways can diversity be valorised? Cohendet and Llerena point out that traditional economics deals with problems of equilibrium and with the mechanisms which make the economy ordered and coherent. Here the idea of diversity (e.g. opportunity costs) is rather limited and it is a rather well-behaved sort of diversity. Diversity primarily becomes important when the focus is on how the equilibrium is disturbed and the economy changes over time, rather than on how it holds together. It is suggested that diversity may be the starting point or a catalyst for an equilibrium process, but it plays no role as a long run mover of the system. (ibid.: 110)

This passive approach to diversity is also a feature of the traditional focus of technology transfer. It is pointed out by Cohendet and Llerena that technology is considered as an information which is available for all and freely floats across national borders. What matters is the availability of the 'best technology', and therefore its adaptation, usage, and diffusion are a matter of time lags rather than industrial and cultural contexts in which technology is developed or implemented. It is argued that since the concept of technology is global, local technologies play a marginal role. Moreover, local technologies are 'deduced' by marginal adaptations from the "ideal" model of the 'best technology'. In this perspective the influence of the local context on the modes and usage of technology can be regarded as 'passive' and marginal, because it consists of local adaptations of the 'best technology' to fit local habits and tastes.

In contrast to the above passive approach to diversity, the evolutionary approach to diversity emphasises a close linkage between diversity of competencies and learning processes. It also recognises that there are intrinsic relationships between technology and institutions. There is however a tension which naturally arises from the interaction between on the one side the functioning of organizations (stimulated by procedures of incentives and coordination) which is a source of diversity, and on the other side processes of diffusion and technological interdependence (lock-in effects, positive feed-backs, path-dependency, cumulative learning, convergence mechanisms, etc. . ..) which are sources of uniformisation. Keeping the right balance between these two processes is certainly the key to economic efficiency. There is a real question of time in this problem of balance. There is a time for experimenting with technologies through standardisation and norms which requires uniformisation. The very problem is to favour the collective capability to assure the transition from diversity to standardisation at the right moment. Should for instance the mechanisms of interdependence (coordination, circulation of information) between agents be lacking, diversity will lead to inefficiency and standardisation would not occur because economic agents refuse to bear the risk of supporting the costs of incompatibility. At the European level, the efficiency should not be appreciated in terms of independence between individuals, but in terms of independence between "local systems of innovation" (Lundvall, 1988 quoted by Cohendet and Llerena, ibid.: 112) which are characterised by a given set of factor endowments, local behaviours, learning processes and institutional frame. The focus has to be on the coordination between the different local systems of innovation.

The problem at the European or even world level, according to Cohendet and Llerena (ibid.: 113) is to specify how such particular local innovation processes and technological trajectories can in some way be coherent themselves. Which mechanisms will allow and generate advantages (or at least no costs) from their simultaneous existence? The advantage of local innovation systems comes from their capacity to mobilise local competencies, to reduce the communication costs and the adaptation costs to local needs and characteristics. The global viability of such a "decentralised" system, with several levels of aggregation and decision centres will depend on its ability to "minimise" the coordination costs, but also and more fundamentally to accumulate (and deccumulate if necessary) the competencies and know-how. In fact, it is an exercise not only of cost minimisation but also of the creation of an adequate "institutional" learning at a more global level.

From an evolutionary perspective, diversity stimulates a dynamic approach to learning and knowledge transfer, thereby providing a broader knowledge base and a spectrum of learning activities. 'This progressive enlargement of the base of knowledge confers to the economic system a better ability to react as quickly as possible to match the speed at which the environmental parameters are changing. It obliges the actors to keep a maximum number of options available (and applicable). The value of diversity as an enlargement of the base of knowledge depends on how the processes of learning are functioning: this may depend on the efficiency of existing institutions. It is clear for instance that without any learning capacity, maintaining of options is of no value.' Information and communication technologies can be used for reducing the costs of storing and processing information as well as for reducing the need for information handling. Producers increase their use of rapidly developing computer and telecommunication technologies. They also change organizational structures in order to reduce the quantity of information that is necessary for them. Flatter organizational structures with more horizontal information flows is sometimes associated with Japanese cultural traits and organizational styles and sometimes with an internationally emerging, new mode of intra-organizational coordination. (ibid.: 115).

It is argued that the diversity-oriented mechanism for technology transfer offers a strong benefit to a diversified community in terms of competitive ability by helping it to master more rapidly the base of knowledge of technology. However, the value of this mechanism is strongly dependent on the ability of each local unit of the community to transform some generic principles into specific knowledge, and then to transmit its own experience of learning and creation to its environment, and more precisely to other units. So the mechanism relies on interactive learning occurring among different local systems of innovation. It also relies on an incentive to exchange information which assumes a collective sharing of the mode of appropriation of the new technology. There are many ways can be used to generate such advantages: on the firm level, it can be through inter-firm agreements, not only in R&D, but also in production. Technological policy, for example at the European level, can facilitate such learning processes. The existence of common institutions, such as collective research centres, can also play a major role in the accumulation of knowledge and know-how (ibid.: 116).

Technology transfer in a diversity oriented framework, however, faces problems of lacking a common language to exploit the potentiality of the new technology, and the risk of incompatibility between different local experiments of technology. If this risk becomes critical, gateways technologies can reduce it. Gateways technologies are technological solutions of compatibility when irreversible processes of adoption of different technologies make the interactive learning mechanism inefficient for allowing natural compatibility. The setting-up of norms is seen as the key to the diffusion process during the process of creation of technology within the network of different local systems of innovation. Norms are considered as a category of public goods: the more producers and consumers respect a given norm, the more one takes advantage of the utilisation of this norm by others. The benefit results in gains on comparability and interchangeability.

Valorising diversity thus implies the development of organisational' devices: norms, gateways technologies, modes of appropriation, 'institutional' gateways like international agencies (ESA, etc. . . .), inter-firm agreements, etc. Cohendet and Llerena propose that the concept of coherence provides a basis for valorising diversity at the European Community level, subject to conditions that some principles of coherence are set-up between the EEC members. They describe a common sense notion of coherence as: "there is a coherence within a network of different local systems of innovation, when the mechanism supporting the exchange of information and experiences between the members of the network and the rules governing the conditions of appropriation of the technologies are sufficient to avoid, at the local and the global level, useless duplication of efforts, misuses of resources and inability to set-up common desirable structures" (ibid.: 119).

Here coherence is said to regulate a 'coherent' network of local systems of innovation at the EC level. It reinforces the ability of each local system to proceed to an interactive learning, defining viable solutions for the collective sharing of the mode of appropriation of new technologies, organising the mechanisms of normalisation and standardisation, anticipating the need for gateways technologies when lock-in mechanisms lead to a non-competitive array of technological solutions. Coherence as a more flexible formulation of cohesion enables the mobilisation of "collective capability to master the tension between the functioning of local organisations, which is a source of diversity and the process of diffusion of innovation which requires standardisation and uniformisation" (ibid.: 119).

Knowledge Networking: a human-centred vision of the Post-industrial Society

The hallmark of the post-industrial society is the accelerating pace at which information and communication technologies are penetrating all facets of societies globally. Although the ICTs may take a much longer time to create social and economic impacts on a scale similar to those of the 'old' technologies such as the car, telephone, radio and television, their impact, is much more multidimensional than these older technologies. The discussion above illustrates some of the dilemmas and paradoxes of the post-industrial society. On the one hand there is talk of the knowledge society and of knowledge as the new social and economic resource, and on the other hand technologies demand and increasing exclusion of both the majority of the world's population (and even nations) and their knowledge from the notions of globalisation. On the one hand there is a talk of the 'local-global nexus' and the creation of common cultural and economic spaces, building upon the notion of the 'valorisation' of diversity, and on the other hand there is an emphasis on standardisation, homogenisation and uniformisation. New technologies, on the one hand, are seen as a medium for social and economic cohesion in Europe, and on the other hand, are seen as an instrument of the 'social market', leading to increasing gaps between the 'haves and 'have-nots' at the individual, local and even regional levels. ICTs and media networks on the one hand provide a social and cultural resource for inclusion of the majority of citizenship in education, training and life long learning, while on the other hand the social market ethos tends to enforce cost effective criteria for technological and social innovations, thereby leading to the exclusion of the majority of citizens from participating in this so called 'information society'. These dilemmas illustrate limitations of the widely shared belief that the *dominant trajectories* of science and technology (S&T) and new forms of information technology and communication systems (in both local, regional and global settings), will shape and determine the 'locality and form' of social and economic progress. We need to reflect on this belief and develop alternative forms of social innovations which transcend the notion that the 'techno-centric' focus of social and economic development is either 'pre-ordained' or predetermined. The human-centred perspective of shaping enables us to view socio-technical innovations within broader societal contexts. Just as technology can be shaped to serve human purpose, so we can shape social and economic innovations to meet the challenges of employment, health, welfare, inequality and poverty. But this requires a fundamental shift in our view of science and technology, a shift from 'causal' science to 'purposive' science (Rosenbrock, 1990). It also requires a fundamental value change on our part, a shift from material wealth to social wealth, a shift from technical innovation to social innovation. Whiston provides an insight into the urgency for such a cultural shift: "This planet and its population are in the very, very early stages of its social evolution: competition and property rights, personal acquisitiveness and self-survival *are* still very much its clarion calls. Hundreds of thousands of individuals starve whilst others worry about whether or not their pension rights are inflation proof. Hundreds of thousands, indeed millions incur almost total blindness when for the cost of a cup of coffee. . . 'Aid' is seen as a donation rather than as a duty (or a return of favour already received)" (ibid.: 109). The complexity of social, economic and political problems is such that a technological fix is no longer either a realistic or a sustainable proposition. "But the mere application of the 'technical fix, approach: via simplistic reliance upon technological solutions to social and economic and even environmental problems is grossly insufficient. For a wider and changed outlook, new institutional structures and possibly a new realpolitik' is necessary" (Herman Kahn, quoted by Whiston, ibid.: 109). This shift will determine our choice of technological and economic trajectories, and thereby the nature of social development itself. The challenge here is how to tame the dominant trajectories of economic and social dualism, and how to shape scientific and technological policies, and turn technological innovations to meet the wider needs of peoples and societies. Could the information society model of the EU be turned into a model of social, economic and cultural networking, a new model of interdependent development both at the EU and global levels? Or, will the Triadic groups, the EU, Japan, and North America, continue to shape economic and technological trajectories to suit their own regional and global circumstances, interests and economic competitiveness? However, the global nature of the post-industrial society, emphasising economies of scope and economies of networks rather than just economies of scale, and emphasising an increasing international networking of information, finance and resources rather than traditional forms of comparative advantage, may also influence the emergence of an interdependent world. In this perspective, innovation, economy of scope and the social shaping of science and technology may become 'controlling and determining' factors of local, regional and global economies and cultures. Whiston argues the case for an interdependent development and notes: "that in the long run the world can neither afford, nor sustain, a system of single minded competitive nations, of local patent rights, of limitation of knowledge, of replicated research at huge cost, Nor can, or should it, seek replicated life styles, replicated cultures, homogenised people and institutions." (ibid.: 110). From this perspective of interdependence, "An integrated-excluded world is not a viable sustainable world; nor is a Regionalised-protectionist one. Knowledge and technology transfer - cutting across existing world barriers can only be favourably improved if all societies maximise their own indigenous educational base. That indigenous educational base simultaneously can lead to the three main requirements of global sustainable developments" (ibid.: 214).

This wider horizon of science and technology transfer reflects a belief in the much wider diffusion of knowledge between societies for mutual benefit. *Whereas the notion of technology transfer has been central to the development of industrial society, knowledge transfer in the wider sense has become a cornerstone of co-development in the post-industrial society.* Just as technical skills and technical training were regarded as determinants for the transfer and use of technology, so are the knowledge and competence now regarded as determinants of knowledge transfer. With "technology *and knowledge transfer.* comes the ability of *all* societies to respond, both in local appropriate -ways and through better, more efficient international collaboration, to the enormous globally-interactive challenges which face the world now and increasingly in the future." (ibid.: 216). There is however a fundamental difference between technology transfer and knowledge transfer. Technology is technically produced and its transfer is explicit and linear. Knowledge is socially produced, it is both objective and tacit, and its transfer is both explicit and non-linear. Knowledge is socially and culturally embedded, it is generative, productive and reproductive; it cannot be codified and explicated as if it were data. Knowledge transfer has to deal with both the objective and the tacit dimensions of knowledge. The tacit dimension consists of both the experiential and personal knowledge, and its transfer is constrained by the social contexts of the experiential knowledge and cultural contexts of the personal knowledge. In many cases the objectified knowledge may not be meaningful without the creation or generation of relevant contexts, and its transfer may again be limited. In general when we talk about knowledge transfer we talk about the transfer of knowledge which is in the public domain, knowledge which is represented and codified in a format which is transferable. We find that even in the case of public knowledge, we create and depend upon informal and formal human networks to facilitate knowledge transfer; both academia and industry facilitate the transfer through formal lectures, tutorial, seminars, workshop and conferences.

This challenge of knowledge networking in the post-industrial society is part of a bigger societal challenge as how to reintegrate technological innovations into the civil society so that technology supports new forms of work life and living environments. Form the perspective of co-development it is also about the valorisation of local and global knowledge and the creation of a local-global nexus of economic and cultural spaces. This requires the innovation of new forms of social structures and organisational cultures which respond and cope with the changing world of work and living.

Chambers (1990: 246-256) notes a shifting of the paradigm among many development researchers from 'blueprint' methods to learning which enshrines participation, sharing of knowledge and experiences, dialogue and empowerment.

Citing Tom Peter's book on *Thriving on Chaos*, and the notions of "delegate and decentralise", Chambers observes a convergent evolution of a new paradigm, decentralisation *and diversity*, which emphasises that development research should be concerned with the socialisation of scientists into participatory approaches. "The challenge is not just to science; it is to see scientists as people". In the same perspective, Castellano (Convergence 19(3), 1986) emphasises the role of participatory research as a systematic effort to expand the pool of knowledge accessible to society. This systematic effort requires a collective engagement of action-reflection, from which knowledge is created. To her, action without reflection is activism. She warns against considering participatory research as a panacea for the multiple problems of development: poverty, political marginality and social breakdown plagues Canadian Native people as well as numerous communities in the Developing countries. Participatory methods, however, can make a major contribution in identifying access points for the community, setting priorities for development, integrating interventions with a variety of factors of community life, and applying the results of laboratory research and surveys.

Morin-Labatut and Akhbar (*Development* 1992:4 - Journal of SID, pp. 24-29) illustrate the complexity of transfer of knowledge between technological cultures and traditional culture and note that the integration of traditional and Western scientific knowledge faces a number of obstacles such as perceptual and language barriers beyond the need to document it and ensure it is widely disseminated. They quote Johnson (1992), "Traditional environmental knowledge is complex, sophisticated, and certainly not homogeneous or "democratic" in itself. It is rooted in specific societies and reflects and affects conflicts and power of struggle of those societies. It is the result of a particular (sometimes very localised) "worldview", and it feeds and nourishes that worldview, reinforcing local beliefs". They argue for wider recognition and application of traditional knowledge beyond environmental problems to issues of health, education and human development. The challenge therefore is how to use ICTs to integrate indigenous knowledge with Western scientific knowledge for development. For example "such a network might facilitate the exchange of data among indigenous organisations, and facilitate their collaboration on research activities and sharing of results, teleconferences to strategize etc., assuming that the technology could be mastered without alienating the users". The integration of traditional knowledge and Western scientific knowledge, however, raises an issue of specificity. Specificity of the traditional knowledge resides in the inter-relationship between knowledge and action. Scientific knowledge on the other hand is characterised by the separation of research and action in time and space, which are the responsibility of different individuals. They stress that the division of labour is fundamental to scientific research, and scientific knowledge lends itself to division into individual components on one hand, and to a high level of abstraction and generalisation on the other. Traditional knowledge, on the contrary, is closely linked to know-how, that of the researcher, practitioner and inventor all rolled into one. ICTs could play an important role in thw virtual globalisation of disparate and geographically mobile communities.

The issues surrounding the integration of indigenous knowledge and scientific knowledge discussed above apply equally to all developmental problems at a conceptual and, in many cases, practical levels, whether they concern developing countries or the developing regions within the European Community. The potential and limitations of ICTs to support the transfer of information and exchange of experiences across cultural and linguistic boundaries again raise issues of local diversities and global integration which are not that conceptually and methodologically distinct for developing countries and the European community. Discussions at a recent European Community sponsored conference, DELTA94 (DGXIII, CEC, Dusseldorf, November 1994) highlighted the importance of the integration of local knowledge and scientific knowledge for developing ICTs for distance learning, distance education and training, for the development of European wide learning organisation, and telecities or learning communities. Participatory research and methodologies of participatory design are regarded as central to the development of developmental ICTs. The irony of ICTs may turn out to be that the participatory approaches of developing countries may provide a potential for applications in the European Community while scientific rationality of the

Western method may retain its potential for collaboration between the developing countries and the European Community.

The cultural shift is already taking place amongst development researchers who treat culture as an inclusive factor in planning rather than as a variable for technology assessment. This culturally rooted participative approach, building on cultural diversity (local specificity and global diversity) is increasingly being seen as a basis for seeking solutions to three core problems - poverty, unemployment, and the marginalisation and disintegration of people and societies. This view of local cultural specificity contributes to the understanding of societies in two ways: i) by providing an "insider" view as against the dominant "outsider" view, which is often distanced from the local culture, and tends to distort reality; and ii) by focusing on the relevance of local problems to local situations, and their social and cultural contexts. However, the challenge is how to create harmony between cultural specificity and global diversity to adapt to the global economic, technological and political changes. This means building local resources and local knowledge bases to deal with global problems which, in an increasingly interdependent world, means sharing models of local experiences and knowledge between and across regions. There is thus a need to develop knowledge networks which enable innovation and sustainability of local knowledge bases while enhancing the process of building a shared common knowledge resource of humanity (Gill, 1995).

This perspective of co-development is as relevant to the European Community, as it is to developing countries. The EU in its Fourth Framework (The EC White Paper, 1993) encompasses social notions such as those of 'valorisation of diversity', cohesion, equality, participation and subsidiarity. These notions situate the European debate on the information society in a broader vision of the knowledge society rather than a popular North American narrow vision of the 'internet society' or 'linking society'. The deep rooted notions of 'harmony', 'sustainability', and 'coherence' provide conceptual tools for the 'valorisation of diversity' in Europe and within pluralistic cultures such as India and China. In a similar way the pluralistic traditions of developing countries such as India and China provide intersecting models of cultural transfer and cultural rationality. The central issue of co-development is that we should recognise that there is both a commonality and diversity in our cultural concepts. It is by gaining a deep understanding of the harmony between these dimensions that we can develop conceptual frameworks for codevelopment and methodological tools for cultural interfaces.

One of the research challenges is to develop the theoretical frameworks and methodologies for transcultural and transnational knowledge transfer. The operational challenge is to establish educational and training frameworks which put into practice the processes of knowledge transfer impacted by the convergences and divergences between economic spaces, cultural spaces and technological systems. Underlying these challenges is a concern that as economic and cultural spaces are becoming more and more interlinked with the globalisation of information, communication and media technologies, there is a danger that the needs, aspirations, interests and hopes of peoples and diverse communities may be determined by the limits of technology rather than by shaping technology for social development. There lies a danger of homogenisation and thereby a danger of conflicts of cultural identity both at the individual, community and societal levels (Gill, 1995).

Knowledge networking is therefore concerned with more than the production and reproduction of knowledge, it is also concerned with the capacity and capabilities of networks to transfer and diffuse this knowledge at local and global levels, in a variety of languages at a variety of competence levels of expression and interpretation. The issue here is to develop a rationality of communication which provides a basis for objectification of diverse knowledge resources residing in the diversity of cultural and social systems. Diversity here is more than a belief in variety; it demands a commitment to a practice of diversity and its 'valorization' (Gill, 1992, 1994).

Diversity within this broader human-centred perspective is about a deep learning experience while sustaining a deep inner coherence of human values, respect, and dignity of human spirit. Without a unique coherence, we cannot agree upon a coherent measurement of technological innovations, and thus cannot achieve 'valorization' of diversity. In the human-centred tradition, this coherence can be achieved through a balance of communication within networks and harmony through networks of relationships; a local-global cultural nexus. This notion of diversity transcends beyond the traditional choice of alternatives and finds coherence in innovation of choices. This coherence of cultural diversity may provide a conceptual framework for knowledge transfer between and across cultural domains.

The notion of human centredness is guided by this coherence and seeks collaboration between human networks and technological networks. It argues that the production and reproduction of knowledge is a social process and is therefore embedded in the culture itself. The ideas and notions underpinning human centredness are the notions of the 'tacit' dimension of knowledge, dialogue, diversity of culture, language, and knowledge, which are also guiding notions of knowledge networking and social innovation.

From this perspective, the common challenge of knowledge networking is sustainable co-development as an alternative to global competitiveness. It is about the social shaping of technological innovations for social and economic cohesion, and laying the foundation for social benefits - education, health and welfare services that flow equitably to all. Universities and research institutes can play a central role to initiate and promote the formulation and articulation of conceptual frameworks and models for knowledge networking. This requires the development of cultural interfacing of society and technology with the purpose of reintegration of technology in civil society.

Some of key issues of human centred perspective of cultural interfacing are:

• *Social Sustainability*
The focus is on the harmonious inter-relationships between the individual, society and the social environment, reflecting the common faiths and diverse hopes, including ambiguities, contradictions and tensions of the social and cultural environments. This dynamic connectivity is central to the social learning and renewal processes. It provides a social framework for the individual while transcending the social boundaries, and thus provides for continuous learning and social renewal.

• *Social Citizenship:*
Tthe idea of social citizenship which regards the citizen not just as a producer and a consumer but also as an active participant in decision making, and a cultural shaper and social assessor of science and technology.

• *'Valorization' of Diversity* :
Social and cultural shaping of science and technology which is based on the notions of the 'valorization' of diversity and coexistence.

• *Social Shaping:*
Instead of the 'separation' view, it is rooted in the idea of mutual exchange. It takes a holistic view in which participants involved in innovation cross their own language, cultural, professional and organisational boundaries in order to exchange knowledge and experiences.

• *Transcendence:*
'Transcendence' is one of the most essential aspects of understanding culturally bounded differences of innovative processes; the understanding of how social innovation process is carried out in different cultures is central to the human-centred approach

• *Multicultural Perspectives*
This perspective enables creativity, cohesion, sustainability and codevelopment; supports education as transmission, exchange and enrichment of cultures rather than as just the transfer of technical skill and competence.

* *Dialogue and human development*
This perspective continually renews the interdependence between personal knowledge, experiential knowledge and explicit knowledge, thus confirming the diversity of knowledges rooted in the social and cultural contexts of peoples rather than one form of objective (scientific) knowledge. Human development from the dialogical perspective is about the realisation of the social potential, both at the individual and collective levels through a process of continuous learning and confirming the dynamic balance and harmony between the individual, society and nature.

Knowledge networks in their wider societal context not only have a role of knowledge transfer, but can also act as actors of 'social critique' in developing the 'social market of ideas, products, and services'. They can act as representatives of plurality, and mediators of the 'valorisation of diversity' at a global level. *Pluralism is a safeguard to societal and individual freedom, but in a world in which we live such pluralism is much compromised and is subject to much distortion* (Whiston, p115). Seen from an optimistic perspective of ICTs, the European Community's debate on the Information Society illustrates an emerging shift in technological innovations from its traditional focus on technical solutions to societal perspectives such as diversity, innovation, learning, diffusion, participation, and cohesion. It underlines the forging of unprecedented links between technological innovation process and economic and social organisation, and notes the inadequacy of the linear model of innovation to deal with the complex mechanism of innovation and the interdependent world of technology and the market. It identifies risks of exclusion and dangers of a two-tier society arising out of the information society, and emphasises the need to mitigate any adverse consequences of individual isolation, intrusion into private life, and moral and ethical problems. While accepting the global character of the information society, and the need for promoting open systems and international standards, the White Paper (ibid.) emphasises that technological developments should "take due account of European characteristics: multilingualism, cultural diversity, economic divergence, and more generally the preservation of its social model" (ibid.: 95). This intertwinement of cultural diversity and technological innovations provides a framework for codevelopment. One of the most significant aspects of the European notion of the information society is that information and communications technologies (ICTs) are seen as resources for European development while at the same time 'valorising' the symbiosis between cultural diversity and European scientific rationality. For example, in a European Community sponsored collaboration of researchers, practitioners or policy makers, diversity enriches participation and interpretation, while rationality provides a common language for collaboration and a shared vision (Gill, 1994). This symbiosis between diversity and rationality is the essence of the debate on knowledge and the post-industrial society.

Conclusions

The paradoxes and dilemmas of the post-industrial society such as those of diversity or homogeneity, cohesion or integration, inclusion or exclusion, are part of a bigger societal challenge about how to reintegrate technological innovations into the civil society, and how to shape new forms of work life and living environments which are *inclusive* rather than *exclusive*. This perspective requires a fundamental shift in our understanding of the relationship between technology, knowledge and development, for example seeing knowledge in terms of social dynamics rather than just aa a scientifically determined entity; diversity as a positive human condition for social and economic cohesion, rather than as a disturbance factor for standardisation and homogenisation; cultural spaces as part of the interdependent world rather than being another component of the virtual reality; knowledge networks as a common cultural resource for co-development rather than technological vehicle for global competitivity. From this developmental perspective, information and communication technologies should be seen as a continuation of social and technological innovations, rather than as a new technical revolution blurring and distorting the social, cultural and economic realities of diverse societies. We should be mindful of confusing the fast pace of information transmission with the dissemination and absorption of knowledge in society, and the cheapness of ICTs infrastructures with the long term sustainability of human organisations. While recognising the change as a fundamental human condition, we must also recognise that change takes place in the real world of work, living and learning, and technological innovations cannot be divorced from the diversities and complexities of these realities. Just as there always is a dynamic symbiosis between language, culture and knowledge, so there should a symbiotic relationship between society and technology. It is this notion of symbiosis which informs knowledge networking for co-development from a human centred perspective.

References

AI & Society; Journal of human-centred systems and machine intelligence, Springer-Verlag.

Bangemann, M., *Europe and the global information society*, DGXII, CEC, Brussels, 1994.

Brant Castellano, Marlene, Collective Wisdom: Participatory Research and Canada's Native People, *Convergence,* 19(3), 1986.

Chambers, R , *Problems of Paradigms*, (available from IDS, University of Sussex), 1990: 246-256.

Castells, M. Crisis, Planning and quality of life: managing new historical relationships between space and society, Environment and Planning D: *Society and space*, 1983.

Cohendet, P., Llerena, P, European diversity in science and technology, *AI & Society*, 1994, vol. 8.2: 107-122.

Commission of the European Communities, The Community of culture, *European file*, CEC, Brussesl, 1983.

Commission of the European Communities, *A fresh boost for culture in the European Community*, CEC, Brussesl, 1987.

Commission of the European Communities, The European community and culture, *European file*, CEC, Brussels, 1988.

Cook, J., One culture, two cultures, three cultures, in B. Goranzon, and F. Florin (Eds.), *Skill and education*, Springer-Verlag, 1992: 233-248.

DELTA94, conference, DGXIII, CEC, Dusseldorf, November 1994.

Drucker, P., *Post-industrial society*, Butterworth, Heinemann, 1993.

Gill K. S., Artificial intelligence and social action: education and training, in B. Goranzon and T. Josefson (eds.), *Knowledge, Skill and Artificial Intelligence*, Springer-Verlag., 1988.

Gill, K. S., Reflections on Participatory Design, *AI & Society*, Vol. 3. No. 4, 1989.

Gill, K. S, A Summary of Human Centred Systems Research in Europe, NTT DATA, Tokyo, Japan, 1990.

Gill, K. S. Artificial intelligence for social citizenship: towards an anthropocentric technology, *Journal of Applied Artificial Intelligence*, Hemisphere, Vol. 5.1, 1991.

Gill, K. S., Human centredness: a 21st century paradigm for industrial cultures in in Masuda, Y. (Ed.),*Human centred systems in the global economy*, Springer-Verlag, London, 1992.

Gill, K. S. (1993), Socially sustainable technology: an agenda for human promotion, in A. Ardigò (Ed.), *le Nuove tecnologie per lepromozione umana*, Angeli, Milano, 1993.
Gill K S, Keynote Paper: Human centred shaping of social innovation, in(eds), F. Schmid, et. al., *Computer Integrated Production Systems and Organisation*, Springer-Verlag, 1994.
Gill K. S., Knowledge networking for co-development in the global information society, Int. Conf. on *Globalisation and IT Networking*, IFIP WG9.4, LSE, London, May 1.6-17, 1994.
Gill, K. S. *Human machine symbiosis*, Springer-Verlag, 1995.
Haraway, D., A manifesto for cyborgs: science, technology, and socialist feminism in the 1980s, in L. Nicolson (Ed.),*Feminism and Postmodernism*, Routledge 1990.
Kennedy, P., *Preparing for the Twenty - First Century*, Vintage Books, New York, 1990.
Hilton, J. Theatricality and technology: Pygmalion and the myth of the intelligent machine, in B. Goranzon, and F. Florin (Eds.), *Dialogue and technology*, Springer-Verlag, 1991:55-72.
Mander, J., Tyranny of Technology, in *Resurgence*, May/June 1994, No164 pp 21-25.
Morin-Labatut, G and Akhbar, S, Traditional Environmental Knowledge: a resource to manage and share, *Development Journal of SID*, 1992.4: 24-29.
Morley, D. and Robins, K., *Spaces of identity: global media, electronic landscapes and cultural boundaries*, Routledge, 1995.
Petrella, R., Three analyses of globalisation technology and economy, in FAST-*Europrospective II*, NAMUR, 1991.
Rosenbrock, H. H, *Machines with a purpose,* OUP, Oxford, 1990.
Sällström, P, The essence of dialogue, in B. Goranzon, and F. Florin (Eds.), *Dialogue and technology*, Springer-Verlag, 1991:27-36.
Telematics Applications Programme 1994-1998, CEC, DGXIII, final draft, December, 1994.
Toulmin S., The dream of the exact language, in B. Goranzon and M. Florin (eds.), *Dialogue and Technology*, Springer-Verlag, 1991.
Whiston, T.G., *Education and employment for a sustainable world*, FAST FOP 333, June 1992, FAST Programme, DGXII, Commission of the European Communities, 200 rue de la Loi, B-1049, Brussels.
Wittrock, B., Polity, Economy and Knowledge in the Age of Modernity in *Europe, AI & Society*, 1992, vol 7.2, pp 127-140.
White Paper, The changing society, the new technologies, Chapter 5, in Growth, competitiveness, employment: the challenges and ways forward into the 21st Century, Brussels, The White Paper, CEC, Brussels, Luxembourg, 1993.
World Bank, World Bank Report 1991: the challenge of development, OUP, Oxford, 1991.

Chapter 2

Media and the Cultural Condition: Language and Education

Inger Lytje

The paper discusses the educational challenges that the transformation of Western societies into post-industrial societies causes. First, the educational challenges that arise from change in the social structures, caused by media and information technology, is analyzed and discussed. Second the cultural conditions of education and training is analyzed and third the conditions caused by re-thinking the notion of knowledge and language is discussed in relation to training and education. Finally, the media education 'humanistisk informatik' is presented briefly.

Introduction

In this paper I shall work from the premise that Western European countries are changing from industrial to post-industrial societies, which are to be conceived as media and information societies. In order to adapt to the new situations and conditions, people's knowledge, skills and competence have to develop accordingly. In this paper, I want to examine some of the transformations our societies are undergoing at the end of the twentieth century, in order to get and understanding of the educational challenges we have to face. Post-industrial societies are among other things characterized by the construction and use of information and media technologies. When discussing educational issues in relation to technological development, we incline to focus on technology, and to forget the human. In accordance with Richard Ennals (Ennals 1988), I believe that we should rather start with an understanding and appreciation of the human, and make the educational environment and educational activities adapt to the social and personal needs of people. When stated from a technology-centred point of view, the salient issue in a debate on education becomes the use of information technology in learning environments, and corresponding issues concerning design, while issues concerning the development of human personality and creativity become second-rate. The technology-centred attitude seemed to be the predominant one in the workshop on Media and Education in Brighton in July 1994. The issues people wanted to discuss were for example educational software, learning environments, class room use of interactive multi-media, media for education, but also issues like 'marginality in relation to knowledge, technology and information' and 'literacy' were suggested for discussion. To me it indicates that although we commit ourselves to a human-centred approach, we are inclined to think of technology first, and only think of humans in the next place. So, I am *not* going to enter into a debate about, how to improve learning environments by the use of information and media technologies, and how to cope with the pedagogical challenges that arise in this connection. What I am going to do, is to try to identify some of the post modern conditions of Western European societies, which have long term educational implications. And I will discuss the educational challenges that we have to face in relation to these conditions.

In the first section, I will focus on the substantial changes of social and political structures at all levels of society, which began in the 1970's - or perhaps before then - and which has appeared to be more radical, than anybody in the seventies even dared to think about. Not only the social structures that have been institutionalized or formalized in one way or the other have changed dramatically during this period, but human relationships in general, such as family structures and gender relationships, and the formation of people's personal identities. The very radical changes of the work place in Western societies has been analysed in great detail by Mike Cooley, Pelle Ehn and many others. De-skilling of workers following from automation of industrial production, and exclusion of people from working life, played a major role in the whole debate during the seventies and the eighties. The skilled (male) worker of industrial production was regarded 'the human' in working life, and 'work' in its present form was regarded something essential to human beings. An alternative, human centred design strategy for skill and democracy was suggested. None of the people that were concerned with information systems design at that time, seemed to realize the profundity of the social changes that were happening, that our societies were changing into postindustrial, postmodern societies. Drawing on Mark Posters theory of 'the mode of information', I will try to encircle some of the characterictics of media and information societies in terms of the commodities, social structures and ways of interacting and communicating that these societies produce, and reconsider the above mentioned issues in relation to that. On this background I will discuss the educational challenges, we are going to face.

The second section is about *culture*. I am going to discuss how people in postmodern societies attach meaning to their every day experiences, and how this meaning creation can be supported by appropriate educational activities. Meaning is created through:

1) the way the world is presented to us through media, information and communication systems and culture products, through
2) our interacting with and being in the natural and social world and through
3) hand down of traditions from past to present.

According to Mark Poster, the post modern world is presented to us through electronic languages, be it images on TV, symbolic or iconic expressions on computer screens, or messages communicated through world wide communication channels. And our being in the world is mediated through cybernetic systems of some kind, that means through some kind of symbolic interaction. Language and symbolic interaction becomes 'the real thing'. What is reality, and what is virtual reality? That is the question. Massimo Negrotti (1991) analyses Western culture from a historical point of view as a 'culture of the artificial'. He finds that the technological development in Western societies now and in the past, that means since Medieval times, has been aiming at creating machines and artefacts that imitate human capabilities. The question now is whether artificial intelligence has brought this culture to its limits? What does it mean to be human, when machines can imitate human intellectual capabilities?

The third section is about *knowledge*. Within the *artificial intelligence* debate, the notion of knowledge has been widely discussed, and it has been claimed that knowledge based systems, that means the representation of knowledge in computers, ignore anything but propositional knowledge. I think that this opinion is based on a conception of knowledge that separates, in a well defined way, the knowing subject from the object that is known about. But in media and information societies, in the computer age, this conception of knowledge is inadequate. Knowledge has to be seen as interaction and exchange between a knowing subject and an object. Artificial intelligence make us reconsider conceptual schemes and thought figures, and catalyzes the whole process of de-and reconstructing basic ways of thinking and knowing in Western societies today.

Göranzon (1988) stresses *the practical intellect*, and claims that the use of computers emphasizes the close relationships between three kinds of knowledge namely: 1) propositional knowledge, 2) practical knowledge and 3) knowledge of familarity. This claim is consistent with my personal experiences from computing: knowledge about computers and about computer based systems is created through interacting with the system, whether we talk about the designer, who creates a software system through an experimental, innovative processes, or we talk about the end user, who interprets a system in a specific environment.

Different educational purposes are managed by different institutions such as primary school, secondary school, universities & colleges for further education etc. It is my opinion that the way educational systems are organized and institutionalized need not be appropriate for ever, but I am not going to enter into a debate about these matters. Rather I will focus more substantially on educational matters. My personal experience of training and education, comes from higher education at Aalborg University in Denmark where I teach 'humanistisk informatik'- a training program, that integrates *computing* with 'media and communication' studies and studies in linguistics and philosophy. Throughout this chapter I will refer to practical experiences from 'humanistisk informatik', and finally the contribution will include a brief presentation of the course.

Education and social structure

The transformation of industrial into post-industrial information and media societies causes dramatic change in their social and political structures. One important aspect of this transformation is the introduction of information and media technologies. Richard Ennals suggests that we regard technology as "the partial realization of particular defined human skills, as implementations of the extension of man" (Ennals 1988:73). I think that this conception of the relationship between technology and humans can be used to explain basic differences between industrial and postindustrial societies: In industrial societies, technology extends the human *body*, and in present media and information societies technology extends the human *mind* and the *linguistic capabilities* of human beings, this means the capabilities to communicate and understand. The relationship between technology and human beings in industrial societies has been analyzed by marxist sociologists and social scientists (such as Braverman) in great detail, and I am not going into this debate here, as my interest concerns post-industrial societies.

In post-industrial Western European societies, the production, distribution and consumption of commodities is regulated by a capitalist market economy, as was the case for industrial societies. But new kinds of commodities characterize the market, namely *media* products. I use the term 'media' for things that on the one hand are experienced as physical objects, but on the other hand becomes meaningful to people, not as physical objects, but as *text*. The software aspect of media products makes up the media text, and this media text is implemented in hardware, that represents the *commodity* regarded as a physical object. According to Jens F. Jensen (Jensen 1993), the production-circulation-consumption chain has to be understood as *communication*. During the production phase, the media text is encoded and implemented by teams of designers and producers, and during consumption, the message is decoded by the consumer. Consumption can be characterized as reception, as a kind of reading, during which the media text is interpreted. It implies that the receiver, interact (in a bodily manner) with the hardware that implements the media text. Although this model is not worked out with computer software in mind, I think that the production-circulation-consumption chain fits the life cycle of *computer software* very nicely, when we think of 'reading' as "implementating and interpreting the system in a social context". But there are some problems with regarding information systems as comodities, that can be consumed. One example of this is the use of expert systems for knowledge transfer, which is discussed by Richard Ennals (Ennals 1988). The idea of using expert systems for knowledge transfer comes from the conception of knowledge as a marketable commodity. It implies that expert knowledge can be encoded into an expert system, and to people as a commodity in a market. Ennals finds that this idea is based on a mis-understanding of what skill transfer is all about. And I certainly agree with that.

This leads me to consider the theory of 'the mode of information' put forward by Mark Poster (Poster 1990). Poster suggests, that post-industrial information societies cannot be characterized by its mode of production, but should rather be characterized by its mode of information. He argues that *media* and information technologies should not be conceived as commodities that are distributed through a market, but as *electronic language*. He even states that "The principle of private property is threatened in the domain of information" (ibid.:73). Media is defined as "systems of communication that structure an unknown group of receivers, that have, in other words, an abstract audience. In this case the media are centres of information, distributing discourses and images to a broad public " (ibid.:44)

What I find interesting in 'the mode of information' in relation to educational issues and the formation of social structures, is the role of *language*, which, according to Poster, differs significantly from the role of language in industrial societies, where it is common to conceive language as a tool for describing and communicating. Poster phrases it in the following way (ibid.:14):

> "While to some extent language is a tool for intentional action, and as such must be accounted for within the theory of the mode of information, language has another, very different, capacity: it is a figurative, structuring power that constitutes the subject who speaks as well as the one that is spoken to."

Poster maintains that in the case of electronic languages, linguistic expressions do not primarily represent reality, but becomes part of reality themselves (ibid.:15):

> "For the subject in electronically mediated communication, the object tends to become not the material world as represented in language but the flow of signifiers itself. In the mode of information it becomes increasingly difficult, or even pointless, for the subject to distinguish a "real" existing "behind" the flow of signifiers, . . ".

Poster argues (p.22) that "what is new in society is a set of structures of domination that are linguistically based, that one feature of these structures is their reliance on totalizing forms of discourse". This viewpoint is very decisive when discussing educational issues in relation to the formation of social structures and personal identities . To say that structures of domination are linguistically based and to say that the rhetoric, the arguments, the statements etc. become meaningful only within some totalizing form of discourse implies that educational activities at all levels have to develop people's awareness and skills about these matters. This again means to develop a new kind of *literacy*.

I think that it is a very nice idea to think of media as 'electronic languages', and in many cases I also think it is a nice idea to regard computers and their software systems as electronic languages, as has also been suggested by for instance Peter Bøgh Andersen (Andersen 1990). Databases and expert systems are obvious examples. But in some cases computers have to be considered as cybernetic systems, *cyborgs,* that regulate automatic processes. The typical way of interacting with the environment in an information society is through cybernetic mechanisms that can be more or less 'intelligent'. Some obvious examples are automatic opening of doors and stamping a bus ticket. Computers have been introduced in the factories and in the offices. Labour has been transformed from the physical act to the mental operation of interpreting symbols on a monitor.

World wide *communication networks* such as Internet, World Wide Web etc. have made it possible to 'be together in *cyberspace*'. Information is transfered through space in 'no time' or at least in what we experience as 'no time'. These networks challenge the way we collaborate and communicate, and it challenges our educational system, not only because people have to become familiar with using the networks, but because the whole notion of being together, of collaborating etc. changes. Cross cultural communication problems become evident, and also problems concerning communicational forms: how to be polite in cyberspace? Is it possible to be angry in cyberspace? etc. TV shares with communication networks the ability to send and receive messages worldwide in 'no time'. While computers have changed the social structures of working life dramatically, TV has changed the structure of family life. And TV has changed the way the political debate in our societies is organized, because the political matters and discussions are presented to us through TV. The political reality becomes the reality that is presented to us second hand, and without participation, a kind of hyper-reality.

Nowerdays all information can be digitalized, and one of the results is a new kind of electronic language, namely *multimedia* that integrates different modes of presenting information to people.

From a human-centred position the notion of *skill* is of great importance. I like the word, specially because we do not have a similar word in Danish. The word 'færdigheder' is close to it , but the meaning of "færdigheder"is limited to something instrumental. To me, skill means practical knowledge (as opposed to theoretical knowledge). It means to have the competence and the abilities that are necessary to act and interact in the world, and it means to be able to understand. The notion of skill in industrial societies has been closely related to the trades, and a skilled worker is a man belonging to some trade union. From a post-modern point of view this meaning aspect of skill will have to recede into the background, because one of the conditions we live with is that the trades are no longer well defined and delimited from other trades. The borderlines between the trades become blurred, and some trades totally disappear as a consequence of computerization.

In the debate about computerization of working life during the seventies and eighties, Mike Cooley, Pelle Ehn and many others argued that the tendencies of de-skilling of industrial workers should be counteracted through design. The *craftsman* that uses computers as *tools* was the ideal suggested by Pelle Ehn(Ehn 1988), and he suggests how this design ideal should be carried out in practise through cooperative design and experimental prototyping that overcomes the historical division of labour between design and construction processes. The ongoing process of automation implied that "human beings are rendered passive and the systems become more active. . . against this historical background there is an urgent need to view alternative systems, in particular those which may be regarded as human-centred" (Cooley 1988:129).

I believe that the *automation* process that Mike Cooley describes has come to a kind of historical termination. The conclusion is that many industrial processes have been fully automated. De-skilling of industrial workers has been replaced by exclusion of people from the working place. This automation process is not limited to industrial processes, but have dispersed to other sectors of society, e.g. the financial sector. The consequence is unemployment and polarization of the population in our societies. This is the situation at the beginning of the post-industrialism because I think our societies are still regulated by a capitalist economy. This big issue is not discussed by Mark Poster.

And what is the situation today? In a workshop on Information Systems Design run by Randi Markussen and I at University of Brighton in1994, people from many different countries could tell almost univocally that the lack of basic skills in relation to the jobs people had to perform was a very serious problem. We shared the experience that the de-skilling hypothesis is not valid in a post-industrial society. On the contrary, people have to be highly skilled in order to cope with every day situations and challenges. And specially, people have to be able to cope with *change*. This is not to be understood as change from the traditional to the non-traditional, from the ordinary to the extraordinary, from old to new, but change as a basic condition of life, as a condition of uncertainty and ambiguity. This is a consequence of living with soft systems instead of hard systems, and to live with 'presented' reality instead of 'real' reality (whatever it means).

Richard Ennals (1988) suggests that "skills and their transfer are at the centre of contemporary economic and political debate", and "we are faced with a situation where there are a large number of unemployed, many of whom are young people, with a shortage of skills in many walks of life". So developing and transfering skills is a major challenge for the educational system. I agree strongly with Ennal's arguement:

> "There is a clear danger in this technological *advance* that the nature of skill becomes defined in terms of technological and industrial processes, as constituting a human response to the need of the technology, rather than the reverse. When the industrial base collapses, as is happening in the UK at present, it may take with it the narrowly defined human skills which is embodied. Such a drastic form of alienation of the worker from the products of his labour cannot but have explosive effects."
>
> He further reports that,
> "the emphasis of my work is far more on working with groups of people than on working with technology such as information technology".

In continuation of viewing a media text, as electronic language, which is implemented in some kind of machinery, and in continuation of Richard Ennals viewpoints on skill, I will suggest that *skill* is seen as a kind of *literacy*. Usually, we use literacy to denote people's reading and writing abilities that means their ability to read and write natural language texts. This notion of literacy can be extended to other kinds of signifying systems such as computers and TV, and the term *computer literacy* was actually introduced in American journals on computers and learning many years ago. To be litarate in relation to media products means actually being able to recieve the media product, the media text, and also to be able to design and construct such things. People have to be able to *participate* in design and construction processes as an analogue of being able to write a natural language text. In this connection we can learn from Randi Markussen (Markussen 1994) who points at dilemmas in present conceptions of cooperative and participatory design that stems from the totalizing discourse which frame those activities nowadays.

Culture

Jens F. Jensen (1993) defines 'culture' as the structure and processes through which a social communities organize their experiences, relations and actions, and create meaning of the world and of the self. He focuses on the social and mental activity through which culture is permanantly created: 'culture' is seen as the way in which we think and talk about the world , the way in which we create our cultural environment. I like this definition of 'culture' because it focuses on the creation of *meaningfulness*, and because it focuses on the processes that create our cultural environment, and the interaction between ourselves and the environment. Culture is conceived as the self consciousness of society, as the way in which society presents and reflects itself. In this connection *language* is an important issue.

Mark Poster (1990) argues that culture has to be analyzed using language based theories, and he argues that a poststructuralist position is relevant in this connection because it gives priority not only to written language but also to electronic languages. This position takes into consideration the necessary rethinking of the notion of language:

> "Words cannot any longer be located in space and time, whether it be the 'real time' of spoken utterance in a spatial context of presence or the abstract time of documents in a bureaucrat's file cabinet and library's archive. Speech is framed by space/time coordinates and by dramatic action. Writing is framed by space/time coordinates of books and sheets of paper. Both are available to logics of representation. Electronic language, on the contrary, does not lend itself to being so framed. It is everywhere and nowhere, always and never. It is truely immaterial/immaterial".

So according to the mode of information, *language understanding* becomes an ambigous term. It means not only to interpret linguistic utterances in a specific context, but first and foremost to construct a kind of reality, to reinterpret the context from the imagery that the linguistic expressions create in the minds of the participants of the communication process. One of the language based theories I find very useful in this connection is about *metaphors* (Lakoff & Johnsom 1980). Lakoff and Johnson do not conceive metaphors as linguistic phenomena only, but - and I think primarily - as cognitive phenomena. They maintain that the use of metaphors in every day language reflects and constructs the mental images through which we understand and create culture. The computer, for example, has caused the introduction of new metaphors into language. We interprete mind experiences in term of computer metaphors ("it processes very slowly today"), and we interprete computers as bodies, that can be infected by viruses.

I think that the notions of *reality*, *hyper reality*, and *virtual reality* have become very important in present culture. I suggest that *virtual reality* is understood as an experience of the mind which is conceived metaphorically as a *bodily experience*. This definition reflects the feeling of *being in* a world, and not only observing it. The experience of being in the world is also strongly connected to the notion of *real time*. There is no longer such a thing as object time and real time, the system time is experienced as being the real time. People clearly experience the internet as a virtual reality, as a *cyber space*. We talk about 'traveling on the internet' or 'meeting on the internet'. In this case, communication is conceived as a kind of journey, and the interacting between people is seen as something going on in a kind of meeting place for the people's minds. The internet is conceived as a kind of collaborative mental space that is somewhere 'out there'. The verb *travel* literally means to physically move from one place to another by the means of some vehicle. What is moving in this case are people's minds and the vehicle is the signals that are transmitted. The verb *meet* literally means that there are a number of people that physically moves to the same place in physical space. In this case people imagine that people's minds move to the same place which is again 'somewhere out there'. So using the internet is experienced in terms of movement in physical space although nobody moves. The interesting thing is that we also use telephone for distance communication in a similar way, but we do not talk about it in these terms and the telephone system is not considered a virtual reality.

The information mode of signification (as opposed to the representational mode) gives birth to the notion of *hyper reality*. (Poster 1990:61-65). This notion is closely connected to the mass media, especially TV, that creates and constructs reality for people. TV advertisements are nice examples of this phenomenon. I think that also computer language and mathematical language should be seen as vehicles for creating hyper-realities. As a teacher I have experienced that conceiving computer programs not as representations but as hyper realities, enhances the learning process. To work out a computer program means to invent a world consisting of symbols: variables, constants, procedures, predicates, functions etc. I have experienced that many students are afraid of being inventors.

Massimo Negrotti analyzes western culture from a historical point of view, and names it *the culture of the artificial*. He finds that "the whole history of technology is the history of the transfer to particular machines of particular human physical capabilities"(Negrotti 1991:57). According to Negrotti, Western culture has given legitimacy to the ongoing extension of human capabilities. The enhanced capabilities have been used to solve the kind of problems that arise in the highly complex societies that develop from this effort. The human capabability that western culture tries to replicate in the computer age, is the human mind, which we, according to Negrotti, consider the highest level of nature. And Negrotti's interest is to discuss the limit of artificial intelligence, which turns out to be a discussion of the limits of our culture. The conviction that Artificial Intelligence (AI) is able to replicate the human mind is a cultural attitude which is consistent with advanced industrial culture. Computers have improved our capacities to investigate, not only nature but also human and social processes.

Massimo Negrotti argues that the efforts we use to replicate natural prosesses and enhance our physical and mental capabilities in advanced industrial societies, have come to a kind of historical termination. We now have to face what he calls a self limiting process. The question is whether our culture is ready to *sanction* further extension of the individual ego. Negrotti suggests that instead of regarding AI as a replication of the human mind, we should regard it as just *artificial*, different from the natural. Actually he suggests that we introduce a new category: *the artificial.* "AI program a result of human imagination. The outcome of an AI program is a product of our mind and not a mirror of it." (Negrotti 1991:58) This viewpoint parallels my personal viewpoints, and also viewpoints put forward by Richard Ennals: computers should be considered vehicles for studying human mental activity (such as natural language understanding), not machines that replicate the human mind. Through interacting with computers, we can create and implement ideas that go beyond the mechanistic world view of industrial societies. In this way I see artificial intelligence as a technology that is post-modern, deconstructing the logic of its own roots, and leading to a more intellectual and less mechanical culture. I do not agree with Negrotti, who maintains that "computer science and AI have no role in the establishment of the new era, since they are deeply linked to a pragmatic and mechanistic view of man" (Negrotti 1991:59). Negrotti see 'implementatation' as 'ad-hoc methodology', and I rather see implementation as bound to *creativity*, as something qualitatively different from *methodology.*

The educational challenges we have to cope with in relation to culture is related to *meaningfullness* and *understanding*. I have experienced that many young people have a feeling of *alienation* in relation to information technology and media, which often implies that they refuse to learn how to use the systems. The computer, for instance, symbolizes cultural characteristics that happen to be so alien, and even disgusting to people, that the result is total denial. This emotional reaction is very common among women, who, for one reason or the other, do not possess the same innovative curiosity as boys and men do. I think this situation can be explained in terms of *sanctioning*. In Denmark many people and especially women and marginalized groups do not any longer want to sanction the ongoing replication of the human mind and body. This can be seen in computer science departrments, for instance, where more than 90% of the students are male, even in the fields that give priority to systems development issues. One explanation of this could be that the totalizing discourse that control the whole enterprise of computer science education in Denmark has not been questioned. During the last years there has been no debate, only silence, even though the problems that our culture has to face, such as unemployment and marginalization, have grown. One way of changing the discourse is to regard computers as *electronic language* that is part of our culture. But this is a challenge not only to the educational system as such, but to groups and individuals, because people's personal identities and relations to other people will have to change. For example the notion of being male and female, the notion of work etc. This requires debate and dialogue which is totally absent at present.

As a teacher in 'humanistisk informatik' I have experienced that students (about 40% are male and 60 % are female) are eager to discuss how computers affect human language and human ways of thinking . They do not feel confident with what is happening, because - I think - the computer challenges well established conceptions of what it means to be human. These conceptions seem natural at first, but through learning the students find out that they are just cultural creations. Understanding this is frightening because it means that nothing is really stable, that personal identities have to be conctructed every day, because of the lack of well defined contexts. I think that the educational system at all levels should support the learning processes, that make people able to understand and create meaning to their every day experiences.

Knowledge

The notion of knowledge and understanding has to be reconsidered in post-industrial media and information societies. Research in artificial intelligence, for instance, has made us question deeply rooted images of these matters, because artificial intelligence is a technology and a philosophy of the mind. This applies to natural language understanding and expert systems. Compare for instance the famous book 'Mind over Machine' (Dreyfus & Dreyfus 1986). People who believe that knowledge has to be be implemented in machines as knowledge structures limit themselves to propositional knowledge when engaging in computer based or computer supported knowledge representation and understanding. And they limit themselves to a representational view of computer languages. This conception of knowledge reflects, from my point of view, the mechanistic world view of industrial societies, according to which, knowledge was regarded as a kind of machinery. The critics argue that knowledge should not be limited to *propositional knowledge*, and points at other kinds of knowledge such as *tacit knowledge*, *practical knowledge* and *knowledge of familiarity*. But many of the critics do not realize that it is not the computer as such, which limits our conception of knowledge, but culture. My own experience from research in natural language understanding and systems development, make me agree with Bo Göranzon, who maintains that "fundamental to the design of knowledge-based systems is the understanding of the nature of knowledge, and the problems involved in computerizing it". He draws a distinction between three different categories of knowledge: propositional knowledge, practical knowledge and knowledge of familiarity (Göranzon 1987:9). My experience from developing natural language understanding systems that can assist the user in comprehending a natural language text (Lytje 1994) has made me realize that the development and use of artificial intelligence systems, and I think computer software systems in general, brings together the different categories of knowledge, making each of them an indispensable aspect of the concept of knowing. Knowledge about language, for instance, is not limited to the symbolic representation of lexicon and grammar that is obligatory in any natural language understanding system. What I consider knowledge, is the mental activity that humans perform during systems development processes, and, in general, through interacting with the system. This conception of knowledge implies that people engage in mental activity, comprising of personal communication, through which knowledge is created.

Propositional knowledge has something to do with *following rules* while the other types of knowledge, which Bo Göranzon stresses, has something to do with *creativity*. Very often 'creativity' and 'following rules' are seen as contrasts, as two incompatible ways of getting to know something. In Denmark, for instance in the institution where I work, the two types of capabilities are often used to characterize people: the 'following-the-rules' people are the computing, engineering, mathematical type , and the creative people are artists, writers, players, painters type. It is always understood that the first group are the 'formalists', who are necessary for society to function (as a machine!), and the other group, the creative ones, are the people who are the non-functionalists, the people who make life cheerful. This distinction between following-rules and creativity stresses the dualities and dichotomies of the Danish society, and I think, of Northern European societies in general. It is deeply rooted in our culture, and it contributes to, for instance, the constitution of being male and female. Similar things can be said about *responsibility* in relation to propositional knowledge. Naming an association 'computer professionals of social responsipility', for instance, tends to signify, that the computer professionals, who are not members of this association, are not responsible (for the social consequences of using information technology).

As a computer professional I think that these distinctions are obsolete, and have been it for a long time. From systems development experiences I know that design and construction processes are indeed creative processes, and I have had this feeling confirmed by reading the paper by Robert Muller (Muller 1993) in which he draws a 'Creative Thinking Process Model'. Concerning responsibility I think that nobody in this world should practice their profession in a way that can be called irresponsible. The *ethical* dimension is more important than ever. On the other hand, I do not think that anybody should claim to have a monopoly of being responsible.

According to Mark Poster and other post structuralist thinkers, the relations between knowledge and language has changed dramatically through the transformation from industrial to post-industrial societies. Within research and learning in modern societies, language was primarily seen as a tool for representating knowledge about something and reasoning about this 'something'. The language of formal logic was for these reasons considered the most distinguished language for knowledge representation and reasoning. The human subject of the learning process was supposed to be delimited from the object that was studied.

The computer has changed the notion of knowledge dramatically and changed the relation between language and knowledge. In a paragraph on 'Electronic Writing', Mark Poster accounts for the relation between subject and object in electronic writing, and he states the following:

> "Writer and writing, subject and object have a similarity that approaches identity, a simulation of identity that subverts the expectations of the Cartesian subject that the world is composed of rex extensa, beings completely different from the mind". (Poster 1990:111).

I think that this view on electronic writing (which we in Denmark call creative writing) can be generalized: Natural or electronic languages are used as vehicles for knowledge acquisition which is considered a creative process. Once the text has been written, it influences the knowing subject immediately, who then has to rewrite the text, because it is incomplete. When used for developing computer software systems this process is called *prototyping*. The key question is: when does this process finish? Some may say, *never*, others would say, when our *intuition* tells us. Lyotard claims - and I agree that while knowing something in industrial societies was connected to the notion of *truth*, the knowing in post-industrial society is first and foremost connected to performance.

In media and information societies people easily have access to databases and knowledge bases through world wide communication networks and data terminals, and I think that the construction and use of these information ressources has changed our conception of knowledge in a very radical way. Furthermore, the use of media and electronic languages in knowledge processes make the issue of *presentation* of knowledge an important aspect of the knowledge processes. I believe that visualization through graphic interfaces and multimedia will make the presentation aspect of knowledge even more salient.

The understanding of knowledge presented above should be reflected in training environments and educational systems in all Western societies. In Denmark, I think this is far from being the case. In order to be familiar with computers and other kinds of electronic media, it was announced a couple of years ago that teachers in secondary schools have to teach computing as an integrated aspect of any discipline. It means that computers should be used in mathematics, language, history, physics etc. A succesful implementation of this idea would lead to a reorganization of the learning and pedagogical processes in Danish schools, and our children would become familiar with adequate ways of knowing and of acquiring knowledge. But this has not been the case; an exception is 'creative writing', which means using word processors for writing.

Humanistisk Informatik

Finally, I present some of my personal experiences from university training at Aalborg University in Denmark, where I have been a practising teacher and educational manager in 'humanistisk informatik' since 1982. From a historical point of view, 'humanistisk informatik' has developed as:

1) a critique towards the machine-centred and male dominated approach to computer science, which was (and still is) practiced at computer science institutions in Denmark,
2) a way of introducing computer science issues to the human sciences: media and cultural studies, linguistics, philosophy, logic etc., from the point of view that the human sciences, methodologically and epistemologically, do not remain unaffected by computer and information technology.

I find that the first of these two 'historical missions' represents a human-centred approach to the creation and transfer of computer science knowledge, in the way Karamjit Gill and others conceive human-centredness: "The human-centred approach allows a collaboration between the user and the computer in such a way that they complement each other's capabilities", and, the human-centred approach "should reject neither human judgement, tacit knowledge, intuition and imagination, nor the scientific or the rule based methods" (Gill 1988:81).

'Humanistisk informatik' is neither a *human science*, nor a *computer or information science*, but something else (which very often is considered 'something in between'). 'Humanistisk Informatik' is not about, either 'the human', or 'the computer', but about the *interaction* between the two, in a very broad sense. These viewpoints parallel to those of Massimo Negrotti on artificial intelligence: "AI is really intelligence and, at the same time really artificial. It is a new field of technological research, and not a human science. Its advances are constrained by intrinsic limits in reproducing human faculties, but *they could be of great concern if cultural evolution were to reject or modify the early and unfounded premises of AI*" (Negrotti 1991: 61, my italics). I think that 'humanisk informatik' represents such a modification of the unfounded premises of AI. This modification consists in regarding the collaboration between human and machine as knowledge, and not the propositional structures as such. Knowledge is created through interaction with software systems that perform tasks that we do not normally expect that machines are able to perform.

The Scandinavian tradition in systems development, that means the collective ressource /participatory design approach has had considerable influence on the way human-centredness is practiced in 'humanistisk informatik' in Aalborg. This tradition has been modified by the artificial intelligence debate, that means the debate on knowledge, skill and learning, and by the HCI and CSCW field that comprise the use of semiotic and cognitive theories in the study of human-computer interaction (Bøgh 1990). 'Humanistisk informatik' focuses on the *interaction* between humans and computers at all levels, while the Scandinavian tradition tends to encourage the separation between 'soft' and 'hard' aspects, and between the human aspects and the formal and technical aspects.

The learning environment of educational practices has to reflect an understanding of knowledge and learning that is shared by students and teachers. We believe that different categories of knowledge interact, namely propositional knowledge, practical knowledge and knowledge of familiarity. Practical knowledge about media including computers and multimedia and about inter-personal communication is learnt through laboratory work, and theoretical knowledge is acquired through course work and project work. The students become familiar with the subjects by studying them in project groups in a problem oriented way. The cultural dimension related to 'humanistisk informatik' is studied through technology history and technology theory.

Conclusion

I have discussed some of the educational challenges that are caused by the transformation of Western countries into postindustrial media and information societies. Social structures change dramatically, and in this connection the role of language and information becomes important. From a post-structuralist position, society has to be analyzed using language based theories focusing on the totalizing discources that control people's way of thinking and acting. From this position the notion of literacy together with a renewed conception of reading and writing capabilities and skills become important. Computerization of work processes has implied that former industrial workers have been excluded from the work place, and one of the educational challenges we have to face is re-skilling in order to cope with unemployment, poverty and polarization.

An important aim of training and education is to support the construction of culture, cultural identity, and cross cultural communication. We no longer live in well defined contexts with well defined traditions and conventions. Consequently, meaning and understanding has to be created through debate and discussion in learning environments. Many, especially young people, feel alien to information technology, and in this connection the question af sanctioning 'the culture of the artificial' is a crucial one. The notion of being human, the notion of knowledge, language and reality have changed because of computers and other electronic languages, and it has to be reflected in the curriculae and in the way learning environments are organized.

References

Bøgh, Andersen Peter. *A Theory of Computer Semiotics*, Cambridge University Press, 1990.

Bødker, Susanne. Creating conditions for participation: Conflicts and resources in systems design, in Proceedings of the Participatory Design Conference, p.13-20, Palo Alto:Computer Professionals for Social Responsibility, 1994.

Cooley, Mike. Creativity, Skill and Human-Centred Systems, in Bo Göranzon and Ingela Josephson (eds.) *Knowledge, Skill and Artificial Intelligence*, London: Springer-Verlag, 1988.

Dreyfus, Hubert L. and Dreyfus, Stuart E. *Mind over Machine*, New York: Macmillan, 1986.

Dreyfus, Hubert L. and Dreyfus, Stuart E. Making a Mind Versus Modelling the Brain: Artificial Intelligence Back at the Branchpoint, in Massimo Negrotti(ed.) *Understanding the Artificial*, London: Springer-Verlag, 1991.

Ehn, Pelle. *Work Oriented Design of Computer Artefacts*, Swedish Centre of Working Life, Stockholm, 1988.

Ennals, Richard. Can Skills be Transferable? in Bo Göranzon and Ingela Josephson (eds.) *Knowledge, Skill and Artificial Intelligence*, London:Springer-Verlag, 1988.

Gill; Karamjit S. Artificial Intelligence and Social Action: Education and Training, in Bo Göranzon and Ingela Josephson (eds.) *Knowledge, Skill and Artificial Intelligence*, London:Springer-Verlag, 1988.

Göranzon, Bo. The Practice of the Use of Computers. A Paradoxical Encounter between Different Traditions of Knowledge, in Bo Göranzon and Ingela Josephson (eds.) *Knowledge, Skill and Artificial Intelligence*, London:Springer-Verlag, 1988.

Jensen, Jens F. Computer Culture: The Meaning of Technology and the Technology of Meaning. A triadic essay on the semiotics of technology, in Peter Bøgh Andersen, Berit Holmqvist and Jens F. Jensen (eds.) *The Computer as Medium*, Cambridge University Press, 1993.

Lakoff & Johnson. *Metaphors we live by*, Chicago:Chicago University Press, 1980.

Lyotard, Jean-Francois. The Postmodern Condition: A Report on Knowledge, Minneapolis: University of Minnesota Press, 1979, 1984,1989.

Lytje, Inger. A humanistic approach to systems development, in Office. *Technology and People*,4:147-155, England: Elsevier, 1989.

Lytje, Inger. Knowledge Acquisition from Text, in Inger Lytje(ed.) *Logic, Knowledge and Meaning*, TOPICS, Denmark: Roskilde University, Cognitive Science Centre, 1994.

Markussen, Randi. Dilemmas in Cooperative Design, in Proceedings of the Participatory Design Conference p.59-66, Palo Alto:Computer Professionals for Social Responsibility, 1994.

Muller, Robert C. Enhancing Creativity, Innovation and Cooperation, in *AI & Society* ,1993; 7:4-39.

Negrotti, Massimo. Alternative Intelligence, in Massimo Negrotti(ed.) *Understanding the Artificial*, London: Springer-Verlag, 1991.

Poster, Mark. *The Mode of Information. Poststructuralism and Social Context*, Great Britain: Polity Press, 1990.

Searle, John. Cognitive Science and the Computer Metaphor, in *Understanding the Artificial*, London: Springer-Verlag, 1991.

Chapter 3

Knowledge and Sustainable Development: Towards the furtherance of a global communication system*

Tom Whiston

Education and training is for a purpose. In global terms one of the prime purposes must be to reduce the gap between the world's rich and poor. This is critical if a global sustainable environment is to ensue. That in turn implies one of the main aims should be improvement of the circumstances determining, *'technology and knowledge transfer'*. With that transfer comes the ability of *all* societies to respond, both in local appropriate ways and through better, more efficient international collaboration, to the enormous globally interactive challenges which face the world now and increasingly in the future.

Now, an enormous literature exists relating to Technology Transfer. It is not our intention to review that literature here. Rather our aim is to discuss some issues of *global* importance relevant to the transfer of 'knowledge'. Subsequently we will attempt to relate the more specific (and tangible) area of technology transfer to the much wider concept of knowledge transfer. We must also recognise that to talk of 'knowledge' as if it is a codified, 'once and for all', concept is highly misleading. That idea must be dismissed at once. Knowledge is open ended, developing, self creative. Equally some knowledge can become 'obsolescent', or at least superseded by more contemporary gains. Thus to talk of knowledge as if it is a static, stationary concept is not only wrong, but can also lead to counterproductive or less than optimal activity or policies, especially in relation to education.

Knowledge and Technology Transfer Seen as a Communication Process

Knowledge, the distribution, creation, further development has therefore to be seen as a dynamic process. In the same way that an individual may be viewed as an information-processing entity (Lindsay and Norman, 1972) so educational establishments, government agencies, industrial and commercial organisations, national systems (agricultural, energy generation and distribution', innovation policy endeavour, research networks) are all knowledge processors, information processors. In that wide 'meta' sense the *cybernetics* literature (Wiener, 1948) has much to offer in terms of understanding the ways in which information, 'knowledge flow, is organised, feeds-back upon itself. As such it then -becomes useful to use the language of information and communication theory (Shannon and Weaver, 1949) which suggests such concepts as 'channel-capacity', 'systems overload', information handling-rate, information-bottlenecks, switching capacity and the like. Indeed if one goes one step further from the passivity (and reductionism) of information and communication theory to the world of *cognitive psychology* then a whole range of concepts more related to volition, intention, meaning emerge. Knowledge is then viewed in a more experiential, learning, meaningful sense and discussion of knowledge transfer takes on a more useful guise of which technology transfer is only but a narrower more observable facet, viz. the applicative exemplar. Though even here it may not be a 'physical entity' (e.g. computer software programming is a 'technology, but not physical'; similarly with applied mathematics or many aspects of chemical engineering).

Another qualification which is necessary regarding 'knowledge' (and subsequently knowledge transfer) is the distinction between public observable, communicable knowledge with that of tacit or heuristic knowledge. The latter is much more difficult to describe or formulate. As a consequence it is not easily codified or communicable: and therefore may be difficult to 'transfer'. (No doubt an artist, a creative scientist, a pottery maker, a gymnast . . have much skill and 'knowledge', but much of this is of a 'heuristic' form and therefore not readily reducible to communicable algorithms. We can read Einstein's papers, look at a Rembrandt painting, watch an artist at work, talk with a scientist about his views on the stereochemistry of a complex natural product but that does not mean we can ourselves reproduce the same ability or codify the knowledge or skill).

In one sense this difficulty (of abstract or theoretical leaning) is attempted to be, overcome by a combination of 'intellectual osmosis' and 'learning by doing'. That is why artists have workshop studies; it is why people imitate and modify earlier innovations, thereby learning internally - *not* in an instructional sense, from the act of doing and undoing. This accounts for much of Japanese industry's success in the decades following World War II; and also for India's failure in several areas. It is why science professors have research assistants and why in earlier decades (and centuries) the apprenticeship and journeyman approach was *so* important as a means of learning, improvement, the diffusion of skills and the transfer and emulation of knowledge. In contemporary times the German 'Technical-Foreman' is of tremendous conceptual and practical importance in that respect.

What we are leading to in all of this is that 'knowledge', knowledge transfer (and if you will technology, and technology transfer) are by *no means* simple concepts that can be easily handled or discussed by policy makers or economists. 'Knowledge' has defeated many philosophical interpretations, frustrated considerable psychological analysis and in many ways remains an enigma. Indeed knowledge, like wisdom, can most probably *not be taught* although paradoxically it may be transferred! How so? If knowledge and wisdom cannot be 'taught' what is going on in all the world's schools, and universities and international seminars, and UNESCO workshops and 'knowledge-transfer agencies'? What are they doing? What function or role do they serve? The answer to that (and it is the key to the paradox that knowledge cannot be taught, but can be transferred) is that: schools, universities, international bodies (many of which directly or indirectly are concerned with knowledge transfer) are *facilitators*. They are the mechanics, providing the mechanism of transfer. But to be *taught,* one must learn. And to learn one must possess the appropriate absorptive capacity (If the absorptive capacity is inappropriate then on occasions a more creative type of learning may occur. I once observed this as a child when on my frequent visits to the Birmingham Museum I used to marvel at a bicycle built completely out of bamboo and wood - chain, spokes, wheels, everything. it had been made by an African native who had never seen a metal-bike, just a photograph, and possessed only the materials to hand. *That* is knowledge transfer; much greater than 'mere' technology transfer. Full knowledge transfer, by the way, would have included an understanding of the means of mass production of bicycles, plus the sociology of the bicycles use in yesterday's society. Economics concerns itself with the former, social anthropology with the latter. For an effective understanding of what knowledge transfer and technology transfer is about we need both types of concern and much else).

So for knowledge to be absorbed - to be transferred - we require a 'receiver' who has the intellectual, the social means of 'receiving' the transmitted information. The 'capability of receiving' then, and only then, converts, transforms the transmitted data into knowledge. In short, he or she then learns. Equally the 'sender' of the transmitted data must be capable of encoding *his* own knowledge into a suitably codified form for transmission; he must also want (viz. 'volition') to transmit the knowledge. Often both the volition and the ability to encode is missing, or much less than optimal. Some of this is caught in the series of diagrams itemised below.

Now against the scale of world problems which we are examining here, much of the above regarding the transmission of data, and the transformation into 'knowledge' and thereby demonstrating learning must appear excessively pedantic. Far from that it is, I would suggest of crucial importance. For, if we tease out the concepts more fully (which implies only giving the underlying mechanisms greater *macro* emphasis, viz. one individual learning is not too much of interest to the economist or to the 'top-down' policy-maker, but if we repeat the argument in a purely algebraic sense whereby the one individual becomes a hundred million individuals then we have a 'nation' and suddenly the economist or the policy-maker wakes up and takes interest). We then arrive at a much wider area of application and more clearly understand the importance of, for example:

- Indigenous capability (at *all* levels)
- Indigenous infrastructures
- Local learning institutions and networking
- The restrictive importance of IPR
- The problem of translating 'appropriate' knowledge from one culture to another
- The restricting influence of self-serving bureaucracies
- The influence of tacit knowledge
- The often long time scale of learning
- Knowledge embedded in organisational structures and social relationships
- The relative 'location' of knowledge in the public and private sector
- The role of international technology and knowledge transfer agencies
- The role of collaborative international S&T
- The exchange in an international setting of scientists, engineers and policy makers
- The need of common global concern and mutually dependent economic, commercial and technological policies
- The interdependency of development
- The lack of volition to communicate
- S&T primarily. defined by the North's needs

We will examine the above list more fully in a little while. In so doing we will attempt to relate the importance of that list to a fuller understanding of 'knowledge transfer' and 'technology transfer' and in so doing emphasise the critical importance of the overall concept (and restrictions) of knowledge transfer and technology transfer to the ultimate aim of our study. viz. *Global Sustainability.*

However, in examining 'knowledge and technology transfer' from the perspective of the more generic concept of a communication system one further step has to be made. Therefore the rather simplistic (and reductionistic) diagrams referred to earlier (see Figures 1-7) require to be translated into the more worldly representations demonstrated in Figure (8). In so doing an examination of Figure (9) to which we will

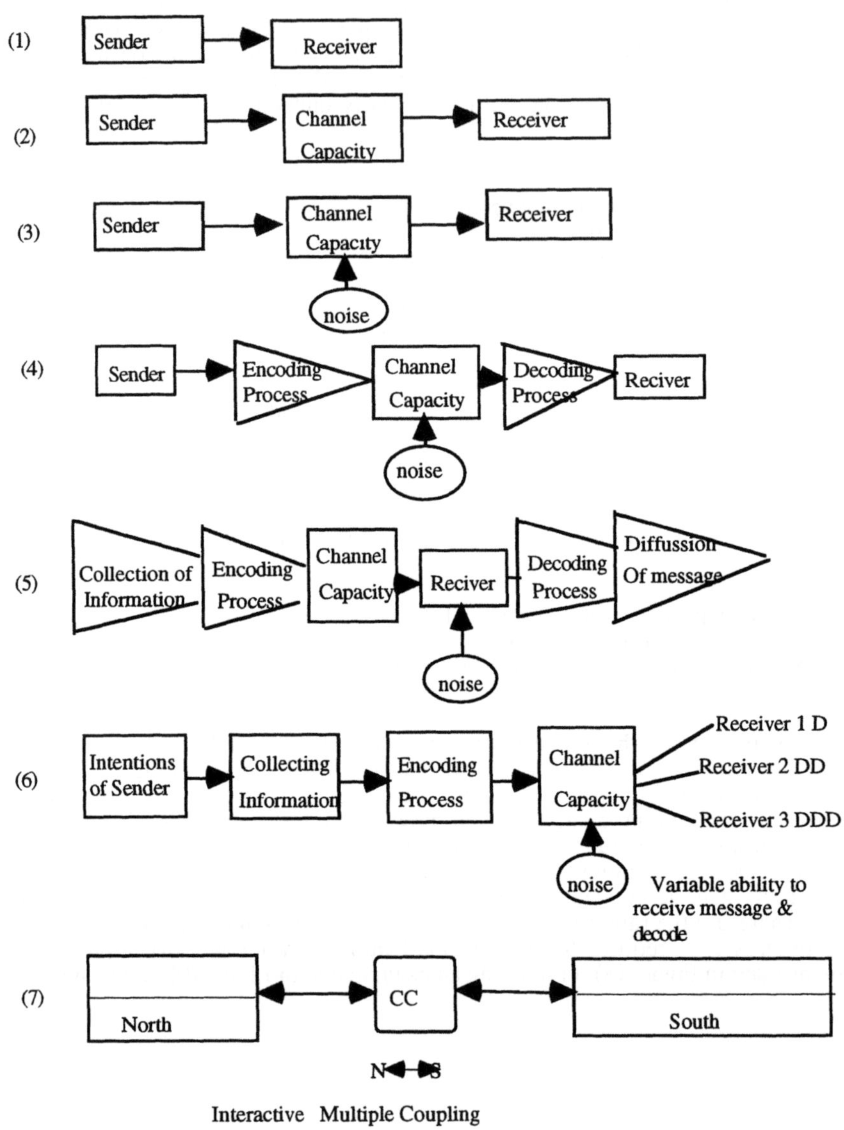

Figures 1-7 Stages of sophistication in understanding the communication process

later refer, reveals that the list of topics given earlier (i.e. indigenous capability, indigenous infrastructure etc.) take on a more specific and *inter-related, interdependent meaning* if we group those separate items, or rather interlink them into a total 'global communication' picture or model.

Global Communication

In making the jump from a theoretical communication model to the actual world scene it is worth while to briefly recap upon the problems that the world faces. For if they remain unameliorated it will almost certainly ensure that a state of global sustainability, let alone partial stability is never attained. Thus we might summarise the world scene as follows: The world may be divided, somewhat crudely into developed and less developed regimes - at least in industrial and economic, if not cultural terms. Usually referred to as N-S divide; or OECD and less developed regimes; Triadic grouping (North America, Europe and Japan) and the rest of the world or whatever[1]. Such a division is overly simplistic in as much as NICs LDCs; *least* developed countries; 'Four Tigers', second world etc. imply the need of requiring many qualifications. Nevertheless the distinction has some use. A considerable economic divide separates the two main blocs. There is much partial integration (viz. N-N trade and industrial, commercial, scientific and technological linking primarily between OECD nations) and considerable 'exclusion' whereby less industrially developed regions do not intimately partake in the economic, scientific, technological, trade exchanges which partly personify the OECD 'Club' (see diagram 8).

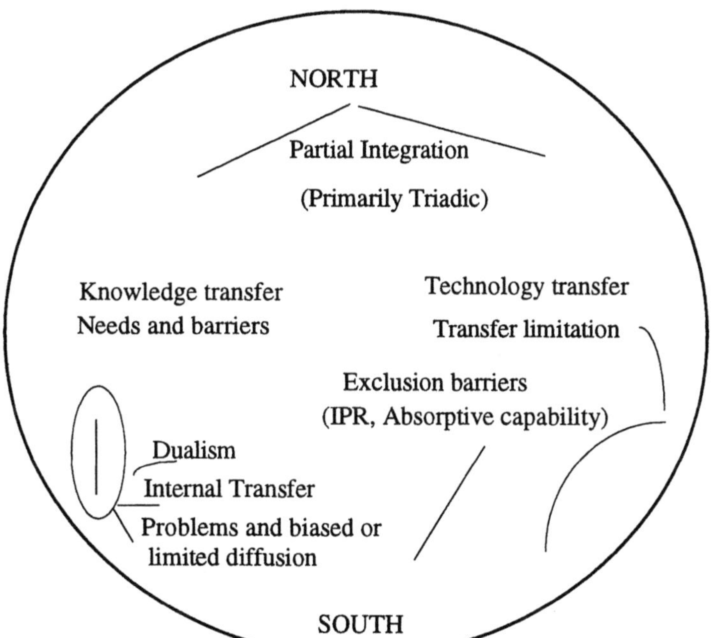

Figure 8 The Global Knowledge Divide

Figure 9

GLOBAL COMMUNICATION FOR SUSTAINABLE DEVELOPMENT
FACTORS INFLUENCING KNOWLEDGE AND TECHNOLOGY TRANSFER
(see text)

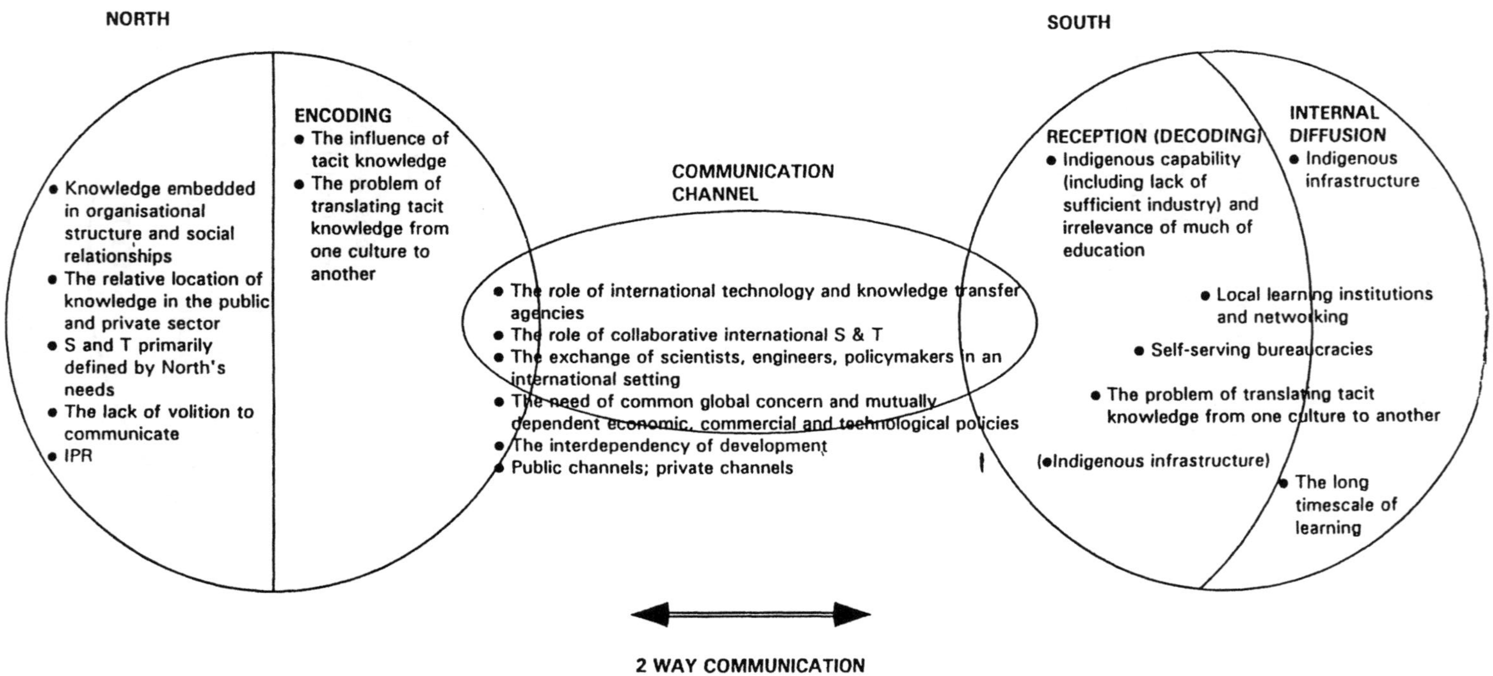

Thus knowledge and technology transfer from N-S is not considerable. A gross economic gap continues to widen despite partial localised gains made in some NICs. These economic gaps are not limited to that between 'North' and 'South' for *within* the South the problem of so called 'dualism' - in part deified by a rural/urban divide but more complicated than that - reflects an equally tragic division of the populace, even *within* less developed countries.

In global terms the division of the North and South has led to several problems which go beyond borders. Thus the 'global warming' problem, the ozone-depletion problem, the numerous ecological loss patterns which flow from much of the North's activities nevertheless compromise the whole planet. And whilst in terms of material appetite the 20% of the world's population who compromise the North are utilising in excess of 80% of the worlds material and energy output which contains its own global penalties, the poorer and much larger population in the South understandably seek to develop and trade in whatever way the global economy permits them. Single crop production, single-metal mining and ore extraction, development trajectories implicitly or explicitly imposed by World Bank or IMF perspectives serve, ultimately, to compound the global dilemma in that environmental problems of the 'South' also feed back into the Global Equation.

Added to this the partial integration/excluded divide, or rather the relative infrastructural conditions which characterise and differentiate those two worlds *ensures* in different ways that technology transfer, knowledge transfer is neither as fast, or on a scale of sufficiency or urgency as to allow the poorer less developed nations to attain the means of attending to their present - or future - industrial/environmental problems. Thus whilst the 'North' may be moving toward an era which seeks (say) greater material and energy efficiency, improved environmental technology, technical 'fixes' and legislative standards which try to stem the unwanted tide of environmental and ecological damage which has accrued to date, the 'South' has neither the means, or the full diffusion of best practice technology. There are many technology transfer, knowledge transfer, and economic-dependency factors which play a strong part in all of this. Such a state of affairs is further complicated by the fact that whilst much *(but by no means all)* 'scientific knowledge 'is in the public domain, technological knowledge is primarily in the private domain. Transfer from the latter is therefore subject to the usual economic forces. And *even* if potential transfer is available or permissible then utilisation and diffusion of that knowledge is *often compromised* by lack of 'absorptive capacity or capability' in the South (see diagram 9 opposite).

In global communication terms, if we now explore our earlier analogy, the dire need is to' improve all forms of data transmission between 'North' and 'South', between 'public' and 'private' sectors, between the 'two levels of internal dualism' viz. to undo the communication blockages indicated in figures 8 and 9. But that need implies *much else.* For if 'data-transmission' is to be transformed into effective knowledge *transfer,* effective technology *transfer,* then the means of decoding data into a meaningful message is necessary. That implies the capacity to *absorb* and utilise 'information' and to revert to our earlier analogy it means that 'communication theory' is not enough. It is not only the transmission of data but the intention of the sender of the message, his willingness to release information and his willingness to participate in *mutual learning* (since as argued earlier much knowledge is 'tacit', embedded in organisational structures, even social structure) which ensures that knowledge transfer actually occurs. This, of course, also requires that the 'receiver' of the potential knowledge transfer can absorb or decode the transmitted information. *Hence the need of extensive indigenous capability and the importance of indigenous infrastructure.*

In global communication terms, therefore, the factors of knowledge transfer and technology transfer which were arbitrarily listed earlier can now be more systematically reorganised into the form shown in figure (9) below. And we can now comment upon the individual significance of each item and the global significance of the totality. In so doing we then have at least the basis of discussion by future generations for the achievement of a sustainable social and physical environment. The appropriate international and national agencies and the supporting policy mechanisms will then require further exploration.

Comments on Figure (9) (Global Communication for sustainable development: factors influencing knowledge and technology transfer):

The global 'communication system' indicated in figure (9) can be reproduced in a simplified form as shown in Figure 10 below and the influence of the various sub-parts more clearly elicited.

Components A and B comprise the industrialised nations communication capacity; D and E that of the less developed nations 'receiving-power'. Area C we will refer to as the main communication channel. Sub-factors have been indicated in Figure 9 where many of the more important features are listed.

Now the North's communication capacity (or capability) is divided into two main characteristic Area 'A' relates to both the 'location' of knowledge and the propensity to transmit knowledge. It can therefore be subdivided as shown in figure 11.

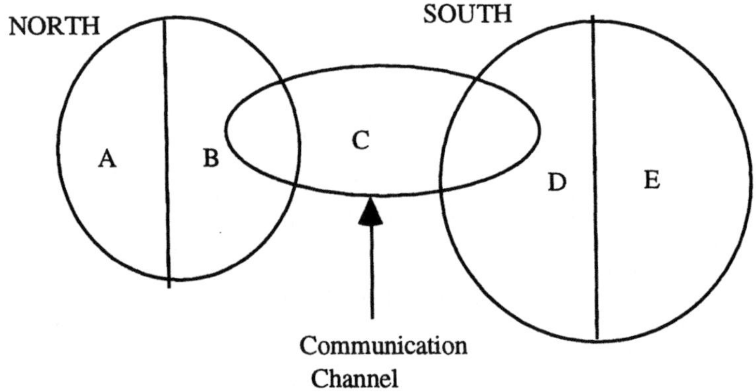

Figure 10 Simplified Global Communication System

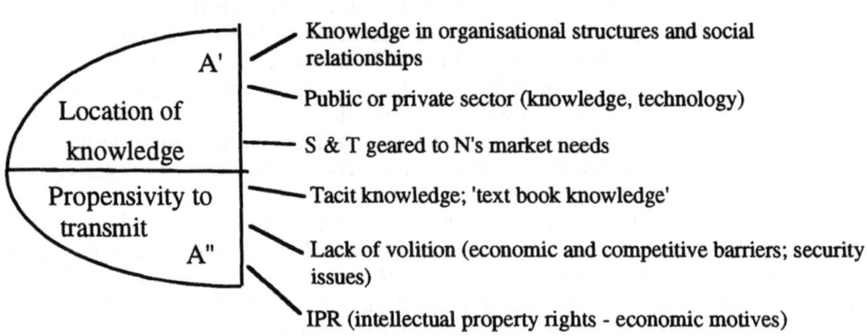

Figure 11 Location of knowledge and propensity to transmit

The distinction of A' and A" is important in a global policy sense (as are the other categories C, D and E etc.) in that we can more clearly classify macro policy needs; make appropriate groupings and clustering. This ultimately is much more satisfactory than a long 'shopping-list' of arbitrary recommendations. In addition the point can be more clearly made that as with *any* communication system failure of any sub-component this leads to total failure of successful transmission, encoding or reception. Thus, if either A', A", B, C, D or E 'fails' then the whole communication system is compromised. But to return to A' and A": A' refers to the 'location' of knowledge. This is not as simple a concept as it at first appears. Not all knowledge is "in a textbook" or drawn on a blueprint. Much knowledge is effectively in 'peoples heads' or embedded an organisational structures (or even social structures). This is 'tacit' knowledge. Assuming that there are no *external* barriers *to* communication *(viz.* region A" - IPR etc.) then the policy task is to *translate* that embedded or tacit knowledge into a suitably encoded form which takes as to region B. Not only that, but it has to be in a form that can be assimilated from one culture to another. Many mistakes are made here and hence the whole topic of *appropriate technology* etc. But even without recourse to the special case of appropriate (or culturally bound) technology many technologies require different plant, a factory farm often requires to address very different technical and organisational solutions to the differing problems of say Germany, Brazil and India. Translating much of this tacit (or even observable knowledge) which corresponds to region B in the diagram is therefore often a formidable task. There have been very many historical failures.

Region or Area D and E constitutes the reception and internal diffusion components of the receiving countries - in this case the less developed world. The initial reception, or rather its decoding of the S&T knowledge (and related organisational features which attend that knowledge. viz. tacit knowledge again!) depends crucially upon the local indigenous capacity and related infrastructure. This implies not only the need of many scientists, academics, institutes, but also commerce and industry itself. All of the latter plays a part both in decoding and later internal diffusion. Indeed if we make our model dynamic then reception and later diffusion ought to constantly interact via two-way feedback. Such 'attenuation of signal' then leads to extra information being sought where necessary and redundant or misleading information being discarded. Also region E can be subdivided into E' and E", where this time E' corresponds to *urban sector* and E" to the rural sector since each requires different diffusion characteristics. In fact E" (the rural sector) can take as many patterns, as one wishes to recognise in relation to local or sub-regional requirements which permits a heterogeneity of policy response analysis or whatever. This is demonstrated in Figure (12) below.

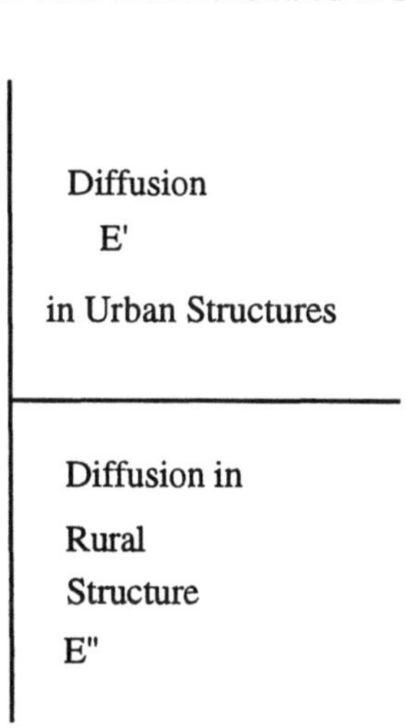

Figure 12 (a) A bimodal diffusion of knowledge and technology scene

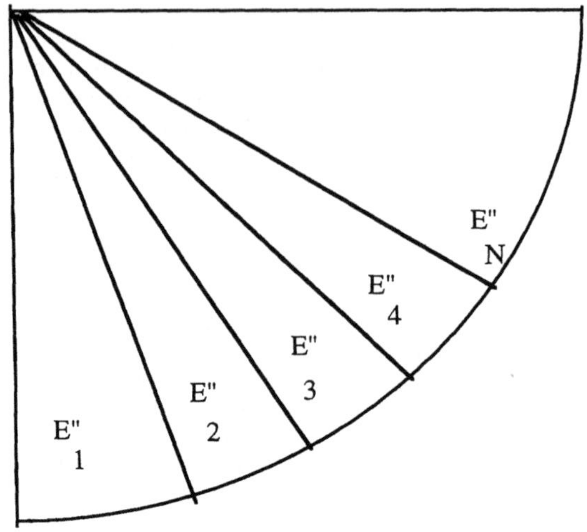

Figure 12 (b) Heterogeneity of rural circumstances and knowledge transfer needs

Finally, the communication channel, C, covers the mechanisms and agencies, the public and private channels for the transmission of knowledge, technological know-how etc. In communication theory parlance the 'bandwidth' of that all-important channel is determined by first, its terms of reference, and second, by the efficiency and power of the relevant actors or agencies. Thus in figure (9) earlier we find listed in the communication channel area two items of extreme importance. These are: 1) the need of common global concern; and 2) the interdependency of development. Both of these aspects can control what it is considered appropriate or legitimate to communicate. Failure at either of these two levels in policy terms, can severely compromise the whole world communication scene. It should also be noted that as shown in Figure (9) the communication' system has a two-way requirement. This should not be N-S dominated or vice versa. Dominance in either direction is undesirable.

Barriers to Communication

Having made the above points what are the major barriers to the achievement of a global communication system which leads to sustainable development? It is necessary to keep them in mind in order to see what has to be done and what has to be overcome; I would suggest the following play a large part:

(1) The vast majority of the citizenry of the 'North' do not fully accept that their lifestyles impose a straight-jacket on the possibility of the South developing in more fully or that many of the conditions of the South derive from the conditions of the North, or that the conditions of the North depends in several important ways on the conditions of the South.

(2) If the South does manage over forthcoming decades to develop (considerably) its economic and industrial potential (and thereby probably solves its population problems - which are world problems) there has been insufficient analysis or attention to what this would imply for the global economy or the physical environment. Earlier literature was woefully inadequate. Having said that the gap between North and South continues to grow; the dominant development trajectories of the South are defined by three factors (one internal and two external, although the internal factor is a derivation of the external). The internal factor is dualism: an elite

minority, a formal urban sector which tends to set the economic and social policy agenda in a myriad of ways. The two external factors include (a) the 'imposed' development trajectory which derive from the nature of the world -economy (dependency theory, if you will); (b) Special requirements from the World Bank, IMP and other less 'public' loan agencies. Thus part of the South follows the development trajectory of the' North, whilst much 6o the South remains essentially in limbo.

(3) Assuming that 'the global environmental problems are, or become, so enormous that a massive, radical change in the relationship of the private sector to the public world at large is called for, our economies (and ownership) are presently structured in a way which may inhibit that radical change.

(4) An ethos of 'private competition' compromises much transfer of knowledge and the possibilities of development of poorer economies and the majority of the world's population.

(5) An era which is sceptical of centralisation, centralised government planning, provides its own systemic barriers

(6) Dualism, elitism, localised self-interest in the South (which only mirrors a slightly less distorted condition in the North) induces its own problems of societal irrelevance in policy and unsatisfied need of the majority.

(7) As capital-intensive techniques progress, as the transfer of labour from the primary to other sectors ensues there emerges an ever increasing problem regarding full global employment.

(8) Regionalised protectionism remains just as potent a force as calls for integrated open world economy thereby reinforcing existing world geo-economic and geo-political problems.

(9) Despite an apparent increase in the power and authority of the UN the main influence upon its outlook comes from the world's most powerful economic and military nations, not the most populace or needy.

(10) Though there is much literature, much discussion of alternative life-styles, more environmentally benign environmental policies, and the need for large scale R&D programmes into alternative, energy schemes, decentralisation etc., little of this has been translated into large scale programmes of action or explanation.

(11) Local Recessions, calls for employment and growth (all understandable), reinforce past trajectories not new pathways.

(12) The power of private industry: its remit, its perception of market needs and its definition of the market-place continues to grow. Legislative boundaries, social containment is not that strong.

Conclusions

What does all of this imply in policy terms, with *respect to knowledge and technology transfer in a global setting* and with respect to the solving of contemporary and future world problems? We would suggest the following:

First, with respect, to macro-policy it is useful if the world agencies examine in detail the five areas or dominant facets of global communication shown in figure (10) [viz. A, B, C, D and E] in order to establish a clear picture of the difficulties, barriers to communication which exists in each of the five levels of the communication process. Agencies must then seek to ensure that each level functions in a way commensurate with *global* need.

Second, the 'responsibility' for each level will vary. To a large degree the developed economies (and within that the EC are largely responsible for levels 'A' and 'B' and to some extent level 'C'. At present the developed economies control and set the terms of reference of 'channel' C'. *This should change.* The less developed reforms need to determine the characteristics of C to an equal, or even greater, degree than the developed economies. [In our model we have not commented upon S-S communication links, that are equally important and would shadow much of our discussion so far - excepting 'that the 'translation' problem between developing countries themselves might not be so great since many problems and needs are shared]. On the other hand the less developed regions are responsible for policies which determine the effectiveness of levels D and E. But here we encounter a problem. This is because the rate and form of development of indigenous capacity and indigenous infrastructure in LDCs is indirectly controlled by the developed countries (viz. world economic policy; terms of trade; commodity prices; development 'requirements' imposed by World Banks, and IMF etc.). Nevertheless much can and has been done to develop local infrastructural and indigenous development in LDCs by their own interventionist policies: witness the comparatively successful development of the so called 'four tigers' and especially the educational policies of South Korea for example.

Third, as mentioned earlier failure of any one of the stages of 'communication' in A to E compromises, indeed may even totally defeat successful knowledge or technological transfer. The strength and importance of the 'model' is therefore *to view it in its entirety*: to see it is a completely functionally interacting system. The policy aim is then to either ensure the total communication system functions and/or to note which are the weakest links and to exert maximum policy' pressure on the weakest links.

Fourth, each level requires to be broken down into more detailed constituent parts (see figure 9 which suggests *some* of the factors) and to further understand how the sub-components interact.

Fifth, it is necessary to assess if improvement of the knowledge transfer system (the communication) is primarily dependent upon (say) economic factors, sociological factors, manpower requirements, institutional structure or whatever.

Sixth, the model we have put forward - viewing the world knowledge and technology transfer problem as a communication issue - allows the EC to see its part in a global perspective. Thus the communication system A to E could be redrawn in a more specific manner for the EC 'linkage' with (say) East Europe; Asian; Africa; South America. The effectiveness, problems and needs for each sub-mapping of the world economy could (and should) be undertaken in order to elicit new technology and knowledge transfer links. Each mapping would be (is) different. East Europe's receptive capability (D and subsequent diffusion E) would no doubt be different from that between (say) the EC and African nations. There are many reasons for this which will not be discussed here. But it indicates the need of such global and regional communication mapping - and the potential importance of braking down into functional terms the five critical stages of communication or 'transfer' of knowledge.

Seventh, So far we have put forward the model purely in logistical or functional terms but there is an urgent need to provide a quantitative *picture.* This applies to each stage (A to E) of the overall process. In particular the world (and the EC) need to know many details concerning the 'channel capacity' of 'C', the communication channel. Thus, for example, how many international, technology or development agencies *does* the world need? On what scale, what manpower, and with what resources? Ten times or a hundred times that which presently exist? Similarly what number of exchange arrangements between scientists, engineers, policy makers? How ('numerically') can this be supplemented by a myriad of advanced, multi-media techniques? What scale of finance, and over what time period, is implied by analysing the world in such terms? Or yet again, in terms of indigenous capability, indigenous development, or infrastructural development (whether this be energy provision, transport system, shelter, communication systems or whatever)... then what financial scale of commitment is implied to ensure less developed regions are 'above threshold'. Here we may refer to Critical Industrial Mass (CIM) in the sense that many less developed economies have yet to develop their own internal industrial and urban infrastructure on a scale commensurate with need. Each dimension of infrastructure - road, rail, water, energy system, food supply and distribution implies a quantitative technological 'critical mass need' that is if levels D and E of our global communication model are to function satisfactorily. All of that implies, a quantitative analytical need - and subsequent derivation of global (and EC) policy requirements.

Eight, In terms of 'critical mass' and the ability of individual nations to prosper in the global economy there remains the issue of the problems of the weakest nations - the so called 'Least Developed Nations'. Thus, in all of our discussion we have, in the most simplistic terms referred to the world as 'North' and South'. This has been of course purely for ease of discussion. It misses much. It misses the contemporary East-West détente, the restructuring of the USSR, the differences between S E Asia and Latin America. It misses the declining economic force of the USA, the migratory pressures on the EC, the fact that the EC might 'dissolve' somewhat with the 'German problem', the incorporation, of East Europe, the pressure of the South. It misses the rise of the Pacific Rim nations, the rise of Asian fundamentalism. It misses China.

In particular it misses as we have just noted the *'Least* Developed Countries'. Those countries, depending upon our criteria, constitute about 50 nations with a significant proportion of the world's total population. They have special problems: low per capita income, often small nations, highly vulnerable economies and local environments. Viewed as single economies they may be 'unviable' in geo-political terms if not with respect to local culture. For such nations in order to achieve 'critical-mass', new forms of linkage - new patterns of international partnership will become necessary. And with that it may then be possible to make their absorptive capacity, their ability to fully benefit from greater international knowledge exchange, a more viable proposition. Overall the policy implications in a world setting (and the place of the EC within this) can now be seen more clearly. It is to address each of the eight factors listed above. It is to encourage quantitative commitment and the political will to alleviate the failings of present patterns of global-communication of knowledge in both its pure and applied sense.

It requires changes in attitude to IPR, to the translation and encoding of knowledge; it requires larger and wider terms of reference for each 'communication channel' available (whether this be transfer agency, exchange of scientists and engineers, global telecommunication systems, international networking, collaborative research or whatever); it requires assistance in relation to local infrastructure development. All of that implies a role for the EC, a new set of protocols. At the same time it demands inputs and changes on the part of less developed economies: patterns of self-development; in particular a single minded commitment to *all* members of their own societies rather than a distortion of policy interest to the urban or elite 'minority of the greater majority of humankind'.

However, technology and knowledge transfer does not stand alone: many wider economic and geo-political changes are also required within which knowledge transfer (or lack of) is embedded. The recent UNDP report 'Human Development Report 1992 indicates some of the required changes: e.g. reduction in military expenditure by 3% per year for the rest of the 1990s and creation of a $1500 billion 'peace divided'; opening up of global markets which could give a $500 billion boost for poorer nations, a new arrangement regarding foreign debt and interest rates to reduce the $50 billion current net transfer from S-N; a global income tax on GNP to be spent on environmental programmes; a restructured UN and the formation of a Development Security Council with strong 'South' representation which would coordinate global development policies; and finally the monitoring of corruption.

Much of this reflects the point of view regarding international S&T and economic cooperation. Knowledge, Trade, Economic, Environment - all are seen to stand as interdependent forces. Failure on any one suggests, ultimately, total system failure.

References

Brandt Commission (1983), Common Crises: North-South cooperation for world recovery, Pan Books, London

Rahman, A. (1972), Science, technology and development in a new social order, in Goldsmith, M and King, A (eds), *Issues of Development,* Oxford, Pergamon Press. p 57-70.
Lindsay, P and Norman, D (1972), *Human information processing*, Academic Press, New York.
Shannon, C and Weaver, W. (1949), The mathematical theory of communication, Illinois: University of Illinois Press.
Whiston, T G, (1991), Forecasting the world's problems - the last empire: the corporatisation of society and the diminution of self, *Futures,* March 1991, p 163-178.
Whiston, T G (1988), Coordinating educational policies and plans with those of science and technology: developing and Western developed countries, *Bulletin of the International Bureau of Education* No 247, UNESCO, April-June 1988, p 1-144.
Wiener, N. (1948), *Cybernetics*, Wiley, New York.
World Bank (1991), World Development Report 1991: The Challenge of Development, University Press, Oxford.

Notes

* Appeared in Whiston, T Education and employment for a sustainable world, an EC- FAST report, FOP 323, European Commission, June 1992

Chapter 4

The Keyboard Blues: Modern technology and the rights and risks of people at work*

Patricia Shipley

Health and safety at work is a moral imperative, but the debates emphasise only the economic and legal sides. Autonomy and freedom in work process control enhances the power that responsibly-minded workers may need to protect their health. Drawing on case material from working with VDUs and other forms of modern technology, it is shown, on the other hand, that loss of control over their immediate work processes can be stressful and potentially harmful to them. It is suggested that unquestioned divisive and dualistic practices at workplaces are a potent and unnecessary reason for this problem.

Introduction

> "A human being can only survive in the Age of Machinery if the ethical norms of life are held sacred. This Shamanist protest at the destructive power of evil, as expressed in the Curse upon iron, stands forth prominently in a society in moral crisis."

[Extracts from programme notes accompanying the performance by the Danish National Radio Choir of this piece by the Estonian composer, Veljo Tormis, at St Johns Smith Square, December 1994.]

I begin my paper by asserting the moral rights of working people for health protection at work. I continue with a discussion of workers' legal health and safety rights in the UK today, followed by a consideration of the risks accompanying modern industry and technology. Then the state of occupational health and safety services in the UK is summarised, and an illustration of the limitations of current provisions is given through a description of an experimental worker health advisory project based in doctors' surgeries in a local community in London. Stress at work was found to be a major health problem for workers of both sexes seen in the project, but particularly for those workers doing clerical and secretarial/word-processing jobs.

The use of machinery and equipment was a major job hazard or risk reported by many women interviewed in the project, and the problem of intensive, repetitive work with VDUs was highlighted in case studies of women presenting in the clinic with serious 'repetitive strain' injuries. The problem of perceived lack of control at work is discussed next in relation to the division of labour, particularly occupational divisions on gender lines, and to externally paced work, along with the current emphasis within stress psychology on individual coping. The control problem is adumbrated with a case study from air traffic control. It is then suggested that *'deep dualism'* (unquestioned dualisic attitudes in practice), is one insidious and major reason for problems with the health and safety protection of workers and members of the public affected by industry, and the role of modern technology is touched on here. The paper finishes with suggested examples for dealing with dualism, in the belief that ordinary goodness will prevail in the end.

Health and Safety Rights at Work

There isn't much written about the health and safety *rights* of working people, - or, for that matter, of the public who are affected by business practices in some way or other. There are two sorts of rights I have in mind; one is legal and the other is moral or ethical. It is the latter, in particular, about which there is scant discussion. 'Business ethics' is fashionable in academia and in business and management schools, but it is unclear how far such thinking has penetrated the real world of business and commerce. Indeed, there is a traditional view that the welfare and *moral* rights of their workforce or the public affected by that business are not the bosses' legitimate concern, except insofar as this bears upon the business 'owner's' interests in the long term. In her book 'Just Business' one contemporary exponent of this view, the American author Elaine Sternberg - no doubt inspired by Aristotle's doctrine about the essence or nature of things and their fundamental or essential purpose or telos - argues that "the correct ethical concern of business is *just business* - nothing but business but business which is just", and that "altruism is out of place in business and the trendy demands for corporate social responsibility should not be taken seriously." (Sternberg, 1994).

But what is 'just' business? The main premise of my paper is that working people do have an intrinsic moral right to the protection of their health and safety on the job; and that this is part of a more general moral good, that of the unconditional maximisation of human health and minimisation of distress. I do not believe we should put a price on health. It is also my contention that all man-made artefacts can be turned against the human race if they are used without concern for their ethical implications.

There is also a *legal* right in the UK to such protection, as worker or as an affected member of the public - up to a point - ie the law requires employers to exercise a general duty of care of their workforce, and the public in their vicinity, only "as far as is reasonably practicable" (Health & Safety at Work Act, 1974). This is a pragmatic clause which tends to boil down in practice to a combination of what is economically feasible to that enterprise and to acting within the bounds of current knowledge and technology. This law is backed up by the few available codes of practice and is in the British tradition of prioritising the voluntary conduct of affairs before legal enforcement. Deep down in our culture there is an engrained liberal fear of outside interference in our business as well as our private lives, and our way of conducting business perhaps reflects our emphasis on individual freedom over more presciptive external regulation. The law is presumed realistic about the limits to state intervention in such a complex area; enterprise, after all, generates the wealth to pay for the health, and goodheartedness without solvency is business suicide. In its publicity package to industry as part of Europe's 1993 campaign for health and safety protection at work the UK government's Health & Safety Executive, which 'polices' the law, includes the following slogan: "In today's competitive world, good health is good business." Clearly, economic values and indicators take priority over other considerations in the rhetoric of those who have official responsibility for the health and wellbeing of the nation's workforce.

Furthermore, the State, it is implied, cannot keep an eye on everything that might go wrong; and perfect health and safety, like perfect happiness, are impossible pipedreams. People also need the right incentives to change. Better that those who generate the risks and those who work with those risks share the responsibility, our law dictates. Furthermore, it is recognised that the technology of risk control is still in a state of infancy. The law, therefore, expects a culture of health and safety-mindedness, of prevention, to be promoted in workplaces.

But many of our organizations fall well short of this expectation. The result is that the high costs of workplace injury and ill-health are at least as much borne by those directly injured, and indirectly their families and the communities in which they live, as they are by the employer. The State - the tax payer - also picks up a large portion of the tab, in sick pay benefits and National Health Service costs resulting from workplace injuries and ill health.

As with other bodies of our legislation, this sovereign law on health and safety is now challenged by legislation from the European Union which has recently adopted a 'Framework Directive' on health and safety at work. The European Union hopes to encourage member states to improve workplace health and safety through this means. Worker participation and worker rights for information, consultation, training, and representation in health and safety matters, are seen as an important route to achieving such a goal. The EU law is more explicit in the setting of standards than the UK law where the underlying principle is more one of *self-regulation*. The British government succeeded, however, in getting some of the draft EU regulations watered down and, as a result, it was agreed that member states could interpret and implement the Directive in accordance with their own national, local laws and practices. The UK has continually resisted the continental model of formal worker democracy, with its structures for worker representation on Works' Councils, which are to be found in Germany and the Netherlands, for example, preferring to leave such issues to local negotiation instead. We wait to see how effective the new European law will be in practice.

My concern, therefore, is that of the equal rights all workers should have to good health and safety provisions and facilities, including access to relevant advice and information to help them to protect themselves and to understand the nature and extent of the risks they take in earning their living. It follows, that it is encumbent on us all in the workplace to seek to protect the rights of others there, not only our own rights, insofar as we have the power to do so. Free trade and the free market are all very well but freedom in the market, as in society at large, has always carried obligations. Freedom always did have limits and responsibilities.

Health and Safety Risks at Work

Even so, risks to worker health do not abate in an increasingly industrialised and competitive world. As one set of risks comes under control it is replaced by a new set accompanying a new technology, the adverse effects of which often coming to light only after that technology has been in operation for a while. Each year, for example, some 1000 new chemicals are added to the risks generated by industry, and many of these could put the public outside the factory gates at risk from pollutant emissions. As I write it is the tenth anniversary of that tragic and costly Bhopal Chemical Plant disaster in India, where 7000 died and 20,000 were harmed with chemical injuries, many of them grave, which raises as many moral as it does economic and legal questions about the citing and operation of the plant. Most of the victims were not workers in the plant, but local residents. Consumers of the products of chemical industries may also be put at risk because of inadequately-tested dangerous chemical additives to food, drink and domestic goods. I was stunned to learn of the enormous range of ordinary Western household products that are implicated in the possible genesis of cancer (Clark, 1993). Some 200 substances, also, are recognised as causing occupational asthma, from flour and other dusts to solders used in the *e lectronic* s industry.

These days there are rapid changes in work processes, and the introduction of new technology is a major part of this scenario - from computer mainframes, E-mail, desktop PCs (Personal Computers), and 'Internet', to 'super information highways', and supercomputers. In an increasingly complex and technologically-driven world of global communications where business fights for survival by struggling to maintain the competitive edge, and where technological innovations and technological solutions to problems are preferred to the alternatives, it may be tempting to take the risks first and ask questions afterwards. Even the most socially and environmentally-conscious employer and innovator may be unable, moreover, to answer all the questions about the risks in advance. The technology of control is unable, if you like, to match the technology of innovation in this 'technological fix'. It feels like a technological juggernaut that has run out of control and we cannot climb off. I have resisted, moreover, citing the seemingly insoluble safety problems associated with the nuclear industrial/military complex, an example of which was the disaster to the Chernobyl nuclear power plant in the Ukraine, where the consequences stretched far beyond the locality responsible for its failure.

The UK has a long tradition of health and welfare legislation and of philanthropic employers, for sure; the first of its many Factories Acts became law in 1802. But there is little room for complacency in the UK as in any industrialised country in an increasingly technologically-complex world. Working people need ready access to freely available and intelligible information about the risks they run while at work.

The 'new technology' (based on computers and micro-electronics), is also a new source of health problems, particularly in the workplace. I shall expand on this below with reference to case studies from the electronic office in which one form of the new technology is in common use, the keyboard VDU, but before that I shall summarise the picture of occupational health and safety services in this country, given that the first industrialised country in the world has had longer than others to develop such facilities, and should serve as a model for those countries which have become or are becoming newly-industrialised and technocised.

This focus on the potential adverse effects of new technology does not imply, however, that I am against such innovation in principle. I am no Luddite; on the contrary, I am mindful of the many social benefits that accrue from it. It has, for example, improved the quality of life of some disabled people; such as in the use of PCs as enhanced means of communication for those unfortunate enough to have severely-impaired or total loss of hearing or speech and, despite the worrying case studies of the abuse of computers in the health service there is plenty of evidence of good use of the new technology which benefits patient care. There is a pioneering project in Belfast, for example, based on a clinic-to-hospital video link through which clinic nurses can show difficult cases to a hospital consultant with the minimum of delay. And in The Netherlands there is a successful computerised ambulance service with the control room staffed by experienced paramedicals.

I maintain that problems reside more with the tool users than the tools, and that this may account for much of the seeming ambiguity of technology. Technology can be a two-edged sword. The fact that something may be put to bad use, either intentionally or unintentionally, does not mean that it is in itself bad. I am all in favour, though, of the introduction of appropriate technology in the right way. Yet this is a sophisticated process. The ambiguous clause in the UK Health and Safety at Work Act, for instance, about what is 'reasonably practicable', should not depend on one-sided interpretation. All those seriouly affected should have a say; workers as well as managers and sometimes consumers and other members of the public.

And I do not believe we should divorce technology from the socio-organisational side of a system. But my view is rather different from that propounded for some years by the London-based Tavisock Institute of Human Relations, the 'socio-technical systems' view, which is that of the *joint optimisation* of the technical and social dimensions of an organisation, where one organisational feature such as the social is not prioritised at the expense of the other. There is an ethical, as well as ergonomic, argument for putting the people first - at the centre of the design map - and building the technological aids around them - their needs and interests (Oborne *et al* , 1993).

Occupational Health and Safety Services and Facilities in the UK

Occupational health services in the workplace have never been mandatory in the UK, although many large companies voluntarily offer such a service. The best of these company schemes seek to reduce or prevent workplace risks to health and safety but in reality others do not go further than providing a service to management for the screening of individual workers for recruitment purposes. At the national level there is some limited official state protection of worker health. This takes the form of a central health and safety inspectorate in a 'health and safety policemen' role whose duty is to try to enforce the law (currently the Health and Safety at Work etc Act of 1974). Local Authorities are delegated this responsibility at regional levels for some workplaces, such as retail shops, and employ community environmental health officers who are the local equivalent of the national inspectorate. Both bodies are expected to fulfil their duties proactively through unannounced inspections of workplaces, and reactively by following up reported accidents and complaints made about a particular employer. In practice unannounced visits by health and safety inspectors are infrequent. A reason for this must be the substantial (13%) cuts to inspectorate staffing imposed by this country's government over the past 15 years; a government which it is argued (see, for example, Dalton, 1992) has proved itself hostile to labour protection laws.

Occupational health facilities in the UK are still patchy and thin on the ground despite our long industrial history. Furthermore, there is a large number of small to medium sized enterprises in the UK, many of which are invisible to the state's health and safety inspectorate and sometimes to local environmental officers too, and lacking in the knowledge and facilities for good health and safety practice at work. So there is considerable room for improvement. In a survey of occupational health and safety provisions in a sample of comparatively large companies a few years ago, for example, we found that industrial physicians employed by these companies could sometimes feel compromised by the ambiguity of their role; by a conflict of interests - managers' and workers'; the company health doctor is employed by management and typically identifies with the status of management, (Orlans and Shipley, 1983). Who, then, is serving our workforce's health care interests unambiguously?

The Camden and Islington Occupational Health Project in London

Since January 1990, the Camden and Islington Occupational Health Project (C&IOHP) has offered a specialist information, support and advisory service to working people, and their community doctors (ie their GPs or 'general practitioners' working at the level of 'primary care'). There are two such Projects in London but they cover only a fraction of the capital's workforce, and there are only a handful of them nationwide. Advice is given on occupational risks and diseases and their prevention and alleviation. Although the Project is active in the community in several ways, its main focus has been in the small number of GP surgeries in the community which volunteered to participate in the experiment. Project workers who are trained in health and safety, not medicine, have so far interviewed over 3000 workers attending there as patients. Occupational histories are taken and patients' reports of job risks and health problems at work are noted (see Dalton 1993). Individual reports are then aggregated anonymously and compiled into local job health and risk profiles on a computer data-base. These Projects are independent of employers and all are funded insecurely; 'on a shoestring' as it were.

I recently did a formal evaluation of the Camden Project some three years after its inception, to guage how far it had raised awareness in patients and their GPs about issues concerning health and safety at work, and how far it had provided support to working patients and to GP practice staff in dealing with health and safety problems brought to light in the practice clinics (Shipley, 1993). Among other activities I collected opinions about the Project from the patients and doctors participating and examined the computer data-base for frequency of reported workplace problems. As many as one patient in two interviewed by Project workers reported a personal occupational health problem.

There are comparatively few occupational health specialists in the UK and the medical referral rate of patients to such consultants by GPs is therefore correspondingly low. Several of the GPs in the volunteer practices said they did not know to whom to turn for appropriate advice on occupational health problems of patients, seeing themselves in more of a back-up than an interventionist role in this respect; employers and government official inspectors were the people seen by them to be more properly responsible here. The latter, it was believed, have the power to monitor and change the workplace to meet required standards of health and safety, not community doctors. Besides, the GPs did not wish to betray patient confidence or put a patient's job at risk by intervening at the level of the patient's employer. The doctors appeared not to appreciate the limitations imposed by an under-resourced official inspectorate, or by the vested interests or lack of imagination of some of the employers. Instead, the GPs saw their responsibilities for health promotion in terms of the medical screening of individual patients and of offering patients lifestyle advice.

Such Projects are one tiny step in the direction of trying to meet the needs of working people for proper and *independent* care of their health at the workplace, although what they are able to achieve in practice is severely limited because of scarcity of resources and lack of influence. They are at best a thin 'finger in the dyke'. Even their hold in primary care in the community is tiny and precarious. Nearly half of the country's workforce has no occupational health cover at all, neither the protection offered by an employer through some kind of occupational health service on or off site, nor help from a Project like the Camden one (see, for example, DoH, 1993). A few of these workers may find help from a well-informed trade union representative, and even fewer will feel able to protect themselves at work.

About half of the patients I interviewed in the C&IOHP reported having an occupational health service at work, but some thought it appeared to be a first aid facility only, or was mainly used for employment screening purposes. Less than half of the patients interviewed said that they had been aware of health and safety matters beforehand, and many told me they felt their GPs should take an interest in such issues but did not seem to have the time or training to deal with them in the surgery.

Two VDU case studies from the Project

It should be said at the outset that these case study patients were working for large companies which are household names; one, a high street bank. Both case studies are of female workers doing intensive VDU work who had complained to their doctors of 'work related upper limb disorder' or 'repetitive strain injury (RSI)'. It is not proposed to discuss here the many other health problems, such as eye, neck and shoulder complaints, that may be associated with work on VDUs.

It has been estimated that some 10 million workers, about 40% of the total workforce in the UK, now use VDUs on the job (London Hazards Centre, 1993). It is also reported that RSI is the largest source of work-related ill health in Britain, with an annual cost to industry from lost working days alone of 1.2 billion pounds ('The Guardian' newspaper, 1994). Many of these cases come from heavy older industry such as from car assembly, and from other, lighter older industries, such as turkey plucking. Many come from new forms of work using electronic check-in and check-out workstations. Others are generated by bad working practices in electronics offices with intensive VDU use. Many in the new groups of workers affected are women.

RSI is thought to be irreversible if not treated in time and much can be done to the workplace and to working practices to prevent it arising in the first place through ergonomically well-designed equipment and realistic workloads. RSI is a generic term which covers many muskulo-skeletal conditions, some well defined, others more diffuse. Workers at risk are those whose work includes repetitive movements in an awkward position with insufficient rest for recovery. The picture is complicated because there may be no external sign of injury. Occupational stress was found to be the main health problem reported to the Project workers by both males and females in my analysis of the C&IOHP records collected over the previous two years (Shipley, *op.cit.*), and the issue of work stress is to be discussed later in this paper. The greatest reason, however, for referral by GPs or patients and practice nurses to the Camden Project over the past year has been for RSI (C&IOHP, 1994).

As a worker health risk RSI predates the advent of the VDU, but there is little doubt that it is now a more prevalent health problem because of the careless use of the new technology (see Carter and Banister 1994, for a review of musculoskeletal problems in VDU work and how to deal with them). RSI is a recognised 'work-related' disorder where, unlike an occupational disease whose cause can be linked without question to a particular job or task, it is assumed that there are pre-existing physical and medical conditions which are exacerbated by work (World Health Organisation, 1985). In a recent official UK survey of worker health (Hodgson *et al* , 1993), covering 75,000 working people in England and Wales, about 6% of the sample questioned - implying over 2 million people out of the total UK workforce - reported they had illnesses they believed to have been caused or made worse by their work. Musculo-skeletal problems were much greater in reported prevalence than any other category of disease, of which over 8% 'caused' by work fell into the RSI category. Male rates were lower than for females for RSI, and a higher than average proportion of cases of RSI, compared with other complaints we are told, were reported as work-related. Now, on to the case studies.

Case 1

This female clerical worker had suffered a back injury on a previous job and reported to the Project worker that she now had wristache, headache and 'stress' in her current job. She cited VDUs, the repetitive nature of the work, and lifting, as current job risks or hazards to health from the job. She had taken 12 weeks off work for the back injury and she worked 8 hours daily on the VDU.

The purpose of her visit to the GP at the time of the interview was for the administration of what she referred to as a "painful" cortisone injection in one wrist to help relieve pain and her forearm and wrist were encased in plaster. Both limbs had been affected and the GP told the Project worker that the injury was "almost certainly occupational" but did not think it was helpful to contact the employer; that such problems were an inevitable part of the job. The patient was referred to hospital specialists, however. The Project worker advised the patient to try and ensure her medical records referred to the occupational cause of her injury in case she were to apply for state compensation in the future, and urged her to consult her workplace health and safety representative, if there was one, warning her that the condition could worsen and lead to the loss of the use of her arms if she carried on working in that way. The Project worker contacted the relevant trade union on the patient' s behalf and gave the patient the phone number of the Repetitive Strain Injury (RSI) Association. One of the consultants to whom the patient had been referred by her GP contacted the employer for details about the furniture used on the job and recommended suitable rest breaks from VDU use. A year later the patient reported that the employer had made improvements to the job, but this was too late for her benefit; she felt the workstation should have been ergonomically designed properly in the first place to help prevent her injury, which she described as "VDU-induced bi-lateral tenosynovitis". She was back on the job with one limb having been treated surgically and the other awaiting an operation. She had not tried to claim compensation as such but had been awarded State 'industrial injury benefit' for three months, and then put on light duties at work for a time.

Case 2

This is another, and less successful, case of a woman with tenosynovitis similarly exposed to prolonged, intensive and repetitive, but unergonomically-designed VDU work. The Project worker gave her a leaflet on managing the health risks of VDUs and details of the people she might contact for more specialist advice. The local government environmental health officer was also contacted on her behalf. The latter, however, was recorded as having said about her job that "It is not an onerous activity", and that he was very busy dealing with more serious matters such as deaths at work! He also suggested that the particular worker concerned must have been particularly susceptible to the disease. The GP had diagnosed her condition as "bi-lateral wrist tenosynovitis", and by then the woman was incapable of lifting a few books. The patient told the Project worker that work colleagues suffered similar complaints but were afraid to join her in making a formal complaint because they were in fear of being made redundant at a time of staff cuts. The union representative informed the Project worker that the company did have a manual of guidelines on VDU use but no specific rest breaks were laid down in it. The patient was subsequently transferred to cashier and filing duties but these were too much for her (she was by then wearing splints on her wrists). She had to take sick leave and pay for help from a physiotherapist outside work. She then had to leave the job altogether because of the disability, had applied for State benefits and was looking into the possibility of a claim for compensation under the Project's guidance.

The office manager had seen her as a 'troublemaker'. Her work culture had not been consistent with her doctor's advice to take the job at a slower pace. That option was simply not open to her, she thought. There was "too much pressure", and "they crashed down on you hard if you had a day off . . . they really grilled you". She added that working intensively without regular breaks worsened her condition. "You had to keep at it and get everything done each day, often working without a proper break and doing overtime". There was no time to think about adjusting the workstation to make it more ergonomic. She had been referred to a hospital orthopaedic surgeon who "did not know about RSI", and was told by him that she was lucky it wasn't arthritis! She changed her GP because her GP at that time did not know anything about RSI.

Stress, Coping and Control

Several of the doctors and patients I personally interviewed in the evaluation of the Camden Project reported that health and safety complaints to employers by patients had become fewer in recent years because of fears of job loss created by the economic climate of redundancies, staff cut backs and high unemployment. On the other hand, work had become more stressful, intensive and demanding for those remaining in employment, with, they thought, greater risks to worker health as a consequence. Patients generally did not feel powerful enough to tackle management on these issues, and, although some had enlisted the support of their workplace health and safety representatives, labour unions had been substantially weakened through government changes to labour legislation in comparatively recent years. In the UK labour force survey reported above (Hodgson *et al* , *op.cit.*) 'stress and depression' was the third largest category of work-related complaints after musculo-skeletal and lower respiratory diseases.

Of the many men and women interviewed by the C&IOHP workers themselves who reported *stress* to be their main health problem at work, uncertainty of employment was a source of stress, but the nature of the work itself was also a major problem. From the Project records of surgery interviews of working women patients I noticed that the next biggest reported work-related health problem after stress for the women was 'headaches', then 'backache', followed by problems with their 'joints/muscles/eyes'. Many of these health concerns resulted from using the new technology. Several of the women were employed in low grade clerical jobs, ie semi-skilled office jobs and general office work. Clerical workers of both sexes reported the most stress out of the several non-management job types represented in the total sample interviewed. Women doing secretarial and word processing jobs, and unemployed men, were the next most stressed. For both men and women 'lifting' was the main reported job *risk*, followed by 'machines/equipment' for women and 'general dust' for men (Shipley, 1993, *op. cit.*).

Stress

By 'stress' is meant 'distress' in this paper, or uncontrollable stress, which will be elaborated below. It is not proposed here that life and work should be devoid of stress as a morally good thing or goal, if that were indeed possible. Indeed, there is much to be said for the opportunity to have challenges to meet in the workplace, which, in the right conditions, can be stimulating and growthful, affording a sense of mastery and the chance to develop one's skill, resourcefulness and self-confidence. Rather is it maintained that conscious attempts should be made by employers and management to try to prevent and reduce distressing work-related experiences for the staff under their care, where it is possible that such stress could lead to injury, *mental* injury even. The prevention of mental injury at work is in fact required by the UK law, but it is also a moral right of workers even if it were not.

Although it patently is not responsible for all ill-health, injuries, errors and accidents at work, the extent to which stress does play a part in their aetiology is considerably under-estimated. There are at least theoretical grounds for this assertion. This is partly because stress is not a well-understood problem, largely on account of its complexity. The complexity includes what people mean by stress. This definitional ambiguity permits all kinds of prejudice about stress to surface, including that of arguing that we are entitled to do nothing about stress control and prevention because people cannot agree over what stress is and how to assess it, or, because sometimes it can seem to lead to positive, healthy and beneficial effects. Until comparatively recently stress was not part of the language, 'the discourse,' of business here in the West. The current fashion for 'stress control' in the workplace and 'stress management', furthermore, is not because the generating of distress is seen as morally wrong. Or if it is, then it is not written about, because any standard text putting the case for it usually cites the economic advantages; rarely the legal side to the case, and never the ethical.

The current fashion within the stress field which focusses on how people *cope* with stress and how to improve their coping (outlined below) is another reason, I suspect, why there is an underestimation of the size and gravity of the stress problem. But, where there is stress perpetrated by me that I could have avoided which leads to someone else's distress and injury then isn't that stress-inducing conduct morally wrong? A further point: if stress was not implicated in the cause of an injury or accident the latter usually have distressing *effect* s, for the victim if not the perpetrator.

Coping

Changing the environment to prevent or reduce stress is a topic which is rather less in evidence than that of coping with the status quo; see, for example, the themes of the contributions to the special issue on 'Coping with Stress at Work', of the international journal "Work & Stress" (1993). The underlying philosophy is that we should employ or develop the 'hardy worker', or, to draw attention to possible Darwinian undertones, that of the survival of the fittest in an era of unprecedented change. Does this thought resonate with the American and British liberal traditions? This idea is conveyed in the contribution by Rosenbaum to the above special issue (Rosenbaum, 1993). The key words published with his article are: "Self-control, coping, experiential self-control, resourcefulness". To quote him (p43):

> "During the past two decades there has been a notable shift in behavioural technology from the study of environmental contingencies that control behaviour to the study of the processes by which people control their own behaviour."

The kind of person to exhibit what Rosenberg calls 'learned resourcefulness' has acquired the necessary repertoire of skills and 'cognitions' such that, on the one hand, they are , he suggests, "capable of maintaining stability in the face of stressful events" and, on the other hand, are "open to new experiences that promote change and development" (p44). 'Learned resourcefulness' is a comparatively new gimmick in the coping literature and has come to supersede the older notion of 'learned helplessness' of the 1960s. Presumably, the hardy copers in the Camden Project are the ones who enlist the support of their health and safety representatives, (should they have them on the spot), to get the job changed; or who just pace themselves simply refusing to adhere to all of management's demands; or who get out of the job before the damage is done to their health. Unfortunately, in these days of high unemployment alternative jobs to escape to are quite scarce.

This is not to deny the evidence for differential susceptibility to stress and differences in coping ability between people; the different levels of vulnerability that people bring to the job, given roughly comparable conditions. Marsella (1994), for example, accepts this point, but he, nontheless, cites the Japanese concept of *karoshi* which, we are told, means 'death from overwork'. Quite a common problem apparently among contemporary Japanese businessmen, since, we are also told that the Japanese Ministry of Labour has invested in a "two million dollar study of job-related illness" because of it, (p154). Research evidence also grows apace confirming that it is the relationship between effort and reward which is implicated in health. It is the sustained and chronic "effort-reward imbalance", "immersion" or "exhaustive coping", in the words of Siegrist and Peter (1994) in their study of cardiovascular pathology, which ". . .elicits those recurrent episodes of distress and autonomic arousal. . .", episodes which do the damage in the long run. The effort and the costs have to be high and the rewards low for this to happen.

Control

Stress, then, is a complex process. In *externally* -paced work the sense of *control* felt by the worker may be diminished or non-existent. Although loss of control is not the only cause of stress, and stress is not always the only consequence of loss of control which by itself may lead to injury, such a state of affairs ca be, and often is, stressful. It is a feeling of being out of control when one needs to be in control; when *perceived* demands are perceived also to outstrip *perceived* resources for coping, and success at coping is seen as important to that person. It is stressful if the *perceived* consequences are anticipated by them to lead to a threat to health or performance, not only one's own health but that of others affected by one's performance on the job, others one cares about or is responsible for, as in air traffic control, for instance. It could be just as acute for the VDU operator doing paced work who fears for her health and its effects on her care of her dependants at home as for the air traffic controller for whom public and passenger safety is an over-riding concern. Lack of sufficient control over their immediate work processes, where that control is seen by them as valuable, to protect health and safety at work, is to deprive workers of a fundamental right or freedom, and this, I suggest, is morally wrong.

Granted that it is clearly not the only cause of errors, stress, near-misses, accidents and injuries, the loss of control, or perceived threat of it, is an abiding theme in the scientific and professional literature on stress, including stress at the workplace. There are degrees of consciousness or shades of awareness, of how much control one has at any one time. This adds to the complexity of the subject. It may sometimes only be feasible to measure stress by taking account of, possibly vague, feelings of *felt distress* , of something being 'not quite right' (see Levi, 1994). We may find it difficult to articulate the problem. We often know more than we can tell. Trying to keep a measure of control over their life events in general is indubitably important, indeed is a necessary skill, to ordinary people. Behind stress and distress there always lurks some degree of real or perceived lack of control, when having control really matters (see, for example, Fisher, 1985, and Gaillard and Wientjes, 1994).

In a study of mainly women telephone switchboard operators, (Babb and Shipley, 1994), new technology leading to impaired control was a major stress. While overcoming many of the technical problems associated with the older cordboards, computerised systems resulted in operator boredom and monotony and loss of control on the task. The operator was able to control the length of the call, but the actual degree of personal control was severely restricted by the organisational emphasis on speed and efficiency, and by the system's demands. The work demand was comparatively low at the time of the study but there was little operator involvement in decision-making around the job, along with a high degree of control by the system. Activities were determined by the rules of the switchboard; if breaks were taken and for how long, for example, and performance was monitored by the computer. Not only did the operators have very little control over the task and equipment, and actually felt controlled by the computer, they were also under the strict control of management. Following are some of the negative things the operators said about their new job:

> "The system is a machine that needs a person rather than the other way around".
>
> "Operators have no control; just go along with it. It controls you."
>
> "Not too little work, just boring. Before we were operators; we were in charge. Now the computer is in charge - we're not".

This study is a good example of the ambiguity and narrow use of the new technology. The case study that follows is of interest because it demonstrates a number of relevant issues: everyday coping of operators in a demanding technology-dependent system where important parts of the local technology are not up-to-scratch, and are incompatible with the more advanced technology in operation in other parts of a multinational network; the disastrous potential of the loss of control in such a complex and dangerous modern socio-technical system where demands outstrip the capacity to cope; and the unethical tendency for some individuals to scapegoat a defenceless colleague (to blame the victim) when things do go drastically wrong, to get themselves "off the hook".

A case study from air traffic control (ATC)

The job of 'air traffic control' is something of a paradox. How can a controller run out of control? Well, it does happen and the air travelling public rarely learns about it. The skill of ensuring the safe and expeditious flow of modern air traffic is 4-dimensional. Variations in 3-D space, in geographic position and height, are compounded with variations in time. Everything is in fluid continuous movement with a constantly changing dynamic picture whose essence is time. The controller is continuously planning ahead and revising those plans. A multi-variable mental model of the future is built up. There are often many aircraft in the sector, or expected to arrive in the sector, and each has different parameters, such as actual and potential velocity, which have to be accounted for in the controller's mental model. The stressful image of the modern air traffic controller's job has now assumed a myth-like quality, but there are grains of truth. Weston and Hurst (1982) decribe the controller's mental model by analogy with a house of cards; a pyramid of playing cards. Like other stressful jobs ATC has its own stress vocabulary. Controllers fear 'losing my scan' and 'losing the picture'. This can happen when there is too heavy a workload. It is the unexpected event, the unplanned contingency, like an unexpected aircraft arriving in the sector, which can be the one card too many, that leads to the whole pack - the picture - collapsing. Because of these problems a controller is typically on duty for no more than two hours at a time before taking an hour's break.

Fortunately, it very rarely happens these days that a failure in air traffic control results in a nasty accident. But that one chance in ten million did occur over Zagreb in former Yugoslavia on the morning of September 10, 1976, when things did get out of control at the busy airport control centre, resulting in the complete loss of life of the passengers and crew of two airliners which collided in midair in conditions of good visibility at 33,000 feet. The direct, measurable costs alone were estimated at nearly 18 million dollars, and the youngest controller on the job at the time, who was responsible for directing these two particular aircraft, was imprisoned for criminal negligence with his career, and his peace of mind certainly in ruins. Weston and Hurst 1982, who did a thorough analysis of the accident, with Weston (a lawyer) himself testifying in the Yugoslav court, make the case that the controller had been scapegoated to cover up for what they refer to as a "ramshackel system", in which controllers and supervisors frantically tried to 'pass the buck' rather than assist in establishing the truth in order to help prevent future such tragedies.

Weston and Hurst (*ibid*) paint an astonishing picture of organisational ineptitude and negligence; of misunderstandings, irresponsibility, confusion, overwork and undermanning, several breaches of ATC rules and a history of unauthorised controller absenteeism and lateness on the job. There were no official workload limits and the blamed controller's own hours had been excessive and higher than his colleagues in the previous week. Thirty controllers were doing the work of the forty specified for work at that centre, a busy international air crossroads, and he was working alone at that console when he should have had an assistant with him. There had been an increase of 85% overall in air traffic at that centre in the past 10 years. There had also been 32 recorded 'near misses' there in the past five years, and two controllers dismissed for incompetence.

The scapegoated man was unable to use his radar set because it had not been properly adjusted since it was installed three years earlier, and he believed it to be unreliable. The unexpected aircraft arriving in his sector at a time of heavy workload was his downfall. About 15 minutes before the accident happened he was supposed to have taken a break for an hour. Instead he was left alone handling two jobs at a very busy time. There was confusion and misunderstanding around the handover to him of instructions about this unexpected aircraft to which he could not give his full attention. The recordings show that he made two verbal slips on radio telephony at that critical time. Calculations show that he only had about four seconds to alert the pilot that he was on a collision course. One expert view is that it was just about enough time to have got the captain to change his bearing, but, in a state of panic, the controller did not think of that and instructed the captain to hold to his fateful course and height, instead.

If stress was a cause of the accident it must have resided in the mind of this controller a few seconds beforehand with the ghastly realisation of the position. There is also evidence of flight deck stress within seconds of the crash. After the event, however, the stress must have been collossal and widespread, from the guilt shared amongst the ATC staff to the grieving among the mourners. Other valuable source material are: Air Safety Review (1983) and Accident Investigation Board Aircraft Report 9/82 (1982) for analysis of the Zagreb accident; and Moore-Ede (1993) is an excellent text for an analysis of problems of conflict between human biological rhythms and the hours of work demanded of controllers in modern complex socio-technical systems which incorporate costly and rapidly obsolete technologies. It is not known how far modern computerisation at Zagreb would have prevented this particular disaster. Without question the incriminated controller (a Serb from Belgrade working in Croatia, incidentally) had been deprived of appropriate support by his team and by the State bureaucrats in the conduct of a difficult and highly responsible job; support to which I would argue he had a moral right.

The case study is also sobering testimony to our worldwide dependence on exquisitely fine time margins and ultratight schedules at the critical interfaces within modern socio-technical systems, made possible by computers in the first place. There is plenty of other case study material to be found which dramatically documents the failure of similar systems; (see for example, Kopec and Michie, 1983). In some of these we find evidence of 'near misses' occurring when the computer system fails; in others there are psychosocial reasons for the problems, such as communications failures and other problems of relationship between people working in teams where good cooperation is essential to avoid 'losing the picture'.

Division of Labour

There is a strong economic argument why employers in a fast-changing world should empower their workforces by giving them more flexibility and discretion - more control - in their jobs. The current fad for employee involvement in decision-making on the job, on 'Japanese -style 'quality circles', and worker participation, is rooted as much in anticipated productivity gains as it is in humanitarian considerations (see Shipley, 1990, for a discussion on worker participation as ideology or methodology), but such policies, based as they are on enlightened self-interest are not my concern here, except where worker participation and consultation practices constitute some of the possible tools or technology for promoting health and safety at work, and where such policies and practices in themselves constitute a desirable moral good .

Division of labour as a longstanding management tactic for promoting efficiency has led to undoubted economic benefits and has been a major social tool for managing complexity. Like other tools, however, it has a 'downside' resulting in adverse effects for many people. Lack of control can be a consequence of dualism in organisations. For the sake of simplicity two main job types using modern technology may be distinguished. There is the technology used in high discretion jobs, usually occupied by men, in creative computer-aided design, for example, and there are data entry jobs which are usually done by women at the bottom of the organization's hierarchy. The distinguishing criterion is where the locus of control lies. In the latter it is generally outside, and the job is externally paced. The former are typically complex, self-paced and of comparatively high status where the new technology is used as a sophisticated job aid or support as, for example, in modern stock exchange dealing, and up-to-date, computerised ATC.

Now, it is not always the woman user who contracts the disease of RSI, although it usually is. It is not always the low status worker, either, who suffers from it; freelance writers can inflict it upon themselves, and journalists working in newspaper houses get it too. The common factor is repetitive intensive *paced* work in unergonomic conditions. The fact is women mostly are found to be doing such work under such conditions. It is the modern equivalent of the 'belt burn-out' suffered by men working on car assembly (much of it now automated) in piecework conditions not so long ago. It is a product of management's application of the philosophy of Fordism or Taylorism, of 'rationalised' work, to the modern office -to get the job done as fast as possible for reasons of 'efficiency and productivity'. And the pace is often driven remotely by some central computer system to which a battery of VDU workstations is tied. For Garson (1988) it is the 'electronic sweatshop'.

People do normally have a measure of control over their lives, but there is also a strong influence over many people's lives of external control and authority; of 'environmental contingencies'. Both are true. To over-emphasise the environment may foster a dependency culture of 'learned helplessness' deplored by our current government in the UK which is so anxious to cut public expenditure, but an over-emphasis on the power of individual control and choice may equally let off the hook those with a responsibility for the promotion of health and safety at work and the minimisation of stress and its damaging effects. The two RSI case studies are of low status jobs in modern offices usually occupied by comparatively powerless women.

The plain fact is that the occupants of such jobs *are*, to a large extent, dependent on those responsible for designing the jobs in the first place and those capable of getting them changed if they are not.

This problem is not confined to the conventional workplace, as reports on conditions of work in the home for the growing number of homeworkers testify. 'Telework' is just one (rather autonomous) occupation for both sexes, in this new breed of cottage industry, but in her survey of homeworkers Huws (1994), confronts us with a rather different picture -of low status, low-paid work with the work paced from outside. Over 90% of her sample were women, most of them caring for school-aged children. The women assemble printed circuit boards, fill envelopes, sew and pack, and are unable to pace themselves and plan ahead because work arrives irregularly and has to be done in a hurry. They often work weekends and at night to get the jobs out, and have no job security. They certainly do not fall under the auspices of any company health and safety service.

It is not my intention to debate here why women are discriminated against in such division of labour. The least one can say is that the 'electronic sweatshop' appears to be a logical/technological extension of the typing pool. VDU work in the sweatshop differs in crucial ways, however, from the latter. One crucial distinction is that many of these workstations have a built-in electronic performance measuring/monitoring facility which puts the worker under added pressure from management. Furthermore, activities ancillary to typing such as filing, which once afforded a rest break, are no longer available in a job in which all the tasks are integral to the VDU. In the worst case, then, the operator has lost almost total control, or, to use current jargon from stress psychology research, 'job latitude/discretion/autonomy'. She is in a sense 'chained' to the VDU with little respite; a scenario for biophysiological overload at least, and possibly mental and emotional stress and strain also.

Deep Dualism

Emanating from European initiatives VDU workstations in the UK now have to comply with minimum standards laid down by recent health and safety regulations (Health & Safety Executive 1992). But published guidelines by ergonomists on the design and use of modern technology are not particularly new. See for example, Damodaran, Simpson and Wilson (1980), whose guidebook was intended specifically for computer personnel and management. Why, therefore, do users continue to get hurt despite this available knowledge and despite the legal pressures for worker protection? There is no single answer. The whole area is under-researched and under-theorised. Clearly social problems, such as discrimination practices at work, associated with division of labour, are part of the problem. For sure, there are unscrupulous marketeers and consultants and ruthless employers and managers but there are employers, too, who do not want to hurt their staff. Many staff no doubt work healthily and perhaps happily in their well-designed VDU jobs. Certainly, it is probable that the patients in the GP's surgery in the Camden Project were not all that representative of the general working population; they presumably, most of them, perceived they had a health problem, because they were in attendance at the surgery, and many of the problems would have had little or nothing directly to do with work. True that smaller firms may not have the resources to manage the technology well. Also true that those who do have discretion and control on the job will not always use it carefully. It may be a failure of management's imagination that leads to the mis-use of new technology with unfortunate unintended consequences. Research work at Nottingham University in the UK suggests that stress may be a crucial mediating factor for the onset of RSI; i.e. that workers under stress may not engage/be allowed to engage in healthy work practices - are working too fast or too intensively in order to meet deadlines, for example (see Griffiths, 1994). There are many contradictions.

One other reason for the above contradictory state of affairs may be the pervasive degree of *dualism* in the modern world; or 'deep dualism', (see Leal and Shipley, 1992). In that paper we argued that dualism takes many forms and that ordinary folk go about their everyday lives without giving it a thought. The dualism is enshrined in many of our habitual practices and customs. To quote from Leal and Shipley (*ibid*, p 34-35):

> "Let's start with a bald assertion of our thesis. All philosophical dualisms are a reflex of one very deep tendency in human beings, viz. the tendency to make an unbridgeable gap between themselves and everything else, particularly other people; in abstract, and somewhat psychoanalytical language, a split between self and not-self. This split has been partially spotted by social psychologists in what they call the "actor-observer paradox", which means briefly that if you make a mistake, external circumstances (including other people) should be blamed for that, whereas if other people make a mistake, it is their own fault. . . . [T]he split is not just a matter of attributions, but a matter of actual power. . . . We propose calling this attitude *deep dualism*. It is not a theoretical attitude; it is a practical attitude. The point is not that I am *viewing* other people as different, but that I am *treating* them as different. . .. [D]eep dualism is not just a speech; it is real. By calling it "deep" we allude not only to the fact that it is so natural and has such a profound grip on us, but also to the idea, which we want to argue for, that it underlies all other dualisms. . .. And its implications are *ethical* rather than metaphysical. But it is all the more insidious; and it takes many forms in social life."

We are aware that it is common practice to think dualistically, in either/or opposites, as distinct from, say, in more continuous terms. Howard (1992) claims that in all Indo-European languages like English verbs can be expressed only in two 'voices', the 'active' voice of the 'I jumped' kind, and the passive 'I was pushed' kind. Other languages possess 'middle voices' with graduations of activity, Howard argues. The importance of linguistic structures for influencing how we think, and therefore our conduct, is well accepted by us. Our emphasis, however, is on the embodiment of such thinking, as it were in everyday external structures, such as in the structures and functions of employing institutions. In modern complex organisations there is typically a hierarchy of dualisms which is, for example, embodied in various levels of management, but which probably all boils down to a form of deep dualism.

Feminists are especially interested in the adverse effects for women of male-female dualism, ie in sex discrimination and the segregation of work, which is the division of labour on gender lines. This has, along with their domestic circumstances, trapped many women in low status work. In the Zagreb courtroom, Weston and Hurst (*op cit*) give us a graphic account of the actor-observer paradox at work, as the various actors in this particular drama hurled recriminations, accusations and blame at each other, and the scape-goated controller was not powerful enough to protect himself from carrying most of the blame. Lack of control is a consequence of dualisms in organisations. Dualistic attitudes may not be deliberate but can have profoundly immoral consequences. By definition, deep dualism is largely unconscious and unintentional. In spite of the undeniable greed and competitiveness of the modern world it would be absurd to maintain that managers and engineers are actually trying to hurt workers.

The hallmark of deep dualism, then, is unselfconscious or unintended immoral conduct; the 'zeitgeist' of the modern materialistic, consumerist world. This pervasive 'unconscious' dualism is a major problem for modernity as organizations and states have got bigger. An important feature of modernity is the growth of specialisation, which is part of the division of labour. Whatever its merits specialisation can also create a psychological distance between people. It can do so, not simply as a result of professional specialists jostling for place in an elitist social hierarchy and failing to communicate with each other in team projects because of differences in ideas and jargons (ie lateral separation, see Shipley 1990, *op.cit.*), but also by distancing specialist professionals from their users or clients (ie vertical separation).

Ordinary Goodness and Personal and Impersonal Relationships

Our world is growing exponentially in complexity because of modern technology. One paradox is that not all those involved in the production of this technology and its use in industry and commerce will benefit from it in proportion. Indeed, many will pay a disproportionate price in terms of their lost health and other life opportunities. Many technological innovations and changes are well intended but have unintended and negative side effects; unforeseen noxious effects on worker and public health, for example.

In our 'post-modern', 'post-industrial' world technological solutions are seen uncritically as the solution to everything. In his 1953-54 Gifford lectures at the University of Glasgow on the philosophy of community, John Macmurray (1961) proposed that the fundamental unit of being for mankind/womankind is that of the *person in relation*, not the individual self, or, if I may be more up-to-date, not the self at the personal computer interface. His starting point is anti-Cartesian in that it presupposes a *'heterocentric '*, rather than an *'egocentric'* view of human life. This dissolves the linguistic and psychological 'space' between self and other. The point here is not that we are either/or; we are clearly both -solitary and group animals- with the potential for both selfishness and self sacrifice. The issue, rather, is how far we value these conditions - mutuality and sharing or privacy and self interest. What Macmurray refers to as the 'practical' or 'personal' or social self is primary and the reflective self is secondary and subordinate to it. A dualistic Cartesian emphasis on the solitary self is to assert the self primarily as an isolated thinker withdrawn from practical and interpersonal engagement in the world. Other people become objects to be known rather than *persons* with whom one already has some sort of relationship. It follows, therefore, that a side effect of modern professionalisation is that such *direct* relationships with clients and users of one's products and services becomes increasingingly difficult to achieve; indeed, it probably doesn't occur to most professionals that they have such a problem. To quote Macmurray (p16):

> "In reflection we isolate ourselves from dynamic relations with the other; we withdraw into ourselves, adopting the attitude of spectators, not of participants."

In Cartesian dualism the self is divided into mind-body, thinker-doer. In the dualist analysis of the self these irreconcilable aspects of thinker versus agent, are 'theoretical' and 'defensive', in Macmurrian terms. We are both subject and object to ourselves and to others and, for Macmurray (p28), "I can know another person as a person only by entering into personal relations with him." Technology, for Macmurray, is *pragmatic*, not personal or moral. Specialists, therefore, need to be fully rounded - as thinkers and doers. More than ever the modern world needs reflective practitioners and involved and committed practically-minded thinkers.

The 'americanisation' of the modern, consumerist, technologically-driven world is deeply egocentric, on the other hand, and its underlying materialist philosophy has driven wedges between people. It is a world in which morals (in their fullest sense) have gone underground; a world in which ethics is 'fragile' (F.Leal, personal communication), and the language of moral philosophy is rendered potentially powerless. For Macmurray, moral conduct is meaningless outside relationship, and ipso facto vice versa. We develop our moral sense primarily through interaction with others and in direct and personal relationship with them. It follows that modern technology can enhance moral relating by breaking down barriers between people, possibly in interactive and genuinely participative tele-networking for example, or it can impair or inhibit it by putting more distance between people. In the modern world of work many problems emanate from people being in *indirect* relationships which are broadly economic, rather than social and moral. Efficiency is the aim and the relationships are pragmatic, between people qua workers not people qua persons. Here people are a means to an end and reciprocal rights and obligations depend more on formal contract than informal and direct interrelating.

Indeed, there may be a modern form of psychopathology, a form of computer addiction which may serve to augment a narcisistic neurosis grounded in social isolation and the fear of, and lack of skill, for direct relationships. The seduction and magic of computer games may reside in this escape from reality and the nor-adrenalin kick to be got from the illusory sense of mastery the games offer. Struck by the visible helplessness of the crack NASA space controllers witnessing the breakup in mid air of their spacecraft supposedly under their sophisticated control, displayed on millions of televisions around the world, Branton and Shipley (1986) proposed a new breed of individual which they called 'Houston Man', in their discussion of the disaster to the American space shuttle 'Challenger'. Provenzo (1991), in an analysis of children and video games, uncovers the predominance of aggression and violence against an anonymous enemy in a video game culture; there is no teamwork in the software, no objectives, no communications. These games also, incidently, reinforce and propogate sexual stereotypes.

The new technology has become a sacred cow; an ikon. It plays into a deep desire in us for speed, mastery and novelty; for fantasy and escape from reality. We over-rely on technological solutions to problems. What, after all is the status of this 'information' with which we are so obsessed in today's 'information society'? For much of it its validity, it's truth, is here today and gone tomorrow, as in the ever-changing picture of share values on the stockmarket.

The Ethical Imperative and Overcoming Deep Dualism

But all is not lost. To reiterate, the central value of this paper is the promotion of health, safety and wellbeing at work as a moral imperative, not only a legal and economic concern. This issue has to do with the fundamental goodness of ordinary people and what they themselves would wish for. It is an appeal to something important and taken-for-granted by us all; a strong personal sense of the moral and ethical. The moral imperative consists of obligations, responsibilities and duties, not just rights and entitlements. All ordinary people possess a capacity for conscience, for compassion, for a sense of responsibility; they all participate in the moral struggle of everyday life. It is a testimony to the ordinary human capacity for reliability, for *reasonableness*, , that workers continue to do their jobs on those 'off days' we all have when our health and strength are a bit impaired. Workers often also do much better at the job than they are given credit for by professional observers, particularly in situations calling for more than routine knowledge and skill. Grosdeva and de Montmollin (1994) found this out in their study of nuclear power plant operators in France. People simply rise to the occasion. This is a major reason why the many 'near misses' do not turn into real disasters. Furthermore, it is common human experience to feel discomfort or even outrage where there is injustice done to oneself and to others.

Ordinary working people and designers and managers do their own practical ethics without depending on philosophers for this. After all, the problems are theirs and not the philosophers. The best of managers do not hide away behind their desks or fraternise only in the executive dining room; they walk the factory floor and get to know their staff, sometimes rolling up their sleeves to work alongside them. Company doctors and nurses also get out on the shopfloor so that their staff rarely need to solicit help from their community GP for workplace health problems. The position of the engineer is somewhat different. S/he usually serves his/her employer or sponsor directly, and this is often not the individual end user of the product. Systems analyists and engineers who work outside the company to which they sell their ideas and their products do, however, have a number of strategies for ethical conduct open to them. They can , for example, first ensure that the sale is based on a full survey of workplace needs. Equipment designers may refuse to design VDUs with a built-in operator checking device, for example. In so doing they will be bridging some of that gulf that exists between themselves and the end users of their products.

The end user, the client or patient, this 'other', then ceases to be just an object, or an instrument for the 'egocentric' purposes of the professional. Many professionals are like ordinary folk, people of goodwill but, like ordinary people too, can be victims of unconscious dualism. Most would be shocked to think that their work resulted in harming others. But the greater the distance between specialist and layperson, the greater the degree of impersonal relating, the less visible the moral issues, and the greater the risks of those unintended adverse consequences arising. Professional codes of practice and statutory laws are major tools for protecting people's health and safety at work. But these codes are insufficient in themselves. We have to live out in actual practice, have first hand and preferably face-to-face experience, in the ethics of direct interpersonal relationships. It is the mutual exchange that occurs in that process which enables us to fully know ourselves - including our capacity for deep dualism.

To distance ourselves, either geographically or psychologically, may be a secret wish to escape from moral commitment. Ethical and moral conduct is a property of persons in relation; it is not a property of a firm, a state, a code of practice, the law, a profession, or a technology. Professionals are indeed people in direct relationships at their own professional level. These days, however, their relationships with their end users are *indirect.* We ought not to rely solely on the power of external authorities, rules, regulations and codes to solve those relationship problems for us. We are related to each other as equals which, to Macmurray, is an *intentional,* rather than a *de facto* equality: "it is an aspect of the mutuality of the relation." (Macmurray, *op cit,* p158) To quote Macmurray further (p201): "It rests upon an intention to see to it that my freedom of action does not directly or indirectly injure anyone who is affected by it." Professional humility depends on the acknowledgement that all knowledge is hypothetical and problematic which needs to be verified in action and interaction (see Macmurray, *op cit,*, p216).

On a final, somewhat Kantian note, in a further quotation from Leal and Shipley (*op cit,* p40):

> "As opposed to deep dualism we propose a practical and ethical imperative.
> *We have a duty to treat other people in the very same way that we treat ourselves." (our italics)*

We mean by this, in particular, that we stop treating other people as if they were objects, and with reference to the workplace this means specifically that we stop treating them as machines. Or even less than machines; since it appears to be part of modern psychopathology to treat machines, such as cars and computers, with more tender loving care than spouse, children, friends and colleagues. More specifically, in the classical demand for gender equality that 'women should be treated in the same way as men', this means they should be treated very seriously indeed. Women's pain and distress is not less important than men's.

This equality will never be achieved if low-grade clerical and secretarial work is almost the sole province of women, which may be one reason why such workers continue to get hurt by the new technology. Their stresses may not be seen as important as the stresses of men in higher status occupations. The executive's stress (usually male) is taken very seriously, much more than the stress on his secretary (usually female). Could this be because the executive's work is seen to be related to the real 'big' heroic issues such as sales volumes and productivity levels, whereas the secretary is only concerned with the little matters such as not being able to fulfil the daily word-processing quota (under the stern vigilance of 'big brother'; the keytouch-counting computer perhaps), or not managing to do the job and feed and care for the children back home properly? Women do not, after all, die of RSI, as the Camden district environmental officer reminded us above, but men die or get crippled all the time from real, onerous work, such as mining, building and truck-driving, and perhaps from heart attacks from the stress of top-level decision-making.

It is also part of modern psychopathology, paradoxically, to mistreat, to hate ourselves. To understand oneself better, our capacity for both callousness and deep dualism and for conscience and caring for others, is part way to loving and caring for oneself. How can we love and care for others as *persons* if we cannot love and care for ourselves? Moreover, the business executive who is a moral being at home but leaves his ethics behind when he gets to the office is a split personality. Is this a mild, non-clinical and common form of schizophrenia, for which we all have the potential? To live and work with such a grave contradiction is a form of fragmentation. Such inner, intrapsychic, divisions may also constitute a source of stress to the divided individual, whether conscious of them or but dimly aware that something does not feel quite right. The new technology may potentially contribute to the prevention and management of such problems, but that is the subject of another paper. In the meantime, managers, engineers, and designers, I respectfully suggest, may wish to consider reclaiming their social and moral responsibilities for the undesired and unintentional side-effects of the new technology.

Acknowledgments

I am grateful to Dr Morva Fordham, Professor Sally Redfern, and Dr Fernando Leal for their generous ideas and help in the preparation of this paper, and for financial support from the Society for the Furtherance of the Critical Philosophy, London. I am also indebted to Dr Anne Cockcroft, Consultant in Occupational Health at the Royal Free Hospital, London, for her help with the occupational health and risks sections of the paper.

References

Accident Investigation Board Aircraft Report 9/82. On the Collision in the Zagreb Area Yugoslavia, between British Airways Trident G-AWZT and Inex Adria DC-9 Yu-AJR on 10 September 1976. H.M.S.O. London.

Air Safety Review. (1983). Air Safety Review (No. 7). July. British Airways. London.

Babb, P. and P. Shipley. (1994). A Study of Stress in Telephone Switchboard Operation. Paper submitted to Applied Ergonomics.

Branton, P. and P. Shipley. (1986). VDU Stress: is Houston Man addicted, bored or mystic? In Knave, B. and P. Widebæck. (eds.) Proceedings of International Scientific Conference on Work with Display Units. Stockholm. Sweden.

Camden & Islington Occupational Health Project. (1994). Occupational Health News. **3**. Autumn. C&IOHP. London.

Carter, J. B. and E. W. Banister. (1994). Musculo-skeletal Problems in VDT Work: a Review. Ergonomics. **37** (10). 1623-1648.

Clark, H. (1993). The Cure For All Cancers. Promotion Publishing. San Diego, California.

Dalton, A. J. P. (1992). Lessons from the United Kingdom: fightback on workplace hazards, 1979-1992. International Journal of Health Services. **22** (3). 489-495.

Dalton, A. J. P. (1993). It's My Job, Doc! Occupational Health Review. Jan./Feb.

Damodaran, L., A. S. Simpson and P. A. Wilson (1980). Designing Systems For People. National Computing Centre. Manchester, U.K.

Department of Health (1993) Workplace Taskforce Report . Department of Health (DoH). London.

Fisher, S. (1985). Control and Blue-collar Work. In Cooper, C. L. and M. J. Smith (eds.) Job Stress and Blue Collar Work. Wiley. Chichester, UK.

Gaillard, A. W. K. and C. J. E. Wientjes. (1994). Mental Load and Two Types of Energy Mobilization. Work and Stress. Special issue: A Healthier Work Environment. **8** (2). 141-152.

Garson, B. (1988). The Electronic Sweatshop: how computers are transforming the office of the future into the factory of the past. Simon & Schuster. New York.

Griffiths, A. (1994). The Management of Muskulo-skeletal Upper Limb Disorders and White-collar Work in the UK. Work & Stress. **8** (1). 1-3.

Grosdeva, T. and M. de Montmollin. (1994). Reasoning and Knowledge of Nuclear Power Plant Operators in Case of Accidents. Applied Ergonomics. **25** (5). 305-308.

Health & Safety Executive. (1992). Display Screen Equipment at Work: guidance on regulations. H.M.S.O. London.

Hodgson, J.T., J.R. Jones, R. C. Elliott and J. Osman. (1993). Self-reported Work-related Illness. Health & Safety Executive, Research Paper 33. H.M.S.O. London.

Howard, G.S. (1992). No Middle Voice. Theoretical and Philosophical Psychology. **12** . 12-26.

Huws, U. (1994). Home Truths. National Group on Homeworking Report. London.

Kopec, D. and D. Michie. (1983). Mismatch Between Machine Representations and Human Concepts: Dangers and Remedies. FAST Series No. 9, Science and Technology Policy. Commission of the European Communities. Brussels.

Leal, F. and P. Shipley. (1992). Deep dualism. Int. Journal of Applied Philosophy. **7** (2). 33-44.

Levi, L. (1994). Work, Worker and Wellbeing: an overview. Work and Stress. Special issue: A Healthier Work Environment. **8** (2). 79-83.

London Hazards Centre Trust. (1993). VDU Work and the Hazards to Health. L.H.C. London.

Macmurray, J. (1961). Persons in Relation. Reprinted by Humanities Press 1991. New Jersey, USA.

Marsella, A. J. (1994). The Measurement of Emotional Reactions to Work: conceptual, methodological and research issues. Work and Stress. Special issue: A Healthier Work Environment. **8** (2). 153-176.

Moore-Ede, M. (1993). The 24-hour Society: the risks, costs and challenges of a world that never stops. Piatkus. London.

Oborne, D. J., R. Branton. F. Leal, P. Shipley and T. Stewart. (eds.) (1993). Person-centred Ergonomics: a Brantonian view of human factors. Taylor & Francis. London.

Orlans, V. and P. Shipley. (1983). A Survey of Stress Management and Prevention Facilities in a Sample of UK Organisations. A Report for the Stress Research and Control Centre, Birkbeck College, University of London.

Provenzo, E. (1991). Video Kids: making sense of Nintendo. Harvard University Press. Harvard. USA.

Rosenbaum, M. (1993). The Three Functions of Self-control Behaviour: redressive, reformative and experiential. Work & Stress. **7** (1). 33-46.

Shipley, P. (1990). Participation Ideology and Methodology in Ergonomics Practice. In Wilson J. R. and E. N. Corlett Evaluation of Human Work: a practical ergonomics methodology. Taylor & Francis. London. 819-834.

Shipley, P. (1993). An Evaluation of the Camden Occupational Health Project. A Report for the King's Fund Institute. London.

Siegrist, J. and R. Peter. (1994). Job Stressors and Coping Characteristics in Work-related Disease: issues of validity. Work and Stress. Special issue: A Healthier WorkEnvironment. **8** (2). 130-140.

Special Issue ofWork and Stress. (1993). Coping with Stress at Work. Work and Stress. Issue. **7** (1).
Sternberg, E. (1994). Just Business. Little Brown. London.
The Guardian. (1994). Pain of the Strain Costs £1.25 bn a Year. The Guardian. November 22, p20.
Weston, R. and R. Hurst. (1982). Zagreb One Four: cleared to collide? Granada. London.
World Health Organization. (1985). Identification and Control of Work-related Diseases. Technical Report 174. 7-11. WHO. Geneva.

Notes

* This paper has also been scheduled to appear in *AI & Society*; 1996 9 1 (editor)

Chapter 5

Ethics is Fragile, Goodness is Not*

Fernando Leal

This paper first illustrates what kind of ethical issues arise from the new information, communication and automation technology. It then argues that we may embrace the popular idea that technology is ethically neutral or even ambivalent without having to close our eyes to those issues, and in fact that the ethical neutrality of technology makes them all the more urgent. Finally, it suggests that the widely ignored fact of normal responsible behaviour offers a new and fruitful starting point for any future thinking about such issues.

Introduction

> Graham: *Harry doesn't know any better. He's never thought of anybody in the world but himself.*
> Billie: *Who does?*
> Graham: *Oh God, Billie, millions of people do.*
>
> [Born Yesterday, *the film.*]

Although the prestige philosophers once enjoyed in general society is pretty worn out by now, a kind of secret hope sometimes lingers that they may still be able to offer good advice or even answer the big questions about what the good life is (Williams 1986). This hope is bound to be disappointed for several reasons, not the least among which is that there are no ethical recipes and never have been. On the other hand, even if I would like to maintain that there is some useful work for philosophers to do in our increasingly complex societies, if only we pull ourselves together and dare see what is in front of our eyes, nonetheless I would also like to persuade iy readers that they should not wait for philosophers to build an ethical theory free from any possible objection or immune to abuse. Ethical issues always arise in concrete settings and nobody is better qualified to attend to them with the required subtlety and feeling for detail than the persons directly acquainted with those settings. Remote managers and bureaucrats, let alone philosophers, are in comparison rather like the proverbial elephant in the china shop. But doesn't ethical knowledge and moral thinking require professional skills? All classical moral philosophers, most famously among did them Immanuel Kant, didn't think it did.[1] And they were right. Only the insidious dualisms mushrooming in our modern industrial life could produce the absurd idea of 'ethical expertise'[2]

The particular subject of this paper is the new information, communication and automation technology, or ICA tecnology for short; and its argument runs as follows: (1) ICA technology is related to a lot of ethical issues, some of which are wholly new and all of which are at least partly new; (2) we may embrace the popular idea that technology is ethically neutral or even ambivalent without having to close our eyes to those issues, in fact the ethical neutrality of technology makes them all the more urgent;

and (3) the starting point for a new thinking about them has to be the widely ignored fact of normal responsible behaviour.

Dr Frankenstein's Ethical Legacy: Five Examples

Different writers may want to classify the ethical issues arising front ICA technology in different ways (see e.g. Ermann *et* al. 1990). My favourite five categories are all in terms of *loss:* what we are losing are skills, communication, privacy, control, and last but not least our own sense of self (or our identity, to use the more fashionable expression in the social sciences). Although each one of these complex ethical issues can be said to be a direct consequence of (some use of) ICA technologies, it could be argued that there are also causal connections between some of them, which reinforce the original impact of technology. Figure 1 suggests some of those further connections. For lack of space, the following shall be a very brief review of the issues when considered in isolation.

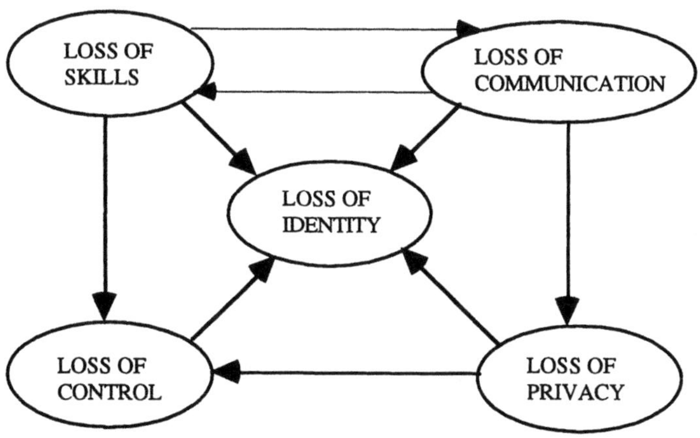

Figure 1. Some causal connections between the five identified complex ethical issues arising from the new ICA technology. (The dotted lines are rather more tentative than the continuous ones). [

Perhaps the most widely publicized ethical issue is that associated with the concept of *deskilling*. Ever since Bravermann published his famous book there has been a great debate as to whether ICA technology has effectively destroyed the old skills of workers by first incorporating them in ever more sophisticated systems and then letting these be run or supervised by unskilled operators (Wood 1982, 1989). But the arguments purporting to show that technological developments are unethical show a great deal of diversity. The simplest argument just says that through ICA technologies jobs are lost, unemployment rises and more people become welfare dependent and their lives lose the meaning associated with working. On the other hand, it is also said that automation creates a new kind of dualism: some people get the more interesting work of, say, designing the systems, whereas other people have to perform the unskilled jobs, such as entering data routinely into computers or thoughtlessly following the instructions issued by the system at ever higher speeds (Garson, 1988). This dualism is considered to be bad in itself, because it reinforces old or fosters new divisions in society, some of which are based on differences of class, race or gender. But it also has the consequence that the particular jobs in the lower ranges are soul-destroying, inhumane and debasing. A yet different line of argument says that the products of such new division of labour tend to be of a much poorer quality than in the good old days. This might be considered bad in itself, but it has yet another consequence which is sometimes mentioned, viz. that the standards of excellence of the consumer or 'end-user' become lowered in the process. Finally, at a slightly more philosophical level it might even be argued that creating systems, such as expert systems, which incorporate the knowledge and skills of real people coping with real situations effectively destroys such knowledge and skills (Cooley 1987, Dreyfus & Dreyfus 1986). Some argue that this is bad in itself, whilst others point out the terrible consequences which might ensue if in the future there should be a shortage of energy preventing the new systems from working properly. As far as I can see, these are the arguments purporting to show the unethical consequences of deskilling. There are of course other people who claim it is all very much exaggerated, and that automation actually eliminates only jobs which were uninteresting in the first place, and also that all deskilling is accompanied by processes of reskilling, whereby new knowledge and skills are born into the world (Wood 1982, 1989; Hirschhorn 1984; Ropohl 1985). Wherever the truth may lie, moral philosophers manageto keep very quiet about these debates.[3]

New *communication* technologies have arguably a paradoxical effect in that they either change the actual process of communication or even destroy it. This sort of problem was probably first experienced when the very first communication technology appeared, viz. writing (Havelock 1982). We know that writing and reading are acquired tastes and demand the development of special skills to cope with them. These skills go hand in hand with the creation of new codes, registers and jargons; written language is very different from spoken language, a fact which has a particular effect upon ordinary human communication by speech. And this effect becomes even more marked when writing is supported by printing. We all know from United Nations reports, how widely spread functional illiteracy is, even in industrial societies, and what the consequences for education, training and cultural division and discrimination are. Now the temporal distance between the invention of writing and the invention of printing embraces more than two millennia, whereas the distance between the invention of printing and the development of the new communication technologies spans only about three centuries. First we had the telegraph, the gramophone and the daguerreotype, then the telephone, the radio and moving pictures, later the television. And now we have all these as enhanced by satellite telecommunications plus the personal computer, the modem, the fax, the e-mail, the video, and so on and so forth. Communication and thereby human life itself has been changing at an incredible pace. It can be argued that our very being, character and personality are changing. There is talk also of new varieties of artificial 'autism', and of the inability to cope with so much information as is being produced by the minute. There is talk of the effects of visual violence on the souls of children and young people. There is talk of visual and acoustic pollution in our town and cities. All these and other things can be said to be very relevant to ethics, but they have been and still are by and large ignored by our moral philosophers.A third complex of issues has to do with *privacy* - or rather the loss thereof. It has been known for many years now that ICA technologies allow for a rapid transfer of information, some of which used to be the property of individual people in the old days. Thus you subscribe to a journal like M *and Society* and in some mysterious way you start receiving all sorts of offers from all sorts of people who know who you are, where you live and what you do. This may be mildly annoying in some cases, and words like 'junk mail' have been coined to talk about them. Yet quite a few people are worried about what might happen if some of this private information ends up in the wrong hands. There is a new mistrust growing in industrial societies about answering polls and surveys. New laws have been passed to prevent the worst, but it may not be enough. When communication technologies enter into the picture, you even see things like sexual harassment via electronic mail. Finally, at the workplace we find quite a lot of monitoring of people's work. The new managers are capable of not only counting one's keystrokes and phonecalls but also listening in when one is talking to clients to see whether one is really following the instructions of the newest expert system; why, they can even analyze one's general patterns of performance! Up to a few years ago, this sort of monitoring affected workers only on the shopfloor or at the counter, then it reached middle management, but recently it has begun to affect the work of the big bosses themselves. They don't like it, naturally, but they were rather naive if they thought they were going to be exempt. Absolutely no job is safe from this kind of sophisticated surveillance. So the invasion of privacy is something moral philosophers should be worrying about, but they don't seem to be much interested.

The invasion of privacy is of course only the beginning. The information gained about people can of course be used to manipulate and control them (Garson 1988, Ermann et al. 1990). On the other hand, people are supposed to *control* things themselves and this is becoming increasingly difficult because of the sheer complexity of some of the tasks assigned. First of all, a breakdown in power supply might disrupt the functioning of the new system and thereby cause lots of trouble, sometimes suddenly forcing operators to take desperate steps to remedy the situation for which they are scarcely prepared. When such things happen at critical moments, such as during heavy traffic in sophisticated transportation systems, accidents may occur resulting in loss of lives and property (for further elaboration of this problem see Shipley, this issue). Yet it has been powerfully argued that human beings are not 'biologically designed' to cope with these or similar situations which are becoming increasingly common in the 'nonstop society'. The new ICA technology makes it possible and even imperative, at least under capitalism, for workers all over the world to labour under extremely stressful conditions and at times of the day which may run counter to their own internal clocks. This creates an unprecedented danger which the economy does not address, preferring as it does to invest in systems rather than in people (Moore-Ede 1993). And if it escapes the economy, it is no wonder that it also escapes professional philosophy.

Finally, one of our most cherished values has to do with our *sense of self.* It can be argued that all the things listed in the above have an impact on our identity going well beyond the changes they effect in the ways we communicate and gather or transfer information, and even beyond the ways we work (hence the middle position of the 'loss of identity' circle in Figure 1). Namely, it can be argued that the very fact that our computers and systems are so clever makes for comparison. On the one hand, people can get quite intimidated by ever more complicated software, faulty design of control buttons or levers, and hard-to-read instruction manuals (Norman, 1989). Their self-confidence falters and they may be prey to depression and stress. But there may be a more direct, probably deeper and partly independent influence of ICA technologies on our sense of self. Comparison between people and systems produces, as we know, the so-called computer metaphor, which is a sophisticated elaboration of the older machine metaphor. Now the machine metaphor as such was rather harmless in comparison. After all, it is difficult to feel jealous of a motorcycle or a car because they can run faster than us or of an airplane because it can fly and we can't. But when machines start to think - or at least when we believe they do, it is far more difficult to retain our poise. We are tempted to describe ourselves in a new way. The point is of course that, according to some authors, this redescription is all wrong and has tremendous ethical implications. It has even been argued that the unethical aspects of information, automation, and communication here briefly reviewed are ultimately dependent on the computer metaphor; that we could never design the jobs we are designing or pry into people's lives the way we do or suffer the television programmes we suffer if we didn't think of people as machines, and particulary as computers (Rosenbrock 1989, 1990) If this is so, then a certain loss of identity will not only be influenced by the above-mentioned four losses but will actually have an impact upon them through the peculiar kind of technology we have (Figure 2 is a possible partial representation of this). For the purposes of this essay, it doesn't matter whether these claims are true or not.[4] The important thing is that our smartest pundits and gurus working in artificial intelligence and cognitive science - and of course also their philosophical allies - do not give a damn about ethical issues. So their use of the computer metaphor can be safely described as ethically neutral. This leads us to the general question of the ethical neutrality of technology.

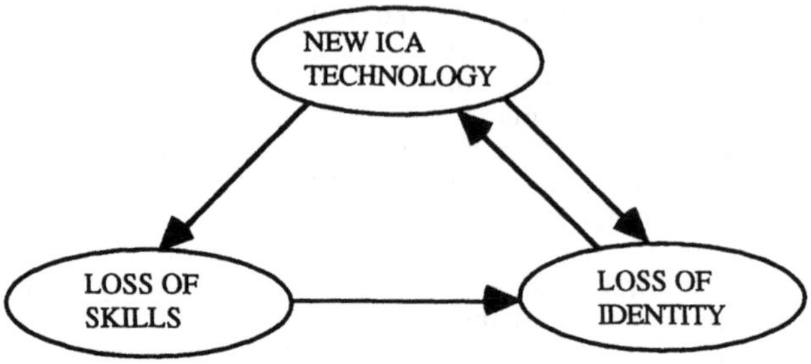

Figure 2. Possible causal connection between loss of skills and loss of identity in relation to the new ICA technology.

Is Technology Neutral?

A thesis that has been defended by politicians, business persons, scientists and engineers is that 'there is nothing wrong with tools per se', or, to put it in a terminology which has become familiar from an old debate in the social sciences, that technology is value-free. The social science debate actually didn't revolve around a statement but rather around the demand that social science *should* be value-free, a demand which was designed to prevent political commitments interfering with scientific objectivity. I suppose the thesis as related to technology could be also framed as a demand that technology should be value-free, because politics would otherwise prevent it from *working*. So 'working' in technology would be the equivalent of objectivity in science. Sham technology which doesn't do what it is supposed to do but only benef its politicians is not what we want. We want it to work, but of course how we use it is a completely different thing: we can use atomic technology to kill people or to cure cancer. This is up to us and the politicians.

Regardless of whether it is a statement or a demand, the following discussion might become easier if we refer to the above thesis as *neutralism.* By far the most popular argument against neutralism counters that there are at least some technologies, like those specifically pertaining to nuclear weapons, which can only be used wrongly. Inasmuch as this argument depends on the further premise that nuclear weapons are inherently destructive, One could argue that it is just a particular application of the standard philosophical argument against neutralism, viz. that our technologies embody our values, whether we are aware of the fact or not. In a parallel fashion, some people might be prepared to argue that, say, expert systems will destroy existing knowledge and skills however we design them. Thus nuclear weapons and expert systems would be ethically wrong in themselves. The counter-argument would of course be that expert systems may destroy knowledge but do not have to. We can find a better use for them and design them so that human life and work is enhanced instead. If we generalize this position, we would then say that any technology can be used *both rightly or wrongly.* This corresponds to the most popular form of neutralism; but it seems to me to be a bit too strong. Maybe there are inherently bad technologies after all. And anyway, I don't want to go into debates as to whether the atom bomb or expert systems are capable of ethically impeccable application. So I propose to settle for a weaker version, viz. that any technology can be used *wrongly*. According to standard philosophical jargon we might call this position *weak neutralism*.

Now, enemies of neutralism, as I mentioned before, want to insist that technologies have inbuilt values. Although they usually have in mind values they disagree with, unless they are totally opposed to any kind of technology, they necessarily imply that there might be technologies which embody the right values. An example might be a computer program built in such a way as to save effort when completing our annual income tax return. The point is that such a program may eventually be used to deskill people, to destroy valuable knowledge or even to put an innocent person in prison. It is clear that both the good and the bad guys can use practically any technology for their own purposes, which will eventually result in good and bad (or wrong) uses made of it. In fact, technology is not only independent of the high ethical standards and integrity of its designers or inventors, it is also independent of the moral qualities of its users, because, as we know, any action can have bad consequences for all or some of the people affected by that action. Indeed, given the vagaries of human intentions and the reality of unintended and perverse effects I suggest that we have to accept that weak neutralism is true.

However, there is a further consideration emerging from an unprejudiced acceptance of weak neutralism. Even weak neutralism presupposes that we can distinguish good and bad consequences of technology. The question is whether we can do that in a way that really satisfies everyone involved. I said before that any action can have bad consequences for all or some of the people affected by that action. But what very commonly happens is that some actions have good consequences for some people and bad consequences for other people. This is a question which has to be addressed when considering the ethical issues raised by technology.

Barbara Garson's book, *The Electronic Sweatshop* (1988), is an impressive source for examples of job design and expert systems which destroy skills and cause anxiety, stress and loss of self-confidence. Some of her cases have to do with ICA technology and some do not. But even these latter, she argues, obey the same kind of logic. For Garson, a certain kind of job design is always the harbinger of technological changes: you first change the job, then you introduce the systems. Her case is powerfully argued and profusely illustrated, so that one wonders whether she can see any positive effect accruing from ICA technology. She presents findings from interviews with all sorts of people and at all levels, who either explicitly articulate their anger at the workplaces made possible by ICA technology or else unwittingly in some other way betray the horrors of those new jobs. But there is a very interesting exception - her interview with former secretary Sophia Crandall in chapter 7. The topic of this chapter is the changes in the office which started taking place in the 1980s, when the personal secretaries of managers were separated from the latter and integrated into a secretarial department of their own - a rearrangement of jobs made possible by the introduction of word processing. Managers who thus lost their 'office wife' and personalized assistance, and quite a bit of status, complained just a little bit louder than the secretaries themselves who became more strictly monitored and controlled under the new system. But then Sophia Crandall's interview makes visible a hitherto unnoticed aspect of the new arrangements in the office. She says that managers resent the fact that women have their own department - usually run by one Qf them instead of by a male - so that bosses can no longer impose extra-official duties on secretaries or harass them any more. The secretarial department, on the other hand, gives women a new sense of their own power and importance with respect to the general output of the company; at the same time, they now have more control over their own time and duties than they ever had when 'monogamically' attached to just one manager.

This relatively simple example proves that we shouldn't be too quick in judging whether a given consequence of the new ICA technology is good or bad. There may be cases in which a group of people will find that ICA technology has displaced them or made their work more difficult, whereas another group of people will instantly welcome it because it benefits them enormously. Recent ethical theories which say moral philosophy should be based on what is called 'discourse' (Habermas 1983) are relevant here. By that they iean a kind of discussion which does not seek to control or manipulate other people but to bring genuine differences of opinion to full expression; reasoning instead of force is then used to achieve some form of reconciliation which respects as fairly as possible all interests involved in a given situation.There is of course no unique method for reaching agreement or even compromise, say in the workplace, when the system gets very complicated (Cropanzano 1993). And the deeper one looks, the more complicated things get. Thus, most conflicts and controversies which have a moral edge are doubtless connected with the relatively simple clash of particular personal or corporate interests, but it is becoming increasingly clear that at least some of them have to do with a deeper struggle between different or even incompatible value systems. The most obvious of these differences emerge from the multiethnic and multicultural nature of today's societies, which is caused by global communication as well as by migration; migration being in its turn not only caused by politics but also by economic factors connected with technological progress.[5] Less obvious but immensely important are the differences within what would appear to be a single culture, as was first argued by Macchiavelli in the 16th century (Berlin 1955), then by Montesquieu and Steuart in the 18th century (Hirschman 1977), and more recently by several authors writing from quite diverse perspectives (see e.g.Hampshire 1989, Klein & Eason 1991, Jacobs 1995).[6] Clearly, "discourse' isn't easy and we shouldn't be naive about that or believe good will is all we need. Tolerance and good judgement are rare skills, which we will have to cultivate much farther before we can make any real progress. In this context, I think that we still have much to learn from the kind of discourse which Socrates introduced into general philosophy. But a discussion of this topic would go far beyond the limits of this paper."[7]

But can ethical reasoning and ethical discussion deliver the goods by themselves? In trying to promote them, we may easily forget the most important lesson which weak neutralism can teach us. Bad consequences of our actions and our use of tools may be just a contingency we have to learn to live with, but the same thing is true of ethics as long as we think of it as a kind of *theory*. It makes no difference whether the inventor or user of a new technology is not just an ordinary human being but actually a moral philosopher, even a professor of ethics. Even if the theory be somehow part of a master plan underlying our technology, weak neutralism warns us that such a technology, like any other one, is liable to misuse of one sort or another. Yet, technologies are not always misused. We have not yet said anything about why this should be so, although it is, in my opinion, the other half of the ethical story and by far the most vital one.

Normal Responsible Behaviour: A Neglected Quantity

Third world countries are famous for a kind of corruption which seems to be endemic to the social system. There may or may not be a significant difference in the amount of corruption actually existent in a third world country such as Mexico and a first world country such as Britain, but bad reputation has at least one consequence which often escapes notice. I was once teaching logic to a group of high-school students in Mexico when something they said made it clear to me that they actually thought that *nobody* in our country abides by the law. I was amazed by the idea and spent the rest of the hour trying to prove by means of examples that such a state of affairs could simply not be true, that social life is impossible unless the majority of people's actions are in conformity to the writen law and also obey all sorts of implicit norms and rules. Thus I pointed out to them that they would have been unable to come to school if it hadn't been for a bus driver who for the most part obeyed public regulations; in fact, it was necessary for most people driving that morning to do so; otherwise the traffic would have been in chaos. I also pointed out to them that even before going out to take the bus, all sorts of other people would have had to do their jobs, starting with those workers who made the alarm clock, continuing with those who collected the garbage from the streets and their own parents who woke them up and prepared breakfast for them, and ending with the farmers who produced the food their parents then prepared, the merchants and grocers who made sure that food was of good quality, transported it across the country and put it on sale in the right places, and so on. After an hour or so of describing all those things, they had to accept that, in spite of all the corruption there might otherwise be, such a statement as 'nobody abides by the law in Mexico' is simply outrageous. Most people must just be doing their duty most of the time, even in Mexico.

Simple as this statement might appear to be, no moral philosopher has given it the weight it should have. As the celebrated zoologist, J.Z. Young (1951), once said, it is not rationality or consciousness which make us the peculiar biological species that we are but rather that intricate network of cooperation, on a steadily increasing space-time scale, which constitutes social life. What I am calling 'cooperation' seems to have two aspects, a collective aspect and an individual one. The collective aspect is what social scientists commonly refer to as cooperation but which I would prefer to call 'coordination' (Argyle 1991). Coordination ranges from the intricacies of face-to-face conversation to the complexities of telecommunication and from simple localized division of labour in a workshop to the international transfer of capital and human resources. It is an amazing thing to look at and trying to understand how it works can be very difficult indeed. But it does work; and it does make us human. On the other hand, there is an individual aspect to cooperation without which coordination would not be possible. I propose to call this 'normal responsible behaviour'.[8]

Of course, it could equally well be argued that normal responsible behaviour is also impossible without coordination. I am ready to concede that; but the fact is that coordination is something which at least social scientists are ready to recognize and research into, whereas normal responsible behaviour is receiving much less attention than it should. However that may be, the fact that coordination and normal responsible behaviour necessitate each other and are mutually dependent does not affect the argument.

I would like to suggest that normal responsible behaviour should be the centrepiece of ethical consideration. There was a famous writer who once said that all great literature is about human misfortune, and that nobody writes about happiness because it is so terribly boring. A similar gestalt effect applies to normal responsible behaviour. It is always bad conduct which makes the headlines (no news is good news, as they say). The result is that we become blind to the normality of cooperative social life, viz. to that which happens most of the time. We are obsessed with evil1 sin and human error. This is as true of literature as it is true of moral philosophy and even of psychology and social science. And goodness strikes us only under the guise of heroism, even if it is a tragic failure. I don't want to dismiss heroic deeds, but I think that we need heroes only insofar as the system has broken down. Thus we should be thinking more of how to design systems so as to make heroism as unnecessary as possible. But we can only do that if we pay sufficient attention to normal responsible behaviour.

To push my argument a bit further, I would like to say that normal responsible behaviour embodies *human goodness* at its best. Normal responsible behaviour is very robust and very reliable, so reliable in fact that badly designed systems are sometimes prevented from breaking down only because responsible human operators save the situation by doing the right thing at the right time.[9]9 But of course, normal responsible behaviour, as all things human, is not infallible. It works most of the time but not always. And one of the reasons why it sometimes doesn't work is the way we design the system (Moore-Ede 1993, nd almost all contributions to this issue). To see this more clearly, I think we have to go into a bit of philosophizing, for which I offer my apologies in advance.

My main thesis then is that the embodiment of human goodness in normal responsible behaviour makes it invisible to the usual ethical theorizing and psychological or sociological analysis. As far as I can tell, there was only one philosopher who actually tried to make the right connection here, viz. Socrates, who having been a skilled craftsman himself, pointed out again and again that human goodness was akin to a skill. This point was partially recovered by Aristotle when he distinguished the practical philosopher from the theoretical philosopher. The theoretical philosopher is a person who can think her way through mazes of argument, dissect pros and cons, and come up at the end of all this with a neat well-grounded logical solution to some philosophical question, say how movement is possible, what ultimate components of matter there are, or whether the universe has a beginning in time. The practical philosopher, by contrast, is a person who has become wise, i.e. who hasn't just thought about philosophical problems or knows the right solutions to such problems, but a person who *incarnates* philosophy in all her *dealings* with the social and political world around her; a person who *enacts* philosophy, who makes it work in the real world. The problem is that this insight was drowned by Aristotle's own vision of the good life as contemplative and intellectual. In fact, we scholars and scientists have inherited this prejudice, which in some way or other infects all current models underlying cognitive science and their practical applications within the new technology (Shipley & Leal 1991, Leal & Shipley 1992).

What I therefore would like to suggest is that we should reassess Socrates and even perhaps go beyond him in saying that goodness is not just a skill among others, but that it is an integral part of all human skills, effectively embedded in any one of them. I don't think we can extricate ordinary goodness from ordinary skills. Of course, there is slipshod craftmanship, skills *can* occasionally be misused, and ordinary goodness as embedded in a skill is far from infallible. However, a familiar point from the psychology of skills is that skills are not supposed to hit the target all the time but only most of the time (Singleton 1978). I want to suggest that what is true of ordinary skills is also true of human goodness. In fact, that is bound to be the case if my suggestion that they belong together is anywhere near the mark. The important thing is that such limited success is usually enough. Being able to hit the target most of the time doesn't make ordinary skills and ordinary goodness fragile, except if the system puts inordinate pressure upon them. Which leads to the importance of keeping the reality of normal responsible behaviour in mind when applying the new technologies.

One of the old philosophical dreams was the attainment of absolute certainty and absolute perfection. The whole history of philosophical thinking can be read that way (Dewey 1929). Now the form in which such certainty and perfection was to be attained was the theoretical form. Practice and experience was just too accidental and variegated to serve the purposes of such a magnificent dream. Our own century has seen such revolutions in theory that it is nowadays a commonplace to think of theories as fallible and replaceable. But it hasn't quite taught us to think of ordinary human experience and practice, of ordinary human judgement and skill, in one word of ordinary human *goodness* as the only genuine article. I think that by doing so we might yet be able to design better systems - systems, that is, which better enable people to do what they would try to do anyway. Doctors, psychologists and ergonomists are fond of depicting themselves as in a perpetual struggle with engineers to protect human operators from unnecessary hazards (Oborne et al. 1993, Moore-Ede 1993). This is of course largely, although not completely true. On the one hand, some engineers have put up a valiant fight to advance human-centred technology (Rosenbrock 1989, 1990; Cooley 1987). On the other hand, the truth is that *most* people involved in human factors, whether they are engineers or not, have the deplorable habit of describing the human operator as a worrisome 'source of error' and/or 'the weakest link' in the system; consequently they constantly strive to 'close the loop' and 'design the man out' of the system. At the same time, however, designers and consultants implicitly and even unthinkingly take for granted what I've been calling normal responsible behaviour. When all is said and done, this means that they rely on the common decency of human operators, who will indeed do their sometimes desperate best to protect the health, safety or even life of the people immediately affected by any malfunctioning of their precious systems. I wonder how many of them really obey the Golden Rule of putting themselves in other people's shoes.

Conclusion

In conclusion, if technology is ethically neutral in the sense that it is liable to misuse, then ethics under the dispensation of powerful new technologies is a very fragile thing indeed.[10] This makes ethics all the more precious -meaning by 'ethics' not only ethical theory in the abstract*but also* the 'moral' structures and the inbuilt 'values' of, say, technology.[11] Nevertheless, I want to insist here that it is ethics and not human goodness which is fragile, as has recently been suggested (Nussbaum 1986). Believing in the fragility of goodness comes, I think, from the strong influence that the tragic vision of humankind and human life still has upon our imaginations.[12] 12As against this tragic vision, I would like to insist that people - ordinary real people - do not normally lead tragic lives and so their goodness is a firm rock upon which we can build and use ever better technologies.

Acknowledgements

Part of the above material was used in a seminar I gave on "Language, Ethics, and the Philosophy of Work" at the Organizational Studies Area (Department of Economics) of the Metropolitan University in Mexico City in November 1993. My heartfelt thanks go to all participants and especially to the organizers, Dr. Luis Montano and Eduardo Ibarra, for their helpful comments. I am also very grateful to Dr. Rene Saran and Dr. Patricia Shipley for reading the first draft of this paper and improving both its form and its content. The Society for the Furtherance of the Critical Philosophy (London) provided financial assistance and acongenial environment which allowed me to finish the work in leisure.

References

Argyle, Michael (1991) Cooperation: the basis of sociability.
London: Routledge.
Berlin, Isaiah (1955) Against the current: essays in the history of ideas. London: The Hogarth Press.
Cooley, Mike (1987) Architect or bee? The human price of technology. New edition. London: The Hogarth Press.
Cropanzano, Russell, ed. (1993) Justice in the workplace: approaching fairness in human resource management. Hillsdale, NJ: Lawrence Erlbaui Associates.
Dewey, John (1929) The quest for certainty: a study of the relation of knowledge and action. London: Allen & Unwin.
Dreyfus, Hubert L. & Dreyfus, Stuart E. (1986) Mind over machine: the power of human intuition and expertise in the era of the computer. New York: The Free Press.
Ermann, M. David, Williams, Mary B. & Gutierrez, Claudio (1990) Computers, ethics, and society. New York: Oxford University Press.
Garson, Barbara (1988) The electronic sweatshop: how computers are transforming the office of the future into the factory of the past. New York: Simon & Schuster.
Habermas, Jurgen (1983) Theorie des kommunikativen Handelns. Frankfurt: Suhrkamp.
Hampshire, Stuart (1989) Innocence and experience. Harvard University Press.
Havelock, Eric (1982) The literate revolution in Greece and its cultural consequences. Princeton, NJ: Princeton University Press.

Hirschhorn, Larry (1984) Beyond mechanization: work and technology in a postindustrial age. Cambridge, MA: The MIT Press.
Hirschman, Albert 0. (1977) The passions and the interests: political arguments for capitalism before its triumph. Princeton, NJ: Princeton University Press.
Jacobs, Jane (1993) Systems of survival: a dialogue on the moral foundations of commerce and politics. London: Hodder & Stoughton.
Kant, Immanuel (1786) Critik der practischen Vernunft. (Critique of Practical Reason.) Hartknoch: Riga.
Klein, Lisl & Eason, Ken (1991) Putting social science to work: the ground between theory and use explored through case studies in organisations. Cambridge, UK: Cambridge University Press.
Leal, fernando & Shipley, Patricia (1992) 'Deep dualism.' International Journal of Applied Philosophy, 7, 33-44.
Moore-Ede, Martin (1993) The 24-hour society: the risks, costs and challenges of a world that never stops. London: Piatkus.
Mothersill, Mary (1984) Beauty restored. Oxford: ClarendonPress.
Norman, Donald A. (1989) The design of everyday things. New York: Doubleday.
Nussbaum, Martha (1986) The fragility of goodness: luck and ethics in Greek tragedy and philosophy. Cambridge, UK: Cambridge University Press.
Oborne, D.J., Branton, R., Leal, F., Shipley, P. & Stewart, T., eds. (1993) Person-centred ergonomics: a Brantonian view of human factors. London: Taylor & Francis.
Ropohl, Gunter (1985) Die unvolikommene Technik. Frankfurt am Main: Suhrkamp.
Rosenbrock, Howard (1990) Machines with a purpose. Oxford: Oxford University Press.
Rosenbrock, Howard, ed. (1989) Designing human-centred technology: a cross-disciplinary project in computer-aided manufacturing. London: Springer-Verlag.
Shipley, Patricia & Leal, Fernando (1991) 'The active self: beyond dualism.' Newsletter of the British Psychological Society, History and Philosophy of Psychology Section, 13, 4-16.
Singleton, W.T., ed. (1978) The analysis of practical skills. Lancaster: MTP Press.
Young, J.Z. (1951) Doubt and certainty in science. Oxford: Clarendon Press.
Williams, Bernard (1986) Ethics and the limits of philosophy. London: Fontana.
Wood, Stephen, ed. (1982) The degradation of work? London: Hutchinson.
Wood, Stephen, ed. (1989) The transformation of work? London: Routledge.

Notes

* This paper has also been scheduled to appear in *AI & Society*; 1996: 9.1 (editor)

[1] When someone tried to criticize Kant by saying that his 'categorical imperative' was only a formulation of conon human knowledge, he replied that he never intended it to be anything else, and that it would be ridiculous to try to pose as a moral master to humankind, as though ethics was something a philosopher could invent from scratch (Kant 1786, Preface).

[2] These dualisms have been explored in recent papers by the guest-editors of this special issue (Shipley & Leal 1991, Leal & Shipley 1992; see Shipley, this volume).

[3] The reader will remark that this as well as the next four paragraphs reviewing the ethical issues arising from ICA technology always finish by indicating that contemporary moral philosophy is guilty of neglect. This theme is developed further in the introduction to this special issue.

[4] Thus, Kenneth Gergen has interestingly argued that we shouldn't mourn the loss of a "stable center of identity" -by losing it the world stands a fair chance to get rid of self-righteousness, bigotry and jingoism. For a popular summary of Gergen's ideas, see "The decline and fall of personality[1] in *Psychology Today,* vol. 25, no. 6, November-December 1992, pp.59-63.

[5] People working at what might be called the 'cultural interface' - social workers, educators, and so on - thus acquire a particular relevance in helping us to sort things out and achieve 'discourse'. Like engineers, doctors and ergonomists in system design, those persons are best qualified to think about the ethical issues arising from ICA technology in their particular workplaces.

[6] I suspect that the distinctions between the right and the good, or between duties and virtues, or between justice and care, are "splits of (ethical) truth[1], if I may be allowed to use a phrase used in classical German

philosophy. This would explain the increasingly acrimonious tone of many recent debates in moral philosophy, in which people tend to conceive of each other as ethical morons. But this whole subject goes beyond the scope of this paper.

[7]The contributions by Eason et al. and Ord to this issue are in this context exemplary, as observed in the Introduction to this special issue.

[8]This theme is explored in several chapters of Oborne et al. 1993, even if the term 'normal responsible behaviour' does not explicitly appear in any of them (see also Shipley & Leal 1991, Leal & Shipley 1992).

[9]Notice that I am not asking the question why (most) people are (for the most part, most of the time) good. I don't know the answer to that question and probably no one else does. However, it is *not* necessary either to ask that question or to answer it in order to see that (a) as a matter of fact, people are good; (b) things in general run relatively smoothly fo everyone because people are good; (c) people "save the situation" very often *because* they persist in being good despite inhuman arrangements; (d) everyone would be better served if people should be enabled to persist in being good without having to "save the situation", i.e. if inhuman arrangements would be improved. That is all we need to know.

[10]A good example is genetic screening as presented by Sanmartin in this issue.

[11]It should be clear by now that by 'ethics' I understand a framework or structure within which things are done. Such a framework is constituted by ideas, values, precepts, codes, and whatnot; and so is an *intellectual* structure, or rather several intellectual structures, in Roseribrock's sense of the word (see his contribution to this volume). Calling such a structure "fragile" means first of all that it is liable to abuse at any given time. One example among many is the value shift in hospital life examined by Ord in this issue.

[12]"Only in a *very* wicked world would decency inspire *awe*", says quite justly Mary Mothersill (1984) when criticizing Kant's temporary lapse into estheticizing ethics. Anyone can succumb to this ever-present temptation; and maybe it is a good thing, too, or even unavoidable when dealing with literary works of art (such as those Nussbaum analyzes in her beautiful book); but we should resist it when discussing real-life issues.

Chapter 6

Organisational Spaces and Intelligent Machines: A metaphorical approach to ethics*

Luis Montaño Hirose

This paper tackles the main changes that have taken place in the mechanical worldview -of simple, self-regulating and intelligent machines- and studies their repercussions at the ethical and organisational level. These views of machines agree with the scientific, human-relations and postmodern proposals in organisation theory, in that they are in fact reflections on human nature which depend on metaphorical devices within which the machine metaphor is central.

Introduction

> "If we were only to govern our actions by the reflection of the inert world's irrevocable laws in our own consciousness, we would be completely unmoral, or to put it better, amoral; Good and Bad would lack meaning for us. . ." (A. Caso)
>
> "A system is an imaginary machine. . . (A. Smith)

The problem of ethics within organisations is an old concern. it even precedes the very formation of the discipline which studies them -Organisational Analysis. This fact is in no way surprising since every organisation which emerges into the social spectrum does so under the influence of other institutional conventions (Castoriadis 1975), taking from those institutions a blend of values which, during a certain period of time, justify and give direction to the organisation's future conduct. in this sense, the organisation does not exist in a pure form, but in factappears as a meeting place-and a place of confusion- where diverse social discourses coexist (Montaño 1994). This bringing up-to-date of institutional spaces, similar to that which occurs in the individual sub-conscious over the years, is rooted in the metaphorical dimension within which individuals redefine their perception of the world, overlapping it with a variety of themes. However, this metaphorical process is not confined exclusively to the sphere of institutional spaces but reaches deeper down into the great narratives which guide collective conduct.

The machine has been the central metaphor in the formal definition of organisations (Montaño 1993). This has had a profound influence on the determination of organisational structures and processes, giving direction to important changes in the moral conception not only of organisations but also of society. Nevertheless, it is also important to show that the conception of "the machine" in turn has undergone significant changes, in accordance with the spectacular advances achieved by science and technology, up to our current wondering about the real possibilities of constructing an intelligent machine. Two important antecedents of this project, which have given form toorganisational views, are the simple machine, present in Scientific Management, and the self regulating machine, central to the Human Relations School of Organisational Analysis. Without doubt, one of the fundamental aspects of the view of machines in organisations rests upon the division of labour. The latter is not, as is generally supposed, an effect of the increasing mechanisation of work, but is a result of man's conception of machines.

Thus, perhaps one of the most relevant ethical precedents for the study of organisations would be the division of labour. For this, let us begin by taking up again the argument put forward by Adam Smith and Emile Durkheirn on the subject, highlighting the patterns which social solidarity assumes. in the second section we shall examine some of the ideas *establishied* by Frederic Taylor in his well-known *Scientific Management.* We shall attempt to treat the idea of the machine as a mere appliance, separate from any conception of intelligence, and its repercussions, both organisational and ethical. in the third section we shall apply interpretive analysis to proposals of the Human Relations School in order to underline the importance of the *informal* aspects of organisations, as well as the constituent elements of the metaphorical process, deeply rooted within the analytical framework of Cybernetics. These two earlier movements -Scientific Management and Human Relations-, are central to understanding of so-called postmodern organisations, which incorporate the most advanced technological developments, including the possibility of the intelligent machine. This will be the subject of the fourth section. Finally, by way of conclusion, we shall outline some comments which allow Organisational Analysis to enlarge the debate. To this end we shall introduce some elements of the most significant transformations in the metaphorical process.

Division of labour: the forms of solidarity

Division of labour has been widely studied. it has been treated from the beginning as a moral problem. Adam Smith, in his well-known work An *Inquiry into the* Nature *and Causes of the Wealth of Nations,* published in 1776, was astonished by the advances achieved by the division of labour in the already famous pin factory, and placed this in the foreground of economic analysis. Nevertheless, the author warned of the grave dangers implied in terms of the deterioration of intellectual faculties and even requested the government to intervene in the matter:

> "The man whose life is spent in performing a few simple operations, of which the effects too are, perhaps, always the same, has no occasion to exert his understanding, or to exercise his invention in finding out expedients for removing difficulties which never occur. He naturally loses, therefore, the habit of such exertion, and generally becomes as stupid and ignorant as it is possible for a human creature to become. (...) His dexterity at his own particular trade seems in this manner, to be acquired at the expense of his intellectual, social, and martial virtues. But in every improved and civilized society this is the state into which the labouring poor, that is, the great body of the people, must necessarily fall, unless government takes some pains to prevent it." (Smith 1937: 734-735).

Nevertheless, Smith fought throughout his work for the division of labour as the source of wealth. For this author, the division precedes the development of machines, since it is the exclusive attention to a task which gives rise to the discovery of new methods of work wich could be later mechanised. We can say that, from this perspective the machine *incorporates* the functions of the human being.

From an economic point of view it is the choice of the individual in pursuit of his own interests which causes the emergence of the division of labour. Against this view Emile Durkheim set up his proposals. For him the division of labour implies a moral basis which goes further than personal egoism; it is morality that leads to the division of labour. For Smith progress results from individual action, which can nevertheless be restrained by "general rules" of morality, derived from the individual faculties of "fellow feeling", reflection and imagination (Smith 1976).

Durkheim approaches the problem of the division of labour from another ethical perspective by considering it to be one of the foundations of social order. *The Division of Social Labour,* his doctoral thesis, published in 1893, represents the first great work of this sociologist. Unlike the Scottish economist, for him the central value of the division of labour does not reside in economic achievement but in its potential as a mechanism of solidarity. This is not automatically derived from self-interest; it is the birth of a new morality, which has cooperation as its origin. The author distinguishes two types of solidarity: the mechanical, based on the similarities of individuals, and the organic, which is based on their differences. In the former, the individuals attract one another through their similarities and they find themselves linked to a common collective interest, which ensures that the individuals reproduce their fundamental similarities. On the other hand, organic solidarity, considered to be morally superior, is based on individual differentiation, and promotes more complex forms of collaboration. Cooperation, in general terms, is understood to be the distribution of roles for the carrying out of common tasks, which can be maintained by the division of simple work within which the tasks are similar, or of complex work characterised by the heterogenity of the activities to be performed. The latter implies the idea of specialisation which acquires a higher moral status; not only solidarity, but also social progress depends on it. As for the mechanical and organic content of the forms of solidarity, the author is quite explicit. Thus, referring to the former, he says:

> "This word does not mean produced by mechanical and artificial means. We do not give it this name if not by analogy of the cohesion which unites within itself the elements of inert bodies, in opposition to that which constitutes the unity of living bodies. This naming has been justified by the fact that the link which thus unites the individual to society is identical to that which links the object to the person. Individual consciousness, considered in this aspect is simple dependence from the collective type (...) . In those societies where this kind of solidarity is more developed, the individual does not own himself (...); he is literally a thing which society makes use of."
>
> (Durkheim 1987: 141).

In its turn, organic solidarity gets its name from the analogy with superior animals in which every organ has a level of autonomy and specific functions. Durkheim aestablishes the superiority of the organic over the mechanical. Mechanical solidarity corresponds to primitive societies, dominated by feelings and common values. Individual rationality, incorporated into society, set itself up as the motive of progress. This improvement implied the development of a superior form of solidarity, the organic.

There are at least three criticisms to be made. Firstly, there is the concept of an evolutionism which does not take into consideration certain pre-modern collective forms based on the individuality of society (Starkey 1992). Secondly, there is a clear dualism between society and individual, which has made it difficult to understand the concrete forms of the social/individual, as well as groups, classes (Giddens 1978), and organisations. Finally, the idea of a harmonious progressive social order confuses the social with the economic.

However, the economic ideal of progress based on the detailed division of labour raised its head, which left both general rules of morality and the organic nature of society out of consideration, taking up individualism -rationality and self-interesed pursuits- as a source of development within society.

Scientific Management Man-machine or Machine-man?

No other proposition of Organizational Analysis has met with such fierce criticism because of its mechanical nature as Taylorism (March and Simon 1958). The image of the worker reduced to a mere appendage of a machine has been a source of inspiration for the rejection of these practices. Let us remember the famous film *Modern Times* in which Charles Chaplin is swallowed up in the complex workings of the productive machine, not with the intention of crushing or destroying him, but of simply *incorporating* him into the machinery. This criticism is raised not only because of the economic intentions of the new practices -exploitation(Coriat 1979), *nor* because of the effects of the detailed division of labour -deskilling- (Braverman 1974), nor because of the loss of meaning in the workplace -alienation-(Friedman 1963), nor because of the imposition of a new political project -discipline- (Clegg 1981), but also because of human resistance to being relegated to the inert status of a machine. In reality it is a double process of incorporation. The first consists in giving the machine a body, in copying the movements of the worker and in reproducing them, in the most efficient manner, in an inert object. In this way, every machine has an "organic" structure, by representing an extension of the bodily functions:

> "The condition of possibility of using artefacts, as a last resort of machines, of mobile bodies in space, is the prior reduction of the movements of the bodily organs, mobile in space, to mechanical movements, or to movements which, although natural, because movements of the human body, turn up to be artificial or contrived in terms of the way they work."
>
> (Gaos 1992: 649)

The second moment signals man's increasing dependence on machines, given the high degree of efficiency reached in terms of strength, precision, speed and capacity which machines possess in relation to some human capacities. So the relationship is inverted; the organisational capacity of the machine is such that man has to adapt himself to it, in a sense mechanise himself, generating at the same time specific forms of organisation aimed at this end. The most frequent example of this tendency can be observed nowadays in some of the most outstanding Japanese companies, where quality has ceased to represent an important problem, and where Total Quality Programmes have given way to those of Total Maintenance: i.e. total attention to the machine.

This Management, which called itself "Scientific", was not only so because of the systematisation of tasks, as Taylor claimed, but also because deep down it shared this determined search for irreducible elements, essential material, the ultimate reality. It was also because it professed to be universal, reproducible, without any consideration for the concepts of space and time. On ethical grounds it presented a moral orientation tending to the achievement of social harmony. In the first sentence of his book *The Principles of Scientific Management,* published in 1911, the author specifies the objective of management: "To ensure maximum prosperity for the owner, together with the maximum prosperity for each of the employees" (Taylor 1972: 19). This prosperity, however, is not restricted to a mere question of salary, but is seen as an opportunity for every individual to reach his maximum efficiency in diverse spheres of life. Nevertheless, this division of labour was aimed at increasing productive efficiency to the detriment of the development of intellectual activities. A worker is not paid to think but to work -as Taylor used to say. This image of a human being reduced to the machine's condition of existence, as an object, reflects the forms taken by the organisation of production. The mechanical aspect is not exclusively due to everyday interaction with the machine but to the fact that man is the subject of a fortf!al administration which in fact denies him the opportunities which the project of modernity had promised: i.e. access to reason.

On the other hand, we can say that to this mechanical conception of work corresponds an organic view of organisational structures. The establishment of a *Thinking Department* (Friedman 1977), responsible for carrying out planning activities, far away from the machine room, signified another division of labour, now in terms of a wider organisational structure. The functional collaboration of both parts then came about as the primordial objective of Scientific Management; but this lacked the moral value for qt'ich Smith and Durkheim fought.

Human Relations: Towards Self-Regulation?

The School of Human Relations has generally been reduced to a code of good conduct, to a model of public relations, to the recognition of spontaneous behaviour or to the discovery of small work groups. It is true that it has also been criticized for being a poor analytical scheme (Clegg 1990), behind which is concealed a political project capable of establishing a powerful disciplinary system, based on manipulation (Baritz 1974; Montaño 1985). On the other hand, it has also been interpreted as a break with or as a complement to Scientific Management. In spite of it being very tempting to review all of these topics, it is necessary to limit our consideration to the Cybernetic view which underlies it (Desmarèz 1983; Montaño 1987), and to introduce the metaphorical mechanisms which lie at the origins of self-regulation (Montafio 1994).

Human Relations management has built upon a systematic base very close to the Cybernetic conception of self regulation. Amidst these ideas, we must single out Joseph Lawrence Henderson. This physiologist, a professor of the Philosophy of Science at Harvard University, was as strongly influenced by the work *of* tile French doctor Claude Bernard as by that of the Italian writer Vilfredo Pareto, from whom he acquired the concepts of 'internal environment' and 'equilibrium'. The former is taken from Bernard and has to do with the discovery of the constancy and conservation of the composition of blood, and was evidence for an internal environment *-milieu intérieur-* which constitutes the "condition of a free and independent life" (Henderson 1970: 153). The latter is taken from Pareto, originally developed in a thesis on the subject of solid objects and later transferred to economics and finally to sociology. Henderson worked out a model using these ideas, on the subject of which one of his prominent students, Norbert Wiener, commented:

> "There was also Professor Lawrence J. Henderson, the physiologist, who combined some really brilliant ideas about the fitness of the environment with what seemed to me to be a distressing inability to place them in any philosophical structure. . ."
>
> (Wiener 1966: 166) .

This Wienerian perspective, influenced by Henderson's developments, placed the emphasis on the concept of homeostasis, in other words on the ability of a system to resist the process of corruption and degeneration. We know that information plays a central part in the acquisition and maintenance of Cybernetic equilibrium. This is a "negative entropy" and is a measure of the degree of system organisation (Wiener 1969: 11). There then arises a symbiotic process: organisation as a cybernetic machine and cybernetics as an organisational conception. In this way, self regulation and organisation would appear inseparable and act as an important foundation for the Artificial Intelligence project. The study of the organisational aspects of the machine hence became a privileged focal point in understanding the world just as it does in many of later technological developments:

> "Cybernetics is the first science which, after western science's advances of the seventeenth century has established its method, has brought about its operational success, and has achieved the recognition of other sciences through its treatment of a physical system, the machine, not in the operation of its constitutive elements, but in the operation of its organisational features"
>
> (Morin 1981: 285) .

Within this theoretical framework of self-regulation, the concepts of internal environment and equilibrium are developed. Perhaps the most consummated proposal on the Human Relations School is that expounded by Fritz Roethlisberger and William Dickson in their well-known work *Management and the Worker,* published in 1936. For these authors, organisation consists of an alliance of dual structures -or suborganisations. 'Technical' organisation is complemented by 'human' organisation, which in turn is divided into 'individual' and 'social' organisation. The social is then subdivided into the 'formal' and 'informal' organisations (Roethlisberger and Dickson 1976). The first alliance accepts the distinction between the material and the human fields, always emphasising their close links. The second attempts to differentiate the strictly personal from the social; finally, the third stresses the lack of connection between the planned a organisation and that which in fact emerges from unexpected behaviour. So the project basically derives from an attempt to achieve an articulation between these two later organisations.

Hence an imbalance appears in this organisational duality, since the content of each of them varies in different ways and each of them requires different methods of qualitative control. So, for example, the change in the formal organisation can be very rapid and can meet few obstacles, while the informal organisation requires much longer periods of adjustment, during which time workers' resistance to change plays a dominant role. Thus Roethlisberger and Dickson implicitly raise the question of the adequacy of the forms of social organisation to meet the technological advances, in which the establishment of disciplinary mechanisms plays a fundamental role.

The relative autonomy required by the organisational system was achieved by means of the psychological process of internalization of these external spaces. Thus, schematically speaking, we can say that informal organisation does not abstractly represent spontaneous behaviour. The authors of this movement (Roethlisberger and Dickson 1976; Mayo 1933; Mayo 1945; Homans 1959) realised that cooperation, as a joint aoperation, was not achieved exclusively in the formal organisation but that the informal one also played a fundamental role. Informal relations represent, from our point of view, institutional spaces which the individual has internalised over the years of her/his everyday life, such as religion, school, family and army. S/he possesses a set of values, beliefs, of manners of participation and of behavioural guidelines, derived from specific ethical spheres, each one controlled by diverse disciplinary mechanisms.

Thus, the individual passes daily through different social environments. When s/he enters the workplace, for example, s/he finds her/himself not exclusively in a place of work but s/he also reproduces at the same time a set of practices from other environments. By way of example, in the company from which these studies originated, the Hawthorne works of the Western Electric Company in Chicago, employee relations policies, had been renamed *The Ten Commandments* by the employees. However let us not forget that the informal organisation also shelters a set of defensive practices which hinder the smooth running of the formal administration. This constant movement linking the formal and informal organisations prevents, from our point of view, the workplace from becoming solely a productive place:

> "For most of the supervisors the company represents more than the 'big bosses', New York, the stockholders, or board of directors. It is more than an economic unit with merely economic functions. The company is also an entity onto which they project their greatest hopes and fears"
> (Roethlisberger and Dickson 1976: 368)

Organisational modernism separates the formal and the informal, not only in order to control those informal spaces which infringe the formal rules and hinder the progress of productivity, but also with the aim of taking advantage of them, rendering them the repositories of efficient diciplinary schemes. The family, the school, the prison, the church and the army are examples of social spaces with a very high disciplinary content. Through this movement we became aware of the need to anticipate open conflict through symbolic compensation (Pagès et al 1979).

Thus, we find a double metaphor in this movement. Firstly, that which views the organisation as a self-regulating machine, a precursor of the intelligent machine. Secondly, a process which makes the first possible, starting with the manipulation of social environments in the organisation, whose goal is to encourage a certain type of conduct through the promotion of a set of values which would diminish the negative aspects of the company and would import disciplinary aspects from the outside. "This isn't a company, but a big family" is a slogan from the 193Os which exemplifies this process well. In this sense, we may say that the capacity for self-regulation was directly associated with the degree of relative autonomy reached through the "internalization of the external". It was not necessary to think about adapting to the external environment since it was possible to reproduce it, in functional terms, at the heart of the company. The idea of a company as a small society is perhaps the most representative metaphoric form of this second process. It later facilitated the operation of corporate culture.

The development of the Japanese productive system of *Just in Time* was formulated in order to accommodate the needs of the market in real time and the growing capacity of productive diversification, both being results of technological innovations. It encouraged the emergence of new organisational forms which tended to overlap the formal and informal spaces of the company (Montaño 1994). The moral values resulting from the organisational process of modernisation, which originated mainly from the wider social field and were redefined in the informal organisation, will no longer have the leading role which they once held in most industrialised countries. Nowadays, owing to the spectacular advances in technology -mainly in big companies where the development of applied research holds a privileged position-the company has set itself up as *the* organisational model for all other social spaces -previously internalized. In other words it sets itself up as a promoter of wider social values. So, the school, the hospital, the state and even society itself have been the objects of profound restructurations which try to imitate the organisational forms originated in the productive model of the private sector (Ouchi 1984).

Postmodern organisations: An ordered intelligence?

Few concepts are as attractive and fashionable as that of the "postmodern organisation". However, this must be approached with caution so as not to fall into stereotyped ideas. The concept forms a central part of the contemporary debate about new organisational forms and their social implications (Parker 1992a; Parker 1992b; Tsoukas 1992; Cooper and Burrel 1988; Cooper 1989).

The idea of social progress that strongly encouraged the division of labour, as much in its international versions (Smith 1937) as in its social (Durkheim 1987) and detailed aversions (Taylor 1972), now receives a new stimulus, starting from the study of industrial organisation. A new idea of organisation is proposed to substitute for the inflexibilities of the Scientific Management model. Although we could quote a whole set of characteristic elements of these new forms, we can synthesize them into one: their capacity for reprogramming, which is the basis of one of the most frequently mentioned concepts in the present process of restructuration; their flexibility.

This was the pioneering attempt carried out by Tom Burns and G. M. Stalker in their book *The Management of Innovation,* published in 1961. The authors suggest that the mechanical and organic managerial concepts are extreme poles of a continum of possibilities. Both types represent rational forms of organisation. The first is characterised, amongst other things, by a specialised differentiation of functional tasks, which are constantly subject to technical improvements without any consideration of rights or obligations, and a set of technical procedures necessary to perform each task, as well as a hierarchical structure of control, authority and communication. The authors consider that this mechanical organisational form is adequate under conditions of relative stability. In contrast, the authors suggest the organic model a is better when confronted with situations of change. This model is characterised, amongst other things, by the following elements: the contribution of specialised knowledge to global tasks, continual adjustment to individual tasks, a more collective responsibility, and a much more open network of control, authority and communication (Burns and Stalker 1961: 120-121).

In this proposal we can clearly observe the introduction of the concept of structural flexibility, preceeding the discourse on post-Fordism put forward by the School of Regulation (Aglietta 1979, Leborgne and Lipietz 1988), and foreshadowing some of the central characteristics of the socalled 'postmodern organisation'.

Along the same lines of argument, Heydebrand sets his proposal within the context of post-industrial capitalism. This writer conceptualises the new organisational forms as the result of a transition process from an industrial capitalism to a post-industrial one. in a synthetical manner, the author characterises this new form in the following way:

> "it would tend to be small or tend to be located in small units of larger organisations; its object is typically service or information, if not automated production; its technology is computerized; its division of labour is informal and flexible; and its managerial structure is functionally decentralized, eclectic, and participative, overlapping in many ways with nonmanagerial functions. in short, post-industrial organisations or those emerging from the transition tend to have a postbureaucratic control structure even though prebureaucratic elements such as clanlike personalism, informalism and corporate culture may be used to integrate an otherwise loosely coupled, centrifugal system"
> (Heydebrand 1989: 327).

We are currently witnessing a huge development of so-called *information technology* (Lyotard 1989), which has substantially modified the forms taken by organisations, above all in the highly industrialised countries. On the one hand, there is the increasingly generalised use of these machines, and on the other, the high capacity they have for reducing the time of response. The introduction of industrial robots, expert systems, computer - assisted design and production, among others, have facilitated the emergence of the production system *Just in Time.* This, in turn, has required significant structural changes in the organisational field, promoting with it the materialisation of a new type of worker, called *polivalent,* who is characterised by being highly qualified in the achievement of diverse tasks and who has a high level of interaction with the machine. This polivalence is positively correlated with the development of a general-purpose machines, which present a higher level of productive flexibility than their predecessors, special-purpose machines. March and Simon (1958) comment that the second type gave rise to the Taylorist view of the worker as a labouring machine, whilst the first type corresponds to the modern view of the worker i.e computer man.

Productive flexibility, based on the high speed of response of *Just in Time,* facilitates the surpassing of the limitations produced by traditional systems of production, sometimes called *Just in Case*. This is based on the development of inventories as a central procedure in the combating of uncertainties, emanating from changes in demand from disarrangements in production lines caused by tile difficulties of managerial coordination in the detailed division of labour.

Polivalence in no way causes harm to the division of labour in the factory. it is a question of a new modality, however This polivalence facilitates a greater rotation of posts and a continual reassignation of tasks. it provokes a greater capacity for adaptation to constant technological change, it allows the mitigation of the rigidities in the production plan, and causes the generation of mechanisms of consensus to give rise to collective responsibilities in a order to meet production requirements. The division of labour does not reside more in the object of transformation than in organisational identification. in fact, the rotation of posts not only encourages the development of interpersonal relations which reduce the cost of interdepartmental transactions (Aoki 1990), but it also generates knowledge of the diverse components of the organisation, achieving, not an identification with the single post or job as would be the case in the detailed division of labour, but an identification with the organisation as a whole.

Artificial intelligence has played an exceedingly outstanding part in the aforementioned changes. As its name suggests, it is an ambitious project; undoubtedly one of the most ambitious projects that human rationality has ever been able to conceive. it is, however, not a recent project since we find the first signals of it in a very distant past. One could, for instance, say that the modern version of Cartesian dualism of the body and mind, is computer hardware and software (McCorduck 1993). Nevertheless, the project is still in its first stages, and diverse contradictory positions present possible future scenarios. These vary between those which predict a realisation date of 2017 (Waltz 1993) and those which maintain a sceptical attitude about its future a (Putnam 1993). The first group contemplates two different procedures, though not mutually exclusive: the *heuristic search,* based on the hypothesis of the *physical system of symbols* of Newell and Simon (1972) and the theory of *neuron networks* (Waltz 1993). in the past, the notion of Artificial intelligence seems to have advanced more via the first procedure; perhaps its most spectacular results have been called expert systems, characterised by the handling of large volumes of information, dynamic searching processes and high processing speeds. This is far, of course, from being a true concept of Artificial intelligence. However, both the utilisation of these advances and the prospects of a project of such magnitude have greatly contributed to modifying not only our everyday practices but also the way in which we observe ourselves, and therefore, our own values.

In the field of Organisational Analysis, we locate the proposal of March and Simon (1958) as a pioneer of a new approach. Some of the Taylorist man-machine restrictions were apparently overcome by the updating of the mechanical metaphor. These authors advanced the previously mentioned concept of computing-man in order to characterise *functionally* the limited rational behaviour of human beings:

> "March and Simon do not a make the mistake of claiming that the human being -the grey matter inside the skull- is built like a computer. Their basic assumption is that the human mind functions like a computing machine, just as Taylor's assumption was that the human body functions like a labouring machine."
>
> (Kilduff 1993: 21) .

Simon tried to apply the developments in this form of Artificial intelligence to the study of managerial decisions, basically in the field of so-called "unprogrammed decisions". These correspond in a big way to the decisions about which there is no archive of past experiences and in which the procedures of heuristic search acquire a significant relevance. This is made possible, as the author mentions, by the ease of imitating the logical functions of the brain which are, according to Simon, one of the most easiest to duplicate (Simon 1977: 22) .

The machine's capacity for facing new situations, the opportunity for constant reprogramming and its high speed of response have all contributed to the development of new organisational forms. Nevertheless, in spite of the fact that the metaphoric evolution of machines has known a certain continuity, it is also important to point to some basic ruptures which imply fundamental changes in social values. This, however, belongs to the concluding chapter.

Conclusions

All metaphor, as a vision of the world and startpoint of a discursive project (Foucault 1971), establishes specific forms of behaviour. The machine has been one of the great narratives which has left a deep imprint on the development of society and its organisations (Montao 1993; Montaño 1994). However, the metaphoric process has met with a whole set of accidents linked to the changes caused by the advance of technology. in this last section we will comment on three aspects which seem fundamental to this investigation.

a) Firstly, it should be pointed out that if it is indeed true that every analysed movement contains a certain mechanical view -the simple machine, the self-regulating machine and finally, the intelligent machine-, each one of these assumes a certain organic form, and implies both a specific organisational form and a variation of the mechanical metaphor. The real organic metaphor in fact existed before the appearance of the mechanical option. This was one of the conditions of social existence, predominant during the Medieval era, blurred by the arrival of rationality, as Merchant reminds us:

> "The image of the earth as a living organism and nurturing mother served as a cultural constraint, restricting the actions of human beings. One does not readily slay a mother, dig into her entrails for gold, or mutilate her body. . .. As long as the earth was considered to be alive and sensitive, it could be considered a breach of human ethical behavior to carry out destructive acts against it."
>
> (Quoted in Capra 1982: 61) .

b) On the other hand, we are currently witnessing the development of another metaphoric reversal, which, from our point of view, characterises the nature of postmodern organisation. This refers to the drastic reversal of the metaphor, which sees the company as a small society. Society no longer finds itself incorporated into the company, but the company is that which establishes itself as a social model to imitate. The advances achieved, not only in terms of productive efficiency but also in terms of speed of response and ability to adapt, have placed the company at the very heart of current social development, forcing the other social protagonists to imitate its performance. it is no longer only the school, for instance, which is internalized in the informal area of the company, but it is the company which sets the behavioural guidelines of the school. The premodern duality of values par excellence, the sacred and the profane, which had a limited and partial influence over the project of organisational modernity in Human Relations, has been replaced by the duality efficiency/inefficiency (Alberoni 1992) in the postmodern project.

c) Finally, as Baudrillard (1983) reminds us, there is an important change of those elements of the discourse that "become more real than reality" and thus deny validating their representations, without realising the emerging absurdity of its new function. We are surely referring here to an "hyper-real" ethical concept which could even promote irrational actions. Such are the cases[1] for example, of the rush of nuclear weapons production, of the *Excellence Programms,* interpreted as an endless process (Aubert and Gaulejac 1991), and of the speed of the machine, as Gaos points out:

> "Such an image is that of the driver of a vehicle (...) The concept of a journey becomes an integral part of two others: that of a goal and that of a route towards it. Then the image taken to the extreme, is that of the cancellation of the route and the goal; therefore of the journey itself, it is another contradiction; it cancels itself out"
>
> (Gaos 1992: 653) .

Some consequences for social life, including some ethical aspects, must also be mentioned. First of all, the development of new technologies seems not to have kept its promise about the reduction of working time. High prices of new technologies and their elevated rate of obsolescence has provoked an increase of the number of hours dedicated to work -a reduction of holidays, and a growing overtime work and work done at home- because of the economic interest, by big companies, of having the greatest productivity from their investments. Spare time, which should be translated into privacy and freedom for enjoying life -music, reading, sports, family life and other activities-, becomes more and more just an occasional distraction. This increasing time consecrated to work has had a very important effect not only in tile living schedule but also in the manner we observe ourselves, by emphasizing the workplace as the central aspect of our life, and then reinforcing the idea of the company as the model of social organisation.

Secondly, there are some ethical contradictions that derive from this metaphorical view of living organisations. We want to underline some primary aspects of selfregulating and intelligent machines. in the first case, as was already mentioned, there is a daily transit of the worker through different social spaces inside organisations. Organisation members must then reconcile different discourses which in some cases are greatly divergent, which can be emotionally destabilising . The second metaphor emphasizes the speed of response to new environmental conditions through flexibility, and contracts formal and informal spaces. This trend is, however, led by the formal restrictions of production, giving rise to an ideal image of efficiency in which all organisation members are supposed to participate. This image has been quickly transferred to many other institutional spaces -for instance, the introduction of quality and excellence discourses in educational organisations.

The intelligent machine is certainly a project. We anticipate that in its future development it will face unavoidable conceptual and technical problems. it will also surely have to meet with problems of economics and implementation, which we think it will overcome because of the benefits which it promises. And not only because of those which it promises, but also because of those which it unconsciously brings about, as in the case of Biology:

> "The new Biology . . . borrows the fundamental concepts which have caused its theoretical advances . . . from the information sciences and artificial organisms (programmable and automated machines)"
>
> (Atlan 1991: 52) .

It is true that this has probably limited other projects, again without realising it. The intelligent machine is probably still not a reality. However, the simple fact of announcing it modifies not only our expectations but also our ways of behaving. it deals with a project which both fascinates and terrifies us. Of all the problems in its path, there is one which worries us because it does not represent a visible obstacle. We mean ethics. Opening the doors to this discussion represents an act of "non artificial intelligence". Or, better still, it implies the potential to restore real meaning to the term "artificial", not as something foreign and antagonist to mankind, but as something produced by us for our own benefit

[Translated by Joanna Coutler.]

References

Aglietta, Michel. Regulacion y crisis del capitalismo, Siglo XXI, Mexico, 1979.
Alberoni, Francesco. Las razones del bien y del mal, Gedisa, Barcelona, 1992.
Aoki, Masahiko. La estructura de la economia Japonesa, Fondo de Cultura Economica, Mexico, 1990.
At lan, Henri. Con razon y sin ella. lntercritica de la Ciencia y del Nito, Tusguets, Barcelona, 1991.
Aubert Nicole and Vincent de Gaulejac. Le cout de l'excellence, Seuil, Paris, 1991.
Baritz, Loren. The Servants of Power: A History of the Use of Social Science in American industry, Greenwood Press, Connecticut, 1974.
Baudrillard, Jean. Les strategies fatales, Bernard Grasset, Paris, 1983.
Braverman, Harry. Labor and Monopoly Capital, *Monthly Review*, New York, 1974.
Burns, Tom and G. M. Stalker. The Management of innovation, Tavistock Publications, London, 1961.
Capra, Fritjof. The Turning Point: science, society1 and the rising culture, Simon & Schuster, New York, 1982.
Caso, Antonio. 11La filosofia moral de don Eugenio M. de Hostos", in Conferencias del Ateneo de la Juventud, Mexico, 1910. Quoted by Zea, Leopoldo (1993), El postitivismo en Mexico: nacimiento, apogeo y decadencia, Fondo de Cultura Economica, Mexico.
Castoriadis, Cornelius. L'institution imaginaire de la Societe, Seuil, Paris, 1975.
Clegg, Stewart R. "organization and Control", in *Administrative Science Quarterly*, 1981; Vol. 26, No. 4, pp. 546-562.
Clegg, Stewart R. *Modern organizations. Organization Studies in the Postmodern World*, Sage, London, 1990.
Cooper, Robert. "Modernism, Post Modernism and Organizational Analysis 3: The Contribution of Jacque Derrida" in *Organization Studios*, 1989; 10/4, pp. 479-502.
Cooper, Robert and Gibson Burrel. "Modernism, Postmodernism and organizational Analysis: An introduction", in *Organization Studies*; 1988; 9/1, pp. 91-112.
Coriat, Benjamin. L'atalier et le chronometre. lssai sur le taylorisme, le fordisme et la production de masse, Christian Bourgois Editeur, Paris, 1979.
Desmarez, Pierre. "La sociologie industrielle. Fille de la thermodynamique d'equilibre?, in *Sociologie du Travail*, 1983; No. 3, pp. 261-274.
Durkheim, Emile. La division social del trabajo, Colofon, Mexico, 1979.
Foucault, Michel. L'ordre du discoursing Gallimard, Paris, 1971.
Friedman, Georges. ou va le travail humain?, Idees/Gallimard, Paris, 1973.
Friedman, Georges. La crisis del progreso, Laia, Barcelona, 1977.
Gaos, Jose Historia de nuestra idea del mundo, Fondo de Cultura Economica/El Colegio de Mexico, Mexico, 1992.
Giddens, Anthony. Durkheim, Fontana, Glasgow, 1978.
Henderson, Lawrence J. On the Social System, The University of Chicago Press, Chicago, 1970.1989;
Heydebrand, Wolf V. New Organizational Forms", in *Work and Occupations*, Vol. 16, No. 3, pp. 323-357.
Homans, George C. The Human Group, Harcourt Brace, New York, 1959.
Kilduff, Martin. "Deconstructing Organizations", in Academy of Management Review, 1993; Vol. 18, No. 1, pp.13-31.
Leborgne, Danile and Alain Lipietz. "L'apres-fordisme et son espace", in *Les Temps Modernes*, 1988, No. 501, abril, pp. 75-110.
Lyotard, Jean-Francois. La condition postmoderne, Editions du Minuit, Paris, 1989.

March, James G. and Herbert A. Simon. Organizations, Wiley, New York, 1958.
Mayo, Elton. The Human Problems of an Industrial Civilization, Viking, New York, 1933.
Mayo, Elton. The Social Problems of an Industrial Civilization, Harvard University, Boston, 1945.
McCorduk, Pamela. "Inteligencia artificial: an aperc'u", in Graubard, Stephen R. (ed.), El nuevo debate sobre la inteligencia artificial. Sistemas simbolicos y redes neuronales, Gedisa, Barcelona, 1993, pp. 81-101.
Montaño Hirose, Luis. "La escuela de las relaciones humanas: premisas para un debate", in Ibarra Colado, Eduardo and Luis Montaño Hirose (eds.), Historia del pensamiento administrativo, Vol. 1, Universidad Aut6noma Metropolitana-Iztapalapa, Mexico, 1985, pp. 351-356.
Montaño Hirose, Luis. "Las nuevas relaciones-humanas: un falso reto a la democracia", in Ensayos criticos para el 'studio de las organizaciones en Mexico, Universidad Autonoma Metropolitana-Iztapalapa, Mexico, 1985, pp. 63-102.
Montaño Hirose, Luis. "El orden sistemico: algunos avatares del paradigma organizacional", in Ibarra colado, Eduardo and Luis Montaño Hirose (eds.), El orden organizacional: poder, estrategia y contradiccion, Universidad Autonoma Metropolitana-Iztapalapa, Mexico, 1987, pp. 1-58.
Montaño Hirose, Luis. "De la metafora al poder. Algunas reflexiones acerca de las aproximaciones organizacionales a la educaci6n superior", in Ibarra Colado, Eduardo (ed.), La universidad ante el espejodo la excelencia. Enjuegos organizacionales, Universidad Aut6noma Metropolitana-Iztapalapa, Mexico, 1993, pp. 1-17.
Montaño Hirose, Luis "At the Edge of Modernity: Boundaries, Mediations and Overlappings. The Lessons of the Japanese Organization" in *Osaka City University Business Journal*, 1994, pp. 35-57.
Morin, Edgar. El Metodo: la naturaleza do la naturaleza, Catedra, Madrid, 1981.
Newell, Allan and Herbert A. Simon. Human Problems Solving, Prentice-Hall, New Jersey, 1972.
Ouchi, William. The N-Form Society: How American Teamwork Can Recapture the Competitive Edge, Addison-Weley Massachusetts, 1984.
Pagès, Max, Michel Bonetti, Vincent de Gaulejac and Daniel Descendre. L'emprise do l'organisation, Presses Universitaires de France, Paris, 1971.
Parker, Martin. "Post-Modern Organizations or Post-Modern Organization Theory?", in *Organization Studies*, 1992a; 13/1, pp. 1-17.
Parker, Martin. "Getting Down from the Fence: A Reply to Haridimos Tsoukas", in *Organization Studies*, 1992b; 13/4, pp. 51-653.
Putnam, Hilary. "Mucho ruido por muy poco" in Graubard, Stephen R. (ed.), El nuevo debate sobre la inteligencia artificial. Sistemas simbolicos y redes neuronales, Gedisa, Barcelona, 1993, pp. 306-319.
Roethlisberger, Fritz and William Dickson, Nanagement and the Worker, Harvard University Press, Cambridge, 1976.
Simon, Herbert A. La nueva ciencia do la decision gerencial, El Ateneo, Buenos Aires, 1977.
Smith, Adam. An Inquiry into the Nature and Causes of the Wealth of Nations, The Modern Library, New York, 1937.
Smith, Adam. The Theory of Noral Sentiments, Liberty Classics, Indianapolis, 1976.
Starkey, Ken. "Durkheim and Organizational Analysis", in *Organization Studies,* 1992; 13/4, p. 627-642.
Taylor, Frederick W. Scientific Nanagement: Shop Management. The Principles of Scientific Management. Testimony Before the Special Committee, Greenwood, Connecticut, 1972.
Tsuokas, Haridimos. "Postmodernism, Reflexive Rationalism and Organizational Studies: A Reply to Martin Parker", in *Organization Studies*, 1992; 13/4, pp. 643-649.
Waltz, David L. "Perspectivas de la construccion de maquinas verdaderamente inteligentes" in Graubard, Stephen R. (ed.), El nuevo debate sobre la inteligencia

artificial. Sistemas simbolicos y redes neuronales, Gedisa, Barcelona, 1993, pp. 218-242.
Wiener, Norbert. Cybernetics. Or Control and Communication in the Animal and the Machine, Massachusetts Intitute of Technology, Massachusetts, 1969.
Wiener, Norbert. Ex-prodigy My childhood and youth, Massachusetts Institute of Technology, Cambridge, 1966.

Notes

* This paper has also been scheduled to appear in *AI & Society*; 1996: 9.1 (editor)

Chapter 7

Information System Design: Human Centred Approaches

Jim Thorpe

Distinguishing marks of Human Centred system designers are to be found more in the range of concerns brought to the activity of information system design than in a predilection for particular techniques of software engineering. If not partnered by an account of the themes central to the Human Centred tradition, notably the social context in which IT artefacts exist, the cultural and personal realities of people using technology or subject to its pervasive activity, and an acknowledgement of the forms taken by knowledge as a social phenomenon, Human Centred design could be dismissed as simple pragmatism.

The Human Centred designer may exclude methods of design which are unable to match the richness of the information environment of which the proposed artefacts are to be a part; other methods will be judged according to their value in supporting human judgement: the methods themselves will not dominate. On occasions certain methods of system development may be particularly compatible with insights into knowledge, communication, and organisations promoted by the Human Centred tradition. This point will be expanded below with reference to making judgements and to the social nature of the information environment.

The Human Centred design tradition emphasises the context in which IT is to be used. The functioning of organisations and how people interact with one another and with machines are considered a proper concern of the system developer. Hence the term 'information environment' is favoured, more effectively to highlight that space in which humans and machines touch one another than if information systems and the situation of their use were spoken of as if no profound interplay existed between them. This profundity is ignored when people constituting the information environment are referred to simply as 'users'.

Human Centred perspectives counter the prevailing bias towards an over-strong belief in rationality and the dominant metaphor of the machine, which encourage IT designers to reduce design issues too slickly to ones of simple functionality. We speak of 'the social machinery' and may be misled into believing that society is a machine. The undoubted value in the past of the Enlightenment faith in rationality to free us from the dogma of tradition released a force which empowered the Industrial Age and its successor the Information Age, but the power of the rational to remove uncertainty, and likewise the value of doing so, was exaggerated. Now overarching rationality is attacked by critiques from a variety of often opposing camps. In particular we see the rise of the post-modern critique with its view of the world as multi-faceted rather than governed by a single rationality. There are here, we believe, lessons for us as designers.

Introduction

Advocates are to be found for a diversity of methods of developing information systems. Distinguishing marks of Human Centred system designers are to be found more in the range of concerns brought to the activity of information system design than in a predilection for particular techniques of software engineering. If not partnered by an account of the themes central to the Human Centred tradition, notably the social context in which IT artefacts exist, the cultural and personal realities of people using technology or subject to its pervasive activity, and an acknowledgement of the forms taken by knowledge as a social phenomenon, Human Centred design could be dismissed as simple pragmatism.

The Human Centred designer may exclude methods of design which are unable to match the richness of the information environment of which the proposed artefacts are to be a part; other methods will be judged according to their value in supporting human judgement: the methods themselves will not dominate. On occasions certain methods of system development may be particularly compatible with insights into knowledge, communication, and organisations promoted by the Human Centred tradition. This point will be expanded below with reference to making judgements and to the social nature of the information environment.

The Human Centred design tradition emphasises the context in which IT is to be used. The functioning of organisations and how people interact with one another and with machines are considered a proper concern of the system developer. Hence the term 'information environment' is favoured, more effectively to highlight that space in which humans and machines touch one another than if information systems and the situation of their use were spoken of as if no profound interplay existed between them. This profundity is ignored when people constituting the information environment are referred to simply as 'users'.

Human Centred perspectives counter the prevailing bias towards an over-strong belief in rationality and the dominant metaphor of the machine, which encourage IT designers to reduce design issues too slickly to ones of simple functionality. We speak of 'the social machinery' and may be misled into believing that society is a machine. The undoubted value in the past of the Enlightenment faith in rationality to free us from the dogma of tradition released a force which empowered the Industrial Age and its successor the Information Age, but the power of the rational to remove uncertainty, and likewise the value of doing so, was exaggerated. Now overarching rationality is attacked by critiques from a variety of often opposing camps. In particular we see the rise of the post-modern[1] critique with its view of the world as multi-faceted rather than governed by a single rationality. There are here, we believe, lessons for us as designers. There is an innate limitation on the ability of people to understand one another. The place of rational discourse and the activity of making definitions only goes some way to removing the limitation. As Johansson reminds us,

> Because it is possible to temporarily reduce the intrinsic vagueness of the words we speak and read, by using conscious reason to impose temporary constraints on meaning, it was inevitable that someone would dream up the possibility of using reason to end vagueness, and thus banish the need for interpretation once and for all. This is the Western dream of reason which captivated Leibnitz: two philosophers who disagreed about what words meant would sit and calculate together, until the error which caused their disagreement would be discovered, and their dispute would evaporate.
>
> Johansson (1993)

We are divided in spite of a common language because meanings are to an extent defined by the context in which language is used and by the different meaning people associate with their words as a consequence of the different ways in which those people accommodate to the activities they carry out. Those in the information environment havetheir context-specific knowledge of the problem situation and a designer, imported from outside the problematic context from which the design brief arose, possesses general, context-independent knowledge. In lieu of complete understanding designers need to form working relationships and to become trusted by those in the information environment.

Because of communication limitations the tendency of the designer is, according to Bell and Wood-Harper (1992) to create theoretically sound rather than contextually appropriate systems. The conflict of values and objectives between designers and clients or stakeholders leads to the development of ineffective systems. The key to avoiding such conflict according to those authors is 'The lesson to be learned is that *irrespective of professionalism the planner/analyst must have the humility and common sense to see the client as central to a working system..'* We would argue for designers to possess these personal virtues, but would emphasise the need to consider the centrality of the client from a systemic perspective, taking into account skills, knowledge-in-context, and allowing for values, and acknowledging the diversity of understanding among stakeholders, an understanding of which only a only part will be held in common. Efforts to work with, rather than attempt to overcome or remove the communication gap include what are becoming known as 'participatory design' or 'collaborative design'. The support and involvement of stakeholders inherently offer opportunity for relevance of design practice to perceived problem.

Limitations of awareness and skill beset attempts at design and implementation, as do constraints of budget and time. There is always a struggle to attend to the range of issues in design, but even partial awareness resulting from merely meagre consideration may lead to better design than to ignore the context of design, the space in which IT artefacts are implemented: at least expectation of the outcome of design may be tempered and less ambitious goals may lead to better systems.

The Human Centred tradition is not a method of design but a movement, even though that description suggests more coherence than actually exists. Those within the tradition attempt to promote and contribute to such wider awareness about the way design is carried out and its outcomes as have been sketched above. This chapter stops short of instructing would-be designers. Its focus is on the context of design and on perspectives which may contribute to an emerging tradition of design which is more relevant to wider human needs than less culturally aware IT design practice.

Human Centred Systems or Machine Centred Systems

The term 'Human-Centred Systems' is used in contrast to 'machine-centred systems', and as far as IT system design is concerned the contrast is between design undertaken in the light of social and cultural need and design approaches which owe much to design of engineering artefacts and the simplistic scientism of 'scientific management'[2] with its view of the person as a machine or system with defined functionality. The metaphor of the machine[3] and the associated notion of causality underpin Western technology and the organisation of production, but are dangerous when they lead us to view systems of human activity with the simplifying clarity with which we analyse machine systems.

The pressure to achieve certainty provides a powerful motivation to drive out human variability by inventing technology to enact uniformity, and the very means of creating such technology themselves tend to be reduced to uniform procedure. Unfortunately human intelligence, the human quality of making judgements is thereby lost, and human control over the processes is threatened[4].

Seen as a movement, the Human Centred design tradition undertakes, as a first step towards encouraging more effective human and socially sensitive design practice, to expose the underlying biases in our society which give machine-centred design its plausibility and to encourage more effective human and socially sensitive design practice. As a second step it is important to consider such major issues as Gill (1989) refers to as *knowledge transfer* and the *quality of skills*. 'We therefore need to fully understand' claims Gill 'the social and cultural factors of complex wider social and organisational systems in order to provide software engineers with practical design models', and, we may add, support for developing their own.

The contrast between Machine Centred design and Human Centred design, may be epitomised, at the risk of distortion. (See Table 1)

Design Issues

Issues commonly used to describe the context of information system design are not in themselves contentious: it is in its dealing with the issues from a wider view that marks out Human Centred design. Selection of such issues and a consideration of how they relate to one another is a matter of whatever seems relevant to the case in handThe issues relate to activities taking place within organisations, typically clerical, financial, management and production.The sort of issues to which we refer are indicated in figure 1, shown interlinked and with a suggestion of levels of analysis and the enveloping cultural context. It is not so much the issues themselves, although the issue of *culture* would often be regarded as too refractory to be dealt with in system design, but how they are taken into account which distinguish Human Centred design

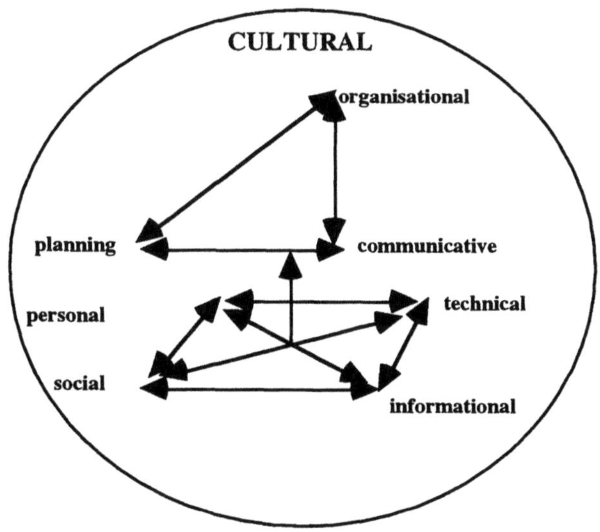

Figure 1: Related Issues in Systems Development

	Human Centred design	Machine Centred design
knowledge	—cannot always be made entirely explicit yet retain validity; Is often embedded in action. —multiple views possible that may not be validly reduced to a single view —explicit or implicit/tacit	—can be made explicit by representation in language or other formalism —a single truth —explicit, e.g. facts and rules
approaches to reasoning	—although accepting the place of manipulation representations by means of formal procedures (logic), also acknowledges judgement based on experience —affirms human judgement, assisted where appropriate by automated reasoning	—consists of manipulating representations by means of formal procedures such as first order predicate logic —favours automated reasoning
design approach	—socio-technical activity —multi-disciplinary, incorporating perspectives of social science research	—technical activity, defined by brief —engineering design approach
design process	—a process involving reason but also a creative encounter between stakeholders to redesign the information environment	—a process in which needs are identified and met by a technological or organisational artefact determined by rational activity
nature of domain	—diverse understandings of domain held by stakeholders of the information environment	—a single reality, potentially knowable although often too complicated to know other than approximately
human involvement	—involvement optimised —people as creators and sustainers of the information environment	—involvement minimised —people as users and as system components
place of values	—acknowledged	—ignored as far as possible

knowledge representation	—metaphorical structures helping understanding. They can be called 'models' but no presumption is made about the certainty of relation between conceived structure and the world that inspired the structure	—models providing an approximate image of reality
knowledge elicitation	—avoids complete elicitation, prefers to work with knowledge in its context	—encourages complete verbalisation
belief in particular method	—provisional in the light of enabling awareness and agreed action	—provisional in the light of effectiveness of model space in creating a system conforming to needs as made explicit
information environment	—people and systems	—people as systems
technology in human affairs	—skill-enhancing tool	—machine replacement for people

Table 1: Differences between Machine Centred and Human Centred design

Limitations to communicative ability have been referred to above and thus, with the exception of design so unproblematic as to deserve the accolade 'routine design', traditional attempts to carry out design by a designer identifying the relevant components, 'decomposing' the problem are in general doomed to failure. *We are faced once more*, writes Bijl (1989), *with our fundamental uncertainty about the completeness of overt knowledge, even when we try to isolate tasks into discrete processes.* Only for tasks which can be declared context-free, isolated by the boundary of agreed definition, is the concept of well-formedness of use. Alternative ways of developing systems referred to as participatory design, referred to below, involve the designer as part of the design situation rather than being a detached organiser of it, and work from personal views of reality rather than presume an absolute reality. The term holistic is sometimes used to refer to forms of design which involve more than formal knowledge-representation, acknowledging and accommodating intuitive understanding in the design activity.

Design in the Formal and in the Semi-Formal Context

In the practice of engineering design there is a traditional division of labour between *engineering design* and *industrial design*, corresponding to activities directed towards providing an artefact with specified functionality (see Hopgood 1993), and on the other hand a concern for presentation. '*Industrial design seeks to rectify the omissions of engineering, a conscious attempt to bring form and visual order to engineering hardware where technology does not of itself provide these features.*' (Open University 1986, in Hopgood 1993). The plausibility of designing separately for function may arise from the uniformity of need for which many engineering products are required. *Electrical and electronic engineering have*, according to Hopgood (1993), *been most amenable to the application of decision support tools, as designs are often routine rather than innovative and can often be treated as optimisation problems.* However, this disjunction between the designing of *form* separately from *function* is not unchallenged even within engineering: the view of one industrial design department in a large electrical engineering company in which the present writer worked regarded their work as about better design. Appearance was part of the department's work but so was—as the department would have to explain it to enquirers— ergonomics.

Design reduced to routine is economical design. But design by routine is ineffective in meeting the needs of people who are takers of purposeful action not programmable machines. When the context for which a design is intended can be modelled exactly, it is what Whitley (1991) refers to as a 'formal domain' and in principle design may be routine although in practice neither methods nor materials may exist. How do we know we have a formal domain? In the end we do not: but we may know enough to anticipate a sufficiently good match between designed artefact and context of its use. A completely non-formal domain is one for which design is impossible: the context we face as designers is at worst the semi-formal domain.

Human Centred design is appropriate to semi-formal domains and thus to *innovative* rather than *routine* design. Given its acknowledgement of the place of the social and the regard for a variety of ways of knowing, notably intuitive and tacit knowledge, the tradition naturally favours the emerging practice of engaging users in the activity of design not merely consulting them, and the term user-involved design is gaining currency. In an attempt to make the sweep of design more comprehensive, talk of 'users' has moved on to refer to 'stakeholders', hopefully a transient move. Another attempt to engender relevance, described as user-modifiable technology, springs from disbelief in the possibility in general of designing context-relevant technology even with the involvement of users.

Relevant technology may emerge which is not the outcome of careful design. It would be incomplete to ignore the fortuitous in successful technology: whether the technology met a need or whether it created a need is up for debate. The Sony Walkman for instance, an inspiration of Sony's chairman, was not the outcome of market research.

The consideration of relevant technology suggests the question of whether a technological artefact itself may be considered Human Centred, or whether to reserve the term only for the process of design. The question might be explored by considering technology which however designed, leads to the amplification of human opportunity. A suggested example is the humble pencil. The word 'humble' might seem a merely rhetorical inclusion, but it might be argued that only artefacts available and accessible enough to merit the accolade can be regarded as able to enhance opportunity for society, and counter-argued that this is to view opportunity for all as synonymous with availability to each member of society.

Language, Action and Social Context

Social structures which are stable are so because they are continuously renewed[5] by recurrent action reinforced by corresponding viewpoints. Neither society nor individuals has ontological priority. That social reality which is 'above' or 'independent' of individuals provides structure within which action is taken by the people belonging to that social reality: and that action contributes to the structure. Its suitability lies in that it is 'created and manipulated by individuals through their activities.'[6]

The mutually sustaining characteristics of action, belief and structure mean that the 'empirical facts' of what takes place are not clearly differentiable from the ideas and belief surrounding everyday practice although the distinction is familiar enough. This mutually sustaining, or self-referential structure, is referred to as *autopoiesis*. For recent work see for example Qvortrup (1991). The information system developer is enters a social world, an information environment, held stable by forces which those within the environment more-or-less unconsciously work to sustain. The developer must tread carefully in disturbing this conservative structure, and must not expect to be liked.

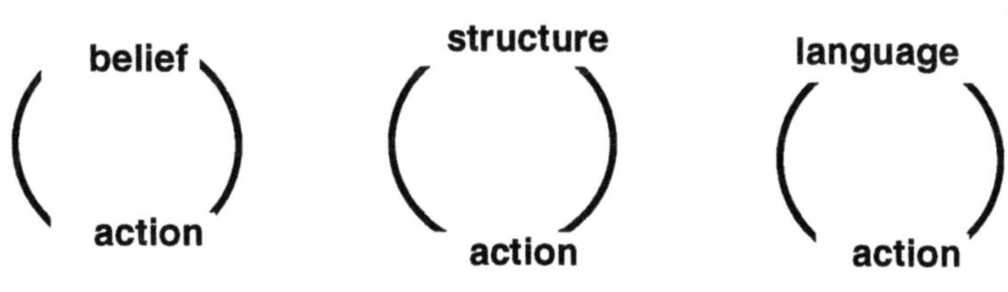

Figure 2: Mutual dependence of action, belief and structure

The relationship between language and action, language and reality is not as clear-cut as we might wish. This is why we must often work with the 'communications gap':

we cannot always remove it. The act of giving definitions only really works in a context in which people already understand one another: the definitions in mathematical papers, by appearing at the head of the papers falsely hint at the point of their creation. The essential uncertainty in language has been well documented and Johansson (1993) urges us to acknowledge that 'vagueness is central to the social construction of meaning'. Language and action are mutually sustaining: meaning is not simply a linguistic matter.

As to design, the rationalistic presumption that design is about reducing uncertainty, rather than about meeting human purposes, about enabling action, needs to be disturbed by the non-rational world in which design actually takes place. Mike Cooley[7] has noted the disregard for intuition and human judgement implicit in the rationalist presumption.

Expanded Criteria for Design

Consideration of Human Centred design methods for technology should be preceded by the establishment of enhanced design goals. We can consider, for instance, the relationship between machine and the activity of workers with such machines, and we can contemplate design goals concerned with the contribution of new technology to interpersonal relationships and satisfactory working conditions.

Human Judgement: Supported or Replaced

An increasing use of IT is to assist with decision making, but its use is problematic for reasons alluded to above and the following points are noted.

- When acts of judgement are made by cognitive technology they will be fair and consistent, it may be argued. Two computers using the same facts and rules may come up with the same answer to a problem—but only *perhaps*, since the outcome also depends upon how the program is constructed, for example how its control structures determines the order in which rules will 'fire'.
- Decision-making IT is only as good as the criteria according to which it operates. Self-consistency of the computer model is no guarantee of relevance.
- Consistency is not the only virtue: appropriateness, validity, relevance are also important. Surrendering decision-making to technology and to formal methods denies the place of human capacities for judgement other than rule-based reasoning.
- A decision taken is something the decision takers may simply have to live with, and it is important that the changes planned by them are compatible with their capabilities and insights: thus a decision seen as a sub-optimal solution by outsiders may be well suit the participants.
- It is not only from the foibles of human behaviour but also from human experience and learning that cognitive technology may insulate us. People take decisions and from them two sorts of outcome flow: an action and a learning by the decision maker. Cognitive technology may lose us control of our decisions.
- Generally IT is safer when it helps us organise our knowledge to support rather than to replace human judgement.

The encroachment into human affairs of mechanised judgement is becoming well understood. We believe that it is not always beneficial but convincing others of its pitfalls meets resistance from the prevalent world view. The rise of mechanised judgement is not simply an inevitable outcome of the development of the means for carrying it out, viz. computer-based information systems. The prevalent presumption that thought, or more loosely, judgement, is only about rational process and not about reflection upon the observed, together with the inexorable tendency to replace inconstant human activity with a cheaper and more reliable mechanical process provides plausibility and motive. Referring to cognitive technologies Kennedy (1989) has described the replacement of human judgement by automated reasoning under the title 'The Industrialisation of Intelligence'.

The economic benefits to an organisation, as commonly measured, of increasing automation are undeniable. The replacement of physical labour by mechanised procedure has been high in profile with us since the days of Henry Ford so the move to reduce acts of judgement to rules and algorithms and replace human decision-making activity by computer processing is in concept but a short step forwards. Questions are posed about the human cost of such economic benefits and at a more local level we can ask about the impact within organisations when the work of people is restructured or done away with, as distinct from the immediate benefit to the company of one computer and one worker doing the work of three people.

Against such a global back-cloth the opportunity for individual designers to work in ways which cut across the mechanisation of mental activity seems slight. Opposing mechanisation may be a hard case to argue as the danger of loss of control in human affairs attributable to over-mechanisation may not emerge immediately, although quality and efficiency can be reduced in the short-term by careless mechanisation.

The impact of a computer based information system cannot be predicted especially in the long-term, but undesirable side-effects will not be anticipated if there is no systemic or organisational perspective in the design process. A thought-experiment offered by Bjørn-Anderson (1984) concerns a medical Expert System intended to diagnose illness with the accuracy of an experienced doctor. A doctor who overrules the System, but who happens to give an erroneous alternative diagnosis is at risk of censure for ignoring the 'advice' it provided. If the doctor had surrendered authority to the Expert System there would be the computer to blame in the event of a tragedy. There is thus social pressure to accept automated diagnosis, and so deny doctors their own power of judgement and the ability to develop their professional skills by learning through experience. Technocentric design ignores the social and organisational implications, the organisational consequences of the new technology are not foreseen, and only ad hoc attempts are made to anticipate possible dangers.

Information is not an end-product in the functioning of organisations: information is the precursor to action. Information systems which support human judgement facilitate informed decision making and action. Information systems which replace human judgement deny the opportunity for informed action-taking by reducing human activity to a choice between alternatives offered by the information system or to mere enactment of an automated decision process.

Enhanced Goals for Office Technology Design

It is claimed by Bjørn-Anderson (1984) that the 'socio-technical' design principles for new office technology promoted particularly in Scandinavia lead to greater efficiency and better systems for both customers/clients and employees. Work with computer based technology, claims Bjørn-Anderson, who lists desirable characteristics for office information systems, should not be a surrender of human initiative. Work should be a symbiotic partnership between user and computer based system.

Office computer systems should

- not continuously monitor human activities
- make use of the substantial knowledge possessed by users rather than assume the users have no knowledge
- not detract from the human powers of discretion and autonomy
- be comprehensible ('transparent') to users who are not computer experts
- be modifiable by users, and the users trained to modify systems
- enhance skills and stimulate users to learn better ways of performing their jobs

- respect and assist not only the rational abilities but other qualities such as intuition and creativity
- enhance rather than inhibit social contact

These socio-technical design criteria illustrate the sort of expanded goals considered by Human Centred design.

Human-Machine Activity

Work continues in making a considering how to make more effective a technology which is by its ability to offer cognitive support less external to human activity than former technology. The already referred to notion of 'user' harks back to a former age and is not always a revealing metaphor. What follows merely hints at what is an on-going discussion.

Machine Metaphor versus Tool Metaphor of Information Systems

Reference was made above to the contrast between using information systems as a substitute for human activity or using them to support that activity i.e., replacing people with machines which do their work or providing tools which enable them to work more effectively. Systems designed in the light of the *tool* metaphor preserve existing skills or allow users of the IT artefact to retain control oftheir activity. Part of the human activity may be automated, for example calculation, but a choice is made about what to automate, rather than presume the inherent advantages of automation. The metaphor of the *tool* is deliberately used by those with the design goal of support for, or amplification of, skilled activity in contrast to design carried out in the image of the *machine* with no concern about making existing skills redundant.

We are accustomed to the de-skilling effects of technology and the corresponding social effects but have heard less about 'de-knowledging'. Yet it is a matter of concern that knowledge encapsulated in computer systems is isolated from that known by people. If knowledge is power, it is a design as well a social issue to consider the locus of that knowledge if we are to be aware of the opportunities and constraints which information systems bring to the information environment.

Human-Machine Symbiosis

With less symmetry than in its biological counterpart, Human-Machine Symbiosis as referred to by Bjørn-Anderson (1984) is about systems which combine human skills and computing power to carry out a task more effectively than could be done by the human or computer alone.

> Symbiotic systems exist in many different areas. For example, computerised axial tomogaphy is a computer-controlled scanning technique which can present three-dimensional X-ray images of the body. It operates as a partnership between the computer, which performs an immense amount of mathematical calculations, and the doctor, whose experience and visual perception enable the information to be interpreted in ways which discriminate between subtle differences in aspects of the image.

Methodology of Design

Why Is Design Often Ineffective?

It is outside the scope of this chapter to attempt an extensive account of systems failures attributable to the design stages. The intention here is rather to cast light on the nature of Human Centred design by reference to endemic failure arising from too narrow a view of human activity and inadequate ways of describing its manifestation. One account of the failure of systems to meet the needs of users given by Bell and Wood-Harper (1992) is framed in terms of information which is poorly gathered and sorted, inadequately edited, incorrectly analysed, analysed for the wrong things, and badly presented. Agreed, and in their experience many systems fail because they do not take into account the views and worries of the end users. It is the contention here that it is not enough merely to consider the adequacy of information: we must consider the ways in which information is made available by information systems to those who use them.

Activities Misconstrued

The recognition that computer support for human activities is not neutral leads naturally to questions about how people work. By 'not neutral' I mean that the action taken by someone who uses an information system is constrained by the form of the support system. In the context of CAD systems Bijl (1989) describes the constraining effect of one system because its design had not taken proper account of the nature of the professional activity it was intended to support, incorrectly seeing the activity as knowledge-based, rather than as an experience-based activity. The table below, adapted from Bijl (1989), illustrates in general terms the contrast between the two forms of activity.

	Knowledge Based Activity	Experience Based Activity
Knowledge in Activity	—explicit knowledge chiefly used in the path from problem to solution	—explicit knowledge and practitioner's reflexive judgement
Accountability	—to peers who share a basis of knowledge	—to public which does not share the same knowledge
Discipline	—formal and detached	—ad hoc in response to demands
Procedures	—systematic and stable; exclude the intuitive	—idiosyncratic or systemic; mixture of knowledge and experience

Table 2: Differences between knowledge based activity and experience based activity

The sort of questions that a systems designer might ask in order to design more appropriate technology could well include ones revealing the extent to which the activity to be supported by technology is knowledge based, and how far experience based.

Another type of system criticised by Bijl is intended to provide the designer with specialist knowledge, to undertake the functions of a specialist. These systems are criticised for their inability to provide the information that an architect, say, would need about how strictly standards have to be applied, i.e. the system is not able to enact a crucial feature of discussions commonly taking place between an architect and a specialist concerned with negotiating constraints applicable to the project in hand.

This omission was transparent: but the same sort of error in other contexts may go unnoticed: the ill-effects may be subtle or long-term, or the operation of the software may not be so open to scrutiny. The CAD software Bijl criticises would be used by professionals in a creative profession who are of necessity critical of their performance and as a matter of survival ever seeking to improve the quality of their work and are accordingly vigilant about the quality of their tools.

Limited View of Knowledge and Action

The problems about the two CAD systems described above by Bijl reflect a prevalent bias about knowledge. We ignore much of what knowing is about when we see it as only about explicit knowledge such as statements and rules, and we ignore the ways in which people take action from their different modes of knowing, thereby reducing action to the enactment of rules. We know that learning from experience exists, the outcome of learning by doing and by attending to things, but we perhaps ignore it because we do not know how to talk about it, and conversely. The need of programmers to work from a supplied functional specification leads naturally to stress knowledge as explicit formulation and a corresponding discomfort with the notion of implicit and tacit knowledge.

The increasingly high profile attained by the 'information society' reflects a move away from manufacture of physical products but status accorfded to the myth or concept of 'information' tends to reduce the act of informing to message-passing, encouraging the belief that action has to be preceded or accompanied by explicit rather than tacit knowing, including that form of knowing which is only evident when action takes place. The view of knowledge that makes possible the information society (at least in the form we know of it) is, according to Gill (1992) the Platonic view that knowledge is only that which can be precisely stated. It is but a short step to believe that knowledge can in general be meaningfully exchanged and used separate from the context in which it has arisen and made it valid.

> 'In recent years an historical transition has taken place, from activity involving the creation and manipulation of artefacts to activity based on something called 'information', and that this activity takes place in an 'information society . . .This view of knowledge separates knowledge from its social and cultural contexts in which it is constructed, interpreted and maintained through its practical use in context.
>
> Gill (1992)

In addition to the issue of the universality of knowledge to which Gill alludes, if we are to be comprehensive in our approach to design the place of personal knowledge must be acknowledged. Personal knowledge may include what one person but not another knows, but the aspect to which I am refer is the forms of knowing which cannot be formulated as procedures or rendered as statements. Those forms of knowing are attested to by terms such as tacit knowledge, the tacit dimension, or intuition. Bijl (1989) describes intuition and the kind of knowledge called common sense, the commonality of a shared life-world. These less public forms of knowing Bijl contrasts with formal knowledge.

> 'Intuition is our knowledge of ourselves in our world in a form we cannot externalise objectively in overt expressions. Intuition is knowledge by virtue of the fact that we use it to condition our actions in response to experience.'
>
> Common sense ' . . . refers to knowledge shard between people which constitutes our inter-subjective reality and is evident in our shared practical ability to do things. Common sense requires people to be able to externalise what they know, but this knowledge is not fully overt in that people do not necessarily know how their externalisations work. Typically, common sense is expressed informally in natural language . . .'
>
> Formal knowledge . . . refers to knowledge about formal structures of abstract worlds which is used to construct overt representations of people's experience . . .Typically, formalisms employ classical logic and its derivatives which . . . are formally treatable aspects of human logic. It is this kind of knowledge which is used mostly by scientists and theoreticians when they seek to explain common sense and innate knowledge. This is the only kind of knowledge we are able to recreate in computers.
>
> Bijl (1989)

Frequently articulated, common sense is often uttered in words referring to lived events more through image than structured as symbolic form. Common sense expressions, Bijl reminds us, employ metaphors which draw upon words to do with the animal senses—sight, sound, etc.—thereby reminding us of our bodily existence and the connection of common sense with the world as we perceive it.

Questions about knowledge that may be asked in the context of designing technology would be to do with the appropriate interaction between the formal, or purposive, action of computers and the intuitive and social purposeful activity of the intended users of the technology.

Inflexibility of System

Machine Centred design ignores the tolerance in the space of human activity. The inevitable inexactness of formulation and the incompleteness of the planners of the human system to be able to anticipate all eventualities meant that those involved always had to interpret their instructions. The formal structure is always partnered by an informal functioning. IT systems which presume for their efficacy a particular human organisation obstruct proper human functioning.

> The relentless logic of computers allows no grey areas. It can reveal various arrangements between individuals and groups as being totally 'irrational', although they may play an important role in oiling the wheels of working life. The programming of work procedures into the software may make social control more meticulous and more rigid.
>
> Crozier and Pavé (1984)

The need to be consistent conflicts with the requirements of adaptability and accordingly poses a potential threat to the organisation.

Ordering the Stages of Design

A typical list of the stages in the development of an information system includes the following elements.

1. Identify the information problems
2. Establish the context of the problems
3. Identify resources and constraints
4. Establish components of the information problems
5. Structure the problems into a model
6. Design model solutions to the problems
7. Implement the model

A vast array of different methods, point out Bell and Wood-Harper (1992), are available for fulfilling this sequence of tasks. Without further qualification, it would be reasonable to assume that the design process was an orderly trek through the list of elements, but not all methods concur. Another list of design phases offered by Hopgood (1993) who claims to present a more-or-less consensus view, also suggests a linear march, here from needs analysis to selling.

Phase 1	Market	i.e.	needs analysis, problem identification, and identifying end-users
Phase 2	Product design specification	i.e.	functional specification
Phase 3	Conceptual design	i.e.	determining the general form of the product
Phase 4	Optimisation and evaluation	i.e.	refinement and consistency with product design specification
Phase 5	Detailed design	i.e.	refinement to ensure satisfaction of all constraints
Phase 6	Manufacture		
Phase 7	Selling		

On closer reading it is acknowledged by Hopgood (1993) that the design process he portrays as a chronological sequence of events involves a considerable interaction between the phases in the light of changes in design constraints taking place whilst design is in progress. A difference between a Human Centred account of design and the consensus view Hopgood reports would be in the attention given to the 'considerable interaction between the phases'.

The contention that a more flexible and iterative sequence of design activities is needed to reflect the complexity of the information environment is supported by the view sketched in section 4.1 about language and action and the part they jointly play in establishing and maintaining the stability of social space. An attempt to combine order and flexibility is the Helical Project Lifecycle described below.

Following a linear sequence of design stages has been described as the 'waterfall approach' starting with a *statement of requirements* followed by *functional specification* followed by *design specification* followed by *prototype* etc. After many years of working on software projects following this approach the poor success rate of projects based upon it became apparent. One attempt to improve the situation, was to ask the users to sign-off the various documents: but this is to view communication problems in a simple light, ignoring the complex interlinking of language and action. Other attempts were made to improve the waterfall approach, but to no avail. However, during the ESPRIT 1199 project, where engineers met social scientists, a new approach was formulated. This new approach to software development draws from both the engineering and social science fields. The approach was termed, by one of the partners in the ESPRIT project, the *Helical Project Lifecycle*.

The Helical approach attacked the weakest element of the old approach, the Requirements Specification. The first action to be taken when using this new approach is to devise a scenario followed by a form of role-play. When the scenario has been firmed up and agreed to by all parties the next move round and up the Helix is taken, returning to the same issues at a higher level: at each turn round the Helix, the model of the system becomes clearer until, during the final phase, the traditional waterfall model is entered into. When this point is reached the participants would have reached agreement (explicit) and a working understanding (in part implicit or tacit) of what to do.

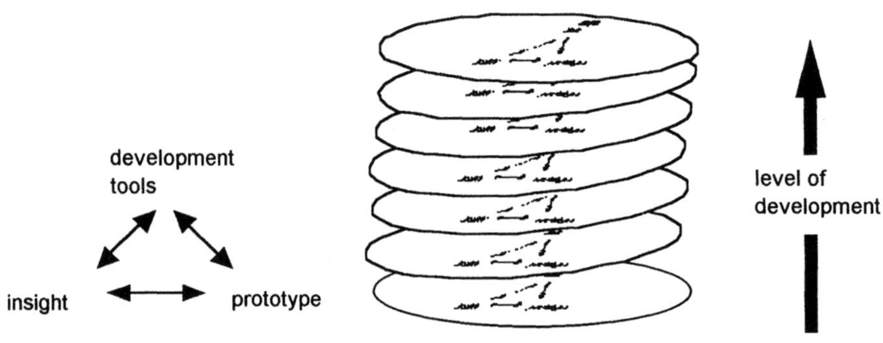

Figure 3: A Helical Design Scenario

The helical design scenario illustrated in Figure 4 does not replicate that in the ESPRIT project. The intention is to illuminate an iterative process in which insight by participants in the design process, the development of prototypes and the employment and construction of development tools all grow in course of development in which the same issues are revisited at increasing levels of sophistication.

Two Definitions of 'Methodology'

These contrasting definitions quoted in Avison & Fitzgerald (1988) refer to different levels:

> 'a recommended collection of philosophies, phases, procedures, rules, techniques, tools, documentation, management and training for developers of information systems'
>
> Maddison (1983)

> '. . . a set of principles of method, which in any particular situation has to be reduced to a method uniquely suited to that particular situation.'
>
> Checkland (1981)

The situation to which the definition according to Checkland applies could be seen as the precursor to the adoption of procedures, rules, techniques and tools, to which Maddison refers. There is a hint in Checkland's words of a situation-driven approach to design in contrast to that of Maddison's which seems more impelled by procedure.

I suggest *methodology* is about the reduction from the complexity or messiness of the total situation to procedures to enable change to take place in the information environment. This description is compatible with the 'soft systems' methodology alluded to below but is in contrast to 'hard systems' approaches.

Hard systems methodology is reductionist, believing in a reality that may in principle be known through techniques such as measurement. In non-reductionist methodology reductive activity is carried out from the 'mess' to the conceptual, but the metaphors or models derived in the process of design and their links with reality are viewed differently. The following contrasting features between typical elements in hard and soft systems methodology are respectively noted.

soft systems approach

- diverse perceptions acknowledged
- personal and interpersonal view of reality accepted as basic
- participatory design
- qualitative research

hard systems approach

- world consists of objective facts
- reality is measurable
- objectivity/independence of researcher
- quantitative research

Soft Systems Methodology

Soft systems approaches are more compatible with Human Centred design than hard systems methodology because of their acknowledgement of the social space and their attitude to technique. Checkland (1981) in a book the title of which well reveals his agenda, *Systems Thinking, Systems Practice* introduced the notion of soft systems methodologies. The underlying standpoint is sometimes called the *systems* or *holistic paradigm* and its aim is to acknowledge inter-subjectivity of the information environment by not assuming it is valid to leap directly into formal information collecting. In Checkland's 'soft systems analysis' the initial phase is to form a 'rich picture' formulated in user's terms, from which 'problem themes' are consequently extracted. Then the cycle of activities leads to resolution of the problem.

Checkland starts from the position that we engage with the world by using concepts themselves derived from the world, a position which supports the Kantian view that the regularity we observe in the experienced world is put there ourselves by our intrinsic and learned pattern making capacity. This 'constructive character of human perception' is supported by recent psychological research into perception (Imbert, M, Bertelson, P et al. (Eds.) 1987) and supports the view that 'the way we see is in terms of our human purposes in the environment' (Oatley, K 1979).

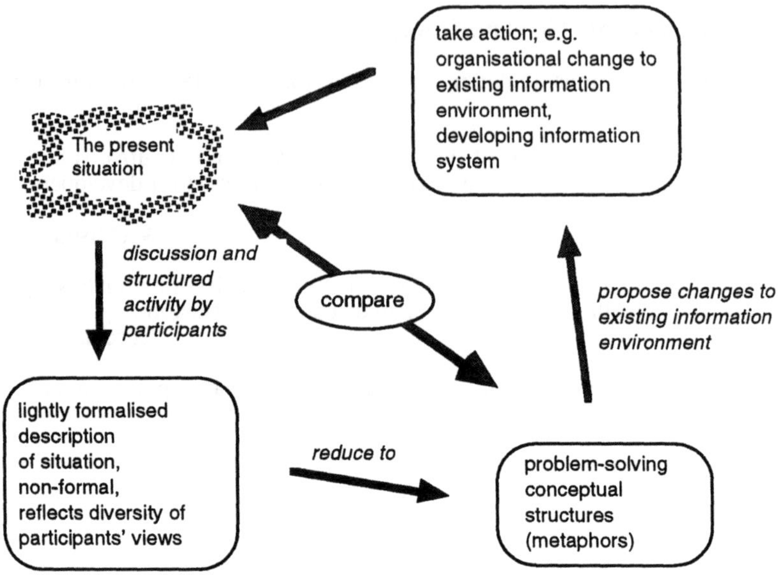

Figure 4: A Soft Systems Design Cycle

Checkland and Scholes soft systems methodology exempifies what Reason (1988) calls the paradigm of co-operative enquiry where instead of making the assumption of the reductionist paradigm that problems can be reduced to a set of components which can be attended to separately and which lead to a picture of a fixed reality independent of the people involved, the inquirer attempts to stay with the real world complexity by acting as participant and to negotiate a discourse on which to base intersubjective pictures of the problem situation. The outcome is 'descriptive and systemic', claims Reason who refers to the product as a 'pattern model' (Reason, P. 1988). The methodology of soft systems is participatory and involves action in the 'real world' and in the world of systems thinking.

Soft systems methodology is in accord with the view of the present writer that the value of particular methods of systems analysis lie in the contribution they make to turning the initial disturbance in the information environment into a problem evident to the designers as one needing solution. Particular methods are more natural allies of Human Centred design: qualitative methods will be favoured for their revelatory qualities. The quantitative, as Renée Thom once pointed out in a lecture[8] on Catastrophe Theory, must follow the qualitative. That is to say establishing a conceptual framework is a matter for human judgement not for statistical methods.

The Personal State of the Designer

> Advances in knowledge and associated technological development should not be divorced from the individuals who promote them. Accordingly, here follows a brief sketch of myself as a person, a designer, and a computer technologist . . .As a designer wishing to defend the sensitivities that I believed were important to myself and other people, I remember being resistant to what I saw as impersonal technological change . . .This reluctance to accept technological advance rested on a wish to preserve idiosyncratic control of expression . . .The attraction of technology was the power it afforded in enabling me to process more information. I was able

to produce more of my own drawings...Computers as implementations of ideas are interesting, and we can explore these ideas without knowing much about the physical devices. My intention here is to raise these ideas up to a level of common sense, so that ordinary people can judge what computers should be able to do.'

Aart Bijl (1989)

There is an evolving tradition of experience in fields of design other than information technology. The involvement of the designer is recognised in those traditions and the personal state of the designer accordingly acknowledged. Such acknowledgement as there is in the field of IT design tends to be oblique reference rather than an attempt to consider the designer in relation to the activity of design.

Hopgood (1993) restricts his comments on the place of the designer to the single statement 'The human designer remains at the centre of the design process and a range of decision support tools are being developed which will assist rather than replace him or her': there is no discussion by Hopgood of how the designer should occupy that place which he describes as central. This omission is not surprising given Hopgood's claim that engineering designs are 'often routine'.

Other writers on IT design are not lacking in their endorsement of the importance of the personal state of the designers. However there is no clarification of the links with the design activity. It may be that skilled designers restrict themselves to writing about the explicit side of their design skills because the personal side belongs to their—less available to description—intuitive knowledge. Barker (1990) is an advocate of the information engineering technique known as Entity Relationship Modelling as a means to improve system quality and increase the software productivity, by providing 'good modelling techniques and supported by rigorous standards and conventions to remove ambiguity and aid communication.' He partners his advocacy by strongly recommending a particular personal approach.

'In this book I am implicitly recommending that (systems) analysts must discard their egos, and instead recognise that there is strength in human fallibility. In practical terms it means seeking out the most thorough and accurate understanding of the business, and then exposing that to your users and peers so they can help you gain even more accuracy. I have seen this 'egoless' team approach not only enable teams to build far more appropriate systems but act as a catalyst, knitting together users, systems development staff and even accountants.' Barker (1990)

The need for architects to be innovative and to relate to other people and their activities means, according to Bijl (1989), that they are necessarily idiosyncratic and innovative. Correspondingly, the activity of design will place demands on their resources of established knowledge and intuition. 'Intuition may be less dominant in those fields where functionality of objects plays a greater part in defining designed artefacts. But the role of intuition does not disappear even when designing aeroplanes or electric kettles.' The view taken by Bell and Wood-Harper (1992) of the place of the personal in the activity of design is that the preferences of designers will unavoidably affect the way the activity is carried out, which will include attempts by the designer to influence stakeholders towards pre-set ideas about what is right. The authors identify four types of analyst, described here in paraphrase.

Technocratic	**Radical**	**Teacher**	**Emancipator**
• technical expert	• agent for social change	• facilitator, assisting problem solution	• catalyst to assist others to change
• imposes expert advice	• 'warrior'	• encourages client involvement	• assertive/ confrontational
• fixes problem with objectivity and rigour	• asserts radical reform	• seeks meanings of problem	• seeks to change minds and behaviour

Table 3: Types of Analyst—adapted from Bell and Wood-Harper (1992)

The authors note that the third image is the one that most would wish to be associated with. Both as a precursor to research, and in relation to changing tack should the initial approach to analysis and design fail, the authors claim that the designer would benefit from answering the following questions. *Am I seeking change or meaning? Am I planning a technical fix to the problem in hand or am I assisting others to recognise existing problems and develop internal solutions? What is my self-perception? How will this affect the way in which I carry out my analysis and design?*

The establishment of effective structures for education and professional development affect the growth of the individual designer and relate to developing supportive traditions of design in which experience may be embodied. Potter (1980), arguing for designers to be educated not merely trained, points out that training emphasises technical competence—'how' questions and tidy answers, but education encourages asking 'why' questions.

> 'Skills ought to keep pace with understanding and thus emerge organically; and the spread of lateral thinking must be complemented by vertical thinking (and dreaming) of a quite different kind, if understanding is to grow from strong roots.'
>
> 'There is a good sense in which any designer worth the name will be a student for the whole of his working life. This is not only a function of creative resource, but also of rapid technological change which a designer must meet in his work'
>
> 'A design capability proceeds from a fusion of skills, knowledge, understanding and imagination; consolidated by experience.'
>
> 'If the gap between technical capability and social imagination is to be bridged, or if that problem is to be energetically appraised, education must lose much of its formality in pursuit of a new warmth and flexibility of outlook.'
>
> Potter (1980)

At the personal level designers should be encouraged to be researchers: researchers into their own practice. The notion of the reflective practitioner—if kept as a term of stimulation rather than a fixed state into which all must enter—may prove rewarding and has been taken up by Schon (1984) under this title. Issues of personal knowledge have been addressed by Polanyi (1957, 1967) and taken up by other writers. In the context of IT design the journal AI & Society is a focus for these issues. For an account of question of subjectivity and objectivity in enquiry see among others Myrdal (1966). Designers need a combination of intuitive and technical strengths and an ability to draw upon or ignore parts of their experience. If they cannot be thought of as technicians applying a rational skill, designers must be relied upon because they are dependable.

Concluding Remarks

This chapter has aspired to offer insight into the design approaches of the emerging Human Centred tradition of computer-based system design. The present writer sees this growing approach as paradigm shift away from over-formal design methods, towards design infused with a rich understanding of communication, action, and their embedding in a social context, and thus we are promoting a vital element in the move to make the design of technology more relevant to the way we live and work. Researchers in the Human Centred tradition are concerned with a background philosophy and a necessary critique of existing traditions since they see much that is lacking in existing design as a result of too narrow an understanding of human activity and planning.

A Human Centred approach is particularly relevant to the design of computer-enhanced systems for supporting decision-making processes. The failure to adopt such design approaches would be more likely to result in less effective design than, say, in the design of a more technically centred design project such as an Expert System for engineering of heat exchangers. Even there the caution urged by the Human Centred tradition regarding the accessibility of the knowledge needed to design such an Expert System would not be out of place.

The Human Centred design tradition has emerged in response to the challenge implied by claim of Artificial Intelligence to mechanise those activities which if done by people would be manifestations of human intelligence. Mechanisation is not new: Ned Ludd responded violently to earlier moves to economise on people by replacing them with machines. Whatever the benefits accruing to succeeding generations the Luddites were correct in seeing the threat of machines to their livelihood. What is new is the mechanisation of the mind. The debate about whether we can create artificial minds continues, and how it will be when we share our world with non-human intelligence.

What is particularly worrying at the present time is the reverse process: the human imitating the artificial—the reduction of human judgement to the reductive processes of computer systems. Whether a bank will grant a loan is increasingly reduced from human interchange to an automated points scoring system; less subject to whim but also less sensitive to the diversity of the human situation. The economic benefits to the bank of a computerised system and the uniformity of treatment meted out by the bank to its customers brought about by a fixed set of criteria need to be weighed against the questionable validity of such automated judgement.

Opponents of the Human Centred tradition sometimes denounce its advocates for being anti-technology: but this is to exaggerate what is intended as a caution about the uncritical use of technological artefacts which cannot deliver what they promise, and a failure to join in the discussion about appropriate methods of design. But we have to say that the too eager giving over of human judgement to mechanical decision-making should be resisted and design methods advocated which are more likely to provide appropriate cognitive support tools.

Once it is seen that the investigative side of design has a social science aspect, the behaviour of the designer is as much anthropologist as engineer and has to be appropriate to the social context and not simply as someone undertaking a merely technical project with defined functionality. As a person among others, positions must be negotiated and values acknowledged, although sometimes tacitly through the format of the ways in which users and other stakeholders share in the development. The designer is not a neutral gatherer of facts. Even if neutral to begin with the designer will move from neutrality to commitment as research gives rise to viewpoints that will enable changes in the information environment. Designers need to acknowledge albeit quietly their valuations and standpoints.

The demise of the 'industrial society' is linked to talk of post-modernism because the industrial society is founded it is claimed on rational principles an belief in a unity of knowledge, a single world we may all view.

The issues raised by the Human Centred movement are ones we must always probe because every society is a technological society and technology profoundly influences our ways of being and doing. Once enshrined, after its initial disturbance, our new technology is hard to remove and its effects on our action and consciousness pervasive. Design must be carried out in acknowledgement of this if it is to be socially responsible. The constraints on action imposed by technology will not trouble us if we restrict our consciousness to machines which only help us do a little better what we ordinarily do: but not all technology is like that, and if we must speak about 'using technology', we should also talk of technology using us. There is an especial urgency in our society to evaluate the increasing automation of mental activity because of our inclination to expect too much of abstract rationality in decision making and action.

Bibliography

Avison D. E. & Fitzgerald G. (1988), *Information Systems Development*, Blackwell

Barker, R. (1990) *CASE*METHOD™; Entity Relationship Modelling*, Wokingham, England: Addison-Wesley

Bell, S. and Wood-Harper, T. (1992) *Rapid Information Systems Development*; London: McGraw-Hill

Bijl, A. (1989)*Computer Discipline and Design Practice*. Edinburgh: Edinburgh University Press

Bjørn-Anderson, N. (1984) Management use of new office technology; in Otway, H. J. & Peltu, M. (Eds.) *The Managerial Challenge of New Office Technology*; London: Butterworths

Checkland, P. (1981) *Systems Thinking, Systems Practice* Chichester: Wiley

Checkland, P & Scholes J (1990) *Soft Systems Methodology in Action* Wiley

Cooley, M (1987) *Architect or Bee?: the human price of technology*; London: Hogarth Press

Crozier, M. and Pavé, F. (1984) Managing the Changing Organiastion; in Otway, H. J. & Peltu, M. (Eds.) *The Managerial Challenge of New Office Technology*; London: Butterworths

Gill, K. S. (1989) *Editorial*, AI & Society, 3:2; London: Springer-Verlag

Holy, L. and Stuchlik, M. (1983) *Actions, norms and representations* Cambridge: University Press

Hopgood, A. A. (1993) *Knowledge Based Systems for Engineers and Scientists*; CRC Press

Imbert, M., Bertelson, P. et al. (Eds.) (1987) *Cognitive Science in Europe*; Springer Verlag

Karlqvist, A, and Svedin, U. (1993) *The Machine as Metaphor and Tool*; Springer-Verlag

Johansson, R. S. (1993) the Brain's Software: The Natural Languages and Poetic Information Processing; in Haken, H. Karlqvist, A. and Svedin, U. (Eds.) *The Machine as Metaphor and Tool*; Springer-Verlag

Kennedy, N. (1989) *The Industrialisation Of Intelligence*. London: Unwin

Lyon, D. (1994) *Postmodernity*; Buckingham: Open University Press

Maddison, R. N. (Ed.) (1983) *Information System Methodologies* Wiley Heyden

Moore, S. F. (1975) Epilogue: uncertainties in situations. Indeterminacy in culture. In S. F. Moore, S. F. and Myerhoff, G. (eds.) *Symbols and politics in communal ideology* Ithaca: Cornell University Press

Myrdal, G. (1969) *Objectivity in Social Research*, New York: Pantheon

Oatley, K (1979) *Perceptions and Representations: the theoretical bases of brain research and psychology*; Methuen

Open University (1986) *PT610: Manufacture, Materials, Design - Unit 7*; Open University Press

Polanyi, M. (1957) *Personal Knowledge*; London: RKP

Polanyi, M. (1967) *The Tacit Dimension*; New York: Doubleday & Co.

Potter, N. (1980) *What is a designer: things. places. message Hyphen* Press

Qvortrup, L. (1991) *Hi-Tech Network Organisations as Self-Referential Systems - New Paradigms in Organisational Communication Theory*; Denmark: Odense University

Reason, P (1988) Introduction. In (Ed.) Reason, P (1988) *Human Enquiry in Action - Developments in New Paradigm Research*;Sage

Schon, D. (1984) *The Reflective Practitioner*, Temple Smith

Whitley, E. A. (1991) Two Approaches to Developing Expert Systems: A consideration of Formal and Semi-Formal Domains; in *AI & Society* Vol. 5: No. 2. London: Springer-Verlag

Notes

1 'Many writers and artists', declares Lyon (1994), also expressed misgivings about the march of the machine and its accompanying social organization...In the twentieth century the anti-rationalization cry would be taken up by critical theorists such as Theodor Adorno - 'the administered society' – or Herbert Marcuse – 'one-dimensional man' and by the French sociologist Jacques Ellul in his devastating critique of a world reduced to 'technique' alone.'

2 see Cooley (1987)

3 see Karlqvist and Svedin (1993)

4 Issues of autonomy and control in the context of universal rationality and of the machine have been raised under, *inter alia*, the notions of autonomy and that of control. Lyon (1994) remarks that

> 'For Max Weber and, later, for critical theorists the Enlightenment promise of freedom as a product of rationality was a hollow one. Supposedly autonomous individuals, liberated from the authorities of tradition to forge their own destiny, find themselves mocked by the machine-like systems they now inhabit. According to Charles Taylor, it is just here that we see the three 'malaises of modernity'. Individualism, though it does emancipate us from given social orders, proceeds to confine us to 'the solitude of our own hearts' (de Tocqueville) and removes the heroic dimension of life, the purpose worth dying for. Then instrumental reason, that reduces everything to a level of cost-benefit analysis, represents further loss of autonomy. And the two are combined in the fear that 'soft despotism' will take over political power, bureaucratically organised, and unhindered by disinterested individuals busy seeking their own.'

5 see, for example, Moore (1975)

6 see Holy and Stuchlik (1983)

7 ...we begin to regard design as something that reduces or eliminates uncertainty, and since human judgement, as distinct form calculation, is itself held to constitute an uncertainty, it follows some kind of Jesuitical logic that good design is about eliminating human judgement and intuition.

Cooley (1987)

8 London 1978

Section II
Information Society: Working and Learning Dimensions

Chapter 8

Technological Change, Social Innovation, and Employment

Peter van den Besselaar & Teresa Mom

Policy statements about the future of the European welfare state and about the emerging European information society emphasise that, apart from technological innovation, there is an urgent need to support social innovation. Social innovation is generally defined in terms of the adaptation of society to the needs of a globalising economy and to the development and diffusion of the so called 'information superhighway'. This notion of social innovation focuses on more market and less government regulation, for liberalisation of markets and for flexibilisation of the labour market. Perceived in this way, social innovation is not any more based on political values and decision making, but it is reduced to the mere adaptation of social institutions to the one and only possible development left for society: a market dominated information society.

This paper argues that this view of social innovation is seriously flawed. It is argues that the future is open, and that very different types of information societies are possible. Therefore, there is a need for various visions of the future, and for a conscious decisionmaking within the political arena about the developments we want to bring about, and about the developments we want to prevent from occurring. It emphasises that in the recent past no fundamental differences existed between the various developed countries on this issue. The concept of the 'post-industrial society' does not cover one type of society, but various types of societies, that did differ in important respects. More specifically, underlying the growing share of service employment, post-industrial societies do have very different employment structures. Also the role of unpaid work is different in the different post-industrial societies. These differences are strongly related to political (i.e., normative) choices that were made during the processes of building the various 'welfare states'. This indicates that, despite some general tendencies, political choices do matter. The same holds true, in our view, for the information society. Although the role of information, knowledge and communication, and the related technologies, will increase everywhere, there is no one best way of organising the information society. Therefore, we need alternative designs for the institutional make up of the information society, based on equality, inclusion of all, social security, and cultural diversity. The dominant political (and technocratic) paradigm of more technology, more market, more flexibility, and, consequently, less equality, has to be read as it is: only one possible view of the future.Introduction

---

The first decades after WW2 were characterised by an unprecedented high level of economic growth, and, in most European countries, by a very low level of unemployment. Based on enduring prosperity, the welfare state was created, and the role played by governments and public institutions increased, partly replacing the market as a co-ordinating mechanism for social and economic processes. According to dominant Keynesian views, government was expected to stabilise economic growth at a full employment level, using the instrument of counter-cyclical spending. After two oil-crises in the seventies, however, awareness grew that developed societies were facing a *structural* crisis. Traditional economic sectors and the technologies they were based on, had gradually lost their growth potential, leading to much lower growth rates and a sharply rising unemployment. As many governments experienced in the early eighties, traditional stimulation of demand did not work anymore. Schumpeter, who explicitly related long term growth of advanced economies with innovation and technological change, replaced Keynes as the main source of inspiration. In the same period, new

traditional stimulation of demand did not work anymore. Schumpeter, who explicitly related long term growth of advanced economies with innovation and technological change, replaced Keynes as the main source of inspiration. In the same period, new microelectronics based information and communication technologies started to diffuse, leading to a theoretical and political debate about the effects of technological change on economic structure, on globalization and on unemployment. Although no consensus emerged about the effects of technological development on unemployment, the view that became dominant was that technological innovation was necessary for the long term economic and social development. Large scale R&D programs were launched by national governments and by the European Union, all focusing on the same technologies: micro electronics and information technology, new materials, energy, and biotechnology. This reflects the view that modern technological and economic developments take place at a world scale: only countries that succeed in competing with advanced technologies on the world market will be able to retain a high level of income and growth. However, despite the efforts in the field of R&D, and despite two periods of high economic growth - the second half of the eighties and the mid nineties - unemployment remains at a high level, especially in the European Union. Awareness has grown that the mere availability of new technologies is insufficient. To gain economic effects, new technologies have to be used on a large scale. As a consequence, a country's position in the world economy does not only depend on the level of its technological knowledge, but also on its capabilities to use the technology in economy and society. Where in the eighties the building up of technological knowledge dominated, we now witness an increasing attention upon problems related to the implementation, diffusion and use of new technologies. This is reflected in the application oriented nature of many R&D programs, e.g., the *Fourth Framework* of the European Union. However, large scale diffusion of radical new technologies requires social change of institutions and of practices. It is therefore no surprise that recent policy statements, like Delors' *White Paper on Growth, Competition and Employment*, and the Bangemann committee's *Report on Europe and the global information society* (Bangemann, 1994), do emphasise the required social conditions for Europe to transform into an *information society* and to benefit from the possibilities new information and communication technologies create.

It is true that the enduring unemployment crisis asks for structural change, however, the question is in which direction. From the *White Paper*, and the *Bangemann Report*, one gets the impression that there is only one possible future: an information society based on the intensive use of modern information and telecommunication technology, on privatisation of many traditional public services, on liberalisation of many markets, and on flexibilisation of the labour market. If that is true, no room for politics is left. Politics is reduced to a matter of adaptating to the pressures of economic and technological development, achieved by changing regulation, the provision of infrastructures, stimulation of R&D, and by financial support for projects that show the possibilities of the new technology. In other words, a greater market orientation and an increase in technology are supposed to be the main carriers for employment creating economic growth[1].

This paper proposes an alternative view. We argue that technological innovation has to be accompanied by social innovation, but that this leaves room for social and political choice. There is no*one and only* road to the information society; there are various paths. Our future is not mere adaptation to technological development and globalization of the economy. In our view, the critical role of social research is to show the possibility of functionally equivalent social arrangements, with different structural properties, and different normative implications. In this way, social research enlarges the scope of options, rather than being a legitimisation of dominant politics.

Technological change and long waves in the economic development

The increasing awareness of the role of technological development for economic growth and for employment, resulted into a renewed interest in the ideas of Joseph Schumpeter about the so called *long waves* of economic development. (Mensch 1979; Mandel 1980; Freeman, Clark & Soete 1982; Kleinknecht 1987). It was the Russian economist Kondratiev[2], who discovered long waves in time series of prices and interest rates. Schumpeter emphasised that also real (non-monetary) economic developments exhibit such a long wave pattern, in which periods of fast economic growth are alternating with periods of stagnation. The 'Kondratiev wave' has been strongly disputed, as well its existence, its duration, as its explanation. However, Kleinknecht (1987) convincingly showed that the long wave pattern does exist, at least for the phase of late capitalism, since 1870. Various explanations for the long wave pattern have been (similar to the occurrence of war) changes in the growth of fixed capital and the speed of technological innovation. (Van Duijn 1983) According to Schumpeter, the long waves are produced by clusters of related innovations that appear irregularly and therefore revolutionise the economy, leading to structural economic change. The new technological system creates many new possibilities for entrepreneurs. The emerging markets for new products and services, together with the huge investments necessary to produce the new technologies and the supporting infrastructure, induce a period of high economic growth. Other entrepreneurs enter the new fast growing market to get a share of the high profits. Competition leads to many larger and smaller innovations, resulting in a permanent improvement of the quality of products and an increasing labour productivity. The economic effects are not limited to the sectors that produce the new technology, but also other sectors are affected. Some, because they are able to use new technologies for both product and process innovations, and others, because the demand for their products and services is increasing, due to technology based economic growth. The result is a high and stable growth rate for a longer period. After some time, however, the new technological system matures and new product innovations become scarce. At the same time, the growth of the markets starts to slow down because of saturation. This also affects growth in other economic sectors and a long period of stagnation begins, until a new technological paradigm becomes available and makes an economic impact.

The history of capitalist economies can be described in several subsequent long waves, each depending on specific technologies. The first Kondratiev wave (1782-1845) was based on the steam engine and textiles; the second (1845-1892) on railroads, iron, coal; the third (1892-1948) on electricity, chemical technology, the automobile and steel; and the fourth (1948-1985) on semiconductors, electronics, aerospace, automobile (Europe and Japan) and pharmaceutics. The fifth Kondratiev wave is expected to be based on microelectronics and related information and communication technologies (possibly with biotechnology, new materials and energy technology). Policy makers in almost all countries are nowadays focusing on the 'information highway', based on telecommunications technology, media, and electronic services.

The upper turning point of the long wave, which is the transition from the upswing into the downswing, is explained by the maturing of the technological system, resulting in a lack of new product innovations, saturation of many markets, and a dominant role for process innovations. The explanation of the lower turning point of the long wave is more difficult. Why should entrepreneurs start with developing and using new technologies, a risky adventure in the depth of the crisis? If new technologies already existed in the previous prosperity phase, why were they not used already then? And, if they have to be produced in the crisis, why would someone invest in risky R&D when the economic prospects are bad? At this point, the issue of social innovation becomes crucial. It is insufficient to have a new technological system available; the new technological system, the economic system, and the social system have to be adjusted to each other. This issue is actually the core of the *White Paper* and the *Bangemann*

Report. The new technological system, based on the new information and telecommunication technology, is only a necessary, but not a sufficient condition for high economic growth. According to both reports we have to get rid of all kinds of existing social and institutional arrangements that are perceived as barriers to the diffusion of the new techno-economic paradigm: regulations with respect to the telecommunication market, the dominant role of governments in the provision of many services, labour regulations that hinder commercial service provision, existing patterns of consumption of educational, health and recreational services, and so on. In the words of the *Bangemann Report*: we need a market-driven revolution, and a break with the past. The older literature on technological innovation and employment did focus on the interaction between technology and the economic subsystem only (e.g., Freeman, Clark Soete 1982), but more recently, authors like Perez (1983; 1985) and Boyer (1988) emphasise that stable long term upswings do not only depend on a techno-economic paradigm, but also on the mutual adaptation of technology, the organisation of production, consumption patterns, and especially the way society is regulated: labour regulation, social security, the monetary and credit system, the regulatory environment affecting competition and the operation of markets, and so on. The mode of regulation is institutionalised in a specific combination of the various co-ordination mechanisms of social action: the market, the state (hierarchies), and social networks (e.g., the family; local communities).

The fit between the various subsystems does not emerge spontaneously, but requires conscious interventions, as we can learn from studies in the history of technological development, e.g., Thomas Hughes' study of the electrification of the US. Hughes (1987) describes Edison not only as an inventor, who produced the necessary technological innovations needed or the construction of the electric power system. Edison was a 'heterogeneous' manager, who also created the organisational forms, the political conditions, and the economic linkages, that ultimately resulted in an enormous social and techno-economic change: the electrification of the world.

We will not continue a theoretical discussion of the co-evolution of the techno-economic and the social system. For the purpose of this article, it is enough to formulate as a the conclusion that the creation of socio-technical systems, and their mode of regulation requires conscious (political) intervention. Here, we are interested in the question whether alternative views on the post-industrial society can be formulated: Is it possible to formulate *social alternatives* for the dominant *technocratic paradigm* of the position of work in the information society? And if so, does this require *different* political interventions?

In the next section, we will discuss briefly the relation between long term technological change and unemployment. After showing that since the late nineteenth century, technological change has resulted in a net decline of employment levels, we turn to a discussion of the largest sector of the post-industrial information economy: the service sector. We will show that the size and composition of the service sector in the various countries differ very much, and this depends heavily on social and institutional factors. The same holds for the size of the 'unpaid economy', which is discussed in a later section. The inclusion of the unpaid economy in the discussion about technology, economic development, and employment, however, creates a much broader perspective on possible future developments.

Technological change and long waves in unemployment

If one accepts the idea that the economy is developing in long waves, the unemployment problem can be conceptualised within the same theoretical framework. Freeman et. al. (1982) suggest the following 'Schumpetarian' dynamics of unemployment: "In the major boom periods new industries and technological systems tend to generate a great deal of new employment, as the form that expansion takes is the installation of completely new capacity and the building up of associated capital goods industries. Since the technology is still in a relatively fluid state and standardised special plant and machinery is not yet available, the new factories and plants are often fairly labour-intensive." (ibid. 1982, p.75). "Over time, however, these new 'technological systems' mature and their investment and employment consequences tend to change. The combination of standardisation, growing capital intensity and scale economies means that the employment generated per unit of investment tends to diminish. . ." (ibid. 1982, p.189-190). Together with market saturation for the products that did induce the upswing, this will result in a low growth of output and a major improvement of productivity, implying a decreasing employment. In terms of the relation between output growth and productivity growth: in the first phase the growth of output will exceed the growth of productivity, where in the second phase it is just the other way round. This phenomenon is reflected in innovation patterns: there exists evidence that during the long wave upswing, a shift from product innovations towards process innovations occurs (Blackburn et. al., 1985). Of course, a large increase of productivity may result in a strong fall of prices, leading eventually to an increase in demand, and, as a consequence, to a stabilisation of employment. Market saturation, however, can prevent this from occurring. Moreover, in the later phases the number of radical product innovations decreases, and as a consequence no new markets will emerge. Summarising, in the upswing periods, unemployment is decreasing to a low level, where the opposite trend will be dominating the long downswing periods.

A weak point in the argument is the lack of systematic empirical evidence. Of course, examples of fast growing 'high-tech' firms and setors, as well in terms of output as of employment, are provided. However, nobody will deny that new technologies create new economic possibilities, and as a consequence, new employment. For the problem of unemployment, however, developments in individual firms and setors are not very relevant; what counts is the net effect of the creation of new jobs and rationalisation, compared to the changes in total labour force. This brings us to another point of criticism. The "fairly labour-intensive ways of producing goods in the beginning of the upswing" is supposed to result into an increasing employment during the upswing of the long wave. The quantitative impact of this remains doubtful, because the new technology is labour intensive compared with the possible labour productivity of the current technology at a later stage, and not necessarily (and even improbably) comparable to the technology of the former long wave. This, now, is exactly the case.

If one wants to compare employment between periods and between countries, available figures have been corrected in order to take account of changes in the length of the working week, for cross national variation in the share of part-time work, and for variation in demographic changes. This has been done not by studying the number of workers or jobs, but by looking at the *average number of hours annually worked per capita* (Van den Besselaar 1993). Using this indicator, we find an almost permanent declining amount of work done per capita in all developed countries. This decline is stronger in the downswing phases than in the upswing phases, and the main difference between the countries is the *level* at which this process does take place (Van den Besselaar 1988, 1991, 1996). We think that this downward tendency is the result of technological change leading to a growing output, especially in agriculture and the manufacturing industry, with a decreasing labour input.

Will this tendency continue in the future? Developments in 'knowledge technology' and in computer-communication technologies may result in strong increases of labour productivity, and subsequently in job losses in office work as well as in professional work. On the other hand, the decrease of the amount of work available may be confronted with limits. Firstly, the higher labour productivity is, the smaller are the possible additional labour savings. Secondly, parts of the service economy may be less vulnerable for rationalisation, because they are labour intensive by nature. One can think of personal services (recreational services; household services, etc.), educational services and the so-called 'caring services' (health care, care for the elderly people etc.)[3]. The final services are already now the main sector in terms of employment, and in the future this will probably be even more pronounced. Therefore, we will look a little more detailed at employment patterns in the final services.

Employment in the Services Sector

According to the so called 'stage theories' of economic development (Clark 1940; Fischer 1939; Fourastie 1950), technical change will result in a changing sectoral composition of the workforce, namely an increase of employment in the service sector and a decrease of employment in manufacturing industry and in agriculture. Also, these days, economists and politicians expect the service sector to be the main source of new employment. Contrary to the common sense ideas about the 'transition to the service society', size, structure and trends in service employment have been shown to differ considerably between countries(Van den Besselaar, 1993). The findings can be summarised as follows.

The service sector consists of three broad classes based on the economic nature of the services: the intermediate producer services, the final commercial services, and the final public services. Using various statistical sources, employment in the three classes can be estimated for various years. Labour input in the intermediate producer services increases everywhere. Because they are strongly related to the manufacturing industry, we focus here on the changes in industry and producer services together. Table 1 exhibits the figures for seven countries. We see a decrease of labour input in manufacturing industry plus producer services in all countries except Japan, however, at different rates and different levels. Another striking observation is that the differences between the countries are becoming larger: the coefficient of variance (the ratio of standard deviation and the mean, a standardised measure for the spread of the observations) does increase.

Similar differences can be found in the service sector. Three out of seven countries show an increasing labour input per capita, but four other countries show an opposite development. Here, also, we see increasing differences and the coefficient of variance almost doubles. Finally, in all seven countries, labour input in manufacturing industry shows a more negative pattern than in the service sector. As a consequence, the share of the final services in total employment is clearly rising everywhere, and the variance decreases. In this relative sense, we see a post-industrial society emerging. But, as noted above, the developments in the individual countries are diverging and very different.

	Industry+Producer Services			Final Services			Share Final Services	
Country	1960	1984	Annual Growth	1960	1984	Annual Growth	1960	1984
France	599	414	-1.5%	450	426	-0.25%	34	46
FRG	85	533	-1.8%	436	419	-0.17%	35	44
Japan	707	744	+0.21%	487	637	+1.13%	28	42
Holland	695	339	-2.95%	475	395	-0.75%	41	54
Sweden	654	504	-1.0%	419	579	+1.36%	39	54
UK	834	483	-2.3%	493	459	-0.3%	38	50
US	543	516	-0.2%	604	655	+0.34%	53	56
Average	694	505	-1.3%	481	510	0.24%	38	49
Coeff of Variance	0,16	0,25		0,13	0,22		0,19	0,10

In hours worked per capita (in the working age) per year. Source: Van den Besselaar (1993); Maddison (1982, p280, 1987 p686); Elfring (1988, p59); Petterson (1989, p126); OECD, National Accounts, 1989.

Share of final services in total employment. Source: Calculated from Van den Besselaar, 1993, table 2 and table 6.

Table 1: Labour input in the services*

In a next step, we break down the service sector into the final *public* services and the *commercial* services, and again we find a large variation (table 2). In Sweden, the public services are the largest, where in the US and Japan employment in the commercial services is more important. In the Netherlands, France and Germany, both the public as the commercial final services are at a low level. Finally, the UK shows the effects of the Thatcher period: the share of the commercial services is growing, and the share of the public services is declining.

Figures 1 and 2 depict the development of theservice sector over a somewhat longer period. Three groups of countries emerge. First, we see countries (US and Japan) with high and increasing employment in the commercial services. Second we see a country (Sweden) with high and increasing employment in the final public services between 1960 and 1987. These three countries also show an increasing labour input per capita during the eighties. The third group of countries (Germany, France, Netherlands, UK) shows a relatively low employment in both parts of the service sector. Even more importantly, the labour input in the service sector is decreasing. These results suggest that the high developed service society has many different forms. In some countries, service sector employment compensates for a decreasing employment in other sectors. In other countries this is clearly not so.

Final Commercial Services			Final Public Services		
1975	1987	annual growth	1975	1987	annual growth
210	194	-0.7%	210	225	+0.6%
235	217	-0.7%	232	233	0
419	475	+1.1%	175	200	+1.1%
236	196	-1.5%	185	171	-0.7%
221	212	-0.4%	342	416	+1.7%
259	274	+0.5%	269	255	-0.4%
349	393	+1%	280	278	0
276	280	+0.1%	242	254	+0.4%
0,26	0,37		0,23	0,29	

* In hours worked per capita (in the working age) per year. Source: Van den Besselaar (1993); Maddison (1982, p280, 1987 p686);

Table 2: Labour input in the final services*

Can we find the factors that explain the differences between countries? And, in the light of the *Bangemann report* and the *White Paper*, do differences in the organisation of welfare state institutions and in the nature of the labour market play a role here?

The different patterns in service employment are usually explained in terms of substitution-processes (Skolka 1976; Gershuny, Miles 1983). Elsewhere we argued that this is not adequate. We show that the variance in service employment is related to differences in the social and institutional structures of countries, which can be seen in terms of the level of inequality and the share of public sector spending[4]. Using these two structural variables, three groups of countries could be discerned:

1. The 'market dominated' economies, characterised by relatively low taxes and social security contributions and by relatively high levels of inequality.
2. The 'social democratic' welfare states, with a large state sector and relative high level of equality.
3. The third group of countries do not have a very pronounced structure in terms of the two mentioned variables, and are characterised by moderate or low levels of inequality and moderate levels of taxation.

The countries within each of these three categories also resemble each other in terms of service employment. The 'market dominated' countries have a high level of employment in the commercial services and a relatively low level of employment in the public services. The group of 'social democratic welfare states' show the opposite pattern: a high level of public services and a low employment in the commercial services. The countries in the third group are characterised by a low level of employment in the public services, as well as in the commercial services part of it. Using multiple regression, about 76% (in 1975) and 82% (in 1987) of the variance in employment in the commercial services can be explained by the independent structural variables, and about 46% (in 1975) and 62% (in 1987) of the variance of employment in the public services.

What can we learn from the analysis above? First, technological development results in a decreasing amount of work available per capita. Second, this process takes place at different levels in various countries. Third, the type of institutional make-up of a society can possibly counteract this tendency of decreasing employment. Fourth, we are faced with the dilemma that 'equal' societies can only create employment in the public sector (e.g., Sweden in the eighties) or will face a permanent decline of the amount of work available. Currently, the increase of the public sector is a politically closed door. In such a situation, 'equal' societies seem to be unable to bring together the still unmet needs of citizens and the many unused or underused resources, especially (unemployed) labour. Solving this dilemma is one of the main goals of the *White Paper* and the *Bangemann Report*:. Lowering the price of low and unskilled labour (that is, increasing inequality) and reducing the size of the public sector are expected to result in a strong increase of low paid jobs, especially in the commercial services.

Production in social networks

The production of commercial services is co-ordinated through the market. The production of public services is co-ordinated through the state, through bureaucracies. In this section we will discuss a third way of providing services, namely the production of services within social networks: the unpaid economy. We will compare various developed countries in terms of the size of their respective unpaid sectors. Additionally, we will compare the size of unpaid sector with the size of the public and commercial service sectors. The question here is whether and to which extent differences in service provision through the formal economy is compensated by the unpaid economy.

Unpaid work is a part of the informal economy, that also consists of the 'black' (or 'grey') sector. The black sector consists of a very broad set of activities, ranging from small jobs for which people get a wage but without paying taxes, to earning money with illegal activities. As far as statistics are available, the size of the black economy is much smaller than the size of the unpaid sector. Estimates of the size of the black economy range from a few to 10 percent, with some extreme values up to a quarter of GNP and employment (Van Eck & Kazemir 1990, pp. 123-5). We will not go deeper into the size and the dynamics of the black sector, but focus on the sector of unpaid work.

Unpaid work can be defined as those activities people undertake without payment, which might also be done as paid work in the private or the public sector. Unpaid work consists of home work, voluntary work, and 'do it yourself' activities. Although unpaid work is not included in the National Accounts, it does produce 'value'. The contribution of the unpaid sector can be estimated by counting time spent in this type of activities, and by estimating the wages that should have been paid if these activities had been undertaken within the formal economy. Estimations of the value of unpaid work in several countries go up to more than 50% of the official GNP (Frerk 1990; Bruyn Hunt et al. 1982).

The largest part of the unpaid sector consists of activities in and around the household: Cooking and dish washing, housework, odd jobs and do it yourself jobs, gardening, shopping, child care, household related travel, medical care, knitting and sewing. For example, cooking one's own food is unpaid work, because alternatives do exist in the formal economy: e.g., going to a restaurant or to a domestic caterer. Another example is cleaning one's own house, that also could be done by hiring a house cleaner. Also parents who are helping their children with the homework are performing unpaid work, because the alternative in the formal economy is a homework-class after school with paid teachers. A second category of unpaid work is voluntary work, unpaid activities in churches, trade unions, political parties, social organisations, etc. These activities can be undertaken (and are partly done) as paid jobs. Therefore, we include it in unpaid work. On the other hand, time spent on activities like walking, watching TV, or going to a party, is not unpaid work, because people do it for leisure. It makes no sense to hire somebody to do those things for you.

Although this classification seems straightforward, some remarks need to be made. First, it should be remembered that applying the above classification is sometimes ambiguous. Although the definition of unpaid work makes sense, in practice it is not always that clear to which category an activity belongs. For example cooking may be classified as 'unpaid work' but also as a 'hobby'. Second, some categories might be partly 'unpaid work' and partly not. For example, if someone visits a friend to help him or her with something, we may want to classify this partly as 'unpaid work' and partly as 'visiting friends', which is a form of 'leisure'. Third, people may not see some of their activities as unpaid work because they like the activities. For example, some people might perceive 'child care' as unpaid work, where others might see it (at least partly) as something you do because it pleases you. The other way around, some people consider their work as a hobby. In our analysis, we classify activities in terms of a *possible* (and *sensible*) inclusion in the economy, without referring to the values involved.

To measure the size of the unpaid sector we use time budget studies. The European Foundation of the Improvement of Working Life has developed an 'international time budget archive' (ITBA), based on many national surveys. (Gershuny & Jones, 1986; O'Conghaile & Köhler, 1991) The current ITBA consists of data on 17 countries and between 1955 and 1985, however, without providing a complete coverage.

Time budget studies are not easily comparable, because in the various countries different methodologies are used with respect of the categories of time use, the research techniques, the number of respondents, the information gathered about the respondents, etc. One of the main advantages of the ITBA is that the national data are re-estimated and reordered in a way that makes cross national and longitudinal comparisons possible. This, of course incurs a price of using more aggregated information than available in the individual studies. Consequently, one has less information about the respondents[5] and less time-use categories than in the various national surveys. Whereas some national studies distinguish 200 categories of time use, the ITBA uses a 40-categories grouping, based upon the work of Szalai (1972). It is exhibited in table 3. By using our definition, unpaid work can be defined by the categories 6, 7, 8, 9, 10, 11, 12, 15, 23, and 38. A comparison with the detailed 200 categories system (Knulst, Van Beek 1991) shows that this is an adequate operationalisation for enabling us to distinguish unpaid work from paid work. Our analysis is based on a 21-categories classification of the ITBA data, and therefore we need to compare it with the 40-categories classification (table 3). Obviously, our data are usable. Only 'civic duties' (category 23) is included in the more heterogeneous category XIV 'passive recreation', and 'knitting & sewing' (category 38) in the larger category XXI 'hobbies'. We estimated the proportion of civic duties in category XIV and of knitting & sewing in category XXI on the basis of the detailed Dutch data.[6]

type	40 categories	21 categories
paid	1. at work	I. paid work
paid	2. at home	I
paid	3. second job	I
	4. school	I
paid	5. work related travel	I
housework	6. cooking, dishwashing	II. cooking
housework	7. housework	III. housework
diys	8. odd jobs	IV. odd jobs
diys	9. gardening	IV
housework	10. shopping	V. domestic travel
housework	11. child care	VI. child care
housework	12. domestic travel	VII. domestic travel
	13. dressing, toilet	VIII. personal care
	14. sleep, naps	VIII
	15. personal services	IX. medical care
	16. meals, snacks	X. eating
	17. leisure travel	XI. other travel
	18. excursions	XI
	19. active sports	XII. sports
	20. walks	XIII. walks
	21. passive sport	XIV. passive recreation
	22. at church	XIV
voluntary	23. civic duties	XIV
	24. cinema, theatre	XIV
	25. dance, party	XIV
	26. social club	XV. pub, club
	27. pub	XV
	28. restaurant	XVI. eat out
	29. visit to friends	XVII. visits
	30. entertaining friends	XVII
	39. listening to radio	XVIII. tv, radio
	31. watching tv	XVIII
	32. listening to tapes	XVIII
	33. study	XIX. reading
	34. reading books	XIX
	35. read. papers/mag.	XIX
	36. relaxing	XX. chat
	37. conversation	XX
diys	38. knitting, sewing	XXI. hobbies
	40. other past-time	XXI

diys: do it your self activities
unpaid work: housework + voluntary + diys

Table 3: Categories of time use

About year:	1965	1975	1980	1987
Denmark	na	160	160	154
Germany	260	na	na	na
Finland	na	na	201	188
France	275	248	na	na
Italy	na	na	242	nb
Netherlands	na	245	245	250
Norway	na	244	223	na
UK	280	203	217	231
US	270	241	235	232
Average**	271	224	217	212
Coeff. of Variance.***	0,03	0,14	0,13	0,16

*	Average per person between 20 and 60 year, in minutes per day.
**	Without Denmark: resp. 271; 236; 228; 223.
***	Without Denmark: resp. 0.3; 0.7; 0.7; 0.10.
na	Not available
source:	International Time Budget Archive; Knulst, van Beek 1985. Some figures are estimated by interpolation.

Table 4:: Onbetaalde arbeid* in 9 landen, 1965-1987

Our data cover the following countries and years: Denmark (1975), Finland (1979 & 1987), France (1965 & 1974), Germany (1965), Italy (1980), the Netherlands (1975 & 1980), Norway (1971 & 1981), UK (1961, 1975 & 1987), and US (1965, 1975 & 1985)[7]. Additionally, the Dutch raw data file on time use in 1985 was used to estimate the Dutch figures for that year. Because we want to compare unpaid work with paid work in the service sector in 1975 and 1987, we occasionally estimate the time use figures for the two years by interpolation and extrapolation.

Table 4 give the results for several countries in 1965, 1975, 1980 and 1987. We also calculated the annual averages and the coefficients of variation. It becomes clear that the amount of unpaid work seems to decrease slightly. In 1965, people between 20 and 60 years of age spent on average 271 minutes per day for unpaid work. In 1975 this number had declined to 224 minutes per day and in 1987 even further to 212 minutes. On the other hand, the coefficient of variation increases considerably: from 0.7 in 1975 to 0.13 in 1986, implying that the cross national differences in the amount of unpaid work are have grown much larger. This matches the patterns of labour input to the service sector, analysed in the preceding section. There we see an increase of the coefficient of variation between 1975 and 1987 from 0.13 to 0.22 (table 1).

Are unpaid work and paid work related, and if so, how? Are the differences between countries in labour input per capita in the service sector (partly) compensated by differences in unpaid work? Figure 3 shows total paid and unpaid work in the nine countries, suggesting a relation between the two types of work: a high labour input per capita in the formal economy corresponds clearly with a low labour input in unpaid work, and vice versa. The curves in figure 3 that represent the amount of paid work, form more or less the mirror image of the curves that represent the amount of unpaid work. The curves representing the sum of paid work and unpaid work, are 'flatter' than the other curves, indicating that paid work and unpaid work are substitutes for each other. Statistics underscore this visual inspection of the graphs: the coefficient of variation is 0.07, 0.12, and 0.15 for paid work in 1974/76, 1979/81 and 1985/87 respectively, and 0.14, 0.13 and 0.16 for unpaid work in the same years. However, for total (paid plus unpaid) work, the coefficient of variation is 0.05, 0.03, and 0.04.

Pursuing the analysis a little bit further, it becomes clear that unpaid work is more specifically a substitute for the public services. Figure 4 exhibits the relation between labour input in the public services, and labour input in unpaid work. The graph suggests a strong (negative) relation between the two variables, which is corroborated by statistics: 71% of total variance in time used for unpaid work can be explained by differences in the labour input to public services. On the other hand, the relation between 'paid work in the commercial services' and 'unpaid work' is very weak. Only 7% of the total variance in unpaid work is explained by differences in the labour input in the final commercial services.

The analysis of employment in the services, and of time used for unpaid work, show that we have three types of 'post industrial societies'. The social democratic and the market oriented variants have been described above. There, we defined the third variant in a rather negative way: not so very pronounced in institutional and political terms, and characterised by a low level of labour input in the service sector. Although the data available are not very complete, we find that the countries with the low level of paid work in the service sector seem to have a larger sector of unpaid work in the household and in the community. Furthermore, the evidence suggests that unpaid work especially compensates the low level of public service provision. The distribution of work over the formal economy and the household-sector proves to be very different in the various developed countries. The mere existence of these diverging economic structures creates an alternative perspective on the unemployment problem. The consequences will be discussed briefly in the following section.

Social innovation and political choice in the transition towards the information society

As demonstrated in the preceeding sections, we can discern at least three different types of post-industrial service societies. But that is based on an analysis of the past. What can we learn from this about the future of the information society? Before answering this question, we need to address another issue: Can we discern a post-industrial 'information society', different from the post-industrial service society. Daniel Bell (1979) distinguished between agriculture, manufacturing industry, services, and the information sector, and he shows that since the mid-1950s in the US, employment in the service sector has been larger than in the other sectors. Consequentially, the US can be called an information society since then. Also other indicators show the increasing importance of information, knowledge and communication, in society and economy. To mention several:

- The telecommunication sector has become larger that the automobile sector.
- The share of information occupations in the total work force has increased considerably, and since the early eighties, the majority of the US-workforce is in information occupations. (Kling 1993) Other developed countries follow a little behind.
- The use of information and communication technologies that support these information, knowledge and communication intensive processes is steadily growing, and since 1990 in the US, capital spending related to these technologies exceeds the capital spending on equipment, plant, and physical transportation (Zuboff 1996).
- An increasing emphasis on the development of appropriate infrastructures for the operation of these technologies: the electronic superhighway.
- An increasing role of research, development, and design in the economy.

The main difference between the post-industrial service society and the information society probably is the transformation of information and knowledge into commodities. It is not anymore the delivery of the service, but its information and knowledge content that is central. In the information society, information and knowledge as such are becoming the commodity that can be traded, and it is the development of information and communication technologies that enable this process. This also explains, for example, why intellectual property rights are such a dominant policy issue in the transition to the information society. Electronic information services are perceived as the innovative commodities that can give an new impetus to economic growth.

On various places in the White Paper, it is explicitly stated that a shift of services from the public sector to the private sector has to result into an increasing supply of final commercial information services, and, hopefully, of many new jobs. Also a considerable part of the applications that are proposed in the Bangemann report are in the same spirit of privatization. In the fields of training, education, culture, health care, and safety, we will be faced with a change from public to private production and consumption of (electronic) services, based not any more on taxation but on 'pay per view'. The Bangemann report, and the White Paper on Growth, Competition and Employment therefore can be interpreted as one deliberate effort to restructure European societies in the direction of more market, more marketable technology, and less public sector. That privatization of public services will and its impct on the loss of many jobs, and that private final services can only be viable if wages are low, or if the production of those services is labour extensive, is not discussed at all. The building of the information infrastructure requires enormous investments from the telecommunication operators and electronic service providers, and the White Paper estimates 150 billion ECU in the period 1994- 2000. The only thing that really seems to count is the need for appropriate returns on this huge investment. This, of course, requires European citizens to consume many electronic services and to make extensively use of the infrastructure.

But why is this social progress? Why will the extension of the market place result in an improvement of the quality of living and working? Why is economic growth through the market better than public provision of new services? And why is selling your labour power better than doing voluntary work? Current market idiology is very short-sighted: also public institutions, and unpaid activities produce value. It is also disputable whether all the proposed electronic services can be considered as progress. Consider, for example, the issue of telewoking. Both discussed reports claim that teleworking is good for employment, but there is no argument to support this claim. Also the other claim, that teleworking will contribute to the reduction traffic problems, is very disputable. If we continue with reducing the weekly working hours, this traffic reducing effect of teleworking - if real at all - withers away: with shorter the working week, people will be inclined to go a large part of those hours to their offices/factory, to meet colleagues. And, from an ecological point of view it is probably better to reduce distances between places where people live and places where people work, and to improve the quality of public transport, than introducing telework on a large scale. Similar questions can be posed with respect to the distance learning, connecting the private house to the information superhighway, and so on. Under what conditions do these developments add to the quality of peoples lives? Also the more professional applications have to be evaluated carefully. Is the coupling of research institutions and universities the most important thing to do? Or should the system of higher eductation confronted with financial problems seek other solutions? Is the relatively low level of knowledge intensity of small and medium sized firms a question of access to knowledge sources, that can be solved by linking these SME's electronicaly with research institutions?

The issue here is that it is increasingly understood that the introduction of information technologies in organizations needs the involvement of the end users, who have to specify their information needs and their interests, which have to be reflected in the design and redesign of the information infrastructures within the organization. This insight has been acquired through many experiences of failed implementations of inforamtion technology in organzations. As far as electronic information services are concerned, it is even more pronounced. Telematics projects like videotext did fail almost everywhere, because they did not fit into peoples information needs. The only exeption, the French Minitel system, was primarily a substitution for the paper version of the telephone-directory, that was not delivered anymore: so people are forced to use Minitel. These critical remarks do not imply that we do not see any positive aspects of the information superhighway - on the contrary. But what is going on now is a technology push development, not at all based on consumer needs. Fundamental issue is that if the new technology offers additional options, it may increase quality of life. But if the new technology results in replacing the old modes of service provision, the change may be result into deterioration. In case of large infrastructural developments, like the information superhighway, this is a substantial risk. As infrastructural developments are often irreverible, this kind of developments ask for careful and participative decision making.

We now return to the question we started this section with: What does the analysis of the various forms of the service society teach us for the design of the information society? Above, we focussed on several new issues raised by the development of the information society. However, also important similarities between the post-industrial service society and the information society do exist. In the view of Daniel Bell, that was referred to above, there has never been a service society: the service sector never was the largest in terms of employment. This is, of course, due to Bell's inclusion of a large part of the service sector in the information sector. In other words, the information society is at the same time a service society, and operates according to the same logic, that underlies the development of the service society. This makes our analysis of the preceeding sections relevant for future developments. Also in the information society, an extensive growth of final commercial and labour intensive information services requires large income differences; also in the information society, expensive final information services will tendentially be replaced by cheaper information commodities; and so on. If we read the White Paper on Growth, Competition and Employment as a proposal to redesign the post-industrial service society, it is not difficult to see that the EU has chosen to adopt the market dominated model. The report wants to fight the persisting high levels of unemployment in the EU by making the labour market more flexible, to enable employers to hire (and fire) workers easier and cheaper. Especially the lower wages should become even lower, social security should become more sober, especially the unemployment benefits, and the protection of workers against dismissals should become less. On the other hand, the extension of the public sector is not considered at all, and the non-paid economy does not seem to exist within the EU's way of thinking. Because most unemployed are whithin the category of people with no or little formal education, the EU-commission wants the number of unskilled jobs to grow considerably, especially in the commercial services. This, as has been showed, requires lower wages for the unskilled, and a higher level of inequality. In other words, the choice has been made to adopt the US-model, in which the market and private investments have to do the job of creating new (full) employment.

Although the White Paper of Delors does also emphasize the traditional European values of equality and social security, it does not systematically relate this to the proposed direction of techno-economic change. In the contrary, the White Paper asks for the development of a new regulatory and legal framework for the European information society, but the basic techno-economic structure of the European information society already is taken for granted. As our analysis in the preceeding sections showed, it does not seem possible to combine a market-oriented development with an acceptable level of equality and a reasonable social policy. In discussing the unemployment problem, policy makers too easily look at the US, with its high level of employment, and, compared with Europe, low level of unemployment. However, this employment is of a very unequal nature, in terms of the quality of jobs, in terms of wages, and in terms of the distribution of paid and unpaid work. In the US, hourly wages are declining, as is leisure for those people who occupy a job. (Schorr 1992). The result is a decreasing quality of life.

Like the post-industrial service society, information societies will share several general characteristics. At the same time, however, these commonalities may be embedded in very different social structures in the various countries. As it was with service societies, information societies do not need to share a similar social or institutional structure. Thus, we have a design problem with respect to the the information society: Are we going to develop a market dominated system, a system with a large public sector, or a system with a large unpaid sector? To rephrase the question a little more subtley, which combination of state, market and social networks do we prefer, because of political and normative considerations? The diffusion and use of modern information and communication technology is not necessary coupled to the market as dominant mechanism of coordination in society. Social systems may depend on various coordination mechanisms, and the market is only one. The future of society can take various forms, as did the past. And, the alternatives do not differ in terms of sophistication, but in terms of underlying normative principles.

Here, the issue of social innovation as a basis for technological innovation is relevant again. For example, if we include unpaid work and its product in the analysis, because it is normatively valuated as important, social issues like the unemployment problem look different. The unemployment problem is then not any more a problem of the number of jobs. As a consequence, we do not strive for social changes like the White Paper does, i.e., flexibilization of the labour market and lowering the labour costs of the unskilled and low skilled workers, so that markets can emerge for services that have been disappeared because currently labour is too expensive in the EU to produce these services for a price consumers are willing to pay. However, one thinks of unpaid work as a valuable way of producing certain services, one asks for social innovations at the interface of the formal and the unpaid economy, so that the unpaid economy is not any more a marginal phenomenon. How do we coordinate the relations between the market, the public sector and the unpaid economy? How do we distribute the available amount of paid work and of unpaid work in a equal manner? What mechanisms for income distribution are needed? In other words, if one perceives the unemployment problem in a different way, there is a need for other social innovations. If one broadens the scope of possible social innovations, of possible future directions of the information society, this has also implication for technological development. The information highway ands the application technologies, like multimedia, are complex technological systems, that for their operations are heavily dependent on the social and institutional framework they will be implemented in. Therefore, public funding of R&D in advanced information technologies and telematics should, at least partly, reflect the non-market developments within the information society.

What can an alternative model of social and technological innovation for the information society look like? The main social characteristics could be the following:

1. First, against the current dominant market-ideology, we need to revalue the public sector. As is still clear in the Scandinavian countries, a large public sector is able to provide many important social services, while retaining a high level of equality. An extension of public services and public investment may create many new jobs in the European Community, especially in education, caring services, health care, culture and so on. Much useful work in social organisations is done as voluntary work, that partly can be transformed in public sector jobs. At the same time, because jobs in the public sector are relatively high skilled, this contributes to the improvement of the structure of the demand for labour too.
2. Second, after two decades of discussing issues like 'human centred systems', 'anthropocentric technology', and 'humanizing working life', it sounds a little curious that there is a need for more unskilled jobs. It is true that unemployment is concentrated in the segment of the low skilled and unskilled, but this is because they are crowded out by higher skilled workers, who cannot find a job on their own level of education. So, actually there is a lack of jobs for the high and semi-high educated, and progress would be to create those jobs.
3. Third, a radical reduction of weekly working hours is a major instrument against unemployment - as it always has been. Also other forms of reducing working hours can he very helpful here: e.g., sabatical leaves for learning, or for recovering from stressful work.
4. Fourth, a reduction of working hours also creates more possibilities for unpaid work within social networks: in the family, in social organisations and in the local community. An interesting innovation in this field are the 'local employment and trading systems' and similar initiatives that are emerging in many countries. Although this kind of organisations generally are associated with low developed societies, or with unemployed people seeking to improve their existence, we think that in the future they will become more and more relevant for developed countries as well, as an serious counterpart of the formal economy. (Offe & Heinze, 1990)

5. Finally, the inclusion of non-market, and especially of non- paid activities in National Accounts is an important step to counteract current dominant market-ideology.

The goal of this paper is to clarify some issues related to the social structure of theinformation society. A more detailed analysis of how information and communication technology may support the various models of the information society, lies outside the scope of this article. Nevertheless, social experiments with information and communication technology, currently taking place, show some possible directions. We see a lot of effort put into the creation of local information and communication networks. These are focussing much more on support of local community development, than on participation in the global cyberspace. Examples are digital cities, community networks, and so on. Additionally, we see various social organizations startingwith the use of information and communication technology, like developmental organizations. In many developing countries, and in situations of war, electronic mail is a much more accessible communication media than telephone or letters. Another example is the HIV-NET for distributing medical information about AIDS and AIDS-related issues. Also technologies for the unpaid economy could be developed, like support-systems for the already mentioned 'local exchange and trading systems', or expert and support systems that help people doing things they now can ony do with professional support that they probably cannot effort. (Polman, Van der Pouw Kraan, 1995)

If we accept that society is more than the market, public technology policy and R&D funding should reflect this. Techological innovation should reflect the importance of the public sector and of thee unpaid economy, and public technology policys should therefore not be dominated by 'the market'. A 'human centred' agenda for the information highway urgently needs to be developed, so that we do not end up in a similar situation as with physical transport: a good public transport system, that from an ecomlogical point of view is urgently needed, has not been developed (but even deliberately destroyed) because in the dominant view on the future there was only place for private (automobile) transport. From this perspective, policy recommendations like the Bangemann report are not value-free statements of 'high level specialists'. De facto, it is a political program full of normative presuppositions, that calls for alternatives.

References

Bangemann M, et. al., *Europe and the global information society ('Bangemann report)*. Cordis Focus, supplement 2, 15 July 1994.

Bell, The social framework of the information society. In: Forrester,*The microelectronics revolution.* 1979

Blackburn, P., R. Coombs, K. Green, T*echnology, economic growth and the labour process*. London: Macmillan, 1985.

Boyer, R., Technical change and the theory of 'regulation'. In: Dosi et.al, (eds.) Technical change and economic theory. London: Pinter, 1988.

Bruyn Hunt, M., W. Driehuis, Y.M. Koot, L. Mossel (1982) *Changes in the relation between paid and unpaid work* (Dutch). Amsterdam: SEO/UvA.

Clark, C., *The conditions of economic progress*. London, 1940.

Elfring, Tom, *Service sector employment in advanced economies; a comparative analysis of its implications for economic growth*. Aldershot: Gower, 1988.

European Commission, *White paper on economic growth, competition and employment*. Luxembourg, EU, 1994;

Fischer, A.G.B., Production: primary, secondary and tertiary. In: *The Economic Record*, **15** (1939) pp. 24-38.

Fourastié, J., *Le grand espoir de XXe siecle*. Paris, 1950.

Freeman, C., J. Clark, L. Soete, *Unemployment and technical innovation*. London: Frances Pinter, 1982.

Freeman, C., L. Soete, (1987) *Technical change and Full employment* London: Pinter.Freeman, Soete 1987;

Frerk, G. (1990) Economic effects of the use of new information technologies in private households. *Intern. Journ. of Information and Library Research* **2**. pp.11-21.

Gershuny, Jonathan, Ian Miles *The new service economy*. London: Pinter, 1983.

Gershuny, J., S. Jones, *Time use in seven countries 1961-1984*. Dublin: European Foundation, 1986.

Gershuny,J., J.P. Robinson, Historical changes in the household division of labour. In *Demography*, 25 (1988) 537-552.

Hughes, T.P., The evolution of large technological systems. In: Bijker, Hughes, Pinch (eds), *The social construction of technological systems*. Cambridge, Mass.: MIT Press, 1987.

Kleinknecht, A., *Innovation patterns in crisis and prosperity: Schumpeter's long cycle reconsidered*. London: MacMillan, 1987.

Knulst, W.P., & P. Van Beek, 1985 *Timebudget research 1985. Computerfile (P0926)*. Amsterdam Steinmetz Archive

Knulst, W.P., & P. van Beek, *Tijd komt met de jaren*. Den Haag: SDU, 1991.

Maddison, A., *Phases in capitalist development*. Oxford. 1982, 1987.

Mandel, E., Long waves in capitalist development. Cambridge: CUP, 1980.

Mensch, G., Stalemate in technology. Ballinger, 1979.

O'Conghaile, W., E. Köhler, *The changing use of time*. Dublin: European Foundation 1991

OECD, *National Accounts*. Paris: OECD, various years.

Perez, C., Structural change and the assimilation of new technologies in the economic and social system. In: *Futures 15 (1983), 357-375*.

Perez, C., Microelectronics, long waves and world structural change. In: *World Development* **13** (1985), pp 441-63.

Petterson, G. *Zeit-Puzzle; Modell Schweden: Arbeitszeit und Familienpolitiek*. Hamburg: VSA, (1990) .

Scharpf, Fritz, Strukturen der Post-Industrielle Gesellschaft; verschwindet die Massenarbeits-losigkeit in der Dienstleistungs- und Informations-ökonomie? IN: *Soziale Welt* **37** (1986) pp. 3-24.

Schorr, J., *The overworked American, the unexpected decline of leisure*. New York: Basic Books, 1992

Schumpeter, J.A., *Business cycles*. New York: McGraw Hill, 1939.

Skolka, V., Long term effects of unbalanced productivity growth. In: Solari, Du Pasquier (eds), *Private and enlarged consumption*. Amsterdam, 1976.

Szalai, A. (ed) *The use of time*. Den Haag: Mouton, 1972.

Van den Besselaar, Peter, Technological innovation: rationalization and compensating effects. In: *Tijdschrift voor Politieke Economie* **11** (1988) 1, pp. 8-30. (in Dutch)

Van den Besselaar, Peter, Assessing the impact of information technology on employment. In: Berleur, Drumm (eds), *Information Technology Assessment*. Amsterdam: North Holland, 1991.

Van den Besselaar, Peter, National differnces in service employment - trends, causes, consequences. In: C. Verhaar et. al. (eds.), *On the mysteries of unemployment*. Dordrecht: Kluwer Science Publishers, 1993.

Van den Besselaar., Peter, Technological change and Employment. In: *Proceedings Symposium Computers and the Quality of Life*, New York: ACM, 1996.

Van Duijn, J.J., The long wave in economic life. London: Allen & Unwin, 1983.

Van Eck, R., & B. Kazimir, *Income form hidden labour, an analysis of survey results*. (Dutch) Den Haag: CBS, 1990 .

Polman, M. & P. Van der Pouw Kraan, Van bolwrken naar netwerken, *datacommunicatie door maatschappelijke organisaties*. Amsterdam: Ravijn, 1995.

Zuboff, S., The emperor's new inforamtion economy. In: W. Orlikowsli, et al, (eds.), *Information technology and changes in organizational work*. London: Chapman & Hall, 1996.

Notes

[1] It is interesting to note that among politicians and economists, the majority thinks that the use of information technology will result in increasing employment. On the other hand, very few European citizens (about 5%) believe that computers and factory automation will create new jobs (Source: CEC, Eurobarometer 38.1, 1993).

[2] However, the Dutch marxist economists De Wolff and Van Gelderen probably discovered the long waves before Kondratiev (Kleinknecht 1987; Van Duijn 1983).

[3] If the services are less vulnerable for jobs destroying technological change, it might be a source for real employment growth. As technological change results in economic growth, a growing demand for services - and therefore a growth in employment in the service sector- may be the result. However, in the personal and social services, labour saving technological development does also take place. An example of this is 'self-diagnosis equipment', that may replace jobs of nurses.

[4] Of course, other explanations can be formulated. First, one could argue that various countries are in a different stage in the development towards a service society. The differences in labour input in the services could reflect these different stages. If that is true, one would expect a relation between er capita service employment and the per capita national income. This is not the case. Countries with the same income per capita show very different levels of labour input in the services. Other explanations refer to possible cross national differences in labour productivity in the services. Of course, similar services may be produced much less labour intensive in some countries than in others. We are not able to discuss this issue here more detailed, but we think that it is more plausible to relate the differences in labour input in the services with differences in the structure of the service sector.

5 Another effect is that the figures in this article are based on the population between 20 and 60 years only.

[6] the 'civic duties' and 'sewing/knitting' categories are estimated by taking 50% of the larger class they belong to in the 21-categories system. This is of course not without risks, especially in a cross national comparison. On the other hand, the proportion of these two categories in total unpaid work is relatively small, and therefore the effect of possible wrong estimations will be small too.

[7] We are grateful to Jonathan Gershuny for providing the data.

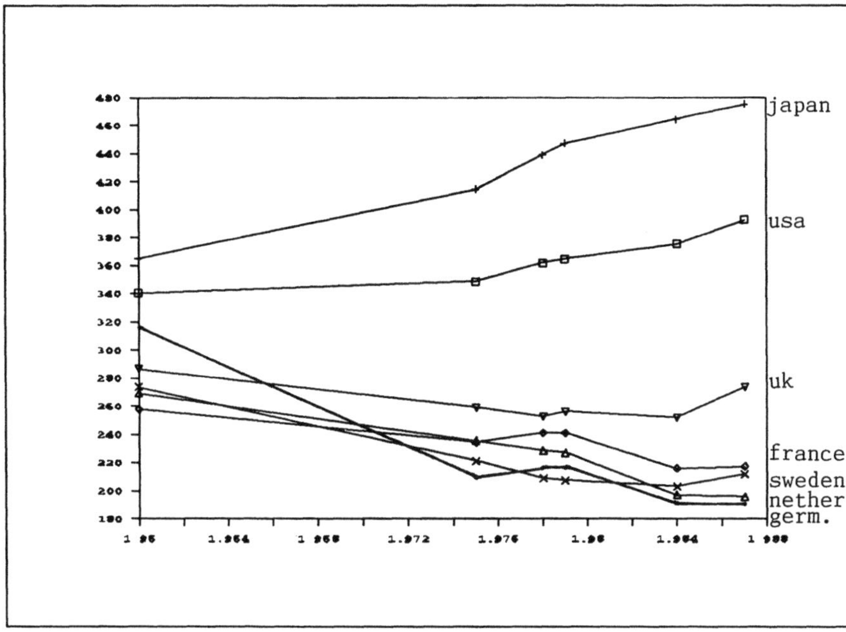

Figure 1: Labour input in the final commercial services
(hours per capita 16-65 yr)

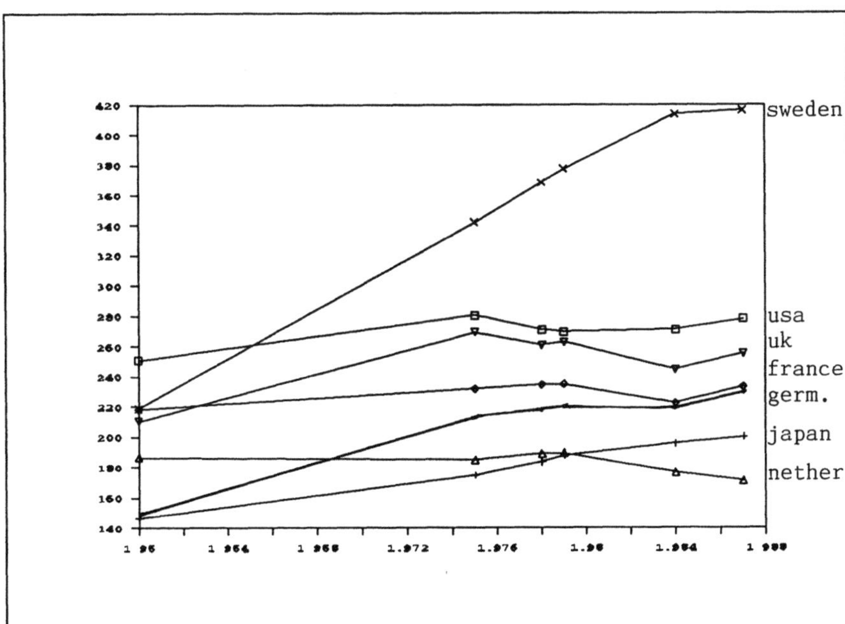

Figure 2: Labour input in the final public services
(hours per capita 16-65 yr)

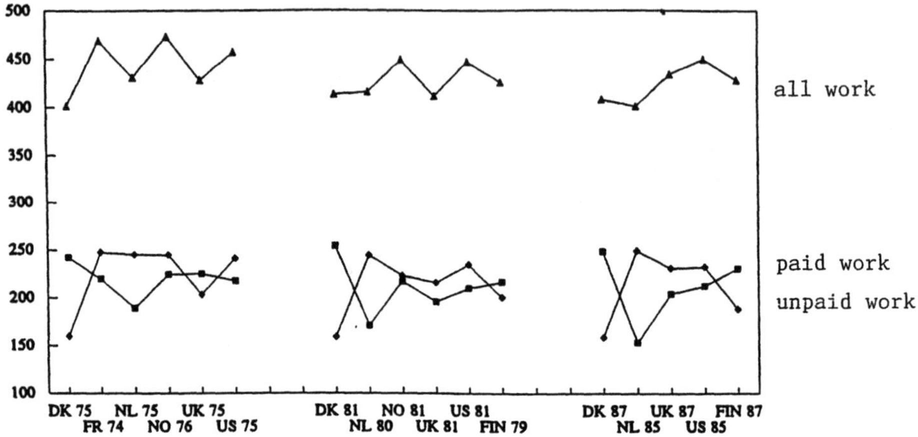

Figure 3: Paid and unpaid work in minutes per day

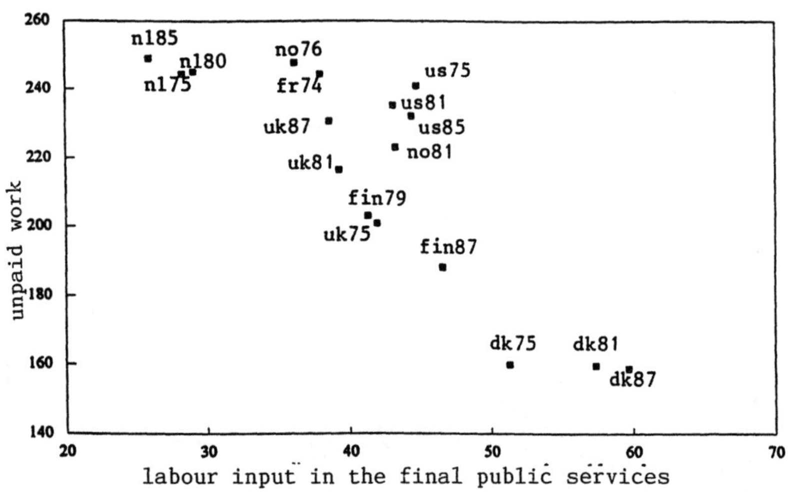

Figure 4: The relation between public services and unpaid work (minutes per day)

Chapter 9

Empowerment and Enslavement: Business process reengineering and the transformation of work

Matthew Jones

Business Process Reengineering (BPR) is currently attracting immense interest in the management field as a means of achieving dramatic improvements in organisational productivity. It is widely seen as providing the blueprint for the future development of organisations in developed capitalist economies. Many of its features may be seen as similar to other influential models of organisational change such as the network organisation or the horizontal organisation.

One of the main elements of BPR is the promotion of a fundamental transformation of organisational work which is presented as inexorable, novel and emancipatory. A critical analysis of the literature, however, indicates that each of these claims may be questioned. BPR may be seen as part of a broader discourse of social transformation with particular disciplinary effects. Despite the protestations of some of its main proponents, many of its features may be seen as being based on well-established approaches to work organisation. The emancipatory character of BPR may be seen to be based on an impoverished model of organisational power relationships. The implications of the influence of the BPR model of organisations for the nature of the 'Information Society' are discusssion.

Introduction

According to its proponents, Business Process Reengineering (BPR) is *the* major breakthrough in management thinking since Adam Smith's *Wealth of Nations*. Application of its principles, they suggest, will enable companies to achieve dramatic improvements in productivity. Reengineering, Hammer & Champy (1993) claim, "isn't about making marginal or incremental improvements, but about achieving quantum leaps in performance". The BPR literature is full of stories of companies that cut a seven-day turnround to four hours, reduced the number of people involved in a process by 75%, halved the time from design to production and reduced tooling and manufacturing costs by 25%. What is more, its proponents argue, there is no choice in the matter - "the alternative is for corporate America to close its doors and go out of business" (Hammer & Champy, 1993). Faced with such threats and promises, many companies have rushed to embrace reengineering, creating a market for BPR consultancy which is reported to be growing at 46% per annum (Fintech, 1992b). Evidence of the popularity of the concept is also provided by the flood of articles on the topic (nearly 1000 in the last 3 years at a recent count), particularly in the popular management literature. Despite all this interest in the topic, there has been surprisingly little critical analysis of its content and principles. In this paper we will focus on the model of organisation on which BPR is based and will compare this with other currently influential perspectives. Before doing so, however, it may be helpful to sketch out the key features of reengineering to set this model in context.

The Nature of BPR

The concept of BPR is generally identified as originating with a *Harvard Business Review* article by Michael Hammer (Hammer, 1990) entitled "Reengineering Work: Don't Automate, Obliterate". Another article in the *Sloan Management Review* of the same year (Davenport & Short, 1990) is also widely cited as another influential early contribution. While differing in some respects, Hammer and Davenport & Short advanced a broadly similar argument. Organisations, they argued, should seek to transform themselves from an orientation around functional specialisms, such as marketing, finance or purchasing, to one based around processes. This would require a fundamental reappraisal of the organisations' activities, but would be the only way to achieve dramatic performance improvements. Both articles also suggested that recent developments in Information Technology (IT) were essential factors 'enabling' such reorganisation.

The subsequent literature on BPR has generally retained these three features: process orientation, fundamental redesign and the enabling role of IT, although with some differences of emphasis and interpretation.

Process orientation

Hammer & Champy (1993) define a process as "the collection of activities that takes one or more kinds of input and creates an output that is of value to the customer". There is some disagreement, however, about the scope of processes to be redesigned. Venkatraman (1992) suggests that there four levels of processes, each of which is taken by different authors to be the appropriate focus for reengineering. At the lowest level are individual work tasks, such as answering a customer enquiry. Harrington (1991) argues that reengineering may be applied to such activities. Morris & Brandon (1993), adopt a slightly broader view, arguing that a process is "larger than a task . . . [but] smaller than an area of business such as operations, human resources or shipping". The majority of writers on BPR, however, follow Hammer (1990) in focusing on organisation-wide processes that operate across traditional functional boundaries, especially those "core processes [that] define a company's strategic competitive advantage" (Kaplan & Murdock, 1991). Finally, Short &Venkatraman (1992) suggest that processes to be reengineered may extend beyond a company's boundaries to include the whole of its supply chain.

Fundamental Redesign

Hammer & Champy (1993) describe reengineering as a "new beginning"; it means "disregarding all existing structures and procedures and inventing completely new ways of accomplishing work". They also claim that it is an entirely new concept which "has little or nothing in common with any of these other (process improvement) programs and differs in significant ways even from those with which it does share some common premises". In particular, they deny any link with quality programmes which they see as addressing only incremental improvement of established processes. Rather reengineering "seeks breakthroughs, not by enhancing existing processes, but by discarding them and replacing them with entirely new ones".

Other writers on BPR, however, are much keener to emphasise the links with Total Quality Management and other Japanese initiatives such as Just-in-Time. Thus Johannson *et al* (1993) argue that TQM, JIT and BPR are all members of the same family, and that the first two are necessary prerequisites of the last. Some writers such as Shillingford (1992) and Lopes (1993) even argue that "business reengineering is fundamentally akin to Just in Time production programs - only it promises to reach all the way from the factory floor to the front office". Perhaps a yet more extreme position is adopted by Klein (1993) who argues that the US Navy was engaged in reengineering at around the turn of the century and that "what Henry Ford did to automobile manufacturing around 1910 was also BPR".

The Role of IT

Klein's view of BPR as a new label for traditional work reorganisation programmes would seem to clash with many writers on the subject who emphasise the pivotal role of Information Technology in reengineering. Thus Hammer & Champy (1993) describe the contribution of IT as "difficult to overstate". Again, however, there are a range of views on what BPR means in this context.

Some writers such as Heygate & Brebach (1991), Aikins (1993) or Lopes (1993) appear to start with specific technologies, such as decision support systems, expert systems or workflow systems and see BPR in terms of the organisational changes these promote. Hammer's position is that technology is only an "enabler", albeit an "essential" one. Much of the discussion of IT in Hammer & Champy (1993), however, is also focused on specific technologies, such as shared databases or interactive videodisks, and describes how they "break the rules that limit how we conduct our work". The difference between IT as an "enabler" and "IT-induced" (Guha et al, 1993) or "IT-driven" (Davenport & Short, 1990) reengineering may therefore be rather smaller than might at first appear to be the case.

A more limited rôle for IT in reengineering is envisaged by other writers, for example Grover *et al* (1993) state that "BPR ... does not need to be associated with IT", rather it is "the common-sense practice of redesigning business processes before bringing in technology" (Fintech, 1992a). In principle, therefore, BPR "does not have to involve IT at all" (Fintech, 1992b), although, in practice, a number of these authors suggest, many redesigned processes will do so. In such circumstances, however, the rôle of IT may be seen as secondary - just one among a number of resources to be reengineered (Morris & Brandon, 1993).

BPR and Organisational Change

Hammer & Champy (1993) argue that reengineering means that "practically every aspect of the organisation is transformed, often beyond recognition", and identify a number of specific implications as shown in Table 1.

These changes may be compared with those identified as characterising other emerging organisational forms such as the 'Organization of the 90s' (Dichter, 1991), the 'Horizontal Organization' (Ostroff & Smith, 1992), and the 'Network Organization' (Coulson-Thomas, 1993).

As may be seen from Table 2, there is considerable similarity between these different concepts.

That BPR is aligned with these other popular models of organisation would not seem altogether surprising as the later papers, while drawing attention to their own distinctive contribution, are generally based on the earlier ones. What would seem more interesting, however, is to consider the assumptions underlying some of their common themes and the extent to which they represent a new and distinctive perspective on organisations.

Key Themes of the Reengineered Organisation

Team working

Stewart (1992) suggests that the "Organization of tomorrow" will be a "high-involvement workplace" based on self-managing teams. These, according to Ostroff & Smith (1992), will be made up of "people with complementary skills, . . . committed to a common purpose and to specific and measurable performance goals for which they hold themselves mutually accountable". Hammer & Champy (1993) claim that it is possible to have a team of one, although for Ostroff & Smith (1992) it "usually comprises between two and twenty people". Proponents of teamworking argue that it leads to improvements in employee motivation and job satisfaction and consequent rises in productivity, for which Stewart quotes a 'typical' figure of 40%.

As Stewart (1992) acknowledges, however, this is not a new idea. Proposals for teamworking go back at least as far as the socio-technical theories of the Tavistock Institute in the 1950s (Trist & Bamforth, 1951) and may be argued to correspond to forms of work which pre-date the industrial revolution. The managers of a number of the plants cited by Stewart as pioneers of teamworking also express frustration that their success has not lead to the widespread adoption of such forms of work organisation, even within their own companies. This is attributed to excessive caution on the part of senior executives who are only willing to consider such 'radical' experiments for relatively unimportant company sites, where "failure won't be fatal". Team working also makes the linking of pay to individual performance more difficult and therefore runs counter to another of the recommendations of Hammer & Champy (1993).

The adoption of teamwork does not mean that job design in the reengineered organisation is necessarily more 'human-centred'. Indeed, the intensification of work implicit in the productivity gains advertised as the outcome of successful BPR, and evident in many of the case histories of BPR in the literature, would seem to bear a greater resemblance to the'democratic Taylorism' of Japanese lean production, than to the Scandinavian model (Berggren, 1994). While a shift from functional to process-oriented work organisation may significantly improve efficiency, the elimination of 75% of the original staff numbers would seem likely to mean increased pressures on those who remain. Reengineering would thus seem to lead us towards the sort of 1/2 X 2 X 3 organisation described by Handy (1994), in which half as many people earn twice as much for three times the effort.

- work units change - from functional departments to process teams
- jobs change - from simple tasks to multi-dimensional work
- people's roles change - from controlled to empowered;
- job preparation changes - from training to education
- the focus of performance measures and compensation shifts - from activity to results
- advancement criteria change - from performance to ability
- values change - from protective to productive
- managers change - from supervisors to coaches
- organisational structures change - from hierarchical to flat
- executives change - from scorekeepers to leaders

Table 1: Organisational changes associated with reengineering (Hammer & Champy, 1993)

The Organisation of the 90s (Dichter, 1991)	*The Horizontal Organisation* (Ostroff & Smith, 1992)	*The Networked Organisation* (Coulson-Thomas, 1993)
• Customer (*vs* supervisor) focus	• Maximise supplier and customer contact	• Blurred boundary with customers, suppliers and partners
• Team (*vs* hierarchical) relationships	• Make teams, not individuals the principal building block	• Growth of teamwork
• Flat, flexible (*vs* vertical, static) structures	• Flatten hierarchy	• Flatter, leaner, tighter
• Vision and value-driven (*vs* control-oriented) leadership	• Combine managerial and non-managerial activities	• Facilitating networks, rather than bureaucracy
• Continuous performance improvement (*vs* meeting periodically-defined objectives)		• Processes for continuous change
• Empowerment (*vs* compliance)		•Greater accountability and responsibility
	• Organise around process not task	• Processes rather than procedures
	• Link performance objectives to customer satisfaction	• Remuneration related to value added
	• Treat multiple competencies as the rule, not the exception	• Need for flexibility and adaptability
	• Inform and train people on a "Just-in-time to perform" basis	• Continuous development and updating
	• Reward individual skill development and team performance	•Integration of individuals into teams
	• Assign ownership of processes	
		• Use of facilitating technology

Table 2: Characteristics of new organisational forms

Flexibility

A corollary of teamworking is generally seen to be employee flexibility. Teams may consist of individuals from many 'specialisms', but members are often expected to become multi-skilled so that they can substitute for one another and adjust quickly to changing requirements. This is seen to improve job satisfaction as work becomes more substantive and employees achieve a greater sense of completion, closure and accomplishment from their jobs. It may also have implications for reward systems and promotion criteria as employees come to be rewarded for the skills they acquire and for their contribution to team performance rather than on the basis of seniority. The promotion of a "learning organisation" in which employees are encouraged to continuously update their expertise is presented as the ultimate goal of such an approach.

There are tensions, however, between this multi-skilling and the need for functional expertise. Despite the argument of Ostroff & Smith (1992) that the value of specialised task expertise is "illusory" in most organisations and that it is more than compensated by increased understanding of the broader picture of importance to the customer, they do not deny the need to maintain functional excellence in areas critical to the organisation's overall goals. Similarly, Hammer & Champy (1993) suggest that not all process teams may be sufficiently permanent to justify multi-skilling. Instead, these virtual teams may bring together domain experts to work together on a specific project, such as a new product design, who will then disperse again when their task is completed. Individuals may be involved in several such projects simultaneously. Such forms of work organisation are familiar from management consultancy and the software industry, but it is argued, may be expected to be adopted more widely in reengineered organisations.

Empowerment

Teamworking, multi-skilling, the promotion of learning, are all presented in the BPR literature as manifestations of employee empowerment. Teams are given the authority to make the decisions needed to complete the processes for which they are responsible and are "inevitably self-directing" (Hammer & Champy, 1993). Process team workers are therefore "both permitted and required to think, use judgements and make decisions". This is seen by Ostroff & Smith (1992) as dissolving the distinction between managing and working. "Teams who do the real work", they argue, " must also do real management".

The scope of this autonomy is not unlimited, however, as Dichter (1991) argues - "by bounding behaviour with broader concepts such as business objectives and shared values the team or individual has greater opportunity to improve performance". The main concern of empowerment in the reengineered organisation may thus be seen to be productivity rather than emancipation. Moreover, as the quote from Hammer & Champy above illustrates, power is not seen in terms of the relationship between managers and their subordinates, (cf Clegg, 1989) but as something which managers may dispose at their discretion - permitting employees to think! The implicit assumption about the contribution of employees to organisational performance in more hierarchical structures would also seem naive. As Wynne & Otway (1982) discuss, the effective day-to-day operation of organisations depends not on obedience to instructions from the "top", but on the active, creative participation of all their members (as the paralysis induced by 'working to rule' illustrates).

These problems with empowerment may be attributed, Clement (1994) argues, to the conflation of two disparate concepts under the one term. Thus empowerment in the reengineering literature is usually seen in functional terms, i.e. "it is oriented to improving performance in the interests of organizational goals that are assumed to be shared, unproblematically by all participants". The alternative is described as "democratic" empowerment, which emphasises the "rights and abilities of people to participate as equals in decisions about affairs that affect them". As argued above, this empowerment is not something which is bestowed by those at the "top", but is achieved "through ongoing individual and collective action". Clement (1994) argues, however, that much of the "potency and appeal" of "functional" empowerment derives from its association with this more political tradition. Notwithstanding the predominantly "functional" approach to empowerment adopted by Hammer & Champy (1993), therefore, reengineering may be seen as benefiting from the evocation of this emancipatory image.

Customer Orientation

This is addressed by Hammer & Champy (1993) under the rubric of changing values. The traditional culture in many organisations, they argue, tends to promote an inward-looking, bureaucratic approach to work. Rather than seeking to please the customer, employees focus on securing their position within the organisational hierarchy. To overcome this, therefore, reward systems need to be altered to make an explicit link between customer satisfaction and individual pay. Appropriate performance measures will also be needed, Ostroff & Smith (1992) argue, to enable employees to monitor their achievements. Similarly, contact with customers and suppliers, who may often be internal to the organisation, should be maximised.

Such arguments may be seen as promoting an atomising model of organisations as markets which is potentially at odds with the team-orientation described above. Individuals are also presented as crude reward maximisers - according to Hammer & Champy (1993) "the ways in which people are paid, the measures by which their performance is evaluated . . . are the primary shapers of employees values & beliefs". This "cult(ure) of the customer" is argued by DuGay & Salaman (1992) as affecting not just the employee's work role, but their personal identity. Thus through envisaging the organisation as a network of customers and suppliers, individuals learn to see themselves as autonomous agents engaged in transactions with their fellow citizens rather than as members of some broader collective based on their economic position or social setting.

In this respect, BPR may be seen as part of a broader development in business thinking, exemplified by the *Excellence* literature based on the writings of Peters & Waterman (1982), which envisages organisational culture as a new domain of management action. Thus Hammer & Champy (1993) identify "values and beliefs" as a key aspect of the organisation to be reengineered, and state that this involves changing "what goes on in workers" heads". Such claims would seem to support the argument of Willmott (1993) that there are significant 'subjugating and totalitarian' implications to this project. No longer is it simply the labour power of the worker that management seeks to appropriate, but their 'souls' (DuGay & Salaman, 1992). Employees are required to adopt and internalise the values of the organisation such that its success becomes a measure of their own. The benign and liberating image of reengineering with its promise of a reconciliation of individual autonomy and corporate interests may thus be seen as altogether more questionable.

The Organisation of the Future

Despite the claims of Hammer & Champy (1993) that reengineering is an entirely novel and atheoretical concept, it has similarities with a much wider range of models of organisation than simply those propounded in the popular management literature. Themes of flexibility, empowerment and customer orientation, for example, are discussed in theories such as the Second Industrial Divide (Piore & Sabel, 1984), Flexible Accumulation (Boyer, 1988) and PostModernism (Harvey, 1989). We may therefore see reengineering not just as a product of current managerial fashion, but as a manifestation of broader social changes. This is not to say that all these theories are in agreement about the nature of, and reasons for, the emergence of new organisational forms, but that the phenomena that reengineering is seeking to explain and promote are not its sole invention, and need to be located within a broader societal picture.

Piore & Sabel (1984) are perhaps closest to reengineering in their analysis of organisational change, which they describe in terms of the model of Flexible Specialisation. This is seen as developing within networks of federated enterprises, often using information technology to integrate their operations and achieve high levels of customer responsiveness. Phillimore (1989) identifies the organisational implications of Flexible Specialisation as including a shift from fragmentation of work processes and skills to task flexibility, and the replacement of managerial hierarchies by networks. As with reengineering, these developments are largely explained in economic terms involving increasing competition and customer power.

Boyer (1988) and writers of the French regulation school, also offer an economic explanation of the organisational changes, attributing these to the emergence of a new 'regime of accumulation', that of 'Flexible Accumulation'. This is seen as replacing the Fordist system of mass-production and mass consumption which dominated the developed capitalist economies in the post-war period. Linked with these economic changes, however, they also identify a shift in the "mode of social and political regulation" leading to the reemergence of entrepreneurialism and neo-conservatism, as was evident in the UK and US in the 1980s. At the organisational level the changes are often described as 'Post-Fordism'. Wood (1989) identifies a significant shift away from traditional Taylorite division of labour and the merging of direct and indirect work as characteristics of these developments.

The immense diversity of theories brought together by Harvey (1989) under the banner of Post-Modernism includes those of Post-Fordism and Flexible Specialisation. What Harvey particularly draws attention to however, is the contribution of a number of theories which adopt the anti-foundationalism and indeterminacy of philosophical post-modernism, especially of French post-structuralists such as Baudrillard and Lyotard. The organisational implications of this are identified by Berg (1989) as including a shift towards 'loosely coupled' corporate structures, a move from 'grand strategies' to micro-decisions, and a growth in the importance of organisational symbolism for example in corporate identity programmes.

A number of writers such as Miller & Rose (1990), Willmott (1993), Kerfoot & Knights (1994) have sought to explain a variety of recent organisational restructuring initiatives as involving changes not just in the economy or in the dominant ideology or epistemology, but in the whole way we think about work. Entrepreneurialism, "Excellence" and Total Quality Management are seen not as isolated developments, but as manifestations of a common "discourse of enterprise". Although DuGay & Salaman (1992) link the emergence of this discourse with attempts to promote an "enterprise culture" in the UK in the 1980s, they also argue that it is essentially a global phenomenon.

The concept of discourse, derived from the work of Foucault, is described by Knights & Morgan (1991) as "a set of ideas and practices which condition our ways of relating to, and acting upon particular phenomena". They also emphasise that discourse is embedded in social practices which serve to reproduce the interpretations which validate it. Hence we need to see reengineering not just in terms of a "set of procedures for effecting radical change" as Hammer & Champy (1993) present it, but also as a set beliefs about the nature of organisation and a language through which the whole concept may be explained and justified. In addition, through the performance of these 'sets of procedures' individuals will help to reinforce the discourses of which reengineering is a part.

The correspondence between the view of organisational change presented by Hammer & Champy (1993) as characteristic of reengineered organisations and that of other theories of social change may therefore be seen as reflecting a common discourse. Hammer's achievement was therefore perhaps to provide a persuasive, popular articulation of these ideas rather than to invent a new management concept from scratch. That BPR "showed up just as disappointment was growing with Total Quality Management's ability to transform companies" (Klein, 1993) may consequently be more than fortuitous. That this also coincided with an economic recession which drove many companies to "downsize", might also seem to support the views of cynics who claim that it is "little more than euphemism for laying people off" (Byrne, 1993). Even if this was not the primary concern of most companies engaging in reengineering, though, the recession may be seen as having helped to promote an atmosphere of uncertainty, if not crisis, in established management beliefs and increased the receptiveness of companies towards new and radical solutions.

More significantly perhaps, Rose (1990) argues that the discourse of enterprise has an important role in shaping individual subjectivity. As was discussed above in relation to empowerment and customer focus, entrepreneurialism seeks a rapprochement between individual self-actualisation and the competitive advancement of the company. "For the entrepreneurial self", therefore, "work is no longer necessarily a constraint upon the freedom of the individual to fulfil his or her potential through striving for autonomy, creativity and responsibility. Work is an essential element in the path to self-realization" (Miller & Rose, 1990). Reengineering may therefore be seen as sustaining this new self-disciplinary regime.

In suggesting that managers and employees may have fallen sway to this seductive, but arguably repressive, discourse, it would be easy to appear patronising towards them. Yet the implication of the concept of discourse, is that we are engaged in it too. In discussing reengineering and its effects on organisations in terms of entrepreneurialism, we are contributing to the reproduction of the discourse ourselves. More than that, our own subjectivity is permeated by its effects. We too are drawn into seeing ourselves as enterprising individuals, striving for autonomy through self expression (perhaps through writing conference papers!). This is not to say that the discourse of enterprise is permanent or immutable (or that it has necessarily been correctly characterised in this paper), but that it is sustained not by dupes or dictators but by the social practices of us all.

BPR and the Information Society

Viewing BPR, then, not as a "conceptually new business model" (Hammer & Champy, 1993), but as another "managerial attempt to reconstruct work organization" (DuGay & Salaman, 1992), we may consider the vision of the Information Society it offers. Hammer and the great majority of writers on BPR, however, give little consideration to the social effects of reengineering, other than its effect on the ability of (USA) companies to compete in global markets and passing remarks on the potential to 'slash' staffing levels. For example there is no consideration of the social dualism implicit in the flexible firm model it promotes. Enough may be gleaned from its description of organisational changes, however, to suggest that it tends towards the more technically-oriented, optimistic and rationalistic perspective of Post-Industrialism identified by Jones (1991).

Although Bell (1973) eschews technological determinism in presenting his theory of the Post-Industrial society, his discussion of the 'social framework of the information society' (Bell, 1980) is strongly tied to consideration of the implications of developments in information technology. 'The major determinant of policy issues', he argues, 'is the question of what kind of infrastructure will be created out of the merging technologies of computers and communications' (Bell, 1980). This view of technology may be seen to have many similarities with the role of enabler identified by Hammer & Champy (1993).

Perhaps the most striking feature of Bell's Post-Industrialism from the present standpoint is its faith in the contribution of 'intellectual technology', particularly in national-level planning. While there are clearly ideological reasons for the present rejection of any role for the government in planning the economy, the crisis of Operational Research (Dando & Bennett, 1981; Rosenhead, 1989) would seem to be indicative of a more deep-rooted loss of confidence in organisational and social modelling. Postmodernism would also seem to represent a profound challenge to the whole rationalist project.

The position of reengineering on rationalism is ambivalent (Jones, 1994). On the one hand, Hammer (1990) argues that reengineering "cannot be planned meticulously". Rather it depends on "commitment, consistency - maybe even a touch of fanaticism" by leaders who must provide inspiration to their empowered workers. This has lead Klein to complain that "some writers assert that it is impossible to be prescriptive about BPR . . . they describe it as a creative act in almost mystical terms". On the other hand, there is an important strand of the BPR literature which stresses its association with the "power of (F.W.) Taylor's mechanising vision" (Davenport & Short, 1990). For these writers reengineering is the "new industrial engineering" (Davenport & Short, 1990) for which a "clear cut procedure" (Wilkinson, 1991) or a "comprehensive methodology" (Guha *et al*, 1993) can be provided. Hammer, for all his visionary rhetoric may also be argued to be esentially a rationalist, believing there is a 'right way' to restore "the competitive vigor of American business" (the choice of re*engineering* to describe the concept may not be entirely accidental either). This leads Wheatley (1994) to criticise BPR as "another attempt, usually by people at the top ... to take one set of rigid guidelines and impose them on the rest of the organisation . . . it's a mechanical view of organisations and people".

Another parallel between Post-Industrialism and Reengineering is the argument that we are in an era of revolutionary change, a turning point in history. The new forms of society or organisations which are now emerging, it is argued, will not be extensions of the present models, but based on radically different principles. Success in the new society or organisation will go to those who can master these principles. At the same time, however, the basic 'order' of society or organisations is not seen as being changed by these revolutions. There may be international agreements on "the space time framework of communications" (Bell, 1980), or the rise of successfully reengineered organisations and the demise of some of their competitors, but the basic global or organisational political order remains relatively stable.

Reengineering would thus appear to fit better with the technological rather than the humanistic vision of the Information Society. Viewing BPR as itself a form of organisational technology, the absence of a social dimension in the reengineering literature may be seen as further evidence of its orientation. BPR, however, is not just a theoretical concept, but a practical guide to management action, which, given its current popularity, may be expected to have a significant impact on the nature of the 'organisation of tomorrow' and hence of society as a whole. If the argument of this paper is correct, therefore, then reengineering and the other models of organisation with which we have sought to illustrate its connection may be seen as powerful factors contributing to the emergence of the technological paradigm.

Conclusion

From a reading of Hammer & Champy (1993), or indeed almost any other writer on reengineering, it would appear that in the future all organisations will be designed according to its principles. Those that ignore its precepts are doomed to extinction. What is more, this development should be welcomed, since it heralds a new age of organisational harmony in which empowered workers, inspired by visionary leaders, will break all previous performance records.

In this paper, however, we have sought to argue that reengineering may be seen as part of broader organisational and social developments. This leads us to suggest that its vision of the reengineered workplace is overly optimistic, largely neglecting any negative effects, and myopic, lacking any significant social dimension. A more critical approach to reengineering would therefore appear to be needed, seeing it not as an entirely new phenomenon, but as an element of currently-influential social discourses which are contributing to the emergence of a more "technological" society.

References

Aikins, J. (1993) Business process reengineering: where do knowledge-based systems fit? *IEEE Expert*, **8**,2.

Bell, D. (1973) *The Coming of Post-Industrial Society*. New York: Basic Books.

Bell, D. (1980) The social framework of the information society. In: Forester, T. (Ed) *the Microelectronics Revolution.*. Oxford: Blackwell, pp. 500-549.

Berg, P.O. (1989) Postmodern management? From facts to fiction in theory and practice. *Scandinavian Journal of Management*, **5**, 210-217.

Berggren, C. (1994) NUMMI vs. Uddevalla. *Sloan Management Review*, Winter, 37-49.

Boyer, R. (1988)*The Search for Labour Market Flexibility*. Oxford: Clarendon.

Byrne, J.A. (1993) Reengineering: beyond the buzzword. *Business Week*, May 24, 5-6.

Clegg, S. (1989) *Frameworks of Power.* London: Sage.

Clement, A. (1994) Computing at work: empowering action by 'low-level users'. *Communications of the ACM*, **37** (1), 53-63.

Coulson-Thomas, C.J. (1993) Corporate transformation and Business Process Reengineering. *Executive Development.*, **6**, 14-20.

Dando, M.R. & Bennett, P. G. (1981) A Kuhnian crisis in management science? *Journal of the Operational Research Society*, **32**, 91-103.

Davenport, T.E. & Short, J.E. (1990) The new industrial engineering: information technology and business process redesign. *Sloan Management Review*, Summer, 11-27.

Dichter, S.F. (1991) The organization of the 90s. *McKinsey Quarterly*, 145-155.

Du Gay, P. & Salaman, G. (1992) The cult(ure) of the customer. *Journal of Management Studies*, **29**, 615-633.

Fintech (1992a) Business Process Redesign: IT suppliers take lessons from users. *FinTech Electronic Office*, 9 September, p. 1.

Fintech (1992b) Spotlight: Business Process Redesign brings big benefits. *FinTech Electronic Office*, 2 December, p. 4.

Guha, S.; Kettinger, W.J. & Teng, J.T.C. (1993) Business process reengineering: building a comprehensive methodology. *Information Systems Management*, Summer, 13-22.

Grover, V.; Teng, J.T.C. & Fiedler, K.D. (1993) Information technology enabled business process redesign: an integrated planning framework. *Omega*, **21** (4), 433-447.

Hammer, M. (1990) Reengineering work: don't automate, obliterate. *Harvard Business Review*, July-August, 104-112.

Hammer, M. & Champy, J. (1993) *Reengineering the Corporation: a Manifesto for Business Revolution.* London: Nicholas Brealey.

Handy, C. (1994) *The Empty Raincoat: Making Sense of the Future.* London: Hutchinson

Harrington, H.J. (1991) *Business Process Improvement.* London: McGraw Hill.

Harvey, D. (1989) *The Condition of Post-Modernity*, Blackwell, Oxford.

Heygate, R. & Brebach, G. (1991) Corporate Reengineering. *McKinsey Quarterly*, 44-55.

Johannson, H.J.; McHugh, P.; Pendlebury, A.J. & Wheeler, W.A. (1993) *Business Process Reengineering: Breakpoint Strategies for Market Dominance.* Chichester: John Wiley.

Jones, M.R. (1991) Post-Industrial and Post-Fordist perspectives on information systems *European Journal of Information Systems*, **1**, 171-182.

Jones, M.R. (1994) *The Contradictions of Reengineering.* Paper presented at the "Management Challenges in IS" Conference, Cranfield University, 12-13 July.

Kaplan, R.B. & Murdock, L. (1991) Core process redesign. *McKinsey Quarterly*, 27-43.

Kerfoot, D. & Knights, D. (1994) Empowering the quality worker? The seduction and contradiction of the total quality phenomenon. In: Wilkinson, A. & Willmott, H. (Eds) *Quality and the Labour Process*, London: Routledge.

Klein, M. M. (1993) IEs fill facilitator role in benchmarking operations to improve performance
Industrial Engineering, September, 40-42.

Knights, D. & Morgan, G. (1991) Corporate strategy, organizations and subjectivity: a critique. *Organisation Studies*, **12**, 251-273.

Lopes, P.F. (1993) Fine-tuning reengineering with workflow automation: blueprint and tool. *Industrial Engineering*, August, 51-53.

Miller, P. & Rose, N. (1990) Governing economic life. *Economy & Society*, **19**, 1-31.

Morris, D. & Brandon, J. (1993) *Reengineering Your Business.* London: McGraw Hill.

Ostroff, F. & Smith, D. (1992) The horizontal organization. *McKinsey Quarterly*, 148-168.

Peters, T.J. & Waterman, R.H. (1982) *In Search of Excellence*. New York: Harper & Row

Piore, M.J. & Sabel, C.F. (1984) *The Second Industrial Divide: Possibilities for Prosperity*, New York: Basic Books.

Phillimore, A.J. (1989) Flexible specialisation, work organisation and skills: approaching the Second Industrial Divide, *New technology, Work and Employment*, **4**, 79-91.

Rose, N. (1990) *Governing the Soul*. London: Routledge

Rosenhead, J. (1989) Introduction: old and new paradigms of analysis. In: Rosenhead, J. (Ed) *Rational Analysis for a Problematic World*. Chichester: John Wiley, pp. 1-20.

Shillingford, J. (1992) Offices follow the factory's example. *Financial Times*, 19 March, p. 20.

Short, J.E. & Venkatraman, N. (1992) Beyond Business Process Redesign: redefining Baxter's business network. *Sloan Management Review*, Fall, 7-21.

Stewart, T.A. (1992) The search for the organization of tomorrow. *Fortune*, **125**, May 18, 92-98.

Trist, E.L. & Emery, K.W. (1951) Some social and psychological consequences of the longwall method of coal getting. *Human Relations*, **4**, 3-38.

Venkatraman, N. (1992) IT-induced business reconfiguration. In M. Scott-Morton (ed.), *The Corporation of the 1990s - IT and Organizational Transformation*. Oxford: Oxford University Press, pp. 122-158.

Warren, L. (1993) Streamlining from the outside in. *Informatics* , May, 23-28.

Wilkinson, R. (1991) Reengineering: Industrial Engineering in action. *Industrial Engineering*, August, 47-49.

Wheatley, M. (1994) De-engineering the corporation. *Industry Week*, April 18, 18-26.

Willmott, H. (1993) Strength is ignorance; slavery is freedom: managing culture in modern organisations. *Journal of Management Studies*, **30**, 515-552.

Wood, S. (1989) The transformation of work? In : Wood, S. (Ed)*The Transformation of Work?*. London: Unwin Hyman, pp. 1-43.

Wynne, B. & Otway, H.J. (1982) Information Technology, power and managers (1). In: Bjørn-Andersen, N.; Earl, M.; Holst, O. & Mumford, E. (Eds) *Information Society: For Richer, for Poorer*, Amsterdam: North Holland, pp 207-217.

Chapter 10

The Role of Creativity in Post-Industrial Society: Exploring the implications of non-conventional technologies for work and management organisation

Paul Levy

Competitive industrial markets demand state of the art use of new emerging technologies and manufacturing processes. To use new technologies effectively the dimension of human responsibility has to be explored and properly managed. Work has been carried out at CENTRIM in the area of the human implications associated with the management of conventional technologies. However, non-conventional technologies and their associated organisational problems pose new challenges for the technology managers of the future. In this paper the problems of acquiring new knowledge of the worker and integration of technology and work and management processes is discussed drawing on comparative case data from the UK and Slovenia. Issues of creativity and motivation are stressed as being key factors in realising maximum human potential. The paper presents a tool for analysing the 'non-conventional' organisational design required to support exploitation of non-conventional technologies. This tool - the *'creativity matrix'* examines the differing levels of creativity present in organisations and acts as a catalyst to organisational re-design. Environmental and organisational conditions of Factory 2000 are analysed in order to facilitate best practice exploitation of new non-conventional technologies, particularly the flexibility required to cope with increasing rates of market turbulence.

Introduction

The importance of organisation design in the effective management of technological change is increasingly recognised as key to competitive success. Elsewhere we have supported the view of writers such as Bessant (1991) that a paradigm shift taking place in manufacturing requires changes in organisation design at incremental and step-function levels to cope with changing market requirements and new technology developments. Characteristics of what is often termed the 'post Fordist' paradigm are a shift away from mass production models, a move to greater emphasis on market-pull rather than supply push and a massive increase in the importance of non-price factors. (Bessant et al, 1990, 1992) The key requirement of firms operating under these conditions is to become highly flexible and responsive - and this can be achieved through both technological innovation and through organisational development (Bessant, 1991).

Work in the past has been carried out by a number of writers (including ourselves) in the area of the human implications associated with the management of *conventional technologies*. Such work has focused on a wide range of issues in the areas of selection of appropriate technological processes, impacts on job design, skills implications and user-interface issues, as well as on the process of implementation itself. However, the emerging generation of *non-conventional technologies* and their associated organisational problems pose new challenges for the technology managers of the future.

Arguably the challenge for firms as they move into what is (in our view, inadequately) termed the 'post-industrial' paradigm, is to find more appropriate combinations of technology and organisation which can deliver such flexibility. Many organisations are turning to a mixture of advanced technologies (often based around non-conventional processes), and new organisational techniques such as Just-in-Time and Total quality Management (underpinned by emerging developments in management development and empowerment programmes).

Bancroft (1992) points out: "Clearly most business are still based primarily on the hierarchical model of organisation. Even the matrix and interfacing forms coming into existence are not distinct states, but rather are overlaid on the hierarchical format. At the heart of the problem is the need for management and workers to break away from the traditional mindset of how organisations should best be structured. The relationship among business, its organisation, and its technology must be reconceptualised."

Warner et al (1990) support the view that the hierarchical approach is becoming inappropriate:

> "It is precisely the new technologies, from industrial robots to flexible production systems and digitalised screen steering of processes, which in the first instance represent only a potential for efficient manufacture. In order to employ this potential on the shop floor and above all to guarantee and optimise the now technically feasible flexibility, the traditional work design based on the division of labour is proving increasingly dysfunctional."

This is of particular relevance when considering the high complexity of non-conventional technologies. Warner et al underline this suggesting: ". . . it is becoming harder to understand the way in which new generation systems function. Nevertheless, people must have frames of reference if they are to cope with the jobs they will be called to do. This means that technology should be an integral part of everyone's basic education, creating what is often called 'technical mindedness'."

The worker in Factory 2000 may, in many cases have to employ this 'technical mindedness' in a creative dialogue with the technology systems they are interfacing with. Warner et al echo this view:

> "Operatives and their supervisors are today expected not just to react to events and single incidents but to anticipate them and take action. This broadening of the abilities demanded is radically changing the basic skills needed. Operatives must be capable of analysing and thinking for themselves. In addition to their basic technical knowledge, they must be capable of lateral thinking so that they can apply that knowledge within certain frames of action."

Such a picture is simplistic to say the least. However, according to Bessant et al (1992), such an organisational form represents part of the emergence of a new manufacturing paradigm yet to be fully realised.

In several companies we have studied, the implementation of advanced, non-conventional technologies was either seen as an opportunity to raise the scope of individual creative input, or in several cases, was seen as a stumbling block due to its complexity. In one example, the implementation of a laser welder onto a microelectronics assembly line had caused significant problems due to its 'unwieldyness', safety issues, the problems of scheduling work from several lines through such an expensive machine. Problems had not been resolved and the laser welder now lies virtually idle.

A major benefit to emerge from this turbulent period has been the recognition of the importance of manufacturing as a *strategic function* within the firm. In turn this means that manufacturing as a function has to be aware of the range of challenges and the emergence of a new set of competitive priorities for the 1990s - priorities which will require a very different set of technologies and organisational frameworks.

Increasing evidence suggests that despite extensive investment in computer-integrated technologies (CITs), many firms are failing to obtain the full benefits offered by such innovation. (see, for example, Kearney, 1990, Bessant , 1991) Although technical problems play some role in slowing the effective implementation of CITs, much of the difficulty appears to lie in the lack of recognition amongst user firms of the need for accompanying organisational development and change. (Ettlie, 1988). Essentially attempts which implement new technologies using outdated assumptions and models leads to failure.

According to Lievegoed (1991):". . . every science is a prisoner of the systems and models it has itself created." In characterising the process of analysing systems in terms of simple models Lievegoed says:

> "... from any portion of reality various types of system can be used, and in turn it is possible to make various models out of these systems. One and the same system can give occasion for various models; and one and the same model can serve for the examination of various systems. A model is a further abstraction of a system. Having decided upon the system, one can then proceed to choose a model for a particular problem ."

However, much of the literature on organisation design has tended to view individuals, groups, organisations and even societies in a 'static' way, as closed systems, or, at best, as open systems in 'static' environments. Lievegoed presents a typology of systems as follows concluding that the emrging post-industrial view of organisations is as "dynamic open systems in changing environments." (Lievegoed 1991)

Lievegoed claims that ". . . An industrial organisation is an example of a system which is dynamically open, operating in a changing environment. Changes in the economic, technical and social environment affect it. Control and innovation are therefore basic essentials for the life of an industrial organisation." However, much of the literature, particularly from the classical and behaviourist schools of organisation theory, (which still predominate in much organisational thinking) does not progress beyond a systems perspective at Lievegoed's level 4 - the Dynamic Open System (where the changing nature of the environment is ignored).

The requirements for competitive products in the market place require new approaches to the basic activities of manufacturing. (Bessant 1991). Rapid rates of change in the sphere of technology and the development of evermore innovative generations of technology are forcing organisations to re-evaluate their approaches to control, coordination and decision making. Today's technology Manager increasingly is become an integrative manager combining an awareness of strategic and production engineering considerations in the quest for optimising the timing and management of new technological innovation. The technology manager of the 1990s must be aware that no technological solution is permanent and, in an environment where "the only constant is change", such a manager must use all his motivation to exploit new technological opportunities and commit all his creativity to newer, increasingly non-conventional solutions and decisions, without the burden of traditional ways of thinking and reacting.

This requires an ability to shift 'taken for granted assumptions' about the enterprise, that is, psychologically embedded (and often hidden) beliefs about the basic purpose, values and behaviours of commercial enterprises and the role of technology and organisation in managing these enterprises. The modern era of new achievements can no longer be measured in terms of 'revolutions', 'milestones', or 'water-shed events', but rather a continuous stream of permanent transient development. Looking from the mechanical engineering stand-point we must be aware that our profession is becoming an integrative part of technology in society as a whole, requiring ever closer cooperation between and across traditionally separate disciplines. Non-conventional processes and technologies are the result of such trends towards integration. However, it is our belief that the potential of these processes and technologies will only be fully realised through an organisation design which facilitates integration into the overall production/manufacturing system.

Non-conventional Processes

The term non-conventional process is used to denote those processes which emerged at the beginning of the Forties when new fabrication processes using different types of energy, such as electrical, chemical, thermal, electromagnetic, nuclear etc. were developed as an answer to the challenge of machining new materials which could no longer be satisfactorily machined with conventional machining techniques using wedge cutting tools as indirect objects of energy transfer (Peklenik, 1992).

Taking into account some specific attributes which are common for most of the so called non-conventional processes the following specific characteristics can be summarised:

- high speed of surface generation
- high specific energy
- atomic scale processing
- metal removal is based on several complex physical and chemical phenomena
- their development and applications are still increasing
- they are suitable for machining hard, brittle and the so called 'exotic' materials
- the are suitable for work pieces with high shape complexity
- they are suitable for automation of data communication
- they fulfil high surface integrity and precision requirements
- they meet miniaturisation requirements

(Peklenik 1982, Taniguchi 1990, Gunther 1975, Snoeys 1986)

According to the type of applied energy, non-conventional processes are classified by Snoeys (1986) as:

- mechanical processes
- chemical processes
- electro-chemical processes
- electro-thermal processes

In general non-conventional processes provide manufacturing engineers with additional choices or alternatives to the traditional conventional mechanical or abrasive material removal processes They are already well established in modern technologies such as micro-machining, nanotechnology, biotechnology and will be indispensable in the Factory of the Future. The generic designation of whether the process in non-conventional or conventional is open to discussion, since some of the so called non-conventional processes are already well established in different branches of industry. Electrical Discharge Machining, for example, is nowadays traditionally used for the manufacturing of tools and dies in the tool manufacturing industry. As such, it can no longer be described as a non-conventional process since its application is widely diffused and conventionally used for a wide range of machining operations. To avoid this, reflecting a high degree of subjectivity, the systematic approach for classification of new processes has been proposed by P. Rosenthal and H.T. McAdams (Peklenik 1982).

In summary, non-conventional processes and the technologies which underpin them move towards 'conventional' as they become established in a particular industry. In general, however, non-conventional processes in the current environment often comprise those which help to facilitate the moving away from the traditional 'mass production model towards a model based on increasing flexibility in product and process design, increasing process capability and higher precision in the delivery and quality control of products. In our view, the post-industrial era will be characterised by an exponential increase in the development of non-conventional technologies and this, combined with increasing hyperturbulence, will render even current organisational arrangements (often termed in the literature as 'new paradigm' organisational forms) obsolete. In the post-industrial organisation in a potential scenario where 'the only constant is change' organisations will need to operate as dynamic open systems which 'cope with chaos'. As such, we believe the current penchant for recipes for organisation design, will not hold good. Indeed organisational configurations around non-conventional technology arrangements will be at best, temporary, coordinated through what Mintzberg (1989) terms a 'shared ideology' of flexibility, creativity and proactivity.

In general non-conventional processes and the technologies which underpin them provide manufacturing engineers with additional choices or alternatives, for example, to the traditional conventional mechanical or abrasive material removal processes.(Junkar and Levy 1992) They are already well established in modern technologies such as micro-machining, nanotechnology, biotechnology and will be indispensable in the Factory of the Future.

The implications for 'creativity' and non-conventional technologies

Rickards (1985, 1990) suggests that ". . . creativity is a gift which we all possess, and which can be developed by appropriate training and application." He goes on to state: "A poor climate for creativity would be one which leads people to avoid risks, be over-critical of new ideas, and resist attempts to introduce change. A creative climate would be one in which people trust each other so that they can take the psychological risks of being open and revealing their deeper needs and fears."

Rickards also suggests a basic definition of creativity: "Hundreds of definitions have been suggested. In this book we have taken the simple one of 'escape from mental stuckness'. Many of the more formal definitions imply a process which leads to a sudden and significant discovery. Novelty and usefulness of the product are emphasised."

According to Langrish (1988): "Most technological change involves organisations; most new ideas come from individuals or the interaction between two or three individuals. The management of organisations is often concerned with preserving the present rather than creating the future, but creative individuals usually need access to the resources of organisations in order to turn their ideas into reality. There is therefore a problem - how to harness the creativity of individuals to the resources of organisations."

Whitfield (1975) highlights the importance of creativity in the technological innovation process suggesting that innovation is ". . . a complex problem-solving sequence which in some way produces something novel yet tangible and complete." Its full cycle includes seven steps:

1. Perceiving some need or problem.
2. Gathering relevant facts and classifying the true nature of the problem.
3. Seeking new information and analysing the whole picture.
4. Proposing alternative ideas for a solution.
5. Evaluating and selecting a final solution for implementation.
6. Implementing the solution.
7. Verifying that the solution is satisfactory.

"Creativity, while essential in step 4 to provide the novelty demanded by the word 'innovation', is by no means necessarily confined to this part of the sequence. Considerable ingenuity and downright creativity may be needed to achieve progress at any stage of the proceedings." The importance of creativity in managing technology is further echoed in the work of Junkar (1991,1992) who compares the traditional 'Tayloristic' view of technology systems and organisational structures with the emerging creative approaches to manufacturing organisation inherent in experts systems approaches and Artificial Intelligence.

In our view, the above writers on creativity will increasingly be seen as having something of relevance to say to the implementers of non-conventional technologies. New generations of technology create capability but also complexity. Experience in the 1980s and 1990s with non-conventional technologies points to significant organisational problems and the need for increased worker participation in problem identification and solution. In Mintzberg's (1989) terms this constitutes a shift in the way an organisation is coordinated from standardised work processes (i.e. through standard pieces of technology with minimal operator control) towards coordination through a shared purposed and standardised skills and knowledge, with emphasis on developing in operators a broader set of transferable skills and competences to cope with increasingly complex processes. Mintzberg characterises such an organisation as an 'adhocracy.' (Bessant et al. 1992)

Our initial work with several companies in the UK supports the above view: that the broadened view of work at the operator level helps to explain best practice in the use of advanced non-conventional technologies. Below is an attempt to describe the 'levels of creativity' we found in several UK companies who have currently engaged in attempts to implement advanced technologies. We have, for want of a better phrase, termed this the 'creativity matrix'!

	1	2	3	4
1st level	C	C	C	O
2nd level	C	C	O	O
3rd level	C	O	O	O

Figure 1 <u>Creativity Matrix</u>

1 - Traditional Control Organisation
2 - Process Improvement Organisation
3 - Process Management Organisation
4 - Transformational Organisation

In the matrix, C denotes closed, ie. designed and fixed by either a higher level in the organisation or by a specialist department. O denotes open, where creative input is obtained from a broader base in the organisation.

In the matrix, the first level concerns creativity at the level of product design, the second level is about 'process design and technology choice', and the third level is at the level of process control and improvement.

Organisation 1 we term the *Traditional Control Form.* In this organisation, (identified in our research) the key assumptions about management were based on the Fordist model. Product design was exclusively carried out by specialists in the design department using a CAD system with visual display only available to designers. No creative input to product design was allowed from production or engineering personnel except at a very minor, technical level and then, only from those at managerial level. Organisation 1 held the taken for granted assumption that operator-technology interfaces should be tightly defined and controlled and that products flowing through the systems were under the exclusive control of specialists.

Organisation 2 we term the *Process Improvement Organisation.* Many organisations which 'open up' their processes to a wider range of creative input are engaged in 'continuous improvement' philosophies. We identified several companies in our research which were in this category. In these organisations, problem solving forms a regular part of operator daily routine. In the Japanese model operators are empowered to stop the production lines when problems arise. In several firms we studied in the UK operators were members of process improvement teams and were empowered to self-inspect and carry out limited maintenance and adjustment of the technologies they were using. In the case of non-conventional technologies however, this was posing more of a problem, often due to safety aspects and the reluctance of technology specialists to 'let go' of their control of the technology system.

Organisation 3 could be termed the *Process Management Organisation*. In this organisation production lines were usually organised into cellular forms, group technology layouts, product based teams etc. Multi skilling, operator self inspect, on-line maintenance was common. In several cases engineering functions were also located on the product line. Several best practice organisation were developing the concept of a 'factory within a factory' consisting of operators responsibility for the complete manufacture of the product. Operators were trained in basic problem solving techniques and were thus able to creatively input into process design and the setting of process control parameters. Once again, however, in the case of non-conventional technologies this was more of a problem with such technologies and processes still being viewed as 'black boxes' where the core process was often physically hidden from view by protective casing ! In one example however, a manufacturer of high quality hi-fi equipment comprised 'product builders' who were technically very conversant with the product design, were responsible individually for the entire assembly of the product, inputed to its process control and improvement and even personally dealt with product complaints and queries. Many organisations in this category termed this approach 'total quality management'.

Organisation 4 is at present theoretical (in terms of our own research, yet suggested in the Literature eg. Lievegoed (1991)) and included for completeness of the matrix. Whether such a form will be realised in manufacturing is open to question. That such a form exists in other sectors is beyond question. However, it is a form currently confined to small, highly skilled' 'craft' based businesses and not high-tech manufacturing. In this form, even the design of products and specification of technology would be open to a broad creative input from a large employee base inside the organisation and across its boundaries into the customer and supplier base. In one company studied operators had inputed into the choice of new press machines and one quality improvement team had actually suggested a redesign to a feeder track to a press machine which saved the company tens of thousands of pounds ! Progress in this area had been more effective in inter-organisation relationships with the concepts of -'comakership' and strategic alliances emerging in recent years. Organisation 4 could be termed *'transformational'* in that creative input can generate changes which can transform the organisations products and processes, and thus performance.

A simple selection of quotes taken from interviews from a manufacturing firm undergoing transformation suggests the heightened creative activity taking place:

"much informal face to face problem solving"

"wider range of skills - to cope with flexible machinery, self-inspection, robotics etc."

"the company has always regarded its employees as its most precious asset at all levels and will continue to do so."

"increases in multi-skilling - including self-inspect, adjustment etc."

"the team approach has been key to successful implementation - full involvement and harnessing all the expertise in the organisation - and rewarding that expertise"

monthly payments, right across the plant - not payment by output."

"blurred boundaries between quality control and production, sharper boundaries in more traditional areas eg. accounting, sales etc."

"we have a suggestion scheme with significant rewards for improvements"

"the organisation is quite flat in terms of structure with only three or four levels"

"counselling is continually practiced at all levels"

"reduction in the number of personnel in the computing department as more people on the line take on computer work"

"high amounts of training at all levels - people must know what's going on"

In our view, companies adopting non-conventional technologies successfully experience a significant shift away from the traditional control form in our creativity matrix towards the process control and management forms. This is essentially characterised by the development of an increased level of holism in the view of stakeholders in non-conventional technologies. Such technologies are contextualised as forming parts of the overall dynamic open system in a changing environment. This can be characterised as an increased level of creative interaction at all levels of the organisation (see figure 2).

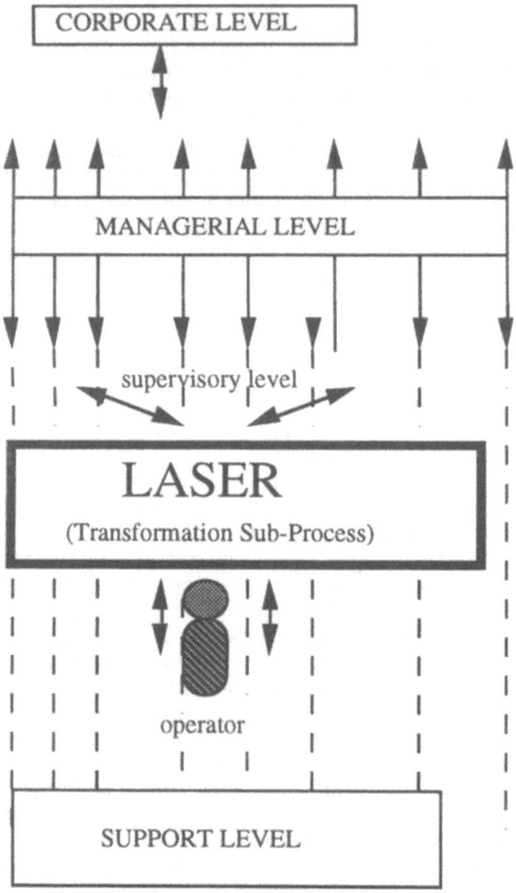

Figure 2 - The Contextualisation of Laser Technology in the Overall Organisation Picture

This enables effective organisation to occur which best supports successful use of the non-convetional technologies being adopted. In several cases, traditionally unskilled operators have made suggestions which have yielded significant improvements in quality and utilisation. This has occured through the recognition and harnessing of operator skills and creativity.

Conclusion

Our work with the creativity matrix is just beginning to uncover some interesting issues around the issue of creativity and advanced technology, which we believe may make a contribution to the post-industrial debate. The level of creative input in today's organisations varies in quantity and scope across functions. The best practice picture emerging in the UK is emerging as a shift away from the 'traditional control' form towards the 'transformational' form characterised by increasing involvement and input of operators in the design and management of products and processes. We intend to develop the matrix, and are continuing our research in the UK and carrying out comparative work in Slovenia. However, despite the innovation taking place in the development of non-conventional technologies, as a 'technology push' response to increasing hyperturbulence, there still remains a significant gap between the 'inventors', the implementers, and the operators, which is required to make these technologies fully effective on the shop-floor level. Creativity, is only one, but a fundamental element in this equation.

References

Bancroft, N.H., (1992), Managing Technological Change, John Wiley and Sons, New York.

Bessant J (1991), Fifth Wave Manufacturing: Management Implications of Advanced Manufacturing Technology, Basil Blackwell, Oxford.

Bessant J, Levy P, Tranfield D, Smith S and Ley C, (1990), Management and Organisation for Computer Integrated Technologies. Proceedings of UK Operations Management Association Conference, June 1990, Warwick University.

Bessant, J., Levy, P., Ley, C., Tranfield, D and Smith, S (1992), Coping with Chaos: Designing the Organisation for Factory 2000, paper presented to the Annual Conference of the Institute for Electrical Engineers, University of York, UK.

Bessant J, Levy P, Tranfield D, Smith S and Ley C, (1990) Management and Organisation for Computer Integrated Technologies. Proceedings of UK Operations Management Association Conference, June 1990, Warwick University.

Bessant J , P. Levy, P., Levy, C., Tranfield, D and Smith, S., (1992), Organisation Design for Factory 2000, International Journal of Human Factors in Manufacturing, Vol 2,2, JOHN WILEY AND SONS, INC., pp. 95-125.

Ettlie J (1988), Taking Charge of Manufacturing, Hossey Bass, San Francisco

Guenther, K.G., (1975), Anwendungsgebiete nicht-Koventioneller Formsgebungsverfahren, Annals of the CIRP, Vol 24/2/1975, pp. 533-538.

Hayes, R.H., Wheelwright, S.C., and Clark, K.B., (1988), Dynamic Manufacturing: Creating the Learning Organisation, The Free Press, New York, p 250

Hayes, R.H., and Jaikumar R., (1988), Manufacturing's Crisis: New Technologies, Obsolete Organisations, Harvard Business Review, September-October.

Junkar, M (1992), Kreativnost in Technologija , Business and Product Trends in the Developed World and Us (Slovenia), 5th Seminar, Machinatores - association of Mechanical Engineers, November 1992.

Junkar, M and Levy P., (1992), Non-Conventional Processes Integrated Into Manufacturing Systems, proceedings of the 25th CIRP International Seminar on Manufacturing Systems, 22-23 April, Bled, Slovenia pp. 221-235.

Junkar, M, Filipic, B, and Bratko, I., (1991), Identifying the Grinding Process by Means of Inductive Machine Learning, Computers in Industry, 17 (1991), pp 147-153, Elsevier.

Kearney A T (1990), Computer Integrated Manufacturing - Competitive Advantage or Technological Dead End?, London.

Langrish, J., (1988), Innovation Management: The Role of Creativity, in Rickards T., and

Moger, S., (1988), Creativity and Innovation Yearbook, University of Manchester, ISSN 09534199, Manchester, UK, p. 7, vol 1.

Liu M, Denis H, Kolodny H and Stymne B (1990), Organisation Design for Technological Change, *Human Relations*, 43, (1).

Lievegoed, B.C, (1991), :Managing the Developing Organisation, Basil Blackwell, ch.2.

Mintzberg. H., (1989), Mintzberg on Management, The Free Press.

Peklenik, J., (1992), FMS: A Complex Object of Control - The Extrapolation of an European View into the 21st Century, Presented at the IFIP Transactions, Tokyo, Japan, 24-26 June.

Peklenik. J., (1982), Round Table: The Impact of Engineering Materials on the Development of Fabrication Processes, Annals of the CIRP, Vol 31/2/1982, pp. 471-475.

Rickards T., (1985), Stimulating Innovation: A Systems View, Francis Pinter (Publishers) Limited, London, ch.3.

Rickards, T., (1990), Creativity and Problem Solving at Work, Gower Publishing Company, Aldershot, UK., ch.1.

Snoeys R., Staelens F., and Dekeyser W., (1986), Current Trends in Non-Conventional Material Removal Processes, Annals of the CIRP, Vol 35/2/1986, pp. 6467-6480.

Warner, M., Wobbe, W., and Brodner, P., (eds.)(1990), New Technology and Manufacturing Management, John Wiley and Sons, New York, ch.4.

Whitfield, P.R., (1975) ,Creativity in Industry, Penguin Books , Middlesex, UK, ch.1.

Chapter 11

The Global Information Society and Rural Economies

Arild Jansen

What does the development towards the 'post-industrial' society mean to rural areas? Will it imply an increase in information and knowledge based jobs locally, and stimulate an indigenous development? Or will it just lead to a new form of a branch plant, 'fordist' economy, characterized by a high level of external control and a narrow range of technical skill? This chapter reports some findings from a study of the diffusion of information technology in rural areas in Norway. It shows that this diffusion leads to a stronger integration of the local industries into the national economy through the development of vertical linkages, and to an increased import of services into the region. However, we also see substantial improvements of the quality and availability of private and public services, and that the competence and skills have increased in many sectors of the economy. During the years to come, we expect to see dramatic changes in the telematic infrastructure and their use, both technically, organisationally and economically. From the present experiences with IT diffusion, the question is discussed: is it likely that initiatives like 'a national information infrastructure' will serve the interests of rural societies, or will we see more of a branch plant economy?

Introduction

The development of microcomputers and extensive telecommunication networks has resulted in promising scenarios for regional areas. Among others, Toffler, with his vision of the electronic cottage, has contributed strongly to the belief that information technology (IT) leads to a more decentralised society (Toffler, 1980). Later experiences have shown that IT represents both opportunities and threats for the rural periphery, as economic realities have falsified these optimistic visions. The overall goal for the Norwegian regional politics has been to maintain our very decentralised demographic structure. Deriving from the promising visions, various policies and measures have been initiated to stimulate the diffusion of IT in rural[1] areas. In particular, a number of social experiments with the applications of new telecommunication services have been accomplished.

This paper presents some empirical findings from a study of IT diffusion in a remote area of Norway. The primary aim is to examine more closely some of the experiences with IT usage in a rural context[2]. The main conclusion is that we need a better understanding of the implications of the development towards the 'information society' for rural areas. The informatisation processes is making the integration of the local economy into national and international structures possible. This may increase the differences rather that closing the gaps, if adequate counterstrategies are not implemented.

The rest of this paper is structured as follows. The first section discusses the background and some relevant work, including an outline of the research issues. The second section briefly presents the empirical findings. The third section introduces a model that may help understand the role of information in value-adding processes in the economy. Finally, the fourth section discusses some important aspects of the national information infrastructure.

IT and Regional Transformation

From being a tool for cost reductions and increased effectiveness in organisations, we now see that the use of IT causes pervasive changes in the whole economy. It creates new ways of interlinking production, distribution and consumption processes of the economy, which implies new forms of information flow and transfer of knowledge, the basis for the network economy.

There is an increasing emphasis on the need for a flexible response to rapid shifts in the marketplace. One such response is the 'virtual company', which is a temporary network of independent companies; suppliers, customers, even rivals, linked by IT to share skills, resources and costs. Small specialised firms can establish close collaboration and provide complete solutions. In this way they may compete with larger companies, but in a more flexible way. ITs, and in particular telecommunications, play a crucial role in helping to overcome geographic and organisational barriers, and allow for the sharing of resources in flexible ways.

We also see a significant shift away from the traditional view of physical and material resources towards knowledge-based economic activities, where IT plays an key role. Zuboff (1988) describes two opposing strategies for computerisation: automating and informating. *Automating* means to use IT to collect information for surveillance and enhancing the control of the employees, and IT is used for automating the work processes. *Informating*, on the other hand, means to distribute information to individuals in an organisation to enhance their ability to do more competent work. The former is a continuation of a tayloristic management style, based on more advanced forms of control (Schulz-Wild,1991). The latter implies an increase in competence and skill which can challenge this traditional patterns of hierarchical control (Boyer,1988). Networking technologies can support both strategies.

What is an information infrastructure

The infrastructure dimension of IT is becoming increasingly important, not at least due to the various initiatives for building a national information infrastructure, as e.g. the Clinton and Gore initiative (U.S. Government, 1993) and the Bangeman report to the European Commission (Bangeman, 1994).

In general, infrastructure refers to the aspects of the physical and human environment that are shared for the public good: streets, bridges, sewers, schools, and furthermore language, monetary systems etc. An information infrastructure (INI) is the part of IT capabilities that is intended to be shared, including hardware, software and services, in particular communication and information services. This infrastructure thus consists of both technical and human components in a layered system, where the uppermost components are the technical capabilities related to service provision along with general available skills and competence necessary to provide these services (Davenpost and Linder, 1994).

Infrastructure can be viewed from many different levels. Here it will be focused on infrastructure at the local community and regional level, but with a strong link to the national level. Monteiro et al claim that the meaning of communicative artefact like INI, is completely dependent on joint, concerted actions. INI requires, in a strong sense, the co-operation of the involved parties for the system to function at all; it establishes a kind of mutual dependence among the involved parties as the system locks previously independent work routines together (Monteiro et al, 1995). Star and Ruhleder extend this perspective in claiming that infrastructure is fundamentally and always a relation, never a thing, and where choices and politics embedded in such a system become articulated components (Star and Ruhleder 1994:p 1). This view on infrastructure implies that organisations act or react to it in different ways, depending on both the quality of the infrastructure, and on the specific characteristics of the involved organisations' internal factors.

Centralisation or decentralisation?

Whether IT promotes centralisation or decentralisation has been a hot issue for a long time. George and King (1991) conclude that IT can support either, depending on what the most powerful group wants in the various cases. They hold that 'what emerges is a strong tendency toward the use of computing technology to reinforce the decision authority status quo: in other words, the reinforcement of political interpretation'.

Decentralisation itself is a blurred concept. Firstly, it can just mean *administrative decentralisation*, implying that operations and resources to carry them out are moved down in an organisation, while the decision making power is kept centrally. Secondly, one can emphasise the *political* dimension of decentralisation, which implies that the authority to define goals is moved from higher to lower levels of authority. Thirdly, it may just mean *deconcentration or distribution* of resources, e.g. businesses, departments, etc. from centres to the periphery. A special case is 'selective decentralisation 'in that a corporation is split into separate production units (divisions), which are all integrated into a centralized governing structure. The primary task of the division leaders is to achieve optimal results, in accordance with the goals and strategy defined by the headquarters (Andersen & Petterson,1989).

Goodman captures the basic idea of the political dimension by saying that "decentralisation is increasing the numbers of centers of decision-making and the number of initiators of policy; increasing the awareness of the whole function in which they are involved; and establish as much face-to-face association with decision making-makers as possible" (in Winner, 1986, p 88).

In the discussion of the different aspects of decentralisation, we therefore need to ask: decentralisation for whom, where and for what purpose? It raises question about the number, location, power, diversity and vitality of centers, which are key issues in regional politics (Winner, 1986).

Many will think of networking as a way of decentralisation, implying cooperation between more or less autonomous actors, as e.g. in the case of virtual organisations. This may create a conflict between centralisation and the need for standardisation versus the need for locally developed solutions that are better suited for their use of IT. Hanseth et al point to that the current trends of networking towards integration, within and across organisational barriers, implies that an increasing number of actors across groups and organisations are involved. Networking is not just another word for cooperation (Hanseth et al,1994). While cooperation is often based on work towards common goals, networking means to encounter incompatible beliefs and values. In this context, it is important to study how increased networking will influence rural economies.

Are we entering the Information Society?

Following Machlup's study of the information resources in the US (Machlup,1962), Porat coined the concept of information economy, aiming at describing a new phase of economic development, wherein the production of information goods and services dominate wealth and job creation (Porat,1977). Their work was devoted to establish the scale of information work in the economies, based on the high proportion of the workforce employed in the 'information' or 'knowledge' sector.

Quinn et al. claim in a major study that 'over the next two decades most of US's growth and many of its greatest opportunities for entrepreneurship and application of new technologies will arise in the service sector, as they have in the past 20 years' (Quinn, 1987). Cohen and Zysman (1987) reject the notion of the post-industrial society. They show that the manufacturing in the US has in fact maintained its share of GNP, if not employment over the past 40 years and that there is a 'direct linkage' between at least half of the jobs in the service sector to manufacturing production. They argue that: "the transition we are experiencing is not of industry into service, but from one kind of industrial society to another". In a regional perspective, the consequence of this view is that relying on the information sector to create new jobs and wealth may not be an adequate strategy. One should rather aim at linking information activities to the existing local industrial structures.

Is it a real disagreement in the analysis of the current development trends, or are we witnessing a pseudo-disagreement where different actors use different words? Miles (1991) advocates for a new understanding of this term, claiming that most jobs require some sort of information processing. He argues that we should define the 'information economy' in terms of IT-related activities, as it is the use of IT that represents the new development within industrial societies. This means shifting focus from the information sector and extending it to include other than those yielding 'information products' or employing 'information workers'. Miles thus offers a new macro-economic framework for analysing technological change, which requires examining the specific use of different classes of information, and the role of technical change in these processes.

Technology and rural development

There is an ongoing scientific discussion concerning the theoretical concept of rural development. It is important to differentiate "development in a rural region" from "development of a rural region." The first is a reduced concept, defining a rural area as a place of development, i.e., modernization, markets, businesses, etc. The latter implies "defining rural as a specific rural community that has a political and cultural identity, and is more than an arena of trends that are ubiquitous" (Storgaard et al.,1993).

A key question is whether diffusion of new technology will lead to more locally based, indigenous development, by creating a basis for more sustainable local economies. Closely related to this is self-reliance. According to Galtung, the strategy for selfreliance is based on three ideas (in Johannisson and Spilling,1983):

- to work for development of people, and not things
- to develop a region through autonomy, by the use of its own resources, capital, creativeness, etc.
- to aim at breaking down outside controlled structures, and define own goals for development.

According to Parker et al, every concrete situation is unique: "There is no single process by which a region can use telecommunications for enhancing rural development. So much depends on the specific region's political culture, economic base, existing telecommunication infrastructure, and myriad's of other factors" (Parker et al, 1992).

In his survey of telematics and regional development, Qvortrup claims that there are at least 4 possible scenarios (or strategies) for regional development (Qvortrup,1994):

- *dependent development*, where external industries are locating in rural areas, seeing rural labour as a resource which can be deployed by an urban-based organisation
- *transition management*, intending to enable rural communities to cope with sudden changes in their economy when facing decline, and to minimise pain
- *urbanisation,* with the intention to bring rural life as close as possible to urban norms
- *indigenous development.* Here the aim is to support communities and enhance their control over the development process, which demands a long-term process of change.

Rather than seeing these scenarios as distinct categories, they should be located along a continuum, running from dependent development based on mobile, external capital, rapid employment creation, low-skilled jobs, few prerequisites and low internal integration. At the other end, indigenous development should be based on incremental employment creation, high skilled jobs, extensive prerequisites and high economic integration. The latter strategy is, from a rural point of view, to be preferred, but of course harder to achieve.

Research issues

This brief literature survey shows a number of possible scenarios for regional development, and illustrates that many different issues related to the application in rural areas need to be studied. My particular focus in this article is whether the diffusion of IT in rural areas leads to stronger centralisation, or if it can strengthen decentralisation efforts. The following questions are being addressed:

1) Has the diffusion of computer networks created new information and communication services locally? If so, what type of services do we find?
2) To what extent do we see the establishment of IT-based jobs locally?
3) Has the role of information and information work changed in the local economy?
4) Has this development implied an increase in export of services from the region, or do we see an import of services into the region?
5) Are the consequences for women of this development different than for men?

The empirical data reported here are collected through a study of the diffusion and use of information technology in the northernmost region of Norway (Jansen, 1995b). Two different trajectories of technology diffusion are being analysed:

1. The effects of national and regional IT-policies carried out in the region (top-down strategies).
2. The impact of user-driven diffusion, caused by a general economic development (bottom-up strategies).

The Case Of Diffusion Of IT In The North Of Norway

Finnmark, the northernmost county in Norway, has a very scattered population and great distances. Characteristic features of the region's economy are:

- small local market and long distance to national/international markets
- small labor markets, low competence and difficulty in recruiting skilled workers
- easy access to rich natural resources, in particular fish from the Barents Sea. But economic and trade regulations have favoured export of raw material.

This has created a one-sided and vulnerable industrial structure, dominated by the fishing industry and some mining companies. Private and in particular public services account for a large part of the employment. Many small communities along the coast are completely dependent of one or two fish-processing plants.

Policy-initiated diffusion of technology in Finnmark

Earlier studies have shown that the use of IT in Finnmark has been lagging behind other parts of Norway. The number of IT-companies in the region is still small. The proportion of the population with higher education in this region is lower than in the rest of Norway. There are few job opportunities for well educated women, in particular along the coast (St.mld 32:1989-90). To stimulate the diffusion of IT in the region , a 5-year IT programme has been carried out. A brief summary of these efforts is given below, for details, see Jansen (1995b).

a) Infrastructure and telematic service development, which included these elements:

i) The establishment of a computer network (FUNN) between regional research centers in Finnmark and other parts of the country. It turned out that very few centers were able to provide profitable information services (Hetland, 1994). A major reason was the lack of support from local authorities, and that there was little demand for the services being offered.

ii) Support for the development of 10 telematic centers which provided to-way video communication services. These services have been important for other parts of the program. However, many of the centers have economic problems, due to the changed charging policy by Norwegian Telecom.

iii) The development of user applications based on this infrastructure, as telemedicine, teleteaching and video-conferencing. The telemedicine project has been successful, and such services are now an integral part of the health services in the region. The other applications, as video-conferencing and teleteaching have not been similar successes, and their usage is almost non-existing.

b) Support for telecottages and other IT-service providers

The goal was to support the establishment of five Community Teleservice Centers (CTCs). To day, none are in operation. Support has also been given to other businesses offering distance work using PC and telecommunications, or general software development. Only a couple of these businesses have survived. This illustrates a typical problem when establishing a small, service-providing firm in a rural area. It faces a small, low-competent local market, a staff with little experience in economic planning and business operation, and long distances to larger markets.

c) Support for IT-investments and development of user competence

The last elements of the program have been to give financial support to a number of export-oriented companies for the renewal of their technical solutions, in order to increase the efficiency in production and administrative routines, and to improve the quality of services and sales operation. Some of these projects have been rather successful. However, a report summarising these efforts states that there have been few examples of organisational changes, and that many of the companies lacked the competence required to take full advantage of the potential created by the IT investments (Christensen, 1993).

The effects of the plan on the development in the region.

Most of the efforts in the plan were oriented towards infrastructure and subsidising service provision (supply-side efforts). No efforts have been made to integrate the enterprises into the local economy, and the program lacked initiatives that would stimulate the demand for the services that were developed. Only the telemedicine project was both supply- and demand-oriented, as the project included the introduction of new applications, and support for users of the corresponding services. This has not been the case for the teleconference facilities, as the demand for such services has been low. To day, only those telematic centers providing telemedicine services are in daily operation. The effects of these efforts may be summarised as follows (Jansen,1995).

Table 1: ***The effects of the IT-program***

	Technical skill	Quality of functional service	Sosio-economic strategic factors	Organisational/ Regional impact
Telecottage	poor	poor	lacking	negligible
New IT services	poor/fair	poor/fair	poor	negligible
Video-conferences	good	fair/good	poor	small
IT-investments	good	fair/good	poor/fair	small/medium
Telemedicine	good	good	good	significant

[1])The ratings are estimated by the author, based on personal interviews and written reports from the different projects. These estimates are average for each group, some organisations within each group may have higher or lower scores.

This table shows that a necessary condition for organisational and regional impact is that all factors, both technical skill, operational services and socio-economic factors are fulfilled.

In conclusion, these efforts have succeeded in creating technical functioning systems, but the services that were offered have to a large extent not been integrated into the local economy. Few links between service providers and users are established, and few new jobs or services have been created. We must note that it takes a long time to gain full effect of such infrastructure development.

User-driven technology diffusion in the region

The other trajectory of the diffusion of IT is closely linked to the economic development and changes in production life in general. Storgaard et al. (1993) claim that we can identify three forms of technology diffusion in a regional context:

i) Consumer-driven transfer of technology, mainly because most people can afford to buy advanced equipment, e.g., mobile telephones, TV/video and other electronic equipment.

ii) Through organisational transformations where businesses have changed work routines and through interregional collaboration have adapted themselves to higher technical standards, e.g., as (sub)providers,

iii) Technology transfer mediated by larger corporations, in particular in the utilization of raw materials in the fishing industry, in service provision, communication, etc.

To provide more insight into such processes, some small scale investigations have been carried out. The data have been collected as part of student projects, where the aim is to analyse the actual use of IT in the regional economy in Finnmark (Jansen, 1995b). The data are collected from a selection of businesses, which represent only a few sectors in the local economy. Some of the finding are:

In most branches of the economy , we find that the local technical solutions are compatible with those found elsewhere in Norway. The quality of private as well as public services have been improved substantially during the last 10-15 years. Modern telecommunications provide easy access to information and knowledge outside the region, and provides better tools for co-operation and knowledge exchange. The skill development have been positive in a number of sectors (as e.g. in banks, insurance companies, transportation and building/construction and other service-providing companies, public sector, etc.).

But we do find a number of negative trends:

Most enterprises are linked to computer networks operated from outside which opens for external control and increased local vulnerability through dependence of remote information systems (vertical integration). Most computer systems in use are developed and maintained outside the region. This may create a dependency of external expertise, and delay competence build-up locally. Many local offices (or branches) are mainly importing IT-services into the region through the networks, and few are buying these services locally. The use of networks has increased specialisation and division of labour in some sectors (e.g. in office work, retail trade, manufacturing industry), which implies that the job content for lower-level employees has been reduced, not at least part workers. It may also imply that the region's share of the value-adding activity are being reduced.

A comparison of the two different types of technology diffusion

When breaking down these data into a number of factors[3], we can compare the effects of the user-driven development with those of the IT-plan. This can be summarized in the following table (see Table 2).

It should be emphasized that these ratings are based on qualitative assessment of the data collected through interviews in the organizations that are studied. Some comments to these findings may be needed.

1) *Competence development* means that employees have increased their knowledge and capabilities to meet higher job qualification requirements. We found that telemedicine implies a positive competence develop-ment In the case of banking and insurance, increased use of IT has implied automation of routine tasks, while the employees are left with more consulting and management type of work. On the other hand, in e.g. parts of the trade sector, we find that work on the shop floor have become more routine, while managerial tasks are more demanding.

Table 2: *Some of the effects of the IT-policy compared to the impact of general IT diffusion*

	1 Compe-tence devel.	2 Oppor-tunity for women	3 Employme nt Impact	4 Use of local IT suppliers	5 Export/ import services	6 Strength of vertical integra-tion	7 Devel horizon network	8 Type of devel achieved
IT policy								
Tele-medicine	yes	yes	positive	some	import	no	no	indigenous
Tele-cottages	-	no	-	no	exp/imp	no	no	-
New IT services	-/yes	no	positive	no	export	no	no	urban
IT invest-ments	-/yes	no	positive	no	import	yes	no	urban/ indigenous
TI[4]	yes	yes	positive	no	export	no	no	urban/ indigenous
General IT diffu-sion								
Power supply	-	-	-	no	import	yes	no	urban
Retail trade	-/neg	no	negative	no	import	yes	no	dependent
Hotel/ Travels	-	yes	-	no	exp/imp	yes	yes	urban
Bank/ insurance	yes	yes	negative	no	import	yes	no	dependant/ urban
Printing/ publ	yes	no	some	no	export	yes	yes	indigenous
Consult. services	yes	no	some	no	exp/imp	no	some	urban/ indigenous
State agency	-/yes	yes	negative	some	import	yes	no	dependant/ urban
Local admin	yes	yes	-	some	import	no	no	urban

- : Means that amigous trends are identified, and that it is difficult to specify any specific value

2) *Opportunities for women.* We found in a number of cases that changes in job organisation at work places typical for women may imply competence development and the possibilities for stimulating upward mobility. Examples are routine clerical work which is being transformed to provision of services. We see a tendency of polarisation: those who have education and experience may foresee a job carrier, while those lacking adequate education and practice are the losers, and will most likely be laid off.

3) *Employment impact*: There has been created some new work places, mainly in service providing businesses. But the most likely effect is that jobs are

vanishing. E.g. in banking, it is that a staff reduction of about 30-40% has taken place during the last 5-6 years. We see a similar trend in the public sector, where cost reduction is a main reason for increased IT-use, which usually implies fewer employees.

4) *Local IT-suppliers*: This factor concerns if IT equipment or services are purchased from a local or regional supplier. We find rather few cases in which a significant part of the acquisitions are made locally.

5) *Export or import of IT-based services.* The major trend for many multi-locational organisations is that improved telecommunications offer the possibilities importing services, e.g. that branch offices are accessing central databases, or that they use standardised payroll and accounting systems offered from the main office, instead of maintaining local systems. This applies both to private and public organisations, in industry as well as in the service sector. We find few cases of successful export of locally produced services.

6) *Vertical integration.* There is a significant tendency that improved telecommunication implies the a stronger integration of local offices into the central organisation, and that a larger part of the value-adding activities are carried out centrally.

7) *Horizontal network.* The new IT infrastructure may provide an excellent support for improved local cooperation, which can increase value-adding activities locally. So far, we have found few such cases.

8) *The type of development is observed*.We have estimated the development type, related to the categories defined by Qvortrup. It seems that the 'urban development type' is the most typical one, and that there are very few cases supporting an indigenous development.

In spite of the bias in the data, this table indicates that even in a highly developed economy as the Norwegian, the diffusion of IT may imply negative development trends for rural areas. The impact for employment and value-adding activities has in general not been positive, and local IT-suppliers are not able to get a larger share of the market. It seems to be difficult to develop IT-based information services locally that are competitive on a remote market.

However, the findings show that private and public services have been improved, and that the connection to IT networks makes various types of information more easily accessible, which may provide a good basis for local innovations. The case of TI illustrates very well that it is feasible to create public work places locally, if it exist a political priority for doing so. But there are not many such cases. These conclusions do no give any unambiguous picture, but seem to offer interesting perspectives that should be studied further.

Other findings

Other studies of diffusion of IT in rural areas provide corresponding results. Hetland (1991) have studied the Norwegian experiments with telecottages and telematic centers, and points to the difficulties that remote service providing businesses experience in gaining entry into a remote market. He concludes: 'The more standardised a service is, the more important it is that the transaction cost is low, whereas the more unique a service being provided is, the less effect such cost exerts on its profitability. The experience shows that when a rural community tries to establish an enterprise based on local competent personnel, it demands an extensive degree of networking and a long period to become accepted in the market".

Gillespie & Robins(1989) conclude "improved communication and better trade relations with fewer barriers provide a better competitive climate for stronger rather than weaker economies. For the districts that have a weak economy, greater openness will only render their weakness more obvious. In this negative scenario, the main applications of communication services are as delivery mechanisms for externally-produced goods and services, so that the region concerned will have little roles to play in shaping the infrastructure or the services run over it, because it is designed primarily to serve the interest of external organisations."

Vendramin and Valenduc report from a study of the developments in retail trade in European countries, and claim that "the organisational changes lead to more interdependence within the trade sector. A consequence is an increased organisational flexibility, with the risk of deterioration of worker condition, and their jobs have become standardized" (Vendramin and Valenduc, 1993).

In an analysis of the potentials for teleworking in Europe, Qvortrup points to important barriers which hamper rural communities to benefit fully from the wide range of existing telecommunication and information services:

- barriers in the *organizational systems*, in that centrally located organisations do not integrate local service providers if not being rather competitive
- barriers in the *rural economic system,* in that the local infrastructure and basic support services is not adequate.
- barriers at *the user level* , which can be *technical* matters that requires specific support services, or *cost and price* structures that do not favour local user, or lack of *qualification*, in that the skill requirement are not met rurally.

Preliminary reports from the Accorde-project indicate that the development of telecommunication infra-structure in remote areas does increase the dependency development trend (Qvortrup, 1995). He concludes by saying that teleworking is not ‘the magic word in a remote region context’, and that remote regions can be supported in different ways, implying different results.

How Can IT Support Indigenous Development?

The preceding analysis clearly illustrates that there has been a massive diffusion of IT into the northern regions of Norway. However, the analysis also shows that the technology policy was not based on an adequate understanding of the actual mechanisms in the local economy. This conclusion, however, gives little insight into what factors that should be changed to influence this development. It is necessary to look into the innovation and learning processes in order to understand the factors that can stimulate a more positive development.

Lundvall (1992) underlines that an important factor in the innovation and diffusion processes is the interaction between users and producers of product innovations. The diffusion processes result in further innovations and the diffusion process cannot be understood without reference to the ongoing changes in the characteristics of the original innovation. This user-producer approach implies an emphasis on innovation as an interactive learning process.

It seems that the economy in this region, as in most rural areas, can be characterized by strong vertical integration, controlled from the outside, and that we find few examples of horizontal integration across the sectors. The geographical distances are large, both inside the region and to the outside markets. The cultural differences between the region and the markets or central authorities also cause obstacles.

These long distances along various dimensions imply that interactive learning can be difficult to achieve locally and the interaction between information providers and users is particularly low. The fragmentation of the production system between central and local locations most likely weakens the rural economy, as the knowledge buildup will not take place locally. Since most of the IT-systems and networks are developed and operated outside the region, the possibility for knowledge buildup in the region may seem to be limited. We need, accordingly, a strategy that can change the structures that control the information flow and by that stimulate the local knowledge buildup.

Controlling information flow as a strategy for indigenous development

Krogh (1993) has developed a model that may be used to understand these processes, where he focuses on the role of information in the *value-adding processes*. His basic assumption is that information is an input factor in production, corresponding to physical resources, as information is required in all business activities. The main point is that information work is not a separate activity, but an integrated activity in all parts of the value adding system. The information work in the production process has three important characteristics:

* Every step in the production processes creates data that can be converted into knowledge and action
* The information handling processes are directed towards all links in the value-adding activity, starting with the harvesting of natural resources, and ending with market and sales operations
* These processes may take place at large distances from the physical processes.

The model may de described in this way:

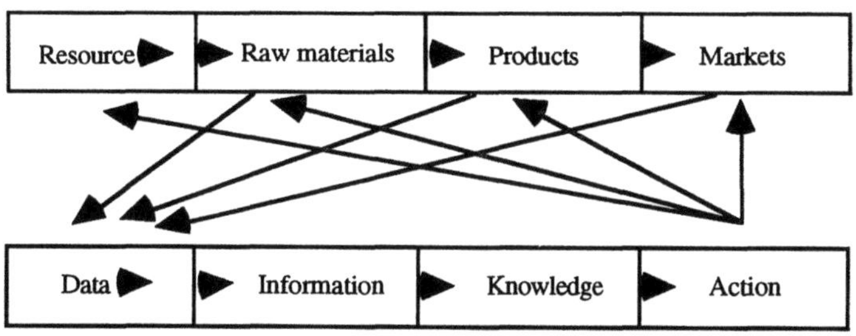

Figure 3: A model of value adding processes in a resource based production (Krogh,1993).

The value-adding processes in the fishing industry can illustrate this model. Data are collected through the catching of fish in the ocean, in the production, distribution and marketing processes, and finally in the negotiations with the customers. If a local fish plant belongs to a national or international corporation, a large part of these operations are carried out outside the region, and the corresponding data accumulation, e.g. about market needs, are not available locally. This inhibits local actors in developing new knowledge, e.g. how to adapt production according to user needs.

In spite of the vast use of IT in all parts of society, people are still the most important factor in transforming data to actions, as actions are initiated by people who interpret the data and integrate the data into their existing knowledge framework. Weizenbaum (1987) claims that data becomes information in the light of a hypothesis, and says "the way knowledge is put into a computer clearly reflects someone's hypothesis". He continues on by saying: "What happens with the organisation of knowledge in the computer is that the organisation itself, that is the whole system, very rapidly becomes incomprehensible. This is because a large scale organisation's data, information and knowledge is a function of its history, and its history gets lost in the very act of its construction". People's background, culture and values are thus essential, as well as their network relations with other people. It is of great importance that people locally participate in such processes, to achieve successful innovations.

The challenge for the local economy is to get access to the basic data in all parts of the production chain. One way to achieve this is to stimulate horizontal cooperation in such a way that more information flows internally in the region. This and other studies(e.g. Hetland, 1994) have clearly shown that direct contacts with actors in the market are essential for local service providers). Hepworth (1989) emphasizes ". . .that it is a major question for rural development policy to discover ways of helping small-scale operations to connect into the information economy. Rather than continuing a dependency form of development associated with branch-plant economies, there is a need for a strategy that would result in greater regional autonomy, based on creating a networking culture between small and medium-sized enterprises (SMEs) in remote areas, such that locally based service offerings can stimulate indigenous development."

We may find such examples, as e.g. in the furniture industry, which is a successful export-oriented business sector in Norway. A majority of the enterprises are found in a small, remote region at the west coast (Møre and Romsdal), and they have established well developed horizontal networks and locally based cooperation patterns (Wiig, 1994).

The Political Vision Of The Information Economy

The National Information Infrastructure

The United States president B. Clinton have spoken frequently about the promise to develop a *National Information Infrastructure (NII)*, a nationwide high capacity computer and information network. Their vision is to create an information highway connecting academia, educational and R&D-institutions and the industry. Vice president A.Gore envisions a future, in which oceans of data, libraries of movies, books and other creative work would be readily available in every home, and he hold forth the image of classrooms without walls, sophisticated medical collaboration and globally competitive small businesses (Abernathy, 1993).

The European response to this American initiative is the Bangemann Report '*Europe and the Global information society*, commissioned by the European Council in December 93 (Bangeman, 1994). Their vision is clear: "the information society has the potential to improve the quality of life of Europe's citizens, the efficiency of our society and to reinforce cohesion". They furthermore state "Preparing Europeans for the advent of the information society is a priority task. Education, training and promotion will necessarily play a central role"

NII and the Information Age: A market-driven technological imperative

Both the US initiative and EU response seem to be based on a view which can be seen as a kind of techno-economic 'determinism'. Gore claims that "NII is at all odds the most important and lucrative marketplace of the 21st century". Chapman and Rosenberg of CPSR (Computer Scientist for Social Responsibility) on the other hand see NII as "a bandwagon for very powerful economic interests, including telephone and telecommuni-cations companies, cable television operators, computer manufacturers, software developers, acolytes of an emerging 'computer culture', and a wide variety of other people".

The Bangeman group states (page 7): "The information revolution prompts profound changes in the way we view our societies and structures. This presents us with a major challenge: either we grasp the opportunities before us and master the risks, or we bow to them, together with all the uncertainties this may entail. *The tide waits for no man, it is a revolutionary tide, sweeping through economic and social life"*(my emphasis). The report is clearly based on a perspective of an open market in which competitive suppliers of network and services are increasingly active, as the group "urges the European Union to put its faith in market mechanisms as the motive power to carry us into information age" and their recommendations focus on ending monopoly, and to relieve the providers of political constraints.

Shaping the NII through a process of social construction of technology

Others have a different view of the forces that influence the design of this infrastructure. Rather than having the infrastructure as a result of market driven developments only, CSPR want to intervene in this process of social construction so that the range of interests and opinions participating in the discourse of choice is as broad as possible. Among other they have therefor made these recommendations:

- to consider the social impact of NII development
- to guarantee equitable and universal access to network services
- to provide access to government services via NII
- to protect public space and think globally, not nationally
- and provide full services at home, at workplaces, and in community centers
- democratic participation in design and development, and encourage experimentation.

It is most likely that their general concern and recommendations are relevant for the European initiatives. The question we must ask in addition is: are these requirements enough to secure a positive rural development?

Can NII really serve the interests of local communities?

The EU ORA[5] project is based on the assumption that information and telecommunications technologies offer opportunities for rural areas to *compete on equal basis*, providing that the necessary telecommunications infrastructure is in place (ORA, 1993). In the project report, it is claimed that employment in rural areas can be created or secured by expansion of existing small enterprises to rural areas by better access to markets. This can also be achieved by enabling "information intensive" enterprises to re-establish in rural areas, or enabling small manufacturing units to become viable through better communications with other components in design, production and marketing organisation. Their main strategy seems to be to create information work and educate information workers in rural areas. However, they express some concern, as it is clearly stated that "if positive steps are not taken, the enabling telematic systems will be available only in cities and core regions, and the opportunities for rural revitalisation through application of these technologies may be delayed or lost".

Some of the Norwegian experiments with developing a telematic infrastructure in rural areas may provide relevant experiences. Neither the R&D-network project, nor the social experiments with telematic centers and telecottage have been any success, as nearly all were closed down when the subsidising ended (Jansen,1995). Hetland explains these failures by the rather strong technological focus in these initiatives, and the lack of capability to build allies and networks with different user groups (Hetland 1994). To little attention was paid to type of information and the information services to be provided, and the local market was too small. Similar experiences are reported from two Minitel experiments (Ødegård 1991; Bjørkås 1992).

Meier-Dallach et al report from experiments with the diffusion of telecommunication services in Swiss rural areas, including an initiative to establish telecottages. The telecottages are now closed down, and no new jobs was created. They state that the project neither managed to involve important actors locally, nor did they succeed in gaining entry into remote markets (Meier-Dallach et al, 1994).

On the other hand, the Norwegian telemedicine project provides an excellent example of successful social construction of technology. Telemedicine corresponds to an indigenous development scenario as it offers the same services in rural areas as is done centrally, and that emphasis has been put on developing experience and competence locally. It could very well have been organised in another, more centralised way, as other telemedicine experiments (Fosse, 1992).

Conclusions

A preliminary conclusion from the empirical findings presented here do not provide us with a unambiguous picture of the future for rural communities in the information age. The results from this study emphasise the need for better understanding of telecommunications and the information economy in a rural context Rather than focusing on information workers and information work as specialized activities, it seems to be more fruitful to focus on all types of information handling, and the role of IT in such activities. It is important to study what type of information that is being processed and the information services that are provided. Some suggestions may thus be made as premises for future regional technology policies.

1) Information is the key strategic resource on which production and delivery of goods and services in all sectors of the world economy will depend. Far from a transformation to a post-industrial society which emphasises a shift from manufacturing to services, an information economy perspective would suggest that manufacturing and service activities are becoming equally dependent on effective information management.
2) This economic transformation is being underpinned by a technical transformation, dominated by the development of computer and telecommunication networks, where the cities will become the nodes in a network based economy. The liberalisation of the telecommunication market, implying more differenciated services and tariff structures, may not favour peripheral areas. A regional counter-strategy is required, which focuses on defining requirements to the infrastructure development, and on to develop skills and competence in order to utilise the corresponding services.
3) This "informatisation" of the economy is making the global integration of national and regional economies possible. Far from eliminating differences between places, the use of IT can permit exploitation of differences between areas, for example in terms of labour market conditions, the nature of cultural facilities, and of institutional structures.
4) Accordingly, the belief that IT causes decentralisation may be misleading. Our findings indicate that the development of IT networks more often implies increased import of services from the centers to rural areas, rather than an increase in value-adding activities locally. IT *may* enable distribution or deconcentration of organisational units or even entire enterprises.. But that is more likely to be the result of deliberate political decision than caused by economic reasoning alone.
5) Increased knowledge and competence is the most important factor in order to benefit from the potential of new technology. The vertical integration of the local businesses may imply that essential knowledge about important processes in the value adding chain is lost locally. A critical factor for rural economies is therefor access to *information*, and to stimulate the development of *knowledge and competence* from this information through various types of learning processes. A key strategy for a regional economy is to get access to, and to control the information (properly speaking data) that are created in the utilisation of the resources in the region.
6) The information processing activities are, however, not the end in itself, but an integrated part of the production and distribution systems. It is then important to maintain and develop an organisational and cultural context which can act as a basis for local innovations on their own terms. Structuring of data, and formalising of tacit knowledge should be part of local innovation processes.
7) Special focus should be paid to incorporating small-scale enterprises into local networks. It is particularly important to focus on businesses in which typical women jobs are dominating, as lack of women is a serious problem for many rural communities.

These conclusions do not imply that vertical links and connecting to centrally controlled networks do only have negative implications for rural economies. As is clearly shown by many of the examples mentioned in this paper, such relationship's are necessary for rural development. But they should not be the dominant type of development, as several trajectories for rural areas should be supported.

Hepworth (1989) put it this way 'a new geography of economy is unfolding, where it is necessary to 'get inside' the firm. Consideration should be given to both the geographical and social location of information, and how the division of labor within and between firms is determined by the locational dynamics of the new technologies'.

At the same time, Goddard points to: .'While IT permits an increase volume of inter-organisational transactions, it seems that interpersonal contact remain sufficiently important, particularly in relation to the development of new services and relationships, that the role of the cities is further enhanced' (in Hepworth,1989). Similarly, local and regional actors should maintain, and even extend their strong (horizontal) networks for information acquisition as basis for cooperation and interactive learning.

References

Abernathy, Joe: *National Information Infrastructure Story*. Houston Chronicle, April 4, 1993.

Bangeman, M: *Europe and the global information society. Recommendation to the European Council.* CD-84-94-290-En-C. Brussels, May, 1994.

Bjørkås, S.: *Minitel -Rjukan* (in Norwegian). Report nr. 49/1992, Telemark Research Foundation, Bø. ISBN 82-7401-050-7.

Boyer, R: *New Directions in Management Practices and Work Organisation.* At OECD Conference: Technology as a Social Process. Helsinki 11-13.12.1989.

Christensen, R: *Informasjonsteknologi i Finnmark.* Sluttrapport. (IN Norwegian) FINNUT, Vadsø, 1993.

Chapman, G, Rotenberg, M: *The national information infrastructure. A public interest opportunity.* CPSR Newsletter, 11(2), 1-5, 16-23, 1993.

Cohen, Stephen S., and Zysman, John: *Manufacturing Matters: The Myth of The Post-industrial Economy.* (Basic Book, New York, 1987).

Fosse, G: *Telemedisin:En studie av innføring av telematikk i helsevesenet.* Phd.thesis, Bergen University. 1995

Gillespie, A, & Goddard J: *In Report of the seminar on regional Impact of Telecommunications services*, Kiruna, 19-21 June 1990. DSTI/ICCP/TISP/90.19, OECD, Paris, 1990.

Gillespie, A. and Robins, K.: *Geographical In equalities. The Spatial bias of New Communication Technologies.*, Journal of Communication, 1989.

Hanseth, O, Thoresen, K & Winner, L: *The Politics of NetWorking in Health Care.* In Clement et al (eds.) NetWorking: Connecting Workers In and Between Organisations. North Holland, 1994.

Hepworth, M.: *The Geography of Technical Change in the Informaion Economy.* Regional Studies, London, 1986.

Hepworth, M: *Geography of Infromation Economy.* Belhaven, London, 1989.

Hetland, P.: *The social Construction of Telecommunications.* Aalborg-seminar 20-22.11, 1991.

Hetland, P.: *Exploring Hybrid Communities - telecommunications on Trial.* Dr. thesis, Dept. of Economics and Planning, University of Roskilde, Roskilde, 1994

Jansen, A: *Rural development through diffusion of New Technology*? In Scaninavian Journal for Information System, Vol 7 (1) Aalborg, 1995

Jansen, A.: *Informasjonsteknologi som vekstfaktor i utkantstrøk. En analyse av satsingen på IT i Finnmark.*
(In Norwegian) HiF Researh Report 1995:4. Alta. 2-7541-187-4

Johannison and Spilling: *Strategier for lokal och regional sjølutvekling.* NORDREFO, Oslo, 1983.

Krogh, L: *Informasjonsforvaltning - et avgjørende område for naturbasserte regioner.* Paper at 1.International Barents Symposium, Kirkenes 21-24.10.1993.

George, J & King, J. *Examining the Computing and centralisation debate.*CACM, vol.34(7),Juli 91

Lundvall, B. Å.: *User-Poducer Relationship.* In Lundvall (ed.) National Systems of Innovation. Pinter Publisher, London, 1992.

Machlup, F. *The Production and Distribution of Knowledge in the United States.* Princeton, NJ, Princeton University Press. 1986.

Meier-Dallach, Gloor, Meyer Hohermuth: *Der Computer in der Bergregion, Soziokulturelle Auswirkungen von Computern und der Telematik am Fallbeispie Goms, IVT, ETH, Zürich, 1993* .
Miles, I: *The Information Economy. A New Framework Is Needed.* Proceeding from an Int. Seminar in Oslo, 1991 FDH-report 82-7541-06-2, Alta, 1991.
NoU 83:32 Telematics. *The telecommision report II.* (In Norwegian) The Ministry of Transport, Oslo, 1982.
ORA'93: *R& D on Telematic Systems for Rural Areas.* Commision of EU, DG XIII, Brussels, 1993 OECD: *IT and Economic Growth.* ICCP report nr. 19. OECD Paris, 1989
Parker, E. &, Hudson, H: *Electronic Byways. State Policies for Rural Development through Telecommunications.* The Aspen Institute, Westview Press, Boulder et al, 1992,
Porat, M: *The Information Economy. Definition and Measurement.* Washington, DC. Office of Telecommunication, US Department of Commerce. 1970
Quinn, Baruch & Cushman Paquette:*Technology in Services.* Scientific American, vol 257 (6), 1987
Qvortrup,L: *Flexiwork Perspectives in the European and Nordic Labor Markets.* 18-19.5.1993, Helsinki, Finland.
Qvortrup, L: *Telematics and Regional development: A research Literature Review.* Report to the EU-ACCORD project, Odense University, 1994
Qvortrup, L: *Telework, the Trend Towards Networking.* Presented at Telework'94. Sydney, Australia, dec. 1994. CCS, Odense University, Denmark,
Schulz-Wild, R: *CIM and future factory structures in Germany.* Futures 23, nr. 10, Oxford, 1991.
Storgaard, K, Hetland, P. Meier-Dallach, H-P.:*Social Shaping of Telematics and Rural Development.* Proposal to the COST-Committee. Copenhangen, sept.1993.
St.meld. 32:1989-90 (In Norwegian, Parliament White Paper). Universitetetsforlaget, Oslo, 1989.
Toffler, A: *Th e Third Wave.* New York, Morrow, 1980
U.S. Government. '*Technology for America's Economic GrowthA New Direction to build Economic Strength.* White House Office of Communications, Executive Office of the President, February 22, 1993
Vendramin,P.& Valenduc,G.:*Networking in Services. Organisational and professional changes.* In Clement(ed):*NetWorking, Connecting Workers In and Between Organizations.* North-Holland, 1994.
Weizenbaum, J: *On the status of Knowledge in Information Society.* In Forchenheimer, C: Proceedings from Knowledge in the Computers age. Nov. 2-3, Linkøping, 1987.
Winner, L: *The Whale and the Reactor.* University of Chicago Press, Chicago, 1986.
Zuboff, S: *In the Age of the smart machine.* Heinemann Prof. Publishing Ltd. Oxford, England, 1988.
Ødegård, O: MINITEL på Lillehammer, (In Norwegian) Easternm Research Institute, report 24/91. ISBN 82-7356-193-3.
Wiig, H. and Wood, M: *Innovation activity and the regional economic environment. A quantitative analysis of innovation in a Norwegian Region: Møre og Romsdal* STEP report 10/94. Oslo

Notes

[1] This study was part of the 'Rural Development Programme', whish was funded by the Norwegian Research Council.

[2] Rurality is here used for remote, less populated areas in the context of the highly industrialised Norwegian economy.

[3] The factors correspond partly to 8 cohesion issues that are defined in the EU ACCORDE project (Advanced Communication and Regional development).

[4] TI Health Insurance Collecting Agency, which was established in a small, rural community to compensate for loss of work places in a large mining company IT has to day 107 employees.

[5] The ORA program (Opportunities for Rural Areas) is the European Union's programme for research and deve-lopment on telematic systems It aims at exploiting the potentials of IT for rural areas and was initiated in 1992.

Chapter 12

Information Communication Technology and Society: A community-based approach

Peter Day

This chapter focuses on the issue of social exclusion from the developing information infrastructure. It discusses the need for guaranteed public spaces as a means of addressing the problems of social exclusion, and proposes a model of tripartite collaboration as a way of creating these public spaces on the 'infostructure'. The chapter argues that urgent consideration must be given to the social implications of information communication technology (ICT) and their relationship to the broader information society debate. It discusses European Union and UK government approaches to the development of the information infrastructure, and how this development is often interpreted as being the sole information society issue. It examines deficiencies of the techno-economic approach to the information society, and suggests universal participation as an alternative to the current paradigm. Community networks and community telecentres are used as exemplars of this alternative.

Introduction: Information Infrastructure ~ an 'Infostructure'

The focus of the current information society debate centres on the development of what has become known as the information superhighway or infobahn. The metaphor provides a useful conceptual image because of the similarity between a network of motorways as a means of transportation (and therefore communication) and the development of a network of digital telecommunication networks for communication purposes. As both are forms of infrastructure the information superhighway is best described as an information infrastructure or 'infostructure' (Day & Horner, 1995). A belief in market forces combined with a techno-centric policy approach currently drives the development of the European 'infostructure'. If society as a whole is to benefit from such infrastructure development then its social impacts and how people might participate fully in the process must also be considered.

An interesting issue in the 'infostructure' debate is how policy makers promote its development in terms of socio-economic impact (CEC, 1994a, b, c). Applications such as telemedicine and distance learning are frequently portrayed in policy documents, political speeches and the marketing of commercial products to indicate to the public that the brave new world of telematics will provide answers to a number of social problems such as unemployment and the environment. However, closer inspection shows these tactics often to be attempts to secure future markets for commercial organisations, or to show policy makers as being at the cutting edge of technological development. Very little consideration is paid to how technology shapes the life of individuals and communities at the micro level. There is also a serious lack of discussion on how individuals and communities can participate in the shaping of these applications, thereby improving their lives and environments.

Current arguments claim that the transition to an information society opens a period of unlimited possibilities; a time of both opportunities and challenges. The development of the 'infostructure', it is argued will provide tools for social, as well as economic and technological innovation (Bangemann, 1995), and a resource for the creation of wealth and jobs. However, these arguments either ignore real life issues such as social exclusion, isolation and unemployment, or at best, only partially address important themes such as citizenship and participation in an information society. The development of the social economy (Corbett, 1994), where an empowered citizenship harness ICT to meet hither to unmet social needs, highlights some potential uses that can obviate social exclusion and isolation.

Discussion of the 'infostructure' is often confused with the broader issues involved in the information society debate, and the terms information superhighway and information society are now increasingly used interchangeably. This might partially explain why both focus on a techno-economic paradigm that neither fully reflects society's present structure, nor the wider needs of a future information society. According to Delors, human activities in the new information society are underpinned by ICT services (op. cit.). Longhorn (1994) suggests that the driving force behind the information society is the desire of governments world-wide to improve the use of ICT products and make the best possible use of the opportunities they create. The Federal Trust (1995) develops this theme further by suggesting the need for a policy framework which establishes both an industrial climate in which European IT and telecoms companies can vie on more or less equal terms with international competitors, and educates Europeans to use widespread applications of newer IT tools emerging in a broadband era.

An example of one of the applications currently being considered, by both the EC and UK government, as demonstrating citizens' access to information services, is the kiosk (CEC, 1995a). An interactive, multimedia system which can be used by people with no previous computer skills, as well as the computer literate. The kiosk is most likely to be situated in key public areas, use a touch-sensitive screen and offer 'what, when and where' type information (CEC, 1995b). The meaning of interactivity in this sense is somewhat limited, in that the person using the kiosk only makes choices as to which information s/he selects. In other words, the technology leads people only to information that the owner of the kiosk wishes them to see and does not permit dialogue. This is not to suggest that all such applications are entirely limited and will not benefit society. Indeed, to use the example of the kiosk once again, it is easy to see how such an application would benefit a citizen searching for the type of information they deliver. The limitations of the kiosk system is that it represents only one of a number of delivery channels and types, and there appears to be little in the way of participative alternatives being developed, however, there are signs of lateral thinking on the subject. According to a recent workshop on kiosks, design and development should consider workplace, schools and the home as potential access channels (CCTA, 1995a).

The interpretation of interactivity in the kiosk application does not support a participatory process, but offers a restricted choice of information and response. As a 'social' application, the mode of interactivity facilitated by the kiosk illustrates the techno-centric nature of the 'infostructure' and that the policies pursued by both the European Union and the UK government, are often similar in content, if not description, to those of the United States (IITF, 1993 & 1994). That is to say, somewhat limited in their approach to active and participative citizenship in an information society. As if to reinforce this point, an ISPO report defines the information society in terms of:

- Basic network (physical network + basic functions)
- Generic Services (e-mail, data base access, interactive video)
- Applications (telework, telemedicine, telebanking, etc.)

(CEC, 1995c).

Despite this techno-economic approach, the European Commission, makes a distinction between its view of the information society, and what it considers to be a concentration on the infrastructure in the form of information highways by the United States (CEC, 1995d). The Commission emphasizes that the European approach is more concerned with social and organisational changes that arise from ICT developments. To reinforce this concern for the social dimension, the Commission's Information Society Project Office (ISPO) identifies: health care; teleworking; traffic management; education; videoconferencing; consumer information and democracy as areas where telematics will improve the lives of EU citizens. ISPO claims its social awareness priority by stating the importance of a public acceptance of new technologies. It proposes that ICTs will give people more control over their lives rather than becoming slaves to technology. The danger is however, that policy makers may perceive citizen participation in technical terms of interactivity and focus on the technological aspects of 'infostructure' development.

The Commission reasons that the 'infostructure' is only a means to achieving the information society and asserts that the European Union is anxious to prevent the emergence of a two-tier society (CEC, 1995e). To this end, a group of 'experts', in the form of the Information Society Forum have been charged with assessing the social and cultural aspects of the information society (CEC, 1995f). A recent Forum theme paper recognized the risk of the emergence of "info-elitism" and the threat of reinforcing, or even creating new forms of social exclusion. It suggests open and easy access to information and the 'infostructure' as a solution to such problems but fails to define what this means (CEC, 1995g).

Social exclusion is not simply a rhetorical term used by people of social conscience. It is a harsh fact of life that spells hardship and suffering for the excluded. It is a term that can be used to describe many states of the human condition, ranging from the unemployed or the homeless to the disabled or the elderly. It can include single-parents; those on low-incomes; ethnic minorities; or members of other minority groups. However, the phrase social exclusion can equally be applied to those living in rural and peripheral communities also. To address social exclusion, policies need to tackle its root causes. To understand these causes, policy makers need to engage in dialogue with, and learn from, those that experience forms of exclusion.

Information Society: society or technology?

The interchangeability of the terms information society and the 'infostructure' has been referred to earlier but it is important to explain why focusing on technological, economic and information issues at the expense of people is an error. The following section deals with issues that identify the information society as the genus to the 'infostructure' species.

If the raison d'être of the 'infostructure' is economic competition, and the bulk of the information society policy debate follows the same thread, then there appears to be much in the conclusion that, while there has undoubtedly been an information explosion, it is premature to conceive of an information society (Webster, 1995). Webster argues that we should emphasize the 'informatisation' of established relations instead. That is to say that the techno-economic approach to the development of an 'infostructure' serves to reinforce the societal status quo and does little to address wider social issues such as social exclusion and isolation.

Lyon (1988) follows a similar line of reasoning and suggests an 'informatizing' society. He criticises Tofler's (1980) notion of a 'Third Wave' of evolutionary progress as 'sociological simplism'. He does not however, dismiss the idea of an information society, describing it instead as a problematic, or a field which presents problems for investigation. He suggests alternative approaches to socially appropriate development of IT. Making user need, for example, the driving force behind innovative development might be a departure from the present practice of commercial potential but Lyon reasons it highlights the extent to which technologically determinist views dominate the current policy debate and research focus on the information society.

If the concept of an information society is to ever be fully realized, then policy makers must recognize its people as participative citizens of that society. Citizens, who in a democracy have the right to choose, and a need to be confident that such a society will address their concerns. Herman (1995) reasons that to approach the information society as though the information component was of most importance is a mistake. He argues that there is no shortage of information but people do suffer from too much disease, too few resources, too little money and food, not enough time, and perhaps most importantly, too little control over the levers of power. The question is not whether the 'infobahn' allows citizens access to numerous archives of interesting information but does it enable them to address their social needs? Does it empower its citizenship and allow them to enrich their lives? Or is it simply a means to boost consumerism among one section of society whilst increasing social exclusion among another?

Recent research in the United States indicates that many of the most disadvantaged groups in terms of computer and modem penetration are the most enthusiastic users of on-line services that might enable 'economic uplift and empowerment' (NTIA, 1995). That is to say, low-income, minority, young and less educated citizens in rural and inner city areas, when given the opportunity, form the majority in on-line classes. The research not only shows a willingness on the part of the disadvantaged to learn and use the technology, it also highlights the problem of access for these social groups.

The NTIA report highlights the need to identify those in need and target support to them. Only then, the report continues, can all those who desire to access the 'infostructure' be accommodated. NTIA suggest libraries, schools and other 'community access centres' could provide a means of electronic access during the interim period when universal household connectivity is achieved. Ratan, in an exposé of the haves and have-nots on the information highway, suggests that many of the early approaches may be local and small scale but point the direction for the future (Ratan, 1995).

If the information society is to become a society in fact, then there is a need to address social issues at both micro and macro levels. The social view of the information society will still present opportunities for techno-economic activity but will do so by addressing the needs of all its citizens.

One of the main thrusts of the seminal Delors White Paper (op. cit.) (as it relates to the information society) is that it prioritises teleworking and telepartnership as a means of developing disadvantaged areas of Europe. Indeed, telework and telepartnerships are seen by some as a paradigm case for socio-economic development in all areas. However, as Day and Horner (1994) explain, it is important to note that thus far much of the debate lacks any substantial social analysis.

An extension of the teleworking concept is the notion of the telecottage (telecentre) (Gray *et al*, 1993, pp. 11-15). If, as both Delors and Bangemann (op. cit.) suggest, the policy of creating 'common information areas' will help regenerate rural/peripheral areas then issues other than connectivity must be addressed. It has been argued that creative partnerships between private, public and voluntary sectors can act as the driving force for development and regeneration (Landry and Bianchini, 1995, pp. 51-54). MacShane (1994, pp. 90-93) approaches this argument from a slightly different angle by suggesting a need to re-pluralise economic ownership and control. Applying this approach to the development and evolution of the 'infostructure' requires a more socially representative and receptive means of development than the current market forces paradigm.

The European Commission has attempted to move partially in this direction through its Community Financial Instruments. It recognizes that some projects will have a clear socio-economic benefit but may not be immediately commercially viable (CEC, 1995e). Whilst moving a little way in the suggested direction, implicit in the Commission's approach is that it still views ICT applications as the long term preserve of the private sector. In this respect the US might be ahead of the EU in its line of thought. At a PICT Policy Research Forum in 1994, Michael Nelson of the US Office of Science and Technology Policy, accepted that some not-for-profit services might need to be subsidised by tax dollars and ride on the network (Dutton *et al*, 1994, p.37).

Paradoxically, the Commission argues the primacy of the private sector in constructing the information infrastructure and providing applications, whilst requiring the public sector to support the private sector, through finance, regulation and legislation, in achieving this aim in less profitable areas. There is clearly a need for private investment, and the theory of partnership is valid but it must be meaningful. The partnership should involve not only the private and public sectors, but should also recognizes the dynamic contribution the not-for-profit sector has to make to society. Day and Horner (1995) promote this tripartite approach to collaboration in a paper focusing on social innovation in rural areas. Tripartite collaboration is defined as a partnership, based on equity, between public, private and not-for-profit sectors. It enables each sector to bring there own strengths, skills, expertise and knowledge to the partnership. Landry and Bianchini, (op. cit.) argue that the private sector is usually good at getting things done efficiently; the not-for-profit sector is good at articulating local views, communicating with users, and developing a sense of citizen ownership; whilst the public sector's key strength is in ensuring the broader public objectives of the partnership are achieved by maintaining a strategic overview. Tripartite collaboration facilitates flexible and fluid partnerships to meet the challenges of a changing socio-economic landscape. The participatory and collaborative nature of tripartite partnerships is both reflective of, and complimentary to, the potential networking nature of the modern 'infostructure'. By adopting the tripartite approach of partnership to the development of the 'infostructure' a more accurate representation of the needs of citizens in an evolving information society can be achieved, as the PACE94 report argued,

> "ICT cannot be expected to solve societal problems by themselves (only social solutions can do that) but to provide the platforms that are required for the efficient support of effective solutions."
>
> (CEC, 1994d)

Community Led Applications

The above discussion highlights the limitations of the current techno-economic focus of the 'infostructure' and argues that a social dimension is lacking from the current debates and policies relating to the information society. The following sections focus on applications rooted within their communities that have successfully harnessed social and cultural aspects through their evolution. Community networks and telecottages (telecentres) are used as exemplars of alternative models for information society development.

Community Networks

Community networks are known by many names (Beamish, 1995).[1] Regardless of their name, they always consist of a network of computers interconnected via a telecommunication link to form a distributed system which provides community information and a means for the community to communicate electronically.

As has already been suggested, the problem surrounding the current information society debate is that it focuses on the infrastructure, when the issues of prime importance are social in nature; such as equity and universal participation. How do social groups such as the poor, non-English speakers, the illiterate, the elderly and the disabled participate in the evolving information society? Can men and women participate equally in the development and uses of the 'infostructure'? How does society pull down barriers to access that inevitably lead to social exclusion in an information society? By focusing on the technology in terms of markets, profits and commodifying citizens as consumers, policy makers miss the broader implications of the social transformation taking place.

This then posses the question, what makes community networks different from other applications of the 'infostructure'? Beamish shows how, in terms of the technology used, there is very little difference. A resident of a neighbourhood, town or city dials into a central computer using a personal computer/telecoms link. A series of menus appear on screen and the user selects the information or communication system they wish to use. They can access information provided by local government; business; the not-for-profit sector, etc. They can participate in public discussion on local issues with others in their community or, they can communicate via e-mail with others in their community.

Community networks offer a variety of information and communication resources appropriate to their local community. Some are non-profit and free to users, others are non-profit but charge access fees and a few are run for profit. All operate on a low budget, relying heavily on private and public donations/grants, and volunteer labour. This is a key issue for community networks as Cisler (1995) explains, many of them are labours of love, drawing from the voluntary spirit of technical and non-technical citizens alike to contribute their time, effort and expertise in providing the information and maintaining the system. Beamish has classified four main types of Community Network:-

1. The term Free-Net is often used as a generic term for a community network but is actually a very specific type of network. Free-Nets are members of the National Public Telecomputing Network (NPTN), a non-profit corporation established in 1989 to disseminate software and methodology for establishing community networks. They follow NPTN policies and procedures and are consequently amongst the most organised and widespread of community network systems. Free-Nets, as suggested by their name, are free to the user, and seek to develop local information sources, these are then backed-up by national information feeds from NPTN. They have been characterised as attempting to make the information age available to as many people as possible (Grunder, 1993).
2. Neighbourhood Bulletin Boards on the other hand tend to be much smaller and focus on a specific neighbourhood rather than a city. They are often scaled-down versions of city networks and can be stand alone or a part of a larger city-wide network. They are usually established by an individual running the system from home, or run by a small group of community activists. Users often know each other personally and as a consequence tend to result in much face-to-face social interaction.
3. Government-Sponsored Networks are sponsored by state or local government and their primary purpose is to make city records and municipal information available to the local populace. Residents can access the system through read-only boards with information provided by city government; private e-mail between residents or between city hall and residents; or public conferences (mail-lists) on a wide range of topics. Problems exist in creating a system that people value and use. According to Beamish there has been some evidence of internal resistance by some departments and elected officials not wanting to be readily accessible to public.
4. Wired Cities (Dutton *et al*, 1987) are described in the literature in one of two ways. The first is a futuristic view of community in which a multiplicity of electronic communication services are available to households and businesses. The second focuses on experimental projects involving the provision of ICT services to households and businesses such as those found in the European Telecities project.

Community networks are based in a physical location and as such are unlike 'on-line communities' or 'virtual communities', which are groups of people congregating electronically to discuss specific issues but who are not bound by geographical boundaries. The commonality of interest to participants of community networks is their neighbourhood, town or city, rather than a discipline, or discussion topic on an electronic mailing list.

Beamish shows how community networks have the potential to benefit many groups. They offer residents of communities and local schools access to information and communication services. In line with G7 policy (CCTA, 1995b), all levels of government can provide citizens with information, and residents can communicate with elected officials quickly and cheaply. SMEs can gain access to information and communication services that are normally only available to large firms either because smaller, more localised companies/co-operatives cannot afford to buy the technology platforms necessary to get on-line; or employ an information worker who could add value to retrieved information, making the company more competitive in the process. Telecommunication providers can offer services to a much larger demographic group, and strategically can create future demand for commercial services by supporting community networks in training and educating people to use the technology. In terms of the social economy, community organisations use the networks to communicate with each other, develop collaborative policies and strategies to deal with community needs. The networks also facilitate direct communication between community organisations and their clients in the community, when personal contact is not imperative.

Each community network is unique in as much as it reflects the culture and identity of its own community, but they do tend to share three main areas of commonality. The most distinguishing characteristic is the focus on local issues. Beamish describes how the ethos of community networks emphasizes local culture, local relevance, local pride and community ownership. In addition to this, community networks provide fora for residents to discuss local issues. There is always a concern about representation, and community networkers make every effort to ensure that the network reflects and includes all members of the local community who wish to participate and not simply traditional ICT users. This means that community networks are frequently involved in placing equipment in publicly accessible places such as community centres and libraries. Initiatives such as these may well provide a future role for community telecottages/telecentres, and see a merging of the community network and telecottage movements, or at least a forging of closer links.

There is a strong belief within community networks that systems of communications and information can strengthen and vitalize existing communities. They are often seen by their organizers as tools for community organisation, in much the same way that traditional tools such as - printers, photocopiers, telephones, computers, community radio and television (Clement, 1981) have been in the past . Beamish asserts that community networks are used by local communities to find and build solutions to local problems. It is the nature and effectiveness of networks, together with an overwhelming belief in community action that gives the pioneers of civic networks so much faith in their potential. This faith is manifest in the three main goals common to most networks, that Beamish identifies in her research.

The first is a desire to strengthen a sense of community. Networks operate on the principal that increased communication and information increases a sense of community, and serves as a tool to solve some of the problems facing the community at grass-roots level. Utilisation of the networks by community volunteers enables them to make new contacts and, as a consequence, to form new coalitions with other groups and individuals for positive community action.

It is important to note that community networks are not substitutes for face-to-face contact but they do create electronic 'third places', providing an additional environment where people can get together, meet, talk and arrange face-to-face meetings. In this respect they encourage interaction within the community, both electronically and in the real world. However, the goal of creating places to talk and interact, which strengthens a sense of belonging and community, is often more difficult to achieve than getting local information on the network. This remains a major challenge for the networks to achieve.

The second goal is to improve democracy by empowering citizens to become more active and informed. Whilst public discussion of important issues clearly takes place on the networks, how this feeds into democratic participation and the process of government is less clear. Too often government participation is interpreted to mean providing city information such as bus time-tables and other local government information (Campbell, 1995). Whilst this is clearly a useful service to provide, in no way can it be described as dialogue, or the active participation of communities in the democratic process. Access to, or the active participation of government officials is rare on community networks. Participation in the information society must be about dialogue. To put it at its most basic in communication terms, it should mean the ability to send as well as receive signals. Interactivity should mean that everyone can be a broadcaster as well as receiver, or that they can talk back and be heard.

The main problem with 'Infostructure' policy direction is that people are viewed as passive consumers and interactivity is restricted to making choices from a pre-determined number of services on offer (Graham, 1994). A classic example of this is video-on-demand, where bandwidth capacity coming into a house is large enough to carry text, sound and images, yet bandwidth capacity going out is just large enough to select a video and send payment details. Universal access and interactivity, if they are to have any relevance, should mean the ability of citizens to participate in the shaping of applications to improve their lives and environments. This in turn must be based upon access to and dialogue with all levels of government.

The third and final goal is to ensure inclusion, that is to say that all those in the community who wish to, regardless of income, can participate in the evolving National Information Infrastructure (NII). The aims and objectives of most community networks set this as a priority, and for this reason the movement participates in placing equipment in public places. However, despite strongly encouraging people to join community networks Beamish claims that a broad-cross section of the community does not participate. It is not uncommon for library and information services to discover that they are actively providing a service to only part of their intended user population. Its crucial that community networks, if they are to reflect the make-up of their local community, need to adopt pro-active strategies to remedy this situation. They must find out who uses the network and what their needs are, to ensure continued use. They need to establish why others are not using the system, and devise strategies for correcting the problems. None of this is any different from what good and successful information services do already, and in this respect community networks can benefit from the experiences and knowledge built up by more traditional information networks.

Community networks are about people not technology! They possess the potential to enable people to learn how to live in an information society. Unlike other organisations, community networks are not struggling to come to terms with the information society, they have developed as a result of it. They are distributed forms of social organisation which provide a space for people to explore learning about life in an information society (Graham, 1995). They are principally about community development through the use of communications media, but as Avis (1995) explains they are also about education and democratic participation.

In his work on the social purposes of community networks, Graham (op. cit.) introduces an important cultural reason for such initiatives. The ability of CMC networks to transcend geographical boundaries has led to a globalizing of society. Based primarily on satellite and broadband, fibre optic technology, this global society is driven by a market-forces led rush to conquer the home-entertainment market, which often reduces broadcast output to its lowest common denominator. By saturating homes across the globe with the same programme content, broadcast companies maximise their profit margins but at what cost to local culture? This global 'Disneyfication' (Taylor, 1994) of cultural output has resulted in an erosion of cultural diversity (Gill, 1995). The threat of such a downgrading to an amorphous global cultural identity serves to highlight why preserving a sense of community has become increasingly important. If the richly diverse nature of communities at both micro and macro levels is to continue, then it is important to view culture as identity and not as a commodity.

Community networks present a global expression of local culture by reflecting and preserving local identity. Community networks help maintain this sense of identity and create grass-roots control by placing in juxtaposition, the local and global. In this way, geographically remote users of the 'infostructure' might learn of the local culture/history/identity of a specific community. This in turn can contribute to communication and dialogue between communities that might otherwise never come into contact. The facilitation of a process of social learning between communities presents a more positive image of globalization than does the present mechanistic reality of cultural erosion.

Today there exist conflicting perspectives about goals in the information society. Graham (op. cit.) poses the contrast of value as profit versus value of self identity in community, and universal access to technology versus universal participation in an information society. These then are the real issues to be discussed by policy makers when looking at the role of community networks in terms of developing the 'infostructure'.

It could be argued that community networks have a long way to go before they begin to address the ambitious goals they have set themselves. They are underfunded, use volunteer labour, face escalating demands from their users and often with donated or orphaned equipment. However, the fact that they satisfy a very real and deeply felt need for information, together with a way of communicating in and between neighbourhoods/cities, etc., indicates a future for them. Cisler (1993) argues that the information contained in the networks combined with the relationships that develop between participants, reinforce and add value to their communities. He likens them to an electronic greenbelt, or what Surman (1994) defines as an electronic commons, a concept similar to the important open spaces addressed later in the chapter.

Community networks generate and tap an incredible amount of energy and enthusiasm within communities. They show that people care about their communities and are looking for ways of participating in them more fully. As Beamish reasons, it is too early to decide whether these networks will succeed in their goals of creating a greater sense of community; increasing democratic debate; and ensuring access for all, who want it, to the NII. What is clear is that they are purposeful attempts by local people, against all the odds, to participate, and make a difference to their lives, their communities and society in general. Furthermore, they introduce a social dimension, together with a sense of community that has thus far been missing from an information society debate that still reflects the individualistic and consumerist nature of the 1980s.

Rural Planning and Development: The Importance of ICT

In an oft cited FAST Commission report, Cooley (1989) suggested that by the new millennium some 100,000 small towns and villages in peripheral and rural areas will cease to exist. This depopulation poses serious cultural, industrial, political and social problems, not only for the areas themselves but for the human and financial resources of urban areas affected by this phenomenon. Qvortrup (1994) contests that for rural communities to survive as indigenous societies, rural economies must be diversified. This is a development of an earlier theme where Qvortrup (1991) argues that rural areas are not simply places where people live, or increasingly where they do not live; they fulfil a vital function for society as a whole. They produce food, maintain an ecological balance, and provide much of our cultural identity. He suggests that the countryside must be preserved, not simply as agricultural production areas, or for recreational purposes but as areas with many business and cultural options based on the social structure of village communities with a variety of private and public services. The private sector alone cannot act as the driving force for this much needed regeneration. The current move toward deregulation and the liberalisation of ICT markets has resulted in the development of what Gibbs (1993) terms "urban areas of importance", often at the cost of the less commercially attractive rural and small town communities.

The Delors White Paper prioritises teleworking and telepartnership as a means of developing disadvantaged areas of Europe. Teleworking can be seen as the paradigm case of the combination of the application of ICTs, new forms of work organisation and economic development. New impetus has been given to the adoption of telework as employers seek to reduce overheads by adopting flexible working patterns (Wilson, 1991). It has recently been estimated that if the development of new organisational structures can de-centralise only 10% of new employment, then some of the problems of regional and rural economic development could be eased, whilst making a significant contribution to the de-congestion of major cities at the same time (Johnston, 1995). One such model for the regeneration of rural, peripheral and low-income communities is the telecottage.

Telecottages: A brief history

The telecottage (or Community Teleservice Centre), although Danish in origin, was first established in Sweden at Vemdalen in 1985 (Albrechsten, 1988). Its conceptual background was the Nordic working-life traditions of co-operation and fellowship built upon trade union traditions, corporate democracy and a belief that everyone in the workplace has the right to influence and shape the future (Berg and Lie, 1988). The prime function of Vemdalen's telecottage or Information and Community Service Centre (ICSC) as it was then known, was to train people from this rural area to exploit information using ICT and thereby enhance their lives economically, socially and culturally. It was a co-operative venture of local residents, government representatives (from various levels of governance), educators and the private sector. What began as an attempt to solve the problems of unemployment and depopulation, soon developed a dynamic focus concerned with growth and development, together with the enhancement of the quality of individual and community life alike (Inez and Sperr, 1988).

One of the interesting facets of the initiative was that it encouraged self-reliance by stimulating individual initiative. Individuals participated freely in the governing and management committees, this coupled with education and training programmes in the exploitation of information for business, citizenship and communication purposes helped nurture active participation in community affairs. As participation in training courses was voluntary, people developed at their own pace.

Telecottage initiatives developed swiftly and successfully throughout the Nordic countries for several years. As with the Vemdalen ICSC, these telecottage initiatives provided their communities with five basic services: information retrieval; consultancy services; distance working; training and education; and electronic village hall facilities (Qvortrup, 1987). Such initiatives were not confined to rural areas however. Many experiments of innovative Community Teleservice Centres have also taken place in urban areas (Storgaard, 1993).

However, a number of factors contributed to some initiatives struggling to survive or closing altogether: e.g. the temporary nature of pump priming finance (EC grants or national/local government funding); poor management; changes in the sympathetic charging policies of telecommunication providers (Jansen, 1994); and exaggerated claims regarding the demand for teleworking at that time. That said, it is useful to note that a significant number survived and still prosper today.

The determination of European policy makers to develop an inter-operable, inter-connective network of 'infostructures' which comply to an appropriate international regulatory and legal framework, combined with the Corfu Summit endorsement of the application priority areas proposed by the Bangemann group,[2] and the growing demand for greater access to information signifies a qualitative growth in demand for new and innovative models of socio-economic development. As a result many new telecottage initiatives, drawing on the lessons of the past, are adopting new approaches and foci.

The idea of a Telecottage

As with the related concept of telework, the literature reveals many definitions, which tend to vary according to contextual use. Indeed, often there is no consistency in the terms used to describe a telecottage by the people who run them. In the UK, for example they are also known as: Telecentre, Information Technology Centre,

Teleworking Centre, Business Centre and also Electronic Village Hall (Burt, 1995). In Scandinavian countries they are often described as Community Teleservice Centres (CTSCs).

Qvortrup claims that the success of CTSCs is due to the fact that they help overcome four barriers hampering access to teleservices in rural and low-income areas. The answer to the network barrier, where individual connections are not financially viable (e.g. a remote rural village) is to provide access in one place such as a CTSC with communal use of facilities. The service barrier is best overcome by providing not only telephone services, but computer and multimedia services such as distance training courses, oriented toward local needs. Communal access to IT equipment reduces the cost to individuals and overcomes the cost barrier which often precludes small farms, family-based enterprises and individuals from connectivity because the necessary equipment and services charges do not warrant the expense. Finally, the qualification barrier can be overcome by incorporating on-site training courses and advisory services within CTSC activities. Qvortrup explains that whilst not all these barriers can be overcome by teleservices *per se*, some are more likely to be met by the teleservices and support provided by CTSCs.

This is certainly true in the UK where, in some areas, the telecottage movement has had to face similar problems to the Scandinavian telecottage pioneers. With the help of the Telecottage Association (Denbigh, 1995), an organisation whose specific purpose is to advise initiatives by offering training and support, many UK telecottages are facing the challenges of the current economic climate by maximising the opportunities presented by the information society. One such initiative is the telecentre established by the Standon Parish Council in rural Hertfordshire. Standon Parish Electronic Centre's (SPEC) Business Plan describes the project as an attempt to establish a teleworking and business support centre that provides access to and training on networked IT (SPEC, 1994). SPEC's three main objectives are to meet the social, economic, and local decision making needs of residents, visitors, businesses, voluntary and statutory bodies by enabling them to share the use of public facilities for community development.

The holistic community-based approach of the SPEC telecentre, represents an example of the tripartite collaboration between public, private and not-for-profit sectors in partnership. Local people, clubs, societies and voluntary organisations are entitled to use the facilities for free; and the services at cost price. The self-employed, home workers and small businesses get access to the facilities and business services at a higher rate but this is still advantageous when compared to the cost of buying hardware and software platforms, and maintaining service charges. Concessions operate for the unemployed, students, school leavers using these services.

SPEC shows one way for the local business community to utilise the services available at the local telecentre. As has already been stated, many small businesses and self-employed people do not possess the appropriate IT platforms, or telecommunication links to allow them to exploit the wide range of commercial and economic information existing on-line. The advent of Electronic Data Interchange (EDI) has meant that much business today is conducted on-line and local companies that do not have access will lose out on business opportunities as a consequence, with a negative impact on the local economy and employment in the community. The Single European Market and transborder data flows mean that access to ICT can present local companies with greater opportunities to do business in an extended market place. For a charge, a telecottage can make the technology available when small businesses need it, and without prohibitive purchase and service costs. Because of their size, most small businesses cannot employ a skilled information worker with the knowledge and expertise to locate, access, retrieve and add-value to on-line business information. A telecottage is one way of sharing resources, thus making crucial information available. Such a dynamic approach can stimulate income generation and facilitate the support of other social services provided by the telecottage.

IT training and educational courses can be a significant generator of income, fulfilling both a need in the commercial sector, and a social need within the community at large. From a social perspective there is much to be gained from allowing otherwise excluded groups such as the elderly, the unwaged, and community groups, access to cheap, off-peak IT training and services. There are a number of successful initiative throughout the UK (Wright, 1995) and many in the USA and Canada that highlight the social benefits of such an approach (Beamish, 1995, Graham, 1995).

Electronic networks can be utilised as a tool for extending democracy and giving the local community access to local government at an additional level. SPEC has provided remote access facilities to local government service departments which enable communication with local government and provide local people with information from the authorities. An extension of this provision could be the use of e-mail to provide 24 hours a day virtual councillor's surgeries. Councillors, as elected members of local government, have a heavy demand on their time. Accessibility to constituents has proven difficult in the past. The surgery has been an attempt by some councillors to guarantee a time and a place where constituents could meet elected representatives and discuss issues of local concern. The problem has been that the usefulness of the surgery depends on constituents being able to attend the location, at a specified time. For those many local people unable to do so, councillors still remain inaccessible. The use of e-mail can circumvent such problems and improve representation by allowing local citizens access to elected representatives that might otherwise be denied due to domestic, work or social commitments. As well as improving contact with constituents, an extra advantage for elected representatives might be that whilst the public have 24 hour access to register needs, opinions, complaints, etc.; the councillor can respond at their own convenience. This means they can determine the use of their time more effectively, e.g. choosing when they spend quality time with their families and when they are available to constituents.

Telecentres could also be used as first-stop shops to council services and information. The political process can be improved by making council agenda, minutes and reports available. All non-confidential documents which have to be word-processed, could be made automatically available on-line.

One of the major impediments to the regeneration of rural areas is the lack of adequate teleservices. Qvortrup (1994) asserts that telecommunications give access to markets and decision makers, and are an essential condition for economic diversification. He argues that many rural communities have virtually no access to telephony and other teleservices, and that Community Teleservice Centres might be one way of bridging this gap. It is important to remember though that CTSCs are social as well economic initiatives. If they are to succeed, the criteria for support must be founded on more than short-term economic returns.

A recent research proposal sums up the required approach best by distinguishing between "development in a rural area" and "development of a rural area". The former is a reduced concept, defining a rural area as a place of development: i.e. markets; businesses and modernization, whilst the latter recognizes a rural area as a specific community that possess its own political and cultural identity; something more than an arena of ubiquitous trends (Storgaard, *et al*, 1993). By using this approach as a basis for establishing CTSCs as a model of rural regeneration, the participation of the local community in developing a successful initiative can be harnessed. Failure to adopt such an approach runs the risk of the local community viewing the teleservice centre as an external entity that just happens to be situated in their locality, but in which they play little or no part.

UK Models of the Telecottage

Telecottages tend to focus on five basic areas: information retrieval; consultancy services; teleworking; training and education; and electronic village hall facilities. They can best be described as giving local access to ICT by providing training and education; skills and expertise; information services and facilities for small businesses and community use. A recent seminar (ACRE, 1995) run by the Telecottage Association in association with Action with Communities in Rural England (ACRE) determined that there are three main categories of telecottage in the UK: commercial; community; and a hybrid.

The commercial telecottage focuses primarily on income generation. It is generally an entrepreneurial enterprise run as a small business, using private money or sponsorship to cover set-up and initial running costs. It can be argued that these initiatives fulfil a community as well as economic role and whilst this is often the case, the prime motivation is commercial gain or income generation. An example of this type of telecottage is the Boon Telecentre in West Dorset, which focuses on four key areas of work: Direct telecentre activities (word processing, faxing, copying and DTP, etc.); IT support service; hire of computer equipment to local users; and contracts and services for individual pieces of work. Boon is a non-profit making initiative whose business partners are a combination of the public and private sectors, but primarily public. It operates a successful model of disability employment programme, employing between ten and twenty-five people, so it clearly fulfils a social or community purpose. However, it is run as a business with a commercial ethos and does not believe that a mixture of commercial and community work well together.

The community telecottage on the other hand is often publicly owned/financed, or might take the form of a co-operative venture between the public (often local government) and the not-for-profit sectors. Here the prime motivation is the social and cultural benefit the centre brings to the local community. Economic considerations are, of course, a priority but it is generally a case of off-setting minimal losses against the societal benefits gained, or aiming to become self financing. Occasionally successful initiatives generate a small profit through sale of value-added services, expertise and training. Examples of community initiatives are the electronic village halls (EVH) found on the Manchester Host (Leach, 1992). These consist of education and training programmes for various sections of the community, e.g. women, the disabled and the unemployed, together with community resource provision.

Training courses in IT skills are often tailor made to fit the needs of individuals with a view to improving potential employability and developing business skills. Crèche facilities are provided in a 'drop-in' environment, where flexibility in terms of tuition and time is crucial. Affordability, a supportive, informal and non-threatening atmosphere are also important. Burt (1995) cites the example of the Manchester EVH which in 1992/93 had more than two hundred women attend its courses. Of this number, 44% are now employed, 32% went onto further training courses, and 14% now undertake voluntary work. Only 10% were either unemployed, or no information regarding their status could be found. This is clearly a sign of marked success and indicates the potential of the community telecentre.

As can be seen above, there is often some cross over between the commercial and community telecottage and this is sometimes taken to represent the hybrid initiative. However, to be successful, as the BOON Telecentre makes clear, both initiatives should have clearly defined mission statements, a business plan, and aims and objectives. For the purpose of this chapter, such a definition is excluded. The hybrid telecottage is taken to mean a collaborative venture between public, private and not-for-profit sectors, each bringing its own peculiar set of strengths, knowledge and experience to an innovative initiative. A partnership based on co-operation and collaboration and designed to regenerate the socio-economic quality of local community life.

The SPEC initiative was outlined earlier as an example of this hybrid or collaborative approach, another is the Highlands and Islands Project. This initiative seeks to strike a balance between community and commercial interests by adopting a culture of co-operation and collaboration within the network (Craig, 1992). The geographical remoteness of the area; its topographical ruggedness (mountain ranges and groups of islands); and sparse population all combine to create both service and goods provision problems. However, as a result of the Highlands & Islands Initiative the key telecommunications actors in the area (BT & the Highlands and Islands Development Board) were brought together in partnership to deliver an enhanced telecommunications infrastructure. The provision of the telecommunications infrastructure and the characteristics of the area have resulted in the community seeking to develop teletraining and distance-learning initiatives that take into account the risk of social isolation. This bringing together of the best parts of commercial and community enterprise suggests a way forward for future development and regeneration in rural and peripheral areas.

A Guaranteed Public Space

The commercially driven expansion of the 'infostructure' and the race to secure a competitive edge, whether at global, national, regional or local levels, poses a very real problem to the development and evolution of community networks and telecentres as models of socio-economic regeneration. In the techno-economic model of the information society, the provision of public spaces on the 'infostructure' is at best, considered only as an afterthought, and at worst, is not considered at all.

It has been argued that cyberspace should be treated as an extension of, rather than an alternative to, the space we live in (Shapiro, 1995). Shapiro presents two models of cyberspace: The first reflects life as it really is, so that once on-line, the citizen navigates a virtual world full of all the rich and diverse activities encountered when walking through any town in any country. In the second model, he describes a vision of a sanitized version of life. Everything is presented in clean boxes where even the graphical representations of people are clean cut, 'respectable' and stereotypical in appearance.

Using an interesting twist to the road metaphor, Shapiro argues that in the real world, pavements, street corners, parks, and the public square are all examples of vibrant public spaces where people come together to discuss issues and interact socially. He explains that in 1939, the Supreme Court of America declared all public spaces to be places for assembly, communicating thoughts between citizens, and discussing public questions. It is an unfortunate fact of life that this speech is now falling silent due to the growth of electronic media and the privatisation of former public spaces. Shapiro stresses the importance of establishing guaranteed public fora in cyberspace. Public spaces which encourage robust debate and act as a counter to dwindling number of spaces in our physical environment.

Continuing this theme, the organisation Computer Professionals for Social Responsibility (CPSR) fear that the NII may fail to provide what they describe as vital public spaces. They consider an erosion of public participation in both the political process and civic life, and suggest that the NII has the potential to reverse this trend by creating a framework for communication and community building (CPSR, 1995).

CPSR contest that if this potential is to be achieved, individuals and groups representing the community must be involved as an integral part of the NII design process. Provision of a full service to homes, workplaces and community centres is en essential element of this process. If the public is offered a restricted, second class service, CPSR reason that the NII will be unable to serve as a medium for individual and community empowerment. Freedom to communicate must be preserved in public spaces which should also act as a venue for communications with all levels of government agencies.

Klein (1995) posits that the Internet is an associative technology which by facilitating association, strengthens democracy. He argues that the process of uniting citizens through association fosters an awareness of the public interest, and of each citizen's role in public affairs. As individuals and community centres learn about the technology they will begin to apply it in their activities, and a broad array of creative uses can be expected to appear . Whilst only a part of the 'infostructure' debate, Klein's views of the Internet could well be applied to the development of the technological infrastructure as a whole.

Increasingly, the role of the public sector these days is seen as regulator and legislator, to ensure that private investment gets a return on its investment in the construction of the NII, its gateways and the services provided (CEC, 1994c). Commercial funding of the 'infostructure' must not be at the expense of guaranteed public spaces and universal participation. Added to the roles of regulator and legislator must then, be added the role of enabler. Indeed, it is the former two roles that will allow the latter to develop. Public policy makers can use legislation and regulation to enable the provision of guaranteed public spaces on the 'infostructure'. It is really a question of rights and responsibility. If the commercial sector has the right to profit from their investment in the 'infostructure', then inherent in that right should be the social responsibility to ensure equity and universal participation through the provision of public spaces.

The leader of the British Labour Party, Tony Blair described recently how the Labour Party has moved partially in this direction (Blair, 1995). He argued for the development of a NII in the UK , in collaboration with the major British Telecommunication provider, BT who are expected to guarantee an element of social connectivity. The argument is that in return for the right of unrestricted entry to the home entertainment market (BT are currently excluded from passing simultaneous entertainment programmes down the existing infrastructure until 2001 at least), BT must shoulder the responsibility of free connectivity for all schools, colleges, hospitals and libraries to the 'infostructure'.

ICT and Social Innovation: an emerging trend

Thus far the chapter has focused on the limitations of both the EC and the UK information policies by highlighting their techno-economic approach to the development of the 'infostructure' and the evolution of an information society. However, two major research programmes have indicated that broader societal issues need to be included in research projects for the new millennium.

The EC's Fourth Framework, Telematics Applications Programme has two aims. The first is to promote the competitiveness of European industry and the efficiency of services of public interest and to stimulate job creation through the development of new telematics systems and services in such areas as telework and teleservices. The second is to promote research activities necessary for other common policies (DGXIII, 1995). The programme's work sectors cover five main areas.[3] The aims of Sector 6, Telematics for Urban and Rural Areas, in Area C permit the establishment of new economic activities, the reinforcement of traditional activities and the improvement of living conditions in the interests of rural and urban areas with inadequate socio-economic and cultural infrastructure.

In the UK, the Economic and Social Research Council (ESRC) has recently announced its nine thematic priorities[4] which will direct its research and training portfolio for the next ten years. Priority 5, Human Communication and the Social Shaping of Technology aims to increase the understanding of how ICT are both shaped by human activities, and have an impact on society and the individual. Priority 9, Social Integration and Exclusion aims to address the causes and implications of divisions within society; and develop an understanding of the sources of social stability and the mechanisms whereby individuals are integrated into society (ESRC, 1995).

It is clear from these programmes that broader societal issues are about to reappear on the policy makers agenda. As the results from such major research projects begin to filter through, so policy makers will develop policy based upon the symbiotic relationship between people, technology and the economy, rather than current techno-economic approach. However, in many respects, research programmes such as the EC's Telematics Applications Programme and the UK's new ESRC Programme are merely reflecting what is already happening within society in general.

The Social Economy

A factor behind the shaping of new socio-economic relationships has been the development of tripartite social partnerships between public, private and not-for-profit sectors. The collaborative and co-operative nature of this new approach is seen as providing a catalyst for the socio-economic regeneration of local communities. Initiatives such as those being developed in the Telecities project (European Telematics Partnership, 1995) are testament to the practical and positive results of such a tripartite coalition. It is not often recognised that a rich and diverse source of social creativity exists in local communities. These newly formed social partnerships posses an endemic potential capable of unlocking untapped sources of local creativity, enabling them to thrive and flourish in myriad forms of social innovation.

By providing the expertise, resources and support for the social creative processes of local communities, a bridge can be built between the formal institutions and the informal networks that characterise the everyday life of local communities. It is the process of social partnership which harnesses the knowledge and creativity of the informal local community with the professional skills and expertise of the formal agencies that facilitates social innovation. Social innovation is defined in this context as social initiatives designed and driven by local people to solve the problems and meet the needs of the local community, which in turn can create new forms of social employment. The processes and activities resulting as a result of social partnership and social innovation are quite distinct from the more structured approach found in the formal economy and are best described as components of the social economy.

In a social economy, community life is based on the principles of participation and self-empowerment. That is to say that individuals have the right to self-actualisation (Maslow, 1943) whilst at the same time having social responsibilities to the rest of the community (Etzioni, 1993). It is the ability of the individual to participate in a full, active and democratic manner in the information society; designing and developing social applications, and thereby addressing the issue of social exclusion that transcends the passive participation of the current techno-economic paradigm.

Social Innovation in the UK

In the UK much of the innovative work relating to the development of the information infrastructure is oriented toward software applications and as such is influenced by economic criteria. There are however a growing number of social applications developing. Local community and regional socio-economic initiatives concerned with socially innovative uses of the information infrastructure are growing in prominence throughout the UK. These include: the Manchester Women's Electronic Village Hall (EVH); the Disabled People's EVH in Dewsbury; Community Organisations in Batley; and a Body positive HIV/AIDS information network. Many of these initiatives are sited on Poptel, an electronic network for the not-for-profit sector, developed by Soft Solution which is a workers co-operative committed to the growth of popular telematics.

The Manchester Women's Electronic Village Hall provides skills and confidence for women returning to work by training in areas such as networking and computing (WEVH, 1994). The Disabled People's Electronic Village Hall (DP-EVH) in Dewsbury runs IT training courses for disabled people (Director, 1994). It also provides access to a full range of Host services, and is concerned with the disabled user input into the design of user-interfaces and software applications. The DP-EVH provides group-based telework option as an alternative to the isolation of low value-added, home-based computer work for disabled people. It also acts as a meeting place for social interaction, the exchange of ideas, and a source of information and innovation. Through the work at Dewsbury a network has been created to provide services for, and campaign on behalf of members of the various disability forums and organisations that make up the network.

Chorlton EVH works with the Worker's Educational Association (WEA) and Manchester TEC (Training and Enterprise Council) to provide training and IT based education for unemployed and unwaged adults (Robinson, 1994). The Chorlton EVH used telematics to establish the LETS (Local Exchange Trade System) online directory. The Greater Manchester Bangladeshi Association (GMBA) EVH has developed a range of courses in IT and telematics applications (MTP, 1994, p.21). It has a high take-up rate for its training amongst ethnic minority communities throughout the city. The Association EVH also runs specialised training for small businesses. Batley community organisations have developed a widespread telematics 'community' of voluntary and community-based organisations and groups (Gasse, 1994). The 'community' uses networked information services to make their organisations more effective in meeting local social needs. Several produce online newsletters and have established bulletin boards to promote their activities. The Body positive HIV/AIDS information network is a self-help group run by and for people with HIV related diseases (MTP, 1994, p.26). The centre uses telematics to develop the more effective networking of HIV/AIDS information.

The Citizen's Advice Bureaux (CABx) network links all Manchester's CABx to distribute welfare rights information (East, 1994). They have their own bulletin board which contains brief updates on law as well as other items that might be of interest. The network is used to ensure that people in local communities do not suffer as a result of ignorance of their rights and responsibilities; and equally; to influence the development of social policies both locally and nationally.

ICTs and the Trade Unions

The Labour Telematics Centre supports the development of information services for the trades union movement. A number of unions are now developing electronic news services which distribute news to members, affiliates, other union members and broader labour movement. Most use Bulletin Boards - electronic notice boards containing news of interest. Instantly available, they can be browsed and read by union members using the service world-wide. Many unions are constructing mailing lists for affiliates and fraternal organisations using e-mail, fax, and telex, all of which has had a major impact on the speed and ease of dispatching urgent news. Telematics can be a powerful tool for organisation and co-ordination of solidarity actions. Requests for assistance can be received, internationally distributed and responded to via computer.

Collective Bargaining

The break up of national bargaining; the introduction of market mechanisms; and competition in public services has had the affect of curbing the activity of many trade unions. Compulsory Competitive Tendering (CCT) in NHS and local government has taken large numbers of workers out of national agreements, resulting in local level bargaining. The public service union UNISON has responded by drawing up plans for computer-based bargaining support system (Opie, 1994). The aim is to develop services for negotiators at all levels of the union, providing a similar level of support enjoyed by national negotiators. Regional and head office staff are given access to an unprecedented quality of data about the state of collective bargaining across public services. UNISON are introducing an integrated database and communication systems linking branches, regions and head office. The information includes details of the labour market; private and public pay and conditions; CCT; as well as instantaneous updates on negotiations, management tactics and union successes. UNISON is determined to ensure that union negotiators have access to better information than employers. In the future unions will no longer have to accept management's arguments because of a lack of information.

Trends of Social Innovation in the UK

The current trends of social innovation in the UK can be summarised as:

- Social and Community Networks: based on the traditional networking of the not-for profit sector (i.e. voluntary, community and cultural groups) and local communities in general.
- Social Economy: collaboration between local authorities, community network organisations (e.g. community groups, voluntary organisations) and local industry for social and economic regeneration.
- Cultural Enterprise: social innovation models and practices rooted in the ethnic cultural traditions of family and social networking
- ICTs and Social and Economic Regeneration: Collaboration between local councils, local industries and social actors for employment and training schemes
- Telecottages for both urban and rural development, new forms of working and community development.

Examples of more top-down initiatives can be summarised as:

- Enterprise Schemes: sponsored by the central government and regional enterprise boards, linked to regional and local industries
- City Regeneration Schemes: linked to local industries, local universities and training sectors
- Cultural Industries: linked to local heritage and tourist industries, local councils, and the service sector

Summary: A Scenario for Research

Both Delors and Bangemann (op. cit.) view telework and telepartnership as a paradigm case for developing disadvantaged areas of Europe. Current policy debate as it relates to the use of ICT as tools of development misses two crucial perspectives. The first is what Storgaard *et al* (op. cit.) define as the difference between "development in" and "development of" rural, or in this case, all disadvantaged areas. The second is any clear evaluation of the profound role of technology in altering the texture of daily life (Sclove, 1995, p. 5). The former has already been discussed in respect of telecottages. The latter forms the locus of this section.

Johnston's observation (op. cit.), that the development of new organisational structures associated with telework could lead to the decentralisation of 10% of new employment to rural areas, forms the cornerstone of the European Commission's policies for rural and peripheral development and regeneration. In an attempt to counter the depopulation of rural areas described by Cooley (op. cit.), the European Commission have, in effect, developed a model of organisational decentralisation from urban to rural areas. If such policies for the use of telematics are to be successful, it is crucial that an evaluation of the role of these technologies in altering the texture of daily life is undertaken. It is important to emphasize that the impacts are to be found at many points of this model and not simply in the rural areas. That is to say that if traditionally structured organisations are adopting policies of decentralisation as they adopt new technologies and work practices, then the logical starting point for such evaluations is here.

A strong relationship has developed between telework and flexible work patterns. As organisations seek to reduce overheads, so flexible working and telework hold more appeal to them. This relationship has implications for manager and employee alike, yet much of the current research and associated literature focuses on the manager's perspective to telework (Burch, 1991; Stanworth and Stanworth, 1991; Huws, 1993; NCC, 1993). Organisations consist of more than the community of management. Indeed, they are compound structures made up of different communities with complex social relationships. Qvortrup (1993) links telework to organisational flexibility and right-sizing, a euphemism for organisations making people redundant. As organisations seek greater flexibility through continued organisational restructuring, the impact of these processes on employees, their families, and the communities within which they work and live must be considered. Furthermore, how these communities can participate in, and influence these processes also requires consideration.

Whilst to date, the majority of telework initiatives have tended to concentrate on the high skill, high reward employment sector, this might prove to be a temporary phenomenon. As organisations seek still greater flexibility, and software applications facilitate the deconstruction of formerly skilled jobs, attention might focus on the lower skill, lower reward end of the labour market. An example of an area where this is already happening is that of telesales. The classified sections of newspapers in the UK, are full of job advertisements for people to work using cold teleselling techniques for very small remuneration as piece-rate labour.

The patchwork nature of these initiatives in organisational terms has been met by a similarly uncoordinated response to telework by the trades unions. This piecemeal response is best classified in three broad categories: receptive, defensive and oppositional (Horner and Day, 1995). Receptive unions, tend to be more closely involved with the telecommunications industry and have embraced telework and its potential for increased flexibility of work for their members (NCU, 1992). Defensive unions have adopted a sceptical but technological determinist approach in that they accept that ICT development will continue, and that the pressure for applications such as telework will increase but view these developments against a historical background of the exploitation of homeworkers (Walsh, 1993). Oppositional unions have adopted policies opposing telework in principle as being fundamentally against the interests of members and union alike. However, many of these unions are now adopting a more defensive approach, in order to develop policies that recognize the existence of telecommunities, reflect the changing nature of the workplace, and remain relevant to the needs of their membership (BIFU, 1993).

The study of organisational flexibility forms part of an ongoing research project which focuses on the impact of ICT usage within, and between members of, newly founded telecommunities (Day, 1994). The project uses the European Commission's model of organisational decentralisation from urban to rural/peripheral areas. A comparison of Scandinavian and UK telecottage initiatives will compare and contrast their effectiveness as models of socio-economic development within an information society, and generate knowledge about the social and economic processes that shape their development. The aim is to establish the necessary conditions for sustaining linkages between formal and social economies. A result of this should be the development of a model of socio-economic development that eradicates the problem of social exclusion in rural/peripheral communities by establishing as a right, the opportunity for citizens to participate within an information society. To this end the project contributes to the development of a community network in the Brighton and Hove area of East Sussex. The Community Internet Project is an attempt to make the area a testbed for ways that computer mediated communication systems and local people can interact for the benefit of the local community at large. Whilst experimental in nature, the ultimate goal is long-term sustainability within and by the community itself (CIP, 1995).

The aim of the project is to study the experiences and needs of the subject communities in an open and flexible manner. Another aim is to gain an insight into the nature of tripartite collaboration, universal participation, and the social economy. The threads of these stages are brought together in a research project (Fig 1).

Tripartite collaboration is a major directional shift from the concept of partnership between public and private sectors in development initiatives. Such collaboration forms the basis for a number of existing policy documents, e.g. Delors, Bangemann and IITF (op. cit.). The central thread running through each of these policy documents is that of roles. Current policy has established that the role of the private sector (driven by market forces) is to finance the construction of the information superhighway, and get a return on its investment by offering access and services, with the golden nugget being the home-entertainment market. At the same time the main role of the public sector is seen as that of enabler.

Focus	Objective	Outcome
EC model of organisational decentralisation	Study impact of telematic applications in workplace	Critique of representation for telecommunities models
Community Telecottages	Study socio-economic impact	Analysis of socio-economic development model
Community Networks	Study universal access and participation	Develop models of social innovation and universal participation

Fig. 1: Research Project Stages

That is to say that the public sector enables the private sector to invest in the development of the 'infostructure' through sympathetic legislation and regulation, thereby stimulating economic activity through the private provision of services such as video-on-demand, telebanking and home-shopping. This form of partnership is rooted firmly in the formal economy with its attendant rules of investment, profit and obligations to shareholders.

Tripartite collaboration, on the other hand, recognizes the existence of a social economy (ARIES, 1995), where the not-for-profit sector operates with people in a dynamic and flexible manner. Co-operatives, mutuals, associations, foundations, voluntary organisations and community groups are all parts of the social economy and all make a significant contribution to society in general, through the daily lives of its citizens. Tripartite collaboration is about linking together both formal and social economies in a partnership of equity. Its about recognizing that there is more to life in a society, in this case an information society, than simple economic activity and seeks to give a more holistic approach to development policies by linking social activity with economic.

Tripartite collaboration and the social economies are issues of participation, and this is the third thread which runs throughout the study. It is clear from the ISPO group of experts (op. cit.), that very real dangers exist that will result in a society of information 'haves' and 'have nots'. A crucial element in avoiding this form of social exclusion is by developing policies that facilitate universal access to the 'infostructure'. However, if the 'infostructure' develops on a purely commercial basis and the only services available are those regulated and priced by the service providers, access to the 'infostructure' would be meaningless. Universal participation allows everyone, who wishes to, to participate in the evolution of the information society. The creation of such a democratic ethos can serve only to enrich and empower the lives of citizens in an information society.

Conclusion

This chapter highlights the limitations of current 'infostructure' and information society policies. The hypothesis is that EC and UK models of information society development do not address the wider aspects of social and cultural community evolution, concentrating instead on technological and economic issues. Graham (op. cit.) asserts that the transition to an information society is about social change not technology and that the problem with current policies is that in the name of economic necessity, the practice of citizenship is being translated into the art of shopping on the 'infostructure'.

Social and economic cohesion at micro, as well as macro levels is essential, if as ISPO require, people are to be convinced that new technologies will lead to self-empowerment.

An OECD strategy document for technology in the nineties recognized that market forces alone were insufficient for contemporary socio-economic development. It called for public policy to have as an objective the "active society" in which all members are equipped for, and can perceive themselves and be perceived as, making a useful contribution to socio-economic life (OECD, 1988). Achieving such a target requires a fundamental shift at both research and policy levels. The discussion emphasizes the need to transform the technologically determinist approach inherent in our society to one based on citizens shaping both the evolving 'infostructure' and the information society in general. There is a pressing need for a political sociology of the 'infostructure', but as Lyon posits,

> "Social analysis must remain in, but not of, the information society,"
> (Lyon, 1988, p.158).

The experience of the community network and telecottage movements suggests an alternative route to the development of 'infostructure' and information society which balances economic imperatives with social needs. Community networks and community telecentres are electronic public spaces where ordinary people can meet and converse about common concerns. They are like the parks, pavements and public squares in the real world that Shapiro cites in his first model of cyberspace. Reflecting the diverse and unique nature of their communities, they focus on community development, education and training, and democratic participation. They can, however, also be used to stimulate local economies by providing employment, improving employbility, and facilitating the access of SMEs and the self-employed to on-line business information. By representing community life in this holistic manner, that is to say, as a social experience and not simply as economic and technological processes; community networks and telecentres will emerge as important public spaces on the 'infostructure' where creative, social and economic uses for the technology will emerge.

References

ACRE. *Community Telecottages Seminar,* [Notes from Plenary Sessions]. Cirencester: ACRE. July 6, 1995.

Albrechsten, H. Telecottages in the Nordic Countries, *Information, Knowledge, Evolution:- Proceedings of 44th FID Congress*, Helsinki, FID, 1988.

ARIES, 1995. *The Social Economy.* http://www.poptel.org.uk/aries/socecon.html

Avis, A. *Public Spaces on the Information Highway: The Role of Community Networks,* Calgary: Unpublished Master of Arts Thesis, 1995.
http://www.calgary.ca/~aavis/thesis/thesis.html

Bangemann, M. *Policies for a European Information Society,* [A summary of a speech given at the 1995 Charles Read Lecture on June 20]. PICT, Uxbridge, Middlesex, 1995.

Beamish, A. Communities On-Line: Community-Based Computer Networks. Unpublished Masters in City Planning Thesis, MIT, 1995.
http://alberti.mit.edu/arch/4.207/anneb/thesis/toc.html

Berg, A.-J. & Lie, M. Fjernarbete i Norden. En studie av telematikk og social planlegging (Distance work in the Nordic countries. A study of telematics and social planning) *In* Berg, A.-J. & Lie, M. et al (eds) *Distancearbete i Norden (Distance work in the Nordic Countries).* NordRefo, Helsinki, 1988, pp. 7-58.

BIFU, 1993. *Homeworking: potential applications and possible consequences for BIFU.* London: BIFU, rev. ed. October 1993.
Blair, T. *Speech to National Conference of the Labour Party,* 1995.
http://www.labour.org.uk/speeches/blaireng.htm
Burch, S. *Teleworking - A Strategic Guide for Management.* Kogan Page, London, 1991.
Burt, L. *British and Irish Telecottages - A new phenomenon.* Unpublished Dissertation, University of Edinburgh, 1995.
Campbell, A. Speech made during a debate on Broadband Communications in the House of Commons on the 15th March, 1995.
http://www.worldserver.pipex.com/anne.campbell/house/debate/index.html
CCTA. *Information Superhighways: The First Mile,* Proceedings of CCTA Conference held at QEII Conference Centre, Westminster. July 14, 1995a.
CCTA, *G7 Government On-Line Project,* 1995b.
http://www.open.gov.uk/govoline/golintro.htm
CEC. *Growth, Competitiveness, Employment: The Challenges and Ways Forward into the 21st Century - White Paper,* Luxembourg: Office for Official Publications of the European Communities, 107-115, 1994a.
http://www.ispo.cec.be/infosoc/backg/whitpaper/ch5a_1.html
CEC, *Europe and the global information society: Recommendations to the European Council.* CD-84-94-290-EN. 1994b.
http://www.ispo.cec.be./infosoc/backg/bangeman.html
CEC. *Europe's way to the information society: an action plan,* Brussels: CEC COM(94) 347 final, 19/7/94. 1994c.
http://www.ispo.cec.be/infosoc/backg/action.html
CEC. *Perspectives for economic and social impacts of advanced communications in Europe (PACE 1994): Socio-economic and technology impact assessment and forecast RACE project R-2086 - Synthesis report,* Luxembourg: Office for Official Publications of the European Communities, p10. 1994d.
CEC, 1995a. *Towards the Information Society, Communication from the Commission to the Council, the European Parliament, the Economic and Social Committee and the Committee of the regions on a Methodology for the implementation of information society applications,* Brussels: CEC COM (95) 224, 31/5/95.
http://www.ispo.cec.be/infosoc/legreg/xiii53en.html
CEC, 1995b. *Cap '95 - Luxembourg: European City of Culture 1995,* Luxembourg: Impact. http://www.echo.lu/impact/projects/imm/en/cap.html
CEC, 1995c. *The European Information Society in Action,*
http://www.ispo.cec.be/infosoc/backg/action95.html
CEC, 1995d. *Introduction to the Information Society the European Way,* http://www.ispo.cec.be/infosoc/backg/brochure.html
CEC, 1995e. *The European Information Society in Action,*
http://www.ispo.cec.be/infosoc/backg/action95.html
CEC, 1995f. *Statement: Towards the Information Society,*
http://www.ispo.cec.be/infosoc/backg/statemnt.html
CEC, 1995g. *Information Society Forum Theme Paper,*
http://www.ispo.cec.be/infoforum/pub/themepap.html
CIP, 1995. *Community Internet Project Mission Statement.* e-mail: p.day@bton.ac.uk
Cisler, S. *Community Computer Networks: Building Electronic Greenbelts.* 1993.
http://www.nic-bnc.ca/documents/infopol/community_networks/cisler01.txt
Cisler, S. Can We Keep Community Networks Running? *Computer-Mediated Communications Magazine,* 1995, 2 (1), p. 6.
http://www.nic-bnc/documents/infopol/community_networks/cisler01.htm
Clement, A. Community Computing, *The Journal of Community Communications,* 4, (3) Winter, 1981-82, pp. 10-15.
Cooley, M. *European Competitiveness in the 21st Century: Integration of Work, Culture and Technology,* Brussels: CEC/FAST, 1989.
Corbett, M. Online with ARIES. *ON~Line news,* **4** August/Winter, 1994, p. 13.

CPSR, *Serving the Community: A Public-Interest Vision of the National Information Infrastructure.* 1995. listserv-owner@sunnyside.com, Archive CPSR, file nii_policy.
Craig, C. The Highlands and Islands Experience. *In* Denbigh, A. ed.*Telecottages - the UK Experience: Report of the 1992 seminar*, 1992. ACRE, Cirencester, Glos., pp. 25-29.
Day, P. *Information Policy and the use of ICTs in the socio-economic regeneration of small town and rural communities.* PhD Proposal, Department of Library & Information Studies, University of Brighton, 1994. e-mail: p.day@bton.ac.uk.
Day, P. And Horner, D. Convivial Teleworking for Social and Economic Development, *In* Proceedings *Home-oriented informatics, telematics and automation conference (HOIT94).* Oikos, Copenhagen, 1994, pp.137-143.
Day, P. And Horner, D. Policies for the Information Society: Social Innovation and Rural Communities, *In* Proceedings *Technological Innovation and Global Challenges: IAMOT European Conference on Management of Technology,* Birmingham: Aston University (IAMOT), 1995, pp. 408-415.
Denbigh, A. TCA advises MPs on teleworking policy. *Teleworker,* 1995; 2 (4), p. 2.
DGXIII, 1995. *Telematics Applications Programme (1994-1988),*
http://www.rare.nl/telematics/WorkProgramme/WorkProgramme.html
Director, I. Disabled People and Telematics. *On~Line news,* 1994; 3: 25-26.
Dutton, W. et al (eds). *Wired Cities: Shaping the future of communication.* Communication Library, Washington, 1987.
Dutton, W. et al. *The Information Superhighway: Britain's Respones ~ A Forum Discussion,* Policy Research Paper N0. 29. PICT,ESRC, Uxbridge, Middlesex: 1994.
East, J. Princess launches new CAB Database. *On~Line news,* 1994; 3: 4-5.
ESRC. Thematic priorities: strategic vision for the new millenium, *Social Sciences,* Issue 29, November 1995, p.4.
Etzioni, A. *The Spirit of Community.* Harper Collins, London, 1993.
European Telematics Partnership, 1995. *Telecities,* [Information Pack]. e-mail: telecities@mcr1.poptel.org.uk
Federal Trust. *Network Europe and the Information Society.* Federal Trust, London, 1995.
Gasse, I. Outreach in Action. *On~Line news,* 1994; 4: 10.
Gibbs, D. Telematics and urban economic development policies: Time for caution?. *Telecommunications Policy,* May/June 1993; 250-256.
Gill, K. S. *Information Society and Co-development: designing cultural interfacing for knowledge networking,* [Paper presented to an International Workshop on Human Centred Systems ~ "Revival of Humanity in the Information Society" in Tokyo, Japan, 1995. 30/1/95] e-mail: k.s.gill@brighton.ac.uk
Graham, G. Free-Nets and the Politics of Community in Electronic Networks. *Government Information in Canada,* Electronic Journal, 1994, **1** (1). http://www.nic-bnc.ca/documents/infopol/community_networks/graham01.txt
Graham, G. *A Domain Where Thought is Free to Roam: The Social Purpose of Community Networks,* Carleton: Telecommunities Canada, 1995.
http://www.ncf.carleton.ca/freenet/rootdir/menus/freenet/conference2/crtc.txt
Gray, M. et al. *Teleworking Explained.* John Wiley & Sons, Chichester,1993; 11-15.
Grunder, T. [personal communication] *In* Cisler, S. 1993. *Community Computer Networks: Building Electronic Greenbelts,* 1993.
http://www.nic-bnc.ca/documents/infopol/community_networks/cisler01.txt
Herman, G. An Info Society is also a Society, *Network Policy Briefing,* May 1995, pp. 1-3.
Horner, D. And Day, P. Labour and the information society: trades union policies for teleworking. *Journal of Information Science,* 1995; 21: 5: 333 - 341.
Huws, U. *Teleworking in Britain,* Research Series No. 18, Sheffield: Employment Department, 1993.
IITF, *National Information Infrastructure: Agenda for Action,* Washington DC: National Telecommunications and Information Administraction, 1993.

http://ntiaunix1.ntia.doc.gov:70/0/papers/documents/nii_agenda_for_action.txt
IITF, 1994. *Putting the Information Infrastructure to Work: Report of the Information Infrastructure Task Force Committee on Applications and Technology,* Washington DC: US Government Printing Office - NIST Special Publication 857.
Inez, L. And Sperr, B. Conceptual Framework of the Telecottage Approach to Community Development, *Information, Knowledge, Evolution:- Proceedings of 44th FID Congress,* FID: Helsinki, 1988.
Jansen, A. Information Economy and Rural Development, *In* Proceedings *New visions of the post-industrial society Conference* , Brighton: University of Brighton, 1994.
Johnston, P. *Working on the Infobahn - a European View: Telework development in context of the White paper on Growth, Competitiveness and Employment,* DGXIII-B, CEC: Brussels, 1995.
Klein, H.K. Grassroots Democracy and the Internet: The Telecommunications Policy Roundtable of the Northeast (TPR-NE), *In* Proceedings *INET'95: The 1995 Annual meeting of the Internet Society, Honolulu, Hawaii.* Available URL, 1995.
http://www.isoc.org/HMP/PAPER/164/abst.html
Landry, C. And Bianchini, F. *The Creative City,* London: DEMOS, pp. 51-54.
Leach, B. 1992. The Electronic Village Hall in an Urban Setting, *In* Denbigh, A. ed.*Telecottages - the UK Experience: Report of the 1992 seminar,* Cirencester, Glos: ACRE, 1995; pp. 25-29.
Longhorn, R. The information society: Compaisons in the trio of Europe, North America and Japan, *I&T Magazine,* Winter 1994-5, pp. 5-9.
Lyon, D. *The Information Society: Issues and Illusions,* Cambridge: Polity Press, 1988.
Macshane, D. Living the Issue of Industrial Democracy, *In* Conference Report *Rethinking Worker Democracy: Reclaiming the Rights of Working People,* London: CAITS, 1994, pp. 90-93.
Maslow, A. H. A Theory of Human Motivation, *Psychological Review,* 1943; 50: 370-396.
MTP, 1994. *Manchester: the Information City,* Manchester: MTP.
NCC, 1993. *Integrating Teleworking into the Organisation,* Manchester: NCC.
NCU, 1992. *Teleworking,* Unpublished report RD92/006/2. National Communications Union Research Department, June 1992.
NTIA, 1995. *Falling Through the Net: A Survey of the " Have Nots" in Rural and Urban America,* Washington: NTIA. http://www.ntia.doc.gov/ntiahome/fallingthru.html
OECD, 1988. *New Technologies in the 1990s: A Socio-economic Strategy,* OECD: Paris.
Opie, K. Collective Bargaining by E-mail, *On~Line news,* 1994; 3: 21.
Qvortrup, L. Information and Community Service Centres in Scandinavia: A General Overview, *In* Qvortrup, L. et al (eds) *Social Experiments with Information Technology and the Challenges of Innovation - A Report from the FAST-Programme of the Commission of the European Communities,* Dordrecht: D. Reidel Publishing Company, 1987, pp. 85-92.
Qvortrup, L. Community Teleservice Centres and the Future of Rural Society. *Community Development Journal,* 1991; 26: 2: 124-130.
Qvortrup, L. *Flexiwork and Telework Centres in the Nordic Countries: Trends and Perspectives,* Paper presented at the ECTF International seminar "Flexiwork Policy in the European and Nordic Labour Markets", Helsinki, May 18-19, 1993.
http://www.icbl.hw.ac.uk:80/telep/telework/ttrfolder/typpfolder/ftnc.html
Qvortrup, L. *Community Teleservice Centres: A means to social, cultural and economic development of rural communities and low-income urban settlements,* A document for the World Telecommunication Development Conference (WTDC) on the impact of Community Teleservice Centres (CTSCs) on rural development. Odense: Odense University, 1994.
Ratan, S. A New Divide Between Haves and Have-nots?, *TIME Domestic,* SPECIAL ISSUE, Spring 1995; 145:12.

http://www.pathfinder.com/@@3P@tumH%swEAQII4/time/magazine/domestic/1995/special/special.society.html
Robinson, A. A Round-up from Chorlton. *On~Line news,* 1994; 4: 6.
Sclove, R. E. *Democracy and Technology,* London: Guilford Press, 1995, p. 5.
Shapiro, A.L. Street Corners in Cyberspace, *The Nation,* July 3rd, 1995, pp. 10-14.
SPEC, 1994. *SPEC Business Plan 1994-1995,* Ware, Hertfordshire: Standon Parish Council.
Stanworth, J. And Stanworth, C. *Telework - The Human Resource Implications,* London: IPM, 1991.
Storgaard, K. Telework, the Local Community and Ways of Life. Scandinavian Housing and Planning Research, 1993, 10, pp. 21-35.
Stogaard, K. et al. *Social Shaping of Telematics and Rural Development,* Proposal to the COST-Committee. Copenhagen, 1993.
Surman, M. *From VTR to Cyberspace: Jefferson, Gramsci & the Electronic Commons,* 1994. http://www.web.apc.org/~msurman/ecommons.html
Taylor, J. History, Identity and Democracy: Implications of Community and Domestic Heritage Multimedia, *In* Proceedings *Home-oriented informatics, telematics and automation conference (HOIT94),* Copenhagen: Oikos, 1994, pp. 229-238.
Toffler, A. *The Third Wave,* London: Pan Books, 1980.
Walsh, B. Fraternal warnings. *The European Journal of Teleworking,* 1993; 1: 4: 18-19.
Webster, F. *Theories of the Information Society,* London: Routledge, 1995.
WEVH. Teleworking and Networking. *On~Line news,* 1994; 3: 6-7/
Wilson, A. *Teleworking - Flexibility for a Few,* Report 210, Falmer, Sussex: IMS, 1991.
Wright, P. The Manchester Host Project, *ITs News,* [The Journal of the Library Association Information Technology Group]. March 1995; 31:16-19.

Notes

[1]Community-based computer networks; Community computing;, Community telecomputing; Community bulletin boards; Civic networking; Telecommunity systems; and Community information systems.

[2] Teleworking, distance learning, a network for universities and research centres, telematic services for small and medium-sized enterprises (SMEs), road traffic management, air traffic control, healthcare networks, trans-European public administration network, electronic tendering and city information highways.

[3] Area A: Telematics for Services of Public Interest, Area B: Telematics for Knowledge, Area C: Telematics for Improving Employment and Quality of Life, Area D: Horizontal RTD Activities, Area E: Programme Support Actions.

[4] 1. Economic Performance and Development, 2. Environment and Sustainability, 3. Globalisation, Regions and Emerging Markets, 4. Governance and Regulation, 5. Human Communication and the Social Shaping of technology, 6. Innovation, Organisation and Business processes, 7. Knowledge and Skills, 8. Lifespan, Lifestyles and Health, 9. Social Integration and Exclusion.

Chapter 13

Technology Transfer and Development

Fatima Portela Cysne

The transfer of technology and information systems and information as input and output of technological development are discussed. It is proposed that information services and information providers should play a key role in technology transfer for development. Information services and systems are analysed as an important element of the debate on technology transfer and development through the mechanisms of science parks. A research project of technology transfer for Brazil is used as an example to illustrate the discussion.

Introduction

It is no longer a novelty to say that information has become a valuable resource in all human activities. In particular, it has become a strategic and corporate resource for economic and technological activities and especially, technology transfer. This paper is concerned with the importance and impact of information and the role of information services in the transfer and exploitation of new technology. The inclusion of information services and information systems in the current debate on post-industrial society is crucial. The idea of information as a valuable resource, as an economic and corporate resource, is not yet widely explored, even though there has been an explosion of information and the supporting information technology developed to enhance and facilitate the flow of information.

The paradox of the information society is that, on the one hand, there is an increasing explosion of information being diffused and disseminated by different information mechanisms, and on the other hand, there is an increasing need for more and more knowledge (Engelstad, 1990; Pantry, 1990). A hypothesis for the paradox of the inadequate utilisation of available information is that there is a lack of both appropriate mechanisms and adequate methodology to make this wealth of information more socially and economically useful. In other words, society still needs a service that can transform data and information into socially useful and absorbable knowledge.

For example, the small impact of scientific and technological information on the innovation process is, among other social, cultural and economic factors, a result of the lack of an efficient and specialised information service with information specialist to facilitate and improve the flow of such knowledge between university and industry. Engelstad (1990), suggests that this so-called information society is still dealing with information poverty- "Small industry suffers both lack of information and information overload"(p.257). He believes that one way to cope with this unwanted situation would be the organisation of "information transfer services with a built-in capacity for competence development with end-users themselves. (Concerning the impact of scientific knowledge in innovation see Grant, 1995; Steele, 1995; Faulkner and Senker, 1994; Senker, 1993; Pavit, 1985; Rosenberg, 1991; Barden, 1989; de Solla Price, 1984; Gibbons and Johnston, 1974). The discussion here focuses on different aspects of technology transfer and the associated problems of the transfer of information including:

- the knowledge required in innovation;
- scientific and technological knowledge;

- links between university and industry and science parks;
- a firm's capabilities to access, use and absorb new knowledge; and
- the role of specialised information services to enhance and facilitate the flow of information between various sectors.

The Information Society and Technology Transfer

The 1990s have become known as the "information age", a phrase that has its origins in the microelectronics revolution of the early 1980s. Particular characteristics in the industrial and business fields are the shortening of product cycles and competitive pressure to create new products at an ever increasing rate. These developments have generated a new debate about the real needs of society and the role of business and industry in this new competitive environment.

The problem is thus to develop strategies that will reconcile the need to recoup increasing investment in innovation with customers' needs. To achieve these aims, the economic sector has to pay attention to two important factors: *information and competency*. This suggests that a new structure should be designed to let firms improve their capacity in the changing climate of modern society (Launo, 1993; European Roundtable, 1988; Olaisen and Revang, 1991)

It is undoubtedly the case that information is affecting the nature of competition and company success. It has become an active economic resource and active factor in the innovation process. What is difficult to see and needs further analysis is the nature of the relationship between information and productivity. An important aspect of this is the analysis of the influence of information on firms' performance, and particularly of the relationship between information services and innovation. Here, the interpretation of this relationship is seen through the analysis of technology transfer. It focuses specifically on the transfer of formal codified knowledge and the specific channels through which information flows between organisations. (Osminski, 1991, Montali, 1987; Faulkner, 1994; Bessant, 1993).

Most investigations of innovation do not focus on information as a corporate resource. Furthermore it is not easy to show the full economic value of information. One way to approach this investigation is to evaluate the relationship between information and productivity and test its economic value using specific inputs to analyse its benefits to productivity. This analysis requires an evaluation of the types and formats of information required by the different sectors.

There is a growing literature on the importance and implication of knowledge for innovation and technology transfer. Authors such as Senker (1993) discuss the contribution of tacit knowledge to innovation. Faulkner (1994) categorises the types of knowledge used by industries, Gibbons (1994) discusses in detail the new production of knowledge in the information society, and Grant and Steele, (1995) suggest that the fundamental issue of technology transfer is the identification and analysis of the production and flow of different types of knowledge in the transfer process. This literature provides an important basis for strengthening the emergent debate on the importance of information services as levers of technology transfer and of economic development.

Most literature on technology transfer suggests that the main problem within this process is the lack of a suitable physical, human and socio-economic infrastructure in firms necessary for the full exploitation of technology transfer. This debate also stresses the difficulties in the transfer and absorption of scientific and technological knowledge. (See, for example, Bessant and Rush 1993, Rosenberg 1991, Faulkner, 1994, Faulkner and Senker and Velho 1993, Barbosa 1995, Porter 1990, Grant and Stelle 1995)

However, these investigations make little mention of the lack of suitable information infrastructures or the need for specialised information services, information providers and information professionals to improve the flow of scientific and technical knowledge between research and economic sectors. Grant and Steele (1995, p. 11) discuss technology transfer in the manufacturing realm, and state that documentation, software, and codified knowledge are central to the success of transfer. They also argue that this area has largely been unexplored in technology transfer.

Information networks and systems as a new paradigm of innovation

Current literature on innovation suggests that the main factors that influence technological development can be seen within a policy approach which includes five important elements that determine technological progress:

a) technological paradigm
b) political, economic and institutional context
c) industrial infrastructure
d) technical, human and technological resources
e) company strategy

In trying to understand what has happened in the field of innovation over the last two decades, especially in relation to these five elements, a new paradigm for innovation suggests itself: *information networking is widely being accepted as a crucial element for both innovative activities and the competitiveness of enterprises, sectors and countries.*

There are several factors that may explain the rise of this new paradigm. We can consider, for example, the major changes in international technological dynamics that have arisen from the changes in the paradigm of technologies. Technological dynamics of the 1950's and 1960's was based on cheap energy and materials and also on inflexible mass production. It became intensive, flexible and computerised with the information technologies in the 1970s (Frota and Frota, 1994).

This change occurred as a result of the rapid development and diffusion of information and communication technologies. This technological change offers a new vision of the changing economic sectors and the changing nature of technology transfer for social development in developing countries. Information technologies and information network are a new phenomenon that has become part of everyday life, especially in developed countries. Even though the impact of technological change is limited to large cities in developing countries, this new paradigm has economic and social implications for all societies, including problems of literacy and the skills necessary for coping with new technologies.

The impact of these new paradigms allows us to create a new vision of changing economic sectors. It also offers an opportunity to rethink the technology transfer for development in developing countries.

These changes include:

• intensification of the use of new technologies and, so far, the acceleration of technical development and changes in industrial processes and products;
• the fusion of technological and scientific disciplines which has become a fundamental key to the growth of new industries and the renewal of already established industries;
• the growth in the use of information and communication technology manifested in all economic activities (industria sectors, business, services etc.);
• more rapid, reliable and cheaper acquisition, storage, retrieval, transmission and dissemination of information, especially with the development of the CD-ROM and the internet;
• new methods of production and distribution of knowledge where electronics systems have an important role in the acceleration and generation of new knowledge, in the acquisition of existing knowledge and in the development of new configurations;
• changes in industrial production processes with the introduction of systems that permit automation, flexibility, integration and optimisation of the productive process using on-line monitoring; and
• changes in organisational and managerial structure in companies using information and communication technologies to improve links between different departments

(research, production, management, marketing etc.) and between different enterprises, institutions and countries (LASTRES, 1994).

The intensification of the use of information and communication technology - i.e. information networks - plays an important role in the increasing links between organisations. These new technologies bring new changes in the relationships that exist between enterprises and institutions, and especially between developed and developing countries. These changes in relationship between sectors and countries clearly show the need for a new role for information service provider.

In this context the requirements imposed by this new paradigm for enterprises and information services will need to be analysed. These (requirements) include technical, institutional and organisational changes. An example would be the intensification of collaborative work between organisations with an implied higher increased flow of information, requiring a specific information service provision.

The most important requirement here is the ability of a company to use the available technologies to facilitate and enhance data communication and the use of technical, scientific, market and patent data-bases. These new technologies are already changing the nature and the relationship of research, production, products and commercial structure in developing countries.

In this changing context, the capability of a company to quickly generate, introduce and disseminate innovation has become fundamental. As a consequence, the competitiveness of a specific company is reflected in the range and efficiency of the information systems and information networks it uses. This increased rate of technological innovation is pushing up the level of use of information networks in developed countries. Although developing countries are a long way from this stage, they are already considering information networks as one of the key components for industrial competitiveness and social development.

An example of this can be found in Frota and Frota (1994), who stress the necessity of a National Information Network for Brazil to concentrate efforts to transform and develop its technological and industrial sectors, which include information networks. There is also an important discussion about different countries' information systems supporting technological development (Nelson,1993) where authors discuss the importance of national innovation systems in different countries. In summary we can say that in both developed and developing countries the need to develop and use information networks and systems has become part of company strategy.

The impact of the new paradigm on information services to industry

Given these important and large scale technological changes as a background, we need to understand the role of information services in technology transfer in developing countries, such as Brazil. All these changes have some connection or impact on the traditional public and industrial library's information services. These services therefore need, as a matter of urgency, to take into account the new paradigm, particularly the impact of this paradigm on information service provision.

It is, however, worth noting that automation of information services, even in most developed countries have made very little impact in the industrial sector, and has so far "done very little to change the situation of information poverty in most companies" (Engelstad, 1990). It may be argued that this gap between information services and the economic sector has retarded the establishment of efficient information services to assist the process of innovation in small and medium sized firms in developed countries. This difficulty is further intensified in less developed countries.

To deal with the impact of this new paradigm requires a very careful and systematic analysis of the situation. The understanding derived from a careful analysis of what is required within enterprises in terms of technical and educational programmes, knowledge, skills and adaptation, can enable us to build a theoretical and technical basis for the exploitation of new types of information services.

These services should combine the new technology facilities with human expertise in order to discard, filter, and/or adapt the information for the end-users and prepare them, with the necessary knowledge and skills to evaluate and filter information for themselves. This combination should include the knowledge already produced within the firm's environment, scientific and technological knowledge from university and research institutes as well as knowledge from other related institutions and the firm's partners.

This new perspective of technology transfer implies the development of specific methods and mechanisms to enable information services to become feasible, effective and efficient for the economic sector. This service can then improve information links between different departments within firms, and between different types of organisations and countries. (Montalli, 1987; 1992; Osminski, 1991; Sherwell, 1988, Engelstad, 1990).

Thus it is urgently necessary that information services be re-designed in order to meet the needs of developing countries. The new approach should be rooted in human-centred perspective that emphasises the importance of machines and technologies for social, economic development, and the general development of human life. This view suggests that the new technologies should be used to enhance human relationships through the sharing of ideas, knowledge and skills. It also emphasises the enhancement of social and technological capacity in a more democratic way. This new perspective of social, economic and technological development requires the inclusion of information services, systems and information professionals as part of the innovation and social development process. Their special role is to enhance and facilitate the flow of information between organisations, economic sectors and countries by providing selected and refined strategic and necessary information to end-users.

Innovation and Technology Transfer in Developing Countries: Brazilian Experience

Although Brazil has a relatively large GDP, a wealth of natural resources, a productive agricultural sector and a mature and diversified industrial manufacturing base, it continues to have a faltering competitive position in the world economy. This may be a result of the weak integration between research being done within universities and the needs of the economic sector. In recent decades, the Government, has spent 90% of R & D expenditure in the area of technology transfer. However, it is argued that the dispersal of the R&D efforts of the public sector, and weak linkage between public R & D institutes and the productive sectors has meant that the flow of useful technological services is not commensurate with the extent of public sector resources allocated to technological activities.

The problem of this gap between information and technological services and economic development affects most Third World countries. The links between science and technology and the productive systems or between the government and society still have deep flaws. Barreto (1992) analysing Brazil's context, suggests that the lack of a better link between science, technology and the economic sector arises from the weak and inconsistent relationship between science, technology and society, which allows the perpetuation of the condition of under-development and dependency on developing countries.

The lesson which developing countries can learn from developed countries is that their economic dominance owes much to their ability to develop and organise the production of knowledge and technology in institutions which are specially established for this end. They stimulate the development of research and technological institutes and laboratories, within or outside universities, giving special attention to the development and improvement of their public and university libraries to support their scientific and technological development. In contrast, the importance of this idea has only very recently been recognised in developing countries, where public libraries still offer a very poor information service and university libraries are not well equipped to respond to the demand.

Developing countries have begun to recognise the need to gain, principally for themselves, greater knowledge of technology in order to favour a possibly higher level of integration between technology and development. They also need to strengthen their own scientific and technological capacity. Primarily, they need to break away from the perpetuation of their technological dependency that has characterised their colonial past.

Despite many efforts by national and international organisations (especially in the last decade) to find ways in which developing countries can gain more technological and economical autonomy, it is not clear whether developing countries can benefit from current technology that would stimulate their development according to models adapted to their necessities. This lack of knowledge about the extent of the impact (social, cultural and economic) of imported technology on developing countries highlights the necessity for further studies into methodologies and mechanisms that can bridge the technological gap between developed and developing countries.

It is widely accepted that there is a close relationship between technological and economic autonomy of a country and its capability to develop scientific and technological research and create conditions for solving technical, economic and social problems. This autonomy is fundamental to the development of all levels of society. What is essential is that the result of such research can be easily transferred and absorbed by economic and social sectors. It is necessary to acquire a body of knowledge that can give a country the capability to transfer and absorb technology, and thus generate solutions to their daily problems.

As compared to developing countries, awareness of the importance of information for scientific and technological development is very high in developed countries. Information as a raw material, indispensable for the realisation of scientific and technological development becomes a major concern. This importance of information in economic and technological development leads to the renewal of information policies and the reorganisation of information systems.

Technological developments in this century have become highly sophisticated, being dependent not only on the inventive capacity of man, but also on the existence of a set of previously organised knowledge that is well structured and scientifically and technically accepted. This organisation makes the potential of information central to the economic sector and eventually to the political realm.

Those countries which entered the industrial era early have been able to develop an efficient system for the creation of a knowledge base in the universities and research laboratories which together are the generators of scientific and technological knowledge. These centres create the necessary mechanisms and tools for the use and absorption of this knowledge as well as for understanding industrial research aimed at the production of technology and technological knowledge.

In contrast, industrialisation arrived much later in the developing countries for historical, social and economic reasons. Although technology transfer from developed countries has been an important and necessary contribution for developing countries to reach a certain degree of economic development, they have become technologically dependent on the developed countries, a dependency that greatly affects their social development and is therefore extremely difficult to escape from.

Countries such as Brazil have only recently become aware of this technological dependency, and are now attempting to seek out alternative means for favouring more autonomous development. In Brazil, universities are now being conceived as places for the generation of scientific and technological knowledge. However, in the past they have not been strong in their efforts to fulfil their social role. One reason is that universities have not made serious attempt to develop any significant research in this direction (except for some efforts such as the formation of science parks and individual joint projects).

Even though in the last few decades, research in universities has taken significant steps forward (due to the implementation of post-graduate courses), this increase in research has been mainly directed at fundamental research which is often out of step with national reality and social needs.

Transfer of Knowledge within the Technology Transfer Process

Technology transfer is seen here as the acquisition, understanding, absorption and application of technology. Bessant and Rush, (1993) define technology transfer as: "the set of activities and processes whereby technology (embodied in products and new process or in disembodied forms such as knowledge, skill, legal rights, etc.) is passed from one user to another".

This perspective of technology transfer always "implies some form of learning and adaptation on the part of the receiving organisation". Learning can be take place by using/doing or through technical documents* and scientific and technological literature. This includes acquisition of experiential knowledge, personal and technical skills, creativity and expertise (Senker, 1993), technical ideas, documents, information and data (codified knowledge - Faulkner, 1994) equipment, prototypes, designs and computer codes (machinery)" (Barbosa and Vaidya, 1995).

Technology transfer is thus defined mostly as the transfer of knowledge, especially what is called know-how (see for example Galbraith, 1990 who discusses critical information and know how, Bhattasali, 1972 about transfer of applied scientific methodologies and their operations, Faulkner, 1994 who categorises different types of knowledge used in industry and Senker, 1993 who analyses the role of tacit knowledge in innovation).

Some of these studies state that technology transfer includes the transfer of a combination of tacit, practical and codified knowledge, others argue that tacit knowledge plays a more central role than formal knowledge in the innovation process. In this case, when there is a transfer of machines or processes, the transfer of knowledge will occur through "learning by using" discussed by Rosenberg (1982); Senker (1991), and Faulkner, Senker and Velho (1993).

Grant and Steele (1995) provide a very helpful review of both the nature and process of technology transfer and contribute toward a better understanding of the impact and implication of different types and levels of knowledge on the transfer process. They analyse the four elements of manufacturing technology identified by Ramanathan (1994):

- 'Technoware' that represents object-embodied technology;
- 'Humanware' as person-embodied technology;
- 'Orgaware' as institution-embodied; and
- 'Inforware', document-embodied technology which supports all three categories.

In their review the linkage between knowledge, technology transfer and assimilation capability is very strong as emphasised by Rebentish and Ferreti (1993): "specific knowledge is that which provides a firm with the ability to reproduce another capability". They also consider documentation, software and codified knowledge as "central to transfer success" which requires "control, planning and timing in the transfer process".

The divergence of perspectives on technology transfer illustrates the complexity and diversity of both technological innovation and the innovation process itself. Firstly, this divergence can be seen as the term "technology transfer" itself which is wide-ranging and refers to complex processes. Secondly, when technology transfer includes "hidden knowledge and experience", its transfer is more complicated and difficult, therefore requiring a deeper analysis of all the elements and implications related to the innovation process (Some of these elements and implications are discussed by Bessant; Rush, 1993; Grant; Stele, 1995; Rosenberg, 1982; and Faulkner, Senker, Velho, 1993, among many others)

Technology transfer as the transfer of tacit, practical and codified knowledge, seems to be a more suitable definition for the analysis of the role of scientific and technological information in innovation. This more dynamic perspective of technology transfer "involves a two-way communication process, with learning and change taking place on both sides" (Bessant &Rush, 1993).

However, the sharing of technology, specifically the sharing of tacit knowledge, is very problematic, because it cannot easily be imitated and/or transferred across firms. As the underlying principles (e.g. know-how, know-why) of technology are often hidden, the learning process requires "extensive training or the movement of people". This limitation in transferring knowledge requires attention from different departments of a firm. (See especially Teece (1981) about the complexity of capturing knowledge for transfer; Collet, 1994, about know-how; Rebentish; Ferreti [in Grant and Steele 1995]) about appropriate ways to capture know-how).

The transfer of scientific and technological knowledge is not easy either. Generally the knowledge produced by universities and research laboratories, is registered in a format that is often difficult for companies to use and absorb. Furthermore, in developing countries small and medium size firms do not have people qualified to manage and use information resources. However this kind of knowledge is crucial to the innovation process and it can break through some of the barriers that may limit the transfer of technology.

The limit of technology transfer here is the capability of the receiver to make use of the information that has been transferred. In all the processes of technology transfer it is necessary that the receiving environment has a relevant and responsive cultural, institutional and market infrastructure. This includes the necessity for the 'receiving' company to make the necessary investment, and to develop strategies and education and skills programmes in order to be successful in their ultimate objective of innovation (Barbosa and Vaidya, 1995).

The infrastructure necessary for the transfer of technology should include the information which supports both the activities of a successful transfer of scientific and technological information and the process of innovation itself (such as to select, organise, refine and repackage information in order to make it more useful and absorbable by end-users).

This concept of technology transfer, encompassing the transfer of information, gives a more consistent basis to analyse the role of specialised information services for innovation. However it is still necessary to deepen the analysis of different types of knowledge used in a company. This understanding is necessary to build a body of knowledge body about technology transfer according to the hypothesis:

> Formal codified knowledge can have a more positive impact on the process of technology transfer if there is a specialised information service specially designed and prepared to select, organise, refine and repackage scientific and technological knowledge, making such knowledge more usable and absorbable by firms' end-users.

Firms' Capability to use and Absorb Technological Knowledge

A growing body of literature, discusses firms' capabilities to use, absorb and assimilate new inputs of technology. The literature discusses the successes and failures of technology transfer as a very complex process that requires high levels of "managerial skills and innovative capabilities" from firms". A good example can be found in the following literature: Teece et al (1981); Rumelt (1984), Teece (1986), Voss (1986), Leonard-Barton (1988; 1992), Porter (1990), Irwin & More (1991), Lall (1992), Bessant & Rush (1993; 1993/94) and Barbosa and Vadya (1995).

According to some of these authors, "experience with complex innovation suggests that a period following initial adoption is characterised by a long and difficult learning curve that may extend over a period of months or even years" (Bessant & Rush, 1993). Leonard-Barton calls this period "mutual adaptation" (for technology itself and for the organisation) within which there is a time for learning and a time for implementation.

The possibility of success will depend on an organisation's ability to make the necessary changes to its organisational structures and processes.

Technology transfer as a learning process (which implies a transfer of different kinds of knowledge - e.g. tacit and formal codified), is very complex, with two of many dimensions requiring a more careful analysis: i) the role of science in technological innovation and ii) the skills base of the firms for accessing and applying scientific and technological knowledge. It can be more complex if the transfer is between firms, industrial sectors or nations because it is necessary that the receiving firms have appropriate cultural, institutional and marketing, contexts, strategies, skills, efforts and investment.

Leonard-Barton (1988), discussed in Bessant and Rush (1993), explains part of this learning process as two discrete learning curves: "the *technical learning* curve, which describes the cumulative-knowledge acquisition about the technical aspects of implementing a particular technology, and the *organisation learning* curve, which describes knowledge about the management of organisational issues" (changes in skills, procedures, performance criteria, etc.).

This complex process implies that several levels of technological competence must be developed to give firms the ability to use, absorb, adapt, stretch, develop, design or sell technologies. Some of these variables are described by Irwing & More(1991) as follows:

- the complexity of the technology transfer process resulting in part from the complexity of modern technologies and in part from recent massive growth in the technology industries;
- the environment in which technology transfer is expected to happen is often the very type of environment non-conductive to or even hostile to technology transfer;
- what is being transferred will often not be a completed invention/finished product, but an 'idea in progress', something ambiguous and not easy to disseminate;
- differences between situations involving technology pull (problems looking for solutions) and technology push (solutions looking for problems),
- despite best efforts to map and implement transfer strategies, technology transfer is often a chaotic and disorderly process where chance and serendipity often play an important role;
- a variety of obstacles and barriers operate against easy technology transfer;
- highly specialised vocabularies, with these becoming even more specialised,
- varying personal reward systems, e.g. between universities and industry,
- motivational differences, e.g. between universities' desire to publish results and businesses' desire to create and protect competitive advantages,
- contrasting organisational (and even research)cultures between university and industry,
- licensing and contract procedures,
- users not technically capable of using the technology,
- insufficient R & D funds allocated to technology transfer."

Bessant and Rush (1993/94) have also detailed some aspects of the "innovative capabilities" essential for technology transfer to avoid failures or only partial success:

> firms should have a technology strategy and be able to plan its growth and development; this includes the exploration of the range of technological options available (different machines, technologies, suppliers, etc.) to obtain a good fit with their needs; the comparison between all the options available; the selection of the most appropriate options based upon comparison; extensive negotiation around price, specification, transfer of knowledge, property rights, etc. For the implementation of a transfer of technology extensive project planning and management activities are necessary, which require configuration of both technology and organisation to obtain a good and workable fit. The development of competence to operate and to best use the technology also involves extensive learning.

According to these authors, the lack of what they called "these managerial capabilities" represents one of the main barriers to technology transfer. Each of the activities described above, and those mentioned by Irwin & More, require a very clear specialised information service and system. This kind of service can help a company to break through some of the barriers, not only for technology transfer itself, but for every step of the process (decision-making about which technology to transfer, which infrastructure to build and specialised personnel, until its implementation, production and diffusion).

To design a kind of service to facilitate and stimulate the transfer of scientific and technological information, it is necessary to consider it from the perspective that information services might be developed as a business. Thus, the information sector, department or service, within or outside a firm, created to fulfil a company's information needs, should develop an objective business plan which includes a company's activities and businesses.

Thus, information professionals need to be part of a firm's business team and to have an integral and active participation in the firm's plans, programmes and projects. This can help them to define the firm's information needs according to the different knowledge each department needs, and thus to be able to assist a firm's performance by delivering the right strategic information in time to solve problems and/or for decision- making.

Typology of Knowledge used in Innovation

> At the base of advanced technology is knowledge, especially advanced science(. . .) at the base of all skill, competence and expertise is education. (Stonier,1983. p.12)

This quotation has been chosen to highlight the different types of knowledge used by industry, and the importance of scientific knowledge in the innovation process and the role that information services should play in making this knowledge more useful.

Faulkner (1994) notes that there is a tendency in science and technology (as well as in other areas) to put in a "black box" the knowledge used during R&D leading to innovation. She suggests that it is not easy to transfer scientific knowledge between universities and industries, because there are several barriers to this process. The major barriers being the lack of qualified scientific and technological personnel in firms who are able to access and apply scientific and technological knowledge. It is also difficult to establish and sustain links between industry and universities.

It is generally accepted that a great deal of technological innovation comes from 'learning by using' and many other forms of learning rather than from scientific and technical literature*. Stonier (1983) suggests that a greater use of practical knowledge is characteristic of "earlier times" when the foundation of new science was based on practical experience. For example, experience with the steam engine led to the science of thermodynamics in the nineteenth century.

However, it is important to take into consideration what Stonier means when he says that "the flow of information is now generally in the opposite direction". This suggests a greater importance should be given to previously organised scientific knowledge as a solid basis for the production of new science and technology. For example "the development of the transistor in the middle of the twentieth century [which] was dependent on the solid-state physics conducted decades earlier".

The knowledge used by industry and business

It is not necessary to have a deep knowledge of the sociology of knowledge to understand that its usefulness is socially determined. This means that it involves more than simple cognitive or epistemological constructs. Thus, it is very important to have a more detailed analysis of the role of R&D in a company, and identify the difference between what is called scientific and technological knowledge. It is important also to understand both the extent and impact of the use of different types of knowledge in the innovation process. This knowledge and understanding enables us to analyse the effects of scientific and technical information for industrial improvement. It thus provides good basis for a discussion of the role of information services in industry.

Faulkner (1995) uses the term, "structuring a typology of knowledge used in innovation" in a broad sense including knowledge, expertise, skills, and information. It is used as a tool to investigate the flow of information between various sectors, focusing on the channels of communication and the specialist who can enhance and facilitate the access and use of such knowledge. Analysing the types of knowledge actually used in the innovation process, she acknowledges the role of scientific knowledge in innovation when she says that " ... it is clear that scientific knowledge also contributes to innovation" and explains "the relative contribution of internal and external sources to the knowledge used in innovation".

The discussion above illustrates that there is a wider acceptance of the usefulness of information in different economic activities and in the innovation process. Information has become an essential resource that produces significant changes in different economic, commercial, technical and social activities, especially as a result of the development and wider diffusion of information technology by many companies. For companies that have intensive R&D activities, there is a perception that the preservation and development of an organisation's specific knowledge can play an important managerial role. This knowledge means, for example, knowledge coded as data, documents, technical, confidential and specialised information, information systems and a firm's specific knowledge. (Osminski, 1991; Montali, 1986)

Thus, organisations try to develop their strategic knowledge base by establishing links with universities, research institutes, education, and training centres. Some organisations that have developed the necessary technological infrastructure are in a position to record part of the knowledge that can be stored (through information technology and systems with distinct levels of added value), and are thus able to integrate the strategic use of different types of knowledge (produced and acquired from the external and internal environments) within a unified information resource. However, this crucial information activity is not generally understood by firms and therefore the role of the information specialist in managing the information resource is not recognised

Companies often use knowledge obtained from different sources, produced internally or acquired from outside. Tacit, practical and formal codified knowledge seems to play different and important roles in the activities of a company. It is necessary to know what contribution each type of knowledge makes to innovation. Faulkner (1994) provides an important analysis of the reasons for use of internal and external information sources in the process of innovation, and their impact on he activities of the company.

She suggests that it is not easy to measure the usefulness of the different types of knowledge used by a company. It is very complex, for example, to quantify tacit and codified knowledge used in the development of a new technological process. This analysis requires the identification of the range of knowledge types used in innovation in more specific terms. This implies the use of specific methodologies, such as a mix of quantitative and qualitative methods, to capture the complexity of the process of innovation.

Fortunately there are some studies that contribute towards the production of a body of knowledge that can give a better understanding of this issue. For example, Vicenti (1991), Gibbons and Johnston (1974), Faulkner, Senker and Velho (1994), and most importantly Faulkner (1994) categorise knowledge used in innovation, and Grant and Steele (1995) review important literature related to technology transfer. It is interesting to note that even though they have contributed to a better understanding of the role played by different types of knowledge and of the limitations faced by companies concerning the flow of information in the innovation process, they do not discuss the significance of the information infrastructure which enables and enhances the flow and utilisation of information.

The role of information and knowledge both as input and output of innovation suggests a cause and effect relationship between information and technological development. This cause and effect relationship suggests that technology transfer should be seen as a learning process which takes place first at an individual level, and leads to the acquisition of specific information and the improvement of technological knowledge.

The analysis of technological transfer at company level becomes more complex due to different categories of knowledge and different levels of industrial sectors. It becomes even more complex when we consider technology transfer between developed and developing countries. Furthermore, any analysis of technology transfer between sectors or between countries must consider the different levels of education, skills and training that exist between them, and specifically between developed and developing countries.

National Information Services as a Lever to Strengthen University and Industry Links through Science Parks: A Brazilian Example

Different authors (some mentioned in this paper) have stressed that technological development in a country can be improved through three important scientifc, economic and political components: *research-enterprise-government.* This interface is necessary to build the quality of life of the population rather than to benefit few people.

Accepting this approach and analysing social and technological development we can observe that developing countries are far behind the frontier of international scientific and technological knowledge. Although this situation still persists, these countries are making considerable effort to bridge this knowledge gap.

Medeiros et al (1991) analyse the importance of science parks in the process of innovation and highlight that "the market and productivity units are basic links of the technological chain". A successful innovation requires the other component of technological development - the government - to adequately managed this process. The Government can be a mediator between social, economic and technological problems and science (university) and technologies and technological services (industry). This thus suggests that collaboration between industry and university/research institutes can play the most important role in the innovation process through joint R & D programmes.

It is suggested that Brazil's strategy of technological development has failed to overcome the country's technological dependency (See, for example, a brief description of Brazil's attempt toward self-sufficiency by Gibbons et al. 1994, p. 134-136, and Dahlmman; Frischtak, 1993). However, Brazil has made some important efforts to cope with some problematic political, economic and social barriers, such as the development of the Industrial Competitive Program (PCI) and the Brazilian Quality and Productivity Program (PBQP). A Permanent Commission for Industrial Technological Capacity (CPITC) have been given responsibility for two important actions:

i) to support the formation of adequate human resources, the development and diffusion of technological managerial methods, the development of the required technological infrastructure, and the establishment of information networks;

ii) to directly support small and medium size enterprises in terms of R & D through the establishment of strategic programmes that include the purchase and absorption of technology and the development of science parks.

This last mechanism is based on the assumption that co-operation between enterprises and research institutions, is essential for the interchange of new ideas, knowledge, experience, and therefore the innovation and change process. A mechanism that has been used by industrial countries and newly industrial countries, such as Brazil, to implement this collaboration is the science park.

Brazil has taken important initiatives in improving links between university and industry through the strengthening of science parks. (Medeiros et al 1991; Frota & Frota 1994). These initiatives have led to the establishment of a National Information Network and the development of an integrated information system to enhance the socialisation of knowledge within the country, thereby enhancing the autonomy of technological developments.

Two technology transfer programs have been created to improve the Brazilian innovation process: the Science Parks Program (PROPOTEC) and the Technological Modernisation Poles Program (PMPT). This action is based on the assumption that the geographic proximity of science and technology through university/research laboratory and industry can stimulate, facilitate and enhance the required interchange of knowledge and expertise that favours the development of an adequate technological environment for innovation (Montalli, 1987). In this new age of post-industrial society it is crucial that a developing country can also rapidly create, introduce, adapt and diffuse innovation.

Although Brazil has made a late start in technology transfer, it has taken steps to modernise its technological sector. The supporting programmes for technology transfer developed during the last decade include the Scientific and Technological Support Program (PADCT), the National Industry Confederation - Department to Support Small and Medium Size Firms (CNI-DAMP), the Brazilian Service to Support Micro and Small Size Enterprises (SEBRAE) and the Brazilian Institute of Scientific and technological Information (IBICT). These programmes, among others, are putting Brazilian information systems not too far behind others such as those of Denmark, France, Canada, England, Mexico, Germany and Finland (Montali, 1987).

The Growth and Diversity of Social and Economic Information Needs

Information is increasingly seen as a fundamental resource at all levels of social, cultural and economic activities. There is a growing information need in public and private enterprises, especially in research-intensive companies, where product renewal and product development represent an important part of operations. Information is also a crucial element in the decision-making process, for which personnel, raw materials, capital and knowledge are essential production factors.

However, most enterprises do not perceive the usefulness of information as a fundamental input for improving their technological and commercial capacity in the market. This issue is much more complicated in small and medium size companies. Even though they produce and use different types of information all the time, they do so quite unconsciously, getting information internally and externally, often using informal channels. Often decisions are made without appropriate information support. (Osminski,1991, Montali, 1987)

The problem here is that even though more and more information is available within and across companies(facilitate by information technology) it is not sufficient just to enhance the flow of knowledge between various sectors. It is still difficult for most small companies to know, for example, who holds the information they need and how they can easily select and access the best information for specific problem-solving, decision-making or improving a specific process or a product.

Another concern is how to acquire the information provision when it is needed. Most medium and small companies do not usually receive strategic information on time. However, industrial activities, such as R&D, production, marketing and sales, often depend on having the right information at the right time. This suggests that there is a need for efficient, quick and wide-ranging information services. This also suggests the role of information specialists as knowledge facilitators within a company, particularly in the improvement of the flow of information between departments, different sectors and between countries.

The discussion above implies a need for further analysis of information flow within industry, more specifically concerning the need and use of information in the technology transfer process (Grant and Steele, 1995; Faulkner, 1994; Senker, 1993). This includes the understanding of the value of codified knowledge for innovation and social development, and the effectiveness of the specific information service to select, organise, disseminate and refine information. It is argued that information services play a central role in generating products and services that can fulfil specific and specialised information needs in industry and for technological development (Osminski, 1991; Montalli, 1987).

Special libraries, such as industrial libraries, university libraries and information services for industry and business, already try to provide relevant services for these sectors. However, these services have distinctive objectives and functions and are thus not able to respond properly the firm's information need. In some aspects, these information services are often more information sources (even offering different kind of services) than specialised information services designed to answer specific information questions from a specific client(Osminski, 1991; Montali, 1987). Even though the industrial libraries may be organised along the lines of university libraries to help firms with information provision, they are not equipped to productively anticipate the needs of firms and provide relevant information.

The use of academic information services is not always effective for enterprises. This is because company culture is very different from the culture of academic and research environments. It is suggested by some researchers that small firms often do not make elaborate business plans and do not clearly identify their future problems and needs. Moreover staff are often too busy to think about the problem of technology transfer as an information problem. Thus, if an organisation does not perceive its problem, challenge, and limitations in the term of information, it is unlikely to spend time trying to locate organisations that hold the necessary information sources. It is also unlikely to select appropriate information sources and retrieve information specific to its problems.

Another problem is that traditional industry and university libraries provide a more general service. They may provide specialised services in some areas, but they may not be able to meet the diverse information needs of small firms and therefore fail to create an integrated information resource for different firms. On the one the hand, most small and medium firms do not develop explicit business plans that could enable them to transform their technology transfer problems into information questions, and thereby communicate their information needs effectively to established industry and university libraries. On the other hand, these information services may have insufficient business knowledge to be able to understand the business problems of small firms and thereby provide appropriate information.

This lack of integration between those who need information and those who provide it, suggests that there is a need for a deeper analysis of the relationship between these two sectors and the impact of information services on the activities of the firms. It is necessary to know the type and format of information needed by the economic sector, as well as to know why, when and what information this sector uses, how a firm selects and accesses information, who provides this service, and how information services are seen by the economic sector and how the information needs of firms are understood by information services.

It may be unrealistic to change the current view of the economic sector about the usefulness of specialised information services in the short term. Firms are often concerned with short term risks. They may not be able to give due consideration to how information can make a difference to their activities. There is thus a need to investigate this information gap from the perspective of the end-users.

Information services for industry

Much of information science literature has tended to emphasise the increasingly important function of information within different activities, especially since the emergence of the 'information society' or the 'information revolution'. However, it still neglects to emphasise specialised information services and the role of information specialists within industry and commerce.

Most advances in information services have been concerned with the development and usage of information technology. The focus has been on best use of information technology, the improvement of information management and the use of sophisticated techniques for information storage, retrieval and dissemination, rather than on the impact of the use of information and information technology on business and the daily economic life of society.

The main factor that prevents information organisations from providing more effective information services to different kinds of end-users is the excess of technical specialisation in information techniques and the use of information technology without close linkage to the end-users, such as their environment, needs and interests. It seems that the information activities are still understood as the organisation of the documents, data, and information as an end in itself.

It is important to emphasise that social changes arising from the development of different kinds of technology and the use of information technology have strong implications for the role of information services. This role might change from the traditional role as an 'appendix' to the socio-economic debate, to that of being central to innovation and change in this new age.

Conclusion

The necessity for managerial and technological development to achieve competitiveness in the world market is part of a firm's daily activities.

To reach this objective a firm should acquire technical services which include specialised information services. While it is not possible for every firm to acquire all technical services and information, it can overcome this barrier by the establishment of a specific department which is designed to use different internal and external information resources. Such a department can also develop specialised technical activities in order to assist in a firm's different information needs and, especially those of its R&D department.

Information and technical services are [provided by different kinds of institutions, such as public and private research laboratories, universities, information consultants, technical associations, and libraries. It is, however, important to recognise that specialised information services and information specialists play a central role in collecting knowledge from diverse sources and placing in an accessible and relevant form for organisations.

The challenge for information services and information specialists is to adapt to the new requirements of economically providing specialist information services to end-users in industry, business and commerce. This challenge requires philosophical, educational and technical changes and adaptations in order for specific information services to become part of the thriving business world.

It is the age of the information specialist. This implies better qualified information professionals who are specialist not just in techniques and technology but are also conversant with the wide variety of information activities of the economic sectors, and knowledgeable about new approaches. This requires continuing education and training for acquiring and sustaining skills, knowledge and expertise.

Information services also requires a special attention from business and industrial sectors, in particular in the selection and training of information providers. An effective information service should consist of a qualified information team, consisting of information specialists and scientists whose task is to scan and analyse the literature, produce indexes and specialised information bulletins, and improve the dissemination of selective information services.

Bibliography

Adler, P. Shared Learning. *Management Science*, v.38, n.8, p. 938-957, 1990.

Arrow, K. The Economic implication of Learning by doing. *Review of Economic Studies,* v.29, n.2, p.155-173, 1962.

Barbosa, Francisco and Vadya. Developing Technological Capabilities: The Case of Brazil Steel Company.

Technological Innovation and Global Challenges. Proceedings of the European Conference on Management of Technology, 5-7 July 1995. p. 849-856

Barden, P. and Good, B. *Information flows into industrial research.* London: Centre for Exploitation of

Science and Technology, 1989.

Bhattasali, B. N. *Transfer of technology among developing countries.* Tokyo: Asian Productive organisation, 1972.

Bessant, J. and Rush, H. Government Support of Manufacturing Innovation: Two Country-Level Case Study. IEEE Transactions on Engineering Management, v.40, n. 1, p. 79-91, Feb. 1993. Building Bridges for Innovation; The Role of consultants in Technology (1993) (copy).

Boisot, M.; Griffiths, D. Core Competence and the paradox of value: Managing Evescent Technological Advantage. *Technological Innovation and Global Challenges. Proceedings of the European Conference on Management of Technology, 5-7 July 1995.* p. 633-640.

Carpenter, M P; Cooper, M; Narin, F. Linkage between basic research and patents. *Research Management*, v. 23, n. 2,1980.

Chistensen, Jens Frøslev. The corporate Coherence of the Technology Base. *Technological Innovation and Global Challenges. Proceedings of the European Conference on Management of Technology,* 5-7 July 1995. p. 641-651.

Cohen, W. M; Levinthal D. A. Absorptive Capacity: A New Perspective on Learning and Innovation. *Administrative Science Quarterly,* v.35, p. 128-152, 1990.

Cohen, W.M; Levinthal, D.A. Innovation and Learning: The Two Faces of R & D. *Economic Journal*, v.99, n.397, p. 569-596, 1989.

Cysne, Fatima Portela. Biblioteconomia: Dimenção Social e Educativa. Fortaleza(Brasil): EDUFC, 1993. (Book from MS dissertation about the social and educational role of information provider in Brazilian society).

Cysne, Fatima Portela. Transfer of technology between university and industry: the role of information services and systems. Paper presented at ICAM'95: Anthropocentric Lean Production Systems, Sunderland, 11-13 Sep. 1995.

Dahlmman, C. J; Frischtak, C.R. National systems supporting technical advantage in industry: the Brazilian experience. In: Nelson, R (Ed.) London: Oxford University Press, 1993.

Dickson, Keith; Coles, Anne-Marie. Learning From Experience: Lessons in Managing Inter-Firm R & D Collaboration. *Technological Innovation and Global Challenges. Proceedings of the European Conference on Management of Technology,* 5-7 July 1995.

Dogson, M. T*echnological Collaboration and Organisation Learning.* ISPRU, UK, 1991.

Dogson, M. *Technical Collaboration in Industry*: Strategy, Policy and Internationalisation in Innovation.

London: Routledge, 1993.

Ducan, R; Weiss, A. Organisational Learning: Implications for Organisation Design. In: STAW, B. *Research in Organisational Behaviour*. Greenwich, Conn: JAI Press, 1970. p. 75-123.

Engelstad, Kirsten. Libraries, the knowledge industries and regional industrial development: practical experience in Norway. In Cronin, B; Tudor-Silvic (Eds.).The knowledge of industries: levers of economic and social development in 1990's. Dubrowich, 1990. p. 255-261.

European Roundtable. Information: a challenge for Europe and its industry. In: The Roundtable of European Industrialists. Fifth Youth Conference, Chateau de Limelette, Belgium, Sep. 1988.

Faulkner, Wendy. Conceptualising knowledge used in innovation: a second look at the science-technology distinction and industrial innovation. *Science, Technology, & Human Value,* v. 19, n. 4, p. 425-458, Autumn, 1994.

Faulkner, Wendy;*Knowledge frontiers*: industrial innovation and public sector research in Biotechnology, Engineering Ceramics and Parallel Computing. Oxford, Oxford University Press, 1994.

Faulkner, Wendy. Policy and management issues in company links with academic and government laboratories: a cross-technology study *Edinburgh PICT Working paper,* n.48. (photocopier)

Faulkner, Wendy; Senker, Jacqueline. Making sense of diversity: public-private research linkage in three technology. *Research Policy*, 1994.

Faulkner, Wendy; Senker, Jacqueline; Velho, Léa. *Science and Technology knowledge flows between industrial and public sector research*: a comparative study. 1993.

Fleck, J. The development of information-integration: beyond CIM. Edinburgh PICT working Paper n.9. Edinburgh: Research Centre for Social Science, University of Edinburgh, 1988.

Fleck, J. Expertise: knowledge, tradability and power. Paper presented at PICT Workshop on Exploring Expertise. Edinburgh, Nov. 1992

Fleury, Afonso. On the Issue of Transferability: Diffusion and Adoption of Japanese Modelling Brazilian Industry. *technological innovation and Global Proceedings of the European Conference on Management of Technology, 5-7 July 1995.* p. 841-848.

Frota, M and Frota. Acesso a informacao: estrategia para a competitividade. Sao Paulo, 1994.

Gibbons, M; Johnson, C. Science, technology and the development of the transistor. In: Barnes, B; Edge, D. (Eds.). *Science in context*: readings in the sociology of science, Milton Keynes: Open University, 1982. p. 177-185.

Gibbons, M; Johnston, R. The roles of science in technological innovation. *Research Policy,* v.3, n.3, p.220-242, 1974.

Gibbons M. et al. *The new production of knowledge*: the dynamics of science and research in contemporary societies. London: SAGE Publication, 1994

Galbraith, C.S. Transferring core manufacturing technologies in high-technology firms. *California Management review,* Summer, p. 56-70, 1990

Gee, R.E. Technology transfer effectiveness in university-industry co-operative research. *International ournal of Technology Management,* v.8, n.6-8, p. 652-668.

Gibbons, M; Jonston,R. The role of science in technological innovation. *Research Policy*, v.3, p. 220-242, 1974

Grant, Elliot; Steele, Andrew. International manufacturing transfer: linking context and process. Paper
presented at ICAM'95: Anthropocentric lean production. Sunderland (UK), 11-13 Sept., 1995 (pre-print)

Irwin, Harry; More, Elisabeth. Technology Transfer and Communication: Lessons from Silicon Valley, Route 128, Carolina's Research Triangle and Hi-tec Texas. Journal of information Science, v. 17, p. 273-280, 1991.

Kidd, John B; Stumm, Marielle; Bollo, Daniel. *Technological Innovation and Global Challenges. Proceedings of the European Conference on Management of Technology, 5-7 July 1995.* p. 621-628

Kim, D. H. The link between individual and organisational learning. *Sloan Management Review*, Fall.
p. 37-50, 1993

Kujanpaa, Raimo. Visual Information and Communication Methods Used in a Industrial R & D Project. *Technological Innovation and Global Challenges. Proceedings of the European Conference on Management of Technology, 5-7 July 1995.*

Layton, E. t. technology as knowledge. technology and Culture, v.15, n. 1 p. 31-41, 1974.

Lall, S. Technological Capabilities and Industrialisation. *World Development*, v.20, n.2, p. 65-186, 1992.

Lancaster, F.W. The evaluation of information services: a typology (copy).

Lastres, H. M. M. Acesso à informação: estrategia para conpetitividade: recensões. *Ci Inf.* Brasília, v.23, n. 2 p. 287-288, maio/ago. 1994.

Launo, Ritva. Perspectivas de informação tecnológica/industrial. *Ci.Inf.* Brasília, v.22, n. 2, maio/ago, 1993.

Leonard-Barton, D. Implementation as Mutual Adaptation of Technology Organisation. *Res. Policy,* v.17, n.5, 1988.

Leonardo-Barton, D. The factory as a learning laboratory. *Sloan Management Review*, Fall. p. 23-37, 1992

Lewis, Dennis A. There won't be an information profession in 2000 AD. In: RAFFIN, M.R; Passmore, R. The information worker: identity, image and potential. London: ASLIB, 1977. p. 38-49

Lundqvist, Mats A. *Organising for Cross-Functional Learning in Product Develop In: Technological Innovation and Global Challenges. Proceedings of the European Conference on Management of Technology, 5-7 July 1995.* p. 77-84.

Madeiros, A et al. Plos, incubadora . . . San Paulo, 1991.

Matkin, G.W. Technology transfer and the university. New York: Macmillan, 1990.

Midgley, M. *Wisdom, information and wonder*: what is knowledge for? London: Routledge, 1989.

Montali, Katia M L. Information in the capital goods industry in Brazil. Loughborough, University of Technology, 1987 (DPhil Thesis).

Negus, A. E. *Repackaging of engineering information for manufacturing industry.* London: British research & development, 1982.

Nelson, R. The role of knowledge in R and D efficiency. *Quarterly Journal of Economics,* n. 388, p.453-470, 1982.

Olaisen, Johan; Revang, Oivind. Information management as the main component in the strategy for the 1990s in Scandinavian Airlines Systems (SAS). International Journal of Information Management, v. 11, p. 185-202, 1991.

O'reilly, J. The future of the library/information unit in an industrial/commercial environment. In: International Online Information Meeting, 8th. London, 1984.

Osminski, E. m. *Business information needs of science park companies.* London: The British Library, 1991.

Pantry, Sheila. The changing role of library and information services (copy).

Porter, M. E. *The Competitive Advantage of Nations.* New York, Macmillian Press. 1990.

Pavit, K. Technology transfer among the industrial advanced countries: an overview. In: Rosenberg and

Frischtak (Eds). *International technology transfer.* New York: Praeger, 1985. p. 3-23

Rosenberg, N. *Inside the black box.* Cambridge: Cambridge University Press, 1982

Rosenberg, N. Scientific instrumentation and university research. Policy, n. 21, p. 381-390, 1991

Rumelt, R. P. *"Toward a strategic Theory of the Firms" in Competitive Strategic Management.* Prentice Hall, Eagelwood Cliffs. 1984.

Sbragia, Roberto; Kruglianskas, Isak. R & D at the Firm Level: The Implementation of Data Basein Brazil. *Technological Innovation and Global Challenges. Proceedings of the European Conference on Management of Technology, 5-7 July 1995.* p. 332 340.

Schrader, S; Riggs, W.M; Smith, R.P. Choice over uncertainty and Ambiguity in Technical problem Solving. *Journal of Engineering and Technology management*, v. 10, p. 73-99, 1993.

Schnelling, Reiner. Services for local industry from Constance university library (copy).
Schwartzman, S. *A space for science*: the development of scientific community in Brazil.University Park: Pennsylvania University Press, 1991.
Senker, Jacqueline. The contribution of tacit knowledge to innovation. *AI and Society*, n. 7 p. 208-224,1993.
Senker, Jacqueline; Faulkner, Wendy. Networks, tacit knowledge and innovation, In: COOMBS et al. (Eds.).*Technology Collaboration: causes and Consequence*. Cheltenham, 1995.
Sherwell, John. Design, implementation and evaluation of information systems for the end-users.
Sherwell, John. Information for trade and industry: the state-of-the-art in Great Britain. In: BABAGE, A. et al. Library service to industry: Proceedings of an Anglo-German Conference. London: Anglo-German Foundation for the Study of industrial Society, 1988. p. 12-20.
de Solla Price, D. J. The science/technology relationship, the craft of experimental science, and policyfor improvement of high technology innovation. *Policy,* v. 13, p. 3-20, 1984.
Teece, D.J. The market for know-how and the efficient international transfer technology. The Annuals of the American Academy of Political and Social Science, n. 458, Nov. p. 81-96, 1981.
Teece, D.J. Profiting from Technological Innovation. *Research Policy*, v.5, n.6, p. 285-395, 1986.
Teece, D.J; Pisano, G; Shuen, A. Dynamic capability and strategic management. University of California at Berkeley Working Paper, Feb. 1992.
Vickers, P.H. Common problem of documentary information transfer, storage and retrieval in industrial organisation. *Journal of Documentation,* v.39, n. 4, p. 217-229, 1983.
Vincenti, W. *What Engineers know and How They Know It*: analytical studies from aeronautical history. Baltimore: John Hopkins University Press, 1990.
Von Hippel, E; Tyre, M. How learning by doing is done: problematic identification in novel process equipment. *Research Policy*, v. 24, p. 1-12, 1994.
Voss, C (Ed.). *Management Advanced Manufacturing Technology*. Kempston, UK: IFS Publications, 1986.
Wildavsky, A. Information as an organisational problem. *Journal of Management Studies,* v. 20, n. 1, p. 29-40, 1983.
Winter, S. Knowledge and competence as strategic assets. In: TEECE (Ed.). *The Competitive Challenge*: strategies for industrial innovation and renewal. Ballinger, Cambridge Mass, 1987. p. 159-183.

Notes

* technical documents means here technical manuals, patents, rules, law, etc.

* See for example Rosenberg, Leitão, 1985; Faulkner,1993 and 1995; Senker, 1993; Barbosa, 1995; Grant; Steele, 1995 for further analysis about knowledge used by industry)

Chapter 14

Information, Knowledge and Empowerment: The role of information in rural development

Janet Cooper

This paper is concrned with the role of information as it relates to development in the rural areas of the least developed countries, principally those of sub-Saharan Africa. It points out that the lack of or misleading information has been a major contributory factor in the failure of development projects, indicating the need for dialogue between development personnel and beneficiaries and the importance of involving rural people at every stage of the development process. It argues that the principal objective of rural development is the empowerment of ordinary people to identify and take action to alleviate the conditions which affect their lives. Without this rural people will continue to be dependent on the aid of donor agencies; for development to become sustainable they must be enabled to become self-reliant and to take control of their own development. The discusses emphasises that the information worker has a vital role to play in ensuring that the information needs of both development personnel and rural people are accurately identified and that appropriate measures are taken to supply timely and relevant information in support of development.

Introduction

In this paper I have chosen to consider the role of information as it relates to development in the rural areas of the least developed countries, principally those of sub-Saharan Africa, where are found the highest levels of absolute poverty. Under such circumstances the poorest members of the rural population are virtually powerless to change the conditions that affect their lives. In many cases official development policy has not only failed to meet the needs of these people, but has frequently led to a deterioration in their circumstances. The lack of or misleading information has been a major contributory factor in the failure of development projects, indicating the need for dialogue between development personnel and beneficiaries and the importance of involving rural people at every stage of the development process.

The information worker has a vital role to play in ensuring that the information needs of both development personnel and rural people are accurately identified and that appropriate measures are taken to supply timely and relevant information in support of development. The principal objective of rural development is the empowerment of ordinary people to identify and take action to alleviate the conditions which affect their lives. Without this rural people will continue to be dependent on the aid of donor agencies; for development to become sustainable they must be enabled to become self-reliant and to take control of their own development.

Paradigms and problems

For much of the last forty years the accepted model of development has been modernisation, which involved the complete transformation of economic, cultural, social and political life. Developing countries were encouraged to adopt Western style economic and political systems; it was believed that modernisation of the economy could only come about through industrialisation and export expansion, urbanisation and the technological transformation of agriculture, whilst political modernisation required the rationalisation of authority, bureaucratisation, and democratisation, which was considered not only to be of value in itself but also necessary to maintain economic growth. Culturally, modernisation was defined by the spread of scientific knowledge, resulting in the secularisation of society. (Ingham, 1993)

Opposition to modernisation came from "dependistas" in Latin America in the 1960s, who gave their support to dependency theory, arguing that development and underdevelopment were interrelated processes, to be rectified by a strategy of industrialisation, import substitution, planning and state intervention aimed at achieving self-reliance. (Servaes, 1986)

Other approaches to development included broader considerations in the 1970s of income distribution, poverty and basic needs; absolute poverty being defined as the level of income below which it is impossible to achieve the basic requirements of food, clothing and shelter (Ingham, 1993). Taking this measurement into account, where poverty increased even though the national income had risen, development could not be said to have taken place. In addition economic development also contributed to a reduction of the individual's capabilities and traditional entitlements: for example, family support for the elderly was gradually eroded by modernisation and eventually replaced in developed societies by social security benefit [Ingham,1993].

This is not to say that there have been no improvements to human life as a result of modernisation. For example, in the last 50 years life expectancy in the developing countries has risen on average from 40 to 62 years. Literacy has increased and education has become more accessible at all levels. In cultural terms freedom of choice has expanded with regard to beliefs, values and lifestyles and has led in many societies to greater cultural diversity. However, the benefits to urban areas have generally been double those of rural areas, which have only half their access to health services and safe drinking water. The greatest poverty is found among the rural landless and small farmers and among recent urban migrants from rural areas. In all there are over one billion people living in poverty in the rural areas of developing countries: an estimated 60% of the rural population of sub-Saharan Africa have income and consumption levels which fall below national poverty lines.

Where did the development economists go wrong, and how did their assumptions prove to be so out of line with reality? The principles on which their view of development through modernisation and economic growth were based have come to be known as the "dominant development paradigm", and derive from a set of assumptions which have their origins in the Age of Enlightenment, culminating in the Western scientific method which was claimed to be objective, value-free and universally applicable. Guided by their faith in its infallibility, experts proceeded to impose scientific and economic models of development on cultures and communities very different from their own, in the expectation that they would automatically benefit from embracing Western economic concepts of need, productivity and growth.

Western scientific education has created, through its reductionist, analytical methods of learning, an elite with a monopoly over knowledge; specialists such as scientists and economists whose disciplines overlap but who operate independently of one another, whilst within disciplines specialisms increase. The subject/object relationship within the system results in a hierarchy of teachers/learners, where those at the bottom, i.e. the rural poor, are assumed to have nothing to teach the experts but to be merely passive recipients of both scientific knowledge and development. Since the experts regard the people as objects to be studied rather than as subjects of their own development, much of their academic output has proved to be irrelevant when applied to the problems of the poor, and this in turn has led to a consolidation of views to the extent that 'experts' and 'beneficiaries' have regarded one another as adversaries rather than collaborators (Edwards, 1989).

Rural people became suspicious of those who saw themselves as experts and benefactors, while they in turn looked upon rural people as having negative attitudes to change, being incapable of imagining themselves as other than they are, having low aspirations and reluctance to adopt innovations, and being fatalistic. This theory of 'individual blame', first put forward by Everett Rogers in 1969, became the stereotypical view of uneducated peasants under the dominant development paradigm (Melkote, 1991). That these attitudes have scarcely changed in over twenty years is illustrated by Ken Kampe (1992) in his list of beliefs associated with the 'development culture' which has evolved during 25 years of development practice among the hill tribes of Thailand. They are as follows:

- The only true development is economic development.
- The ignorance of the developee must be taken for granted.
- Understanding of the developee is not necessary for development.
- The relative dependency of the developee must be preserved.
- Development is a tool for winning friends and enhancing developer interests.
- Rhetoric is more important than action, quantity more important than quality (p.11).

Need for a New Development Paradigm

Modern science, or knowledge as power, has prevent people form becoming agents of their own development by retarding the sharing of knowledge and information. Access to knowledge has become a matter of privilege and specialist training only available to those with access to a Western scientific education, including the elites of developing countries who then return to perpetuate the inequalities in their native countries. The control of knowledge by North over South, state over people and educated elites over the rural poor has become the control of power which forms a central component of the development process (Edwards, 1989).

Development has come to mean the transfer of information and knowledge from the 'developed' to the 'underdeveloped', creating a role for the expert who alone is capable of mediating the transfer of skills and technology. It is now time for the development 'expert' to reconsider his or her position, and ask why it is that such technocratic approaches to development research, training and practice have largely failed to address the problems they were intended to solve (Edwards, 1989).

Although development is theoretically directed towards the poor, in practice preference is given to those concerns which are professionally considered of high status, dealing with people who are principally male, educated and more powerful, rather than with those who are weaker, female and of lower status. These people tend to be viewed as ignorant, passive and largely to blame for their conditions as inferior and dependent 'beneficiaries' (Chambers, 1986). An emphasis on economic development has led 'poor' people to perceive themselves as inferior and eventually results in their surrendering their indigenous cultural values and knowledge to 'superior' Western ideas. They lose their sense of cultural identity and their ability to develop indigenously, and become dependent on the dominating structures imposed on them (Rahman, 1989).

A new development paradigm is needed, where these power relations are reversed: the last come before the first in the choice of clients, professional values, research methods and roles. This new approach to development is essentially people-centred, the weak being given preference over the strong, children before adults and women before men; professionals become learners instead of experts and poor people their teachers. Priorities are no longer those of the professionals but those perceived by the poor; the goal of development is no longer seen as being economic growth for its own sake, but well-being as defined by the poor themselves. It involves a continuous search for new ways of understanding how best to meet the needs of the poor, recognising that these can only be discovered through dialogue and experiential learning as partners together with the rural poor. (Chambers, 1986).

Along with this it becomes necessary to redefine the purpose of knowledge as power to ordinary people, reducing the expert's monopolistic control over the commodity of knowledge, democratising the generation of knowledge and by implication shifting the balance of power from the hands of a few experts to the hands of many. Allowing ordinary people greater influence over the generation, utilisation and dissemination of information will enable them to use the power of knowledge to react against trends of oppression against them (Tandon, 1981).

The Importance of Participation

Since the early 1980s when Robert Chambers produced his seminal work "Rural development: putting the last first" (1983), development professionals have identified participation as one of the key ingredients in a successful development project, and participation of the beneficiary has become virtually integral to every development package. However, unless a project is actually owned by the people, i.e. they have a complete say in what will and will not be done and are ultimately responsible for the decisions taken, true participation cannot be said to have taken place; indeed, it is only when development workers learn to become participants in the people's projects that there can be true participation leading to the empowerment of the people. Participation cannot be simply a means used to achieve development but must be seen as an end in itself, the result of which will in fact be development, but on the people's terms and controlled by them. Participation and empowerment are inseparable elements without which truly sustainable development will not occur. Conscientisation, empowerment and liberation may be threatening concepts to development professionals and other experts who have held the reins of power along with the monopoly of knowledge for so long; they challenge established interests, for people's participation requires direct access to the resources necessary for development and the ability to use those resources to influence the course of events in their favour, enabling them to achieve greater control over their circumstances in a collective process of self-improvement (Burkey, 1993).

What emerges from all of this is the fact that development workers have to go into a rural situation being aware that they have information needs which are just as vital if not more so than those of the rural poor, and that they must be prepared to become learners taught by those who were formerly looked on as ignorant beneficiaries, recipients of the 'experts' stock of knowledge. It is now the turn of the poor to become instructors, to identify research priorities, plan agendas, express, analyse and present information, while the professional acts as facilitator and consultant when required. This reversal of roles requires a change of attitudes and behaviour in the professional as listed below by Chambers (1992):

- "participation by the outsiders in rural and village activities
- respect for rural people
- interest in what they have to say and show
- patience, wandering around, not rushing, not interrupting
- humility
- materials and methods that empower rural people to express and analyse their knowledge" (p.10).

Cultural values must be respected instead of viewed as obstacles to progress, since it is from these and their religious beliefs that the people derive meaning for their lives and a sense of identity and cultural integrity. The people must be allowed to build on their present knowledge and to develop new skills and abilities. In this way they will regain confidence in themselves and their ability to change their circumstances. Development workers must show appreciation for the poor as individuals and respect their knowledge and judgement, avoiding such comments and attitudes as will reinforce their sense of inferiority, using language that is easily understood rather than institutional jargon, and always be ready to learn from those with whom they are working (Burkey, 1993). In this way the conventional subject/object relationship will be replaced by one of true participation.

People who have not been used to having their ideas listened to require time to enable them to learn to express themselves and to take part in discussion and decision-making: this is not just a means to an end but an end in itself which must become a continuous process of reflection, analysis and action leading to change and sustainable development (Burkey, 1993). Only when this process is established may the development worker consider that his or her role as change agent has achieved its objective.

The training for development workers will involve a sensitisation process which will enable them to function as facilitators and initiators of the change process, so that they may be able to learn by listening and participation in village activities, and to develop changes in perception towards rural people as well as a critical self-awareness. Owing to the deep rooted dependency relationships of poor rural people, a catalyst is needed to initiate the development process; the development worker as initiator is needed to help the people analyse and understand their problems and to articulate their needs, so setting in motion the action-reflection process (Wignaraja, 1991).

As facilitators they are true 'development' workers, promoting human development by helping people think for themselves and discover that they have the ability and confidence to control their own lives; in short, they are facilitators of people's empowerment.

The Role of Information In Rural Development

Alongside the dominant development paradigm of modernisation for economic growth there emerged in the 1960s and 70s the concept of development communication as the vehicle by which the information needed by developing countries to enable them to modernise could be relayed by 'experts' largely through mass media. The flow of communication of information for development was conceptualised as a simple, mechanistic process of message transmission (Diaz Bordenave, 1977) with the purpose of creating awareness of new ideas and attitudes and changing the attitudes and behaviour of individuals. Mass media were seen as the obvious choice of channel for the unilinear transmission of development information by Daniel Lerner and other communication theorists; by exposing individuals to new ideas and attitudes they accelerated the modernisation process. Lerner saw mass media as both the index and the agent of modernisation, with growth in urbanisation, literacy and mass media systems as indices of social change. Diffusion of innovations theory established the importance of communication in the modernisation process at the local level, as the link by which exogenous ideas infiltrated the local communities (Melkote, 1991).

However, the diffusion model failed to take into account the constraints imposed by social structures in developing countries, assuming as it did that rural people were free to follow or reject development communication as relayed to them by opinion leaders. The theory of individual blame was brought to bear on those who failed to adopt the innovations for reasons assumed to be those of distrust, fatalism, and apathy rather than empathy (Carmen, 1989). The diffusionists failed to recognise that where people's decisions were influenced or negated by social structures in which decisions, values and strategies were imposed by an elite, then access to communication and information was also restricted. Where people did have the necessary information on a particular problem they often lacked the social capability, economic stability or political influence to put their knowledge into practice (Oepen, 1987). Moreover, mass media messages tended to be biased towards the urban population and largely irrelevant to rural people among whom interpersonal communication channels have always predominated (Diaz

Bordenave, 1977). This has resulted in an increasing 'knowledge-gap' between the urban/rich and rural/poor sectors of the population thus reinforcing economic and social disparity as the better-off have been able to benefit from development information while the disadvantaged rural poor fall further behind.

While recognising the importance of information in the development process, by concentrating on the effects of the source, message or channel on the attitudes, knowledge and behaviour of the receiver, communication specialists failed to give enough attention to the content of the messages or to whether the information conveyed was relevant to the receivers' actual problems and needs. No consideration was given to the need for feedback from farmers, in fact communication was seen purely as the unidirectional transmission of information for purposes of persuasion, an approach that was "essentially vertical, directive, aimed at manipulation and indoctrination" (Diaz Bordenave, 1977). A natural consequence of the prevailing view of development as modernisation, this approach assumed that underdeveloped countries needed to adopt the values, institutions and technology of industrialised countries, and that the role of development communication was to speed up the process.

Even within developing countries the top-down message flow continued from the scientists, aid agencies and administrators to the rural and (it was assumed) ignorant peasant. No value was seen in traditional methods of agriculture and so there was no reverse flow of ideas and practices from farmers to scientists; instead resources were concentrated on training farmers in new technology and techniques which were often not applied in the field, since trainees preferred to seek employment as extension agents and government officials. As a result the richer and better educated farmers benefited by the flow of information, and in turn became more successful and increased their information seeking activities, but the expected flow of information to the poorer farmers from the diffusion process did not materialise, and their lack of access to information led to failures and a distrust of extension practices and external agents with little knowledge of their problems and constraints (Melkote, 1991).

Participatory Approaches to Development Communication

One of the most influential critics of top-down methods of communication has been Paulo Freire, Brazilian educator, who in the 1970s described such communication and education systems as tools for the domination of the masses, which contributed nothing to the passive receiver's development as a person capable of contributing to and influencing society, but rather reduced the peasant to the status of an object, the recipient of externally initiated development projects (Carmen, 1989). He emphasised the need to replace such 'banking education' with a 'pedagogy of the oppressed' in which education and communication would be participative and receiver-centred. He first introduced the idea of 'conscientisation', defined as the ability of individuals to see the social system critically (Carmen, 1990) in which communication channels would be used to bring about dialogue through which rural people would arrive at an understanding of their real needs, be able to identify their real constraints and plan to overcome their problems (Melkote, 1991). Instead of being passive recipients rural people would become empowered to become active and informed citizens capable of making decisions regarding community issues, and to regain control of the resources which were rightfully theirs (Carmen, 1990). Kothari (1988) expressed the changing perspectives on development communication thus: "It has to be thought of not as a specialized concern, but as part and parcel of the struggle for human liberation, freedom and justice, strengthening the struggles of communities and cultures, of national entities that are thought to be marginalised, and of already marginalised peoples within these and other societies" (Nair and White, 1993).

The conventional view of knowledge under the dominant development paradigm as the monopoly of the expert is replaced under the participatory development paradigm by 'knowledge empowerment' based on the view that all life styles and cultures are equal, that no-one is totally ignorant (or totally knowledgeable) and that all individuals have the ability to create knowledge through dialogue (Carmen, 1990).

Whereas earlier communication models regarded mass mediated information to be essential whether or not it was of use to the receiver, repeated failures of this approach brought about a realisation that ordinary people should have more access not only to communication media, but also to message development. Instead of top-down communication of development information to rural people it was concluded that there was a great need for reliable and effective assessment of their needs, and that a two-way process of participatory communication could be more effective in bringing about rural development (Melkote, 1991). It was realised that in order for participatory communication to be situated in its overall, complete context it was necessary to view it as an integral part of the movement towards the goal of people-centred development, resulting in social and political empowerment.

The development communication expert must now become facilitator in the participatory process, enabling the sharing of ideas through dialogue in an environment which is supportive, creative, consensual and facilitative (Nair and White, 1987). He or she will link bureaucrats, experts and scientists to rural; people, enabling an exchange of information critical to the rural development process, and must be committed to listening to and enabling people to identify their needs and choose communication media that are appropriate and accessible to the participants (Rodrigo, 1989). The communication priorities of the poor must be recognised and acted upon, and existing channels and methods of communication identified and utilised where possible.

However, as we saw earlier, 'participation' may be interpreted in various ways, and it can be argued that true participation only takes place when the people have complete control of a project and ultimate responsibility for decisions, since this is the only type of participatory development that contributes to their empowerment.

In considering the role of information in the participatory rural development process, three distinct yet complementary and overlapping areas may be identified:

1. The provision of information by participatory communication in specific rural development projects; this is sometimes referred to as 'development support communication'.
2. The democratic generation of knowledge by participatory methods for rural people's empowerment.
3. The provision of information in response to rural people's expressed needs as part of an integrated approach to rural development.

Information for Rural Development Projects

By involving rural people in the planning, implementation and evaluation of their development they are encouraged to contribute their own ideas and knowledge in the decision-making process, but at the same time it has to be recognised that all the information needed is not held by the poor. In "Delivering relevant development information to the rural poor" Dr. Erasmus Monu of the International Institute of Rural Reconstruction (IIRR), the Philippines, writes "meaningful participation depends on availability of adequate and timely information. The rural poor need reliable and timely information. to make rational decisions in project planning, implementation and evaluation" (Monu, 1989). They need the assistance of facilitators to bring together their own sources of information and those of outsiders. Dr. Monu refers to the IIRR's Operational Research Framework which suggests that the development agency should act as catalyst, its principal function being "to facilitate the establishment of functioning people's organisation with adequate capabilities in problem solving, including resource mobilization" (Monu, 1989).

The IIRR has formulated a strategy to facilitate this process, as follows:

1. Legitimisation: this is the first stage in which the RRF gets to know the villagers and collects all available information on the village and surrounding area.

2. Rapport-building: this continues the dialogue during which the RRF collects further information from the villagers on the physical, social and economic characteristics of the village. This information will serve to validate the earlier information and help to identify the poorer villagers. From this the RRF goes on to identify useful technical or service information. He or she will also identify the existing communication channels and their uses.
3. Packaging of information: the RRF will develop a list of technologies and services appropriate to the villagers' needs, which may then be adapted for use in village discussions.
4. Problem identification and prioritisation: the problems of the poorest villagers are given priority.
6 Data information collection: the RRF assists the group in collecting the information they require and may link them to other useful information sources.
6. Formal evaluation: the RRF facilitates the formal identification of problems to be tackled, the possible solutions and ranking of alternatives.
7. Selection of action pathways, once problems and possible solutions have been prioritised.
8. Designing implementation strategy: this may include forming links with similar groups
9. Implementation: this includes the design of a project information system which will collect data/information related to problem solving activities.
10. Monitoring and evaluation: this will involve the documentation of all activities, including interviews and field notes, followed by a summative evaluation to determine the impact of the project, including the extent to which information made available is actually used, and whether any development change results from the use of information in the development projects (Monu, 1989).

This carefully worked out strategy is aimed to providing the rural poor with reliable and adequate information "without unduly influencing their decision-making process" (Monu, 1989). Thus even where the initiative for the project comes from an external agency it is still possible to involve the rural population in every aspect of the process to their maximum benefit, resulting in their increased self-awareness, self-confidence and eventual empowerment.

Democratisation of People's Knowledge

"When a knowledgeable old person dies, a whole library disappears"
African proverb.

The proponents of participatory research emphasise time and again the need to "return knowledge to the people" (Burkey, 1993). Wignaraja (1991) maintains that "connecting people to their knowledge system. is essential in societies where there is the need to decolonise the minds of the people and where repressive institutions continue to prevent the release of the creative energies of the people". People's local knowledge has for so long been despised and mistrusted by the 'experts' for being non-scientific, primitive and based on superstition, that the people themselves have come to consider it inferior to Western scientific knowledge.

Within every culture there is, as we have seen, intrinsic interconnection between knowledge and power, and so the restoration and empowerment process must involve an examination of the social basis of the people's knowledge systems (Wignaraja, 1991). There will be much traditional technology and knowledge which is still of use, and as part of the participatory development process the people themselves need to be encouraged to document, store and disseminate their own knowledge in their own language, through the use of cultural traditions such as story-telling, folk songs and drama. In this way their collective knowledge may be used to build up their collective consciousness, and from there disseminated to neighbouring communities to enable them in their development process: thus they themselves become 'agents of change' (Burkey, 1993). Some of their knowledge may be almost forgotten and will need reviving through participatory research into cultural traditions such as popular stories and ballads, through these people many discover elements in their past which have proved useful in past struggles: Fals Borda (1991) refers to this as the "critical recovery of history".

Collective research and knowledge retrieval will include the collection of information from other sources (with or without the help of facilitators) which then needs to be systematised and validated within the people's own experience and culture. As people investigate their reality there follows a continuous feedback and evaluation process which in turn leads to subsequent action; this releases people's creative energy as part of the reflection, analysis and action process based on their own goals and values. In this way people's knowledge becomes people's power through participatory research and action (Wignaraja, 1991). The people themselves need to gain control over the social power which determines what constitutes useful knowledge, in order that the gap between those who have power over knowledge generation and those who have not may be narrowed, and with it the ability to change the circumstances which affect their lives. This can only happen through endogenous consciousness raising, and knowledge generation and verification processes which are developed collectively through dialogue and social action (Fals Borda, 1991).

Just as approaches to development have changed over the years, so have developmentalists' views on people's indigenous knowledge. From being considered inferior and an obstacle to development in the '60s, it became recognised in the '70s as a 'valuable and under-utilised resource' which might be incorporated into formal research practices to provide sustainable approaches to rural development (Scoones and Thompson, 1993). However, any approach which does not give priority to the empowerment of the people whose development is in question cannot be fully sustainable; it is their knowledge and it is therefore their responsibility to decide how it should be used.

People's knowledge is not static but cumulative and dynamic, continually adapting as it comes into contact with other types of knowledge. There are practical problems for information and development workers trying to translate ideas and concepts from one culture into another, and so it is essential to recognise the differences and similarities of Western and traditional knowledge systems. Indigenous knowledge is orally based, assimilated through action and contact with nature; thus it includes systems of classification and observation about the local environment and the use of resources; in contrast to Western scientific knowledge it is holistic, intuitive, spiritual, qualitative, subjective and experiential, rather than reductionist, analytical, quantitative, objective and positivist. However, indigenous and scientific knowledge are not as incontiguous as might at first appear: both are at the same time general and specific, theoretical and practical, value-laden and context bound and influenced by relations of power (Scoones and Thompson, 1993).

Information scientists who attempt to isolate, document and store indigenous knowledge in national and international resource centres are using Western scientific methods to capture cultural knowledge whose vigour comes from being integrally linked to people's lives. By doing this they are not only separating it from those interactions on which its dynamic depends, and so virtually condemning it to stagnation, but they are failing to recognise the links between power and knowledge; by making it available to all they are in fact undermining people's control over their own knowledge (Agrawal, 1995).

It is therefore vitally important that people should be enabled to collect, analyse, store and disseminate their own knowledge, and be in control of their own research, with assistance from development and information workers acting as catalysts and facilitators in a dialogical, continuous process of learning and action (Scoones and Thompson, 1993).

The Provision of Information as Part of an Integrated Approach to Rural Development

Having considered the way in which the need for information runs through the whole development process, we come to look specifically at the provision of information services, and the role of the information needs of rural people. Taking as our example sub-Saharan Africa, where are found the countries with not only the lowest GNP per capita but also the lowest rates of literacy in the world (IFAD, 1992) we may appreciate the need for information in the people's struggle for empowerment, democracy, literacy, human rights and improved quality of life.

Unfortunately the traditional providers of information, the public library services, have only succeeded in perpetuating the colonial legacy, following service patterns which were originally set up to serve the settler communities: consequently they are ineffective and largely irrelevant to the majority of African rural people (Kantumoya, 1992). If public libraries are to become effective in meeting the needs of rural, and frequently illiterate, people they will need first of all to set aside top-down attitudes to information provision, recognising that information is not just the prerogative of the educated, but an essential resource which should be accessible to all, and set about identifying the variety of information needs of those groups which they aim to serve. They will also need to discover what traditional knowledge resources remain and the ways in which this knowledge is exchanged, since indigenous knowledge systems with their 'information gatekeepers' (often village elders or religious leaders), traditional places or occasions where news and information are exchanged, as well as people's existing reading and radio-listening habits, need to form part of a strategy on which a rural development information service can be based (Mchombu, 1992a).

Experiments by library services to set up rural information services have proved to be successful only to the extent to which local people have been involved in their formation. One-off surveys where people are questioned about their needs have only tended to reveal general areas of information need (Rosenberg, 1993). At the end of a two-month study of rural people's information needs in Malawi, Mchombu (1992b) concluded that people's rural development needs could not be determined simply by questioning them (up to 30% said they had no information needs), but when asked to discuss their needs within a specific context such as health or economic problems they were able to articulate their information needs quite clearly.

Describing a pilot rural library service in Nigeria in which people were offered the opportunity to voice their information needs, Aboyade (1987) states that village people were keen to avail themselves of the facility for making reference and referral requests and in doing so revealed a number of information needs on a variety of matters such as health and diet and the best way to build latrines. Requests were repeatedly made for requests to be passed on to the authorities for the supply of amenities such as piped water, electricity and roads. Many questions revolved around ways to improve village life and work, particularly with regard to obtaining fertiliser, credit facilities and loans. Reading materials were popular, and so were reading sessions of excerpts from books and plays by Yoruba writers. People were politically aware, including the illiterate, and asked for newspaper reports on current events, whilst pamphlets and posters on various topics of interest proved popular.

On the basis of this pilot project Aboyade (1987) envisages a model of a rural development information system (RUDIS). It is designed from the point of view of the recipients of rural development since, the author claims, information provision and use has almost exclusively focused on the needs of policy and decision makers and researchers and those who implement their decisions. It will also take into consideration the information needs of those development workers who have direct contact with rural people. The people will be the most important sources of information on their culture and social conditions, and will have the facility of providing feedback on development projects directed at them. Particular attention will be given to literacy problems: information processing will involve repackaging activities in suitable formats and languages, and a multi-media approach to information dissemination will be adopted.

Documentation activities will involve the identification and collection of materials and information will largely be of the problem-solving type to aid the people in their daily lives.

Ideally Aboyade (1987) maintains that every rural community should have "a library in form of a general information centre under the care or supervision of a professional", and "each community should be able to develop the type of library services that suits and enhances its social goals and development objectives". A network of local libraries would be overseen by a "National Information Centre for Rural Development" which would act as a "central clearing house of information" and "establish a network for existing information sources" which would be available to all.

Unfortunately no more recent information has been forthcoming on Aboyade's enthusiastic if ambitious proposals. As Kantumoya (1992) points out finance is a major problem in the development of rural information services and public libraries which are already underfunded would need to recruit and train extra personnel. In particular where a state-controlled library service operates within a restrictive political, economic and social framework the likelihood of priority being given to establish services where the majority or people are illiterate is very low, nor are such governments likely to endorse the establishment of information centres where activities, whose objectives include promoting the empowerment of the poor, may be construed as political (Rosenberg, 1993).

It is possible therefore that the public library service is not the best agent for promoting rural information centres. Rosenberg (1993) suggests that a stable administration structure is necessary for a sustainable rural development information service, and that local non-governmental organisations such as churches may be able to provide such stability. Mchombu (1992a) also takes the issue of sustainability and reiterates the need to "create services which are market led rather than offering services which are institution centred".

He also stresses the importance of both participation in order that the information products created may reflect the people's needs and that they may be fully involved in the change process, and of empowerment, so that rural people may be enabled to analyse problems, take action and communicate feedback to development agencies, with priority being given to developing their self-confidence and self-awareness.

Mchombu writes as a result of undertaking the 'INFORD' Research Project of which the above-mentioned Malawi study formed a part together with similar studies into rural people's information needs for development in Tanzania and Botswana.

The propositions on which the project was based included the assumption that a link was needed between the indigenous and external knowledge systems and that an information system could not be created in isolation but must form "an organic part of the community's struggle to develop and preserve itself" while "the end-users of information should be involved as main 'actors' and decision makers in the creation and maintenance of an Information System" (Mchombu, 1993).

Mchombu (1992a) stresses the need for information providers to find ways of combining the different knowledge systems found in rural communities: exogenous knowledge supplied by extension services, education, health services, etc; indigenous knowledge developed within each community; and the "knowledge and information generated through the development process, and through experiment carried out by members of the rural community" (p.67). Each knowledge system is distinct from yet convergent on the others; none can alone satisfy the information needs of rural people.

During the INFORD surveys it was found that when rural people were questioned individually about the use of indigenous knowledge the great majority disowned it, but when group discussions were held enthusiasm and excitement was generated as the people collectively shared their experiences of using indigenous knowledge in such fields as medicine, midwifery and the passing on of social skills and behaviour. It appeared that the effects of Western education, particularly on the elite who had taken over most of the functions and powers of chiefs and headmen, had undermined the cultural fabric of the rural communities and conditioned people to deny the efficacy and indigenous knowledge which had virtually been driven underground (Mchombu, 1993).

Ideas for reviewing cultural traditions such as songs, folk tales, poems and dances, as well as ceremonies which were traditional vehicles for passing on knowledge were forthcoming during discussion, and it was realised that such knowledge that remained should be recorded by younger generations before it dies out. It was suggested that skills and technical knowledge should be taught in primary schools by members of the community in order to teach younger people to be self-reliant and appreciate their cultural heritage.

Two types of indigenous knowledge were identified: the common or generalised knowledge which was available to everybody, and specialised information which was the preserve of medicine men, traditional birth attendants, blacksmiths, etc., and was passed on through clans or families through long apprenticeships. Women in particular had specialised knowledge which may only be spoken of to other women, as well as skills and knowledge acquired in food production.

Mchombu (1993) suggests that audio cassettes should be used to record indigenous knowledge experiences as part of the rehabilitation process. Rural people also need encouragement in the creation of local knowledge based on their own experiences and information providers can help by supplying information about innovations, while those who have successfully adopted new ideas should be encouraged to share their experiences through group networking, with the information facility as a contact point (Mchombu, 1992a). Sara Stuart (1987) describes how village women successfully used video as a co-operative information exchange tool to make development solutions available to neighbouring communities, an approach which she maintains values the individual and local experience and builds confidence and a sense of empowerment.

Mchombu, (1992a) avoids making concrete suggestions for a rural development information strategy, since each must be tailored to the specific needs of the community, but the following principles may be derived from his findings:

1. The need to identify the gaps in the existing information transfer/exchange process. Information support must be relevant to the people's needs, and these can only be discovered through dialogue. Both general and location specific needs must be identified.
2. The need to identify how the information exchange/transfer process operates: who are the opinion leaders and information gatekeepers who need to be involved in managing the provision of information, which are the places and occasions where people exchange news and information and what are their usual communication channels.
3. The need to discover the level of literacy in the community so that information may be produced in the most appropriate formats, and also the existing reading and radio listening habits of the villagers.
4. The need to encourage the villagers to revive their own indigenous knowledge and cultural traditions, and to create and share knowledge based on their collective experiences.
5. The need to encourage villagers to experiments and share their successes with others using appropriate media.
6. The need to train community members in the collection, use and storage of endogenous and exogenous information, and in the maintenance of records for use in the rural development process (Mchombu, 1992a, 1993).

Finally Mchombu (1992a) asks "What is the role and function of an information worker, and how does she or he become an effective player in an integrated rural development team?" He suggests the following requirements:

"• an understanding of the basic rural development concepts and its integrated nature.
• an understanding of participative and conscientisation methodologies in community organization.
• an understanding of how to conduct information needs assessment.
• an understanding of how to design, maintain and market a development information support service.

- an understanding of how to facilitate two-way communication of information between individuals, officials, politicians and policy makers.
- an awareness of how the innovation process works in Africa and the role of information sharing in speeding up the adoption proceeds.
- an understanding of the different systems of knowledge operating in rural Africa and how to harness them in support of rural development" (pp.69-70).

Conclusions

The main thesis of this paper is that information is essential to the development process, and that the focus of development should be the empowerment of those people who are lowest on the social scale, whose culture and knowledge systems have been eroded, and who as a result have lost control over the circumstances which affect their lives and the resources on which they depend. It has to be recognised that information is one such resource to which everyone, whatever their social status, should have equal access. All those who are involved in the provision of information to those who are the subjects of development (and this will increasingly include the urban as well as the rural poor as urbanisation continues into the 21st century) have a responsibility to ensure that participatory methods are used to determine the supply of relevant information, and the restoration of control over the knowledge creation process to ordinary people. This does not mean that development projects will always be successful or that participation will always run smoothly since in every community there will always be individuals who attempt to assume power for themselves. It is important however to recognise existing social structures and institutions and to build on these while consciously directing development initiatives to the poorest and least powerful in the community.

Taking these principles into account we may conclude with a summary of the characteristics of a participatory approach to information provision in support of rural development in the form of a model as follows:

Model for Participatory Information Provision in Support of Rural Development

1. Motive for provision: People's empowerment
2. Attitudes towards group Capable of self-development
3. Attitude towards participation A continuous process
4. Learning relationship: Everyone has a contribution to make
5. People seen as: Subjects and actors in development
6. Leaders seen as: Leaders, animators, facilitators and coordinators
7. Selection of leaders: Eventually by people themselves
8. Communication process: Bottom-up, multidirectional
9. Communication methods: Dialogue, using existing channels
10. Planning format: Open ended
11. Time scale: Long term, sustainable by people themselves
12. Indigenous knowledge seen as: people's resource to be used and shared by them
13. Media use: multimedia as appropriate to group
14. Information provision: by information professionals and people themselves
15. Information format: written, oral and visual
16. Information products: problem solving in response to people's expressed needs
17. Monitoring and evaluation: by people themselves
18. Ultimate objective: people's self-reliance

Old development proverb

Go in search of Your People
Love Them;
Learn from Them;
Plan with Them;
Serve Them;
Begin with what They have;
Build on what They know.

But of the best leaders
when their task is accomplished,
their work is done,
The people all remark:
<<We have done it Ourselves.>>

References

Aboyade, B. Olabimpe, Communication potentials of the library for non-literates - an experiment in providing information services in a rural setting *Libri*, 1984, 34 (3), 243-262

Aboyade, B. Olabimpe. *Provision of information for rural development* Ibadan: Fountain Publications. 1987

Agrawal, Arun, Dismantling the divide between indigenous and scientific knowledge *Development and change*;1995, 26 (3), 413-39

Agha, Syed Salim and Akhtar, Shadid., Responsibility and the response: sustaining information systems in developing countries, *Journal of information science*, 1992; 18 (4), 283-92

Alvares, Claude, Science in Sachs, Wolfgang *The development dictionary: a guide to knowledge as power*, London: Zed Books, 1992.

Anacleti, Odhiambo, Research into local culture: implications for participatory development, *Development in practice*; 1993 3 (1), 44-47

Annis, Sheldon, Giving voice to the poor, *Foreign policy*; 1991, 84, 93-106

Bajaj, Jatinder K., Francis Bacon, the first philosopher of modern science: a non-Western view, in Nandy, Ashis *Science, hegemony and violence: a requiem for modernity*, Tokyo: UNU, 1988.

Brindley, Bonita, What is sustainable? Some rules for the development road, *Ceres* ; 1991,128, 35-38

Burkey, Stan. People first: a guide to self-reliant participatory rural development. London: Zed Books, 1993

Carmen, Raff, Development communication: the search for a participatory paradigm, *Community development journal*; 1989, 24 (4), 264-272

Carmen, Raff. *Communication, education and empowerment.* Manchester: Centre for Adult and Higher Education, 1990.

Chambers, Robert. *Normal professionalism, new paradigms and development.* IDS discussion paper 227 Brighton: Institute of Development Studies, 1986.

Chambers, Robert, Rapid and participatory rural appraisal, *Africanus*; 1992,_ 22 (2), 6-15

Davies, Susanna (ed.) et al., Knowledge is power?, *IDS Bulletin*; 1994, 25 (2)

Diaz Bordenave, Juan E. *Communication and rural development* Paris: UNESCO. 1977.

Diener, Richard A.V., Cultural dissolution, a societal information disaster: the case of the Yir Yoront in Australia; in Horton, Forest W. *Great information disasters* London: ASLIB, 1991

Durani, Shiraz, Rural informaton in Kenya, *Information development*; 1985,1 (3), 149-157

Edwards, Michael, The irrelevance of information studies, *Third world quarterly* ; 1989,11 (1), 116-135

Escobar, Arturo (1992) "Planning" in SACHS, Wolfgang op.cit.

Fals-Borda, Orlando, Participatory research and rural social change, *Journal of rural cooperation;* 1982,10 (1), 25-40

Fals-Borda, Orlando. Action and knowledge: breaking the monopoly with participatory action-research London: IT Publications, 1991.

Horton, Forest W. *Great information disasters* London: ASLIB, 1991.

Ingham, Barabara, The meaning of development: interactions between "new" and "old" ideas, *World development;* 1993, 21 (11), 1803-1821

Jazairy, I., Alamgir, M. and Panuccio, T. for IFAD [International Fund for Agricultural Development], *The state of rural world poverty: causes and consequences,* New York: New York UP, 1992.

Johnson, Martha. Lore: capturing traditional environmental knowledge. Ottawa: IDRC, 1992

Kampe, Ken, Development, bureaucracy and life on the margins, *Pacific viewpoint*; 1992,33 (2), 159-164

Kantumoya, Albert, Public libraries and community information services in Africa, *African journal of librarianship, archives and information science;* 1992, 2 (1) 33-38

Kempson, Elaine. Rural community information services: literature review and guidelines for developing services Paris: UNESCO, 1990.

Kivikuru, Ullamaija, Participation or the popular: where to find a nest for the restless minds of rural transition, *Africa media review;* 1994, 8 (3), 40-77

Marglin, F.A. and Marglin, S.A, *Dominating knowledge: development, culture and resistance* Oxford: Clarendon Press, 1990.

Maxmwell, Nicholas. From knowledge to wisdom: a revolution in the aims and methods of science Oxford: Basil Blackwell, 1984.

Mchombu, Kingo J, Rural development information communication in Africa: creating conditions for success, *Information trends* ; 1992a, 5 (2), 51-72

Mchombu, Kingo J., Information needs for rural development: the case study of Malawi" *African journal of librarianship, archives and information science*; (1992b, 2 (1) 17-32

Mchombu, Kingo J. Information needs and seeking patterns for rural people's development in Africa Gaborone: (s.n. PPCB), 1993.

Mehta, S. R. Communication and development, issues and perspectives Jaipur: Rawat, 1992.

Melkote, Srinivas. Communication for development in the Third World. New Delhi: Sage, 1991.

Menike, Karunawathie., People's empowerment from the people's perspective, *Development in practice*; 1993,3 (3), 176-183

Monu, Erasmus, Delivering relevant development information to the rural poor, *Media Asia*; 198,16 (1), 10-15

Morin-Labatut, Gisele and Akhtar, Shahid, Traditional environmental knowledge: a resource to manage and to share, *Development: journal for the Society for International Development* 1992 (4), 24-29

Nair, K.S. and Whie, S.A, Participation is the key to development communication, *Media development*;1987 (3), 36-40

Nair, K.S. and White, S.A. (eds). *Perspectives on development communication* New Delhi: Sage, 1993.

Nandy, Ashis, Science, hegemony and violence: a requiem for modernity Tokyo: UNU, 1988.

Nwagha, Georgiana K.N, Information needs of rural women in Nigeria, *Information development*; 1992, 8 (2). 76-82

Ogun, Bilge, and Smith, Karen Houston. Innocenti Global Seminar: participatory development, : summary report Rome: ICDC, 21-29 May 1991.

Oepen, Manfred (ed.). *Development support communication in Indonesia* Jakarta: Friedrich-Naumann-Stiftung, 1988.
Oepen, Manfred, The barefoot microchip, *Adult education and development* 1990 (34), 3-18
Ojiambo, J.B., Developing human resource capacity for information services in Africa, *African journal of librarianship, archives and information science*; 1992, 2 (2), 83-92
QuebralL, Nora, The application of information and communication technology to development, *Media Asia*; 1992, 19 (4), 213-216
Rodrigo, Milan L., Communication and development: obstacles in implementing development programmes, *Media Asia*; 1989,16 (4), 206-7, 210-14
Rosenberg, Diana, Rural community resource centres: a sustainable option for Africa, *Information development*; 1995, 9 (1/2), 29-35
Sachs, Wolfgang. The development dictionary: a guide to knowledge as power. London: Zed Books, 1992.
Salole, Gerry, Participatory development: the taxation of the beneficiary?", *Journal of social development in Africa*; 1991,6 (2), 5-16
Samad, A., Participatory development: a panacea for rural uplift in the Third World" *Journal of rural development and administration*; 1990, 22 (4), 38-48
Schoenhoff, Doris M. The barefoot expert: the interface of computerized knowledge systems and indigenous knowledge systems. Westport: Greenwood Press, 1993.
Scoones, Ian and Thompson, John. *Challenging the populist perspective: rural people's knowledge, agricultural research and extension practice* Institute of Development Studies Discussion Paper 332. Brighton: IDS. 1993.
Servaes, Jan. Towards an alternative concept of communication and development, *Media development*;1984 (4). 2-5
Servaes, Jan, Communication and development paradigms: an overview" *Media Asia*; 1986,13 (3), 128-136
Shiva, Vandana., Reductionist science as epistemological violence, in Nandy, Ashis op.cit.
Shiva, Vandana. Staying alive: women, ecology and development London: Zed Books. 1988.
Stuart, Sara., The village video network: video as a tool for development and south-south exchange, *Convergence*; 1987, 20 (2), 62-68
Tandon, Rajesh, Participatory research in the empowerment of people, *Convergence*; 1981,14 (3), 20-29
Wignaraja, Ponna et.al. Participatory development learning from South Asia. Karachi: OUP. 1991.

Chapter 15

Participative Citizenry in the Information Age: The role of science and technology towards democratic education in a multicultural society

John Clay

The teaching and learning of science and technology have to be considered carefully if we are to avoid the systematic disenfranchising of many children and young people. Science has to be viewed as a cultural construct with a clear social dimension. The history of `modern science', its philosophical underpinnings and its applications need to be critically examined. The very nature of science has to be explored and questioned.

In this paper I will argue that the aims of science and technology in schools have little to do with empowering future citizens to become scientifically literate but concerns itself primarily with producing a reified work force. This is partly because the prevailing orthodoxy as to what constitutes a valid scientific and technological education for the compulsory school years has continued to foster the notion that there is a single and unproblematic way of doing and knowing. The curriculum thus offered continues to produce outcomes that do little to empower learners but instead seperates and pegeonholes people either as 'experts' or 'non-experts'. Instead this paper argues for a scientifically and technologically literate and participative citizenry for the next century.

Introduction: Epistemology of Science

Science and technology together or as seperate subjects is now a permanent fixture of the school curriculum of most countries. However, the teaching of science and technology has to be carefully considered to avoid the systematic disenfranchisement of many children and young people. Science should be viewed as a cultural construct with a clear social dimension. The birth of `modern science' and the history of its development needs critical examination and re-evaluation. The very nature of science, its epistemolgy, has to be explored and questioned.

The Mertonian concept of the scientific community working to and within the four principal norms of universalism, communality, organized scepticism and disinterestedness helped to portray science as acultural, objective and unfettered by the messy contradictions that pervades other forms of knowledge construction. (Merton, 1949) This view of science also colludes in the separation of science from technology since technology has always been considered culturally embedded.

In this paper, I intentionally link technology with science. I fully acknowledge that many educators have stated that technology should be considered as a distinct epistemology, differently understood in Germany and Sweden. The Sciences vs. Arts dichotomy that currently exists in Anglo Saxon tradition is not mirrored in Germany where there are three subcultures: *Wissenschaft, Kunst and Technik.*(1) It has been argued that:

> Technik is a separate cultural area with codes of behaviour, responses and a dignity of its own. Those working within it do not have constantly to look over their shoulders at `science' or `arts'. `Science' and `arts' do

> not care much for utility, in the way that technik does; furthermore they have a different grasp of the artificial. Technik remains a missing concept in English (Fores and Rey, 1986).

There is the more dominant tradition of viewing science and technology as being both mutually dependent and reinforcing. This position has assumed greater importance since it is the one that has been adopted by the USA. Indeed, science educationalists have argued for technology to be taught in schools as an integral part of school science for some considerable time saying that:

> . . . Science teaching [should move] from merely being a pure 'science for scientists', to embrace more applications in 'science for action', and also more significance as 'science for citizens'. If our science teaching can widen in this way we will have no need for 'technology' as such. Indeed, I believe it is positively harmful to urge that 'technology' should be introduced as a separate subject in the timetable (Woolnough, 1975).

The term technology is defined as, 'the application of scientific and other organized knowledge to practical tasks by hierarchically ordered systems that involve people and machines' (Naughton, 1981). The American Association for the Advancement of Science (AAAS), in launching 'Project 2061: *Science for All Americans*' has been unequivocal about the close relationship between science and technology. The fundamental premise of Project 2061 is that:

> Science for All Americans is based on the belief that the literate person is one who is aware that science, mathematics, and technology are interdependent human enterprises with strengths and limitations; understands key concepts and principles of science; is familiar with the natural world and recognizes both its diversity and unity; and uses scientific knowledge and scientific ways of thinking for individual and social purposes (AAAS, 1989,1990 pp xvi:xvii).

The above project will have a profound effect on the type of science education that millions of young Americans will receive. The project's recommendations include the paradigmmatic view of the way technology draws on science and contributes to it which is pertinent to this paper. It says that:

> Engineering, the systematic application of scientific knowledge in developing and applying technology, has grown from a craft to become a science in itself. . . Scientific knowledge provides a means of estimating what the behaviour of things will be before we make them or observe them. Moreover, science often suggests new kinds of behaviour that had not even been imagined before, and so leads to new technologies. In return, technology provides the eyes and the ears of science - and some of the muscle too. As technologies become more sophisticated, their links to science become stronger. In some fields, such as solid-state physics (which involves transistors and superconductors), the ability to make something and the ability to study it are so interdependent that science and engineering can scarcely be separated (op. cit. pp 26:27).

These understandings of the inseparable links between science and technology lead me to conflate the two for the purposes of this chapter, and any critique of science and/or technology applies to both areas of the curriculum. In addition, the fact that technology is now a foundation subject in the National Curriculum for England and Wales should not be seen as a softening of that approach by science educationalists but more as a pyrrhic victory for the political ideologues that view the inclusion of technology as a separate subject as in part, a `quick fix' solution to British industry's lack of competitiveness.

Science as objective and value-free knowledge has become established orthodoxy. This ideology is deeply rooted and cannot be easily countered because organized science as a body of knowledge and as a way of exploring the world around us has been regarded as neutral, outside the social, economic and political spheres. This portrayal of science as being above the messy everyday existence of day to day living has served a useful purpose in allowing science as a discipline to remain unaccountable to all sections of society, with the possible exception to their own self-selected community of peers and to those with sufficient power to confer patronage and privilege.

The application of privileged scientific knowledge has been the single most important determinant in the maintenance of global power by the USA and its allies that form the G7 group of countries. The Gulf War highlighted the destructive capacity of the applications of science and yet by calling that sharp end of applied science `high-technology', science as a discipline can remain cloaked with the myth of neutrality.

The conflicts over the past forty years have become increasingly brutal and damaging as a result of new advances in all branches of scientific research and in the increasingly sophisticated methods of weapons delivery. We can authoritatively claim that science and mathematics are areas of `powerful knowledge'. Delivery of weapons and their destructive potential have become increasingly sophisticated with the advances in microprocessor technology and accompanying informatics. Where technology becomes too risky or nearing obsolescence, it is exported to other countries as an opportunity for development of their infrastructure. An apposite example of this is the Union Carbide's production plant in Bhopal, and it is a timely reminder for all of us, of the flip side of `progress' in the developed world, ten years on. Many of the workers at that plant and the residents of Bhopal were never appraised of the danger in their midst. Fritjof Capra has encapsulated these concerns eloquently in his book `The Turning Point: Science, Society and the Rising Culture' when he says:

> Twenty five years ago world leaders decided to use `atoms for peace' and presented nuclear power as the reliable, clean and cheap energy source of the future. Today we are becoming painfully aware that nuclear power is neither safe, nor clean, nor cheap. The 360 nuclear reactors now operating world-wide, and the hundreds more planned, have become a major threat to our well-being. The radioactive elements released by nuclear reactors are the same as those making up the fallout of atomic bombs. . . The most toxic of these radioactive poisons, plutonium, is itself fissionable, which means that it can be used to build atomic bombs. Thus nuclear power and nuclear weapons are inextricably linked, being but different aspects of the same threat to humankind. With their continuing proliferation, the likelihood of global extinction becomes greater everyday (1983: 2,3).

The scientific enterprise is carried out by individuals, alone or in groups who bring their own prior understandings and experiences to bear on the way science is practiced and in the way scientific knowledge is accreted and accumulated. Therefore, the culture in which science operates becomes an important factor.

The Cultural Heritage of `Modern Science' and the Resultant Technology

The body of knowledge that has been accumulated, published and widely accepted as the history of science dismisses scientific ideas that pre-date Francis Bacon (17th Century). Science in schools denies through omission, the existence of science before Newton and generally ends with the work of Einstein and Rutherford. School text books acknowledge to varying degrees, the contributions that French, German and other European males have made to science but nowhere do they mention the organized and systematic science that went on in the Arab, Persian, Indian and Chinese worlds. The scientific culture that is transmitted is totally Eurocentric and begins with the Renaissance or Age of Enlightenment. The preceding years were lumped together as the Age of Darkness that conjures up an image of the world before the Renaissance as uncivilized. This is an insult to the civilizations that existed in Africa (the kingdom of Zimbabwe), the Aztec and Maya cultures of the Americas and to the civilizations that were highly advanced in the Indian sub-continent and China. This omission of other cultures and their contribution to scientific knowledge is deeply racist.

The contributions made by women scientists have been grudgingly acknowledged in recent times but usually in a tokenistic way. It is important to recognize however, that the most powerful and persuasive critiques of modern science have come from feminists. There are a plurality of feminist critiques and this has opened up spaces for alternative visions, one of which is that:

> Feminism makes a unique contribution to more traditional studies of science; it encourages the use of expertise that has traditionally belonged to women-not simply as a woman's perspective but as a critical instrument for examining the roots of those dichotomies (subjectivity vs. objectivity; feeling vs. reason) that isolate this perspective and deny its legitimacy. It seeks to enlarge our understanding of the history, philosophy, and sociology of science through the inclusion not only of women and their actual experiences but also of those domains of human experience that have been relegated to women: namely, the personal, the emotional, and the sexual (Keller 1985:9)

The scientific method first expounded by Bacon, and built on by Descartes and re-defined by Kant, sought to provide an epistemology of science that was not only universal but also ahistorical. This positivist approach has in essence been the dominant philosophical tradition with some important modifications made notably by Popper and Lakatos. Even the model offered by Kuhn in his theory of scientific revolutions has not succeeded in influencing school science in taking us beyond crude empiricism. The relativist approach of Feyarabend is dismissed by the scientific establishment as `epistemological anarchy'. Even the important changes that have occurred in the philosophy and sociology of science through Popper's work are not yet reflected in the science taught and learnt in schools.

Evelyn Fox Keller (1985) poses the question;

> 'How much of the nature of science is bound up with the idea of masculinity, and what would it mean for science if it were otherwise?'

The focus of her essays was on the subject of:

> 'not women per se, or even women and science: it is the making of men, women and science, or, more precisely, how the making of men and women has affected the making of science.' (Keller, 1985:4)

In short, she argues for an epistemology of science that:

> '...allows for the productive survival of diverse conceptions of mind and nature, and of correspondingly diverse strategies. In my vision of science, it is not the taming of nature that is sought, but the taming of hegemony.' (op.cit. 1985:178)

In a separate but similar vein, a collection of Indian scientists has critiqued `modern science' for its violence against our planet and all it's living inhabitants. In the book, `Science, Hegemony and Violence: A Requiem for Modernity'; the editor Ashis Nandy summarizes the thrust of the arguments outlined by the contributors as dealing with the issue that:

> Science violates not merely through the super-bombs powered by paranoia and super-greed; [but that] science violates also through bureaucratisation of human suffering and through 'scientization' itself. (Nandy, 1988:21-22)

School Science in England and Wales

The National Curriculum was first introduced into schools in England and Wales as a central plank of the Education Reform Act (1988). As a result, science was elevated to that of a core subject alongside English and Mathematics. There are seven other foundation subjects, which together with the three core subjects listed above, make up a centrally determined curriculum that all children in the UK from the ages of 5 to 16 have to follow. The only schools that are not subjected to such strictures are those in the private sector, which cater for about 8-9% of the school age population in Britain.

As a science educator I should welcome this newly accorded status to science in schools. Nevertheless, my concern is that the aims of science in schools have little to do with empowering future citizens to become scientifically literate but concerns itself primarily with producing a reified work force. This is partly because the shared understanding that existed amongst the constituency of science educators about what constituted a valid science education for the compulsory school years has been disregarded by the ideologues of the radical right and the bureaucrats who have produced instead, a science curriculum that continues to separate and pigeonhole people.

The present situation makes the study of science compulsory to the age of 16. Those deemed suitably `able' at the age of fourteen, study the sciences in a broad and balanced manner leading to a double qualification whilst the rest study a selected diet that gives them a single qualification. The situation is further complicated by the selective high schools and the prestigious private schools that persist with the teaching of biology, chemistry and physics as separate subjects because this provides students with greater factual knowledge to enable them to study the separate sciences for pre-university qualifications (GCE `A' levels). The three differentiated routes outlined above lead to outcomes that afford young people with differing levels of choice that unfortunately have an impact on the kinds of careers open to them. Furthermore, the illusion of choice available to young people at the age of fourteen is often influenced by the guidance offered by science teachers who in turn are influenced by factors unrelated to aptitude, for example gender and non-conforming behaviour.

The current science curriculum for English and Welsh schools has undergone fourteen revisions in five years and the present statutory provisions bear little relation to the original recommendations. The whole tenet and tone have become more instrumental. There is the added concern that as a result of science being a compulsory subject from the age of five, we may be turning off children from science at an even younger age than before as an unintended consequence. Extensive research shows that even before the introduction of compulsory science into primary schools, the science related attitudes of children showed a marked decline between the ages of 11 to 13 in the early years of secondary schooling and this trend may be continuing (Reid and Tracey, 1985, Clay, 1986).

The mechanistic way science is taught in schools is still influenced by the naive inductivism of the Baconian tradition. It starts with the atomistic and microscopic before considering the whole. This reductionist approach runs contrary to how we naturally perceive and make sense of the environment we live in. We do not see things as disconnected parts but usually as inter-related wholes. Therefore the study of school science involves us in `taking leave of our senses'. The role of observation is considered of paramount importance along with measurements and the accumulation of data. Most science teachers, being unaware of the theory-laden nature of observations, do not have the skills and understandings necessary to critically evaluate the limitations of the experimental method.

Vandana Shiva, an Indian physicist and environmentalist has argued forcibly that the monopoly of knowledge informed by and through reductionist science, has resulted in:

> . . .fourfold violence-violence against the subject of knowledge, the object of knowledge, the beneficiary of knowledge, and against knowledge itself...violence is inflicted on the subject socially through the sharp divide between the expert and the non-expert - a divide which converts the vast majority of non-experts into non-knowers even in those areas of life in which the responsibility of practice and action rests with them.
>
> But even the expert is not spared: fragmentation of knowledge converts the expert into a non-knower in fields of knowledge other than his or her specialization.
>
> The *object* of knowledge is violated when modern science, in a mindless effort to transform nature without a thought for the consequences, destroys the innate integrity of nature and thereby robs it of its regenerative capacity. The multidimensional ecological crisis all over the world is an eloquent testimony to the violence that reductionist science perpetrates on nature (1988:233)

In teacher education, many student teachers have themselves had a poor experience of `doing science' during their own schooling and as a consequence, need a framework that enables them to examine the ways in which `scientific knowledge' is structured and legitimated. The understanding of how hierarchies have historically come about within the sciences, with `hard sciences' and `soft sciences' and furthermore, what content within those subjects constitutes legitimate knowledge and how this legitimated and valued knowledge itself is circumscribed by patriarchy and its dominant cultural values is an essential precursor to facilitate the learning of scientific concepts, skills and attitudes at their own level. Without a thorough understanding of the way scientific knowledge is both personally and socially constructed, science teachers will not have the capacity or skills to challenge and transform the dominant scientific discourse. This process allows many student-teachers who have considered themselves failures in school to appreciate that the `science for scientists' model of school science has been a contributory factor in their initial lack of success. I wish to argue further that this dominant discourse in science is informed at the school level by a narrow view of `scientific literacy'.

Ways of knowing

The National Curriculum Council for England and Wales states that:

> 'Scientific literacy is an essential capability for an educated young person. Newspapers, television and magazines, for example, call on knowledge of the function of machines and electrical devices, the effects of chemicals and drugs, the nutritional value of foods, the ecology of different parts of the world and the ethics of transplant surgery and genetics. Part of this literacy is the ability to seek out explanations for things. Pupils need to use their skills to devise ways of testing their ideas

> and the ideas of others, such as advertising claims, and to evaluate possible solutions to problems.....Most of this literacy requires a knowledge of basic science. The National Curriculum provides a broad and balanced range of ideas, skills and contexts through which teachers can structure a curriculum to help prepare an increasingly literate population, capable of dealing with issues of tomorrow. (1993:4).

The NCC's statement would appear to include on a theoretical basis, the acquisition of propositional knowledge and the process skills, supposedly specific to the `scientific method' and to develop critical judgment.

The above model of scientific literacy appears to be firmly based on the premise that the `scientific method' is universal, value-free, objective and totally unproblematic. It could also be viewed as simply arguing for the acquisition of a set of skills necessary for the global tourist and consumer. Regrettably, scientific literacy as seen by the National Curriculum Council is but one model of making sense of the world that we live in, albeit the dominant one that is currently imposed on schools by statute. It would appear to be even less yielding in its claims for hegemony than the model of scientific literacy that is recommended by the AAAS.

This monolithic model of scientific literacy that is embedded in Western science was roundly criticized by Feyarabend amongst others. He says that:

> ...traditions that differ from science are not pockets of wilful disregard of `reality', but are either different ways of dealing with the real or else accounts of parts of reality inaccessible to science (1982:178).

Different models of `scientific and technological literacy' need to be critically examined and furthermore, promoted, if we seek to educate students and citizens of the future to cope with an increasing plurality of views and visions, and to develop a globally equitable and ecologically sustainable economy and technology. In conclusion, I would argue that the mere teaching of `facts' in science is insufficient. However, to teach the scientific method as if it was universal, objective and free from cultural assumptions will only serve to perpetuate the great divide - between experts and non-experts; the rational and the emotional; the `rich' and the poor; the advanced and the backward; the G7 countries and the rest of the world. A curriculum for the 21st Century will need to be less subject bound and should become more learner focused with the present demarcation lines between academic and vocational obliterated. The artificial divide between science and technology cannot be maintained. Michael Young has suggested that:

> What will be needed will be knowledge about how technological choices are enmeshed in organizational, economic and political choices. . .What is needed is a concept of technology as a social phenomenon intimately bound up not only with changes in production but also with every area of social life, and a model of a unified model of the curriculum in which work in its broadest sense is an educational principle for all. . . Technology is important both on account of the enormous ideological power associated with technological expertise, and on account of the way technologies pervade more and more parts of our lives. If it is to become part of a more participative and democratic society, we have to find ways of making explicit how different purposes are involved in its design, its implementation and its use, and how at each stage there are potential choices and decisions to be made. This means a technologically literate population and an increasingly wide debate about the content and meaning of technological literacy (1991: 241,242)

References

Capra, F. *The Turning Point 'Science, Society and the Rising Culture'*. London: Flamingo Press, 1990.

Clay, J.A. 'Science-Related Attitudes of 13 Year Olds in Two Education Systems'. unpublished M.A. dissertation University of London, 1986.

Fores, M.J. and Rey, L. Technik: the relevance of the missing concept , in A. Cross and R. McCormick (eds) *Technology in Schools*. Milton Keynes: Open University Press, 1986.

Feyerabend, P. *Science in a Free Society*. London: Verso, 1982.

Keller, E.F. *Reflections on Gender and Science*. London: Yale University Press, 1985.

National Curriculum Council. Teaching Science at Key Stages 3 and 4. York: NCC. 1993.

Nandy, A. (ed) *Science, Hegemony & Violence: A Requiem for Modernity*. Oxford: Oxford University Press, 1988.

Naughton, J. What is 'technology' anayway? In A. Cross and R. McCormick (eds) *Technology in Schools*. Milton Keynes: Open University Press, 1986.

Reid, D.J and Tracey, D.C. `The evaluation of a school science syllabus through objectives and attitudes', *European Journal of Science Education*. 1985; 7 (4), 375-386

Shiva, V. Reductionist Science as Epistemological Violence in Nandy, A (ed) *Science, Hegemony & Violence: A Requiem for Modernity*. Oxford: Oxford University Press, 1988.

Webster, A. *Science, Technology and Society*: New Directions Basingstoke: Macmillan, 1991.

Woolnough, B.E. The place of technology in schools, in A. Cross and R. McCormick (eds) *Technology in Schools*. Milton Keynes: Open University Press, 1986.

Young, M. 'Technology as an Educational Issue: Why it is so difficult and Why it is so Important' in Mackay, H, Young, M and Beynon, J (ed) *Understanding Technology in Education*, 1991.

Section III

Information Society: Postmodernism Debate

Chapter 16

New Media and Cultural Representation

Jeff Taylor

The debate on postmodernism in this paper is concerned with the tension between global cultural hegemony and local distinctiveness; opportunities for cross-cultural community communication and dangers of cultural homogenisation for consumerism; conflicting new media potentials for both fragmentation and synthesis, for incoherence and holism; reality versus authenticity, 'truth' versus revisionism; the appropriateness of image-driven and experiential media in cultural representation; and broadly, the rhetoric versus the reality of the new media. This discussion is contextualised within a critical postmodern perspective on culture, heritage and the new media, and within a framework that situates and identifies the new media itself as postmodern artefact. The discussion reinforces and raises several issues concerning the representation of culture and heritage through new electronic media, with reference to current examples found on CD-ROM, in museums and on the World Wide Web. These issues concern cultural identity and the role of story versus game; the collision between traditional narrative and new media interactivity, between linearity, multilinearity and non-linearity; and the changing roles of authorship and readership.

Introduction: New Media and Postmodernism

Heralds of the Information Age, from Rousseau through Toffler, provide the cultural and philosophical underpinnings for faith in redemption through technology. The crucible era giving rise to postmodernism is also the birth time of microelectronic, personal computing and the technical and social foundation for multimedia development. Some writers, such as Jameson (1981) regard postmodernism as in fact another name for the Information Age, and Lanham argues that "one might call the personal computer the ultimate postmodern work of art".(Lanham, 1990)

Multimedia computing in turn exhibits so many characteristics of its postmodern genealogy that it can be regarded as a kind of ultimate postmodern artefact to orchestrate the cultural fragments that are so much a feature of the postmodern landscape.(Taylor, 1993)

Cameron notes an "interactivity is post modern" school of thought which regards representations that are interactive as "a liberation from the repressive authority of traditional narrative form", echoing the utopian 60s rhetoric of "avant-garde and anti-narrative movements in cinema and writing" which were symptomatic of the origins of postmodernism itself.(Cameron, 1995)

The postmodern employment of intertextuality throughout its cultural discourses is made manifest in hypermedia systems of linking. Gottdiener defines intertextuality in semiotic terms, as "the relation of signifier to signifier to signifier, the endless deferral of signification"(Gottdiener, 1995:47), which is an apt description of the way hypermedia systems of electronic document linkage such as the World Wide Web function.

Anderson (1990) asserts that under postmodernism "heterogeneity and difference" are seen as "liberative forces"; while Baudrillard emphasises "hyperreality", Gottdiener also highlights "hyperdifferentiation" as a predominant characteristic of postmodernism, listing some "current changes in daily life that might be considered harbingers to postmodernism".(Gottdiener, 1995:50):

"Taking as one dimension of postmodern change the increasing hyperdifferentiation of people's lives, I can briefly suggest some aspects of household commodity use and new technologies that may be significant." "The cornucopia of channels on the family TV set leads to a new kind of freedom and hyperdifferentiation of viewing habits which is further enhanced by the use of VCRs." Similarly microwaves, and "computer modems and 'home' work stations may be considered a further development of postmodern tendencies".(ibid)

Siting even the light bulb as a similar "hyperdifferentiating" technology from modernism, Gottdiener also lists a number of multimedia artefacts as "part of the ideological discourse which regulates consumption".(ibid).

The postmodern idea is that cultural reality is not found 'around' cultural texts but is realised through and in the texts it produces, that a holistic text is composed of the intersection of several texts and discourses.

Foster writes:

> "Derrida considers ... collage/montage as the primary form of postmodern discourse. The inherent heterogeneity of that (be it in painting, writing, architecture) stimulates us, the receivers of the text or image, 'to produce a signification which could be neither univocal nor stable.' Both producers and consumers of 'texts' (cultural artefacts) participate in the production of significations and meanings (hence Hassan's emphasis upon 'process,' 'performance,' 'happening,' and 'participation' in the postmodernist style)."(Foster, 1983)

Foster here is referring to Ihab Hassan"s 1971 essay "POSTmodernISM: A Paracritical Bibliography" which gave name to the era.(Jencks, 1987:19)

Whereas modernism can be characterised by linear progress, fixed truths, "the rational planning of ideal social orders and standardisation of knowledge and production", postmodernism privileges difference and heterogeneity and as liberating forces in redefining cultural discourse.(Anderson, 1990)

Landow, who actively applies Derrida's theories to hypertext which he defines as collage/montage, explains how the new media facilitates postmodernism:

> "Hypertext does not permit a tyrannical, univocal voice. Rather the voice is always that distilled from the combined experience of the momentary focus, the lexia one presently reads, and the continually forming narrative of one's reading path."(Landow, 1992:11)

Barthes speaks of the "lexia" and Derrida the "morceau" as the basic text block for deconstruction, translated by Ulmer as "bit, piece, morsel, fragment; musical composition; snack, mouthful"; similarly Bolter and Landow define lexias in hypermedia as not just print, but visual and all other fragments of linkable data, as well as their joining electronic links.(Landow, 1992:8-9)

Landow continues:

> "Although this absence of a center can create problems for the reader and the writer, it also means that anyone who uses hypertext makes his or her own interests the *de facto* organizing principle (or center) for the investigation at the moment. ..the reader is not locked into any kind of particular organization or hierarchy."(Landow, 1992:12-13)

Literary Machinations

Cameron notes that "Hypertext for Landow is post-structuralism made flesh, transubstantiated - Foucault"s death of the Author a corpse, Derridean débordement actualized as hypertextual annotation...".(Cameron, 1995)

In an ideal open hypertext, the kind defined by Nelson in his Xanadu descriptions of "literary machines", the distinction between author and reader becomes more indistinguishable because anyone has equal access to publish, at low cost. In Derrida's terms, the authority of the producer of culture, the author, is minimised, allowing popular democratic participation in cultural determination via multiple authorship.

In 1967 Barthes proclaimed the death of the author, stating that readers create meanings despite authors' intentions across both sciences and humanities.

As postmodern artifice, multimedia facilitates the erosion of the author as subject, through hypertext systems' capability for multiple authorship and for erasing the author's voice and hand. The hypertext version of Jay D. Bolter's text *Writing Space* plays with this notion and cajoles readers to assume roles of authorship. The introductory screens that appear on launching the application state the following:

> "Writing Space
> The Computer, Hypertext and the History of Writing
> Jay David Bolter
>
> © Jay David Bolter
>
> You may make as many electronic copies of this text as you wish. You may distribute these copies to anyone on any terms. You may give the disks away or sell them. If you can convince someone to pay you for an electronic copy of this text, take the money.
>
> [NEXT SCREEN]
> However, you may not make any hard copy of this text -- that is any copy on paper or a similar material that you can hold in your hand and read by candlelight, flashlight, or reading lamp. You may not make any copy that does not require the use of the computer for presentation and navigation.
>
> [NEXT SCREEN]
> As long as you keep the text in the electronic medium, you may also change it as you see fit, and hand on the changes to others. You may want to indicate that you have changed the text. On the other hand you may not, but then your readers will probably falsely assume that the original author was responsible for the text that you wrote. All readers should be aware that anything in the text may have been added by someone other than the original author. But, of course, this caveat applies in a Borgesian way to the previous sentence as well. Indeed, perhaps this whole crazy copyright notice was added by some mischievous reader. Perhaps the original author had a traditional copyright notice that read as follows:
>
> [NEXT SCREEN]
> Writing Space
> ©Jay David Bolter
>
> All rights reserved. No portion of this text may be reproduced by any means, electronic or mechanical, without the written permission of the author."(Bolter, 1990)

But then, how do we as readers know that the version quoted is an authentic replica, or 'simulacrum' in postmodern lingo, of the hypertext Bolter originally published?

Similarly, virtual environments on the Internet put users "in the position of fiction writers, who compose themselves as characters in the process of writing".(Hay, 1993)

George Landow in his important work *Hypertext : The Convergence of Contemporary Critical Theory and Technology* in 1992 described Xanadu, Nelson's vision of electronic hypertext publishing, "as the embodiment of the sixties News Left thought".(Landow, 1992:169) In his originally self-published text Literary Machines, Nelson calls on us to

> "Imagine a new accessibility and excitement that can unseat the video narcosis that now sits on our land like a fog. Imagine a new libertarian literature with alternative explanations so that anyone can choose the pathway or approach that best suits him or her; with ideas accessible and interesting to everyone, so that a new richness and freedom can come to the human experience; imagine a rebirth of literacy."(Nelson, 1981)

Postmodern literature, as other forms of cultural discourse, has aspired to the disintegration of the notion of a single 'author' with the power to impose meanings or offer a continuous narrative, so that a hallmark of postmodernists is pursuit of the dissolution of narrative, 'metanarrative' and 'meta-theories'. In fact Lyotard defines postmodern theory as "incredulity towards metanarratives". Narrative is seen by Hayden White as a "metacode, a human universal on the basis of which transcultural messages about the nature of a shared reality can be transmitted".(Landow, 1992:103-4) Postmodernism is suspicious of narrative as carriers of such messages, not believing in shared realities that can give similar meaning to such messages, but in solipsism— the theory that 'the self' can only be aware of its own experiences and states.

Borges

Writers working in earlier times are dubbed 'postmodern' posthumously because their work is seen to conform to its characteristics. *Finnegan's Wake* is called postmodern because "it had a plethora of anarchic and disjunctive qualities: no plot, no character, no chronological sequence, no subject, no imitation, no symbolism and no meaning".(Jencks, 1987:19) Proponents of hypertext consider such writers, including William Burroughs, Thomas Pyncheon and even Wittgenstein, as frustrated or virtual 'hypertextualists' (to coin a term), defining their work as hypertext before the possibility of electronic manifestation .

In particular, the work of the late Argentine Jorge Luis Borges, winner of the Nobel Prize for Fiction, has been situated in the hypertext arena by such proponents of hypermedia as Landow, Moulthrop and Bolter who liberally apply the adjective 'Borgesian' to describe attributes of hypertext (e.g. within Bolter's copyright notice on the previous page). Borges in one story describes an 'Aleph' as a point in space containing all other points, without overlapping or transparency. Landow describes a hypertext document as a kind of "travelling Aleph", moving from point to point yet always at the centre.(Landow, 1992:12)

Bolter uses Borges' *The Library of Babel* to highlight limitations of static text: The Library represents "the exhaustion of human symbolic thought. All of the combinations of Gutenberg's letters sit on the shelves waiting for readers. There is nothing left to be written, only discovered, but discovery is impossible because of the crushing number of nonsense books that overwhelm those that are supposed to have meaning".(Bolter, 1990) Borges writes: "Everything is there: The minute history of the future, the autobiography of the archangels, the faithful catalogue of the Library, thousands and thousands of false catalogues, a demonstration of the fallacy of these catalogues, a demonstration of the fallacy of the true catalogue,... a version of each book in all languages, the interpolation of every book in all books."(Borges, 1962:83)

Stuart Moulthrop has even produced a hypertext "interaction after" Borges' *The Garden of the Forking Paths*, the most cited of Borges' works by proponents of the new media. The reader responds to yes-no queries in the text and others that "allow the reader to change directions in the work's hyperspace", as well as perform string searches.(Landow, 1992:111) In this short story Borges fabricates a novel whose story path splits, so that all things are conceivable, and all things occur. Cameron notes that "The author of this story within a story is judged insane and commits suicide, and Borges' narrator is arrested and condemned to death - thus the fate of the narrator and of the author in the interactive era is prefigured."(Cameron, 1995)

Cameron looks to another of Borges' stories, *An examination of the works of Herbert Quain*, in order to highlight some of the problems that accompany loss of authorship and story linearity through its vision of "a banal and meretricious interactive literature".(Cameron, 1995) Borges invents Quain as a multilinear 1930s novelist whose work represents what Borges terms the "regressive, ramified novel", with Quain stating of one of his works: "I lay claim in this novel... to the essential features of all games: symmetry, arbitrary rules, tedium."(Borges, 1962:75) Cameron notes that "Quain was in the habit of arguing that readers were an already extinct species.(Cameron, 1995) "Every European," Borges writes as Quain, "is a writer, potentially or in fact."(Borges, 1962:78) Cameron notes further that "symmetry, arbitrary rules, tedium" are the "depressing qualities in countless CD-roms, computer games and pieces of multimedia", asking rhetorically if this is what interactivity is really all about: the reduction of stories to games.(Cameron, 1995)

In emphasising the importance of story to our cultural representation, Cameron states:

> "The form of the story permeates every aspect of our cultural life. History, politics, memories, even subjectivity, our sense of identity, all are representations in narrative form, signifiers chained together in temporal, spatial, and causal sequence. Narrative is a component of those deep structures with which we construct ourselves and our universe; true stories through which, in the manner of certain Aboriginal legends, the world is dreamed into existence. Narrative enjoys with language the status of a defining characteristic of humanity and its culture - a people without stories seems as absurd an idea as a people without language, (a people with language but no stories even stranger, for what is language for if not to tell stories?)."(Cameron, 1995)

Cameron describes a "collision between a dominant cultural form - narrative, and the technology of interactivity". Increasingly, narrative cinematic experience is being replaced by thrilling virtual rides that new media make possible, with Jurassic Park perhaps the most obvious example to date, with narrative plot almost incidental to special effects. "If the repressed reading of interactivity is that of the game, the preferred reading is interactivity as Post-Modernism come true."(Cameron, 1995)

Borges himself writes of "the simple purity of the unobstructed narrative" and of the dangerous diversions adjectives provide; one should consider similarly the role of hypermedia links: "Any adjective, whether it be pleonastic or equivocal, exercises a power: that of forcing the reader's attention to pause at the substantive to which it refers — a quality which is suitable for description, not for narration."(Christ, 1969:9) Landow, Bolter and Moulthrop focus on *The Garden of the Forking Paths*, reading it as liberating Borges' work's "potential for variation" as Landow describes it, by translating it to hypertext.(Landow, 1992:40)

Moulthrop's *Forking Paths* hypertext, a screenshot of which is published in Landow(1992:111), remains in fact unpublished since to do so would breach Borges' copyright. Moulthrop is credited for providing 'structure and additional text', and there is evidence to suggest that Borges himself, were he alive, would not have agreed with Moulthrop's interpretation of his work's "potential for variation". Borges' own comments on *The South*, another story that seems to bear characteristics of hypertext, places Moulthrop's reading of *The Garden of the Forking Paths* —and the new media proponents' appropriation of Borges — in further question.

Borges says of *The South*, which he thought perhaps his best story: "It is possible to read it as a straight-forward narration of novelistic facts, and also in another way". "The two readings are not ... the result of superimposed levels as might be imagined at first, but the response to two halves of the story arranged in a spatial and chronological sequence."(Christ , 1969:125)

Ronald Christ notes that Borges "... is constantly pushing himself to logical conclusions"(Christ, 1969:13) Most of Borges' stories are in terms of logic and chronology conventionally narrative in nature with ingenius action of plot. As Borges says in *The Aleph* "language is successive" i.e. linear.(Borges, 1971) Such a reading insists that Borges would not approve of the interpretation and transformation of The *Garden of the Forking Paths* into "superimposed levels" of hypertext anymore than he would that of *The South*. It can be argued that Borges means *The South* and *The Garden of the Forking Paths* to be read from beginning to end in a linear fashion, because, he observes, "language and life operate in succession".(Borges, 1971) It is ironic to think of Bolter, Landow and Moulthrop entranced by the illusionary and metaphysical Borges, a powerful seduction carried forth through linear narrative. It could be that the power of such linear narrative to produce such illusions is one of the eternal messages that Borges conveys. Borges himself warns 'The fact that in one of my stories the man is both the dreamer and the dream does not necessarily mean that I am a follower of ...the Buddha.'(Christ, 1969:ix)

The injection of interactivity that new media brings to the traditional linear story so far seems to imply the reduction of story to game. Moulthrop's hypertext *Victory Garden*(Moulthrop, 1991) now available on the Web (1995), though much acclaimed, still lacks the grip of conventional narrative, and his attempt through the Web-based *Hegirascope*(Moulthrop, 1995) to replace this with effects such as Netscape's 'client pull' (meaning the word does not stand still) remain more convincing as game than story. Deena Larsen's *Marble Springs*(Larsen, 1995), seems a more appropriate hybrid candidate inviting users to explore the interconnected lives of the hypertext's 'inhabitants', with its graphical layout undisguised as a kind of game board.

As Cameron reminds us, "The game is frivolous whereas narrative is serious":

> "There is a general assumption here that narrative representation - literature, history, cinema and so on, has a deep and lasting significance which the game lacks. In the end Shakespeare or Proust or Pasolini seem to have more to offer than a game of football or Sonic. The game is outside of history, unworthy of serious remembrance."(Cameron, 1995)

Cameron speculates that 'pornography' represents the resolution of the game-story conflict with its form both narrative and goal-directed, "referring to fictional events and a kind of arousal game with a clearly defined outcome. The pornographic story joins the reader in a cybernetic construct - within this cyborg-text the body of the reader and the body of the text respond to each other."(Cameron, 1995) Will our story-based culture mutate into a culture of equivalents to the kinds of immersive and interactive gaming that early interactive virtual sex products suggest?

Cultural Heritage Multimedia

The documentation of cultural heritage has proceeded from print, through audio and visual media, to our present multimedia. The limitations of print and potential for arrogant bias within the documentary context are exemplified through this entry representing "the Russian character" in the 1830-42 edition of the Encyclopaedia Britannica:

> "The accounts of the Russian character in the works of those who have resided or travelled in the country, are extremely conflicting. He who impartially weighs the evidence will arrive at the conclusion, which might have been suspected before the investigation began, that whilst there are not a few dark stains on the national character, many of them are attributable to the peculiar political system under which the people live, to their general ignorance hitherto, and to the low character and unclerical behaviour of the secular clergy; and that under a proper system of government, instruction, and religious discipline, the Russians would not be far behind some of their continental neighbours who hold much higher place in the scale of civilization and morals."(Smith, 1830)

Even the seemingly innocuous vehicle of children's comics and cartoons can be a media vehicle for imprinting cultural misrepresentations on young minds, as Disney's products exemplify. In *How to Read Donald Duck*, a book coming out of the revolutionary struggle of 1970 Chile shortly before Allende's assassination by the CIA, Dorfman and Mattelart provide a brilliant analysis of Disney as vehicle for 'imperialist ideology' during the two decades prior to publication.(Dorfman & Mattelart, 1971) A cursory look at current images from Donald Duck comics confirms that the very same images of racism, sexism and cultural hegemony persist to pervade young minds as they have for half a century.

Whereas words can so easily deceive, there is a common popular assumption that documentary film is one that tells the truth, or at least attempts to tell the truth, since 'the camera does not lie'. In reality, of course, selectivity and bias begin the moment the camera is picked up and pointed.

Establishing what is the truth of a scene— Is it real? Is it too poetic to be believed? Will it look like propaganda? —are questions that arose for Flaherty on *Nanook of the North* (1922), and are still relevant today. In a sense, non-fiction filmmakers have far more formal, structural, even artistic problems than directors of fictional works. From all that could be shown, their problem is how to decide what relatively little will be shown.

The BBC's *People's Century* television series is judged a success in providing a "clear eyed and dispassionate" view of history. Christopher Dunkley writes,

> "There is a long tradition in television of seeking out the politically correct witness to history - the brave exception who opposed slavery in the deep south, the socialist who went underground to oppose fascism in 1937. That is not what you get here. Pagnamenta and his producers have kept their title in mind and so we hear, for example, not from the dissenters in Nazi Germany of the 1930s but from those who supported and even revered Hitler. Those are the very people you need to hear from if you want to know why things happened in the way they did."(*Financial Times*, Sept. 13, 1995)

Although new media technology allows and encourages an all-inclusive approach foreign to the economics of film production, decisions relevant to structure and coherence, and those relevant to which content will tend to dominate, are as applicable with multimedia as with film. These become still more problematic within a postmodern context that eschews fixed truths or attempts at authoritative representations of reality.

In discussing the postmodern approach to history, Umberto Eco says: "The postmodern reply to the modern consists of recognising that the past, since it cannot really be destroyed, because its destruction leads to silence, must be revisited: but with irony, not innocently...".(Jencks, 1987:20)

Harvey summarises a more cynical agenda of postmodern compromise in its Information Age treatment of history, which articulates concerns relevant to multimedia representation:

> "The assertion of any place-bound identity has to rest at some point on the motivational power of tradition. It is difficult, however, to maintain any sense of historical continuity in the face of all the flux and ephemerality of flexible accumulation. The irony is that tradition is now often preserved by being commodified and marketed as such. The search for roots ends up at works being produced and marketed as an image, as a simulacrum or pastiche (imitation communities constructed to evoke images of some folksy past, the fabric of traditional working-class communities being taken over by an urban gentry). The photograph, the document, the view, and the reproduction become history precisely because they are so overwhelmingly present. The problem, of course, is that none of these are immune from tampering or downright faking for present purposes. At best, historical tradition is reorganised as a museum culture, not necessarily of high modernist art, but of local history, of local production, of how things once upon a time were made, sold, consumed, and integrated into a long-lost and often romanticised daily life (one from which all trace of oppressive social relations may be expunged). Through the presentation of a partially illusory past it becomes possible to signify something of local identity and perhaps to do it profitably".(Harvey, 1989)

Inherent within multimedia, as postmodern artefact, are the conflicting abilities of synthesis and fragmentation. Is the past to be represented as story with depth and empathy with message and lessons that resonate culturally? Or as a fragmented set of superficial borrowings, a heritage patchwork stitched together as game without empathetic commitment to the culture documented, while the receiver only interprets the product by poaching a wide variety of discourses? Critics see these latter as inclinations of our postmodern times.

Roszak describes in his *Cult of Information* (1988) the values of the Information Age as the worship of fragmentary information at the expense of unifying ideas, a reductive approach that the new media is equipped to serve, creating nostalgia-based cultural forms that postmodernism is inclined to favour. Heritage centres, theme-parks and family fun experiences rapidly mummify and 'Disneyfy' our various bygones wholesale. W.W.II becomes, for example, a circus of experiences, such as 'flying' a Hellcats simulator in violent encounters against the Japanese within a simple narrative framework. For 'interactive media environment', read once again 'game', just as cinema becomes thrill ride, pickling versions of the past, editing important aspects of history into two-dimensional half-truths, both shallow and subjective.

Cameron (1995) notes that "What is lost is the complex interplay of signs, Barthes' "weaving of the voices" across different registers, the "perspective of quotations", the "mirage of structures", the "multivalence of the text". These are replaced with a wide band of sensory information referring to specific and schematic aspects of a situation - [in the Hellcats example being] the proairetics of flight, the hermeneutics of battle." This is defined by Cameron (1995) as "the experience of the pilot insofar as he or she is an extension of the machine, that part which keeps the plane in the air and flies this way or that way, presses the trigger and drops bombs, but never that part with a history, a family, skin colour, memories, desire, plans for this evening...".

And of course we are meant to 'enjoy' rather than confront or be challenged, and 'enjoy' rapidly so 'throughput' is maintained and we will pay to visit again in the near future.

As has been noted, the negation of the author, the loss of "authority", is a feature of postmodernism, which multimedia technology and its major proponents accommodate and embrace. Historic 'truth' is shown to be human invention, a social construct, with individual readings equally valid. However, as Foster explains,

> "Minimizing the authority of the cultural producer creates the opportunity for popular participation and democratic determinations of cultural values, but at the price of a certain incoherence or, more problematic, vulnerability to mass-market manipulation."(Foster, 1983)

There is a contiguous relationship between the rhetoric of multimedia and the rhetoric of capitalist postmodernity which positions multimedia as ultimate artifice.

Global Cultural Hegemony

Multimedia in its broadest sense, although presenting new forms for cultural representation and distribution of representation that can increase cross-cultural understanding, is also in commercial hands the latest vehicle for the homogenisation and dilution of culture. It can be seen as the next logical tool of western corporate culture to promote its values through creating and controlling the medium of cultural messages. Visual clues signify meaning, often culturally-derived messages, which become duplicated globally, as culturally imperialistic as Coca-Cola. The appropriateness of its imposition as a pre-cast template of Western cultural values should be critically examined.

Gottdiener notes that postmodernity is an era when "the interplay of sign value dominates cultural logic", and quotes Baudrillard: "the real implodes and disappears in the ideology of hyperreality of the image".(Gottdiener, 1995:47) Gottdiener asserts that "an image-driven culture is undoubtedly a defining characteristic of postmodernism".(Gottdiener, 1995:50)

The potency of media images becomes if anything more intense under postmodernism, less distinguishable from reality by the public. If modernism had produced mass media as a mirror of culture, postmodernism steps beyond to goad multimedia reflection to become reality. The postmodern, market-driven defence arguments run thus: "Disneyworld©®™ is nearer to what people want than what architects have ever given them. Disneyland™®© is the symbolic American utopia." (Appignanesi and Garratt, 1995) The expanding Disney empire — which with its takeover of Capital Cities, owner of ABC, represents the largest media and entertainment collosus — is making still further inroads into reality with its brand of fantasy through the development of Celebration, its first planned residential community. As the embodiment of Walt Disney idealisation of America, this new $2.5 billion community is promoted as "'a special place for families' who wish to flee the incivilities and inconveniences of modern life and return to 'a time of innocence'".(*The Guardian,* Nov. 11, 1995)

Multimedia's predetermined iconography imprinted within the factory of corporate American sensibilities, its postmodern tendency towards fragmentation and incoherence, and its obsession with the experientiality of superficial image over in-depth reflective content — all combine to gravitate against profound diversity and towards the spectre of cultural dilution and homogenisation.

Although it represents a technology that can be appropriated for use at local, community level, developed by and for a particular culture or subculture, and employing its own particular significations, multimedia also can be regarded as culturally biased, a mass-communication product dripping with the values of American technical culture that designed it.

The cultural power and marketing success of Coke is of course not the superiority or irresistibility of the caramel liquid itself. Afterall, the cocaine is no longer an ingredient. Rather it is the power to hook on the icon, to persuade to want to be seen with the logo in hand or on clothing or other apparel. In India for example, the liquid itself is not so much liked by the young people who purchase it rather as fashion, to support identity with Western values. It is appearance, association with the icon that counts rather than any quality of the material product *per se*. The placement of

Mcdonalds on the intersection of Rosa Luxembourg Str., Karl Marx Str., and the bridge and border crossing to Poland across the River Oder in Frankfurt (Oder), Germany is equally symbolic. Gottdiener notes that "cultural hegemony is expressed as the reduction of all objects to sign values".(Gottdiener, 1995:50) Neil Postman recounts that once the Lapps postponed their annual migration at the height of *Dallas* popularity because "they wanted to hang around and see who shot JR".(Postman, 1986)

Critics can see in multimedia as well as egalitarian potential, also a talent and proclivity to serve such cultural imperialism. We witness day to day the relentless McDonaldization, Disneyfication, and Coca-Colonization of global culture. The synergy and vertical integration of megacompanies such as McDonalds, Disney — and increasingly Microsoft— give them enormous scope for global cultural hegemony. The evident intentions of Microsoft to monopolise cyberspace mean not only that users are locked into a rigid pattern of hardware-software consumption, but also into cultural consumption. Like the Coca-Cola Company itself, Microsoft too would like to teach the world to sing its song in perfect harmony with its own cultural vision. Microsoft is very busy purchasing rights to all and sundry multimedia products of cultural representation from around the world, such as London National Gallery's *Art Gallery* (the product of local Brighton firm Cognitive Applications), to be repackaged, and re-presented in Microsoft house style, as well as superficially 'localizing' other products such as its *Encarta* encyclopaedia to better assure global consumption. Will this mean (idealistically) a wider, more democratic access to authentic cultural representation, or (pragmatically) a dilution and homogenisation— a Microsoftening of world cultures?

Landow observes that "One of the most interesting and exciting things about hypertext appears in the way it offers us a means of looking a short way into one or more possible futures, an electronic Pisgah Sight, as it were, a vision of the future that we ourselves will probably not reach."(Landow, 1992:203)

However, critics of the postmodern foresaw already a decade ago a McLuhanesque nightmare unfolding:

> "Under the spell of instantaneous communication, a global culture shuffles together the everyday lives of different continents, weaving around the planet a network of electronic information that offers a continuous world-wide show hooked up to life itself. One has only to surf the technological wave, to miniaturise the instruments and multiply the channels... And yet this bubble of postmodern imagery quickly bursts at the ...slightest contact with reality. For in its description of an imminent future, it jettisons all links with an uncomfortable present."(Mattelart, 1984)

During the BBC radio programme *Desert Island Discs*, author Douglas Adams, best known for his *Hitchhiker's Guide To the Galaxy* series, presented an argument for the development of a 'virtual Bali', a virtual reality representation of Bali, which indicates how 'postmodern imagery' comes to dictate our perceptions of reality. Adams was challenged by the interviewer as to why there should be investment in the development of a virtual Bali instead of encouragement to visit and invest in the infrastructure of the 'real' Bali. Adams replied that the 'real' Bali was littered with Western commercialisation, with Coca-Cola advertisements etc., whereas the virtual Bali would be more "authentic".(BBC, 1994) Again, the rhetoric attests to the hyperreality of the multimedia image.

Passage to Vietnam

In *Passage to Vietnam* (Against All Odds/Interval Research, 1995), a CD-ROM that invites users to "go on assignment with the world's top photographers" and which complements a coffee-table book, Vietnamese culture is represented by photographs taken by mainly Westerns, along with a handful of Vietnamese photographers. The interface allows jumping to specific points of interest, such as the work of specific photographers, photographs of particular regions or themes, and opens up special 'events', such as 'interactive editing sessions', 'virtual galleries' and 'subject loops'. The interface is engaging, 'sexy' in multimedia jargon, and the photographs themselves of the quality one is accustomed to seeing in the *National Geographic*, with video and audio clips sprinkled throughout. Ultimately, though, *Passage* presents an idealised view, a kind of virtual Vietnam in the way that Adams yearned for the virtual Bali. The product of an American company, it is the beauty of the photographs as much as their selective content that seem contrived to present a kind of multimedia wallpaper over the deep scars left by the Vietnam War—providing documentary reassurance to American readers that any residual guilt is unjustified. When the War is dealt with as a theme within the work, it is within a sanitised and anodyne compartment. Although we hear the voices of Western photographers, we never hear the voices of the ordinary Vietnamese themselves, who remain gagged and appear as little more than props to the photographs, as are Benetton advertising's beautifully photographed victims in a marketing strategy that exemplifies how advertising has so cynically embraced postmodernism.

NativeNet

During an Internet conferencing link under the auspices of the conference *The Body in the Virtual World* held at the Institute of Contemporary Arts (London, March 12-13, 1994), I communicated with a group of First Nation Canadian people on NativeNet asking what use the new media might be as a means of representing Native culture. The vehement response — "We want to *make* history, not be it!" — is a challenge to those who would construct such multimedia representations: to avoid the static mausoleum that these people reject, embalming their culture as curious but irrelevant artefact, and instead to exploit the dynamic nature of the technology to capture the dynamism of the culture.

Multimedia becomes a community media when constructed by or with and for the community. One pioneering harbinger of this was Karamjit Gill's *Brighton Parosi* project, based at the University of Brighton (then Brighton Polytechnic) over a decade ago, which aimed to promote language development and intercultural understanding among a diverse immigrant population through pre-computer-based multimedia which portrayed and valued each culture's traditions.(Gill, 1991)

Indications that curricula based on the development of heritage electronic multimedia more modest in scope, which benefits both the student and the community, are beginning, with student multimedia projects developing that work to reinforce the cultural identity of particular indigenous cultures.

A useful model to consider for students of multimedia focusing on public access heritage projects, but who are not themselves necessarily students of social anthropology, is the *Computers and Culture Project* carried out in Burns lake, B.C. through the local high school. The project resulted in the production of a multimedia database of Carrier culture, history and language. The Carrier are the aboriginal inhabitants of central British Columbia. The project is based on the premise that cultures of Canada's First Nations are dying as the elders pass away and younger people "adopt the international mass culture of rock and roll, Nintendo and blue jeans", and aims to be useful as a model for other culture and language preservation projects that can at least "preserve a little of the past before it disappears".(Wilson, 1993:67)

The *Carrier Culture Stack* aims to be a vehicle to combat local non-Native ignorance of and prejudice against the traditions of the native people with whom they share a town. In this instance, native students were cast in the role of content experts, a new and positive experience appropriate for any devalued people. Through their involvement in the *Computers and Culture Project*, the local Native community became more closely involved in the education of their children.(Wilson, 1993:67)

Non-Native students gained a knowledge of local Native culture that they previously lacked. Native and non-Native students shared the positive experience of working together to produce a product in which they could all take pride, and it is conjectured that this reduced prejudicial attitudes on both sides. Among "guidelines for multimedia culture projects" deduced from the *Computers and Culture Project* is listed: "Native people must be involved in production since it is their culture and they are the experts."(Wilson, 1993:68) It would seem arrogant — and undemocratic — in the extreme to attempt a production based upon a community that does not involve closely the ordinary members of that community in the project.(Taylor, 1994a)

My Brighton

Postmodernism denies the possibility of historical and other 'Truth' as reflected by a single objective author, but instead views historic and other truths as social constructs, with all the subjectivity, partiality and pluralism that implies. The postmodern idea that cultural and historic reality is found through the intersection of several texts and discourses calls for the end of historical metanarrative.

The *My Brighton Project* represents in multimedia form the cultural heritage of Brighton, England, from the perspective of both ordinary residents and visitors, and of historic specialists, offering individual and sometimes differing views. In many ways it is congruent with the democratic approach taken by the Carrier project, and with the most democratic premises of postmodernism. Implicit within these assertions is the notion of democracy. It is a feature of postmodernism, according to Jencks, to be "more democratic and accessible"(Jencks, 1987:19), and the pluralist content and construction of the *My Brighton Project* allows readers to traverse the historic landscape from multiple angles.

The project is presented through touch-screen installations within Brighton Museum, which has administered development and held editorial responsibility through John Roles, its Senior Keeper. Its community-based approach is in sharp contrast to the commercial *Passage to Vietnam*. Technical multimedia production has been the responsibility of the small local firm Desktop Display, with considerable volunteer effort beyond their contract supplied by its owners Stella Cardus and Pete Barker, and by Jack Latimer who with Stella Cardus shared the role of Producer/Designer. Financial sponsorship was provided by American Express, whose European headquarters are in Brighton. Interestingly, Desktop Display won the contract in direct competition with more 'prestigious' firms including Epic (which demonstrated its CD-I *Joy of Sex*) and Cognitive Applications (which showed its National Gallery product now marketed as *Art Gallery* by owner Microsoft) by developing and demonstrating a working model of its vision of how the *My Brighton Project* could actually appear.

Instead of professional photographers, a cross section of local volunteers was issued with disposable cameras and instructed to photograph what interested them about Brighton (among a total of 120 who contributed to the project as a whole). Eight photographs were included from each volunteer selected, accompanied by volunteers' stories about each as an audio track.(Cardus & Latimer, 1994) Mathiesen highlights the importance of storytelling for cultural identity within folkloristics in giving local people a sense of cultural identity(Sjöman, 1992), and like the Carrier project, but unlike *Passage to Vietnam*, *My Brighton* is constructed by, about and for its local community, and in this respect is unique among British museums.(Roles, 1995) Striving for ethnographic honesty, it is equally removed from the tourism and marketing 'virtual' cities being erected daily on the Internet. *My Brighton* material currently includes a lesbian tour, and a homeless person's tour has also been announced.

Specialist tours within the product allow the user to cross back and forth between 'ordinary' individual views and in-depth researched information that includes both still and moving image archives, such as that on the early history of filmmaking in Brighton. The personal tours with their photographs, stories and researched histories provide jumping-off points for browsing through galleries of photographs, prints, maps, documents and paintings from the Museum's reference collections. John Roles points out that now thousands of images are available to the public whereas previously only a few of the Museum's vast topographical collections could be seen. Tim Carder's book the *Encyclopaedia of Brighton* is also included within the multimedia as an in-depth reference.

As a dynamic community resource, the *My Brighton Project* is continually expanding, and brings readers back repeatedly to traverse more and more of its terrain. Currently it would take a visitor 50 hours to cover the material. John Roles provides the following statistics: "Initial surveys show that the project has been a popular success with visitors spending an average of 10-12 minutes using *My Brighton*, with 13% spending more than 25 minutes on it. Only 1% were dissatisfied and over 8 out of 10 said they would definitely return to use it again."(Roles, 1995)

Because it is non-profit, it encourages replication of its formula in other communities, and Desktop Display has developed the application Hypmap which runs *My Brighton* through even modest DOS PC's as a template to be duplicated elsewhere by communities that cannot necessarily afford the latest technology. The interface design is therefore kept simple — even proletarian so that anyone can use it without instruction, from school child to punk rocker to nonagenarian — though is as effective as the 'sexy' and far more resource-demanding *Passage to Vietnam.*

It is through the kind of informal social networking that only a community-based project can undertake that *My Brighton* has been able to succeed. Commercial projects of this scale are costing four times the budget of *My Brighton*, and it is only because of commitment to the community by all team members that it could achieve its goals.

Hyperkalevala

The Finnish Ministry of Education noted before Finland joined the EU last year that "Joining the European Economic Area and possible accession to the European Community will open up our country and boost international co-operation, but it will also raise the question of how to preserve our identity, culture and independence".(Ministry of Education, 1994) The *Hyperkalevala Project* developed primarily through the University of Joensuu, with support from the University of Art and Design in Helsinki, and sponsorship from the Finnish Ministry of Education, is an example of folklorists' attempt to rescue a non-linear oral epic (the Finnish 'Kalevala'), from linear text, and to reinstate it as non-linear hypermedia.(Luhtanen, Miettinen and & Wuorisalo, 1994) This project indicates how multimedia technology might go some way towards answering the essentially democratic question posed by the Ministry of Education, and which will be posed by other countries as the EU evolves.

With national conflict, identity and autonomy on the new post-Soviet agenda, hidden histories are emerging from the closet and being delivered by the also emergent multimedia technology. This coincidence of renewed interest in heritage and the development of new media technology imply the potential to deliver cultural and historical messages more powerfully, and more empoweringly, than ever before.

The *Hyperkalevala Project* is a case in point: probably without the annulment of the special Finno-Soviet relationship, even with the availability of sufficiently powerful multimedia technology, it is neither rash nor paranoid to assume this project would never have received public support. The Soviet regime prohibited virtually all research in certain spheres, such as popular conceptions and traditional ideological research. Now in the post-Soviet Baltic countries, a folklorist movement is blossoming, and can be seen as part of the movement towards nationalism.

Generations of schoolchildren have had to endure the inoculation of the linear poem that 19th Century folklorist Elias Lönnrot compiled, a force-feeding of abstract, and generally indigestible high cultural form. The emergence of a multimedia form to include not only the printed text (as hypertext), but recordings of authentic singers, ranging back to some of the earliest sound recordings of 1905, photographs of singers and their Karelian environment from 1895, reproductions of paintings based on the epic, etc. implies a new democratic access based on authenticity and audio-visual interactive motivation. Furthermore, the work attempts to relate historical elements to the modern age, e.g. in what contemporary forms ancient themes and values have managed to endure. Jerome Bruner noted the value of selective historic and remote ethnographic study in order to contextualise and stimulate reflection on the current and familiar.(Bruner, 1967)

The Kalevala, an ancient epic perhaps 6000 years old, after being compiled and transcribed as linear text by Lönnrot and published in 1849 was appropriated by Finnish upper class as high culture, and regurgitated in neutered and sanitised representations which supported the interests and values of that class, e.g. through Sibelius, as well a source of propaganda to bolster the drive for Finnish national independence.

There is today in Finland a renewed interest in Kalevala, linked again to political interests of national identity. What partisan interests might this new electronic version serve, or will it be able to provide democratic access to restored powerful and as yet uncharted messages lost through its appropriation to linear print and the vaults of high culture? Ultimately more significant than the potential nationalistic uses of *Hyperkalevala* or any heritage multimedia artefact, is the choice to fragment and dilute, or to attempt to revive faithfully and amplify ancient powerful archetypal messages implicit within oral epics such as the Kalevala, messages perhaps relevant to our turbulent times.

Texts rich in reference, metaphor and other kinds of associative linking would seem to benefit through the ability to bring forward and make manifest the practical and theoretical linkages through which the text is contextualised. The *Hyperkalevala Project* is well placed for transfer into the non-linear hypermedia world for several reasons. Its origins are in the non-linear performances of oral culture, so there is a valid hypothesis that re-introducing a non-linear structure will produce a more authentic representation. Because the epic has been so faithfully documented by Lönnrot, albeit by necessity in a print-based linear form, because authentic recordings of oral performances were produced, and because of the availability and relevance of a rich source of audio-visual background material, this project would seem well suited for non-linear multimedia consumption.

Political choices surround the selection of songs and rituals to be put forward as representative. Will only the sanitised, even Disneyfied, version be allowed to reach the international market-place? Or will the traditional ethics of ethnographic authenticity and objectivity prevail, exploiting the power of new media technology to give public access to expert knowledge in ways interactive, engaging and informative?(Taylor, 1994b)

The Victorian Web

Cameron notes "a contradiction at the heart of the idea of the interactive narrative - that narrative form appears fundamentally non-interactive", that there are large question marks over this type of multimedia literary representation: "we don't know what an interactive story is like, nor what it is for...".(Cameron, 1995)

But with the *The Victorian Web* — to be found on the World Wide Web(Landow, 1995) — its designer and editor George Landow offers a contrasting approach to literary hypermedia. Containing several thousand documents covering a range of Victorian authors from Charlotte Bronte to Oscar Wilde, and including sections on Victorian religion, arts, science, political and social history, *The Victorian Web* encourages individual explorations, and invites readers to submit material and suggestions for inclusion, a postmodern pluralist dimension of interactivity.

There is no attempt, as with Moulthrop's rendition of Borges, to 'hypertextualise' or render non-linear individual Victorian author's works, which are instead respected as lexias, as are the individual documents or lexias that comprise the Web. Instead the focus is to create a network of links between the various categories that comprise the Victorian context. For example, under Social Context one can explore Racism and Anti-Irish Prejudice in Victorian England and learn from Anthony S. Wohl, Professor of History at Vassar College, that:

> "In much of the pseudo-scientific literature of the day the Irish were held to be inferior, an example of a lower evolutionary form, closer to the apes than their 'superiors', the Anglo-Saxons. Cartoons in *Punch* portrayed the Irish as having bestial, ape-like or demonic features and the Irishman, (especially the political radical) was invariably given a long or prognathous jaw, the stigmata to the phrenologists of a lower evolutionary order, degeneracy or criminality."(Wohl, 1995)

From within the text one can click on the word 'phrenology' in order to learn more about this 'science', or email George Landow to suggest that this lexia would benefit from including actual copies of the *Punch* cartoons to understand better Victorian legacy of scientific racism.

Documenting the Domestic: Home, Hearth, Heritage, Heart

The folkloristic perspective starts from everyday life. Domestic documentation audio-visual media, another manifestation of 'low culture' that has been barely researched, ironically turns out to be one of the most important theoretical foundations to heritage multimedia as natural inheritor of the family album and other domestic recording media, with the ability to orchestrate the fragments of archived domestic audio-visual memorabilia.

Just as with community cultural representations, multimedia claims to bring the ability to orchestrate and readily access the fragments of archived domestic memorabilia amassed in the cupboards and attics of our homes, making shared domestic heritage as available as television.

Prof. Kresten Bjerg quotes the Danish philosopher Peter Sinkernagel (1992): "The multiplicity of private life constitutes an infinitely multidimensional universe."(Bjerg, 1994:330) He deduces that "Therefore the home, considered as a context for such a universe, is a much more subtle and complicated entity than common trivialisation leads us to suspect. Home-contexts are - each home in its own and unique way-:

- A sedimented and sedimenting carrier of past and contemporary cultural forms and meanings
- A highly developed and equipped vessel for navigating through the life-ages
- A reflector of the biographies and extension of the selves of its inhabitants
- A uniquely distributed sedimenting stock of knowledge"(Bjerg, 1994:331)

This notion of domestic 'sedimentation' combines with historic links between home, hearth and heart, and the poor hearth-surrogate television has made, what Ted Nelson has called "the video narcosis that now sits on our land like a fog", or the Hasidic Jews of London have termed "the sewer running through our living rooms". The proposition here is to re-assert the potential centrality of the role of domestic heritage into the 'home' equation — home, heart, hearth, heritage — through new means for archiving and accessing this "sedimenting stock of knowledge".

Pauline Teerehorst speculates that the metamorphosis of home into a working and focal point of the electronic superhighway will encourage positive changes in domestic human relationships. I would submit that meaningful access to shared heritage can also be seen in this context as making coherent a new domestic focus.(Teerehorst, 1994)

Of course there are practical problems associated with our present domestic documentation: of obsolete formats, of access, storage and control. There is a domestic information explosion such that it becomes difficult to locate, for example, particular photos or footage. Older home formats have grown obsolete or lack durability, so in that sense as well have become inaccessible. And our shrinking domestic space poses a practical storage limit on our domestic archives. The importance of 'RVs' in America, the recreational vehicle as mobile retirement home, is one example of the need for VR (virtual reality) as Virtual Roots for those who must leave their 'home' behind, be they in nomadic old age, or like any average American who moves an average of 17 times, or infirm or otherwise so that they must leave loved home and prized possessions and memorabilia.

Tarja Cronberg from the Technology Assessment Unit of the University of Lyngby, speaks of a "domestic technology trajectory" of 5-10 years, whereby new technology of industry, commerce and, I would add, academia, enter the home within a decade.(Cronberg, 1994) Products used at work and to produce the cultural representations discussed earlier in this work will have domestic counterparts developed, while other products are beginning to target the domestic heritage market directly. With cheap digital recording media for home use, huge growth in domestic documentation is predictable, with the multimedia diary offering cheap readily accessible means.

Now it seems we have the opportunity to draw on all these largely unused and inaccessible treasure-troves of domestic observation to make heritage once again a central focus of our home lives. The new technology enables not only access, preservation and control of previous 'traditional' documentation, but also the generation of new forms and combinations. I can easily locate a track of my late father playing, digitised from a fragile aluminium recording, and combine it with a cherished photograph. And I can include my own and others' reminiscences, and link to other sounds and images.

Not just photographs and moving image, but letters and documents can be preserved and made accessible, and further, they can be hypertextualised to link to one another, or to anything else. Past homes can be preserved as virtual homes that can be 'walked through', with cherished objects — memorabilia, paintings, sculpture, furniture — on perpetual display. And all of this can be accessed, for example, via person, place, date or other criteria, including graphical.

What are the implications of this opportunity within a postmodern context that encourages individual reconstructions of the past?

Anttonen notes that postmodernism can be seen as "a demand for cultural and semantic heterogeneity". Instead of seeing additions as cultural material passably inherited from one generation to the next, they should be seen as constructs which people create in the present through a symbolically meaningful reference to the past.(Sjöman, 1992)

Pedro Meyer's CD-ROM *I Photograph to Remember* seems to answer this demand for individual reconstruction, while reaffirming the importance of story and linear narrative as a dramatic means towards creating an impact of shared experience. Meyer photographed the last days of his father's life as he died of cancer, which lasted two years, and incorporated them in a relentless and emotional chronological series. Each photograph is accompanied by a monologue by Meyer himself, with versions in both Spanish and English. The power of the voice that comes through is unexpected in a medium that is normally image-driven, and its sincerity and rhythm — and importantly and unusually for new media, its silences — hypnotically bind the viewer to a narrative that resonates with the shared experience of this intimate human situation. Although individual photos can be accessed individually with accompanying sound, meaning and identity are only derived from their construction as natural story.

The publisher (Voyager) claims that the content could not have been delivered without the technology, but in fact computer adds little beyond convenience to what is essentially an emulation of a sensitive tape-slide presentation, or documentary film of still images. As with film, or tape-slide, or hearth-side tale, the viewer commits her or himself to the authority of a linear and predetermined unfolding story. In the domestic and other spheres, such a traditional approach must not be regarded as a misuse of the technology. As Max Whitby head of the BBC offshoot MultiMedia Corporation notes, "most successful communication involves a great deal of craftsmanship and authorship and point of view and storytelling and narrative."(Cameron, 1995) It is not a game.

Conclusion

Cultural representation through new media as commercial enterprise suggests further questions than have been raised here regarding objectivity and responsibility, as do any in the advertising and marketing arenas, where the tension falls between marketing and authenticity, between nostalgic fabrication and faithful documentation. Heritage is defined as encompassing history and culture, but whose version of history, and whose interpretation of culture? Which history of Richard Nixon will endure? The definition of 'heritage' does not preclude neo-Nazi heritage or other revisionist histories preaching racial supremacy through glittering multimedia. How would Leni Riefenstahl (who filmed Nuremberg rallies 1933-4) have exploited this technology to legitimise fascist and racist politics?

Will the provision of audio-visual interactive access to the past, including virtual realities, provide a democratically balanced and objective liberation of bygone years? Or will only the most audio-visually attractive shards be retained and represented as multimedia glitter, a nostalgic Disneyfied, post-card stroll down a selective memory lane, littered with the booty of plundered adornment? And how real *are* the dangers of promoting a value system built on virtuality, one which abandons commitment to solving the real environmental and social problems of an uncomfortable present?

References

Anderson, W., *Reality Isn't What It Used To Be* San Francisco:Harper & Row, 1990, p42

BBC, *Desert Island Discs* radio programme,1994

Appignanesi, R. & Garratt, C., *Postmodernism for Beginners* Cambridge UK:Icon Books Ltd., 1995, p116

Bjerg K., Domestic Information Dynamics and the Virtual Home. In Bjerg, K. & Borreby K.,(eds.) *HOIT 94:Home-oriented informatics, telematics & automation*: Proceedings of a Cross-disciplinary International Working Conference, University of Copenhagen, June 27th- July 1st, 1994, Copenhagen: Oikos, 1994

Bolter, J., *Writing Space: The Computer, Hypertext and the History of Writing* [Hypertext version], Cambridge, Mass.:Eastgate Systems, 1990 http://www.eastgate.com/products/Cat_Nonfiction.html (Book version: Bolter, J., *Writing Space*, Lawrence Erlbaum, 1990)

Borges, J.L., *Ficciones* New York:Grove Press, 1962

Borges, J.L., *The Aleph and Other Stories, 1933-1969* New York:Bantam, 1971

Cameron, A., *Dissimulations: Illusions of Interactivity* 1995 http://www.wmin.ac.uk/media/VD/Dissimulations.html ,

Christ, R., *The Narrow Act: Borges' Art of Illusion,* New York: New York University Press, 1969

Bruner, J., *Toward a Theory of Instruction* Cambridge Mass.:Belknap Press of Harvard University Press, 1967

Cardus, S. & Latimer, J., Promotional material for *My Brighton interractive community history project* Brighton UK:Brighton Museum, 1994

Cronberg, T., The Social Construction of Home Technology. In Bjerg, K. & Borreby K.,(eds.) *Home-oriented informatics, telematics & automation*: Proceedings of a Cross-disciplinary International Working Conference, University of Copenhagen, June 27th- July 1st, 1994, Copenhagen: Oikos, 1994, p5

Foster, H., (ed.), *The anti-aesthetic essays on postmodern culture* Washington:Port Townsend, 1983, p142

Gill, R. Artificial Intelligence for Social Citizenship: Toward an Anthropocentric Technology. In *Applied Artificial Intelligence* , Hemisphere Publishing Corporation, (1991)5:15-27

Gottdiener, M., *Postmodern Semiotics* Oxford UK & Cambridge USA:Basil Blackwell, 1995, p47
Harvey, D.,*The Condition of Postmodernity: An Enquiry into the Origins of Cultural Change* Cambridge Mass.:Basil Blackwell, 1989, p303
Hay K, A Postmodern Educational Technology. In Estes, N. & Thomas, M. (eds.) *Rethinking the Roles of Technology in Education,* Proceedings of the Tenth ICTE, MIT, March 1993, Vol 2, pp913-15
Jameson, F., *The Political Unconscious* New York:Cornell University Press, 1981
Jencks, C., *Post-Modernism: The New Classicism in Art and Architecture* New York:Rizzoli, 1987
Landow, G., *Hypertext: The Convergence of Contemporary Critical Theory and Technology* Baltimore:John Hopkins University Press, 1992
Landow, G., (ed.), *Victorian Web* 1995 http://twine.stg.brown.edu/projects/hypertext/landow/victorian/victov.html
Lanham, R.A., The Extraordinary Convergence. In *The South Atlantic Quarterly*, Vol. 89, No.1, 1990
Larsen, D., *Marble Springs* Cambridge Mass.:Eastgate Systems, 1993, WWW sampler available at http://www.eastgate.com/MS/Title_184.html
Luhtanen, J., Miettinen, V. & Wuorisalo, J., *Hyperkalevala Proceedings from Complex Learning in Computer Environments Workshop*, Finland:University of Joensuu, 1994, p191
Mattelart, A & M, Axioms For Postmodernisation. In *International Image Markets*, Comedia, 1984
Ministry of Education, *Higher Education Policy in Finland.* Helsinki, 1994
Moulthrop, S., *Victory Garden* Cambridge Mass.:Eastgate Systems 1991 WWW sampler available at http://www.eastgate.com/VG/VGStart.html
Moulthrop, S., *Hegirascope* http://raven.ubalt.edu/Moulthrop/hypertexts/HGS/HGSPropers.html
Nelson, T., *Literary Machines* Self-published, 1981, 1/4
Postman, N., *Amusing Ourselves to Death,* Heinemann, 1986, p.86
Roles, J. *All Change at Brighton Museum*, Brighton:Brighton Museum, 1995
Roszak, T., *The Cult of Information* London:Palladin, 1988
Sjöman, M.,Current research in the Nordic and Baltic countries. In *Nordic Institute of Folklore Newsletter* 4, 1992
Smith, J., Russia. In *Encyclopaedia Britannica* seventh edition 1830-42, reprinted in *An Anthology*, London:Encylopaedia Britannica Ltd., 1963 p38
Taylor, J., Learning in the Nonlinear World: A Critical Postmodernist Reading. In Linna, M. & Ruotsala, P., (eds.)*Hypermedia in Vaasa '93' Conference Proceedings*, May 1993, pp266-73
Taylor, J., [The NativeNet discussion has been substantially published previously within: History, Identity and Democracy: Implications of Community and Domestic Heritage Multimedia. In
Bjerg, K. & Borreby K.,(eds.) *Home-oriented informatics, telematics & automation*: Proceedings of a Cross-disciplinary International Working Conference, University of Copenhagen, June 27th- July 1st, 1994. Copenhagen: Oikos, 1994, pp229-238.
Taylor, J., [The *Hyperkalevala* discussion has been substantially published previously within: Cultural and Democratic Implications of Urban Multimedia: Heritage, Identity and Democracy. In *17th Urban Data Management Symposium Proceedings* Helsinki: Helsinki University of Technology, 1994, pp201-214.
Teerehorst, P., *On the Threshhold of a Post-modern Family-Home* Doors of Perception 2 conference , Amsterdam, Nov. 4-7, 1994 http://www.mediamatic.nl/doors/Doors2/Terreehorst/Terreehorst-Doors2-E.html
Wilson, J., The Computers and Culture Project. In Estes, N. & Thomas, M. (eds.) *Rethinking the Roles of Technology in Education,* Proceedings of the Tenth ICTE, MIT, March 1993, Austin:University of Texas, 1993, Vol 2
[For a longer discussion of this project see: Wilson, J., The computers and culture project: a multimedia approach to the preservation of Native history, language and culture. In *Canadian Journal of Native Education* 19(1), pp7-19]

Wohl, A., Racism and Anti-Irish Prejudice in Victorian England. In *The Victorian Web* 1995
http://twine.stg.brown.edu/projects/hypertext/landow/victorian/race/Racism.html

Chapter 17

Consensus and Authenticity in Representation: Simulation as participative theatre*

Michael T. Black

Representation was invented as an issue during the 17th century in response to specific developments in the technology of simulation. It remains an issue of central importance today in the design of information systems and approaches to artificial intelligence. Our cultural legacy of thought about representation is enormous but as inhibiting as it is productive. The challenge to designers of representative technology is to reshape this legacy by enlarging the politics rather than the technics of simulation.

Introduction

Transport yourself emotionally for a few moments to an unusual society. This is a society obsessed by a newly recognised commodity: symbols. Linguistic symbols in new formally defined languages: architectural symbols in a diversity of innovative styles: musical symbols which are based on recent developments in sound mechanics; artistic symbols which range from the alien and abstract to incredibly life-like illusions.

This society is fascinated - and not a little concerned - about the technologies which promote such symbolic virtuosity. Recently, some rather fundamental advances in science and engineering have allowed symbol generation, manipulation and transmission at low cost, unprecedented speed and with decreasing control by existing authorities. Although revelling in the excitement of symbol-creation, the general attitude among those at the centre of things is one of doubt: the dominant emotion surprise. There is a growing recognition that anticipation of developments - in either the symbols or their technology - is a vain hope.

Does this symbol-oriented society feel familiar? Is this how the well-known extra-terrestrial might describe at least part of life in late 20th century Europe or North America? Perhaps, and with good reason. This is a sketch of Europe - but in the late 16th not late 20th century. It is the beginning of the era we have come to call the Baroque.

The parallels between the Baroque age and our own are rem:trkable: the threatening empire of the East (the Ottoman, not the Soviet) has become incapacitated through internal ossification rather than military defeat. New national boundaries are being established to coincide with language (in France and Germany, not Yugoslavia or The Baltic). Simultaneous strenuous political effort is being made to maintain unity within the continent (the Holy Roman Empire, not the European Community).

Arguably, the most significant root of our commonality with the Baroque is the excitement and the worry we share with that era about symbols and symbol-producing technology. The hardware of 400 years ago was not, of course, electronic circuits and computers; but it was equally important advances in complicated metallurgy and paper production that promoted printing as a major industry for the first time -and as now attracting the best and the brightest to test the possibilities for its application. It was also the invention of precision measuring instruments from the telescope, to the thermometer, to the navigational clock - allowing new sorts of symbol-creation and conversation about the world to take place.

Software developments were equally impressive. Logarithms were invented as a convenient and efficient way to complete otherwise intractable calculations. The special purpose computational device, the slide rule, soon followed, Differential calculus opened up new possibilities for extending the range of hardware applications. Arabic numerals were imported; and the monumentally important symbol discovery - the decimal point - came into general use.

The need for groupware wasn't neglected. The Royal Society, one of several such institutions, was established to organise the discussions about how to develop and most appropriately use the new technologies. Theatres as permanent buildings and enterprises became part of city life nearly everywhere the company of players, rather than the building, was the centre of organisation. National languages became respectable not only in daily informal conversation but in the conduct of technical discussion, coalescing engagement among otherwise unconnected individuals.

The reason that the Baroque is important to us, however, is not its technology. Sociologically, politically, or scientifically there is probably little relevance of the post-Renaissance era in the post-Industrial one. Rather, the Baroque provides us with an intellectual legacy - a legacy of attitudes and prejudices about symbols and their technology. This legacy has become our cultural family seat, a baronial hall to which we feel some vague: but intense obligation. We pour enormous resources into its maintenance without being quite sure about the reasons. There reasons are suspect and selective demolition might be the best way to save the bits worth saving.

Our Baroque Legacy

The Baroque period was a cosmic Big Bang of the symbolic intellect. A technical and manageyial agenda was formed in the heat of its explosion - an agenda the primary concern of which is the authenticity of symbols and the way in which symbolic technology ought to be used. Out of a primal chaos of artistic, literary and scientific symbols energised a specific question that seemed to demand an answer: How can we be sure that the proliferation of symbols is not just a waste of time? Or worse totally misleading and destructive for our way of life?

The answer to this question solidified as the primal elements of the Big Bang cooled. Specific responses varied depending on the view of the terrain once had; but the general message was consistent: authentic generation of symbols could only be achieved by the establishment of a Guarantor outside the community. Without this Guarantor, the slide to anarchy was inevitable - with all the social and political consequences one might expect.

By the 20th century this conclusion had been dissipated as a sofl of background radiation - subtle but pervasive. And the problems of authenticity of representation might have faded completely from all except the most sensitive detectors but for another explosion similar to the first.

Technology had again shifted its focus from producing things to producing symbols. The Infosmation Age had begun. And as symbols and symbol-producing technology proliferated, the cultural residue from the previous symbolic age was noticed and amplified. The questions of the Baroque looked relevant and so did its answers.

Simulation: The Representation of Representation

Artists, not scientists or engineers, were the first to recognise the interesting applications of late 16th Century technology. Cervantes was the first to devise a descriptive simulation - a novel. *Don Quixote; a* true to life story about apparently real people, in believable circumstances and expressed in sufficient detail so that we can imagine ourselves moving within the story as it unfolds.

But neither the greatness of *Don Quixote* nor its status as a simulation rests on its simply being first (and first by a long time). Verbal and literary descriptions are, of course, ancient. The work is ironic (and therefore purposely offensive to those meant to read it). It is, in fact, a study in irony carried to the extreme. The first half is about the enonymous Don Quixote and his unlikely adventures. But the second half of the book is actually 'about' the first half, written as if these adventures were already well-known. It is, in short, totally self-reflexive; and being so raises what subsequently became an obsessive doubt about the authenticity of symbols and their role in representation.

As long as the persona of *Don Quixote* was considered as referring, however obliquely or inaccurately to a class of pompous, archaic individuals, he could be discussed or debated, accepted or rejected by some sort of factual comparisons with that class. His authenticity, in other words, could be assessed. But Cervantes' self-reflexive irony cuts this common-sense route short. The work, he makes clear through his technique, refers to nothing but itself.

Why did Cervantes resort to such a descriptive tactic? political prudence? perversity? prescience? Whatever the reason, in choosing that approach he opened a pandora's Box. By cutting off the symbol from what we have learned to call its referent, he makes his character inherently ambiguous. Real or fictional? Representation or fantasy? Concrete or conceptual? By allowing his symbol to run free, Cervantes may have been a part of the trigger mechanism For the ensuing cultural explosion.

Visual artists (and this is probably decisive for the way the issue of representation was subsequently formulated - as a pictorial problem) picked up Cervantes' cue. A critical mass of talent crystallised around the hint that simulation could produce some interesting results. Starting with fellow Spaniard, Velasquez and extending to an entire school, the Dutch, enormous passion and technical skill was devoted to perfecting visual simulations - paintings so precise, so luminous that they evoke the same: powerful emotions as 'reality'.

But like Cervantes, these artists are not concerned with demonstrating their photographic precision. Bitten by the same bug of perversity, they are also making a point - simulation is not just another technique of the arts. They make this point by becoming totally self-reflexive, by purposely shattering the connections between symbols and anything else - even as they make these connections in paint and canvas.

Velasquez, for example, completes the process of disconnection in his famous Las Meninas[1] which is in itself a complete paradigm of representation. In this, as in dozens of others from the same period and as in *Don Quixote,* the painting is torn loose from any referent - despite the apparent paradox that all those portrayed are identifiable, including the artist himself and the portrait he is painting.

The message of the artists who probed the techniques of simulation is ambiguous, but it was a message picked up by the intellectual and emerging scientific groups in society at large. The interpretation that these groups took from the message was threatening. A basic capability of this new symbol-producing technology is illusion - even worse mass illusion, and the danger of this illusion - of falsehood, of error, of misdirection, of sin - was localised in these representations that represented themselves, these simulations. Society had a problem; distinguishing authentic representation from simulation was indeed an issue. Truth was at stake; and so was the political, moral and economic order built on the integrity and authenticity of the symbol.[2]

The Agenda of Authenticity

Into the middle of this societal crisis steps Rene Descartes. Rebelling against as much as using his Jesuit education, he is keen to articulate the rather vague insight of the artists and to put an end to their threat. His approach is to supply a vocabulary of such clarity that the problem posed by simulation will simply melt away. The important terms in this vocabulary are *minds, things* and *words*. The solution to the doubts raised by simulation is the establishment of the universal rules which connect all three. Any representation not conforming to these rules are false - or at least certifiably fictional.[3]

Of course, these terms of minds, words and things had been around for a long time: but Descartes' intent was not simply to single them out as different from the rest of contemporary French vocabulary. they were, he claimed, not just terms but distinct categories of existence - somehow fundamentally different from one another, and basic to the way the world is. The rest of language might be suspect as invented and manipulated by fallible man. but these three terms were nature's own; the equivalent to the Ten Commandments for an increasingly scientific rather than a religious culture.

We in the Information Age may scoff at Descartes' apparent naivete or reject his rather tortured argumentation. But our dismissal of his formulation is a tribute to his cunning not our superior intellect. 'Mind' has become 'decision-maker'; 'words' strategy and 'things' results. The main difference is that we use our terms with a lot less precision or reflection than Descartes.

Descartes' contemporaries grabbed hold of his fundamental distinction like drowning men to a life-raft. He provided not only the vocabulary but the grammar -the rules necessary for ensuring authentic connections - for eliminating the problem of simulation. And he offered the way to definitively test the authenticity of connections in practice in any and all circumstances. Or so he claimed.

His successors over the next hundred years or so were not so certain of his success about the rules. Each generation produced its own (usually several) definitive, absolute, universal criteria by which minds could authentically make connections between words and things. But they did accept something important from the master -- the essential distinction among minds, things and words. It was this distinction and its puzzles after all which made the debate so interesting and worthwhile. When we design and test neural networks, or analytic computer models, or medical expert systems we track (we think) a symbolic world against a real one to see if it fits - as the latest participants in a long tradition on the Cartesian agenda.

The Rules of Representation

For Descartes the quest for authenticity was not a game. Nor is it for the today's information designer. In both cases, lives and livelihoods depend on the outcome. Perhaps, therefore, it is understandable that so many generations spent so much effort in seeking the key - the final rules of connection - to the Cartesian puzzle.

Or perhaps there is another reason. Behind all the Cartesian-like thinking is a presumption not to be found in the work of the artists who precipitated the debate. This presumption is quite clearly that the rules of authentic representation are not to be found within the community producing and interpreting these representations. Some Archimedian point outside the community - God. Reason, Scientific Method, Absolute Spirit - is necessary to augment human frailty, and this presumption is carried in the Cartesian formulation itself. It is a bird's (or God's) eye view from outside the locus of the problem. It is only from out there that the issues of authenticity can be truly appreciated and resolved. What matters consistently throughout the debate is this need to find security - stability - outside the community.

From this perspective the course of the debate about rules of authenticity - what counts as genuine, reliable, important, valuable, real - follows the societal, or at least personal, concerns about stability. Leibniz (1677) seeks to stabilise relations amongst diverse Christian sects and comes up with rules demonstrating the universal pervasiveness of God. Locke (1690) is worried about the growing rabble calling for mass democracy and formulates rules of representation decided by groups of elite experts. Bishop Berkeley (Daucy, 1987) is worried precisely about the influence of this elite and suggests rules which undermine their credibility in order to preserve existing relationships in society.

Ultimately educated society - the progeny of those seduced by the Cartesian universal model - twigged to the game as it was being played. One.of these - Hegel (1967) - tried to tell the story that the game itself was really real and everything else rotated around it, not many would bite on this hook, however, since while he was trying to meet publisher's deadlines, he sat listening to the cannon of Napoleon on his march across the continent. It is also unlikely that Hegel himself saw the correlation between his circumstances and his message: "Fret not; things look bad but they'll work out in the end".

Beyond the Rules: Privileged Representation

Concern about authenticity seemed to abate during the 19th century. But it only went underground. Marx made the commercial political; Nietzsche made the political competitive; Dewey (1939) made the competitive moral. From then on the criterion of authenticity became pragmatic. If representation 'works' it is right. And competition in free (or at least Anglo-Saxon) markets will let us know if representation works. External guarantees are not needed; our wallets are adequate guides to the authentic. The Cartesian model of mindslthingslwords could be maintained without fruitless debate.

Or could it? Perhaps the most important symbolic development of the 19th century is the industrial corporation. The corporation is (like *Las Meninas* and *Don Quixote)* its own representation. It is a free-floating symbol - or rather complex set of symbols. Its charter gives it life; its organisational structure gives it movement; its reports give it identity; its strategy gives it direction. These, of course, are all representations. They do not simply make the corporation; they are the corporation.

From a social point of view the competitive market, as it turns out, is a superb way for maintaining the Cartesian authenticity of the corporation. The market, constantly expressing the latest fears or desires, does away with the need to articulate universal rules of representation. The corporation is connected to reality as long as it and its representational derivatives are selling better than the competition.

But there is a hitch. While the corporation is guaranteed by the market as authentic. the communities within it - production, finance, marketing, planning - are not, by definition. Functional differentiation - and with this growth - generates an increasingly complex set of representations. The limiting constraints on growth, therefore, is the ability of the corporation to cope with this complexity. A whole new industry was sparked by this need. The objective of this industry was clear: to simulate markets within the corporation. Arguably pride of place within this industry belongs to accounting.

Keeping the proliferating representations of a modern corporation coherent while it grows is no mean feat. Universal laws of representation may have become passe but a new approach - *privileged representation* - provides an alternative. The essential nature of privilege is straightforward. It is the representation against which all others are to be assessed in terms of authenticity. In the case of the corporation accounting - either financial or managerial - this status was achieved almost universally. Once established, even symbol-producing technology can be adopted -or rejected - based on the privileged representation. Privilege allows a degree of representational control never dreamt of during the original Cartesian debates. Even the Catholic Church had sought only to keep Galileo from publisiiing his ideas widely; they never thought of taking away his telescope.

The use of a privileged representation does promote stability during growth. Financial and management accounting systems do facilitate corporate expansion in ways impossible before their introduction. They also promote social cohesion in the corporate community by providing a consistent vocabulary and a set of 'rules of the game' which, if followed, ensure authenticity at every level. Such representation becomes the cornerstone for all decisions in the organisation - particularly those of representation itself.

The Limits of Privilege

Privileged representation is by necessity about value in the commercial corporation. It is the 'final vocabulary' into which we are forced to explain why we do what we do, it must do its job by simulating the dynamics of a market which is external to the corporation within the corporation itself. The problem is that all privileged representations - sooner rather than later - tend to start looking like *Las Meninas*. That is, they become loose symbols with no referent whatsoever.

This phenomenon of the mustang nature of privileged representations is so commonplace as to be unworthy of special notice. Accounting capital, for example - so important to financial institutions for their growth and so obviously concrete to those accustomed to the accounting vocabulary - has no connection with any thing except itself. It is pure representation in most cases not even correlated with any market outside the corporation. Similarly, management cost accounting systems have largely come loose from their moorings of usefulness as allocation of shared costs come to dominate reported results.[5]

Privileged representation does work - in terms which it sets for itself. But not for that reason it claims - connection with market reality - and not without a heavy price. First, privileged representation is expensive to install and maintain. Privilege does not ensure so much as promote; and what it promotes are highly complex reporting, calculating, allocating and management procedures which are in constant need of protection against compromise.

More important, privileged representation causes corporate blindness. By rejecting representations not coherent with itself, the privileged representation prevents any alternative form of representation emerging. It becomes a retro-virus that strikes at the core of the corporation. And this AIDS-like nature of privileged representation is not restricted to accounting or any other simulation. It is a property of privilege not of the quality of the simulation.[6]

From Technics to Politics

Representational restriction - whether through universal law or by privileged representation - is good for community stability and good for allowing community growth. Unfortunately, this tactic also has another consequence - the reduction in adaptability, that is in the ability of the community to respond to change. Our current problems are all precisely those of adaptiveness, not the stability or growth of concern to previous generations. By restricting the range of representation, privileged representation inhibits organisational adaptation and therefore ultimately, stability.

Nevertheless, privileged representation does focus on the issue which is at the root of the representational problem: value. The most important representation in any organisation is this representation of value. It is this representation which is at the heart or the issue of adaptation. In fact the historical debate about representation is parallel to the same debate about value. The attempt to fix a point outside the community to which to attach universal rules of representation is at the same time an attempt to fix the representation of value.

However value like the corporation, is its own representation. Value in other words is what 'we' say it is.[7] Any proposition about the best representation of value is simply a tactic to create community. "Buy DAZ because it makes clothes whiter" is a two-part message. The most important message is the entreaty to use whiteness as the criterion of value and choice for laundry powder. The secondary message, as advertising people know, is that DAZ performs better according to this criterion. Out of infinity of possible criteria of valuelchoice the proposal of whiteness is a straightforward attempt to form a community which agrees on how to assess value -a large part of which will then use the product.

This doesn't mean that the criterion of value proposed can be arbitrary. We are free within a range set by the rest of society, by other overlapping communities, but we are not absolutely free. A representation of value implying racial superiority for the sale of soap powder is unlikely to achieve general community acceptance. Our representations of value must therefore somehow fit within the constraints imposed by a plethora of other representations about value.[8]

There is therefore no absolute representation or value. Privileged representation of value as in corporate accounting or other systems ultimately diverge from what shareholders, customers, debtholders or others with an interest in the corporation represent as value.[9] As long as privileged representation reigns there is no way for the corporation to adapt as this divergency increases.

The Cartesian view of simulation is technical: How do we play the game of minds, words, things? The artistic talent that sparked simulation off was political: Is this the game we want and ought to be playing?[10] Only the latter view can address our problem of adaptation. Simulation is a political not a technical exercise. Its primary uses are in exploring our (often incoherent) beliefs about what is valuable and the way in which these beliefs fit with the beliefs of others. It is a powerful tool for creating new communities rather than stabilising old ones.

Simulation as a Particpative Theatre

Our concern in constructing simulations is of course, with the future not the past. For us the question of representation is not how to formulate the best rules for binding minds, words and things together automatically; or how well do simulation parameters track bits of reality; or how closely are we able to approximate nature's own language. We've learned by now that the answers to these questions don't help much with the future.

Rather, the question is how we can use simulation to evoke and challenge: not only the rules embedded in our psyches by our inherited culture but even the basic models that generate our presumption that there must be such rules. In the vocabulary of Thomas Kuhn(1962), simulation is the vehicle for paradigm shift; a way to rouse us from drowsy intellectual sloth.

Simulating the future means generating new representations - particularly new representations of value to consider, and if appropriate to sell - within our organisations and in general society.[11] From a Cartesian perspective this means purposely confusing the conceptual and the concrete; erasing the distinctions among minds, words and things, eliminating the obsession which some external guarantor of authenticity; living without the need for authenticity at all. In a word simulation means theatre.

Simulation as theatre recognises that the most important interactions are not those among variables; or between one set of representations and another; or even those at the "man/'machine interface". They are the interactions among people stimulated by technology; interactions related to a very particular and notably underdeveloped skill: the articulation and debate about value; what's important (and not), why rather than how a course or action is to be pursued, and what forms are best to represent what's valuable.

Simulation as theatre is inherently disruptive. There seems to be a Cartesian-like presumption in Western organisations that adults entering into reasoned, professional conversation should be able to reach agreement about the nature of commercial value. This presumption is disastrous for adaptation. It is also groundless. It is only because the debate is cut-off by privileged representation that it even looks plausible.

But shouldn't the disruptive quality of simulation as theatre concern corporate managers? Hardly - irreconcilable differences in the criteria of value are precisely the signal needed for divestiture, outsourcing or other organisational reconfiguration. The alternative, common to many organisations, is pervasive guerilla warfare or total incapacitation.

Simulation as theatre is only partly technological. But technology is used in a distinctive mode: as a means of extending the degrees of freedom of expression of participants, not a means of forcing consistent representations, or of 'testing' their validity, or allowing improved communication.[12] In Theatre effect not authenticity is what matters. The only difference with simulation is that there is no audience -effect is pervasive and mutual.

Simulation as theatre is primarily social. It requires placing trust where we've not previously dared in any significant measure - within the community itself.[13] This, not the intellectual relativisation of the Cartesian model, is probably our biggest challenge. It is so because such a shift demands the adoption of a straightforward but unprovable presumption: all human behaviour is purposeful. This may simply be too radical for some of us to bear. Unless we can bootstrap ourselves up to it, however, we re likely to remain stuck using 17th century tools to address 20th century problems.

Creation and Innovation: Dilemmas and Ambiguities

Two lessons from my professional life have impressed themselves on me with the force of law:

1) creation is **a** political act that may have commercial consequences;

2) innovation is a commercial act that may have political consequences.

It seems that our ability to discern the difference has atrophied; and with that ability our language for talking sensibly about either creation or innovation.

Creativity is a godly virtue; in other words a sin for mortals. It is blasphemy. Blasphemy is still punished, not by ecclesiastical courts but by the protectors of the God of rules or conventions that happen to be around. Not all rules and conventions, but those that are obvious, that are taken for granted as the way things are, that are natural. Those who fear or resent the presumption against today's Gods make creativity dangerous. In religion the God of tradition may make women priests dangerous but only for a few. Far more powerful are those who defend the God of change in business, the God of openness in personal relationships. Creativity always implies the politically incorrect. Socrates understood the blasphemy of creativity and still took the risk - knowing what the consequences would be. We are far more casual about the matter. Or have we simply let the idea of creativity deteriorate to the status of a nice thing?

Creation occasionally (I don't think more) leads to something practical, something we can make money from, something which can be used to ease the burden of humanity, something beautiful. Whether this occurs or not has absolutely nothing to do with the intention of the creator - it has everything to do with the response of other people. Is the result of an act accepted, used, valued by us? If so perhaps it was creative. But who is 'us'? 'We', in fact, emerge as a consequence of the creative act. We attest to it, we buy (or sell) its results, we talk about its merits, although, the likelihood is that the more creative the act, the fewer of us there will be, and conversely the more accepted, the less creative the act.

Innovation, on the other hand, is an engineering fact. It is a consequence of playing within accepted rules and conventions, not of inventing new ones. The product of innovation is technology not a community. Innovation has new, often unexpected, consequences but the intention (and this is explicit in innovation) is a confirmation of not a challenge to the rules, mainly the rules of an existing community. Innovation is directed towards the extension of practical knowledge, that is our ability to do more, faster and with less as measured by the standards of an existing community. Innovation is, unlike creation, edifying.

Innovation may of course have political consequences. The invention of the stirrup arguably changed the course of European history by allowing knights on heavy horses to defeat unarmoured opponents at Tours. Naval gunfire control systems may have changed not only the organisation aboard ships but the entire institution of naval forces.

But these effects are accidental. Innovation is accepted as such, in other words, because its metric of value is clearly that of an existing community, although it may change the metric inadvertently.

Information technology by its very nature is innovative not creative, although it may have creative consequences. One of the best examples of this might be the CYC project in Texas. The innovative aspect of the work is the construction of a large scale background database consisting of the millions of 'facts' that most of us take for granted - that the name of an individual, for example, is somehow tied to that individual but does not die when he or she does. The intention is to overcome the 'brittleness' of artificial intelligence by ensuring that the CYC database has enough background information and sufficiently robust rules for using this information that it can approximate human cognition.

In brief, a small army of people input data during the day, at night the machine make inferences (dreams) which are then checked for reasonableness the next day. Inappropriate inferences are then traced to their logical causes and these are used to direct further factual input and to adjust the inferential logic. All very innovative. However the creative aspects of CYC is unpublicised and perhaps even unrecognised. These are the conversations generated among the members of the CYC team about their own presumptions, their own taken-for-granteds in the programming of CYC. As a creative experience in thought it's tough to beat. CYC may be the creative start of what might be called empirical philosophy. It may have accidentally created a new community.

Information technology has made promises it can't keep about creativity. It confuses innovation and creation. Most commercial organisations have been trapped by these promises - last year's innovation has become this year's millstone. Both creativity and innovation are paradoxical, the former because it offends the establishment, whatever the establishment may be; the latter because it flatters the establishment by 'hardwiring' its prejudices and confirming these as natural. Creation produces new communities with new standards; innovation promotes old communities with existing standards. Neither is an unqualified virtue. Without the tension between them creativity degenerates to irrelevance and innovation to paralysis. The risk of creativity is personal, that of innovation corporate. Our judgment is most challenged by the choice of precisely how much of each to tolerate.

Notes

I. See Michael Foucault *On the Order of Things,* Taviatock Publications, London, 1970, for an extensive analysis of Las Meninas in terms of representation and for history of representation different but far more elegant than that presented in this paper.

2. See Keith Thomas, *Religion and the Decline of Magic,* Penguin Books, London, 1971, for a description of the importance of the symbolic in the 16th and 17th centuries and an extensive description of the crises of representation inherent in alchemy, witchcraft, and medicine.

Thomas' remarks on the intellectual changes of the period are particularly appropriate to the theme of this paper (p. 767):

"It is a feature of many systems of thought, and not only primitive thought, that they possess a self-confirming character. Once their initial premisses are accepted no subsequent discovery will shake the believer's faith, for he can explain it away in terms of the existing system. Neither will his convictions be weakened by the failure of some accepted ritual to accomplish its desired end, for this too can be accounted for. Such systems of belief make them virtually immune to external argument."

One plausible explanation of the intentions of visual simulators like Velasquez is that they were attacking just this problem. Unfortunately for us the scientific epiatemologists who followed insisted on substituting one set of iron clad premises for another.

3. See Richard Rorty. *Philosophy and the Mirror of Nature,* Basil Blackwell, Oxford, 1980, for a full critique of the Cartesian model.

4. See Richard Rorty, *Objectivity, Relativism and Truth,* Cambridge University Press, 1991, especially pp. 151-161, for a discussion of the attempt to impose a final vocabulary on the process of inquiry and representation by philosophy; Rorty rejects the problem of representation as classically posed within the Cartesian framework as irrelevant but for different reasons than those given in this paper.

5. See F. Drucker, *Managing for the Future,* Truman Tally Books, New York, 1992, pp. 305-307 for a discussion of the declining usefulness of conventional cost accounting.

6. For example, see Alfred Rappaport, *Creating Shareholder Value,* The Free Press, 1986, in which an alternative privileged representation to accounting is proposed: discounted cash flow analysis. Use of this alternative in practice results in a different sort, but equally destructive, divergency of representations of value.

7. See Richard Rorty, *On the Consequences of Pragmatism,* Harvester Wheataheaf, 1982, for a full discussion on the relevance and effect to claims to speak about the values of the community.

8. See Michael B lack, (unpublished manuscript), *Using Value Metrics for Organisational Transformation.* CSC Index, May 1992.

9. This point is not only relevant to conamercial organisations. The National Gallery in London advertises as "The most representative and balanced" art collection in Europe. Neither representativeness nor balance is an obvious criterion of value for such an enterprise. One can only summarise that these criteria are relevant to both funders and visitors or at least are being marketed as such among important constituencies.

10. See James P. Carse, *Finite and infinite games,* The Free Press, New York, 1986; in Carse's terms the first question is symptomatic of finite game with a clear rule-determined end point; the latter is an infinite game in which the point is to keep the game going - even at the expense of changing the rules.

11. cf C. West Churchman, *The Systems Approach,* Dell Publishing, New York, 1968, especially pp. 119 for a discussion of several approaches to the problem of finding 'representative' representations and the intractability of finding an analytic (rather than synthetic or simulative) solution.

12. See Mark Poster, *The Mode of information.* Polity Press, Oxford, 1990, especially pp. 128-154

13. cf James M. Buchanan, *Liberty, Market and State,* Wheataheaf Books, Brighton, UK, especially pp. 248 for a discussion of the implications of the Cartesian model as basically antithetical to not only liberal democratic principles but to the ability of political systems to adapt in ways analogous to those necessary for the private corporation.

References

Daucy J. (1987). *Berkeley: An introduction,* Basil Blackwell, Oxford.

Dewey, J. (1939). *Theory of Valuation, international Encyclopaedia of Unified Science,* Vol 2, No 4, University of Chicago.

Foster, R. (1986) *innovation:* The Attacker's Advantage, Simon & Schuster, New York.

Hegel, G.W.F. (1967) *The Phenomenology of Mind,* Harper & Row, New York.

Kuhn, T. (1962) *The Structure of Scientific Revolutions,* University of Chicago Press.

Koesther, A. (1964) *The Act of Creation,* Picador, London.

Leibniz, G. (1677) *Dialogue on the Connection Between Words and Things,* (first published 1677) in P. Weiner (ed.), *Liebniz: Selections*, Scribner & Sons, New York, 1951.

Lenat, D. and Guha, R.A. (1990) *Building Large Knowledge - Based Systems: Representation and interference in the CYC Project,* Addison-Wesley, Reading, MA.

Locke, J. *An Essay Concerning Human Understanding,* (first published 1690), Dent, Everyrnan's Library, London 1961, bk.2 Chs. 8-9.
Morison, E. (1966) *Men. Machines and Modern Times,* MIT Press, Cambridge, MA.
White, L. (1962) *Medieval Technology and Social Change,* Oxford Press.

Notes

* This paper first appeared in *AI & Society*; 1993: 7.1

Chapter 18

Cognitive Technology

Barbara Gorayska & Jacob L. Mey

A new programme of research is emerging, called Cognitive Technology (CT). Its main foci of interest are: (a) the role which 'informational artifacts' play in the construction of the human mental world, and (b) the role which this constructed ('fabricated') world must be assigned in the development of new 'informational artifacts'. While 'classical' HCI focuses mainly either on the engineering aspects of information technology, or draws attention to the strictly human problems involved in that technology, in CT we aim at integrating these two trends. Doing that, we emphasize the total world aspect of HCI (and not, say, exclusively such aspects as those gathered under metaphors like 'tool', 'black box', 'machine', etc.). Furthermore, this world is considered not only as something on which humans operate, but something humans work in and with. In particular, we want to stress the aspect of the (computerized) world as a purveyor of guidence, by virtue of its structuredness, rather than as a collector of mere data. CT is presented as sui generis: it has its own direction of enquiry which cannot be reduced to any of the current practices of building Ecological Systems, Cognitive Ergonomics or Cognitive Engineering.

Introduction

In this paper we wish to initiate a new paradigm for research in Human Computer Interaction. Its key focus is a specification of how, and to what extent, human construction of environmental artifacts bears on the operations and structure of the human mind. Investigating this direction of influence between minds and worlds (see also [10]) as well as their symbiotic relationship seems particularly important in the area of Information Technology. The rapid advances in information delivery-systems, such as multimedia, tele-communications or Virtual Reality machines, have amplified the scope for fabrication of the cognitively-manifested environment from its natural physical realm to the realm of imagination at large: we can create fiction which is indistinguishable from, and blends into, our everyday reality (see, e.g., [33] or [18]).

The relationships between such developments and the human mental processes of forming cognitive schemata converge in a new programme for research which we have termed COGNITIVE TECHNOLOGY [2]. The pertinent issues are:

- the nature of, and changes in, the processes of access to information now made available through technological advances;
- how the interaction between humans and technological devices in the realm of information processing influences, from a pragmatic point of view, cognitive developments in humans;
- social and moral issues underlying cognitive developments as affected by modern delivery systems;
- the feedback effect of such influences and interactions on future advances in Information Technology.

In the quest for better, more widespread, and faster delivery of information, it is tempting to focus attention on technological advances for gathering, storing, processing and sending out information, but to disregard the syntactic, semantic and pragmatic properties of information itself and forget about its effects on human recipients. As machines become more and more 'human-like', vice versa, the human operator tends to become more and more 'machine-like'. One of the major aims of Cognitive Technology research is to halt the process of dehumanization which accompanies these technological advances [25] and, instead, produce comfortable and highly adaptable [21, 11] environments for human machine interaction, which not only amplify human cognitive abilities [29, 38] but promote creativity, imagination, self confidence, courage in decision making [11, 5] and better interactions between humans themselves [34].

Relation To Other Current Frameworks

Ecological systems

The main thesis we wish to explore reads:

a. The human mind and the world are interrelated in intricate and inseparable ways, therefore

b. the structure given to the human fabricated environment must have a profound influence on the structure of the mind.

This thesis bears similarity to the principle of the embodiment, by mental interpretation processes, of the environments in which those processes occur (first proposed by Gibson [8,9] for visual systems). Gibson's main claim is that, when humans perceive things, they are not merely responding to raw sensory input data from the environment. Rather, humans are actively searching the data for invariant features of the environment, which they know are relevant to their current recognition purposes and demands for information. In Gibson's model, the environment is a vital and inseparable component upon which, and with which, the human mind operates.

Complementary postulates of such an inseparable relationship between environment and the human processor have recently been echoed by several other authors. For instance, Donald Norman [27:55-6] has argued that "much of the information a person needs to do a task can reside in the world". That is why, "for example, we lack knowledge about common coins even though we recognize them just fine". Rodney Brooks [4:583] has argued that "the world is its own best model." That is also why, e.g., when we construct robots that function in a dynamically changing environment, we do not have to represent, i.e., build an internal model of, that environment in the robot's internal memory. The robot "can use its perception of the world instead." Or, John Haugeland [16:16] has presented "the mind as embodied and embedded in the world". So, e.g., when we drive a car along a road to San Jose, it is possible to contemplate that, in some sense, "the road knows the way to [that place]."

Segal, Campbell and Herskovits [32] have proposed to look at the relationship of the mind to the world from the opposite standpoint by assuming a feedback effect of human artifacts on the human mind. Their Carpentered World Hypothesis conjectures that the regularities present in human constructions, e.g., rectangular but never trapezoidal windows, produce expectations which are the source of geometrical illusions, such as the M¸ller-Lyer effect or the Sander parallelogram (where varied contextual distance interpretations of the same physical length of a line are wrongly assigned), that are present in human conscious experience.

Gorayska and Lindsay [14] have taken the Carpentered World Hypothesis a step further by postulating a much more active and widespread feedback effect of the structure given to the environment upon the human mind. According to their *Fabricated World Hypothesis*, human construction of artifacts provides the means "by which urban man controls behaviour of self and others and releases processing capacity" [emphasis ours]. The human environment tends to be organized around goal satisfaction: e.g. bars, hair salons, kitchens, etc. The principle of this fabrication "makes an immense difference to the processes involved in perception, memory and goal-management. To put it in a challenging way: much of human memory is in the environment. The fabricated environment is such that simple algorithms suffice to generate effective behaviour within it [because the] situations are such as to satisfy the execution conditions of very few actions at any one time" [14: 16-7].

Cognitive Technology research takes the Fabricated World Hypothesis to its extreme. It does not merely accept that most of human memory is in the environment, but proposes to address the issue of how the human fabrication of such memory outlets dictates or prescribes which goals people ought to and will pursue most of the time, and hence changes their behavioural norms.

To date, the main preoccupation of Cognitive Sciences in relation to goal oriented behaviour has been establishing how action sequences are generated once goals are known. The problems no longer seem to lie with the formal structures incorporating goals, but in the substance: what goals are there and where do they come from? [14, 37]. Human factors research has been successful in finding the (types of) human operator's needs or goals, and incorporating these within the human-computer system designs. However, as Schank and Riesbeck [31:39] put it, "[i]f we ask ourselves where [these] goals [and needs] come from, we are [still] left with a very difficult question. Why do people do what they do?"

This new direction of enquiry is intended to shed some light on the sources of human goals and needs. We are proposing to investigate:

a) the cognitive process of adaptation by people to the environment thrust upon them in the Age of Information with its technological advance
b) what people lose or gain in this process.

In particular, we will be looking into the process of ecological integration of multi-agent systems. This integration rests on the functional, and not merely physical, depiction of objects and structures in the environment which ëaffordí, in Gibson's terms, behaviour by interacting with the relevance seeking processes of the human mind. [14, 19, 12, 23, 15] This integration distinguishes itself from most current approaches, in particular Cognitive Ergonomics and Cognitive Engineering. The next two sections will have a closer look at those approaches as compared to CognitiveTechnology.

Cognitive Ergonomics

Cognitive Ergonomics [6] studies human cognitive processing with respect to such factors as eye-movements, spatial proximity of input sources, or degrees of complexity in information displays at any one time. This information is fed into the organization and design of tool equipment for the working environment. This integration of human cognitive functioning within the design of tool organization is intended to prevent the tools, when utilized, from:

a) producing cognitive dissonances in the human agent (such as those which arise when more than one task is competing for the same cognitive resource at any one time, or when people are asked to operate knobs positioned to their right with their left hands), or
b) expecting the human agent to function outside the boundaries of human cognitive closures. (Say, when we require a human response action in less than the physically possible delay threshold of 113 msec [3].)

The overall aim of Cognitive Ergonomics is to maximize the efficiency of human productivity through stimulation of more natural and smoother human cognitive performance. Cognitive Ergonomics proposes to achieve this by concentrating attention on both the physical sides of human cognition and the knowledge dependent aspects of it:

> "Human-computer interaction seeks to support interactions between humans and computers which make computers effective for performing work. Cognitive ergonomics contributes to human-computer interaction by supporting those aspects of the interactions which depend on the

> knowledge, required by the human, to use the computer to perform work effectively" [20:4]

In this case, the outlook on humans appears to be that people are viewed as objects for producing effective, collaborative, human-computer work in organisations. It is a very narrow and dehumanising outlook, geared towards nothing more than task oriented mental activities (see also the section on Cognitive Engineering below).

Cognitive Technology, on the other hand, is primarily interested in how the syntax, semantics and pragmatics of information outputs which such (computerized) tools produce in the cognitively manifested environment with which the human mind interacts, and controls the (representational) adaptation of the mind to its informational environment by forming an ecological niche [22]. Cognitive Technology therefore concentrates its attention on the human side of the 'techne' involved in cognition and Information Technology.

Cognitive Engineering

Cognitive Engineering is a scientific practice of incorporating the human agent as one of the computerized system's components. It is an applied cognitive science which studies human decision making processes and human task performance in an attempt to establish at which points this performance should, and how it ought to, interface with computerized tools [29], so as to maximize the human's effectiveness. As noted in [38], the distinguishing axioms of Cognitive Engineering are:

- Humans function in worlds which are complex.
- Humans function in worlds which are dynamic and open and not artificially bounded.
- Humans perform tasks according to what to them is psychologically real in any domain.
- Humans aim at enhanced performance and error reduction.
- Humans are active cognitive agents and problem solvers. They are not merely using computer software; instead, they interact with other cognitive agents, of which the computer may be considered as one.

In effect, as the authors of [38] appear to claim, Cognitive Engineering takes into account how people combat environmental complexities in their natural settings within cooperative multi-agent worlds. It incorporates these findings into a human-machine problem solving ensemble, to produce systems which increase productivity and decrease human error.

Cognitive Engineering is problem-driven. This means that, in the first place, it analyses and tries to understand problems and problem-solving contexts. It then builds a cognitive description of a problem-solving world which enhances agent performance and reduces sources of agent error. This description often comes in the form of dynamic models of interaction between humans and machines in which the focus falls mainly on human skill acquisition [1]. As its final output, Cognitive Engineering produces tools for people to operate effectively and efficiently in their working environment. In sum, as Donald Norman [26:31] puts it, "[Cognitive Engineering] is a type of applied Cognitive Science, trying to apply what is known from science to the design and construction of machines."

Consequently, it has a machine oriented perception of the human herself:

> "A man is far more than a mechanistic data processor, but in human-machine systems the designer has to consider people as versatile but predictable data processors, and the designer has to plan the data processing allocated to a human and to the instrumentation system as one integrated system. The human machine interface should therefore be based upon compatible models of the data processing in humans and in instruments, and a model of humans drawing heavily upon engineering analogies may be fruitful in this respect." [29:75]

By contrast, Cognitive Technology is human driven. It is primarily interested in people. It proposes to investigate how machine communication tools/aids, once constructed, through the very nature of their outputs,

a) bear on dynamic changes in our human perception of the world and ourselves within it

b) affect natural communication practices between humans.

Justification

The fundamental difference between current approaches to building human-computer-human communication systems and the approach we are proposing is this:

- Current approaches study communication between people and (machine) artifacts in order to produce, primarily, better (human-machine) artifacts and to benefit Information Technology.
- Cognitive Technology studies communication between people and (machine) artifacts in order to produce, primarily, greater socio-cognitive awareness and to benefit people.

We conjecture that this shift in our perception of the main aims of HCI research is vital for the type and the success of the final outcomes, if those outcomes are to preserve universal human values (see also [7]).

It should not (and probably does not) come as a surprise to discover, given current attitudes to progress in Information Technology, that prevalent metaphors permeating system design methodologies are those that identify people with machines [17]. The 'human as machine' metaphors perpetuate the role of human subjects as replaceable instruments which fit in an overall system design. Metaphors of this nature are dangerous, especially if misused and overused. Because metaphors involve identity shifts, the messages they convey are indistinguishable from, and eventually become, reality itself (see also [24, 23]. Consider also the observation of Sherry Turkle " the idea of thinking of the self as a set of computer programs is widespread among students I interviewed at Harvard and MIT who were familiar with large computer systems." [36:289]

By placing the main emphasis on the (socio-cognitive development) of the human operator, we are more likely to prevent dehumanising trends before they even arise.

Secondly, the shift in practices of investigation that endorses the proposed unifying framework of thought, has the potential of bringing together, and to the foreground, distributed efforts of research which have currently been surfacing in HCI, Cognitive Sciences, and the Humanities. Vide a call for papers for the Electronic Journal on Virtual Real Culture:

> " The [. . .] approach which frames this special issue holds that tools embody experiences, biases and worldviews (mental models) of their developers. (Ask any left-handed person who has tried to use a pay telephone in a road booth.) In this view, tools transmit process preferences, procedural models and task sucess criteria from their developers to their users." (Donald L. Day, Syracuse University; electronic message)

Compare also single efforts by individual teams. An example of the latter comes from the report by Calvert et. al. on the development of an interface for choreographers to Life Forms - a compositional tool for the creation of dance choreography:

> "One of the more startling observations we have made in relation to working with choreographers is that not only has the interface evolved in response to user feedback, but that choreographers' method of creating has

evolved or enlarged as a result of working with a computer-based creative tool." [5].

Lastly, and most importantly, we need to remain in full control of what is happening to us as a result of the available technology. This message is similar in spirit to, though larger in scope than, the message put forward by Schank and Jona with regard to computers in education:

"The issue in education is control. Who is in control? Now it is curriculum designers, lecturers, and workbook publishers. In many cases, it ought to be the students. Most students want to learn. When they determine that their questions will be answered, they will keep asking questions. The real role of the teacher, computer or human, is to keep the environment interesting enough to prompt good questions." [30:20]

There is little doubt that technology is going to affect us. Vide the quote from Calvert et. al., or the one below from Mey [21]:

"The consequences of this new mode of access to information [a computerised filing system] are mainly two: In the "medical" domain patients' journals are no longer adapted primarily to the needs of the persons keeping the journal: instead, a rigid format is imposed by the categorizations and systematizations that are inherent in the chosen system of file maintainance. Thus, we have a clear case of "adaptivity", when the nurse making an entry on a particular patient is forced to split her information between what is computer-formattable and what is only expressible in "free form", as a more or less welcome addition in the columns "Other" or "Remarks". And not only do we have adaptivity here: the adaptivity is a forced one." [21: 183]

It is our human right and duty to be fully aware of all the negative and positive conseqences of our interaction with modern technology, and not to be spared the freedom of choice.

Acknowledgements

We wish to express our thanks to NV Balasubramanian, Kevin Cox, Jonathon Marsh, Brian Anderson, Lee Clubb, Victor Mehra, Sophie Hsia, CK Leong, Nick Hamid, Herbert Pick, Albert Yonas, Laurence Goldstein, Ho Mun Chan, and Mike Denny for stimulating and very helpful discussions on the subject, which have led to clarification of many ideas presented in this paper.

References

[1] Ackermann, D. & M.J. Tauber (eds) Mental Models and Human-Computer Interaction 1. Amsterdam: North Holland. 1990

[2] Balasubramanian, N.V., Barbara Gorayska, Jonathon Marsh. Establishing Cognitive Technology Research Group. Technical Report TR-93-04. Department of Computer Science, City Polytechnic of Hong Kong, 1993.

[3] Bailey, Robert W. Human Performance Engineering. Englewood Cliffs, NJ: Prentice Hall, 1989.

[4] Brooks, Rodney A. Intelligence without reason. In: Proc. IJCAI 1991, pp. 569-595.
[5] Calvert, Tom W., Armin Bruderlin, Sang Mah, Thecla Schiphorst, and Chris Welman. The Evolution of An Interface for Choreographers. In: Proc. INTERCHI '93: Human Factors in Computer Systems, Amsterdam, April 24-9, 1993. London: Addison Wesley, 1993, pp. 115-122.
[6] Card, S. K., T.P. Moran and S. Newell The Psychology of Human - Computer Interaction. Hillsdale, NJ: Lawrence Erlbaum Associates, 1983.
[7] Cox, Kevin and David Walker. *Human Interface Design*. 2nd ed. New York: Prentice Hall, 1993.
8] Gibson, James J. *The senses considered as perceptual systems*. Boston: Houghton Mifflin, 1966.
[9] Gibson, James J. *The Ecological Approach to Visual Perception*. Hillsdale, NJ: Lawrence Erlbaum Associates, 1979.
[10] Gorayska, Barbara. Reflections: Commentary on Philosophical Implications of Cognitive Semantics. *Cognitive Linguistics* 4-1, 1993, pp. 47-53.
[11] Gorayska, Barbara and Kevin Cox. Expert Systems as Extensions of the Human Mind. *AI & Society* 6, 1992, pp. 245-262.
[12] Gorayska, Barbara and Kevin Cox. Knowledge Based Systems that Acquire Expertise Autonomously. Research Project 700326. City Polytechnic of Hong Kong. 1993.
[13] Gorayska, Barbara and Kevin Cox. Hidden Meanings in Computer Applications. Presented at the 13th World Computer Congress IFIP'94. Hamburg 28 Aug.-2 Sept 1994.
[14] Gorayska, Barbara, and Roger Lindsay. On Relevance: Goal Dependent Expression & the Control of Action Planning Processes. Research Report 16. School of Computing and Mathematical Sciences, Oxford Brooks University, UK , 1989
[15] Gorayska Barbara and Jonathon Marsh. On Mutual Knowledge, Meta-Puzzles, and Wise Men. A critique of Jones and George's "Why Must the King Speak Out? The meta-puzzle of the wise men." *AISB Quarterly* (under review)
[16] Haugeland, John. Mind Embodied and Embedded. International Symposium on Mind and Cognition, Academia Sinica, Taipei. Taiwan, 28-30 May, 1993 .
[17] Kendall, Julie E. and Kenneth E. Kendall. Metaphors and Methodologies: Living Beyond the Systems Machine. *MIS Quarterly* 17-2, 1993, pp. 149-171.
[18] Laurel, Brenda K. Interface as Mimesis. In: Donald A. Norman. and Stephen W. Draper (eds.), *User Centered System Design*. Hillsdale, NJ: Lawrence Erlbaum Associates, 1986. pp 68-85.
[19] Lindsay, Roger and Barbara Gorayska. Towards a General Theory of Cognition. 1994. Unpublished manuscript.
[20] Long, John. Cognitive Ergonomics and Human-Computer Interaction: An introduction. In J. Long and A. Whitefield (eds.) *Cognitive Ergonomics and Human-Computer Interaction*.Cambridge: CUP, 1989. pp 4-35.
[21] Mey, Jacob. Adaptability: Reflections. AI & Society 6, 1992, pp. 186-191.
[22] Mey, Jacob. Knowledge Organization: The Ecological Niche. Beijing University of Foreign Studies, July, 1993.
[23] Mey, Jacob. Metaphors in Computing: Signs and Realities. Cognitive Technology Lecture Series, No 1. Department of Computer Science, City Polytechnic of Hong Kong, Hong Kong, July, 1993.
[24] Mey, Jacob. Rules, Constraints and Information Technology. Cognitive Technology Lecture Series, No 2. Department of Computer Science, City Polytechnic of Hong Kong, Hong Kong, July, 1993.
[23] Mey, Jacob L. and Barbara Gorayska. Integration in Computing: An Ecological Approach. In: Proceedings of the Third International Conference for System Integration, So Paulo, Brasil, 15-19 August 1994. Los Alamitos, Calif.: IEEE Computer Society. pp 594-599.
[24] Mey, Jacob and Mary Talbot. Computation and the Soul. *Semiotica* 72-3/4, 1988, pp. 291-339.

[25] Mey, Jacob and Hiroshi Tamura. Barriers to Communication in a Computer Age. *AI and Society* 6, 1992, pp. 62-77.

[26] Norman, Donald A. Cognitive Engineering. In: Donald A. Norman and Stephen W. Draper (eds.), User Centered System Design. Hillsdale, NJ: Lawrence Erlbaum Associates, 1986. pp 31-61.

[27] Norman, Donald A. *The Psychology of Everyday Things*. Basic Books, New York, 1988.

[28] Norman, Donald A. and Stephen W. Draper (eds.) *User Centered System Design*. Hillsdale, NJ: Lawrence Erlbaum Associates, 1986.

[29] Rasmussen, Jens. *Information Processing and Human - Machine Interaction: An approach to Cognitive Engineering*. Amsterdam & New York: North Holland/Elsevier, 1988.

[30] Schank, Roger C. and Menachem Y. Jona. Empowering the Student: New Perspectives on the Design of Teaching Systems. Technical Report #4. Institute for the Learning Sciences. Northwestern University, Evanston, Ill., August 1990.

[31] Schank, Roger C. and Christopher Riesbeck. *Inside Computer Understanding*. Hillsdale, NJ: Lawrence Erlbaum Associates, 1981.

32] Segall, Morris H, Donald T. Campbell, and Melvin J. Herskovits. *The influence of culture on visual perception*. New York: Dover, 1966.

[33] Tognazzini, Bruce. Principles, Techniques, and Ethics of Stage Magic and Their Application to Human Interface Design. In: Proc. INTERCHI '93: Human Factors in Computer Systems, Amsterdam, April 24-9, 1993. London: Addison Wesley, 1993. pp. 355-362.

[34] Tamura, Hiroshi. *Human Interface* Tokyo: Corona Publishing, 1987. pp 1-32. (in Japanese)

[35] Tamura, Hiroshi. The concept and practice of Human Interface. *Human Interface* 3, 1988, pp. 149-152.

[36] Turkle, Sherry. *The Second Self: Computers and the Human Spirit*. New York: Simon & Schuster, 1986.

[37] Wilensky, Robert. *Planning and Understanding*. London: Addison-Wesley, 1988.

[38] Woods, D.D. and E. M. Roth. *Cognitive Engineering: Human Problem Solving with Tools*. Human Factors 30-4, 1988, pp.415-430.

Chapter 19

Electronic Mail, IT Productivity and Workplace Culture

C. W. Boyne

Electronic mail is becoming widespread as an aid to organizational efficiency, but the belief that it increases productivity rests on questionable foundations. Organizations have failed to specify how electronic mail systems are supposed to be used, and the way the technology functions also helps to prevent efficient usage. Electronic mail is, however, a significant phenomenon. From the organization's standpoint, it indicates a tendency, or at least a desire, to become in some sense a democratic, participatory institution. More significantly, perhaps, it fosters a more convivial and complete (if less productive) attitude to work from the employee's standpoint. Unless the way organizations use electronic mail alters, it may come to play an important part in shaping the culture of work in the future.

Introduction

Electronic mail (Email) is currently reckoned to be one of the fastest-growing computer applications in use in business situations in the developed world. In a recent article Thackray(1994) reported that virtually all large organizations in the United States now employ Email internally, a quarter of them also having external Email connections. He cites an Electronic Messaging Association estimate which claims that by 1995 some 20 million US workers will have access to Email facilities. These figures are impressive. Even if current estimates err on the optimistic side, and represent connectability rather than actual usage, they still demonstrate a considerable investment in communications technology, suggesting that Email is thought to have an important part to play in US corporate life, and making it likely that other developed economies are, or will soon be, echoing the American pattern of Email expansion.

Yet this explosive growth seems to have aroused very little comment or speculation either in the business and computing press or in academic circles. In some ways this is hardly surprising. Some form of electronic messaging or file transfer facility is an old-established feature of most multi-user programming and development environments; Email has been standardly promoted by all manner of software developers as a part of the 'electronic office' for a good many years; and finally, its introduction across organizations has been gradual, often fragmentary, and generally undramatic in its immediate impact on the user and the organization alike. At first glance, then, Email might well appear to be just another constituent element in office technology, like word processing or electronic file storage. However, I want to suggest that when Email is established on the scale described above, it has very much greater significance than we give it credit for. It has the capacity to exert a radical influence on patterns of human communication within and between organizations, and hence is significant for the future of every form of work-orientated human interaction, from corporate decision-making to the most trivial personal communication that formerly took place around the coffee machine. As such, Email deserves serious consideration. First, and perhaps conventionally, it deserves consideration as an organizational tool which is capable of altering the way the whole organization functions (a process which I believe is already well established, if not widely noted); and second, Email should be examined as a cultural influence on the individual in the world of work, an influence which in turn helps to define reality itself for a sizeable section of the population.

Over the last three decades the growth in the employment of Information Technology has led to great increases in productivity in industrial, commercial and administrative organizations - changes that we now regard as normal. Production-line robotics, which excited so much interest a few years ago, is becoming commonplace, for example; and we all take for granted a society involving so many automated financial transactions per day that it would take the entire workforce to carry them out without computers. These gains in productivity, however, are really all of one kind. They have resulted from lengthy and progressive processes of planned system development. In crude (and perhaps excessively Taylorian) terms, they have stemmed from careful analysis of repetitive work procedures which have then been automated - essentially an extension of the factory system of work management which has been under development in the Western World for two centuries or more and now embraces the 'information production line' as well as the physical production line. The result is that a great number of activities formerly undertaken by factory workers and clerical workers alike have become largely or wholly automated. This tendency is well understood, if not universally welcomed or admired. Yet the routine (hence automatable) productive aspects of any organization's activity are only one side of the coin. There has always been an essential core of non-repetitive, non-structured planning, supervisory and administrative activity in organizations. In general terms, this is the sort of activity which constitutes the role of management, and this in turn requires a penumbra of supporting 'office' activities which are equally hard to automate. As repetitive production becomes less labour intensive and decision-making becomes more intensive and significant, this type of activity is bound to increase. Yet Information Technology cannot in most cases replace these activities. Instead it is required to 'support' them - and this has led to the development of an entirely new type of technology whose essential characteristic is that it is facilitative rather than automative. This difference has not been widely noted, yet it is a fundamental one. The key difference is that facilitative technology is in a very real sense under the user's control, since the user decides where, when and whether to use it; whereas automative technology normally defines and controls the activities of the human worker (where it does not replace him or her entirely). And it is to this new, little understood, but highly significant category of facilitative technology that Email belongs, arguably as the dominant member.

It is difficult to assess the effectiveness of any type of facilitative technology, partly because patterns of usage are bound to vary widely, but partly also, I suspect, because its growth tends to be insidious and passes relatively unnoticed. Yet clearly a good many people must have been led to think that the introduction of Email is worthwhile, and it is interesting to speculate on their reasons. Most obviously, pressure for its introduction is exerted by the increased need to make and support decisions in a fast-changing world, and this pressure leads to the uncritical adoption of any technology which might enhance the decision-making process. There are, it seems, three major arguments which are generally used to support the introduction or extension of Email, two of which are almost certainly mistaken while the third is at best dubious. First, there is the argument by analogy with production; second, the belief that facilitative technology such as Email is relatively cost-free; and third, the belief that it promotes a valuable participatory work culture. Each will be discussed in turn.

It is very widely assumed that because Information Technology has performed so well in increasing productivity on the shop floor that it must be capable of doing the same in the office. Thus for some years now pundits have been asserting that productivity gains to match those of the production line are on the point of being realised through new and more efficient patterns of work, made possible by the introduction of new technology. For example Rowe (1986) wrote "Office work . . . has traditionally been labour-intensive, and this will substantially change, both in quantitative and qualitative terms, with the coming of new information technology." (The same hopeful claim could, I believe, be made in 1996.) This view is characteristic of an assumption, based on what might be called the 'optimistic-generalist' outlook about the effects of Information Technology, that the introduction of devices which promise the possibility of enhanced productivity will (other things being equal) actually result in genuine productivity gains for the employee and the organization. Yet the notion that introducing new office technology will lead directly to improvements in the productivity of those who use the technology is highly questionable - particularly where the technology is facilitative rather than mandatory. While there are bound to be some cases where the introduction of new office technology has led to dramatic productivity improvements, the assumption that this is generally true might be regarded as having the status of a myth. The myth can take various forms. The general form is perhaps that employees will spontaneously develop more productive working practices if they are simply given the facilities to do so. Thus it is thought that the mere provision of Email is sufficient in itself to lead to its effective use as a productivity aid. A more specific form of this myth would be that that the provision of Email automatically leads to improved internal communications, which by their very existence must enhance employee productivity.

It should be obvious that, as they stand, these beliefs are nonsensical. They equate roughly to the idea that by giving a nomadic herdsman a mechanised plough (without explaining what it is for or how to use it), we can expect him to convert himself spontaneously into an arable farmer. Clearly providing the tools themselves is not enough, if they are supplied without considering where (and indeed whether) they are needed, and without the necessary guidance as to their effective use. Yet, by and large, this is what happens when Email is introduced into an organization. The writer has yet to find a major organization that has put up a convincingly reasoned case for company-wide Email prior to implementation (though there is usually plenty of *post hoc* justification available). Nor has the writer ever seen an Email implementation plan which really addressed the question of when and why the system should be used (rather than just how to use it in the technical sense). Something of this has indeed been recognised by one writer of the 'optimistic-generalist' movement, who argues that "the technology does not solve problems solely though its own momentum; end-users must themselves make the effort necessary to grasp the opportunities which technology opens up."(Gunton 1988) The suggestion that the momentum for change must come from the users themselves represents, I believe, a vain hope. Gunton also seems to be implicitly assuming that management cannot or will not provide the momentum - and in my view the most likely reason for this is that management has little or no idea about how facilitative technology is supposed to generate the benefits which are vaguely hoped to accrue from its use. If we now turn to the more specific formulation of the Email-productivity myth, namely that improved communications leads automatically to improved productivity, the fallacy is glaring. By itself, and without some form of strategic guidance as to its use, Email is no doubt likely to generate more communication, but there can be no guarantee that 'more' means 'improved'. Indeed, the opposite is far more likely to be the case. But crucially, even if improved communications are achieved, their equation with improved productivity is highly questionable and requires proof; and the assumption that greater productivity will follow is just another piece of vague optimism about the promise of Information Technology in the office setting.

The second reason put forward for the great growth in the provision of Email is the belief that facilitative technology of this sort is relatively cost-free. This is based on the premiss that since Email normally resides on pc networks which already exist within the organization, and the software is relatively cheap to buy, the costs of the system will be negligible - and they will of course be far outweighed by the (supposed) productivity gains. This, however, is a short-term view, and for a number of reasons. Typically, Email is introduced piecemeal into organizations, but because its role is undefined, it gets used for all sorts of communication, and this is hampered by anything less than 'one-per-desk' connectivity. There is consequently a persistent pressure for the system to be expanded, until a point is reached where the volume of traffic generated requires a battery of file-servers far in excess of original expectations. Often this comes about because users do not store their mail locally, but leave it on the server. The pressure to purge servers leads to the need to archive mail, and I have encountered computer-intensive organizations whose Email archives already rival their formal archives in size. Once created, the problem is intractable - and expensive. Piecemeal expansion has the same effect on maintenance costs. The first small Email system that is set up is virtually self-maintaining, but as it grows, it begins to require full-time management, with a consequent growth of support staff. All these costs, however, are relatively predictable, even if it is rare to find that anyone has actually estimated them in advance. The greatest costs of Email systems are hidden by the optional, facilitative nature of the product, because these costs are tied up in the time and effort expended by users in generating and dealing with Email communications which are in fact of marginal value to the organization. It is widely recognised by students of Human-Computer Interaction that human costs exceed machine costs in virtually all computer-mediated office tasks; and it is widely recognised by users of Email that dealing with the mail is a time-consuming and often tedious process. What is more, it sometimes seems as if Email systems have been specially designed to increase the human costs of usage - a point I shall return to later.

If the two assumptions discussed above - that Email provision spontaneously generates cost-free gains in productivity for the organization - are generally false, there is nevertheless a certain validity in the third assumption - the idea that Email can play a part in promoting a participatory work culture which is valuable to the organization. This is perhaps not the place to try to discuss the value of participation and worker empowerment as a management strategy. (The writer's own observations across a number of organizations, both commercial and non-commercial, tend to suggest that a policy of worker participation in decision-making (where it is not just a facade) often indicates nothing more than the inability of weak management to take decisions. However, such impressionistic evidence may well be misleading.) The relevant question here is whether Email has any value in promoting such a policy, or in fostering participatory attitudes amongst the workforce. On this it is relevant to point out that workers display attitudes and mores in their work which derive from a much wider context than the workplace itself. For example, Morgan (1986) has argued convincingly that the high degree of co-operation and company loyalty exhibited by Japanese employees is culturally dependent on a tradition of agricultural co-operation which was once vital for survival. This cultural outlook has been successfully transplanted into industry and reinforced by Japanese management methods, but significantly, the methods did not create these employee attitudes, which are deeply rooted in the whole cultural basis of Japanese society. It is hardly surprising, therefore, that attempts to copy Japanese management techniques in the West have met with limited success, since here the dominant culture is individualist and group loyalties, where they exist, are fragmented and disparate.

What, then, is to be expected from Email in this respect? The answer is almost certainly that Email usage will in most cases reflect and even amplify the prevailing attitudinal climate that already exists among employees; and where this is not an innately co-operative and participatory climate, it will not be transformed into one just by the provision of a communication tool. This seems to have been the experience of more than one large American corporation which set up Email links to the chief executive and encouraged employees to raise organizational issues directly with the head of the organization. Far from generating a participatory climate, the principal result was to amplify and orchestrate complaints about management. This rare foray into management-directed Email usage cannot be accounted a success. Indeed, I shall suggest later that in Western organizations, Email characteristically becomes a tool of the personal and social culture of the employees rather than the officially-promoted culture of the organization. It is possible that, as part of a well-planned and well-motivated management strategy of promoting participatory attitudes in the workplace, and where employees are already well disposed towards such attitudes, Email could be a valuable enabling technology. However, it is not in itself a strategic weapon, and is no substitute for such a strategy.

The broad assumption that Email aids productivity, then, is highly questionable. Partly it is the software itself which is to blame. Its basic design (together with the lack of organizational direction about what counts as appropriate use) can actually be seen to counteract the notion of helping the workforce to be genuinely more productive. Indeed, when looking at the technical design of Email systems in the context of actual usage, one cannot avoid being struck by the way in which ease of use (at the interface level) works against the deeper value of the system (i.e. its value for efficient organizational communication). Here it may be worth spelling out the technical superiority of Email over alternative systems of internal communication (these being, after all, the very features which make Email appear so attractive as a productivity aid). Email allows near real-time transfer of information between co-workers, irrespective of whether they are physically nearby or distributed over a wide area, and, unlike the telephone, irrespective of whether they are continuously at their base location. Furthermore, the incorporation of mail-lists means that selected groups can be mailed collectively by the Email user in a single operation, and this adds a level of efficiency to the process of *sending* communications that other media cannot easily rival. Documents can be included with, or appended to, a message, and both can be stored as a permanent record. These last two features are worth emphasising, since Voicemail is often described as being a variant form of Email, or else as a viable alternative. However, Voicemail does not allow storable textual material (though verbal messages can of course be stored); and - most significantly - sending messages to large groups of recipients is not as easy or as 'natural' as it is using Email. (Culture plays an important part in this, I think. The telephone is an established medium for one-to-one communication, and Voicemail extends this concept by making the same type of communication time-independent. Email, of course, has no such established pattern of usage to build on, but one of its 'natural' functions is to replace the process of sending the same hard-copy memo to a number of recipients.) The technical superiority of Email over other means of distributing messages to large groups of people is reflected in the ease by which this can be done. Many systems have been set up with large, and overlapping, user groups, so that large numbers of people may be targeted at once (if 'targeted' is the right word for what is often a very loose process of selecting appropriate recipients for one's message!). Some systems allow the sender to select the whole mail-list by highlighting and mouse movement (which often has the interesting effect of printing the whole recipient list on the first few screens of the message as received). One or two Email designers have even been unwise enough to include an 'All users' item in their address lists, so that it actually takes less effort (i.e. fewer keystrokes) to send a message to thousands of different users than it does to send it to one specified one. The creation by the sender of a specific address list is invariably far more cumbersome than using a pre-existing one, so that very precise targeting of recipients becomes the exception rather than the rule. These factors combine to mean that the cost to the individual in time and effort of sending an Email message to large numbers of people (many of whom may have little or no need to receive it) is very small, and accurate targeting of messages is, in practice, penalised by being less convenient to the sender.

If we now look instead at the position of the recipient, however, the situation is markedly different. Let us first note one effect of the bias in favour of the sender which is bound up in the design of Email interfaces - all users receive more mail than they send. Thus the main task for the user of Email is likely to be dealing with mail received, not sending it. (I take it as axiomatic that not all Email received is of value to all recipients. In a study conducted in 1992, I found that normally more than 50% of received messages were judged by their recipients as having no relevance at all to them. The normal proportion of Email judged to be directly relevant to the recipients was in the range 10-20%). All received Email may nevertheless be conscientiously read (which is arguably a great waste of time, and not how we deal efficiently with other types of internal communication). Alternatively, some form of filtering process must take place. However, this is not easy to do both quickly and accurately. Email systems list details of mail received, but few systems require the sender to attach a title to the message sent, which may force the recipient(s) to read the message if they want to know whether it is relevant to them. Where a title is attached, it is often gnomic, due in part to there being no requirement for the sender to be clear in the choice of title, and partly to the fact that most Email systems truncate the titles of received mail in order to fit them into a rather small window on screen. In practice, many Email users seem to find the sender's name a more useful guide to the potential value of the message than the message title - something which suggests that social, political and hierarchical preconceptions are being used to filter out unwanted traffic, which is not the kind of filtering process the organization would probably wish to see used. (Many a chief executive might be surprised to learn that the majority of his subordinates would delete any message from him unread, on the grounds that it would be most unlikely to be relevant to their work!) Where messages contain enclosed documents, these must often be downloaded to a separate application in order to be viewed - a source of annoyance when the purpose of doing so is to determine whether the documents are even worth attending to. Taking all these factors together, therefore, it can be seen that the bias in favour of the sender which is built into Email systems in general must work strongly against the principle of improving efficient and productive communication within the organization. A professor of computing once remarked to me that Email had a positive side - it increased the likelihood that significant communications would be delivered in writing! That, however, was some years ago, when Email was less ubiquitous. Its current use as a normal means of internal document circulation now means that the wheat is likely to be buried amongst the electronic chaff.

The ways in which Email is used are bound to vary with the type of organization employing it, the size and (social) distribution of the workforce, and the rigidity or laxity of the working practices that govern employee activity. In the absence of substantial research, therefore, any generalisations must necessarily be guarded ones, based on the vagaries of personal observation and investigation. However, I think it is safe to say that virtually every Email system carries a large amount of 'chatter' traffic. Some software producers and systems managers have recognised the extent of this traffic by setting up separate 'social mail' categories which users can opt not to receive. This in itself amounts to a recognition that at least one cultural determinant of Email usage is not to further the efficiency of the organization, but to provide the sort of social forum which used to be confined to corridors, washrooms and canteens. However, 'chatter' is not confined to Email systems which specifically cater for it. For example, informal investigations in one large commercial organization revealed a flourishing traffic in discussions of recent TV programmes, which were often (but not always) included in more business-oriented messages. There was a tendency for users to correspond more with other users who watched the same programmes (so that Email traffic patterns formed clusters around groups of TV soap opera addicts, for instance). The resultant blurring of social and work boundaries seen here is unlikely to be an isolated phenomenon. It is surely symptomatic of an employee-centred culture of work which elevates social and personal interests, rather than suppressing them in the way that traditional, and more authoritarian work cultures require - and of course Email is central to this process as the enabling technology. There is some evidence that modern organizations are prepared to tolerate this sort of activity, and even the underlying shift in working patterns that it indicates - though perhaps this is merely through ignorance of its true extent. (Where Email links cross organizational boundaries there may be a risk to commercial integrity or security, and there is evidence that organizations treat this type of traffic more seriously.) More significant still may be the role of Email as an electronic grapevine through which a counter-culture could function. There is (inevitably) little evidence of this except in the few cases already mentioned where management has deliberately promoted Email as a vehicle for what it vainly hoped would be constructive criticism. Nonetheless, users often seem to be adept at identifying and selecting those Email messages which subvert or bypass work issues and deal instead with counter-cultural, social or personal matters. It is a paradox that whereas Email appears in practice to be a relatively inefficient medium for 'official' communication, it can be quite an efficient one for unofficial communication - probably because users select the messages they wish to read by looking at the sender's name, and elect to read messages with a higher social significance in preference to messages which are likely to be wholly work-related. None of this may be inimical to the aims of the organization (which may include making the workplace a sociable environment), but it cannot be rated very highly as an aid to organizational productivity. And if, as I am tentatively suggesting, The social/personal communication culture is seen by many users as taking priority over the communication of purely work-related matters, then Email might be seen as a quite powerful aid to *decreased* productivity in the workplace.

I doubt if the average organization which has installed Email is at all aware of its social significance. But in the event the organization may decide to tolerate a certain amount of Email chatter in working time, just as it does with the telephone - although, due to Email's superior connectivity, the organization may seriously underestimate the total volume of employees' time spent either chatting or dealing with other people's indiscriminate chatter. Yet the organization surely cannot ignore the impact (or lack of it) of the participatory work culture which Email is often intended to promote. There are two interesting aspects to this. One is the understandable human tendency to believe that what is significant in one's own work is important to one's colleagues. This tends to generate global messages of astoundingly low global significance, of which "I've found a new short-cut in Lotus. . ." and "the east car park rubbish bins will now be emptied on Thursdays instead of Wednesdays" are typical examples. Such 'official-but-trivial' communications are the stock-in-trade of the information society, and it is perhaps arrogant of us to assume that they have no value for anyone merely because they rarely have any for us. However, the other aspect of the participatory work culture is the expectation that it can be truly productive, in terms of ideas generated, shared attitudes developed and reinforced, and shared decisions being found acceptable. This is the level at which Email is expected to provide an efficient substitute for lengthy meetings, broaden the range of people consulted, and attract valuable insights from those who would otherwise not be involved. Does any of this in fact happen? In some cases, of course, it must. However, there is very little evidence to suggest that it happens often enough to offset the many negative features of Email I have been describing. For one thing, a great many of the consultative processes which take place are trivial and therefore unproductive. (As an example, the message cited above about emptying the east car park rubbish bins was originally couched in consultative terms. What this consultative process achieved I was unable to discover, since the sender would not tell me anything about the number or quality of the replies, if any. Nevertheless, over a thousand people were 'consulted'.) No doubt this sort of thing has always happened in large organizations, but Email has an unrivalled ability to encourage it, and indeed institutionalise the practice. More significant issues may become invisible amongst quantities of trivial matter. Where genuinely significant matters are laid open for general discussion via Email, the technology allows two possibilities. Either people reply (if they choose to), a process which may or may not elicit any further response from the initiator, so that the impact of the individual's reply is nugatory; or else many people 'discuss' the issue, which means that many send Email to all, so that the sender bias already discussed overloads the recipients and dilutes the effectiveness of the medium. The writer is perhaps unduly biased by his belief that effective decisions tend to be made by, at most, small groups, whilst Email (unless it is very carefully used) tends to enlarge groups to the point of unviability and beyond. In practice, a good deal of what passes for consultation is really a process of informing the users that a decision on such-and-such is being taken. Thus, Email could be said to promote openness rather than consultation (but so could a notice pinned on a notice board).

Although this view of the effectiveness of the consultative process above may be impressionistic, it cannot be denied that general consultation, if carried out properly, is bound to be a slow business. It may seem paradoxical that electronic communications might slow the decision-making process, but it is demonstrably true. If genuine, the consultative process must give time for replies to be sent. Yet my own experiments have shown that in a reasonably typical organization, the median response time from a relatively small group of Email users (about 50 people) was close to three working days. This, of course, makes no allowance for the fact that in a real consultative process, time would have to be taken to evaluate the responses and formulate (or reformulate) the decision accordingly. More substantive consultations involving larger groups are hardly likely to occupy less time. So if those who control organizations wish them to be run on quasi-democratic, consultative, participatory lines, they must accept that this will be a slow and labour-intensive process, even though the technology involved seems to imply that it could be a rapid and effortless one. The rise of Email may well be partly driven by management's desire to make organizations more democratic, participative and internally accountable, but I think it also probable (and in the spirit of facilitative technology) that the *apparent* ease with which Email permits this to happen is the real driving force. In other words, the trend is mainly driven by the availability of the enabling technology, rather than inspired by a real need which the technology is then introduced to satisfy. (And this in spite of the fact that participation in decision-making is often advanced as a reason for the introduction of Email facilities. For the reasoning is rarely thought through, the costs in time and effort are not appreciated in advance, and the resulting participation is, as I have suggested, often illusory.)

Earlier I described the trend towards participation as a fundamental change in the way organizations function. It seems that at present this is not (in most cases) a fundamental change in *practice*. However, I think it does represent a fundamental change in *perspective*, for it implies that organizations would like to see themselves as co-operative entities rather than as autocracies (possibly in spite of the fact that they also continue on the whole to behave like autocracies). The resulting dilution or confusion of organizational direction must have an impact, and it is hardly likely to be in the direction of improved efficiency or productivity, as this is normally understood. If organizations want to enhance efficiency through the use of Email, they must be prescriptive about how the technology is to be used by employees; and if organizations want to empower employees, for whatever reason, they must recognise the costs involved. And this is part (in my view a significant part) of the decision about what sort of entities organizations wish to become in the next century.

If we turn now to the standpoint of the employee, it is apparent that Email is an equally significant phenomenon. Whereas even ten years ago the desktop computer could be portrayed as an alienating and isolating technology, chaining the individual worker to a series of structured but fragmented tasks and separating her from her fellow workers, it can now be seen as a convivial device, allowing work and social activity to merge into a seamless whole. In one sense, the individual responsibility and the power to communicate which Email gives to the average employee can be said to represent an extension of the professional ethos, where one is comparatively free to organise, direct and pace the work for oneself. In another, and perhaps more down-to-earth sense, it offers the permanent possibility of an alternative approach to the task in hand, so that (to put it crudely) one can chat about one's work as a way of doing it, as an alternative to doing it, or as a mixture of the two. In this way Email opens up the possibility of blending formal work and other aspects of one's life - sociability, even the sense of community - into the sort of unity that in some ways echoes the millenial state of society dreamed of by socialism, where work is not seen instrumentally or as an alienating imposition on real life. I do not believe that this is a very productive situation, in the narrow sense of productivity that still formally motivates organizations. However, it may be a significant indication of the way in which the world of work will evolve in the near future, supported by a technology which, though nominally owned by the employer, is really the possession of the employee. If this is a Promethian vision, then Email is the organizational equivalent of the gift of the gods, given to ordinary mortals and virtually impossible to take back once given. This, I suspect, is why the users of Email say they would not wish to be without it, no matter how much they complain about the chore of using it and the quantities of irrelevant material they are forced to deal with.

At present I suspect that understanding the convivial role of Email is at least as significant in gauging its impact on the way the organization functions as its use in improving formal communications and generating a synergy of ideas and information. Much more research needs to be carried out in this area to establish the true picture; but so far, the idea that Email usage constitutes a new, and far more socially orientated, way of embodying human relationships in the work situation has hardly even been recognised. Consequently, while its net effects on organizational efficiency are open to question, its influence in moulding the working practices and attitudes of the employee of the future can scarcely be guessed at. The blind optimistic faith in the beneficial effects of Information Technology could scarcely be better illustrated than by the prevailing management attitude to Email, though it is fair to say that the designers of Email systems are not without their share of responsibility for this attitude. If Email is to contribute to the efficiency and productivity goals that are currently claimed for it, it needs to be better designed, with less bias in favour of ease of sending and more power of selection being given to the recipient; and there is also a real need for more decisive control by management of the nature of the resource, as well as the way it is used. If, however, Email continues (and continues to expand) in substantially its present form, we should recognise that what we see here is the germ of a new form of human relationship in the workplace rather than a mere business tool, and one which changes the nature of what we call work, as opposed to just speeding it up. This is likely to be so significant a change that what we now regard as a productivity aid should be recognised for what it actually is - a cultural phenomenon, shaping the human experience of work, and as rich in its potential significance for the next century as the telephone and the company car have proved to be for the present one.

References

Thakray. 'The Observer' 1st May 1994, p.8.

Rowe C. People and Chips: the Human implications of Information Technology, Paradigm 1986, p67.

Gunton T. End User Focus, Prentice Hall 1988, p43.

Morgan G. Images of organization, Sage 1986, p114 ff.

Chapter 20

Deadly Technology in the Post Industrial Society: A case study of firearms and firearms control

Peter Squires

The invention of the firearm played a vital role in the establishment of modern nation states. In turn, the process of industrialisation reinforced the growing power of these states by equipping their enlarged armies with the firepower to subdue the world. The power of the West was to rest for many years upon the relative monopolisation of access to weapons.

In the post-industrial world, this relative monopoly has been broken, both within the developed nation states themselves, and across the wider world. A dangerous new situation has been created and the gun is causing a new kind of havoc. This article begins with a review of the origins of a debate in the Britain and America about rights, citizenship and access to firearms. It then proceeds to bring these debates up to date with an examination of the problems resulting in these two societies from widespread access to guns, concluding with a review of the seemingly inadequate methods of gun control currently adopted to reverse the dangerous new culture of the gun.

Industrialisation, Civilisation and Firearms.

A spectre is haunting modern civilisation - the spectre of the gun !

The definitive feature of our modern civilisation concerned its new methods of industrial production. It is no less true that these new methods both depended upon and, in turn, gave rise to new forms of social and political power; new forms of accumulation and of accounting, new sciences and new forms of regulating - both of property and of people. Emphasising the connectedness of this technical and social 'progress,' Michel Foucault has described the conditions which gave rise to the take-off of the West in the following terms, 'If the economic take off of the West began with the techniques that made possible the accumulation of capital, it might perhaps be said that the methods for administering the accumulation of men made possible a political take off . . . in fact the two processes - the accumulation of men and the accumulation of capital - cannot be separated . . . . Each makes the other possible and necessary, each provides a model for the other.' (Foucault, 1977, pp.218-221)

And yet, absolutely central to the political and economic power of the West has been its military prowess (Mann, 1986, pp.453-455, 490). In turn, this was dependent upon new ways of exerting military force, in particular, upon new forms of deadly technology - in short, the firearm. As Kiernan has argued, 'firearms were essential to the rise of the modern state.' (Kiernan, 1967, p.136) In due course, new and remarkably 'industrial' methods of first producing, and then using, the gun established the 'military industrial complex' which sustained the power of the West. Foucault again,

> 'The Classical age saw the birth of the great political and military strategy by which nations confronted each other's economic and demographic forces; but it also saw the birth of meticulous military and political tactics by which the control of bodies and individual forces was exercised within states . . . Historians of ideas usually attribute the

dream of a perfect society to the philosophers and jurists of the eighteenth century; but there was also a military dream of society . . . '. (Foucault, 1977, pp. 168-169)

This 'military dream of society' turned into a nightmare as 19th century wars, especially the American Civil War and the Franco-Prussian War, and 20th century wars, the two 'World Wars,' brought a newly rationalised industrial efficiency to the task of mechanised slaughter (Ellis, 1993, chapter 5, Pick, 1993). For Bauman, the inhumane violence represented by the Holocaust, or Hiroshima, is not an aberration of our industrialised modernity but rather very much a legitimate product of our civilisation. (Bauman, 1989)

Only now, in the age of post-industrial society, with the 'balance' of nuclear terror thrown out of alignment, the gun, once the instrument of a new form of social, political and military order in Europe and the West, is coming to wreak new kinds of havoc. There are several dimensions to this. At home our domestic politics are increasingly preoccupied by armed crime and the threat of terrorism, both of which are fuelled by the lucrative trade in illegal weapons. Fear has become an indispensable component of the political barometer, security has become big business. In the third world and, more recently in Eastern Europe, local and regional conflicts have been facilitated, exacerbated and sustained by an abundant supply of firearms, more often than not, obtained from the arsenals of the world's major military and industrial powers. Paradoxically, the 'democratic peace' celebrated by Critchley in *The Conquest of Violence,* (Critchley, 1970) may have been little more than an incidental spin-off of the near monopolisation of firepower in the hands of states and superpowers during the 20th century. In contrast, the 'post-modern' conditions of post industrial society have seen nation-states struggle to maintain 'order' in the face of powerful, economic, political and ideological challenges threatening social disintegration and renewed levels of interpersonal - and frequently armed - violence.

Nevertheless, the political authorities of modern civilisation have devoted relatively little concerted effort towards exorcising - or controlling - the spectre of the gun, and with little apparent success. In a number of cases they appear surprisingly ambivalent about weapons control, in others they even appear vehemently opposed to it. No doubt the very success of this area of economic activity, this branch of technology, and the fact that the weapons industry proves to be one of the more lucrative areas of capitalist activity, insulates it politically. It is so well insulated, of course, that political authorities are often implicated in covert arms transfer operations - in America the 'Arms for hostages' or 'Contragate' scandal, in Britain the Pergau Dam affair. Gun sales around the world are growing at an alarming rate and, equally rapidly, appear to be penetrating into domestic, illegal, underground and third world markets.

Governments, especially when in recession, seem keen to retain the economic activity, the jobs, the exports and the revenues assured by their arms industry. The paradoxes of security and political order in the wider world become ever more apparent with the recognition that the most powerful voices within the United Nations (UN) - the five permanent members of the UN Security Council (USA, Russia, UK, France and China) are themselves responsible for 86% of arms sales to the developing world (Baird, 1994). Yet in the face of the increasing havoc wrought by guns in society, political authorities around the world have attempted markedly contrasting responses to the spectre of the gun.

Later on, this paper seeks to examine these differing responses - the contrasting paradigms of gun control - in order to discover something about social control, citizenship and social order in the context of post-industrial society. The paper will consist of an examination of differing notions of citizenship, rights, and social order in relation to violent crime, weapons control and access to firearms in the UK and the USA but, by way of comparison or illustration, passing reference will be made to other societies around the world. In the section of the paper immediately following, I will begin by addressing some of the philosophical debates and political and historical preconditions concerning the question of firearms and society.

Firearms and Society: Politics, Philosophy and Contexts.

The political and philosophical debate about the role of firearms in society in the UK and the USA, is tied up with a rather contradictory array of principles, duties, freedoms, privileges and rights, which relate to a series of important historical institutions, processes and events. Amongst the most central of these processes, and one which makes the comparative study of firearms control in the USA and UK especially interesting, concerns the fact that the celebrated American 'right to bear arms', the Second Amendment to the US constitution, is itself said to be derived from a corresponding right enshrined in the English Bill of Rights of 1689.

As Joyce Lee Malcolm, the author of an important recent study of the impact of English rights on the US Second Amendment, has noted,

> 'By the late 18th and early 19th century, Parliament, the Courts, and legal opinion were in agreement on the right of Protestant Englishmen to be armed and the place of this right in their nation's delicately balanced constitution. The right to be armed had become, as the Bill of Rights claimed it was, an ancient and indubitable right. It was this heritage that Englishmen took with them to the American colonies and this heritage which Americans fought to protect in 1775.' (Malcolm, 1994 p. 134 Emphasis added.)

But, as she continues, the right to be armed has not stood the test of time very well. In England, 'it has been so gently teased from public use that most Britons have no notion of when or how it came to be withdrawn,' whereas, in the USA, 'a noisy and emotional debate,' surrounds the Second Amendment. It is said to have been 'infringed' by numerous state and federal laws and was under fierce assault, not least, by the Clinton Administration's Crime Control Bill, as recently as 1994. Many in the USA consider that the Second Amendment guarantees an individual right, others regard it as a dangerous anachronism, others insist that no individual right was ever intended.' (Ibid., p.165)

Yet, whilst Americans may have fought hard to retain this 'English' right, 'ancient and indubitable' it certainly was not and no amount of *ex post facto* redrafting of the Bill of rights could make it so. Access to and ownership of firearms had been both a privilege and a duty. It had been restricted by religious affiliation (no Catholics), or according to a property qualification, or by virtue of membership of the local militia. Moreover, if the historical accounts are to be believed, for much of its history, militia membership was experienced primarily as an onerous duty. Although enshrined by Statute, the organisational bases of the militia varied enormously and in many areas it was, at best, informally established and inefficiently supervised. For long periods, in large parts of the country, the practice of mustering the local militia seemed to fall into abeyance. Even so, whenever the practice was revived, militia members had to supply their own arms and ammunition, practice and become proficient with their weapons and attend periodic musters for training and registration. Furthermore, militia members, as ratepayers, had to contribute to the cost of civic defences, support town 'watch' schemes and, when required, assist in raising 'hue and cry' to bring outlaws and felons to justice. Such were the costs and duties associated with the privileged access to firearms enjoyed by a minority of Englishmen (Greenwood, 1972, pp. 7-11). As can be seen, this so called 'right' scarcely adds up to the 'right to bear arms' stoutly defended by the American pioneers in the 18th century and no less vociferously protected in the 20th.

Yet if the 'right to bear arms' has a rather more ambiguous parentage than some of its contemporary supporters are inclined to suggest, neither can militia service and the related access to firearms claim legitimacy in terms of *noblesse oblige*. The social order secured by the militia and the weapons of the (mainly) protestant upper classes was intended to secure their own political, economic and religious interests and privileges alone. Malcolm describes at some length the effect of the series of Game Acts passed during the 17th century, culminating in the Game Act of 1671, which substantially tightened the property qualification applying to the right to hunt game and effectively outlawed the simple possession of firearms by any person not so qualified. Blackstone noted that, under the Act, the property qualification required to hunt was 50 times the amount needed to permit a man to vote. (Malcolm, op cit. p.71, Hay, 1975, p.189.) The immediate result was that less than one per cent of those living on the land were entitled to hunt game, even on their own property. The 1671 Act created a new structure of law enforcement and gave a 'new class of gentry-appointed officials ... direct power over the sport. It gave them a kind of 'private game police'.' (Malcolm, p.70) Gamekeepers or other appointed persons were empowered to search premises on a warrant and seize all 'illegal' weapons or other 'engines of destruction' (Hay, 1975, p. 194).

Malcolm's conclusions about the primary purposes of the game legislation are unequivocal.

> 'The Game Act of 1671 made it no longer necessary to prove that guns and bows had been illegally used; it simply included them in the list of prohibited devices, thus depriving nearly the entire population of a legal right to own them. There can be no doubt that this prohibition was intentional .... [The Act] lowered the standard of proof .... [leaving] much to the discretion of the individual justice, and put more emphasis on confiscating the weapons of tenants on country estates rather than locking up poachers.' (Ibid., pp.72-73)

Later criticism of the Act centred upon it as a feature of class legislation. (Thompson, 1975) The aristocracy's control over the distribution of weapons was substantially tightened. 'Ninety percent of the population ... were forbidden not only to kill a rabbit on their own land but to own a gun for their personal protection.' (Malcolm, pp.74-76)

Whilst enforcement of the Act was rather mixed, with poaching offences reflecting the bulk of the cases unearthed by Malcolm, the major significance of the Act lay in its establishment of a system for the regulation of access to weapons by class and religion in the tumultuous political context of 17th century Britain. The years before the civil war had seen many outbreaks of rioting and, in particular, civil disturbances and protests against the restrictions on hunting and against Commons Land enclosures. The Civil War itself posed important questions about power and authority in society, not the least of which concerned the problems of monopolising access to armed force and the role of an armed militia in peacetime vis a vis the type of new Model Army established by Cromwell. These questions were to preoccupy both King, Parliament and most of the landed and ruling classes for the remainder of the century. With the Restoration of the monarchy in 1660 came much talk of 'popish plots', which was eagerly seized upon as a pretext for launching local militias on a variety of search and seizure forays to disarm both Catholics and their sympathisers as well as any other potential opponents. Finally, the Restoration is sometimes marked as the 'golden age of the highwayman.' Whilst this fact is of rather less political significance than the uprisings and rebellions which followed in the 1680s, however, it marked the arrival of the portable and concealable firearm in an essentially civic, as opposed to military, context.

The broader political tensions of 17th century Britain, the 'delicate balances' referred to by Malcolm (op. cit.) were only settled with the ascendancy of William and Mary. This ensured not only the clear and final establishment of Protestant dominance, but also promised the restoration of the 'traditional' rights and liberties of Englishmen, amongst them, a right to arms and the attempt to resolve the problems concerning the role and authority of the militia. In due course, following substantial drafting and redrafting of clauses, article 7 spelled out the right of Englishmen to have access to weapons in the following terms.

> 'The Subjects which are Protestants may have arms for their defence suitable to their condition and as allowed by Law.' (In Malcolm p.119)

Absent from this final formulation was any reference to the militia or any reference to principles of 'common' or 'collective' defence. The statement remains very conditional. It specifically excludes all bar Protestants, and it refers to 'Subjects' not citizens. Effectively the article implies an individual right to be armed to repel burglars, that is to say, *an individual right for personal defence*. And finally, with the phrase, 'as allowed by Law' it anticipated the need to further limit the right to arms whenever the Law might see fit. (Malcolm, p.119-121)

In subsequent years, the Law went on to do just that. The unsettled political situation at the turn of the 19th century saw the introduction of temporary restrictions on the right of access to firearms although, during the greater part of the 19th century - even after the establishment of a police force - it was asserted that 'any person could purchase and keep in his possession a firearm without any restriction.' However, by the mid 20th century this right had vanished.

As we have seen, the English right to arms had always depended upon what was 'allowed by law' and, in the latter part of the 19th century, concerns began to be raised and pressure for change began to mount. Firstly a system of licensing firearms was introduced, then proposals addressed the carrying of firearms outside the home. Later, following widespread concerns about armed robberies and urban violence in London a number of bills were introduced seeking to restrict access to concealable pistols and revolvers. (Greenwood, 1972, Pearson, 1983) None of these Bills were successful until 1903 when the Pistols Act was passed to prohibit the sale of pistols to minors and felons. By 1920, however, the context had changed enormously. In response to the turbulent domestic and international politics at the end of World War 1 (WW1), parliament passed the Firearms Control Act as a 'comprehensive arms control measure.'

Effectively this act repealed the right to be armed by requiring a firearm certificate, eligibility for which was to be decided by a senior police officer, for anyone wishing to 'Purchase, possess, use or carry any description of firearm or ammunition for the weapon.' (Greenwood, 1972) It was highly significant, according to Malcolm, that 'while the reverberations of the French Revolution left the English right to keep arms intact, the repercussions of WW1 and the Bolshevik Revolution did not.' (Malcolm, p.170)

Whereas the 1689 Bill of Rights had exploited the fiction of an Englishman's 'ancient and indubitable rights' to introduce a qualified and conditional 'permission' regarding access to firearms, the early American colonists were no less creative in establishing a rights claim regarding firearms suitable to their own circumstances. The form of words eventually adopted by the US Congress and sent to the state legislatures for ratification as the Second Amendment to the constitution of the United States declared: '*A well-regulated militia being necessary to the security of a free State, the right of the people to keep and bear arms shall not be infringed.*' (See Malcolm, 1994, Chapter 8)

In contrast to the English right, considered earlier, the limitations of which were plain to see, the especially complicating aspect of the American 'right' is the militia clause, the first part of the statement. The alleged ambiguity has fuelled an exhaustive debate, although, in it, the combatants line up more obviously as advocates or opponents of gun control in the present, rather than as historians. For the supporters of gun control, the militia clause, and the reference to the right of 'the people,' implies a collective right to civil defence rather than individual rights to weapons (Kennett and Anderson, 1975, p. 76; Cress, 1984). Opponents of gun control, refer to the republican conception of citizenship which sees 'the people' as virtually coterminous with 'the militia' and they emphasise the unambiguous phrasing of the main clause about not infringing the people's right to bear arms. From this they argue that no individual should be deprived of weapons. An alternative view, perhaps less concerned about the precise interpretation of the statement, argues that the 18th century conception of a militia is a complete anachronism, as is a personal right to firearms for self defence in a modern society with an efficient police service. For others, however, any references to an efficient police force and its contribution to personal security only begs the question.

The debates about the Second Amendment have ranged far and wide, such that there is insufficient time and space to develop them all here and now. The debates draw upon the political and philosophical ideas of a wide range of commentators, including William Blackstone, Machiavelli, Sir Thomas More, James Harrington, Alexis De Tocqueville and Thomas Jefferson. Out of their writings participants in the more contemporary firearms and society debate have drawn an extensive array of concepts central to our contemporary notions of individual freedom, rights, freedom of choice, duty, equality, security and privacy. In particular, opponents of statutory firearms control have used these ideas to construct a potent discourse of 'Republican Individualism' which effectively dominates the firearms debate in the USA, in effect, according to Larson, 'winning the debate before it even began.' (Larson, 1994, p. 185)

The wider debate on firearms in American society reverberates with the history, folklore and political philosophy of the American past. It draws upon the complex constitutional debates about citizens, freedom and citizen militias from the late 18th century, through to the more practical considerations of personal safety in the wilderness of the early settlers. Later on, patterns of life on the frontier of the developing nation added their own particular emphases and justifications to American attitudes to firearms and violence. (Einstadter, 1978) As Brown puts it, 'A cluster of beliefs mentally programmed westerners to commit violence: the doctrine of no duty to retreat; the imperative of personal self-redress; the homestead ethic; the ethic of individual enterprise; the Code of the West; and the ideology of vigilantism.' (Brown, 1994, p.393) Subsequently, the distorting and glamorising lenses of Hollywood added their own gloss to this 'cowboy culture.' Perhaps, last of all, American experiences of war, from the American Civil War through to 20th century experiences of the two World Wars, the Cold War and, not least, experiences of loss and betrayal in Vietnam, with all that this has entailed for recent American politics and culture. (Hellman, 1986)

As Kennett and Anderson conclude, 'The gun .. [in America] is part of a whole series of traditional attitudes about government, society and the individual. They run, like so many threads, through the tapestry of the national past. In its essence, the gun controversy is a struggle between these attitudes and new ones.' (Kennett and Anderson, 1975, p. 254) And they continue,

> 'But in the long run, time works against the gun. Increased social consciousness finds its excesses intolerable, whereas they were once accepted without thought. The era of thermonuclear war (sic.) has made the citizen soldier harder to defend. The war against crime has mobilised the computer and other sophisticated techniques. Moreover, the police have come to regard the armed citizen more as a hazard than an ally. The city is the enemy of the gun, and the city is growing . . . In megalopolis the gun as necessity seems doomed.' (Kennett and Anderson, 1975, p. 255-6)

Optimistic thoughts for the future of modern civilisation, no doubt. But, as the argument of this paper suggests, the conquest of firearm violence (cf. Critchley, 1970) is far from completed. If anything, the gun is making a comeback: the spectre of the gun has in no way been exorcised. The citizens of Kennett and Anderson's megalopolis have recently been buying their guns in droves.

When the American pioneers agreed with William Blackstone that the triumvirate of 'English freedoms', *Life, Liberty and Property,* meant nothing without an accompanying right to defend these against aggressors they also committed themselves to a wider principle, 'that an armed population was the ultimate check on tyranny.' (Malcolm, 1994, p.157) However, the modern premise of a society founded by the gun was that, ultimately, it could dispense with the gun. By contrast, the uncertainty currently facing many Americans precisely concerns whether 'banning weapons will make their lives more or less dangerous.' (Ibid. p.165) At the moment, many seem to be hedging their bets. According to McCaghy and Cernkovitch, 'A large segment of Americans want something done *about* guns; in the meantime they keep guns in case they have to do something *with* them.' (McCaghy and Cernkovitch, 1987, p. 141.

Emphasis in original. (See also Zimring, 1985). These themes are developed in the sections which follow.

America : Homicide Capitol: New York

Writing in the Observer's *Life* Magazine, John Sweeney remarked that, in the film Casablanca, Humphrey Bogart gave the Nazi Major Strasser a piece of Friendly advice. 'There are certain sections of New York, Major, that I wouldn't advise you to try to invade.' since then little seems to have changed. On one Saturday in the Spring of 1994, he wrote, the NYPD logged the following homicides.

- A corpse wrapped in a carpet, drilled with bullet holes in the front of 1790 Bruckner Boulevard in the Bronx.
- The corpse of an unknown females in her thirties shot repeatedly in.her left side in Ozone Park, Queens. • A husband shot in the chest by his estranged wife in Brooklyn. • A 14 year old shot in the head with a .32 revolver by his brother by mistake. • A 20 year old blown away as he walked with a woman on Southern Boulevard in the Bronx. • A shop assistant in a grocery store zapped in the head in Sheepshead Bay. • A man in his 20s shot in the chest, back and arm at 420 W140th Street in Harlem. • A man in his twenties found with three bullet holes in the head on the rooftop of 510 W135th Street in Harlem.

As Sweeney noted, 'few places in the civilised world, outside America, can match New York for unlawful killing.' Rudy Giuliano was elected as mayor in the Autumn of 1993 on the strength of a promise to put an end to the carnage of unlawful killings on the streets, but no one doubts either the enormity of his task or the size of opposition he faces. (Sweeney, 1994)

However, the bigger picture across North America is hardly more reassuring. In 1970 it was estimated that there were 90 million guns in private hands in the USA, though the researchers went onto remark that other commentators 'supported by some data' were willing to put the figure at anything from as low as 50 million to as high as 200 million. (Morris and Hawkins, 1970 p. 64, Wright and Marston, 1975, Sherrill, 1973, for one, prefers the higher figure, see p.21.) Furthermore, Morris and Hawkins added, 'each year an additional three million guns are purchased, and very few older guns become unusable.' (Morris and Hawkins, op cit.) Sherrill, on the other hand, looks to the supply side of equation noting, in 1973, that each year some 5 million new guns 'come off the proud US assembly lines for domestic consumption,' a rate of arms production which positively dwarfs the rate of civilian armament in the first half of the twentieth century. As Sherrill notes,

> 'The National Commission on the Causes and Prevention of Violence says 10 million firearms on the average were added to our civilian stockpile during each of the first five decades of this century (again this is just their conservative guess), but that an estimated 30 million came into civilian hands between 1958 and 1968. The 1960s saw a doubling of the sales of rifles and shotguns and a quadrupling of the sales of handguns. Between 1966 and 1971 hand gun murders jumped 87 per cent.' (Sherrill, 1973, p.21)

However, even taking Morris and Hawkins' 'best guess' for 1970 as a starting point (90 million), and the rate of gun purchase as roughly constant (though Sherrill provides clear grounds for believing it to have accelerated given the new culture of insecurity and the aggressive marketing of weapons for personal protection and crime prevention in the US firearms magazines) we arrive at a figure close to the 170 million mark. With a population now standing at just over 250 million this makes for a particularly high ratio of privately owned guns to persons.

Reviewing the available data on firearm ownership in the USA in 1978, Williams and McGrath found that the most recent National Opinion Research Survey available suggested that fully one half of sampled households contained at least one firearm. This figure of 50% conformed to the rates of 43% to 50% discovered in the corresponding surveys they re-analysed. Interestingly, in view of much recent panic and press speculation about firearm distribution and violence, in 1978 the rate of legal ownership of firearms by blacks (32%) fell significantly below that of whites. (Williams and McGrath, 1978, pp. 51-56) Of course, data such as this only raises further questions about the extent of illegal ownership and possession of firearms. In any one year over 100,000 guns are stolen from private citizens, with further evidence, from a Police Foundation study, suggesting that 'approximately 25% of the criminal arsenal is made up of expensive handguns that were stolen from private citizens.' (DeZee, 1978, p.42)

Justice Department statistics published recently revealed that in 1992 violent crimes involving handguns broke all previous records, rising almost 50% above the annual average of the past five years. Handguns had been used in a grand total of 931,000 murders, rapes, robberies and assaults in 1992 (up from the previous annual average of 667,000 between 1987-1991). To put these figures into rough perspective across the developed world, the following comparison is revealing, though it comes from a date before the rapid increase in handgun offences noted above. Thus, in 1983, while there were 8 handgun killings in the UK, and 35 in Japan, there were a grand total of 9,014 in the USA. (P. Bromhead, 1988, Living in America, Longman). This rising trend of violent and firearm related crime continued into 1993, a year during which the FBI Unifrom Crime Reports recorded over 23.000 homicides, some 16,189 caused by firearms, of which no less than 13,252 were shootings with handguns (Davis & El Nasser 1994).

Earlier still, in 1968, firearms were used in: 8,870 murders, 64,950 aggravated assaults, and 99,000 armed robberies. (Refer to the graph, figure one.) Guns were also employed in excess of 10,000 suicides and featured in over 2,500 'accidental' deaths. The estimated total of non-fatal gun injuries was 100,000. And finally, guns were used as the murder weapon in 96% of the 475 killings of policemen during the period 1960-68.

As Morris and Hawkins conclude this toll of grim statistics, 'since the beginning of this century some three-quarters of a million people have been killed in the United States by privately owned guns, 30% more than in all the wars in which this country has been involved in its entire history. In sum and in short, the populace is armed with a dangerous weapon.' (Morris and Hawkins, 1970, p.65.)

McCaghy and Cernkovitch demonstrate that in the USA in 1985 approximately 60% of all homicides (including suicides) were firearm-related, whilst in 43% of murders the cause of death is a handgun, in 7% a shotgun and in 4% another form of firearm. They conclude, citing Farley's demographic analysis (*Demography*, 17, 1980) that the evidence on causes of death in the US points to the conclusion that, 'from 1960 to 1975, the increase in the number of homicides was largely the result of an increase in firearm homicides.' (C.H. McCaghy and S.A. Cernkovitch, *Crime in American Society*, Macmillan, 2nd. Edn. New York, 1987.)

The 20th century history of murder and firearm violence in the USA shows some striking continuities, but also, as we have seen, some more alarming recent trends. One of the 'bright sides of homicide,' according to Sherrill in 1973, is that American firearm homicide rates have always been unusually high. In 1929 The New York State Crime Commission estimated (there were no reliable national statistics for a few more years), that 'there is one murder committed in this country every forty minutes and over nine thousand each year ... seemingly the pistol is one of the most popular playthings in

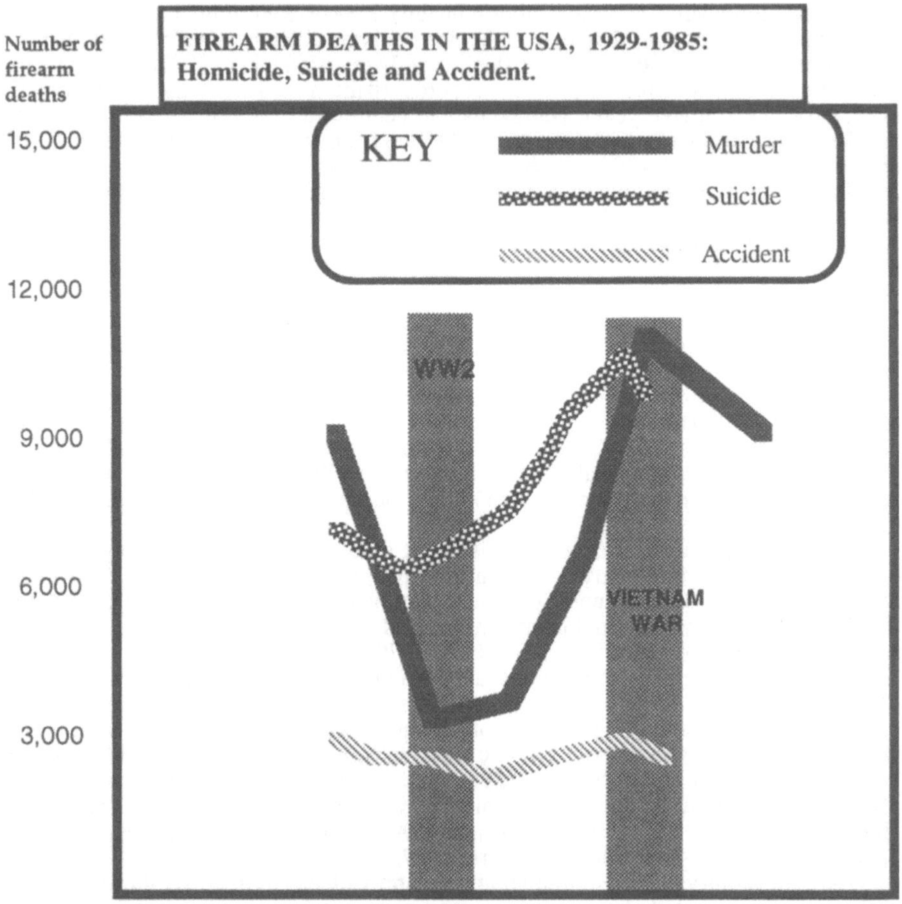

Figure 1

Sources : Morris and Hawkins, 1970, New York State Crime Commission, National Centre for Health Statistics 1933-68, and FBI Statistics, 1970-71 in Sherrill, 1973, and Bromhead, 1988.

America today.' (Baumes Crime Commission, *Annual Report*, 1929, cited in Sherrill, p.20.) If the estimate from 1929 helps put the nine thousand-odd murders in 1985 into appropriate historical perspective then it should also be borne in mind that the US population has more than doubled between the 1920s and the 1980s.

At the end of the 1950s, however, the down-turn in US firearm homicide figures appeared to be over. By the mid-1960s the number of firearm murder victims began to approach, and then exceed, the figures from the late 1920s and early 30s. Between 1966 and 1967, coinciding with American involvement in Vietnam, the firearm homicide rate leapt by over 20% from 6,855 to 8,332, whilst firearm suicides rose slightly to 10,550 and fatal firearm accidents reaching 2,896. The following year, 1968, saw firearm homicides rise to 9,425, suicides to 10,911, but a slight fall in the number of accidents (down to 2,394). Moving into the 1970s and FBI murder statistics, seemingly less precise than those of the NCHS, put the 1971 firearm homicide figure at about 11,500, a figure which, if accurate, marked another 20% increase on the figures of 1968. (Sherrill, 1973, p.21.)

Discussing the wider politics of the American crime problem in 1973, Blumberg identified the roots of America's contemporary law and order crisis. Not only had what he called the 'law and order ideology' fashioned an exclusive and essentially defensive consensus around a supposedly beleaguered (white) middle class, insulating their values and protecting their institutions from attack, it had also led to unprecedented levels of fear and some seemingly drastic forms of self-protection

> 'in cities of over 500,000 inhabitants, the percentage of respondents who feel unsafe rises to 80%. Ominously, 30% indicate that they keep a gun for 'self-defence.' Small wonder, then, that the 'law and order' and 'crime in the streets' themes have such incredible appeal as knee-jerk exclamations of patriotic fervour.' (Blumberg, 1973, p.2)

In practical terms, he continued, the 'law and order crusade' had encouraged the misapplication of existing laws, the creation of repressive new ones and the waiving of suspects rights in a manner designed to intimidate, silence, restrain, detain, search or even imprison US citizens. (Ibid. pp.27-29) He concluded, 'we live in dangerous times and our insecurity mounts because we have failed to invest in people . . . If the slogan of 'law and order' is to mean anything it must be translated into a viable system of judicial and administrative practices . . . The existing system of justice in America promotes and reinforces class warfare by indicating to those at the bottom that they have no real stake in our society.' (Ibid. p.44)

In Los Angeles the symbols of class warfare and exclusion seem to proliferate. The prevalence of threats, sanctions and warnings to 'outsiders' that litter the more up-market commercial and residential districts of Los Angeles are key components in what Davis calls a new 'militarisation of city life grimly visible at street level.' (Davis, 1990, p.223) The most affluent neighbourhoods, he notes, 'isolate themselves behind walls guarded by gun-toting private police and state-of-the-art electronic surveillance.'

Thus, in the LA suburbs, 'residential areas with enough clout are able to privatise local public space, partitioning themselves from the rest of the metropolis, even imposing a variant of neighbourhood 'passport control' on outsiders.' (Davis, p. 246) Next come the fences, the walls and, reflecting the further devaluation of public space and anti-pedestrian bias, coherent urban security design as approved by LAPD architects. Security has become the key 'positional good'. (p.228) 'Downtown, a publicly subsidised 'urban renaissance' has raised the nation's largest corporate citadel, segregated from the poor neighbourhoods around it by a monumental architectural glacis.' (p.223.) As Davis comments, 'even as the walls have come down in Eastern Europe, they are being erected all over Los Angeles,' a form of 'urban apartheid' in the city. (p. 228-230).

On the other side of town, or perhaps just on the 'wrong side of the tracks' in the poorer urban neighbourhoods of American cities, Vergara has noted similar tendencies towards a fortress mentality of crime control. 'Fortification epitomises the ghetto in modern America today,' he remarks.

> 'Buildings grow claws and spikes, their entrances acquire metal plates, their roofs get fenced in, and any additional openings are sealed cutting down on light and ventilation. Glass windowpanes in first floor windows are rare. Instead, windows openings are bricked in or fitted with glass bricks. In schools and in buses, Plexiglas, frosty with scratches blurs the view outside.' (Vergara, 1994a)

The consequences of such dramatic forms of 'target-hardening' are not difficult to detect. The preoccupation with crime takes its toll on civic life, and in its place a kind of privatised urban survivalism prevails. Post-Offices resemble frontier forts, neighbourhoods, warehouses and building sites draped in razor-ribbon wire take on the appearance of military installations and 'churches also turn into fortresses'. The 'new brutalism' evident in fortified urban architecture, whether represented in the DIY survivalism of the ghettos or the more up-market security-styled design of the commercial centres, prompts a rephrasing of Foucault's famous question. In the post-modern city, we now have to ask: 'Why is it that libraries, schools, post-offices, welfare centres, housing projects and office developments so resemble one another, and all resemble military establishments or bunkers?' (see Foucault, 1977) The answer clearly has to do with the fear of crime and the collapse of confidence in public order. Thus, 'in violent neighbourhoods social arrangements have evolved that befit a state of war . . . groups of disabled or elderly residents going from their secure buildings to cheque-cashing outlets and the supermarket require police or security guards for escorts . . . Dogs and security guards protect the few who can afford them. And if one is to believe the residents, just about everybody keeps a gun.' (Vergara, 1994a.)

Vergara's recent work on 'The New American Ghetto' (Rutgers Univ Press, forthcoming 1995), describes 'a special kind of ground, a place set apart from the more pedestrian territory of simple consumers and producers.' In recent years, he notes, such places have acquired rather more obvious signposts because, 'in sections of Chicago, Newark, Detroit and New York City where the murder rate has reached record highs, there are dozens of billboards designed solely to urge people to stop killing and getting killed. Mostly they are sponsored by churches and civic organisations - public service announcements for populations so endangered that they constitute their own macabre advertising niche.' (Vergara, 1994b)

The billboards, which began appearing in poor communities during the late 1980s, carried messages to parents such as 'Don't Let Your Child Be The Next Victim Of Violent Crime,' or 'Its Time for Peace, Stop the Killing,' or simply 'Cease Fire' in large red letters, dripping blood. Another billboard photographed by Vergara on the South Side of Chicago captioned 'Take Crime Out Of Your Child's Life' carried a childlike match stick drawing of one boy shooting another in the head with a huge revolver, although this particular billboard had been 'amended' by the addition of a 'sideways baseball cap on the aggressor, thus identifying him as a gang member.' (Vergara, 1994b)

Nevertheless, the effort to disarm troubled sections of urban American society does not stop at simple billboard advertising. In some disarmament projects positive inducements have been provided. For instance, following high levels of concern about youth gangs and firearm violence in US urban centres, local political administrations in conjunction with city police departments have organised 'amnesties' for anyone handing in an unregistered or otherwise potentially illegal weapon. Some of these amnesties have been sponsored by celebrities. During 1994 the World Heavyweight boxing champion Riddick Bowe agreed to donate $100 to anyone turning in a firearm. It turned out to be a very costly exercise for him, he eventually had to pay out over $360,000. Whilst such schemes are undoubtedly successful in their own terms - every gun handed in is one less lethal weapon on the streets - a question remains, regarding their overall impact on the distribution of illegal weapons. Large numbers of firearms are seized, confiscated or surrendered voluntarily but this activity in no way keeps pace with the supply and it is doubtful as to whether anything other than a rather marginal impact is achieved.

In an effort to take the disarmament message to the young - and bowing to liberal consumer pressure - the giant U.S. marketing chain 'Toys R Us' agreed to cease selling and promoting toy or imitation firearms. The decision followed a spate of news reports about children mistakenly shot and killed by police or neighbours whilst playing with toy guns or killing one another whilst 'playing' with their parents' real firearms. (Larson, 1994)

This issue of firearm control assumes immense significance in the USA where, as we have seen, powerful organisations jealously guard their 'Second Amendment Rights' and gun clubs running 'combat shooting for self defence' classes are increasingly common. (*Guns & Ammo*, Vol. 38, No. 2) Fear of crime has been effectively marketed in the US and, in particular, as one response to the crisis of law and order, it has resulted in a significant upturn in the sale of handguns. As Richard Raynor, discussing the Los Angeles Riots in the wake of the first Rodney King trial verdicts, commented. 'The riots began on Wednesday, 29th April 1992. Monday, 4th of May, was the first day - the first of many - that gun sales topped 2,000 in Southern California, twice the normal figure, a gun sale every forty seconds.' (Raynor, 1992)

This phenomenon is by no means new, for as Sherrill noted in 1973, 'after any serious riot gun sales are said to jump fourfold in that locale,' adding that: 'Doubtless there is some connection between the rise in crime and the increase in gun sales, but there is no way to know to what extent the teetering mound of arms causes crime and to what extent it is simply there as a defensive response.' (Sherrill, 1973, p. 22) However, two years later, from their avowedly more cultural and 'sociological' perspective, Kennett and Anderson drew their conclusion in a particular direction. For them, the purchase of guns by American citizens,

> 'reflects the persistent view that the ultimate defence of the individual American, his final, back-to-the-wall recourse, is his gun. It was a sentiment that was felt in frontier log cabins and in isolated farmhouses and lingers today in city and suburb. The ultimate fear is not that government will tyrannise, but that it will fail to protect. That fear persists; it causes lines to form in front of gun stores after every major riot or atrocity.' (Kennett and Anderson, 1975, pp. 253-54)

Perhaps not surprisingly, given this legacy, the underlying trend suggested by the more recent US crime statistics implied that, year on year, handgun crimes are accounting for an increased proportion of all violent offences committed. (The Times, 16.5.94) The Clinton administration's response to such disturbing statistics involved the introduction, during 1994, of a tough new Anti-Crime Bill, containing new gun control measures, though not addressing the central handgun problem. Even so, the Bill was only passed into law at the second attempt after very close-fought votes in the Senate.

In the USA where the right to carry a gun has been heralded by many as a basic human right, politicians at both state and federal levels have periodically sought to restrict the sale, distribution and availability of guns and the relatively free access of citizens to them. The approach has been one of seeking to regulate the trade in weapons, to license, tax and, in the face of seemingly overwhelming odds, to restrict the supply. Attempts at gun control have typically flown in the face of American history, politics, culture and, not least, Constitution. Something of America's evolution, its War of Independence and its civil and territorial wars gave an immense political credibility to the gun. (Kennett & Anderson, 1975) The gun afforded the people a means of resisting the state, surviving the hostile terrain, conquering the indigenous peoples and deterring external aggression.

Even so, the Clinton administration's recent attempt to remove machine guns from Constitutional protection is only the latest in a long sequence of control measures that the Federal Government, but more usually the state legislatures, have adopted to restrict the supply or regulate the ownership of firearms. Excluding the obvious and historic restrictions denying firearms to Blacks (whether enslaved or free) and American Indians, the first measures involved restrictions in the case of minors and convicted felons (Kennett & Anderson, 1975).

More recent - 20th century - 'controls' have included, high inter-state tariffs on gun sales, state taxes, bans relating to the carrying of concealed weapons and even, in some states such as Oregon, licensing schemes. New York State passed the Sullivan Law in 1911 following the near-fatal shooting of the City Mayor and an upsurge of concern about armed criminal gangs and immigrants. The law was a rather mixed bag of controls, for instance it confirmed existing bans on the carrying of firearms by aliens and minors, but introduced a licensing system for concealable firearms, making unlicensed carrying of concealable firearms a felony and unlicensed possession a misdemeanour. It required firearm dealers only to sell to persons who had already obtained a permit and required them to register all sales and generally toughened the penalties for non compliance with the firearm control laws. By all accounts the new laws were at first vigorously enforced in the city, especially against immigrants and suspected aliens. (Kennett and Anderson, 1975, p.182-4)

A Federal ban was introduced in the 1920s on the purchase of weapons by mail order, and in contrast to many 20th century gun controls the 'mail order sales' ban proceeded with the support of many of the top-line handgun manufacturers in the USA such as Smith & Wesson because it helped cut out an important avenue of sales for the cheap, down-market, pistol manufacturers cashing in on the new mass markets made available by modern methods of industrial production, the advent of mass popular advertising in newspapers and magazines and a cheap and efficient national postal service.

Later in the 20th Century, the mail order restrictions appeared of rather limited effectiveness, for it was a mail-order Italian-made Carcano rifle with which Lee Harvey Oswald is said to have shot President J.F. Kennedy. Ironically, such cheap foreign imported weapons were precisely those that Kennedy, four years before becoming president, had sought unsuccessfully to ban in view of their economic impact upon the important American firearms manufacturing industries in Massachusetts and Connecticut. (Kennett & Anderson, 1975, p. 227, 231)

In turn, however, the assassination of Kennedy led to further efforts at firearms control in Washington. Within one week of the shooting twelve separate firearms control bills had been submitted, fuelling a protracted debate between pro-gun and anti-gun lobbies, albeit heading to a familiar political stalemate. Former Attorney General, Carl Bakal published a savage attack on the fatal consequences of widespread gun ownership in American society, the first systematic analysis of the gun problem. His book contained a summary of the existing - and in many cases non-existent - gun control measures in American states, adding further weight to the arguments against firearms. (Bakal, 1966) Between 1965 and 1968 new gun control measures were introduced in several states including, Connecticut, Illinois, New Jersey and New York, and in cities such as Chicago and Philadelphia. But it seemed to take the killings of Robert Kennedy and Martin Luther King to break the deadlock, and in October 1968 the federal Gun Control Act was signed by President Johnson.

Although the Act was described as 'sweeping' and 'comprehensive' by commentators, (see Kennett & Anderson, 1975) this is only by contrast with the limitations of previous legislation. Essentially the Act established tougher licensing and revenue control powers to regulate the trade in firearms, it restricted the traffic in imported weapons, increased the federal firearm dealer's license fee (but only to ten dollars) and established stricter regulations on the access of young people to firearms and ammunition. Heavier military weapons, such as anti-tank guns and bazookas, were brought within the legislation and federally licensed firearms dealers could not knowingly sell weapons to certain types of known criminals. Finally, anyone caught using a firearm in the commission of a federal felony risked an additional one year prison sentence. (Firearms were the most frequently used weapons by robbers of commercial premises (64%). Skogan, 1978. p.63)

The 1968 Act, the eventual product of much negotiation and manoeuvring, was clearly no panacea for the firearms problem. Hardly surprising, then, to discover in

Murray's multiple regression analysis of the firearm restrictions in a range of states, that few gun control laws, 'however severe' appeared to have any impact upon the homicide problem. A fact, he notes, which may have more to do with the ineffectiveness of the legislation, inadequate enforcement or problems resulting from the 'underlying social conditions' than with gun control per se. (Murray, 1975, see also Zimring, 1985) The debate on gun control thus continued. 'Like the gun itself, it has become a constant in American life,' wrote Kennett & Anderson (p. 245).

More recent controls on the sale and use of weapons have included a 15 day waiting period between payment of a deposit and receipt of the weapon during which time the purchaser's identity and credentials can be checked out by the local Police. In Houston, Texas, a city with a firearm homicide rate averaging 400 a year, a recent city ordinance holds parents responsible for all firearm offences committed by their children with the parents' weapon. Apparently, as one of a series of measures to encourage responsible firearm ownership, the law has had some limited impact upon the numbers of firearm accidents, including suicide and homicide.

During 1994 Arizona became the 40th state to enact a concealed weapons law. The law came into effect in July and allows any legal resident who has obtained a 'concealed carry permit' to carry a concealed handgun. Unlike some other states, however, 'there will be no requirement for the applicant to prove a need to be able to carry a concealed weapon.' To obtain a permit, the applicant has to undergo a 16 hour training course covering such topics as safe gun handling, firearms law and the safe way to carry a concealed gun. Also as part of the course, a number of 'shoot/no shoot' scenarios are set up to test the applicant's judgmental skills. The course concludes with a marksmanship exercise but, perhaps a little worryingly, 'failure to make a minimum score will not be reason enough for the police to refuse issuing the permit.' Such is the character of Second Amendment protection. The right to 'keep and bear arms' extends even to those who appear to have little or no chance of hitting what - or who - they may be aiming at. In any event, so great is the demand for concealed weapon permits in Arizona that in only the first month of their availability there had been over 10,000 applications to join the classes. (T. Walker, 'Stateside', *Guns & Shooting Magazine,* Aug. 1994, p.14)

More recently gun control legislation proposed by the Clinton Administration met the concerted opposition of the weapons industry and a powerful, well-organised gun-lobby, a number of victim movements, the military associations, veterans organisations and, specifically, the National Rifle Association. The Clinton legislation sought to extend some 1986 prohibitions on certain types of automatic weapons (machine guns) and armour piercing bullets in order to remove automatic assault weapons from constitutional protection, (a measure proposed as long ago as 1967) . However, this is considered unlikely to make a significant dent in the relationship between firearms and violent crimes, over 900,000 of which involve handguns. ('The handgun is the greatest contributor to the national homicide rate,' see DeZee, 1978, p.44, National Commission, 1969, p.169) In any event, by December 1994, gun dealers were declaring it had been a 'good year' for sales, 'gun sales soared by as much as 60% nationwide as people rushed to buy weapons on the hit lists.' (Davis & El Nasser, 1994)

The Clinton legislation was opposed on grounds of neo-liberal free market principles, the claims of moral right, the demand for self-defence as self determination, the fear of violent crime and a powerful cultural undercurrent celebrating the gun-toting cowboy-frontiersman ethic. Not surprisingly, attempts to contain, control or restrict the supply of guns has met with limited, if any, success. As we have seen, however, a number of important issues for society, for citizenship, and contemporary culture are raised by the attempt.

Firearms and Crime in the UK

In the UK, by contrast, with a considerably lower level of firearm penetration into society and extensive firearm controls existing since 1920 (Greenwood, 1972) the major question to have surfaced politically has concerned the possible arming of the police. Though as a variety of commentators have made clear, the British Police have never been a completely unarmed force. (Gould & Waldren, 1986, Waddington, 1988) The gun question has not surfaced so strongly in Britain as a supply-side question, although this has not been an entirely absent consideration. For instance, following its election victory in 1970, the Conservative Government, in tandem with a range of new 'law and order' measures, set in motion a 'thorough review of the law on the control of firearms in Great Britain.' A Home Office Working Party was established and its report (never published) led to a Green Paper in 1973. (HMSO, 1973) The underlying philosophy of the Government was outlined in the foreword to the Green Paper:

> 'The extent of firearms use in crime is growing . . . determined criminals will usually manage somehow to acquire firearms [but] society should, through legal controls, nevertheless seek to make this as difficult as possible. The only effective way of doing this is to reduce society's total gun inventory. Consequently, a considerable minority of law-abiding citizens must be subjected to increased regulation and restriction of their firearms ownership and use patterns.' (HMSO, 1973)

In fact no legislation amending the 1968 Firearms Act followed in the course of the decade although the following Labour Government did substantially increase Firearm Licence fees in 1976 and 1978. (Harding, 1979) In contrast to the Home Office view, however, Harding's own research suggested that, during the period covered by the Green Paper and in the years immediately following, 'the rate of firearms use is not in fact increasing any more quickly than is the overall rate of crime in this group of [serious] offences . . . in so far as firearms use in crime can be said to be increasing, it is doing so only as a function of the reasonably slow increase in serious crimes of violence.' (Harding, 1979, pp. 767, 773) However, the more recent data which we review below does suggest that the situation has changed. 'There was a qualitative change in the mid 1970s towards a greatly increased use of firearms,' (Waddington, 1988, pp.52-53) although the particular concern of 1973, increasing use of sawn-off shotguns in robberies, now seems to be taking second place to a concern with the increasing use of handguns.

In the face of such concern about the rising involvement of firearms in crime (particularly the use of firearms in robberies), in the face of reports of armed drug gang rivalries, in response to dramatic one-off incidents such as the killing of police officers or such as the Hungerford shootings in 1985, and with the continuing backcloth of terrorism in Northern Ireland, the question of arming the police on the British mainland, has frequently been visited by politicians and the media.

Of course, 1994 has seen further twists in these ongoing, unresolved, debates. During the year, the Metropolitan Police identified tackling the criminal use of firearms as a core service priority, (Griffiths, 1994) and 'Operation Safety Catch' and the 'Silence a Gun' phoneline campaign, designed to remove illegal weapons from circulation, were launched. ACPO, the Association of Chief Police Officers established a 'national enforcers group' to co-ordinate the activities of Police and Customs agencies in a concerted effort to stem the flow of illegal firearms into the country. Furthermore, in London, important decisions were taken by the Commissioner of the Metropolitan Police, Sir Paul Condon, and by the Chief Constable of the Greater Manchester force, supported by the Home Secretary, to authorise the routine arming of more police officers in specialist response units. An opinion survey, commissioned by the Police

Federation, was published to coincide with the Federation's Annual Conference and seemed to show that the public were even more supportive of arming Police Officers than those officers were themselves. The Police Federation conference of 1994, discussed the question at length.

However, the impression that fuelled the broader public debate of a rising cycle of uncontrollable violence overwhelming both society and its guardians, the police is, at best, uneven and, at worst quite misleading. Between 1990 and 1992 the number of serious assaults on Police officers on duty (GBH) fell by almost half from 1356 in 1990 to 836 in 1992 (data on 1993 suggests a continuation of this downward trend). And likewise, despite the attention devoted by the media to recent incidents, the number of Police Officers killed on duty shows a fairly stable pattern since the mid 1960s.

Table 1. Police Officers Killed Whilst On Duty 1964-1994

1964-1969	1975-1979	1985-1989	1990-1994
11	8	10	10

If the pressure for arming the police - the principle form in which the firearms debate has surfaced politically in the UK - cannot be adequately explained only by reference to violence against the police, we have to look elsewhere. A review of the recent Criminal Statistics relating to firearm offences suggests some interesting patterns. As we shall see later, however, the reliability of such data can been called into question.

During 1991 the police recorded 12,129 offences in which firearms were reported to have been used. (HMSO, Criminal Statistics, 1992) In line with recent years, however, the proportion of all notifiable offences in which firearms were used was only 0.2%. There was an increase of 17% in the number of offences recorded in which firearms were used compared with 1990 but this is consistent with an overall rise of approximately 16.4% between 1990 and 1991 in the overall number of notifiable offences recorded by the police.

Consistent with the USA, the most common category of offence involving firearms was robbery, at 44% of offences (DeZee, 1978). The number of offences of robbery involving firearms in the UK increased by 34% compared with 1990, and the preferred weapon used in such armed robberies is a handgun. Since 1988 the proportion of robberies in which firearms were used has increased. 8.6% of robberies involved firearms in 1988 whereas the figure had reached 11.7% by 1991. The number of bank robberies in which firearms were used has increased by 59% since 1990-1991, and the number of building society raids by 28%. In 1993 shots were fired by robbers during the commission of a robbery on 123 occasions in London compared with two occasions (1 fatal) when the Police returned fire. In the same year, firearms were issued to Flying Squad Officers on 686 occasions. (Griffiths, 1994)

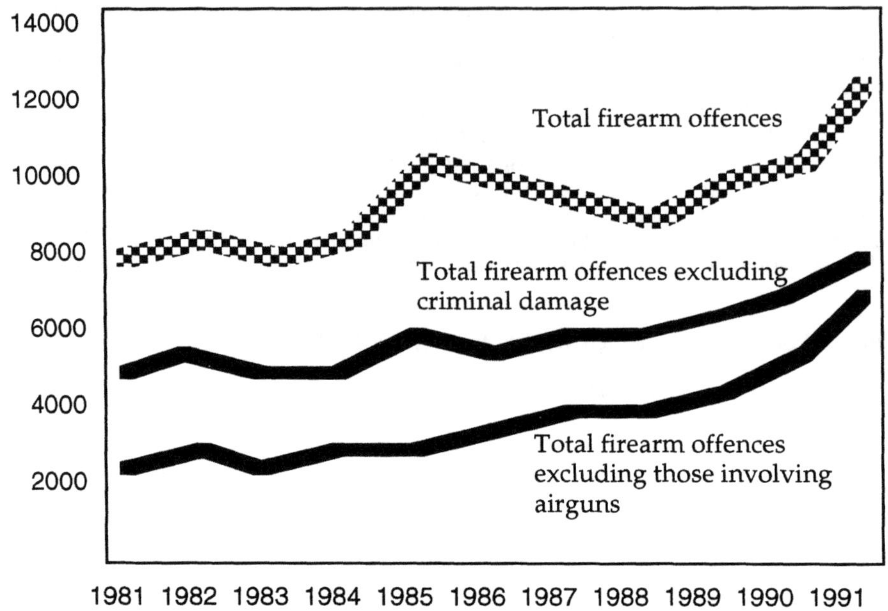

Figure 2 Firearm Offences: 1981-1991

The number of offences of attempted murder and other acts endangering life increased by 30% between 1990 and 1991, although as the table below shows, since 1981 the total number of offences of murder, attempted murder and other acts endangering life has almost trebled.

Table 2 Offences in which firearms were reported to have been used by offence group. Percentages, (actual number in brackets).

	1981	1991
Homicide/Att. Murder & other acts endangering life	4% (311)	8% (916)
Other Violence	33% (2,691)	15% (1,795)
Burglary	2% (126)	3% (345)
Robbery	23% (1,893)	44% (5,296)
Criminal Damage	38% (3,046)	31% (3,771)
Totals	(8,067)	(12,129)

Types of Firearms used

If air weapons are excluded, just over half of offences (51%) involved pistols, 12% involved long-barrelled shot guns and a further 12% sawn-off shot guns. Imitation firearms accounted for 7% of such offences. In more than half of the offences where firearms were employed they were usually displayed to threaten (in 86% of offences) and not fired, and in only 5% of offences were they fired causing injury. The number of offences in which firearms caused injury fell by 23% between 1981 and 1991. The number of fatal and serious injuries has tended to increase, however, to about 4% per

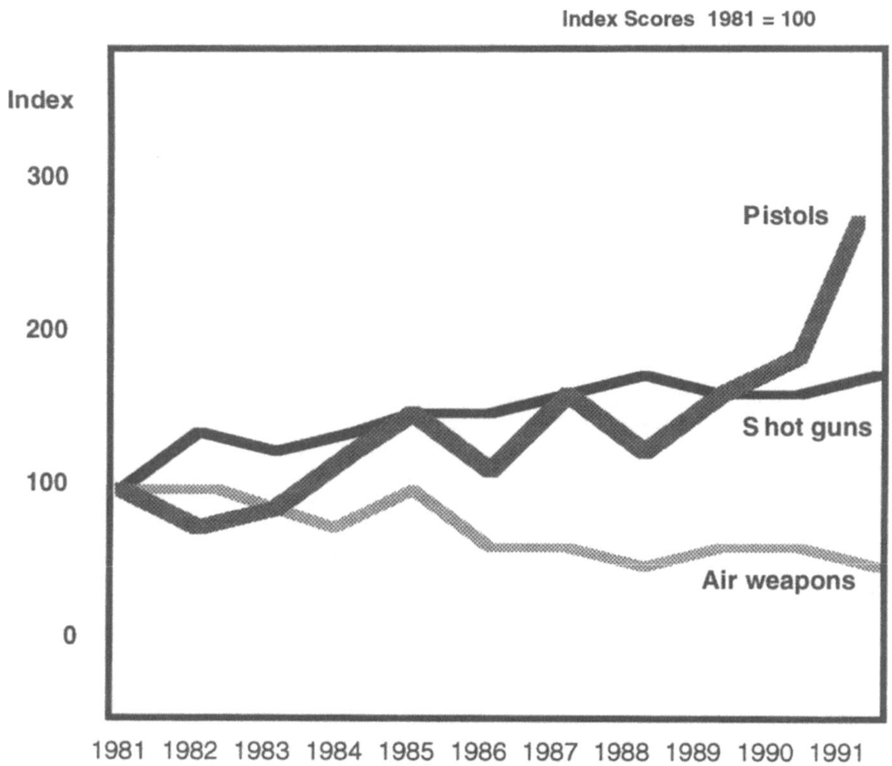

Figure 3 Notifiable offences recorded by the police in which firearms were reported to have caused injury by type of principle weapon: 1981-1991

year. Finally, in 1991 the number of reported thefts of firearms (2,410) increased by 19% compared with 1990.

While the number of minor firearm injuries has fallen, over the last ten years there has been a significant increase in the number of serious and fatal firearm injuries. Between 1981-1986 there were, on average, 370 fatal or serious injuries involving firearms whereas the average for the period 1987-1991 was 451, an increase of almost 22%. The following graph, based upon index scores reworked from the Criminal Statistics, indicates the growing significance of the handgun as the principal 'weapon of injury' in armed crime in the UK.

Arming the Police ?

In the UK, the prospect of more routinely arming the police has been met on the whole with a sense of dismay tempered by a hint of the inevitable. Whenever Police officers are killed 'in the line of duty' the issue invariably resurfaces but, by themselves, such dramatic incidents do not tell the whole story. In any event, no one can doubt that nowadays the British Police, formerly thought to be the best unarmed police service in the world, have ready access to firearms. (Waddington, 1988, pp.113-7)

Arming the British police has been a gradual and incremental process. Nowadays, for example, we might concentrate upon the highly visible Heckler & Koch sub-machine guns openly carried by police officers at Heathrow and Gatwick Airports since 1986. Usually, rather more discrete, are the concealed weapons of officers attached to diplomatic protection or Special Branch, or of the 'trojan' or ARV patrol units ready to make rapid response to firearms incidents throughout London. In one way or another, guns and policing are coming into closer association. The issue seems to emerge as one of equipping the police and security forces to enable them to make more effective response to armed incidents - or, simply put, of augmenting the power of the police.

Some police representatives have expressed concern about the so-called 'ratchet effect', the idea that arming the police will tend to encourage offenders to resort to firearms with increasing regularity. (Panorama June 1994) As we shall see there may be some truth in the observation. Yet it has to be acknowledged that the entire debate takes place in the context of a rather larger 'ratchet effect'. The allegation that offenders are resorting to firearms with increasing regularity is a crucial component in the mounting political and ideological pressure for the police to respond in like manner. Yet despite recent pressures in this direction (May/June 1994) some research published in 1980 seemed to suggest that the Police were clearly leading the 'domestic arms race' (Hoare, 1980). Perhaps there is some small cause for satisfaction here - the alternative is scarcely preferable and, in fact, the Police are fired upon over 100 times more frequently than they fire themselves. (Jacobs and Sanders, 1986) However the particular cause for concern of Benn and Worpole (1986) related to the extent of the police's lead in the domestic arms race, especially in London. (See following table)

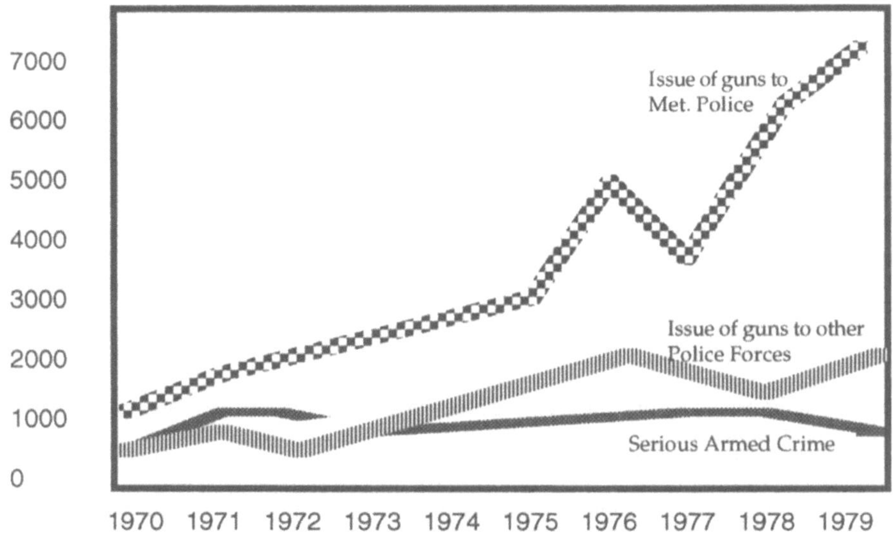

Figure 4 Rates of serious armed crime and the issue of guns to the metropolitan police and to other police forces.

Source: *Hansard* 5.2.1980 and M.A. Hoare , 1980. reproduced in Benn & Worpole, 1986, p.50.

Yet despite the trends suggested in the criminal statistics, there remains some doubt about the reliability of figures on armed crime. As yet unpublished and rather unique Home Office research amongst 100 convicted 'armed' robbers appears to suggest that 60% were not carrying a loaded or unloaded, replica or imitation firearm when they committed the offence for which they were subsequently charged and convicted. In contrast only 30% of those surveyed said that they were carrying a loaded firearm. (*Panorama* June 1994) The issue is clearly a difficult one. The interviewees may not be amongst the most reliable sources of information, yet there is clearly an enormous potential for overstating the frequency of firearm use in crime. After all, despite what the statistics suggest, the only way of knowing that a weapon is genuine is if it is fired. Undoubtedly this is a truth that the victims involved in firearm related incidents would rather not discover. None of this is meant to minimise the significance of firearm incidents - even involving replicas. Replica weapons have the shock value the offender means them to have. Even if they are not used because they are incapable of use, victims will not know this. The 'weapon' invariably generates fear, undermines confidence, and imperils our security just as if it had been real.

Contrasting Traditions : Guns in the Aftermath

The contrasting analyses of firearms control in the USA and the UK raise many important issues for the future of our respective societies. These concern the quality of life afforded to the citizens of these societies, and the conceptions of social justice, social order, citizenship and community they entertain. The two societies may face similar general dilemmas of disorder, violence, disintegration and anomie, but the particular problems they encounter, and the practical ways in which they go about addressing them may be quite different. (The situations of South Africa or Russia maybe different again but there is insufficient space to develop these issues here and now.)

The long term perspective in which I have situated this analysis of firearms and society, has sought to link the relationship between coercive power, industrialisation and the use of firearm violence with the formation of nation states, the establishment of political authorities and the fabrication of the basic conditions for citizenship and social order. But this has always been - and has to be seen as, a dynamic process; citizenship, political authority, industrialisation and so on, were not end-states but parts of a process. The development of a lively discourse on individual rights and freedoms - in the USA - regarding the right to own and possess firearms, is a case in point. This ideology connected so neatly with the establishment of lucrative domestic markets in weapons for the people, and coincided with epidemic levels of fear about violent crime, (Zimring, 1985) itself fuelled by the saturation levels of firearm penetration into American society, such that the foundations of social order and political authority were themselves undermined.

In the UK, by contrast, a more conservative-deferential collectivist tradition facilitated the near monopolisation of the instruments of violence in the hands of the state at a time, shortly after the ending of the First World War, when an intensification of internal and external disorders seemed imminent. A degree of political consensus, sustained by the relatively low salience of the firearm problem kept the issue off the political agenda. Furthermore, generally improving opportunities and standards of living and the, by no means insignificant, fact that participation in 'shooting and field sports' remained, largely, an activity frequented by the rural land-owning upper classes meant that firearms were seldom a live political issue. As we have already seen, this largely privileged access to firearms is very much part of the English tradition - indeed, it is a large part of the explanation for why smooth-bore shotguns remained outside conventional firearms control until the 1960s.

This much is clear from the reassuring tone of the Report of the Bodkin Committee, established in 1934 to advise the Home Office on the 'Statutory Definition and Classification of Firearms and Ammunition,' (Home Office, 1934). Discussing the effect of the 1920 Firearms Control Act, the Committee remarked, that the act, and its enforcement had been remarkably successful, not least because of the stalwart attitudes shown by 'manufacturers of and dealers in firearms [who] have borne their losses with resignation and have loyally co-operated with the authorities in the measures for the restriction of firearms during the past 14 years.' The Committee concluded, 'we are of the opinion that, in view of 14 years experience of the working of the Statute, no alteration of substance . . . is required.' (Bodkin Committee, in Greenwood, 1972, p.60)

Confident words, it seems that before WW2 Britain had no major firearms problem. Things were to change and disturb this conservative consensus, but its persistence is worthy of note. At the end of WW2 fearing that 'souvenir' firearms had been brought home by returning troops the Home Secretary authorised a six week amnesty during 1946 when the 'illegal' weapons could be surrendered without fear of prosecution. In all the exercise netted over 75,000 weapons including, 59,000 pistols and 1,580 machine guns. In the decade following the war there is evidence of a tightening up police policy in relation to the issue and renewal of firearm certificates, with the Home

Secretary commenting that, 'I would not regard the plea that a revolver is wanted for the protection of an applicant's person or property as necessarily justifying the issue of a firearm certificate.' (Home Secretary, 17th Oct. 1946, quoted in Greenwood, 1972, p.72) The implication was clear, protection of persons and property was a collective task to be carried out by the police and the state, not a responsibility discharged by individuals acting in their own interest. The collective providential state had taken upon itself the task of safeguarding the last liberty of individuals, in this sense the British tradition differed significantly from the American.

However the pattern began to change during the late 1950s. In the Metropolitan Police District, firearms were known to have been used or carried in only 19 robberies in 1950 (31% of total robberies), five years later in only 13. By 1960 the number had risen to 53, more than doubling to 114 by 1965. At the end of the decade the figure was 272, representing 42% of all robberies. The six-yearly averages of armed robberies involving firearms are instructive and clearly show the rapid take-off in armed crime after the mid 1960s.

Table 3. Robberies in London in which a firearm was involved - 6 Yearly averages and average percentage of all Robberies.

	1946-1951	1952-1957	1958-1963	1964-1969
No.	**23.5**	**15.3**	**47.1**	**168.3**
%	(31%)	(35%)	(41%)	(42%)

From Greenwood, 1972, p.161, 170.

Likewise, during the 1960s the overall incidence of firearm fatalities began to increase. Between 1960 and 1967 firearm homicides rose from 19 to 48, suicides rose unevenly from 177 to 193, though accidents retained a fairly constant pattern, 65 in 1960, peaking at 83 the following year, falling to 53 in 1966, rising by 10 the following year. (Ibid. p. 177)

Reflecting these rising statistics concern began to grow about violent crime and, especially firearm use in violent crimes although, even in 1965, both the Home Secretary and the Police were still resisting the imposition of additional controls to restrict shotguns in line with other firearms. It took a dramatic shooting incident in August 1966, in which three police officers were killed, to shatter the apparent consensus. Whilst the officers were killed with handguns, Roy Jenkins, as Home Secretary, went on to propose extra controls on shotguns. Two years later, the consolidating 1968 Firearms Act was passed followed, the same year, by the tough new Criminal Justice Act as the Government looked for a hard response to the seemingly growing threat of violent crime. (Greenwood, 1972)

Two years later, amidst continuing concern about violent crime the incoming Conservative Government announced its plans for a review of firearms and their control. Even so, as we have seen, its philosophy remained remarkably consensual, it reiterated the need for tougher controls, and it promised to redraw the balance of arms somewhat, inconveniencing the law abiding and restricting the responsible (shotgun) gun-owner, in order to better control the criminal. Even so, no legislation followed, though it is claimed that, in view of the tougher licensing and higher fees, the number of Firearm Certificates held in Great Britain has fallen from over 255,000 in 1968 to around 168,000 in 1992, a drop of approximately one third. (Cadmus, 1994) As we have seen, in the 1970s the pattern of firearms usage, and the efforts of the police to contain and control it began to change. The tradition of consensual collectivism which had for so long represented the dominant pattern of firearms control in Britain began to fall apart.

Harding predicted that a backlash was likely should the Government seek to lean apparently too heavily upon the rights and freedoms of the law abiding in its efforts to contain the criminal. (Harding, 1979) Reading the commentaries of many of Britain's current Gun and Shooting magazines one gains a definite impression of an seemingly beleaguered minority defending their rights and their sport against the uncaring, alien, heavy handed central state. (Cooper, 1994, Cadmus, 1994) No doubt this impression, the 'Alamo mindset,' is precisely the desired message. Small wonder then, that in the USA, the pro-gun lobby are still able to label gun-controllers as 'Un-American,' latent communists and sympathisers. Firearms are certainly emerging as a critical - and often highly divisive - issue in contempotrary societies.

In the longer term, therefore, whereas firearms and the social relations of firearms control helped create and civilise nations, in many ways they now seem to begin to threaten to de-stabilise them. On either side of the Atlantic the precise processes, factors and issues have differed but the overall result is similar. Industrialism promised technical solutions for social problems, rationality and efficient technical processes. In many respects our security industries are still ploughing that particular furrow in search of the appropriate technical fix for social disorder, witness the enthusiasm for all manner of surveillance systems operating in modern societies (See Lyon, 1991) and the eagerness with which Closed Circuit TV systems have been grasped as a supposed panacea for street crime and disorder.

Likewise, modernism seemed to promise control, the utilitarian training of all that is human, the planning of all that is social, or spontaneous. Industrial society brought us the firearm, modern methods of industrial production gave us ubiquitous handgun. Capitalism turned the latter into a commodity, gave it an image and then went on to create the underlying conditions in which it would find a use and where, paradoxically, it would be sought as a protection when modern, seemingly ineffective, strategies of firearms control began to break down. Effective gun control processes, the safety catch at the heart of modern methods of law enforcement and one of the only real guarantees of social order, are collapsing. Admittedly, the process is that much more advanced in the USA and, as Waldren notes, London is not New York. Shots were fired on three occasions by the Metropolitan Police in London during 1993 compared to 312 incidents in which NYPD officers fired their weapons in New York. (Waldren, 1994) Even so, everyone is 'tooling up'. Gun control, is coming to mean more guns. On both sides of the Atlantic more guns are seen to be the solution for increasing gun violence.

Post-Modern Society and the Post-Industrial Gun: 'Good enough for combat'

If it is true that the apprentice has run off with the sorcerer's piece and has become the scourge of the city, then Smith & Wesson have designed just the weapon for him. The new Smith & Wesson Sigma .40, a polymer framed semi-automatic pistol, was precisely 'designed for the domestic and law enforcement markets.' Its design incorporated the latest research and planning to produce a weapon that is 'low price, . . . lightweight, . . . easy to use and maintain.' Reviewing the gun, Adam noted that the new design, 'meant that S &W could include some features that would not be possible in steel, including light weight, ease of production and low price.' (Adam, 1994)

Indeed the production of the gun marked a near revolution in the Smith & Wesson assembly lines, in that it is the first pistol for which Smith & Wesson, in true post-Fordist fashion, subcontracted the manufacture of most of the weapon components, excluding the barrel. The weapon is then only assembled at the factory, where it travels each stage of the assembly process in its own designer box.

Having 'tested' the weapon Adam's approval is evident. Handgun technology he notes has had to be based upon sound, tried an tested principles, and has 'had to evolve to the most ergonomic and user friendly standards possible.' He continues, 'That is pure Darwinism - if the owner survives and buys them for his children. If they don't it could be fatal and a customer could be lost forever.' Scientific principles are neatly sculptured into the Sigma design, 'to make the grip as ergonomic as possible . . . [with]

a steeper grip angle . . . [so] that the pistol would present better, the frontsight coming up first, essential for close range combat shooting.' These, it seems, are the basic requirements of a 'working gun'. Moreover, while 'not quite up to bullseye standard . . . accuracy is good enough for combat.' But that, it seems, is the point, for, 'while sportsmen shoot their handguns a lot, policemen shoot them very little, but they do carry them for a long time. The light loaded weight of 35 ounces will be a big selling point.' (Adam, 1994)

What could be better, or more bizarre? A post-industrial gun for post-modern society, cheap to buy, requiring minimal skill or maintenance, easy to use, light to carry around, just right for combat and, above all, marketed as 'user-friendly' in the name of social Darwinism. The languages of social defence and community safety are certainly changing, the irony is that this was always part of the process, part of the potential for modern industrial societies. The critical task concerns how we recover some of the lost ground, rebuilding ourselves some security, whilst avoiding the pitfalls of vigilante individualism and authoritarian centralism and the societal conditions which sustain them. That this is a much bigger political and philosophical task than can be tackled here and now almost goes without saying. Yet in the search for the ideas with which to attempt such a task, it has been instructive to try and break free from the relatively narrow debates within which these issues are considered on the separate sides of the Atlantic.

Bibliography

Adam, R. The New Smith & Wesson Sigma Series, *Guns and Shooting Magazine*, Vol. 9, No. 6, June. 1994

Baird, V. Lethal Lies: The Arms Trade, *New Internationalist*, Nov. 1994.

Bakal, C. *The Right to Bear Arms*, McGraw-Hill, New York, 1966

Bauman, Z. *Modernity and the Holocaust*, Polity Press, 1989.

Benn, M &Worpole, K. Death in the City: An examination of Police Related

Deaths in London, Pluto Press, 1986

Blumberg, A.S. Law and Order: *The Scales of Justice*. TransactionBooks NJ, 1973.

Bromhead, P. *Living in America*, Longman 1988.

Brown, R.M. Violence, in Milner et al. (Ed.) *The Oxford History of the American West*, Oxford University Press, 1994.

Cadmus, A Matter of Policy, *Guns Review*, Vol 34, No. 8, August, 1994.

Cooper, N.F. Shotgun Topics: Sight and Sound, *Guns Review*, Vol. 34, No. 6, June 1994

Cress, L. An Armed Community: The Origins and Meaning of the Right to Bear Arms, *Journal of American History*, Vol. 71, No. 1, 1984.

Critchley, T.A. The Conquest of Violence. Constable, 1970.

Davis, M. City of Quartz: Excavating the Future in Los Angeles. Verso, 1991.

Davis, R. & El Nasser, H. New Ammo for Gun Debate, *USA Today*, 28th Dec. 1994

Davis, R. & El Nasser, H. New Ammo for the Gun Debate, *USA Today*, Dec. 28th 1994

DeZee, M.R. Gun Control and Federal Legislation, in J. Inciardi and A. Pottiger, (Ed.) *Violence and American History*. Sage, 1978

Ellis, J. *The Social History of the Machine Gun*, Croom Helm, 1976, 2nd. Edition, Pimlico, Random House, 1993.

Einstadter, W.J. Robbery-Outlawry on the US Frontier, 1863-1890: A Re-examination, in J. Inciardi and A. Pottiger, (Ed.) *Violence and American History*. Sage, 1978

Foucault, M. *Discipline & Punish*, Allen Lane, 1977.

Gould, R.W & Waldren, M.J. *London's Armed Police, Arms and Armour Press*, London, 1986.

Greenwood, C. *Firearms Control: A Study of Armed Crime and Firearms Control in England and Wales*. Routledge, 1972.
Griffiths, W.I. Putting Robbers out of Business, *Criminal Justice Matters*, ISTD, No. 17, Autumn 1994
Guns & Ammo, Vol. 38, No. 2
Harding, R. Firearms Use in Crime, *Criminal Law Review*, 1979, pp.765-774
Hay, D. Poaching and the Game Laws on Cannock Chase, in D.Hay et al (Ed.) *Albion's Fata 18th Century England.* Allen Lane, 1975.
Home Office. The Control of Firearms in Great Britain: A Consultative Green Paper Document, Cmnd. 5297, HMSO. 1973.
Hellman, J. *American Myth and the Legacy of Vietnam*, Columbia University Press, 1986.
Hoare, M.A. *The Pattern of Experience in the Use of Firearms by Criminals and the Police Response*. MSc. Thesis, Cranfield, 1980.
Jacobs, J. & Sanders, A. Should Police Be Armed? *New Society*, July 11th 1986
Jennings, A. Shoot to Kill: The Final Courts of Justice, in Jennings (Ed.) Justice under Fire: The Abuse of Civil Liberties in Northern Ireland, Pluto Press, 1990
Keirnan, V.G. *Foreign Mercenaries and Absolute Monarchy, in Aston (Ed.) Crisis in Europe: 1560-1660*. Anchor Books, New York, 1967
Kennett, L. & Anderson, J.L. *The Gun in America: The Origins of a National Dilemma*. Greenwood Press, 1975
Larson, E. *Fatal Passage*, Crown Publishers, New York, 1994
Leon, H. 'How to be a gun nutter', *Sky Magazine*, Sept. 1994
Mann, M. *The Sources of Social Power, Vol. 1,* Cambridge University Press, 1986.
Mannheim, H. *War and Crime*, Watts & Co. London, 1941.
McCaghy C.H. & Cernkovitch, S.A. *Crime in American Society*, Macmillan, 2nd. Edn. New York, 1987.
Malcolm, J.L. *To Keep and Bear Arms: The Origins of an Anglo-American Righ*t, Harvard University Press, 1994
Morris, N & Hawkins, G. *The Honest Politician's guide to Crime Control*. University of Chicago Press, 1970
Murray, D.R. Handguns, Gun Control Laws and Firearm Violence, *Social Problems*, Vol. 23, No. 1, October 1975
National Commission. On the Causes and Prevention of Violence, Final Report: To Establish Justice, To Insure Domestic Tranquility. US. Government Printing Office, Washington DC. 1969
Pearson, G. *Hooligan: A History of Respectable Fears*. Macmillan, 1983
Pick, D. *War Machine: The Rationalisation of Slaughter in the Modern Age*, Yale University Press, 1993
Raynor, R. Los Angeles, Granta, 1992)
Sherrill. Saturday Night Special, 1973
Skogan, W.J. Weapon Use in Robbery, in J. Inciardi and A. Pottiger, (Ed.) *Violence and American History,* Sage, 1978
Sweeney, J. Day of the Undead, *Observer 'Life' Magazine*, 1st May 1994
The Times. 16.5.94
Thompson, E.P. *Whigs and Hunters: The Origin of the Black Act,* Allen Lane, 1975
Vergara, J.L. Fortress Mentality, *New Statesman & Society*, February, 1994a.
Vergara, J.L. American Graffiti, *New Statesman & Society*, November 18th 1994b
Vergara, J.L. *The New American Ghetto*, Rutgers University Press, forthcoming, 1995.
Waddington, P.J. Arming an Unarmed Police: Policy and Practice in the Metropolitan Police, The Police Foundation, 1988.
Waldren, M. Arming the Police: An Historical Appraisal, Criminal Justice Matters, ISTD, No. 17, Autumn, 1994
Walker, T. 'Stateside', *Guns & Shooting Magazine*, Aug. 1994.
Williams, J.S. & McGrath, J.H. A Social Profile of Urban Gun Owners, in J. Inciardi and
A. Pottiger, (Ed.) *Violence and American History*, Sage, 1978

Wright, J.D. and Marston, L.L. The Ownership of the Means of Destruction: Weapons in the United States, *Social Problems*, Vol. 23, No. 1. 1975

Zimring, F.E. Violence and Firearms Policy, in L. Curtis (Ed.) *American Violence and Public Policy,* Yale University Press, 1985

Chapter 21

Resistance Postmodernism: Emancipatory politics for a new era or academic chic for a defeatist intelligentsia?*

Mike Cole and Dave Hill

In this paper, we attempt an evaluation of what has been described as 'postmodernism or resistance'. We conclude that, while there are clear differences in intention and in emphasis between it and what has described as 'postmodernism of reaction', the 'two postmodernisms' have too much in common to be thought of as separate discourses. It is more accurate, we suggest, to think of a continuum, with 'postmodernism of reaction' at one end and 'postmodernism of resistance' at the other. While one end of the continuum is peopled by reactionaries, engrossed in 'games of despair', the other is composed of defeatist ex-socialists, engaged in a rhetoric of left posturing.

Next, we refer to some key problems with postmodernism per se. Contra the postmodern rejection of the metanarrative, a Marxist analysis, we argue, still has most purchase in explaining economic, political, social and cultural changes and developments in capitalist societies. While recognising the value of some salient features in some aspects of the 'postmodernism of resistance' end of the continuum, we argue that postmodernism analyses, in general, marginalise and/or neglect the determining effects of the relations of production. In particular, we suggest that postmodernism, albeit unwittingly, serves to disempower the oppressed, by denying the notion of 'emancipation in a general sense'.

We argue that recent major processes of restructuring, underpinned by market-led strategies, are in line with the current requirements of capitalist states. This is either denied, ignored or underplayed, or else the changes are designated merely as 'postmodern', in the discourse of postmodernism. In rejecting the determining effects of capital, or in neutralizing capitalism itself, postmodernism, we argue, serves to uphold the Radical Right in their two nation hegemonic project. Ideologically, this project involves the privileging of individualism and greed. Economically, it entails a privatisation programme, incorporating the creation of a hierarchy of provision in the 'public' services.

'Postmodernism of reaction' and 'Postmodernism of resistance'

Lather has distinguished two opposing strands of postmodernism, which she labels `postmodernism of reaction' and `postmodernism of resistance' (1). The former, which she describes as Neo- Nietzschean, she argues, is concerned with the collapse of meaning, with nihilism, and with cynicism. The conception of the individual is of a fractured schizoid consumer, existing in a what Lather describes as `a cultural whirlpool of Baudrillardian simulcra' (1991: 160-161). This vortex is, in fact, captured perfectly by Jean Baudrillard, himself:

> [Postmodernism] is a game with the vestiges of what has been destroyed ... [W]e must move in it, as though it were a kind of circular gravity ... I have the impression with postmodernism that there is an attempt to

> rediscover a certain pleasure in the irony of things, in the game of things. Right now one can tumble into total hopelessness - all the definitions, everything, it's all been done. What can one do? What can one become? And postmodernity is the attempt - perhaps it's desperate, I don't know - to reach a point where one can live with what is left. It is more a survival among the remnants than anything else. (Laughter).(Baudrillard 1984 in Gane 1993: 95)

Writers such as Aronowitz and Giroux (1991); McLaren (1994); McLaren and Hammer (1989); McLaren and Lankshear (1993), however, claim to offer much more than a game. Lather (1991), for example, advocates 'postmodernism of resistance'. This is defined as participatory and dialogic and as encompassing pluralistic structures of authority. It is non- dualistic and anti- hierarchical and celebrates multiple sites from which the word is spoken. Here, the subject is 'in-process' and capable of agency. Unlike the 'postmodernists of reaction', who stress increased normalisation and regulation, `postmodernists of resistance' see difference without opposition, personal autonomy and social relatedness. Whereas the former accept the inevitability of multinational hyperspace, the latter are into ecopolitics (Lather 1991: 160-161). [Postmodern] feminism, is somewhat immodestly described by Lather, following Kroker and Cook (1986), as 'the quantum physics of postmodernism' (ibid: 160).

While we would agree with lather's resume of some of the characteristics of what she describes as postmodernism of reaction', we would like to evaluate her claims about a separate 'postmodernism of resistance', one by one.

First, she states that it is 'participatory and dialogic', encompasses 'pluralistic structures of authority', is 'anti-hierarchical' and `celebrates multiple sites from which the word is spoken'. Our comment would be that, while the celebration of multiple voices (ibid 112), as a methodology, has its strengths, it also has its weaknesses, and that there is nothing inherently 'resistant' or progressive about it. We will develop this argument in the section on 'Methodology'.

Second, it is 'non-dualistic' and sees 'difference without opposition, personal autonomy and social relatedness'. It is indicative of the contradictory nature of postmodernism that Lather includes 'personal autonomy' here, since this is a concept clearly associated with the Enlightenment, an enterprise considered, by the postmodernists, to have been superceded by postmodernism (see below). As far as 'non-dualism' and 'difference without opposition' and 'social relatedness' are concerned, these are, of course, general features of postmodernism and represent, as we will argue, some of its major problems. Postmodernism is unable to recognise a major duality in capitalist societies, that of social class. This has, we believe, profoundly reactionary implications.

Third, the subject is 'in process' and 'capable of agency'. While 'agency' has progressive implications, the fact that the agency advocated by the 'postmodernists of resistance' relates to [localised action only, renders it, over all, reactionary. This argument is developed below.

We would wish to take issue with Lather (and with Aronowitz and Giroux) that postmodernism can be so neatly divide into two and, while we would concur that the well-intentioned project of some (feminist) postmodernists of resistance' stands in stark contrast to the nihilistic and lighthearted desperation of the Baudrillardian gameplayers, we would argue that ultimately, the two postmodernisms lie, in fact, on one continuum. This is not to say that there are not differences in both analysis and approach. In our critique of postmodernism as a whole, we will highlight any differences as they occur. Overall, however, we believe that postmodernism does not deserve the duality afforded to it by these writers. Self- proclaimed 'resistance postmodernist' Peter McLaren suggests that '"resistance postmodernism" and "critical postmodernism" . . . are not alternatives to ludic postmodernism but appropriations and extensions of [the postmodern] critique [of modernity]' (1994: 199). Our response would be that, while recognizing the implication that McLaren accepts the notion of a continuum, we take issue with his assertion that so-called 'postmodernists of resistance' have 'appropriated' postmodernism and thereby purged it of its reactionary essence and have reclaimed it for an 'emancipatory project'. Indeed, in our view, McLaren's notion of such a project may in some respects be liberating for individuals and certain selected small groups, but it fails to set out any visible mass strategy or programme for an emancipated future, in the way that socialism does.

The trouble with postmodernism

> The mass is dumb like beasts, and its silence is equal to the silence of beasts ... it says neither whether the truth is to the left or to the right, nor whether it prefers revolution or repression. It is without truth and without reason. It has been attributed with every arbitrary remark. It is without conscience and without unconscious.
>
> Jean Baudrillard 1983: 28-9 .

We have dealt at length elsewhere with what we perceive to be the central problems with postmodernism (Cole and Hill 1995). Briefly, we take issue with its antifoundationalism, its rejection of the metanarrative, its denial of any 'totalizing' system of thought like Marxism or liberalism; in short, we question its inability to make general statements about society. This point has been made, inter alia, by a number of writers (c.f. Callinicos 1989; Crook 1990; Ainley 1993; Hewitt 1993; Maynard 1993 and, in their pre- postmodern phase, Aronowitz and Giroux 1986).

Contrary to Lyotard, we suggest that the motor of capitalism is still determinant and that the Enlightenment metanarratives of Marxism and neo-Marxism best explain current and ongoing economic, political, social and cultural developments, both in Britain and world-wide.

In addition, we support the arguments of Jurgen Habermas, with respect to the neo-Conservative implications of postmodernist 'theory' (Habermas 1981; 1983; 1987). Postmodernism, we believe, albeit unintentionally for many postmodernists, serves the interests of the current Radical Right hegemonic project, particularly with respect to its interrelated attempts to discredit mass ideologies, such as socialism, to disempower mass groups who are structurally oppressed, and to privilege consumption and greed over production and solidarity.

An acceptance of postmodernist ideas, then, should be a cause for celebration for the Radical Right. If there are no other ways of living, and no alternative to unbridled market-led economic strategies, if no alternative fundamental structural changes in society are possible, then the Left has indeed become an anachronism.

The 'postmodernists of resistance' would, of course, reject the implication that they are playing into the hands of the Radical Right. Lather, for example, asserts that 'there is nothing in postmodernism that makes it intrinsically reactionary' (1991: 49). However, in its `anti-dualism', in its rejection of the possibility of the metanarrative, in its localism (see below) reactionary reverbations are inevitable.

There is another factor which makes postmodernism inherently reactionary. Given postmodernists' insistence on anti-representationalism (the rejection of the view that reality is directly given, without mediation, to subjects), and their consequent reliance on `textualism' (seeing the text as the only source of meaning), it would seem that the possibility of structural analysis and structural change is further removed from the agenda (see, for example, Sarup 1983: 101-102, 153, 157-159 and Jessop 1990: 288-301 for a critique of the textualism of Laclau and Mouffe, and Evans, Davies and Penney 1994 and Troyna and Hatcher 1994 for a critique of Foucauldian and Derridean aspects within Ball 1990 and Bowe, Ball and Gold 1993) (2).

For those at the reactionary end of the continuum, the future seems to consist of some kind of extension, albeit perhaps accelerated, of 'the present'. For the `postmodernism of resistance' end of the continuum, the future is either an open book or a rhetorical 'future' of 'social justice', of 'emancipation' (local' only - presumably) and, that catchword which is all things to all people, 'democracy'. It is in this sense that postmodernism acts as an ideological support for national and global capital.

On the first page of the Preface of *Getting Smart*, Lather declares her `longtime interest in how to turn critical thought into emancipatory action' (1991: xv). However, after over two hundred pages of text, in which indications are made of the need for emancipatory research praxis, in which proclamations are made of how the goals of research should be to understand the maldistribution of power and resources in society, with a view to societal change, we are left wondering how all this is to come about. As other critics have pointed out (c.f. Beyer and Liston 1992; Maynard 1993), the precise nature of this maldistribution and its implications are never made clear. `How', ask the former, `does one identify, locate, and explain structures of oppression, much less structural contradictions' (Beyer and Liston 1992: 385). `How', wonders the latter, can `inequalitiesm . . .be . . . made known through a research process which encourages us to see the social world as a text' (Maynard 1993: 330).

Callinicos has described postmodernism as 'the product of a socially mobile intelligentsia in a climate dominated by the retreat of the Western labour movement and the 'overconsumptionist' dynamic of capitalism in the Reagan- Thatcher era' (1990: 115; see also Green 1994: 74; Skeggs 1991), while Dowling (cited in Lather 1991: 37) views it as 'the opiate of the intelligentsia'. 'From this perspective', Callinicos concludes, 'the term "postmodern" has sought to articulate its political disillusionment and its aspiration to a consumption orientated lifestyle' (1990: 115). Seldom, we would suggest, has this coagulation been more redolently expressed than in the discourse of *New Times* (Hall and Jacques 1989).

Leading *New Times* theorists Stuart Hall and Martin Jacques claim that *New Times* is neither a new orthodoxy nor a finished piece of work. Instead, they define it as 'work in progress' (1989: 13) (3). The project began with a seminar in May 1988, organised by the journal, *Marxism Today's* editorial Board. The *New Times* argument is that the world has changed, both quantitatively and qualitatively, and that the advanced capitalist countries are `increasingly characterised by diversity, differentiation and fragmentation' (Hall and Jacques 1989: 11). `New Times' has a number of recurring themes: the decline of mass production and of the traditional industrial proletariat, the rise of myriad political and social struggles and individualism, style and consumption (4). We have dealt at length elsewhere with our own critique of *New Times* (Cole and Hill 1995; see also Cole 1992). We would accept wholeheartedly the position of A. Sivanandan who has summed up cryptically what *New Times* means for him:

> "a shift in focus from economic determinism, from changing the world to changing the word, from class in and for itself to the individual in and for himself or herself. Use value has ceded to exchange value, need to choice, community to identity, antiimperialism to international humanism. And the self that new timers make so much play about [has] become a small, selfish inward-looking self that finds pride in life-style, exuberance in consumption and commitment in pleasure - and then elevates them all into a politics of this and that, positioning itself this way and that way (with every position a politics and every politics a position) into a 'miscellany of movements and organisations' stretching from hobbies and pleasure to services (1990: 23).

Our argument, resisting 'New Times' and following Marx, is that capitalism can only be adequately theorised if 'the economic' and social class are centrally placed.

Current changes in public health care, in transport, in Initial Teacher Education (marketisation, differentiation, pseudo consumer-choice, so-called quality control data, performance/ test results, a proliferation of new routes into teaching) might well appear to postmodernists to be a vindication and indeed manifestation of postmodern fragmentation, consumerisation and heterogeneity, of the end of mass production, mass control and uniformity in education. But such developments are nor free-floating. Current 'reforms' in these areas can and should be analysed as being part of the Ideological and Repressive Juridico-Legal Apparatuses of the state and are rigidly bounded by strengthened central control (Hartley 1993; Whitty 1993; Apple 1994;

Hargreaves 1994; Cole and Hill 1995). Arguing in a similar vein, and addressing the issue of whether we live in post-capitalist societies, Geoff Whitty suggests that to read 'the espousal of heterogeneity, pluralism and local narratives as the basis of a new social order mistakes phenomenal forms for structural relations (1991: 8-9), while David Harvey (1989) suggests it may be more appropriate to see postmodernist cultural forms and more flexible modes of capital accumulation 'more as shifts in surface appearance rather than as signs of the emergence of some entirely new post-capitalist or even post-industrial society' (cited in Whitty 1991: 8-9) (5). It is important to recognize, we would suggest, that (i) post-Fordist developments in the organistaion of production and consumption have taken and are taking place; (ii) the changes, while developmental, are geographically and sectorally limited and specific; (iii) such changes are not fundamentally altering workers' relations to the means of production; (iv) post-Fordist developments, where they exist, should be conflated neither with post-capitalism nor postmodernism; (v) postmodernist analysis can be seen to be an ideological and theoretical product of those restricted economic change sectors; (vi) postmodernist analysis, with its stress on segmentation, differentiation, collective disempowerment and its telos of individuated desire, serves well the purpose of justifying and adumbrating marketised Radical Right projects.

To reject the 'New Times' analysis and to deny that we live in a post- capitalist society is not of course to refute that capitalism is a dynamic and constantly adapting mode of production. Indeed, Marx and particularly Gramsci were acutely aware of this fact. The 'corporatist' and 'market' strategies that were vying for position between the mid 1970s and the 1980s as alternatives to traditional Social Democratic and Christian Democratic consensual `one nation' policies both demanded, in varying degrees, that the workers pay for the crisis. While (i) recognising contextual, historical, social and economic differences between different capitalist economies (Hill 1990: 1-6), (ii) acknowledging tensions in the wars of position within and between different class fractions and strata (see Ainley 1993 for an analysis of the U.K., and (iii) accepting 'significant variations', e.g. low skill, low wage, U.K., U.S.A. strategies and recent West German and Japanese high skill, high wage strategies (Brown and Lauder 1991), we consider that these are different ways out, different strategies of responding to national and international crises of capital accumulation, different ways of niching into world and regional economies, not indicators of 'New Times'.

Both 'one nation' and 'two nation' strategies (Jessop 1990) demand that some subaltern groups, especially the working classes, have to be yanked into ideological conformity (6). Thatcherism's and Reaganism's 'two nation' project's major break from social democratic consensus requires greater ideological re- structuring, greater vilification and suppression of liberal and socialist opposition, and greater state control over civil society. We see the promotion of individualism, consumerism and marketised 'choice' as an ideological mask for a crisis in capitalism. This mask can be implicit (c.f. Whitty 1991) or it can be explicit, but we refute any notion that it is all part of the postmodern condition. Indeed, it is one of our main contentions that postmodernism acts as an academic support system for these material and ideological developments.

The politics of postmodernism

As far as the possibilities for action are concerned, for the 'postmodernists of reaction', there is, as we have seen, little more to do than 'survive among the remnants' (Baudrillard 1984 in Gane 1993: 95), whereas for the 'postmodernists of resistance', as we have also seen, the subject is capable of agency (Lather 1991: 160; see also Aronowitz and Giroux 1991; Giroux 1992; McLaren 1994). The contentious issue, however, resides in just what the project of that agency consists in.

For postmodernists and postmodern feminists, what should be the task of politics? Consistent with the premises of postmodern 'theory', Judith Butler has stressed the need for an 'antifoundationalist approach to coalitional politics' which assumes neither that 'identity' is a premise nor that the shape or meaning of a coalitional assemblage can be known prior to its achievement' (1990: 15). '[W]hat political possibilities', Butler asks:

> "are the consequences of a radical critique of the categories of identity? What new shape of politics emerges when identity as a common ground no longer constrains the discourse on feminist politics? And to what extent does the effort to locate a common identity as the foundation [sic] for a feminist politics preclude a radical inquiry into the political construction and regulation of identity itself?" (1990: xi)

In order to 'denaturalize gender as such' (1990: 149), Butler proposes 'a strategy to denaturalize and resignify bodily categories', which she describes as 'a set of parodic practices based in a performative theory of gender acts that disrupt the categories of the body, sex, gender, and sexuality and occasion their subversive resignification and proliferation beyond the binary frame' (1990: xii). Her primary political aim, resulting from her (unexceptional) suggestion that `multiple identifications can constitute a non hierarchical configuration of shifting and overlapping identifications that call into question the primacy of any univocal gender attribution' (ibid: 66) is `to make gender trouble' (ibid: 34). In more detail, her text is:

> an effort to think through the possibility of subverting and displacing those naturalized and reified notions of gender that support masculine hegemony and heterosexist power, to make gender trouble, not through strategies that figure a utopian beyond, but through the mobilisation, subversive confusion, and proliferation of precisely those constitutive categories that seek to keep gender in its place by posturing as the foundational illusions of identity (Butler 1990: 34)

We have to ask just how much difference it would make to class nature of economic and political power relationships if the 'gender parody' and drag acts and widespread denaturalization of sex and gender became anti heterosexistly coherent (Butler 1990:138)

Butler herself notes that 'parody by itself is not subversive' and suggests that there must be a way to understand what makes certain kinds of parodic repetitions effectively disruptive, truly troubling (ibid 139). Again, we have to ask, how far does it get us in developing and involving large numbers of individuals in a political project to understand that '[g]ender is an identity tenuously constituted in time, instituted in an exterior space through a stylised repetition of acts' or that it is 'a constructed identity, a performative accomplishment' (ibid: 140, 141)? In fact, transgression of (traditional) gender roles and identities is happening contemporaneously in the material realities of the labour market as more and more women return to work and 'male' work is feminised (c.f. Ainley 1993).

By contrast, Marxism addresses the issue of how the present system operates. The 'postmodernism of resistance' end of the postmodern spectrum can aid in this understanding. But the danger lies in the fact that postmodernism, by definition, lacks the enlightenment project of 'emancipation in a general sense'. In addition, in its rhetoric of resistance, as opposed to a structural analysis of and prescriptions for social change, it undermines progressive social theory and plays into the hands of anti-socialist and indeed anti-feminist forces.

Modernism allows a future to be envisioned and worked towards. This vision can and has been extended beyond the brotherhood of man' concept of early socialists, to include the complex subjectivities (which the postmodernists are so good at bringing centre stage) of all. Socialism can and should be conceived of as a project where subjective identities, such as gender, 'race', ability, non-exploitative sexual preference and age are equally valid. For postmodernists, there is only 'emancipation in a particularist sense'. Here emancipation has a 'minimum profile' (Nederveen Pieterse 1992). This comprises `as regards aims, the concern with autonomy, in terms of organisation, a tendency towards network forms, and, in terms of mentality, a tendency towards self- limitation' (ibid). It provides neither hope for, nor strategies to achieve, a different social order and hence it is essentially reactionary.

In the replacement of 'emancipation in a general sense' by 'emancipation in a particularist sense', in advancing only localised struggle (no Marxist would ever deny the importance of local as well as national and international struggle), postmodernism ultimately plays into the hands of those whose interests lie in the maintenance of national and global systems of exploitation and oppression.

As Beyer and Liston, acknowledging a debt to Svi Shapiro and Jo Anne Pagano, put it with great force and simplicity:

> the postmodern valorization of local and diffused actions, of particular projects, leads to the formation of intellectual enclaves of research and isolated and decontextualised forms of action . . . Local efforts frequently require insight attainable only through the examination and critique of non-local sources of exploitation and oppression, and necessitate directions that are ascertainable through cultural and moral visions that may transcend the immediate situation.The problem with postmodernism in this respect is that it draws too sharp a distinction between the local and the more distant, the particular and the general. We would argue, on the contrary, for a more dialectical relationship between these two things: the sense that the local can illuminate the more general, and that the global can heighten our sensitivity to the more particular (1992: 374).

We should point out here that some 'critical' or `resistance' postmodernists attempt to have it both ways. They criticise 'reactionary' postmodernism, they are scathing of textualism, and assert a belief in a metanarrative of social justice, with Peter McLaren suggesting, for example, 'always totalize' (1994: 206-213). McLaren claims that he is 'not setting up a Manichean contest between the meta recits of liberation and social justice and the polyvocality and positionality of an anti- foundational approach to difference' (ibid: 208) and that 'the invitation posed by critical pedagogy is to bend reality to the requirements of a just world, to decenter, deform, disorient, and ultimately transform modes of authority that domesticate the other' (ibid: 218). However, there is no political strategy set out. There is a fundamental difference between McLaren's self-description and our conception of his theoretical project. To reiterate a point made earlier, whereas, McLaren suggests that he has appropriated postmodernism in a radical project, we believe that he has, in fact, appropriated and thereby neutralized Marxism for postmodernism. In addition to the recognition of a deterministic (and dialectical) relationship between base and superstructure, another defining characteristic of Marxism, is the striving towards a socialist future. This involves more than the rhetoric of social justice and democracy so prevalent in the work of so many postmodernists at the progressive end of the continuum. It involves nothing less that the recognition of and the quest for a democratic socialist world, accompanied by a viable strategy for achieving that aim. The fact that historically, `socialism' has less purchase in north America than Europe is surely a reason for its North American advocates to accentuate and develop the concept, rather than to ditch it (7). The internally incoherent attempt to link Marxism and postmodernism represents another indication of the contradictions within the latter.

Methodology

We referred earlier to the postmodernist notion of anti- representationalism and the consequent reliance on 'textualism'. Textualism, as used here, derives from the work of Jacques Derrida, who once wrote, 'there is no outside text' (Spivak 1976: 158).

Whereas modernists assumed a tight and identifiable relationship between what was being said ('the signified') and how it was being said ('the signifier'), poststructuralism sees these as `continually breaking apart and re-attaching in new combinations'. (Harvey 1989: 49). The task, therefore, is to 'deconstruct the text'. Since 'there is no outside text', cultural life is viewed as a series of texts intersecting with other texts, producing yet more texts (ibid). The cultural producer merely creates raw materials, which can be recombined by consumers in any way they wish. The effect is to beak (deconstruct) the power of the author to impose meanings or to offer a continuous narrative and to call into question all fixed systems of representation (ibid 51).

While there is nothing new in this (it was done by modernist authors like James Joyce and by the surrealists), there are apparent progressive implications here, in calling into question apparently fixed and definitive texts. Moreover, as Ollman (1971) observes, Marx himself deployed his concepts relationally, so that concepts like `value', `labour' and `capital' are `continually breaking apart and reattaching in new combinations' in an open-ended struggle to come to terms with the totalizing processes of capitalism (cited in Harvey 1989: 51).However, perceiving no reality beyond the text is essentially reactionary. This is perhaps best illustrated by a story about Derrida, analysed by Callinicos. Derrida once contributed a piece to a catalogue of an exhibition of anti-apartheid art, which was, in turn, criticized by two American literary theorists for its lack of historical specificity (it was, according to Callinicos, full of banalities, like '[h]asn't apartheid always been the archival record of the unnameable' (Callinicos 1989: 78). This 'silence' was justified by Derrida on the grounds that a 'discourse would compel us to reckon with the present state of force and law. It would draw up contracts, dialecticize itself, let itself be reappropriated' (cited in Callinicos ibid). According to this view, resistance to apartheid must remain inarticulate, must not seek the formulation of a political programme and strategy, since any such attempt would simply involve reincorporation into `the present state of force and law' (Callinicos 1989: 78). As Callinicos concludes, Derrida is unable to rationally ground any political commitments, 'because he denies himself the means either to analyse those existing social arrangements which he rejects or to justify this rejection by outlining some more desirable state of affairs' (ibid 79). The reactionary implications of such a position are once again obvious.

Many postmodern feminists, while largely reliant on discourse/ textual analysis, do not resort to this Derridean 'negative ontology' (Ferry and Renaut, cited in Callinicos (1989: 78). One worthy, though not new, feature of poststructuralist feminist analysis is the shift away from the disadvantage focus. As Alison Jones explains, in the context of educational analysis, `[a]n interest in the unevenness of power means that, while in the past feminist analyses of classrooms have tended uniformly to position girls as having oppressive and negative classroom experience, studies might focus on the ways in which the girls are variously positioned in the classroom' (1993: 160-1: see also Walkerdine 1990). While such an approach is to be welcomed, it is reminiscent of the approach taken by the Marxist feminist Ann-Marie Wolpe (c.f.Wolpe: 1988).

In the final chapter of her book, *Getting Smart,* Lather attempts to demonstrate the praxis which she describes as being 'at the heart of "getting smart" '(1991: 11). It involves a project on 'Student Resistance to Liberatory Curriculum'. Lather asks a series of important questions, not just for feminists but for all engaged in research. These have been neatly summed up by Mary Maynard and include; 1. whether it is possible to develop research techniques which do not involve the researcher in control and surveillance; 2. what does it mean to do empirical research in an unjust world?; 3. how do we explain the lives of others without violating their reality?; 4. how can it be made possible for the people for whom theory is supposed to be emancipatory to take part in its construction and validation?; 5.can this be done without violating the happiness of those, who, retrospectively, might have preferred to remain ignorant and 'unfree'? (Maynard 1993: 329). However, as Maynard points out, not only are these questions, in the main, already part of existing feminist work (ibid) but the result of Lather's endeavours tells us little about student resistance or pedagogy (ibid). For our part, while recognising the importance and validity of the five questions, we fail to see what is pre-eminently 'postmodern' about them. Maynard is critical of Lather's heralding of a new postpositivist era in social research, partly because Lather gives the impression that postmodernism is the only voice to be heard which is critical of positivism (Maynard 1993: 329), but more importantly, because, as many feminists are beginning to realise, quantitative research does have an important role to play (ibid: 330).

Finally given Lather's postmodernist preference for 'multi-voiced, multi-centred discourse' (1991: 112), a valid question that must be asked is, 'assuming that these voices will at least sometimes conflict . . . [must we] confront the stauts and validity of these multiple views - or simply assume they are all equally true (or false), equally revealing (or opaque) (Beyer and Liston 1992: 385). Beyer and Liston's conclusion is that postmodern theory, at least of this type, does not provide an answer (ibid). In addition, an emphasis on making sure that the voices of 'the other' become heard have made some postmodernists even suspicious of or hostile to 'community', which is seen as `necessarily oppressive, patriarchial and limiting' (ibid 380). Writers such as Elizabeth Ellsworth have expressed the fear that 'multiple voices' will be lost or silenced in communities and have therefore suggested that the most that might be hoped for is a gathering of voices within increasingly small and homogenous groups (cited in ibid). Arguing against this position, Beyer and Liston suggest, with considerable efficacy and clarity:

> [W]e agree that personal and social conditions need to be continually created, recreated, and reinforced that will encourage, respect, and value expressions of difference. Yet if the valorization of otherness precludes the search for some common good that can engender solidarity even while it recognizes and respects that difference, we will be left with a cacophony of voices that disallow political and social action that is morally compelling. If a concern for otherness precludes community in any form, how can political action be undertaken, aimed at establishing a common good that disarms patriarchy, racism and social class oppression? What difference can difference then make in the public space? (1992: 380-1).

We are not convinced by those academics who have implicated postmodernism in a new emancipatory politics. Contrary to their claims and hopes, we believe that 'resistance postmodernism' is essentially flawed.

Notes

1. Others have used different formulations. Different ways of describing `postmodernism of resistance' include `oppositional postmodernism' (Foster 1983), `radical critique-al theory' (Zavarzadeh and Morton 1991), `postmodern education' (Aronowitz and Giroux 1991) and `critical postmodernism' (McLaren and Hammer 1989; Giroux 1992; McLaren 1994: 199).

2. Recent work by Stephen Ball, for example Ball 1990 and Bowe, Ball and Gold 1993, can be criticised for underestimating the role and power of the state, and overestimating Foucauldian notions of the dispersion of power, in particular, the power of Radical Right discourse, and for overestimating the relative autonomy of (education) state apparatuses. Such work, in its over- concentration on text and discourse, and on the local and contingent, renders the state too `invisible' and power too `dispersed', thereby failing to acknowledge sufficiently the material power of the ruling coalition of capital. This work can be identified as `quasi- postmodernist'.

3. The `work in progress' continues. In a recent publication, Hall poses the question of whether we are entering a `new constellation of political, economic, social and cultural life' and the `New Times' that we confront. (Hall, Held and McLennan 1992: 4) Andy Green has suggested that the fact that postmodernism serves as the structuring paradigm of several readers for the Open University course,

Understanding Modern Societies (of which this is one) indicates how central it has become to theoretical debates in the U.K. (Green 1994: 3)

4. This postmodern prioritisation of market/ consumption/ lifestyle over production is derived from Max Weber and is commonplace analysis in many sociological accounts of social class. Arguing against too much stress on consumption, Michael Rustin has suggested, correctly in our view,that the Marxist tradition has been right all along in its emphasis on creative work (paid or unpaid) as the central form of human fulfilment and on the importance of the work group, neither of which can be replaced by consumption (1989: 314). This is certainly true in our own experience, and we expect also true in the experiences of the `New Times' writers, who we suspect derive much satisfaction from their creative endeavours.

5. Harvey, however, is somewhat inconsistent; his endorsement of the transition to post- Fordist capitalism (1989: 121-197) indicates more than a mere `surface change'.

6. The move away from the rhetoric that we are all part of `one nation', to a rhetoric which accepts a notion of an undeserving malignant and anti-social `underclass' which threatens the `rest of us' (the `two nation' project) is functional to the economic interests of the ruling class at this particular crisis in capital accumulation, since it justifies the replacement of universal benefits with targeted benefits and further justifies a reduction or withdrawal of these benefits from `the undeserving'. This project entails the scapegoating and vilification of these `enemies within', unlike the `one nation' project, which implies that `we are all in it together'.

7. We would wish to point out that we are restricting our critique to the academic writing , and not the practical activity, of those who describe themselves as `postmodernists of resistance' (or similar). These are not arguments against the person. We laud the involvement on Radical Left politics, inside and outside the academy of many writers that we criticize. We also realize the importance of localised understandings and struggles. Our point remains, however, that, to be politically valid, an analysis must link `the small picture' to `the big picture' of general and generalized analysis and struggles. We maintain that, essentially, postmodernism cannot do this.

Bibliography

Ainley, P. (1993) *Class and Skill: Changing Divisions of Knowledge and Labour*, London: Cassell.

Apple, M. (1994) *Official Knowledge: Democratic Education in a Conservative Age*, London: Routledge.

Aronowitz, S. & Giroux, H. (1986) *Education Under Siege: The Conservative, Liberal and Radical Debate over Schooling*, London: Routledge and Kegan Paul.

Aronowitz, S. & Giroux, H. (1991) *Postmodern Education: Politics, Culture and Social Criticism,* Minneapolis, University of Minnesota Press.

Ball, S. (1990) *Politics and Policy Making in Education: Explorations in Policy Sociology*, London: Routledge.Baudrillard, J. (1983) *In the Shadow of the Silent Majorities...Or the End of the Social and Other Essays*, New York: Semiotext (e), Inc.

Beyer, L. & Liston, D. (1992) Discourse or moral action? a critique of postmodernism, *Educational Theory*, 42,(4) pp 371-393.

Bowe, R., Ball, S. & Gold, A. (1992) *Reforming Education and Changing Schools*, London: Routledge.

Boyne, R. & Rattansi, A. (eds) (1990) *Postmodernism and Society*, London: Macmillan.

Brown, P. & Lauder, H. (1991) Education, Economy and Social Change, in International Studies in *the Sociology of Education*, 1.

Butler, J. (1990) *Gender Trouble: Gender and the Subversion of Identity*, London: Routledge.

Callinicos, A. (1989) *Against Postmodernism: A Marxist Critique*, Cambridge: Polity Press.
Cole, M. (ed) (1988) Bowles and Gintis Revisited: Correspondence and Contradiction in *Educational Theory*, Lewes: Falmer Press.
Cole, M. (1992) Racism, History and Educational Policy: From the Origins of the Welfare State to the Rise of the Radical Right, unpublished PhD thesis: Department of Socio;ogy, University of Essex.
Cole, M. & Hill, D. (1995); Games of Despair and Rhetorics of Resistance: Postmodernism, Education and Reaction, *The British Journal of Sociology of Education*, 16, (2) pp.165-18.
Crook, S. (1990) The End of Radical Social Theory? Notes on Radicalism, Modernism and Postmodernism in R. Boyne & A. Rattansi (eds) (1990) *Postmodernism and Society*, London: Macmillan.
Evans, J., Davies, R. & Penney, D. (1994) Whatever Happened to the Subject and the State? Discourse.Gane, M. (ed) (1993) Baudrillard Live: Selected Interviews, London: Routledge.Giroux, H. (1992) *Border Crossings*, London: Routledge.
Foster, H. (Ed.) (1983). *The anti-aesthetic: essays on postmodern culture*. Poit-Town-Send Wash Bau Press
Giroux, H. (1992) *Border Crossing*. London, Routledge
Giroux, H. (1994) Living dangerously: identity, politics and the new cultural racism. In H. Giroux & P. McLaren (Eds.), *Between borders: pedagogy and politics of cultural studies*. London, Routledge
Green, A. (1994) Postmodernism and State Education, in *Journal of Education Policy*, 9,(1) pp 67-83.Habermas, J. (1981) Modernity vs Postmodernity, New German Critique, (2) pp 3-14.
Habermas, J. (1983) Modernity - an Incomplete Project, in H. Foster (ed) *The Anti-Aesthetic: Essays on Postmodern Culture*, Port Town-send: Wash. Bay Press.
Habermas, J. (1987) *The Philosophical Discourse of Modernity*, Cambridge: MIT Press.Hall, S. & Jacques, M. (eds) (1989) *New Times: The Changing Face of Politics in the 1990s*, London: Lawrence and Wishart.
Hall, S., Held, D. & McLennan, G. (1992) *Introduction to Hall, S., Held. & McGrew, T. Modernity and Its Futures*, Cambridge: Polity Press.
Hargreaves, A. (1994) Restructuring restructuring: postmodern and the prospects for educational change, *Journal of Education Policy* (9)1
Hartley, D. (1993) Confusion in Teacher Education: a postmodern condition? in P. Gilroy & M. Smith (eds) *International Analyses of Teacher Education*, London: Carfax Publishing Company.
Harvey, D. (1989) *The Condition of Postmodernity*, Oxford: Basil Blackwell.
Hewitt, M. (1993) Illusions of Freedom: the regressive implications of `postmodernism' in, R. Miliband and L. Panitch Real Problems, *Raise Solutions Socialist Register*, London: Merlin Press.
Jessop, B. (1990) *State Theory: Putting Capitalist States in their Place*, Cambridge: Polity
Hill, D (1990) Something old, something new, something borrowed, something blue: schooling teacher education and the radical right in Britain and the USA. London, Tufnell Press.
Laclau, E. (1979). *Politics & ideology in marxist theory*. London, Verso
Lather, P. (1991) *Getting smart: feminist research & pedagogy with/in the postmodern*, New York, Routledge.
Maynard, M. (1993) Feminism and the possibilities of a postmodern research practice, *British Journal of Sociology of Education*, 14,(3) pp 327-331.
McLaren, P. (1994) Multiculturalism and the postmodernism critique: towards a pedagogy of resistance and transformation, in H. Giroux and P. McLaren (eds) *Between Borders: Pedagogy and the Politics of Cultural Studies*, London: Routledge.
McLaren, P. & Hammer, R. (1989) Critical Pedagogy and the Postmodern Challenge: Towards a Critical Postmodernist Pedagogy of Liberation, Educational Foundations, 3(3) pp. 29-62.

McLaren, P. & Lankshear, C. (1993) Critical Literacy and the Postmodern turn, in Lankshear, C. & McLaren, P. (eds) *Critical Literacy: Politics, Praxis and the Postmodern*, New York: SUNY Press.
Nederveen Pieterse, (1992) *Emancipations, Modern and Postmodern*, London: Sage
Rustin, M. (1989) The Trouble with New Times in S. Hall & M. Jacques (eds) (1989) New *Times: The Changing Face of Politics in the 1990s*, London: Lawrence and Wishart.
Sarup, M. (1983) *Marxist Structuralism Education*, Lewes: Falmer Press.
Skeggs, B. (1991) Postmodernism: What is all the fuss about?, *British Journal of Sociology of Education*, 12,(2) pp. 255-267.
Sivanandan, A. (1990) All that Melts into Air is Solid: The Hokum of New Times, in *Race and Class*, 31, (3).
Spivak, G. (1976) translation of J. Derrides, Of Grammatology, London: John Hopkins University Press.
Troyna, B. & Hatcher, R. (1994) The Policy Cycle: A Ball by Ball Account, *Journal of Education Policy*.
Walkerdine, V. (1990) *Schoolgirl Fictions*, London: Verso.
Whitty, G. (1991) Recent Educational Reform: Is it a Postmodern phenomenon? Conference Paper to Conference on Reproduction, Social Inequality and Resistance, Germany: University of Bielefeld.
Whitty, G. (1993) Education Reform and Teacher Education in England in the 1990s, in P. Gilfroy and M. Smith (eds). *International Analyses of Teacher Education*, London: Carfax.
Wolpe, A M. (1988) `Experience' as analytical framework: does it account for girls education? in Cole, M. (ed) Bowles and Gintis Revisited: *Correspondence and Contradiction in Educational Theory*, Lewes: Falmer Press.

Notes

* This chapter is a development of some of the arguments set out in Cole, M. and Hill, D. (`Games of Despair and Rhetorics of Resistance: Postmodernism, Education and Reaction', British Journal of Sociology of Education, (1995), 16 (2), pp. 165- 182.

Chapter 22

Postmodernism, Dance and Post-Industrial Society

Graham McFee

The paper explores the meaning of the expression "post-industrial society" and points out that it is not a society whose industry has shut down, but one where industrial activity is no longer needed! It seeks an explanation of Freud's hopes for technology as a solution for human suffering, and explores the the relation of the arts to such a society: in particular, whether arts might fill some of the civilising role identified by Freud? The discussion centres around Freud's 'centrality of reason' and a human being's relation to others. For Freud, in order to ensure a civilisation with a (justified) future what was needed was 'a real change in the relation of human beings to possessions', and what Freud called "the dictatorship of reason".The discussion uses post-modern dance for exploring the role of arts in post-mdern society and concerns itself questions such as: (i) what we can understand and (ii) what concepts are mobilised in doing so (plus how we came by or learned them). It argues that judgements of dance in a post-industrial society are not necessarily subjective, they involve objectivity. But it is crucial to understand that a commitment to objectivity here does not require that there be 'one right answer', only one acceptable judgement of a particular dance. Second, objectivity does not require a check-list, or set of criteria being employed. In other words objectivity can involve a number of acceptable accounts. This perspective of dance within the post-industrial society enables us to reflect on the relationship between the subjective and the objective and between rationality and irrationality.

Preamble

In his book *Civilisation and Its Discontents*[1], Freud, using a hedonist conception of the explanation of action typical of that period, urges that the pain which human kind characteristically must seek to avoid has three chief sources. The first is the person's own body, the second the external world or the world of Nature: these sources of pain might, Freud argued, eventually be overcome or eradicated by technological progress. Or, as he put it, humankind must wait:

> until new discoveries have increased our control over the forces of Nature and so made easier the satisfaction of our needs. (PFL Vol. 2 p. 218)

But the third kind of pain-source is different. It derives, 'as a kind of gratuitous addition' Freud says (PFL Vol. 12. p 264), from a human being's relation to others. It was in this sense that 'our civilisation is largely responsible for our misery' (PFL Vol. 12 p. 274). So that discontent with civilisation might be expected even from those who reaped the maximum (material) benefit from it. For Freud, it was always a constraint on social coherence that societies be organised fairly. As he put it:

It goes without saying that a civilisation which leaves a large number of its participants unsatisfied . . . neither has nor deserves the prospect of a lasting existence. (PFL Vol 12. pp. 191-2)

And further:

> . . . a real change in the relation of human beings to possessions would be of more help in this direction than any ethical commands (PFL Vol. 12 p. 337)

But (for Freud) such changes were not, in themselves, sufficient to ensure a civilisation with a (justified) future. There was needed, in addition, what Freud called 'the dictatorship of reason' (PFL Vol 12 p. 359), expressed also as the hope that '. . . reason . . . [may] establish a dictatorship in the mental life of man' (PFL Vol 2 p. 208).

I mention these (rather unfashionable) ideas to introduce one thesis and the one question that, explored through a concrete case, I will address in what follows. The thesis is a reaffirmation of Freud's commitment to the centrality of reason, although with no more optimism than Freud's that humankind is moving in this direction: as one might say, a commitment to reason in the face of what either is or appears to be a mounting admiration of unreason.

The question assumes that Freud's hopes for technology have been (or are being) fulfilled. And, while I know this is not true, it seems to me what ought to be meant by the expression 'post-industrial society', not a society whose industry has shut down, but one where industrial activity is nolonger needed! And then the question asks about the relation of the arts to such a society: in particular, might they fill some of the civilising role identified by Freud?

To make the question more concrete, let us look at one artform, dance, and one version (or vision) of post-industrial society, namely that urging a postmodern condition. And when I speak of 'dance' here, I mean, of course, roughly theatre dance, the sort of dance plausibly thought art[2].

Postmodern Dance?

I begin with a terminological issue. For it might seem that the way to identify postmodern dance would be as dance of a particular period, since the title suggests dance from the period following the period of modern dance. (This 'chronological' sense to the term is explicitly ascribed to Yvonne Rainer[3]: 'the generation that came after modern dance' [T p. xiii]) But the inadequacy of this strategy can be brought out by considering what its 'blurb' tells us is 'the best book on post-modern dance we have', Sally Banes' *Terpsichore in Sneakers*, which accurately records that, for some sixties dance innovators, there were fundamental questions to be answered about '[t]he nature, history, and function of dance' (T p. xvii). But these are characteristic concerns of *modernists*. At least arguably, therefore:

> ". . . it is post-modern dance that functions as *modernist* art. . . . [It is] in the arena of post-modern dance that issues of modernism in the other arts have arisen." (T p. xv)

Recognising this, we might choose (if it were not so confusing):

> ". . . to call sixties and seventies post-modern dance *post-modern* and dub eighties new dance *post-modernist* "(T p. xv)

But that poses a key problem for accurately describing (and sorting out classifications for) danceworks: post-modern dances on such a classification would not be postmodern!

Banes' remarks fit both my experience of those of these works that I have seen — they are experienced as modernist — and some of their characteristics. Thus, if we wish to consider any dance with genuine postmodern credentials, we must focus on what Banes (T p. xv) considered calling *post-modernist* dance.

With this idea in place, we progress by identifying (as I put it elsewhere: CDE[4] p. 194) the difficulty in deciding precisely which category to consider:

> ". . . should one be thinking about 'post-modern *dance* 'or about post-modern *culture*, with dance merely one manifestation: that is, are we talking about a kind of dance, or a cultural condition?"

In asking this, I did not take my remarks to be original — for example, Joyce Sherlock[5] urges that '[p]ost modern culture must . . . be distinguished from postmodern dance.'

What exactly is at stake here? To understand, consider two dances, *Ghost Dances* (1981) by Christopher Bruce and *Strange Fish* (1992) by DV8[6]. Which, if any, of these is postmodern dance? What makes it so? What does calling a dance 'postmodern' (Banes 'post-modernist') commit us to?

A Postmodern Condition?

Since the expression 'the postmodern condition' achieves prominence through the work of Jean-Francois Lyotard[7], we can usefully begin from him. As has been recognised[8], for Lyotard, the postmodern condition is '. . .. a state of affairs Lyotard claims to be actual' (B p. 4). Moreover, it is '. . .. not simply synonymous with the architectural and artistic movements known as 'postmodernism'.' (B p. 4) Equally, Lyotard *is* concerned with '. . .. the analysis of the contemporary arts' (B p. 4): and is widely recognised to be so — for example, the Appendix: 'Answering the Question: What is Postmodernism?' in *The Postmodern Condition* is explicitly about art.

In his most general (and widely familiar) formulation, Lyotard characterises the postmodern in terms of 'incredulity towards metanarratives' PC p. xxiii [CDE p. 204 fn], and cites Freudianism and Marxism as examples of such metanarratives. Two of the features he takes them to have are relevant for us. First, they seek all-embracing explanation: as Richard Rorty[9] puts it, they 'search for universal commensuration in a final vocabulary'. But (with Lyotard) one might well doubt the possibility of such perfectly general explanation: one might think, instead, of the various descriptions of 'what occurred' when some person performed some action. If we cannot *even* secure agreement as to *the* (single) descriptions of events, it looks unpromising to search for a single explanation. In this vein, postmodernists are seen as giving up this search.

Second, a 'metanarrative' is concerned with 'legitimation with respect to its own status' PC p. 8[10]; giving up the commitment to such general explanation might be seen as giving up the search for legitimation.

Now, one might, with justice, be suspicious about 'one right answer': but nothing *follows* from this idea that *automatically* leads to the 'anything goes' characteristic of subjectivism. . .That is to say, one might give up the grand project *without* concluding that nothing can *ever* be explained. Also, and relatedly, rejecting the grand obsession with justification does not lead inevitably to the conclusion that justification is never either possible or necessary. [I shall return to this idea.] So where exactly does being *incredulous* about metanarratives get you?

Lyotard urges that, once we have put aside the metanarratives (and our longing for them), legitimacy can be seen to reside in what Lyotard calls 'first-order narratives': what people say and do. But, for Lyotard, such narratives:

> . . . determine criteria of competence and/or illustrate how they are to be applied. They thus define what has the right to be said and done in the culture in question, and since they are themselves a part of that culture, they are legitimated by the simple fact that they do. (PC p. 23: see Rorty 1991a p. 167)

What this can seem to mean is that one can say what one likes, offer whatever judgements one likes, and they will be legitimated (roughly, they will be made true) merely by one's saying them. So here 'anything goes': and that is subjectivism.

There is another, though related, thread in Lyotard. For having recognised that we speak and judge as 'the contingent historical selves we find ourselves to be'[11], Lyotard diagnoses a danger in this position: why should such (historically-rooted and contingent) judgements carry any weight for others (much less be compelling on them)? Rather we should, Lyotard thinks, deny any single discourse the right to judge others on its own terms. And his account treats all discourses as equal. It would tempting to search for some tribunal of Pure Reason: but then, as Lyotard asks, 'What language do the judges speak?' It looks as though any answer will import arbitrariness into the heart of human judgement. (Lyotard takes himself to be giving exposition of Wittgenstein at this point: Rorty 1991b p. 217).

Note that this is a good example of a mistake identified earlier: that there was not 'one right answer' was taken to show that anything goes; but this conclusion simply does not follow.

The upshot of this discussion of Lyotard has been the identification of an aspect of our answer to the question about why postmodern theorising is often subjectivist: although, before entering either, it is worth stressing the key word 'often' in the question. For I am not (here) saying that other accounts might not be given; only that subjectivist readings have regularly been given. Why? Our reply has identified a core assumption within such theorising: that what is not independently 'legitimated' is thereby guaranteed to be arbitrary, and such a thought readily supports subjectivist interpretation.

One further example: Lyotard says (about science[12], but that need not concern us) that one difference with the project of modernity is that, in the postmodern condition, social practices may become theorised as discontinuous ('post-modern science . . . is theorising its evolution as discontinuous, catastrophic, non-rectifiable and paradoxical' (Lyotard, PC p. 60)). I will comment on two aspects of this:

(a) 'discontinuous' — with what? To reply, 'with its past' implies continuities also, the place of the rebel etc., and hence makes it less radically different from modernism.

(b) 'theorised' — that is, not so much that it *is* discontinuous, but that it presents itself that way; which is (i) polemical, and (ii) centrally involves the contrast (borrowed from Feyerabend[13]) between the perspectives of the philosopher/theorist and the practitioner: just as a scientist will correctly describe the theoretical judgements of previous scientists as wrong when philosophers might regard the two positions as incommensurable, so the dance critic may think (correctly from his perspective) that a view is being overturned when it is simply being superseded (UD p. 307).

If we accept (from Banes and others) the thought that not all dance called 'postmodern' (or 'post-modern') is actually *postmodern* in the sense of requiring for its understanding 'insights' such as Lyotard's and if, further, we take those 'insights' to be flawed (at least as usually understood), there does not seem much to be learned from postmodernism. But where does that leave postmodern dance?

The upshot of this brief discussion has been to give us two points to take forward. The first concerns the generality of talk of a 'postmodern condition' (even granting the coherence of such talk): what is its special relevance in guiding or explaining artistic production? Unless it is a condition *only* recognised by artists (or centrally recognised by artists) the postmodern condition will not direct artistic enterprises in any particular direction. So postmodern dances would not, of themselves, have any special characteristics. So, is the task to search instead for the characteristics of (roughly) postmodern *vision*? I will come to an example shortly.

The second idea is that the key argumentative strategy employed by, for example, Lyotard is unsound: from a rejection of the search for 'universal commensuration in a final vocabulary' nothing follows about issues of objectivity — or so I shall suggest more fully below (§4) In this way, 'the dictatorship of reason' is compatible with (the justified aspect of) incredulity towards metanarratives.

Postmodernism as a condition of society?

Suppose, for a moment, we put aside key questions about the nature of postmodernism, and ask instead about the upshot for dance of such an idea (however articulated). If postmodernism were a condition of society, then postmodern dances would be any dances produced in a society in that condition: and since (as noted earlier) Lyotard takes the condition to be actual, we can see this as the situation of all recent danceworks. In particular, this view invites us to see dances by Christopher Bruce (for example, *Ghost Dances* [1981]) as postmodern.

There are three main points here. First, this dancework is not experienced as of a distinctive kind, not experienced differently from other works — organisational devices familiar from Classical Ballet and from Modern Dance operate here; for example, cannon. So this is a work for which our existing critical vocabulary seems sufficient.

Second, as noted above, a general social condition can give no (explicit) *direction* to art-making or art appreciation. But, third, it also under-rates the distinctiveness of art. To bring out this point, consider a thesis that, although it is not central to postmodernism, is employed by dance theorists: the idea of the 'death of the author'. For instance, this slogan from literary theory is explicitly invoked by Foster[14] in her explanation of the framework underlying postmodernist thinking for dance (and is recognised to do so: Jordan p. 6), in terms of 'the interpretation of a text (in our case, a dance) based on the codes and conventions that convey meaning', rather than 'a search for the author's intended meaning, recognising 'the arbitrary nature of the relationship between the dance movement, the signifier, and that to which it refers, the signified.'

Now, apart from its obscurity, this formulation commits almost all the errors I can think of in respect of understanding: that is, it (mistakenly) treats understanding (say, understanding language) as rooted in referring, as involving codes or something similar, and (therefore?) as arbitrary in some interesting way. These are the errors (as I call them[15]) associated with structuralist[16] conceptions of understanding, and inherited from structuralism[17].

But suppose we put aside such a line of criticism: there are still at least three ways in which the idea of 'the death of the author' is regularly developed in a fashion inappropriate for those concerned with dance. The first is, again, a fairly general point; namely, that treating one's target as a 'text' can involving ignoring the fact that some texts are, while others are not, artworks[18], or, as we might put it, either ignoring *that*, the activity in question is dance (and not something else), or failing to notice that some dances are, and others are not, suitable objects for *artistic appreciation* (using a technical contrast[19]).

Before introducing the second line of criticism, it is worth noting something appropriate that the expression 'death of the author' might be used to mean. For we *do* want to move away from undue emphasis on the wishes or plans of (in our case) the choreographer: what counts is what he or she *does*, not what is planned, wished or hoped for. But that thought can be introduced with a quite mild thesis about what is relevant to artistic appreciation, of a kind common within philosophical aesthetics.

This leads to the second line of criticism; for rejecting an emphasis on the plans etc. of the choreographer must still involve seeing this dance as *intended* (rather than accidental) and intended *as dance*, and perhaps *as art*. Of course, a choreographer might decide to use chance-based compositional methods, but it is the choosing or deciding here that justifies the choreographer in taking the work as his/her *own*, as something achieved rather than an accident. Further, understanding a dance will typically involve (at least implicitly) locating it within its tradition of composition: for taking a badly composed modern dance for a postmodern, eclectic one would be *mistaking* it, misperceiving it, misunderstanding it. (This was what it means to speak of *categories of art* here: see §4 below.) And, of course, that this is so follows from our commitment to the objectivity of artistic appreciation: one can be wrong, it is not 'anything goes'.

The final line of criticism that I will mention turns on the nature of the argument being employed; and it is a familiar criticism. For the assumption seems to be that *either* the meaning of a 'text' (say, a dancework) is determined be its choreographer's intentions, plans etc. *or* its meaning is arbitrary, that any interpretation is as good as any other. Yet there are other alternatives. As with a multiple-figure (for instance, the duck-rabbit: §5b below), the possibility of being wrong does not require that there be 'one right answer', far less that it be given via a specific intention or plan. What must be seen is how our *practice* of using words[20], and discussing (and performing) dances, can limit what it is appropriate to urge, in this way avoiding a commitment to subjectivism, without necessitating that only one thing could be urged.

Postmodernism in art as (one kind of) eclecticism

If we turn instead to a number of other dance works (the piece by DV8 was our example), we find no such uniformity of organisational devices, there does not seem to be a consistent attitude here: hence no characteristic 'postmodern' attitude. Or perhaps this is the postmodern attitude, such that there is 'a thoroughgoing mixing up of categories'[21]: in a similar vein, Sparshott[22] writes of 'steady-state eclecticism'. We might see this eclecticism as characteristically postmodern.

On the face of it, such eclecticism might generate problems about understanding. We do not know how to go on. And this idea is key for the understanding of artworks. It turns on the need to see dance as in an appropriate category: put extremely bluntly, critics must understand what critical canons to bring to bear on that performance, what categories of art[23] are the appropriate ones here if their judgements of works are to be appropriate, if they are to avoid misperception. And what applies to professional or formal critics applies equally to the rest of us when we come to make sense of a particular performance.

There may also be a parallel problem about how to make art — again, a problem shared with modernism. For if we reject traditional conceptions of structure for artworks, how are we to proceed? The problem is clearly exemplified in some piano works by Morton Feldman, each consisting of notated chords which could be played in whatever order the pianist selected. The reality of these works, in performance, was (first) that pianists tended to always play them in one preferred sequence, the one that made the most sense to the pianist. So the works were not 'liberating' in that way. But (second and more crucial) the works themselves had a 'samey' quality; Feldman selected similar chords for each! In the absence of a structure, artists are often thrown back onto personal resources in just this way. Here two ideas will be developed in the next section: (a) that much of the difficulty is shared with modernists, although we should not overlook the limited nature of the audience for modernist art: as Tom Wolfe[24] charicatured Jackson Pollock as saying 'If I'm so terrific, why ain't I rich?'; (b) that the problem for understanding is solved (in so far as it is) in familiar ways. So that, in effect, we have similar problems and similar solutions for postmodern dance as those for modernist dance. If this idea is accepted, it should mean that any benefits the arts have might be expected to accrue to postmodern dance also.

Appreciating the Postmodern

One issue from postmodernism is whether (or perhaps how), given their 'discontinuities' with the past of dance (with what went on previously as dance), postmodern danceworks can be understood. As we have seen, one key question, (apparently) concerning the credentials of what is presented as dance[25], is [re appreciation] 'Is this dance? . . ..What makes this activity *dance* ?' Asking whether a performance is dance or not is always a good question if it is understood as asking 'what makes this performance (or this work) dance? as opposed to what . . ..?' In context, we can respond. We might see that question posed by, for instance, Yvonne Rainer[26] when she speaks of her *Trio A* — which she calls 'a minimalist work' — as both a exemplification and an investigation of the fact that '[d]ance is hard to see'. [She means of course that it can become hard to make sense of if certain of its traditional 'props' are removed[27].] To see this point more clearly, let us consider a case: the postmodern attitude to narrative

Example: postmodern dance and narrative

To locate a postmodern attitude to narrative, we first need a clear view of the modernist attitude — for modernist works too were not typically narrative. As a typical account[28] of a particular work from the modernist 'phase' of postmodern dance, consider the following, on Rainer's *Trio A* :

> There is no story, character, attitude or action that the movement can be correlated to: thus, *Trio A* forgoes all the traditional narrative devices. . ..

Indeed, we might well agree with Adrian Stokes[29] that one aspect of modernism in ballet involved the replacement of narrative based on 'mimed action', so that 'the action of a modern ballet is expressed in the dancing itself'. But that does not mean that the narrative element is necessarily absent from such dances. A useful parallel may be with a modernist view of the place, within visual art, of representations of peoples, things and places: Clive Bell[30] takes the idea of representation as 'always irrelevant' to artistic merit. In a similar way, in modernism, it is the artistic irrelevance of narrative, not its absence, that is urged.

For postmodernist dance the situation is somewhat different. As Banes notes, 'the narrative, whose death seemed a certainty in the sixties and seventies, has been reborn in the eighties' (T p. xxix). So that if we agree that some dances have a narrative element[31], we must recognise a different attitude to narrative, one more difficult to characterise. And one symptom of such a difficulty is that the characterisations become increasingly theorised[32]. For instances, we are told that such dances 'are different from modern dance . . .. because in important ways they *present* the nondance information (i.e., plot, character, situation), rather than *represent* it. They are not seamless theatrical illusions . . .' (T p. xxxi).

But if, for example, we think that Ian Spink's *Dead Flight* (1980) '. . .. suggested some influence of Pina Bausch' (Jordan p. 187), we are reminded that there are various kinds of theatrical illusions. Equally, we might take Spink's *De Gas* (1981) to be 'theatrical' (Jordan p. 189) or notice the 'raw theatricality' of works by DV8[33] without mistaking either for narrative works of earlier generations. Moreover, as a comparison of critical description[34] of performances/works by DV8 may illustrate, there are many ways of invoking narrative. Consider, first:

. . .. the eight women waited for an agonisingly long time for their lovers, who never showed up. Then, when eight men finally appeared, the women set out to pursue them, chasing them up and down the stage, hobbled by their high heels and tight dresses.

This is described as a straightforward story, posing for the audience questions about 'the ways in which women bind themselves to men' (p. 124). Then, second:

The atmosphere is charged with the desires and demands of clutching hands and convulsed bodies. The dancers portray, from one moment to the next, childish ineptitude and acrobatic virtuosity as they progress and regress through their personal emotional experience.

No hint there of a story-line as such; yet there is, as the critic noted, 'a social and psychological agenda' in the work — as in much of the work of the company. That means that the understanding of this work, as the critic illustrates, can draw on what we know of emotional odysseys; and see this dance as depicting some such. Certainly it cannot easily be treated as the kind of dance dismissed by DV8 in their manifesto[35] for lacking 'personal and political commitment'. So we see both that not all works are committed to narrative and that such commitments may be difficult to identify.

The central difficulty is to experience the unity of such works; here again this is a difficulty shared with modernist works. Moreover, a commitment to narrative might make postmodern dances more readily intelligible. We have learned, from modernist works, that unity may be a complex topic: that the unity of, say, Webern's *Symphonie* Opus 21 may only be easily perceptible when one is analysing the piece, although no doubt any experienced unity in some way depends on it! There is little reason to expect postmodern works to be more transparent.

But might a postmodern work be thought to lack such unity (without this counting as a flaw)? In fact, given that it is a unitary artwork, some sense of unity is guaranteed. But that may not make it easier to identify in practice.

Appreciating postmodernism again

Our primary question was how postmodern dance could be seen as dance. In answer, we notice that the movement-activity must be justified as dance — and this will involve appeal to dance-movements, and to explanations using *dance-reasons* (CDE pp. 84-87; UD p. 253).

"We would need to ask what, precisely, the characteristics of this form of dance are — how does it resemble, and how does it differ from, other things we recognise as dance? Of course, this is . . .. a topic within dance criticism. It is exactly on a par with deciding the characteristics of, say, Romantic Ballet, the one additional difficulty being that one is making the judgements of broadly contemporary works." [CDE p. 196]

So postmodern dance is not escaping dance of the past: at most, it is one way of rebelling against such dance [and explicitly recognised to be so, for instance by DV8[36] in their manifesto]. But the work of rebels can only be correctly understood if it is seen *as* rebellion, and hence understood against a background provided by the ideas etc. against which it is rebelling! In this sense, calling dance 'postmodern' is a polemical stance, rejecting the *answers* that might previously have been given to questions about the nature of dance. Yet rejecting the answer is accepting the *question*. But we have seen that, while there is no formula here, the difficulty is one that we can overcome in broadly the ways that permitted us to understand modernist works (in so far as we did[37]). And there is no reason to suppose that if we had chosen instead a genuinely postmodern dance as our example (rather than what is essentially a modernist one) we would have commented any differently.

But whether or not a particular performance is *dance* (as opposed to something else) is not our practical concern when, say, we go to a performance space to see DV8. Our concern has more to do with (i) what we can understand and (ii) what concepts are mobilised in doing so (plus how we came by or learned them).

Thus, the distinctiveness of postmodern dance is a distinctiveness *within* a familiar framework; that provided by our understanding dances (to the degree that we do), and learned in the way we learned to understand other dances.

As to precisely how we might come to understand danceworks (to the degree that one can) I would mention three features, which elsewhere I illustrated in respect of the understanding of a modernist work[38]:

•It must be 'one step at a time'; hence some steps may prove impossible for a particular person.

•It must operate through 'perceptual engagement' (seeing, hearing) with the work(s)

•It may usefully be supplemented by discussion, drawing parallels etc.

There seems no reason to suppose that this would not succeed as well for postmodern works as modernist ones. But notice too that this is a model of rational process less rationalistic that those sometimes canvassed (by both advocates and enemies).

It is important, at this stage, to recognise that, as I have argued elsewhere[39], judgements of dance are not necessarily subjective[40]. Three points are crucial:

•First, a commitment to objectivity here does not require that there be 'one right answer', only one acceptable judgement of a particular dance. To recognise the general point, consider a multiple-figure from psychology; the duck-rabbit, or the old woman/young woman. Here there is more than one acceptable account of what is depicted, but it is not the case that 'anything goes'; any account must be answerable to the features of the design. I would urge that critical appreciation shares many characteristics with our treatment of this case.

•Second, objectivity does not require a check-list, or set of criteria being employed; to see why, notice that any such list (supposing it accurate) could be made inaccurate by the new creation of a particular choreographer — I like to imagine it being a choreographer who had seen the list of criteria!

•The philosopher John Wisdom[41] provides a helpful way to bring out what *is* required by contrasting what he calls 'the mother's method' of explanation with 'the father's method'. Asked what a greyhound is, the father replies with a kind of 'definition', that a greyhound is 'a dog of such-and-such a type'. (Wisdom comments 'Short, conclusive, the father's procedure. That's more what one might call a proof' (VL p. 48 [52]).) In contrast, the mother says (pointing):

> ". . . that's a greyhound, and you remember your uncle's dog, Entry Badge, well that was a greyhound. But now that (she says, pointing to a Borzoi) is not a greyhound, and even that (she says, pointing to a whippet) is not."

Wisdom also imagines that she might offer the rhyme:

> A foot like a cat, a tail like a rat,
>
> A back like a rake, a head like a snake

He concludes that the mother:

> ". . .. replies with instances of what is and what is not a greyhound or by comparing greyhounds with what they are not, and these two procedures merge into one." (p. 70)

"It seems to me clear, and entirely appropriate, that we learn to understand and to appreciate dance (as most things) by 'the mother's method' or a variant of it. As a result, attempts to force this knowledge and understanding into the straight-jacket of a set of criteria — the sort of thing 'the father's method' offered — seem doomed to failure. But this is no cause for complaint, since the mother's method is the typical route to genuine, public, discussible claims — that is, to objectivity. (Nor should we conclude that sets of candidate criteria (for example, the Assessment of Performance Unit's) are entirely worthless, even though they cannot function as intended. Like the mother's rhyme, they may help us to focus our knowledge.)

What all this means, of course, is that we well understand ways in which judgements might be perfectly objective (where this means that they are public and available for discussion), perfectly well legitimated, without the spectre of 'one right answer' arising. And that is a way of saying that we might accept what postmodernism has *proved* (though it was not the first movement to do so) without adopting what it takes (mistakes) to follow.

But that is not all of the issue. Suppose, on a parallel with (a reading of) Kuhn's view of science[42], the conclusion was that postmodernism involves there not being one integrated or uniform way of proceeding in, for instance, making dances (as though there ever was!) In fact, the situation is even more eclectic — more 'mix-and-match' . . .. Yet every work can be understood by someone, even if few (or no) works can be understood by all. So even this degree of eclecticism does not generate subjectivism (although it might mistakenly be thought to).

Similar treatment can be given to the question, 'Does this postmodern work have meaning in ways appropriate to dance?' [compare Jordan on Foster (quoted earlier), and CDE p. 196.] For recognising it as dance and answering that question should be thought-of as one process, not two. Here again we recognise that difficulties for understanding are in principle soluable within the compass of reason.

The promise of art

To return to our starting point, Freud's own view of the future was not optimistic. Although:

"in the long run, nothing can withstand reason and experience" (PFL Vol 12 p. 238)

Humankind, which needed to attend to rational considerations and arguments if it was to produce civilised society, had a remarkable capacity to fail to do so. In this sense Wollheim[43] was right to characterise Freud's life's work as 'research into the deafness of the mind'. Still, such attention to rational demands was central to becoming a decent human being (as Freud saw it). For the development of the superego, since it was the seat of conscience and morality, carried the demands of civilisation: and it represented 'more than anything the cultural past' (PFL Vol 15 p. 443) from which one acquired not merely one's values but the capacity to discriminate between the claims of certain 'value'. In short, one was on the road to becoming rational.

Initially, I put aside Freud's remarks about the significance for cultural life of matters which, he hoped/assumed, could be settled by technological development. For us, of course, this means that we should take for granted (at least) sufficient levels of facility with high-grade 'Information Technology' to permit its use as a kind of 'black box'; where the emphasis is no longer on the *how* of it. But this is equivalent to assuming (as Freud does) that remaining questions are *not* amenable to technological solution, that they are centrally *normative* questions[44], with a moral dimension. (And such a solution should be seen as importing accounts of information and of knowledge which may differ in important ways from those standardly adopted.)

It was for Freud clear that a culture's art provided one (among many) indices of that culture's health, since that art would have (at least) two key roles: first, it would embody values that could be acquired in acquiring one's superego. Second, the art would provide rational sites for the contestation of dominant values — in coming to understand art works, and ourselves through them, we might move forward[45].

Whether or not we accept the detail of Freud's ideas here, their spirit is clear. But the explanations of artworks and of the nature of art offered by (some) postmodernists and the condition of postmodern dance do not seem conducive to the kinds of development Freud envisaged. That may be, of course, because he was just another fool with a metanarrative. But it might just be that he accurately diagnoses the anti-rationalism of the time: in which case, we may be only too glad if postmodern dance is less of a force for the anti-rational than it is sometimes thought.

Acknowledgements

[Some of this material was presented in a lecture at the Roehampton Institute on 23 May 1994; my thanks to all those who, by their comments on that version, helped make this a clearer presentation.]

Notes

1 Penguin Freud Library Vol 12 — hereafter cited as 'PFL' followed by volume and page number.

2 I will say nothing here about the nature of art, but see Graham McFee *Understanding Dance*, London: Routledge, 1992, cited as 'UD' Ch 3.

3 Sally Banes *Terpsichore in Sneakers (with a new introduction)* Wesleyan Univ Press, 1987, cited as 'T'.

4 Graham McFee *The Concept of Dance Education* London: Routledge, 1994, cited as "CDE"; also UD.

5 Joyce Sherlock "Postmodern Culture and Dance Study" in D. Botterill (ed) *Leisure Participation and Experience: Models and Case Studies* [LSA No 37] Eastbourne: Leisure Studies Association, 1989, p. 116

6 In practice, the excerpts will be from televisual versions of the works: but let us imagine viewing a (genuine) stage performance.

7 Jean-Francois Lyotard *The Postmodern Condition* Manchester: Manchester Univ Press, 1984: cited as 'PC'. [I am conscious that my exclusive concentration on Lyotard here is a weakness; but to have considered other theorists — especially to then have repeated most of the points — would make a long paper even longer.]

8 Geoff Bennington 'Introduction: The Question of Postmodernism' in Lisa Appignanesi (ed) *Postmodernism [ICA Documents]* London: Free Association Books, 1989; cited as 'B'.

9 Richard Rorty *Philosophy and the Mirror of Nature* Princeton: Princeton Univ Press, 1979, p. 368.

10 See Richard Rorty *Essays on Heidegger and Others* Cambridge: Cambridge Univ. Press, 1991a p. 164; p. 166.

11 Richard Rorty *Objectivity, Relativism and Truth* Cambridge: Cambridge Univ Press, 1991b p. 214.

12 Note, too, that Lyotard sees this "not as a repudiation of a bad account of science but as indicating a recent change in the nature of science" (Rorty, 1991a: p.166).

13 Paul Feyerabend *Farewell To Reason* London: Verso, 1987 p. 272.

14 Susan Leigh Foster *Reading Dancing* Berkeley: University of California Press, 1986, p. 242 note 43.

15 For a full treatment of the underlying errors, see G P Baker and P M S Hacker *Language Sense and Nonsense* Oxford: Blackwell, 1984.

16 See Stuart Sim 'Structuralism and Post-structuralism' in Oswald Hanfling (ed) *Philosophical Aesthetics: An Introduction* Oxford: Blackwell, 1992 pp.405-439: esp pp. 422-423.

17 Advice here: concentrate on understanding (that is, on the semantic aspect) and treat it via Wittgenstein's slogan that meaning is what explanation of meaning explains — see UD pp. 113-116.

18 CDE pp. 202-203 (Ch 11 note 1), providing quotation and citation for this idea.

19 *Artistic/ aesthetic* — a fundamental distinction (drawn clearly by David Best *Feeling and Reason in the Arts*, London:George Allen and Unwin, 1985, Ch. 11 [or *The Rationality of Feeling* London: Falmer Press, 1992 Ch 12]) between artistic judgement and appreciation (our judgement of works of art) and aesthetic judgement and appreciation (our judgement of natural beauty, of fountains and firework displays — perhaps better called *merely* aesthetic judgement). Applied to dance, this [technical] artistic/aesthetic distinction means that not all dance will be considered — only that which is art: and further, that when considered, it is considered as dance and not, for example, as movement (See David Carr, 'Though and action in the art of dance', *British Journal of Aesthetics* , 1987, pp. 345-357: also UD, Ch. 2).

20 For exposition (and refutation) of a related mistaken view, see G P Baker and P M S Hacker *Scepticism, Rules and Language* Oxford: Blackwell, 1984 p. 24, where the view is characterised as follows:

> "... you know what 'pain' or 'looks real' means from your exemplar, just as I know from my exemplar. And evolution, or a good angel, has so arranged matters that our exemplars are qualitatively identical .... So thought and action rest firmly on the bedrock of the subjective."

21 Paul Crowther *Critical Aesthetics and Postmodernism* Oxford: Clarendon Press, 1993 p. 94.

22 Francis Sparshott *Off The Ground*, Princeton: Princeton Univ Press, 1988 p. 77.

23 Kendall Walton "Categories of art", reprinted in J. Margolis (ed) *Philosophy Looks at the Arts (Second Edition)*, Philadelphia: Temple Univ. Press, 1978 pp.88-114.

24 Tom Wolfe *The Painted Word*, New York: Farrar, Strauss and Giroux, 1975 p. 65

25 See Francis Sparshott (*Off The Ground*, p. 77) on postmodern dance as "what could not have been dance before"

26 Yvonne Rainer "A Quasi-survey of Some 'Minimalist' Tendencies in the Quantitatively Minimal Dance Activity Midst the Plethora, or an Analysis of *Trio A*" in Roger Copeland and Marshall Cohen (eds) *What Is Dance?* London: Oxford Univ Press, 1983 p. 331.

27 Compare (the easier job of) 'seeing' Mats Ek's *Swan Lake* (1987) as *Swan Lake*: CDE p. 80.

28 Noel Carroll 'Postmodern dance and Expression' in Gordon Fancher and Gerald Myers (eds) *Philosophical Essays on Dance* New York: American Dance Festival, 1981 p. 100.

29 Adrian Stokes *Tonight The Ballet* London: Faber & Faber, 1935 p. 105.

30 Clive Bell *Art* London: Chatto and Windus, 1914 p. 25.

31 Banes' examples here (T p. xxxi) are works I know, if at all, only through film or video; so I have not included them.

32 Compare Foster, quoted earlier (at note 13).

33 From 'DV8's manifesto' included in Judith Mackrell, *Out of Line*, London: Dance Books, 1992 p. 127.

34 The first is from Judith Mackrell *Out of Line* pp. 124-125, describing *My Body Your Body* (1987); the second is from "DV8 — Physical Theatre in Rouen" *Dance Theatre Journal* Vol.8 No 2 Summer 1990 p. 4.

35 "DV8's manifesto" included in Judith Mackrell, *Out of Line* p. 127.

36 From "DV8's manifesto" included in Judith Mackrell, *Out of Line*, p. 127.

37 Note here, for example, the trouble the 'general public' have in making sense of Picasso, let alone Carl Andre or more recent artists (See Ian Ground *Art or Bunk?* Bristol: Bristol Classical Press, 1989 esp pp. 1-7; 25-28) The audience for modernist art should not be overestimated.

38 See my *Much of Jackson Pollock is vivid wallpaper* University Press of America, 1978 Ch. 2, re. Cage's *Four Minutes Thirty Three Seconds*.

39 UD pp. 21-38; 137-145: CDE Ch 9, esp. pp. 87-92; 98-99.

40 The concern is with judgements that are *necessarily* subjective, not merely accidentally so. Thus, a person urging that (our example) judgements of dance were subjective would be urging that they were necessarily subjective — that no matter how carefully they were made, they would still be subjective. Notice that neither colour-perception nor essay-marking is typically thought subjective in this way: we can identify colour-blindness, and would contrast the biased essay-marker (say, me) with my non-biased colleague — indeed, the whole idea of *bias* only makes sense in a framework where there is no *necessary* bias.

41 John Wisdom 'The Metamorphosis of Metaphysics' in his *Paradox and Discovery* Oxford: Blackwell, 1965 p. 69: John Wisdom *Proof and Explanation (The Virginia Lectures)* [ed. S Barker] Washington, DC: University Press of America, 1991, cited as 'VL'.

42 Thomas Kuhn *The Structure of Scientific Revolutions (Second Edition)* Chicago: Chicago Univ Press, 1969 esp. p. 10; p. 189, for accounts of both the period of 'crisis' which Kuhn predicts will precede each scientific revolution and (more important) the idea of 'normal science', where there is a clear idea about 'how to go on' in science. It is the capacity for such "normal science" with its associated *paradigm* that, according to Kuhn (p. vii), social sciences lack: we might urge the same in respect of understanding the arts.

43 Richard Wollheim *Freud* London: Fontana, 1971 p. 234

44 G P Baker and P M S Hacker *Scepticism, Rules and Language* Oxford: Blackwell, 1984 pp. 71-75.

45 PFL Vol 12 p. 268:

At the head of these satisfactions through phantasy stands the enjoyment of works of art....

People who are receptive to the influence of art cannot set too high a value on it as a source of pleasure and consolation in life. (pp. 268-9)

And, for Freud, they were right so to do, for art can both please and (intellectually) challenge; thus it is well-suited to contribute to the development of morality freed from anxiety (W p. 222). In another place (PFL Vol 14 p. 254), he notes that :

Some writers on aesthetics have discovered that this state of intellectual bewilderment is a necessary condition when a work of art is to achieve its greatest effects. It would only be with the greatest reluctance that I could bring myself to believe in any such necessity.

But that was earlier, before he had thought much about the nature of civilisation, or of humans as instinctually aggressive.

Chapter 23

Creativity Constellation for Innovation and Cooperation*

Robert C. Muller

The paper explores the creative thinking process and throws a light on creativity enhancement. From the perspective of possible creativity enhancement both the characteristics of creativity and the creative thinking process are discussed, together with an analysis of the process and its common factors. Constraints on innovation (as a special type of creativity), innovation management and the acceptance of change are discussed; creativity between cooperating individuals is also examined. Some possible computer-based tools to enhance creativity, including innovation, are discussed. A framework of facilities to help promote and support the use of creativity enhancement techniques and tools (SOLI) is proposed. The paper is the result of a study undertaken by the author into creativity, innovation and cooperation.

Introduction

> "He [man] has what no other animal posses, a jigsaw of faculties which alone, over three thousand million years life, make him creative. Every animal leaves traces of what it was; man alone leaves traces of what he created."
>
> J. Bronowski

One of the most challenging, far reaching and greatest attributes of the human mind which, despite a multitude of published literature, remains a contentious black hole attracting more and more of our thoughts, often having nowhere to go; most of us either think we hold the key to the mystery of creativity or can reveal to all that there is no mystery at all. It is my intention to stimulate discussion, particularly on how creativity can be enhanced in individuals and groups of people - and therefore enhance fruitful cooperation, collaboration and sharing - by exploring the creative process.

What motivated me to undertake the study and produce this paper? First, we cannot think of any more important issues facing organisations than creativity, innovation, and cooperation, (the 'scope trinity'). N.B. 'Cooperation' includes sharing and collaboration.

Second, people - whether operating at any time in an organisation or as individuals - continue to miss opportunities through a lack of excellence in the 'scope trinity'; indeed, in one sense the whole paper explores how creativity may enable individuals and organisations to grasp opportunities unselfishly and make a success of them.

Third, every individual has the capability of being creative, yet in most jobs this capability is stifled. There is a percieved need for phased programmes targeting all people in organisations, from top managers to individual workers, to enhance their 'scope trinity', with the help of the appropriate people, focused techniques and tools (including but not restricted to, computers and allied information technology facilities).

Fourth, there is a huge untapped creativity of people outside the workforce in any country, and techniques and tools in local communities could enable people to tap their own creativity - for their own satisfaction and enrichment.

Fifth, particularly in top management, we find an inbuilt caution to invest the amount of time and energy in the necessary innovation and organisational change needed for the healthy future - medium and long term - of the organisation. The situation, particularly in Small to Medium Enterprises (SMEs), is largely due to the organisational culture of senior and top level managers including, a disproportionate time and energy spent on 'protecting their backs' from takeovers and competing managers in the organisation, who have or can wield short term and medium term influence.

Finally, creativity is set to become one of the most important, and potent, focus in the future of work and the community.

Creativity has been my interest and practice for many years. My professional background has been primarily in computing and most of my working expertise has been in dealing creatively with people and concepts. My experience as a computer and management consultant has included work in creativity, innovation, and cooperation.

My current area of interest, 'innovative transfer', led me to undertake a study into creativity, innovation and cooperation, and this paper presents the results of the study.

Outside industry I interviewed many highly creative people who shared with me their creative thinking process, their own techniques and tools. I consider that their methods of working would be of considerable interest to others in their fields and to a wider group of 'creators' (including those in industry).

The Study On Creativity: innovating with creative people

> "What a piece of work is a man! How noble in reason! how infinite in faculty! in form, in moving, how express and admirable! in action how like an angel! in apprehension how like a god! the beauty of the world."
>
> William Shakespeare

During the study I interviewed a cross-section of people on their own creative processes and then checked interim conclusions, primarily by reviewing a small number of publications.

The aim of the study was to draw up findings and propose the means for enhancing creativity, primarily by using computer-based tools. As the study progressed it was decided to draw out innovation due to its importance in meeting the aims. It was during the drafting of the study report, which is fundamentally this paper, that it was realised that a further essence of the study was enhancing cooperation. Thus, the study became creativity, innovation and cooperation enhancement. An interim report on the study was presented at the symposium, 'AI, Reasoning & Creativity' held in August 1991 in Australia

Interviewees and literature were chosen to examine a wide range of creativity, including: problem solving, management, leadership, law, writing, entrepreneurs, innovators, inventors, law, business consulting, Information Technology, Artificial Intelligence, administration, teaching, training and development, psychology, mathematics, physics, chemistry, journalism, copywriting, charity/voluntary/ house work, the retired, acting, directing, accounting, building, creative arts, graphics, film/video making, humour, music, idea-generation, multi-media technologies, broadcasting, daily life, students and school children, theology, and The Creation. Interviewees of study are shown at the end of the paper.

Most interviews were structured according to a questionnaire prepared in advance and were approximately 90 minutes long. After the initial interviews were completed it was found helpful to draw up: a mini-thesaurus for creativity as some interviewees were deterred by the word 'creativity'; and a draft simple model of the creative thinking process which interviewees could relate to. Both these devices proved invaluable; the mini-thesaurus remained unchanged, while the simple model developed as interviews proceeded.

From approximately 100 interviews, most of which were recorded, there emerged a great deal of personal techniques and ideas for tools for creative work. In the confines of the study it has been possible to analyse a small amount.

Once this paper was drafted it was sent to all interviewees welcoming comments from them. The replies received were most helpful and there was time to use some of them.

As befits the subject of creativity, the whole paper is unconventional. In parts it reports specific findings and conclusions but, throughout the paper, poses explicit and implicit questions, leaving many issues purposely open for readers to take further.

Quotations are used extensively. These have been selected by the author from the sayings of famous people and, to a lesser extent, from interviewees. The quotation approach is used as a creative device to stimulate readers to find their own interpretations of creativity. Finally, it has enabled me to add my own personal perspective.

Figures in the paper are hand drawn by me to stress their informal, soft, and tentative contributions to a highly subjective and personal area of human endeavour.

Pattern-Making From Words

> "I feel privileged to be a witness to this primeval enactment of the creative process."
>
> Robert Crumb, cartoonist.

Almost all the interviewees have their personal definition, their own views, and their own mental pattern of 'creativity'. I have no intention of falling into the trap of defining creativity. I went in search of inspiration in published definitions. Many of the books consulted volunteered definitions, sometimes in a short sentence, often in many pages.

Definitions of 'innovate' and 'innovation' are also needed. An admittedly bald but neutral, definition is in the Concise Oxford Dictionary: "Bring in novelties (new or unusual thing or occurrence; novel character of something); make changes". Even this bald definition highlights that a key characteristic of innovation - and much creativity - is its implications for *change.*

This study has been an empirical one, with minimal review of publications. Publications to date on creativity are measured in thousands. Definitions of creativity are measured in millions. One of my favourite recent short description of creativity is given by Peat: *"Human creativity involves a free-flowing play of the mind in which new ideas constantly surface and interact with each other. Ideas are like patterns in a kaleidoscope which move and transform until some new pattern swings into perception."*

Even though the study aimed to cover as wide a range of creativity, people and occupations as possible the words Creativity, Creative Thinking and Creative were daunting to most interviewees; so, I did a 'Thesaurus trawl' and created the 'Creative Thesaurus Trawl Box' which I considered to be a best match for the scope of the study; this was sent or discussed before most interviews. It appeared to work well with interviewees to show facets of creativity and overcome the prejudices associated with the word "creativity".

Creative Thesaurus Trawl Box

----------------------*New Different Distinctive Funny [Ha!Ha! & Peculiar]*----------------------

creative inventive original new unique novel singular different fresh prototype aha! non-standard discovery insight empathy sympathy realise irregular individuality precedent bring-out ingenious distinctive influence innovation motivate impress fertile resourceful imaginative regenerate found conceive give-birth ingenious generate launch start-up pioneer recommence transform extraordinary vivid peculiar revolutionary inspiration intuition transform po humour analogy holistic ambiguous play imaging

----------------------------------*Untried Unknown Uncustomary Untested Unfamiliar*-------------

The negative words at the bottom of the Creative Thesaurus Box, for many people, capture the essence of creativity more than the whole set of positive words. Almost every interviewee had their own definition of and views on "creativity".

Funny Ha!Ha! Or Funny Peculiar?

One word that needs explanation is 'Funny' on the top of the Creative Thesaurus Box. "Funny Ha! Ha!" is crucial to understanding creativity. Well executed humour turns concepts on their head to produce a new, unexpected (funny and often insightful) perspective and often does so by dropping some or all constraints existing before the creation (particularly a joke punchline) is produced. Contraint dropping has been discussed most effectively in a scientific or mathematical discovery context by Boden (1982) in her inaugural address at Sussex University some years ago.

'Funny Peculiar' seems to be another crucial attribute of creativity. Several of the interviewees told of the painful experience of being creative, often their radical creations (whether a business report or a piece of art) being initially rejected, the creators being viewed as peculiar or laughed at behind their backs. Allied to this, some creators may avoid showing their creations to others or they may only show part of their creation to gain some reponse. Some people may hold back from being wholly creative because of their background; the anticipated pain being too much for them. Others will go through the pain or suffering for other reasons.

The influence of background - e.g. experience, knowledge, emotional and psychological experiences gained earlier in life - is discussed in 'The Creative Thinking Process Model' section. People's Funny-Peculiar attributes can give us valuable insights, both to background influence and the pain or suffering from being creative.

The one significant omission from this study on creativity is a detailed look into 'discovery'. For example: how does the creative process in scientific discovery differ from the process in other fields of creativity, and where are the opportunities for it to be enhanced with the help of computer-based tools?

The Creative Thinking Process Model

> "When it comes, will it come without warning just as I'm picking my nose? Will it knock on my door in the morning, or tread in the bus on my toes? Will it come like a change in the weather? Will its greeting be courteous or rough? Will it alter my life altogether? . . ."
>
> W.H.Auden

The study into creativity has led to the development of 'The Creative Thinking Process Model'. Majority of interviewees immediately identified with the features of the model, which helped them in recalling examples of their own creative thinking and in identifying specific stimuli, influences, and conditions in the creative process.

My purpose here was to construct a simple two-dimensional model which could help people to articulate their own creative process and to identify where needs and opportunities for enhancing creativity may exist. N.B. The model does not attempt to describe creativity; a fundamental study of creativity is planned to be researched during the next stage of the study.

However, any simplification of the creative thinking process in an intelligible paper model is bound to lose much of the richness of its subject. Three key features of the creative process are not described explicitly in the model for the sake of simplicity. They include: *problem representaion, parallel thinking;* the (seemingly) *chaotic* element; and the *dynamic iterative* nature of the process. These features together with other key features extrapolated from our own experience and knowledge of creativity should make a potential contribution to creativity enhancement.

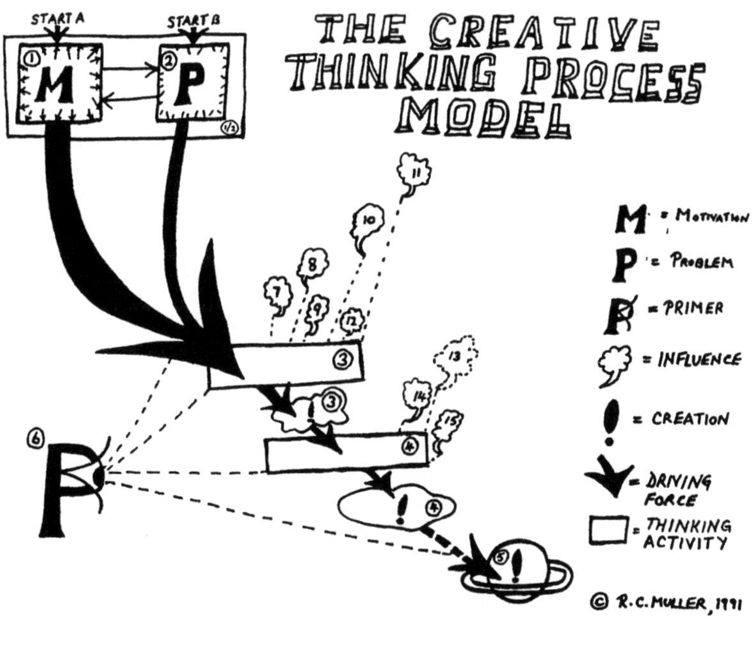

Figure 1. The Creative Thinking Process Model

In this model (Fig 1) all the mental processing occurs within the 'thinking activity' boxes and the increasingly refined mental or physical products of creation are represented by clouds with exclamation marks (representing the 'aha!' or 'eureka!' feeling).

The thought process of a creative 'project' starts either with a creative impulse or *motivation* (1 in the model) to create something (which can be an externally-stimulated motivation, e.g. frustration and a determination to overcome it, or an internally-stimulated motivation, e.g. letting the mind freely wander in a particular mood or subjective state) or with a *thorny problem* (2) to solve. 'Thorny' problems are those which cannot be solved procedurally, one-dimensionally or logically by reasoning alone.

If the start point is motivation then the problem will emerge in trying to realise the aim embodied in the motivation; if the process starts with the problem then motivation must follow for the creative process to continue.

Led by the motivation's *driving force* the creative thinking process (at 3) produces a solution or *creation* (3). There are a number of *influences* (7 onwards) or inputs to the process which, when linked, produce the creation; it is these linkages or associations which are the focus of most computer-based enhancement tool possibilities, with resources including tools, databases and people. Examples of influences include: personal past experience, conversations with other people, observing events (e.g. on TV), personal background, context (e.g. in relation to other problems), and culture.

The process rarely stops there (3). It typically continues and produces further versions or *interim creations* (4), each superseding (ranging from refining to radically changing) the previous creation until the *final creation* (5), which is usually the one on which a decision or action is taken, is produced. At each 'version' of the creation further influences may be brought to bear on the process and further links or associations are made. In some cases, notably for writers of fiction, there are two primary versions, or stages: the first so-called 'inspirational' stage, where the ideas (e.g. key themes of a novel) are created; the second stage, often described by writers as 'crafting' rather than 'creating', (e.g. writing the novel) where the final creation is produced.

There are many permutations, which is not surprising as the creative process is a highly *personal process*. If and how can we enhance a person's creative process? Interviewees' supplied a range of answers to the question on how does the creator know when to stop and bring the creative process to a *successful conclusion* (at 5), possibly becoming an influence in other projects. This is an ability (skill?) which some people have and others lack. Success depends heavily on the correct setting, retention and correct modification in the creator's mind of the project's *constraints* (e.g. timescale, resources, aims, politics etc.).

Other, more minor, items are not shown in the simple model. For instance, when the final creation (5) is reached the creator often finds that (s)he has solved a number of other problems than the main one(2). This is suspicious, as the solution of these sub-problems could be interpreted as the sub-problems helping to justify the final solution! However, it is worth noting.

The final item shown in the model is one of the most interesting findings in the context of enhancing creativity. Once the problem is identified and the driving force is in operation the mind appears to be *primed"*(6) to watch out for or be triggered by anything that could be conceived as a possible link. This feature, arguably above all others, appears to be crucial for creativity and its enhancement. I shall return to this pivotal finding throughout the paper. In the meantime, one of the study's interviewees, Tony Durham, contributed the following searching questions after reviewing the draft of this paper, on the concepts of priming and the primer. Is the primer an external influence, a mental process, a mental state? Is there a special mental state in which the mind searches for analogies and associations and what is the evidence for this? Are there contrary mental states in which the mind is insensitive to analogies and associations? Is this in some way crucial to creativity, and how? Are there times when priming is lost and the creative process stalls? Are there times when you would like to find a link but cannot?

Influences

> "Lucky is he who has been able to understand the causes of things."
> Virgil

Once the mind is suitably primed, potentially relevant influences on any active thinking project (including, but not restricted to creative ones) can be accepted from any conceivable source so that linking of influences can be explored and productive ones made. It is an area of considerable uncertainty and interviewee, George Cochrane, commented that in some cases: "You bring together the pieces and have the feeling that you've got somewhere but find you've got nowhere."

In an individual person's life there have been a multitude of activities, tasks and creative projects, the memory (knowledge) of which can influence the current 'thinking' project. A project, of course, may not have started as a 'creative' one. Usually there are several thinking projects active at any instant, giving opportunities for cross fertilisation. Stand two people side by side with the same given creative projects and one will (at least appear to) be more opportunistic than the other, even though they may both have comparable opportunities. Is this due to the personal influences already owned by each individual - or to the individual's acquired capabilities? Capabilities come from a huge number of sources, proving that creativity is at the heart of every individual's personal, leisure and working lives.

Influences can have a positive (encouraging) or negative (inhibiting) influence on the creative process. A few positive examples shown in the model are: the creator's own knowledge bank (7 in the model); *personal experience* (8) (or patterns of the past) including, but not only, previous successes and failures relevant to the project; received *intellectual, and sensory (all senses) stimulation* (9), e.g. from a book, image on TV, theatre or film visit, discussing the project with other people, overhearing an unrelated conversation. Often these relate to the project by analogy.

Another influence of interest is *'ntentional* (14), where the creator must be aware of and sometimes brings to bear external facts, features, concepts, events etc. on the project in order to strengthen or embellish the result. Satire is a well known example which uses this influence, but we have a wonderful annotated illustration of the intentional influence in *The Annotated Alice* (Lewis Carroll & Martin Gardner). Often, particularly at the later stages of the creative process, the majority of the thinking activity could be more accurately called 'crafting' rather than 'creating' for example the actual writing of some books, where intentional influences are strong. Some intentional influences may not be originally intentional (i.e. unintentional), being brought in 'by accident' like some other influences and links of influences. Two examples are: (1) the puns each of us have produced, many of which have gone unnoticed by us and others, many of which we have been given credit for by others without us noticing them; (2) the intentions, for example in *Hamlet* created by others in addition to Shakespeare's own conscious ones!

In creative thinking we must not overplay intellectual influences at the expense of other psychological, emotional and belief (including spiritual) influences; influences from an individual's early life (part of which is called "background" in this paper) is a powerful example. At the risk of being accused of folk psychology the author singles out a number of findings in this group of influences.

A few interviewees inferred that their creative projects were an excuse for play, particularly at the early creative stages (1,2,3 in the model); the fact that usually they were attempting to solve a real-world problem or to work on a creative project provided sufficient disguise for them to play - with concepts (and sometimes materials) - for their own satisfaction. There is a high correlation between highly creative interviewees and those who could not distinguish between work and leisure when asked for examples of creative thinking from each; they tended to say that they loved their work and always looked forward to Monday mornings. Winnicott (1971) observes "that in playing, and perhaps only in playing, the child or adult is free to be creative". In play and personal acceptance of play could we hold the key to the creative and absorbed person - and therefore the development or enhancement of other (inhibited, less creative or uncreative) people's creativity?

Early life, is a central influence on an individual's capacity to live creatively and to find life worth living. This study's interviews bore this out. Many of the interviewees described, unsolicited, their own childhood and adolescent experiences as an influence on their creative thinking; often these influences are active from the starting motivation (1) of a creative project onwards. Two illuminating cases illustrate the huge differences that can exist between people's psychological *background influences* (10, 11, and 13).

The first case shows an *early background influence* (10). Hughes has written about a forty-two year old man he counselled "who was frantically working himself into exhaustion and it was found that during childhood this man's father repeatedly told him: 'you are not going to amount to anything'. Every time his father lost his temper, he would repeat this statement to the boy. Thirty years later the man still bore the pain of his father's verbal malpractice and was driven to prove his father wrong." In contrast he writes of another man: "He told me that his father used to hug him every day and say: 'You are so special to me. There is no one in this world who could take your place.' That man grew up with aliveness and optimism in his personality."

The first of these men probably would be influenced always by the need to 'prove himself' in each of his creations. All other things being equal (which, as we are aware already, never are in creative thinking!) would the second of these men, being far less 'driven' than the first, have less potential to be creative?

The second case is of what the study calls *Life-Beam background influence* (11). Several of those interviewed were aware that they approached most, if not all, their creative projects under the influence of an overriding aim, mission, cause or interest of their life. Interviewee, David Grubb, was the only one to express this explicitly, calling the influence a 'life-beam'.

There is a great deal more to examine for influences on creativity in the areas of psychology and emotions. Winnicott stresses the great importance of the creative impulse in the contrasted alternatives of living creatively or uncreatively. Interviewees volunteered instances, showing the great power emotion has in the creative process.

When a creator is working on a project (s)he may have other existing or potential projects which could benefit if the current project is executed in a specific way. An example would be for the creator to conceive a more generic creation than is needed for the current project so that it could be re-used for other projects. This influence is called in this study a *Meta-Beambackground influence* (13).

Other background influences cover a wide range of inhibiters, such as "I've always done it that way", and encouragers, such as "I wonder what happens if I try this?". They are generally associated with personal experience, patterns brought forward from the past, upon which the creator has to build the current project; if they are inhibitors anything a computer can do to break the pattern, by creating a new pattern, could lead to a major creativity enhancement.

There is one further influence to highlight, which I have already touched on when asking how the creator knows when to stop creating - or stabilise the patterns. This, the *evaluation and success* influence, is unmarked on the model as it operates, when healthy, at each stage of a successful creation. It includes specific constraints imposed, but also it can be viewed as the creator questioning (both explicitly and tacitly) the feasibility, practicality, and (if it is intended to be so) the success of the creation as it is being conceived. Some creators are good at tapping this influence (wherever its sources); some are weak at it or even do not realise its necessity. This is related to the primer (6) role and could even be considered as part of the priming. Can computer tools be used to enhance the chances of the success of a creation?

Creative Constellations

> "There is, it seems to us, at best, only a limited value in the knowledge derived from experience. The knowledge imposes a pattern, and falsifies, for the pattern is new in every moment and every moment is a new and shocking valuation of all we have been."
>
> T.S.Eliot

Many common factors, or strands, of creative thinking emerged from interviews and from the analysis of types of influences in the creative thinking model.

The common factors were grouped into 'creative constellations', It was found to be productive, particularly when examining factors for computer tools, to group them functionally in this way. Provisional overlapping of constellations is also shown in figure 2 (n.b. overlaps other than those shown would need a three-dimensional representation and are not indicated for the sake of simplicity).

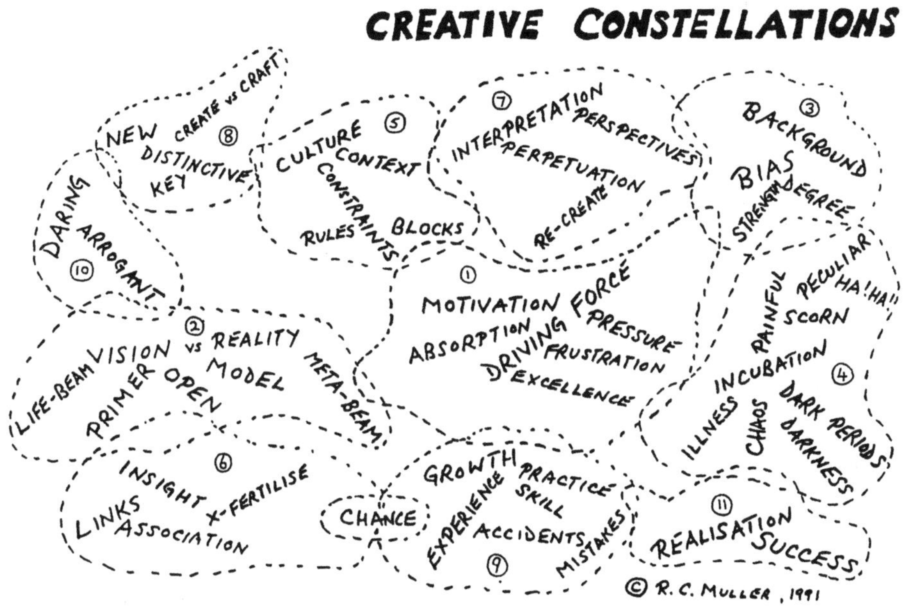

Figure 2. Creative Constellations

The first stage provisional constellations could be represented in a different way to promote other creativity enhancement techniques and tools than the constellation groupings. One option offered by an interviewee after reading the draft paper would be to organise the identified factors into a hierarchy, thus:

- Promoters
    - creative impulse
        - motivation
        - pressure
        - excellence
        - etc.
    - etc.
- Constraints
    - personal
        - inherent
            - bias
            - etc.
        - acquired
            - practice
            - skill
            - etc,
    - etc.
- etc.

I have tried to capture the essence of each constellation through selected quotations, supplemented by a few observations. A couple of the quotations have been selected also to highlight the power of creativity both for good and evil; more than one interviewee highlighted that creative skills can be focused on trivial, worthless, and positively antisocial activities. Also, what is constructive to one creator can be destructive to another creator. Can we find techniques or tools to help self-control avoid the destructive uses of time and give priority to constructive impulses?

Constellation (1): Motivation, Driving Force, Pressure, Frustration, Excellence, Absorption

"You know it's one of the most serious things that can possibly happen to one in a battle - to get one's head cut off." Lewis Carroll

"My dear Tristan, to be an artist at all is like living in Switzerland during a world war" Tom Stoppard

Most creators strive for excellence (in their own eyes), which feeds on itself, or for satisfaction. Unsurprisingly, almost all creators, Shakespeare and Mozart included, produce their best work under the influence of pressure or frustration - and, of course, under the influence of mammon, Wagner and Mozart included. Can we help to invoke or to simulate these influences, particularly pressure, in order to enhance the productivity of creativity. How can we enhance creativity through motivation generation tools? How can we enhance motivation through creativity enhancement tools?

Constellation (2): Vision Vs Reality, Model, Primer, Open, Life-Beam, Meta-Beam

"If a man will begin with certainties, he shall end in doubts; but if he will be content to begin with doubts, he shall end in certainties." Francis Bacon

"This is Minnie B annister, the world-famous poker player - give her a good poker and she'll play any tune you like." Spike Milligan

It seems that many creators (consciously or not) are primed to work on fulfilling or realising a vision, model or life-beam mission. Most creators are primed, on occasions if not at all times, to juggle with more than one creative project simultaneously. All creators become primed in its widest sense, i.e. become open and receptive to any potentially 'productive' (for the intellectual task in hand) influence or stimulus. Can we develop tools to effect, enhance or direct priming? If we can, we may have the key to great capabilitiy stretching abilities with far-reaching implications, and not only for creativity enhancement. Can we even induce the circumstances for pressure? (I am not suggesting that pressure ignites ad hoc creativity. Crises do not create the requisite traits of character: they test and reveal them.)

Constellation (3): Background, Bias, Degree, Strength

"One half of the world cannot understand the pleasures of the other." Jane Austen

"Certainly the growth of the fore-brain has been a success." W.H. Auden

Background influences can be creativity encouragers and inhibitors. The presence of bias, for example whether an individual is particulary good or bad at handling images or words, implies that most people have strengths and weaknesses in specific intellectual and other areas. The degrees to which people have specific intellectual, emotional, and sensory strengths vary greatly; these accumulate to give the sum total impact brought to bear on the creative process. To what extent can these influences be controlled, to the benefit - and, equally importantly, not to their detriment - of individuals and their creativity, with the help of techniques and tools?

Constellation (4): Incubation, Funny-Ha! Ha!, Funny-Peculiar, Painful, Chaos, Darkness, Dark Periods, Illness

"A dissipative structure is a special kind of system which exists far from equilibrium. It does not remain in a balanced state, but 'wobbles', recovering from each fluctuation by an in-built damping down process."
Mark Kidel

"E: But you can see through it. S: Not if you close your eyes."
Spike Milligan

"One of the greatest pains to human nature is the pain of a new idea."
Walter Bagehot

The quotation from Kidel's paper draws attention to the creative *results* of this constellation. As with creativity's incubation, the outcome after an individual's dark periods can be not only just relief but also renewed (sometimes enhanced) creativity. It is a particularly good description of the body politic too, brilliantly applied to current creative events in Eastern Europe. Is it possible to enhance creativity: (a) during dark periods; and (b) by simulating these influences? Is this answered by techniques founded on today's psychology approaches and psychiatry 'treatment'? These are the most challenging questions of the study. As to humour, we could learn a lot by studying the juxtaposition of ideas in the Goon Show scripts of Spike Milligan.

Constellation (5): Constraints, Culture, Context, Blocks, Rules

"I don't mind where people make love, so long as they don't do it in the street and frighten the horses."
Lillian Baylis

"And what my father used to say Is good enough for me."
A.P.Herbert

"Creativity is opting for the <u>second</u> thing that comes to mind."
Peter Sell

Most are creativity inhibitors. Can we build tools to inhibit the inhibitors?

Constellation (6): Links, Association, Cross-Fertilisation, Insight, Chance

"One can live in the shadow of an idea without grasping it."
Elizabeth Bowen

"A moment's insight is sometimes worth a life's experience."
Oliver Holmes

This constellation of influences is at the core of the creativity universe. It addresses how all influences are brought to bear on a creative project, how they are uniquely linked to produce a new creation. It also raises the questions: "what ingredients (including knowledge in different domains) are needed to produce a recipe for 'insight' and is the number of ingredients or the quantity of each ingredient critical?". Three keywords also spring to mind: ambiguity, flexibility and chance. The first two are needed in the extreme. This constellation is very closely linked to the underlying priming influence of constellation 2. Can tools be developed which present external (to the creator) experience, knowledge, information and data in a variety of forms (which can be used by the senses) to feed the creative process? Can tools be built which unlock internal influences to the creator? Can techniques be used (e,g. for giving the lead to the right hemisphere) in conjunction with tools built to encourage the influences in this constellation to be invoked?

Constellation (7): Perpetuation, Interpretation, Perspectives, Re-Create, Perpetual

"The history of art is the history of revivals." Samuel Butler

"Nothing Goes On Forever." Anonymous

Figure 3. Perpetuation

The re-creation and perpetuation of creations is illustrated by creative 'consumers' of creations. Each consumer will have a personal perspective on a creation; many perspectives will be creative, i.e. produce something new, sometimes surprisingly or shockingly new to the creator. Even an incorrect interpretation, at least in the creator's mind, by a consumer can be creative. To some extent we all re-create the creation, e.g. the world we live in, but specific examples of creative consumers include constructive, as opposed to destructive, critics (of music, theatre, film, books, business reports etc.), who interpret creations, and commentators. (Think of Neville Cardus who speedily crafted new creations, his reviews in *The Manchester Guardian*, from interpretations of other peoples'creations in music and cricket). The original creation or creator can often benefit from obtaining creative feedback from consumers of a creation (e.g. a draft proposal for a new venture). Of course, there is a thin line between recreation and re-cycling, but that is a fundamental problem for creativity in general. What would have been the effect on Shakespeare if he had seen Laurence Olivier's film of *Henry V*, where Olivier is interpreter as actor and re-creator as director? The perpetuation of the creation, the play *Henry V* as written, probably would have continued into Shakespeare's next creation and, possibly, caused him to revise his original creation of *Henry V*. How can we build more tools to enhance an individual's ability to build creatively on another creation - with benefits to the individual and, perhaps, the original creator? How can we make these tools widely available?

Constellation (8): New, Distinctive, Key, Create Vs Craft

"There's nothing new in the world." Anon.

"I never think about the purists. They are a breed that has sprung up recently. "

Thomas Beecham

"A tubby little chap who looked as if he had been poured into his clothes and had forgotten to say 'When'."

P.G.Wodehouse

"The artistic temperament is a disease that afflicts amateurs."

G.K.Chesterton

Are there attributes which we can use to evaluate the results of creativity and creativity enhancement? Psychologists, notably Eysenck, have recently worked in the area of creativity measurement. It strikes me that, if there was a Creativity Quotient (CQ), perhaps we could measure the increase in creativity after enhancing it with creativity enhancement tools. However, probably we would not be measuring the CQ increase of individuals but the CQ of the tools! We are tempted to measure 'newness' or 'distinctiveness' and to draw a thick line between 'create' and 'craft'. After all, does it matter that musicologists, AI scientists and others argue whether much of Mozart's output was 'crafted' rather than 'created'? Could we transfer to other people - with the help of techniques and tools - much of the experience, skills and abilities of any highly creative person which he uses to produce his creations? If so, indeed that would be impressive creativity transfer. Would we need to transfer 'much' to achieve a critical mass of knowledge (in the individual and/or computer) for creativity, or would 'some' provide a productive start? Would we need to establish a knowledge base? Could we help creators to find the key which unlocks the door to their creative project's goal? Also, as one interviewee said: "In which ways can we give people opporunities for creative expression?"

Constellation (9): Growth, Experience, Practice, Skill, Accidents, Mistakes, Chance

"We must never forget that most men only learn wisdom by personal experience"

Dietrich Bonhoeffer

"He occasionally stumbled over the truth, but hastily picked himself up and hurried on as if nothing had happened"

A.J.Balfour

"Many claim that 'Citizen Kane' is simply the greatest film ever made and it's hard to disagree with them. . .it is unquestionably a masterpiece. The innovative use of, among other things, sound, deep-focus photography and a fluidly-moving camera had a profound influence, both on Welles' contempories and on every succeeding generation of film-makers."

Barry Norman

First, combine T.S.Elliot in creative constellation presented earlier with Bonhoeffer here. Then add serendipity to produce the potent mixture of this constellation. Orson Welles' stunning move into film from the theatre, directing and playing the lead role in *Citizen Kane* , provides a case study with general lessons for this creative constellation. The lessons apply equally to constellation 8 and touch on other constellations too, but for clarity's sake we shall group the lessons here.

Citizen Kane, known as the film that broke all the rules and invented some new ones, was not only Welles' first film but also - and most interestingly for us - his best. Arguably, the great innovation value of his creation was his total lack of experience in the medium of film; but this only was the chief among several critical success factors. Welles had acquired, through experience in the theatre and radio, an enviable reputation for creativity and, in my opinion, a great capacity for (some may say, reckless) play and showing off. What was the nature of his expertise? The author believes (with only limited supporting facts) the secret of the film's success was Welles' overriding motivation to prove his prowess, for the first time in an enduring form and to a worldwide audience, coupled with his experience of innovation management. The latter is a critical element in all group creative ventures, particularly in high risk situations, where accidents, mistakes and chance need to be exploited, rather than become setbacks that endanger the venture. Can we build tools to stimulate personal creativity growth and to present a spectrum of accidents or mistakes by chance? Can we help raise an individual's capability by knowledge and experience transfer, which is held by some to be critical for highly productive creativity, without generating 'rules' as inhibitors? One could say that, once Welles had learnt the rules, it was downhill all the way.

Constellation (10): Daring/Arrogant

"An idea that is not dangerous is unworthy of being called an idea."

Oscar Wilde

"Very clever, but his brains go to his head."

Margot Asquith

Our case study in constellation 9 could conclude with a terse summary of Welles and his critical creative characteristics which we might wish to induce: Charming, Reckless Arrogance! But it did not. We could describe him as being driven by a consuming passion. But it did not. The Welles case has some strong messages for the possible induction of this constellation's influences, whether to the degree of being larger than life or not. How can techniques and tools help people take risks in the same way that highly creative people do, daring to be daring and (simulating) enough arrogance to overcome what other people think (at the very least during the early stages of their creative process)?

Constellation (11): Realisation/Success

"I have heard that an Englishman's mind works best when it is already too late."

Helmut Schmidt

"Poor man, he's completely unspoiled by failure."

Noel Coward

"The meek may inherit the earth - but not its mineral rights."

J. Paul Getty

"Open Sesame!" Ali Baba

I have discussed the influence of an individual's capability to evaluate his creation. Most creations are produced, at least in part, for the satisfaction of the creator. A 'successful' creation may, of course, be one that satisfies the creator alone or one that, in its making, provides a valuable learning experience for the creator. Some creators may intend or crave for their creations, including innovations, to be accepted, appreciated, applauded and even bought by others. So, we add the influence of realising the success of a creation, particularly if it is to be brought to market. In successful innovation, some marketing is integral to the creative process from an early stage, whilst not inhibiting free-wheeling creativity. What is the best way of capturing and representing these influences (knowledge? expertise?)?

Influence Groupings & Effect; Techniques And Tools

Leading with the Right Brain

"I do not know whether I was then a man dreaming I was a butterfly, or whether I am now a butterfly dreaming I am a man."

Chuang Tse

Creative people interviewed spoke of 'visualising' their creations, even conceptual ones. This dominant characteristic highlights the hypothesis - and it is still a hypothesis - of the right and left brain functions in the creative process. Betty Edwards, an art teacher who developed teaching techniques that forced students to use the right side of the brain, articulates fundamental functions of the right and left hemisphere of the brain in a refreshingly simple way in her book, *Drawing on the Right Side of the Brain* (1982). The following are selected abstracts from her book, selected for their illumination on creativity enhancement.

Using the right hemisphere, we understand metaphors, we dream, we create new combinations of ideas..... and using the right hemisphere we are able to draw pictures of our perceptions. In the right-hemisphere mode of information processing, we use intuition and have leaps of insight - moments when 'everything seems to fall into place' without figuring things out in a logical order.

"One of the marvelous capabilities of the right brain is imaging: seeing an imaginary picture with your mind's eye. The brain is able to conjure up an image and then 'look' at it, 'seeing' it as if it is 'really there'. The terms for this ability, visualising and imaging, are used almost interchangeably."

Edwards includes an astute quote from Levy: "The left hemisphere analyzes over time, whereas the right hemisphere synthesizes over space". Her observation on altering the subjective state of an individual where the right hemisphere 'leads' is telling: "The characteristics of this subjective state are those that artists speak of: a sense of close 'connection' with the work, a sense of timelessness, difficulty in using words or understanding spoken words, a feeling of confidence and a lack of anxiety, a sense of close attention to shapes and forms that remain nameless."

Many people stress the importance of a further factor: the *physical* (spatial) element in human problem solving; i.e. a person's interaction with the world. Some critics assert that the fact that artificial intelligence only handles symbols severely limits its use. Its relevance to creativity enhancement needs to be examined.

Are highly creative people particularly skilled (consciously or unconsciously) at getting their right hemisphere to lead?

Enhancing The Pleasure Of Creators

"Art is not a handicraft, it is the transmission of feeling the artist has experienced."

Leo Tolstoy

One characteristic of creativity which provides a clue to tools for enhancement is that good creations are provided primarily for the creator's own satisfaction.

The fact that good creations are produced for the creator's own satisfaction indicates that tools which enhance creativity, particularly if they help to raise the quality or excellence of its results, help to build a spiral of greater creativity over time. It is also an encouraging sign for the feasibility of re-creating motivation with the help of creativity enhancing tools in de-motivated people and those with low motivation.

Knowledge, Information & The Computer

"If this book helps only one designer get only one original idea,
then all the months I spent putting it together will not have worth it."

Bob Gill (Frontispiece)

In the words of interviewee, Nick Willard: "Some decisions are like the sparks of a car's engine that only have use in the cumulative form but others are like major surges that change the direction or velocity. I suggest to people that decisions are fuelled by information and ignited by knowledge. Information here is recorded information in its various forms. knowledge is the human element", part of which may be recorded in computers, "the combination of memorised information and an understanding of the 'rules' that govern the interpretation of the information and data."

"Where do you keep the books you don't stock?"

The Book Shop, Bicester

This is a good place to outline the capabilities of today's computer to use knowledge held in computers in the interpretation, focusing and filtering of other knowledge, information and data. We live in exciting times for the application of computers and communications (networks) to link them. I believe that the lens is a powerful metaphor which shows the use of knowledge ('inside' the lens).

The figure (Fig.3a) below was inspired by interviewee, George Cochrane, commenting that we lacked a dynamic perspective of the creative constellations and the creation. It shows symbolically the role of each creative constellation in the creative mind. There are two 'lenses' which focus and filter. The lens on the left handles the problem (or whatever is to be the scope of the creative thinking process) and primes the (unconscious?) mind. The lens on the right handles the 'input', mostly information in its various forms. In the centre is the growing creation, on which act the processing constellations using the information focused and filtered by the lens' constellations.

There is some feedback between the two lenses; for example, as time progresses the cumulative affect of the input and the creation may cause the priming to be changed. Many good creators check this aberration by checking back with their terms of reference; many other creators welcome such a creative U-turn! Perhaps many creators decide (unconsciously) to stop when the latest state of the creation equals the latest primer.

In essence the creative constellations can be split into two groups as shown in the figure below. The first group focuses and filters the problem and/or the input (e.g. reading) and those that process (e.g. a technique to improve innovation management). The whole is a highly dynamic process and which, for simplicity's sake, the figure may appear otherwise, has both divergent and convergent elements.

Note that, like the creative thinking model, this figure does not attempt to describe creativity. It is intended to clarify how creative constellations operate to help identify where needs and opportunities for enhancing creativities exist.

1. Motivation: driving force +frustration+prssure+excellence+absorption
2. Primer+open+model+life-beam+meta-beam+vision+reality
3. Background+bias+strength+degree
4. Painful+peculiar+ha!ha!+scorn+illness+dark periods+darkness+chaos
5. Culture+context+constraints+rules+blocks
6. Association+links+insight+cross-fertilise+chance
7. Perpetuation+re-create+perspectives+interpretation
8. New+key+distinctive+create vs craft
9. Experience+growth+skill+practice+mistakes+chance
10. Daring+arrogance
11. Realisation+success

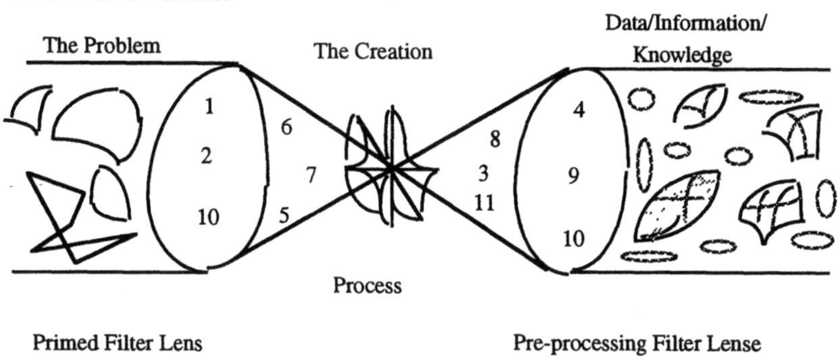

Figure 4. Dynamic Lenses

Techniques & Tools For Creativity Enhancement

> "We know that creativity happens. We can describe it and even attempt to extract some features which seem to recur. All this is very weak. Now, for the first time, we can understand the 'logic' of creativity. The logic arises directly from the asymmetric patterns that inevitably form in a self-organising system. So from the self-organising model we can go directly to understanding creativity in a way which was never possible before."
>
> Edward de Bono

"Creativity is just the envy of other people."
Marvin Minsky

Techniques - including guidance devices and tips - which can be used for enhancing creativity and innovation have many sources, Techniques which can be used for inducing creativity, which are often indistinguishable from those for enhancement, also have many sources. One rich source is the books of Edward de Bono (1987,90,91), who has focused on his 'lateral thinking' ("cutting across patterns instead of moving up and down") techniques. Probably his best known technique is the 'six thinking hats', where the thinker conceptually wears each of six hats in turn and each time considers the situation or problem in a new purposefully different and artificial context, taking steps to change the context, rather than passively waiting for the change.

However, even de Bono's rich set of techniques have not reached or influenced people in industry including senior and top managers, as well as a multitude of potentially very creative people. Some have not read his books; some have remained unchanged by his books.

There has been a gap between writings on creativity and their impact on innovation in industry. Some writers and consultants suggest that the individuals in industry remain uninfluenced by those who offer techniques for inducing or enhancing creativity and innovation and resist the influence. They assert that these people fear the personal consequences of change, they fear the personal threat from creative or innovative people (of whom they are suspicious). Those outside industry may not see the relevance of creativity techniques to them or be unaware of their existence (the techniques, that is!). Presentation of many techniques is unsuitable for many potential users. Accessibility to the range of valuable existing techniques is difficult.

During the study a surprisingly large number of applications were raised by the interviewees; from considering interviews findings, from analysing implications of interviews; triggered by reviewing books; conceived by linking various sources of ideas and needs. As the array of potential computer tools are reviewed in the future, the traps of being technology-led or stretching the technologies too far (except in research) lie in wait. We need to be aware of the dangers to avoid promoting or building computer tools which fail, especially where an existing technique is sufficient. There lies wasted effort and damaged expectations.

Computer Based Creativity Enhancement Tools

The following is a small sample of potential computer-based creativity enhancement tools, sometimes fanciful to stimulate, is given for each of the eleven 'creative constellations'.

Creative Constellation 1

Excellence appears to be a huge motivator for many people. For instance, sitting at a high quality commercial computer-based artist tool, such as Quantel's 'Paintbox', through which the creator - whether artist or not - can produce an excellent visual creation on video or print is an amplifier or liberator of creativity. By this means, rather similar to a very good music synthesiser, huge enhancements can be made by releasing creative capabilities which have remained latent due to a lack of specific skills which were needed up to the time of the new tool becoming available and accessible.

Creative Constellation 2

Given that the computer can be primed (e.g. by using 'demons') in a similar manner to the human mind then it could, via a Knowledge Based System (KBS), filter information and knowledge to bring (possible) relevant ideas to the creator's attention.

This concept elevates the currently fashionable topic of Information Resources Management (IRM) to 'Intelligent' Information Resources Management.

Creative Constellation 3

Bookbanks, Imagebanks, Clipbanks, Videobanks. All these are on CD-ROM (Compact Disk - Read Only Memory), which is revolutionising Information (Knowledge) Resources Management and mass market services. An example used in a networking context would be a 'Smart' Image Bank which could be used to find suitable images, e.g. to illustrate or animate textual information. This example would be particularly valuable as a 'Bias Compensator' for use by people who have a weak visual bias. Imagination is such a potent ingredient of creativity, that its explicit representation could detract from the creative process, for example explicit images of Virtual Valerie, a pornographic item in current CD-ROMs catalogues. Some people's blind spot is numbers and a vital computer tool is graphically representing numbers. People can grasp patterns more easily from pictures (e.g. 3D contouring) than spreadsheets. Tools employing this approach could enhance understanding and creativity in handling numbers.

Creative Constellation 4

Uses of computers as creativity tools perhaps could help de-motivated people or those with low motivation. Creative sessions with the computer could be 'Motivation Re-charging' periods. Some of the early life influences, play and creative impulses which were discussed alongside the creative thinking process model, are crucial considerations here. I may add the fact that many demotivated people, notably amongst the long-term unemployed, have serious social or educational problems (e.g. illiteracy) which also may be helped using computer-based tools.

Any possible hope of success in this area depends on how open to trying new ideas people are and on whether the potential creator can be enticed to use the computer. Tools which could help here include easy to use creativity encouragers (e.g. drawing tools). Once started, the de-motivated person could become creator, which should lead to enhanced motivation.

Creative Constellation 5

Computers can help to clear blocks or other constraints. For instance, people are prepared to "stick their neck out" and attempt to create something by themselves in front of a computer, whereas they are mostly inhibited in front of others or in a shared or 'classroom' environment. Chris Evans (1979) showed in the 1960s that most patients in his experiments were happier being questioned by a computer than by a doctor!

Creative Constellation 6

Computer-activated audio could be used to stimulate assocation. A rather fanciful example may serve to trigger better ideas in reader's minds. Many people are highly creative when attending conferences; they are remote from their day-to-day activities and worries; they can (consciously and unconsciously) work and play with meta views of their projects (for instance, by only half-listening to presentations, the other half of the mind creating and playing with ideas). When reading information on their computer displays at their desk, could specific audio cues be used dynamically at suitable points (e.g. automatic playing of a conference atmosphere, with lots of people talking, gavel, etc) to 'kick-start', by association, individuals into creative mode?

Creative Constellation 7

Virtual Reality (VR), an advance in HCI that produces dynamic three-dimensional images on computer displays and special headsets with integral displays. It gives the user the impression that (s)he is 'immersed' in the environment represented by the computer. Combined with other IT techniques, VR could be used by multi-disciplinary groups to explore possible avenues, in a 'what-if' way, for a number of domains, including scientific and medical modelling. After processing the paths taken in explorations rules could emerge and, with the help of genetic algorithms, 'good', and creative solutions should evolve.

Creative Constellation 8

Using the computer as a mediator for creative work, particularly involving more than one person, will create something new or different as a by-product. It probably will change people's way of working and behaviour, e.g. in the field of Computer Support for Cooperative Working (CSCW), if people want a private conversation with their partners in a negotiating situation they will cover up their microphones (whereas conventionally we wouldn't expect people to turn their backs in the middle of conversation without asking for private consultation). This small example highlights the need for computer tools to be designed so they ensure that groups using CSCW are at least as creative as groups working together physically face-to-face.

Creative Constellation 9

The slogan 'Practice makes perfect' suits the growth of a creative person, especially in developing skills to exploit accidents, mistakes and results of chance linkages. Skilled creators know what *not* to throw away. They have the confidence and skill to Explore & Discover associations with large data, information, and knowledge bases with the help of 'intelligent' navigation tools. Less skilled creators could benefit from computer-mediated associations or linkages, for the project and for the creator's personal development.

Creative Constellation 10

Large numbers of creative people have the lethal combination of daring and arrogance. But how about enabling other people to be daring with pleasure? Or, how about providing facilities for people to be creative in ways previously beyond their reach? Much of the literature reviewed so far in the study show that these issues have been considered and techniques developed, notably by Edward de Bono. But how could computer-based tools help? For instance, creativity enabling tools could help to realise latent creativity in physically handicapped and mentally handicapped people, and, even help some people who are mentally ill, by releasing their creativity. "Imagine the pleasure given to a handicapped person to be able to express himself through a computer that can interpret a few instructions and generate the remainder", David Smith, one of the interviewees, commented.

Creative Constellation 11

An expert system could be developed to help encapsulate some of the expertise in evaluation and success management of successful creative people. Such a tool could be used by creators who do not have strengths in realising a creation or in achieving a successful, perhaps marketed, innovation.

The Universe of Constellations

There is one more example of enhancement tools. This is a family of tools spanning the universe of creative constellations. These 'Creative Management & Administration' tools currently and potentially release the creator from the time-consuming and frustration-generating obstacle course of management and administrative tasks, therefore increasing creative productivity.

There are many administrative and accounting tools already in existence, but their widespread use in contributing to creativity enhancement is barred by deficiencies in ease of use and lingering resistance to computers, the latter being largely due to the lack of awareness and appreciation by most people of how computers can be used, today, as tools to help in areas of interest to them, including creativity enhancement.

Another example could be a tracking tool for tracking ideas, creation version control and reference back to the original problem for each of the creative projects which a creator is juggling with at any one time. Apart from providing 'Creative Juggling Support' this tool would avoid the 'Chinese Whisper' syndrome: by the time many creators have reached an advanced stage of their creative projects they are so absorbed in the creative exercise (the means) that they have lost sight of the original problem (the end).

The final class of tools we shall highlight could help each individual to "know thyself" before exploring capability enhancement tools. This class could take the form of a computer-driven questionnaire to ascertain such personal profiles as learning styles and group working role. In the short term these tools would enable individuals to identify areas which they want to improve (pointing to techniques available to help) and a path to follow if they want to become more all-rounders. In the long term each profile could be held in the computer so that creativity enhancement tools as used are tailored ('user modelling') to the person for optimum ease of use and acceptability in use.

Soli, An Environment To Support The Creative Process

"And always keep a hold of nurse for fear of finding something worse."
Hilaire Belloc

The nineties have been dubbed as the decade of the all-purpose Decision Support System (DSS) on every desk. The next decade could herald what I would like to dubb as the all-purpose Creative Support System (CSS) 'on every desk'. A fast growing appreciation exists in all countries of the need for: focused creativity, innovation and their management at work; and opportunities for creative leisure. A flexible framework is needed to help creative thinking and to realise creativity's full potential through cooperation and collaboration. SOLI, "Solo Or Limitless Innovation", is intended to be a such a framework.

The SOLI framework has three main purposes in the realm of creativity :

[1] Help individuals to be more creative, acting singly and in groups;
[2] Enable innovation from individual, team, and cooperative creative effort;
[3] Encourage cooperation and collaboration.

The major problems and issues chosen as an example set for SOLI are shown in branch 1 of the SOLI meta-map (which is in the form of a Buzan-style mind map). Other branches represent the resources that can be brought to bear on these problems in a human-centred way. Orginally I conceived the SOLI environment in 1989 as an entry to a competition, associated with the 1989 Leonardo exhibition at London's Hayward Gallery, looking for a new design as if it was produced by Leonardo da Vinci had he been alive in 1989. My competition entry put forward the hypothesis that Leonardo would be inspired to solve conceptual, rather than engineering, problems in a 1989 world; in other words he would be a professional creative thinking engineer.

The SOLI mind-map, the new age Leonardo's 'drawing', is based on the premise that if Leonardo were to solve problems of today he would be using today's established tools(from computers, networks, and other converging technologies) to help solve the problems and his first step would be to design a framework for doing this. SOLI is an attempt to lay a foundation for enabling cooperation and collaboration within a world of increasingly self-organising, reflecting complexity and chaos.

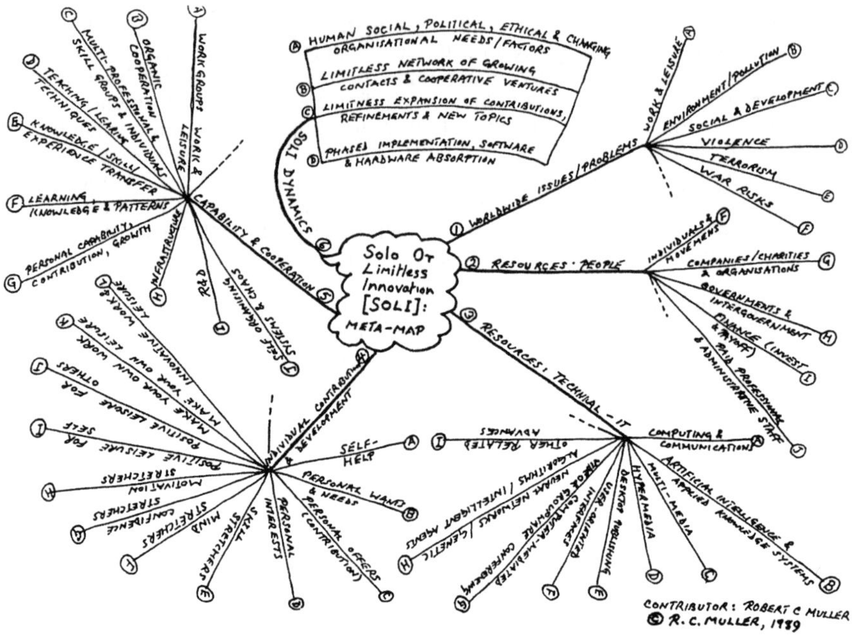

Figure 5. Solo or Limitless Innovation [Soli]: Meta-Map

The mind-map shown is a top level perspective of a framework for a network of individuals, most of whom would be connected via a communications network of personal and corporate computers. Its outline functional specification primarily defines the rules for its operation and use by members of the SOLI network. 'Solo' implies individuals working largely by themselves; 'Limitless' implies people working cooperatively with a limitless number of people through a limitless network. The specially created word, 'Soli', is inspired by music and is intended to convey individual people working with the environment as soloists and as part of the ensemble of individuals in the SOLI network. In other words, SOLI is conceived as a conceptual design for a self-organising innovation machine.

Software Tools Within Soli: A Scenario

> "If you can make the computer accessible it has to be the most powerful tool for enhancing creative ideas available to man."
>
> David Smith

If we move down from the high level conceptual mind-map to more concrete levels of SOLI we reach an integrated set of facilities where specific software tools (including those which can be applied for enhancing creativity) can be accessed so that they combine to produce an organically growing set of tools, many of which will be integrated. Some tools will be mutually dependent, with synergy generated through integration. As all conceptual frameworks, SOLI has many influences. At the network level some models exist, including bulletin boards, computer conferencing, groupware, and the community of Apple Macintosh computer users and software suppliers (with 'shareware'). Clearly, SOLI would need to work within the range of computer environments.

SOLI enables the evolution of facilities in a framework which is based on a range of knowledge and information (accessed on local and remote electronic-bases, together with multiple-copy transportable memories, e.g. CD-ROM). Some primary mechanisms include : HCI, Hypermedia, Groupware, Networking & Global Telecommunications, Database, AI/KBS (including Multiple Agents) , Neural Networks and Genetic Algorithms. Thought-provoking reading incudes: Barr, Brand, Brown, Durham, Engelmore, Feigenbaum & McCorduck & Nii, Forsyth, Hill, Laurel, Michie & Johnston, Nelson, Ovum, Rheingold, Wilson, Winograd & Flores. Also, Dawkins has written a chapter on the application of genetic algorithms.

The environment in which tools are employed to promote and facilitate cooperative practice must be easy to use. We are looking towards developments in Computer Support for Cooperative Work (CSCW) to often non-work-based and non-project-based activities needing Computer Support for Cooperative Creativity (CSCC). Much of CSCC would be of the "what do you think of . ." and "what is your opinion about. . .".

Using existing personal development approaches, supplemented by IT (including applied Artificial Intelligence), communications and other converging technologies, SOLI embraces the concept of stretching people's skills, minds, confidence, and creativity as magnified from the SOLI meta-map shown below (Fig. 5). Techniques and tools to achieve this vision, incorporating self-improvement, would be supported within the SOLI environment.

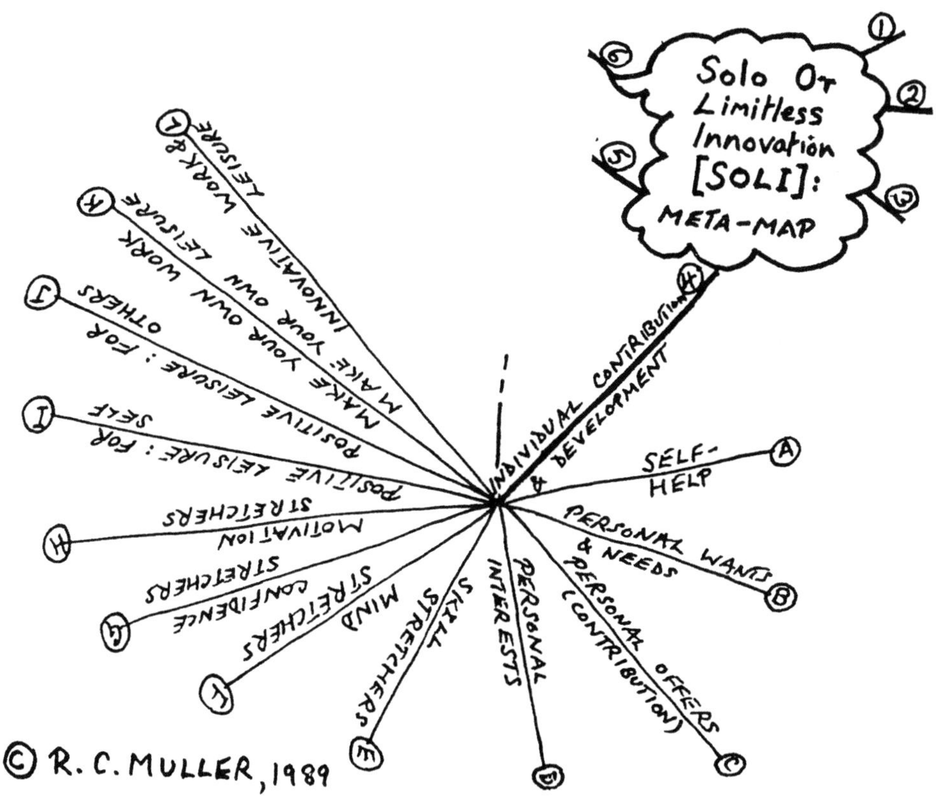

Figure 6. Solo or Limitless Innovation [Soli]: Meta-map

A key element in the model is that the framework and its 'contents' would evolve and be self-organising; it would be impossible to 'engineer' its development. Developments in Groupware, CSCW, and Multimedia Systems suggest that these facilities will find their way to the market and start to be used significantly in the latter half of this decade. SOLI's outline functional specification includes a protocol for use, whereby a user can be a contributor but each contribution is judged in a genetic way (i.e. only if it is productive for a sufficient number of other users is it accepted by the SOLI environment as a global contribution).

Sharing Creativity

"They are ill discoverers that think there is no land, when they can see nothing but sea."

Francis Bacon

Since the early part of the twentieth century there have been innumerable studies into cooperation between individuals, cooperation within and between groups, group dynamics, cooperative solution of problems and groups with competing members (to mention just a few cooperation topics). Sprott's study on social groups has provided a fundamental perpective of SOLI: cooperation of communities, especially small communities. In his classic book on human groups Sprott (1958) shows how the approaches of change agents, notably revolutionaries and reformers - who had thought in terms of 'humanity', the 'workers' and 'the people' - had been overturned through the understanding of the psychology of small groups. Here, the writer of the book's foreword provides unexpected enlightenment for cooperating communities: "the new reformers are more concerned with the power that resides in the small communities of side streets and alleys". That has come full circle with recent changes in Eastern Europe.

Now for the soul searching. How realistic are we in anticipating individuals sharing their creativity? To date in Britain we have a reputation: hiding in academia the latest creations in a locked drawer; in medium to large enterprises (SMEs) wasting opportunities for partnerships because of political manuoeverings of senior and top managers - in small companies, sharing often comes to a poor fraction of time and effort.

If people are becoming less prepared to share without payment - or at least with deferred payment in SOLI's case - things that can be renewed, will they 'share' things which can be exploited by others?

To answer these questions, first, SOLI framework aims to enable a common interest and common ways of communicating. Second, cooperation protocols need to be defined in such a way as to encourage continued sharing. As interviewee, Nick Willard, said *"Each community has its own 'language': semantics, syntax, and classification which would enable community members to communicate, cooperate and share in a SOLI framework today if the framework is established first"*.

Shared Experience

'I am a part of all that I have met;
Yet all experience is an arch wherethro'
Gleams that untravell'd world, whose margin fades
For ever and for ever when I move.'

Alfred, Lord Tennyson

People working, playing and communicating with each other start with a great advantage if they share a relevant common experience. In the area of their shared experience their (level of) assumptions are very similar. They can communicate well with, often far, less information being transmitted between them. This also occurs at the information, as opposed to the experience, level; for instance, like professionals communicate with each other on professional issues in what seems to an outsider to be shared shorthand and jargon-full interactions.

Shared experience of working with each other in a group is part of the preparation process for the most effective group working. For enhanced shared, or group, creativity there would be a significant advantage in being able to acquire shared experience, facilitated by techniques and tools conceived for the purpose of accelerating shared experience. It remains to be seen whether a combination of techniques and computer tools can be researched and developed, perhaps as part of the CSCW tool kit.

Techniques For Problem-Solving

Some well known proven techniques are used to stimulate, direct and enhance creativity; in the management domain they avoid being associated with the 'suspect' word, creativity. These include such techniques as lateral thinking, structured brainstorming, role-playing. They are accompanied by a plethora of advice - again, almost invariably associated for management consumption with anything but 'creativity' ('innovation management', 'change management', 'personal development', 'catalysts' are among the acceptable associations).

An invaluable set of such techniques - adaptations of ideas and practices "found useful in answering the problems presented by a range of solution seekers" - is recorded in a gem of a book on problem solving by Dean Francis Juniper. As Juniper (1989) says in his book the techniques can be personalised: "made the special property of an inventive, new practitioner, and perhaps, by experiment, put to other than the prescribed uses."

The following list of Juniper's techniques indicates the range which could benefit creative thinking. Sorting, Checklists, Ranking & Weighting, Decision Matrices, Algorithms, Prioritising, Sequencing & Terminating (PST), Routines, Intimate Experiential Transfer, Systems-Testing, Problem Limits Technique, Zwicky's Morphological Method, Analogies, Future Scripts, Memory Methods, Twilight Technique, Regressive Thinking, Simberg's Transformation, Two-Way Tabling, Communality Testing Practice, Key Word Searching, Accretion Technique, Interviews, Questionnaires, Scales & Samples, Indices, Brainstorming, Pair-working, Rhythm-Phase and Fragmentation.

Techniques in Juniper's book are in an accessible form. However, most books are not. For instance, Kim's Guide to Tackling Difficult Problems, is a valuable guide that I would recommend, but would need substantial effort to incorporate it for user-friendly access in a techniques compendium (whether on computer or other media).

Industry's Blend Of Creativity & Innovation

I have drawn or inferred some implications of the study's findings and conclusions for business throughout this paper, but some additional negative and positive issues must be raised at this stage to place creativity, innovation and cooperation in the context of business practice.

First, we look at some additional positive issues for the for enhancing creativity in business. This is illustrated through one very lucid response addressed to the author - by interviewee Nick Willard, who specialises in Information Resources Management (IRM) - to the first draft of this paper:

"I think perhaps the best way for me to respond is to discuss your Creative Thinking process Model from a business creativity IRM perpective."

"Does IRM have any relevance?"

If

a. One accepts that managers decisions are at least in part a creative process,

and

b. Decisions as derived come from recorded information and managers' knowledge,

then

c. Better decisions, in the deductive or creative sense, come fom enhancing one or other or both of these components.

IRM is really all about improving the management of an organisation's recorded information so that it can provide better value-for-money information in the pursuit of decisions, including the delivery of it in the most effective form. This is not the place to go into detail of IRM but you could say that it is about the management of the influences in your model."

The use of the word 'understanding' in the context of IRM raises a crucial point, particularly for business. People using a Creative Support System will need to declare in some way their experience and level of assumption so that the interface between them and the computer is tailored to them.

Raudsepp's book, *Managing Creative Scientists and Engineers* (1963) contains outstanding valuable experience and thought on our area of interests of innovation. After all, is it not at the bottom of the economic cycle where the most creative, including innovative, work is needed for the forthcoming upswing? Is it not the supreme business paradox that it is at the bottom of the economic cycle where all the most creative people are jettisoned from dying organisations?

Obstacles To Innovation In Industry

"The past is a foreign country: they do things differently there."
L.P.Hartley

"He that will not apply new remedies must expect new evils; for time is the greatest innovator."
Francis Bacon

Several interviewees expressed their concern about the reluctance of many senior managers in industry - particularly top management - to accept and be prepared to take action on creative solutions, innovation, cooperation, and change.

Unexpectedly, the creative thinking process model proved helpful and the interviewees concurred that top managers who feared change were likely to rely solely on previous successes as their response to new situations without going back to the problem or motivation at the start. They tend to revolve around 5, and possibly 6, in the Creative Process Model (Fig.1); whereas, it was thought, they needed also to start at 1 or 2, giving themselves the opportunity to act on the second (or following) thing that comes to mind and be prepared to take the calculated risks they would have taken when they were younger.

In learning and personal development I am committed to 'experience transfer', particularly in developing and using techniques and tools to achieve long lasting transfer. The challenge is summed up by the quote: "Putting old men's heads on young men's shoulders". In the case of some top and senior managers they have become to learn the "rules" and excel in their use too well. In many cases top managers fear losing face or their jobs more than the medium and long term survival of their organisations. The challenge to help them and their organisations, it seems, can be summed up by a new quote, creatively coined by one of the study's interviewees: "Putting young men's heads on old men's shoulders".

Naturally, many other factors contribute to this problem, including education, culture and context. One revolutionary book, which tackles the predicament of self-centred personal and collective development has the innovative title, Growing Young (Montague, 1981). But these are long term. What achievements can we make to put young men's heads, sometimes, on old men's shoulders in the short and medium term with the help of creativity, innovation and cooperation enhancement facilities (including people. techniques and tools)?

Business's Bad Practice

We may find it productive to examine some negative issues - failures, mistakes and bad practice instruct, often more than good practise. Cooperation and sharing have been explored for now; CSCW within organisations looks set to add value in the future. However, the use of CSCW and SOLI across organisations - each with their own culture - is less certain. This lead us to the question of whether industry is really capable of achieving innovative global collaboration. Most global developments in business appear to the observer to be mergers (which almost invariably means 'acquisition' as one of the organisation's culture swallows up the other).

Theoretically, there should be much room for enhancing innovation in the international business scene. Most unfortunately, the culture of organisations in the West, particularly in Britain and the USA, harbours 'short-termism' and is risk-aversive, i.e. they provide uncomfortable homes for creativity and innovation.

In industry, the culture of the organisation and the cultural mismatches of cooperating and collaborating organisations is of supreme importance for creativity, innovation and cooperation. It therefore comes as no surprise that Britain fairs as badly as, if not worse than the USA. A highly experienced management consultant, Len Saunders, who has specialised in working with Small to Medium Enterprises (SMEs) at chief executive level, says that the great majority of British top managers resist change; they often own the company but mostly place their personal survival much higher than the company's survival. In his experience top management fear the unknown consequences of change, fear the loss of authority, fear loss of respect in the business community or loss of face.

If there is one thing I have learnt from this study it is that each and every one of us is expert at being creative. Without exception each of the people I interviewed were all creative in their own way, and by far the majority of them opened the interview with the statement that they were not creative. With very few exceptions (which were interesting, as we will see), by half way through the interview they were clearly experiencing satisfaction and pleasure talking about their creations; by the end of the interview they were suggesting ways in which their and others' creativity could be enhanced, not always through using computer tools of course.

The exceptions I mentioned earlier as being interesting were all cases where I found it particularly hard to communicate. The 'chemistry' between us wasn't right and, as hard as I tried, the communication lines between the interviewee's mind and mine remained closed. This phenonomen may have been due to many things, including current mood, emotion, language, unshared experiences, culture, 'mind-set'. There may be some relevant issue; but these exceptions showed the rule that human contact and facilitation is vital to help set a person on the track of creativity or innovation enhancement before that person can use computer-based creativity enhancement tools - or even see the relevance of such tools to them.

The key insight I found was the importance of bringing out in people a realisation that they were or could be creative in their work - even if the creative part of their work was a small fraction of the working week.

What of the chances of those who live lives of quiet desperation being given a chance to be creative in mind-shrinking work on the factory floor or in the administration office?

Memories Reactivation & Learning

> "Take hackney'd jokes from Miller, got by rote,
> With just enough of learning to misquote."
>
> Lord Byron

In creative problem solving in business - probably much more than in the arts - we rely on pattern matching with past successful and failed approaches. Our access to and retelling of own 'war stories' can often lead to creative results in the minds of our listeners. One interviewee, George Cochrane, coined the delightful phrase "Memories Reactivation or Reconstruction", which immediately evoked in my mind the possibility of a combination of using the war story technique and a computer-based tool to help, by association, enhance creativity through memories reactivation and reconstruction. Add other people's war stories and memories to produce a superb creativity enhancement tool; the result of adeptly using it is the business edition of a plagiarist, i.e. a first class consultant.

Much risk-taking is a creative act, sometimes highly creative, and it it most important to many creative risk-takers that there is room to fail as well as succeed. This applies in the community just as much as at work, where the recognition of one or more windows of opportunity is often a creative act , and the decision to take the risk is sometimes creative, particularly if the opportunity-taker and risk-taker work in concert to create a better 'creation'.

Highly creative or innovative souls are greedy for opportunities; unless they are managed well or exercise a high degree of self-control they are heading for trouble, which damages them and the organisation for which they work. After all, it is counter-productive for such opportunistic souls to be overwhelmed by attractive opportunities: there lies the way of anti-innovation or manic-depression.

Learning is an integal part of being creative, being innovative, and sharing. It is itself an application of enhanced creativity and innovation. Evans & Russell (1989) provide the foundation for a key conclusion of the study.

> "Today, and in the years to come, we need learning that is relevant to the challenge of the Information Age. First, the speed of change demands that leaning should be continuous and lifelong. And second, there are new, inner skills we need to learn. . . (An) increasing awareness of a new attitude to learning is reflected in a comment from one of the captains of industry interviewed by Francis Kinsman. Speaking of the changes which will come in the 1990's, he emphasised, 'The most serious impact will fall upon those who have given up learning. For them, adopting different attitudes will be a difficult and painful process. In industry this particularly applies to the middle-aged managers.'. . ."

They proceed to discuss the other dimension of learning, self-development, including re-visioning, self-exploration and self-discovery, concluding: *"In short, we are being freed to explore our inner worlds, to develop our thinking and use our minds in a different way. Perhaps this is the real revolution - and the hidden opportunity behind the Information Age."*

A key conclusion of this study for me is that we should be delivering an *integrated* workbench for enhancing creativity, innovation, cooperation, learning, re-visioning, self-exploration, and self-discovery. Not only does this sharing make economic sense but in the long term we may make valuable associations between these activities. I would like to add that the recession of the early 1990s would have: permanently swelled the number of people working on their own and in small groups/networks; raised awareness of people of the need for personal development, in the outer and inner senses; constant re-visioning.

Centres for Creativity & Innovation

> "My father worked for the same firm for twelve years. They fired him. They replaced him with a tiny gadget this big. It does everything my father does, only it does it much better. The depressing thing is my mother ran out and bought one."
>
> *Woody Allen*

My final proposal for the future is the establishment of Creative and Innovation Centres, which would house techniques and tools - including the computer-based creativity workbenches I proposed earlier - to help people enhancce their creativity. The payoff for individuals could be great but the payoff for industry is as great in motivation, productivity and even a rejuvination of loyalty. To lead the way to the 'post-industrial society' I consider that the time is right to establish 'Creation and Innovation Centres', sited in industry or the community, where everyone in work can spend some time (say, each month) enhancing their creativity, innovation and cooperation. These centres would have local or invited people 'on duty' at any one time to help, develop or mentor/coach participant. The centres would also have computing and communications facilities which would give participants access to techniques and tools for enhancing their creativity and innovation.

Such centres need not focus only on creativity and innovation. They could share premises with other industry and community facilities for personal development and counselling. They could be powerful 'Transfer' catalysts to facilitate transfer between participants (including those 'on duty') of skills and experience in: creativity, innovation, cooperation, change, productivity, specific areas of work, etc. Above all, they would provide a 'safe environemnt' for individuals - whether they are chief executive or trainees - to 'play', become children again, make fools of themselves, explore, unlearn, learn and reconstitute their creativity. They could also be designed to encourage individuals to work in groups or cooperatively on their creative 'projects'.

Interviewee Richard Gregory sopke of the 'Explanatory' he founded in Bristol, U.K. Housed in part of Bristol Railway Station built by the great innovator, Brunel, the Explanatory encourages young visitors to explore science 'hands-on' and is highly acclaimed by all its visitors. This was the catalyst that created the concept of Creation and Innovation Centres in my mind, where visitors could explore creativity hands-on. Strictly they ought to be called 'Innovatories' or 'Creativitories', but the temptation to he small-minded to associate with the word 'Lavatories' may be too great to chance calling them such creative names! Creativitorium is similarly too easy to associate with burnt bodies!

Such a concept could be applied to both industry and community centres, either seperate or shared. The Creation and Innovation Centre established for the use of the community could be used in a similar way as the industrial innovation ccentre, but it could also serve the unemployed, ethnic minorities, those who are disabled, those who have become demotivated and those who simply have time on their hands. Participants benefit from the centre, but they could also gain satisfaction form helping others. In fact, the centres could also be called 'Give and Take Centres'.

Conclusion

"Mehr Licht!" "More light!" Attributed dying words of Goethe	"He'd make a lovely corpse" Dickens

What the SOLI environment offers is a conceptual environment for the integration of various support tools for creatvity enhancement. All the technology is in place to develop SOLI further. In this paper I have assumed that innovation is a category of creativity. Tools for enhancing creativity are being used successfully and fairly extensively, now (the word processing tool used to prepare this paper is probably the most ubiquitous example), but I have only scratched the surface. Potential tools for creativity enhancement need further research and development.

Potentially, SOLI adds value in the dissemination and augmentation of creativity enhancement tools and techniques. I see SOLI as a vehicle for achieving creative transfer between people. This leads to one final thought on SOLI and cooperation in a SOLI network. The thought stems from a musical analogy. Members of an orchestra follow a score which has been broken down into parts for the members; in general members are uninterested in what the others are playing; they rely on the conductor for his interpretation and bringing parts together. An opera or concert stuffed with international prima donnas has the inherent danger of individual, stand-alone virtuoso performances. But it is the chamber music group which provides the metaphor for SOLI's potential; individual members have scores (whole or appropriate parts) or improvise, which they work on as a group; in performance the hallmark of chamber groups is that members listen to each other more than themselves. Does the chamber music group metaphor scale up to many, and even limitless, members of a SOLI network?

At this stage there remain four broad questions regarding SOLI which need to be answered - or at least widely discussed:

[1] Is SOLI worth pursuing as a catalyst, as a concept, as a set of protocols and rules in a functional specification for SOLI, or as a specific tool?
[2] What are the positive and negative lessons learnt and what has been achieved - even created - from the catalytic experience of formulating and discussing SOLI?
[3] What are the priorities, what is achievable, and when, by SOLI?
[4] Where do we go from here and what actions are prompted by formulating and considering SOLI?

I hope that this paper proves to be a catalyst for stimulating discussion, ideas, proposals and actions on the issues it raises. I would welcome any comments, contributions and suggestions, particularly on the four questions on SOLI.

However, creativity remains an attribute of the mind which defies superficial explanation. This paper has not aimed to define or explain creativity, but to explore how creativity can be enhanced - essentially by encouraging its practise. Peter Sell, one of the study's interviewees, provides us with a fitting thought-provoking view on creativity!

> "Thought is born of failure. We turn to thought when we don't know what to do or when what we are doing is ineffective. Thinking about creativity is not acting creatively. To me, creativity is a skill, an approach , an attitude of mind. Like other skills, it wants to be practised, not talked about. (I find in golf, that the more someone talks about his swing, the worst he seems to be at it. I also find that very few people talk about how to stay upright on a bicycle.) And practising is a self-sustaining activity:

the more effort you make to become creative, the more new ways of acting creatively you'll find. As the Dodo said, 'The best way to explain it is to do it'.

Epilogue

The concluding paragraphs in Stephen Hawking's phenomally successful book, 'A Brief History of Time' cuts deep into the heart of creativity:

"Einstein once asked the question: "How much choice did God have in constructing the universe?" . . .

"Why does the universe go to all the bother of existing? Is the unified theory so compelling that it brings about its own existence? Or does it need a creator, and, if so, does he have any other effect on the universe? And who created him?

"Up to now, most scientists have been too occupied with the development of new theories that describe what the universe is to ask the question why. On the other hand, the people whose business it is to ask why, the philosophers, have not been able to keep up with the advance of scientific theories. . .

"However, if we do discover a complete theory, it should in time be understandable in broad principle by everyone, not just a few scientists, Then we shall all, philosophers, scientists, and just ordinary people, be able to take part in the discussion of the question of why it is that we and the universe exist. If we find the answer to that, it would be the ultimate triumph of human reason - for then we would know the mind of God."

A further quotation is from Einstein himself, illustrating the need for scientists to step outside logic to create new theories:

"To these elementary laws there leads no logical path, but only intuition, supported by being sympathetically in touch with experience. . .. The state of feeling which makes one capable of such achievements is akin to that of a religious worshipper or of one who is in love".

The second sentence is very similar to that expressed by this study's writers and playwriters interviewed when they spoke of creating their own work; many creators spoke of their total absorption on their creative work.

Carl Jung approaches the subject from different dimensions:

"Now I knew what it was, and knew even more: that man is indispensible for the completion of creation: that, in fact, he himself is the second creator of the world, who alone has given to the world its objective existence - without which, unheard, unseen, silently eating, giving birth, dying, heads nodding through hundreds of millions of years, it would have gone on in the profoundest night of non-being down to its unknown end. Human consciousness created objective existence and meaning, and man found his indispensable place in the great process of being.

M. Scott Peck touches a raw nerve: "It is through the pain of confronting and resolving problems that we learn"; while Benjamin Franklin quotation is short and sharp: "Those things that hurt, instruct".

I now come to my own perspective and personal view of creativity:

We were created by God, simply, in his image, with faculties to freewheel with the freewill he gave to us, to be apprentice creators, where we are free to create new things with his help as mentor, if we wish, and with the help of others. When we have completed successfully our apprenticeship, albeit partly through pain, our soul will be ready to work and play totally creatively with God and others. When we produce something, if we find its production satisfying and instructive, if we find the result new or distinctive and it gives us pleasure - not necessarily long-lasting satisfaction - and, possibly, if we are totally absorbed and embodied part of ourselves in the result, then we can say that we have been using our creativity. The result is a creation and we are the creators. If others disagree, as we showed our creation to them, we need to listen to their criticism and see if we can learn by it, while staying true to our belief in our creation. Above all, the act of creation is a powerful form of loving and learning.

Acknowledgements

"I inherited it brick and left it marble."
Emperor Augustus

I am indebted to each and every one of the creative people interviewed, most of whom are listed in section 12. They answered my awkward questions frankly - especially on their creative thinking process - gave their personal views and definitions of creativity, and offered freely their thoughts on how computers could enhance creativity. In several cases they volunteered the spiritual, emotional and psychological motivation or driving force for their creative acts. I feel most privileged to have discussed with them, what is a supreme and personal characteristic at the centre of being human. Only they have made this paper possible.

Special thanks, go to: Margaret Boden, who originally inspired me to take creativity seriously; Joan Scoons who widened the study's scope by opening up uncharted worlds; Karamjit Gill, who encouraged me to pursue the framework for enhancing individual, group, and shared creativity (SOLI); and an ever-present, super sounding-board Joanna , and Louise, the two Georginas, Betty, Evelyn and creative friends.The paper as published here has gained much from Karamjit Gill's editing and Jeremy Potter's patient wisdom.

Interviewees

N.B. All interviewees are based in the U.K. unless shown otherwise.

Russ Abbott : Commercial Designer, Photographer
Gary Born : Quality Consultant
Kirsty Barker : Self Employed Administrator, Australia
Timothy Barker : Salesman
Melvyn Bragg: Writer, Broadcaster
George Breach : General Builder
Julia Breach: Houseperson
Tony Butler : Playwright, Mathematician
Evelyn Ball : Centenarian, Australia
Mike Barrett : Marketeer, Australia
Alan Benjamin : Companies Chairman

Gordon Bevans : Retired Clinical Psychologist, Inventor
Woody Bledsoe : Mathematician, AI Scientist, USA
Margaret Boden : University Professor
Joni Carter : Computer Artist, USA
Dame Barbara Cartland : Writer, Cause Fighter
Chas Church : Software Development Manager
George Cochrane : Physicist
Douglas Cooling : Retired Pilot & Airline Planning Manager
Alex d'Agapeyeff : Strategic IT Designer
Mike Davidson : Illustrator, Designer, Artist
Tony Durham : Journalist, writer
Ernest Edmonds : University Professor, Artist
Alex Edwards : Analyst /Programmer
Richard Ennals : Business School Professor
Ronald Eyre : Theatre & TV Director, Broadcaster, Writer
Edward Feigenbaum : AI Scientist, USA
Jim Fisher : Retired Managing Director
Susannah Finzi : Copywriter
Tom Gilb : Software Management & Quality Consultant, Norway
Karamjit S. Gill : University Professor , Human Centred Systems
Satinder Gill : Post graduate Doctorate Student
Alex Goodall : IT Consultant
David Gow : Composer, Programme Notes Writer
Pamela Gray : Lawyer, Australia
David Grubb : Charity Director, Writer, Educator
Robert Hardy : Actor, Writer
Herman Hauser : Entrepreneur
Clive Hewitt: Management Consultant , Educationalist
Pat Hill : Retired Agony Aunt Columnist
Peter Holden : Research Fellow
Tim Johnson : Marketing Consultant
Dean Frances Juniper : Writer, Therapist, Educationalist
Kalolaine Lane : Schoolchild, 8, Australia
Doug Lenat : AI Scientist, USA
Rex Malik : Journalist
John McCarthy : AI Scientist, Mathematician, USA
Donald Michie : AI Scientist
Marvin Minsky : AI Scientist, USA
John Morrell : Designer
Betty Muller : Retired Health Visitor
Bob Muller : Management & IT Consultant
Georgina Muller : Student, 16
Joanna Muller : Administrator
Erika Obermeier : Professional Teacher, Germany
Norman Oliver : Voluntary Services Director
Steve Owsianka : Professional (IT) Civil Service
Derek Partridge : IT Professor
Tina Pentes : Third World Health Worker, Australia
Peter Peirce : Church Minister
Robert Pope : Science-Art Artist, Australia
Brian Robson : Communications Security Consultant
Jennifer Richmond-Brown : Journalist
Laureen Roemermann : Schoolchild, 6, Australia
Mark Roemermann : Schoolchild, 9, Australia
Jonathon Rowe : AI Researcher
Len Saunders : Management Consultant
Frances Sell : Chemist
Peter Sell : Computer Researcher

David Smith : Production Manager
Brian Stableford : Writer
Jackie Streeter : Retired Senior Nursing Officer
Helen Taylor : Private School Department Head
Russel Thomas : IT Professional & Manager
Roger Thornton : Public Relations
Mike Thurbon : Electronic Warfare Specialist
Arnold Todd : Retired Farmer & Agricultural Scientist, Australia
Mark Todd : Technician, Australia
Zerneene Todd : Mother, Housewife, Australia
Stanley Turner : Inventor & Innovation Manager
Shunichi Uchida : AI Research Manager, Japan
David Vachel : Management Consultant
Janet Vaux : Journalist
Jeffrey Walton : Accountant
Graeme Ward : Managing Director, Systems Innovation Consultancy
Janet Way : Musician
Lynette Wilkins : Software Manager
Natalie Wilkins : Schoolchild, 6
Tim Wilkins : Marketeer
Nick Willard : Information Management Consultant
Patricia Willard : Artist, Teacher
Philippe Wines : Lloyds Underwriter
David Wood : Actor, Playwright, Composer, Producer, Director
Elizabeth Yauner : Schoolteacher, Potter

References

"Very slowly I began to make a rapid recovery."
John G. Muir

Atkinson, G. The Creation Memos. Collins, 1983

Barr, A., Cohen, R. & Feigenbaum, A. (Editors). The Handbook of Artificial Intelligence Vol. IV. Addison-Wesley, 1990

Belbin, R, Management Teams: Why They Survive or Fail. Heinemann, 1981

Boden, M. Inaugural Lecture: the Mechanism of Creativity. University of Brighton Library (audio cassette). N.A., 1982

Boden, M. The Creative Mind: Myths and Mechanisms. Weiden- feld & Nicolson, 1990

Brand, S. The Media Lab: Inventing the Future at MIT. Viking, 1987

Brown, H. (Editor). HyperMEDIA/HyperTEXT and Object Oriented Databases. Unicom Seminars, Uxbridge, U.K., 1991

Buzan, A. Use Your Head. Ariel, 1982

Callow, S. Being an Actor.Penguin, 1985

Carroll, Lewis & Gardner, Martin (Editor). The Annotated Alice. Penguin Books, 1965

Cleese, J (Direcor). The Life of Brian (Film & video), 1979

Curtiz, M (Director). Casablanca (Film & video) 1942

Dawkins, R. The Blind Watchmaker. Longman, 1986

de Bono, E. Letters to Thinkers. Harrap, 1987

de Bono, E. I am Right - You are Wrong. Viking, 1990

de Bono, E. Handbook for the Positive Revolution. Viking, 1991

Dimond, S. & Beaumont, J. (Eds). Hemisphere Function in the Human Brain. John Wiley, 1974
Durham, A. Computing Horizons. Addison-Wesley, 1988
Edwards, E. Drawing on the Right Side of the Brain. William Collins, 1982
Engelmore, R. & Morgan, A. (Editors). Blackboard Systems. Addison-Wesley, 1988
Evans, C. The Mighty Micro, The Impact of the Micro-Chip Revolution. Victor Gollancz, 1979
Evans, R. & Russell, P. The Creative Manager. Unwin Hyman, 1989
Eysenck, J. The Measurement of Creativity', draft unpublished paper, Institue of Psychiatry, The Maudsley Hospital, London SE5 (1991)
Feigenbaum, E., McCorduck, P. & Nii, P. The Rise of the Expert Company. Times Books, 1988.
Gill, R. Forget all the rules about graphic design. Including the ones in this book. Phaidon Press, 1985
God. The Holy Bible. Living Bible Edition. Kingsway Publications, 1971
Gregory, R. (Editor). The Oxford Companion to the Mind. O. U. P., 1987
Handy, C. Gods of Management. Pan Books, 1985
Hawking. S. A Brief History of Time. Bantum Press, 1988
Hayakawa, S.I. (Editor) & Fletcher, P.J.(Reviser). The Penguin Modern Guide to Synonyms and Related Words. Penguin Books, 1987
Hayward Gallery. Leonardo da Vinci (catalogue). London, 1988
Hill, W.C. 'The Mind at AI: Horseless Carriage to Clock', AI Magazine Vol. 10 No. 2, AAAI (1989)
Hughes, R. The Shock of the New. British Broadcasting Corporation, 1980
Hughes, S. Every Day With Jesus. CWR, 1991
Intel, A. The Everlasting Artificial Intelligent Diary: Illustrated History of Artificial Intelligence Volume 1 - Ai and Expert Systems from 1990 to 1999. Intelligente Publications (R.C.Muller, The Old Stables, Greys Hill, Henley on Thames, Oxfordshire, RG9 1SW, UK), 1986
Jeffries, L (Director). The Railway Children (Film & video), 1972
Jung, C. Memories, Dreams, Reflections.Flamingo, 1983
Juniper, D.F. Successful Problem Solving, The Organised Approach to Creative Solutions. Foulsham, 1989
Kidel, M. & Rowe-Leete, S. (Editors). The Meaning of Illness. Routledge, 1988
Kim, S. Essence of Creativity: a Guide to Tackling Difficult Problems. Oxford University Press, 1990
Kinsman, F. The New Agenda. Spencer Stuart, 1983
Laural, B. The Art of Human-Computer Interface. Addison-Wesley, 1990
Lean, D (Director). Brief Encounter (Film & video), 1945
Leigh, A. Effective Change: twenty ways to make it happen. Institute of Personnel Management (Camp Rd., Wimbledon, SW 19 4UW, UK), 1988
Lenat, D.B.. 'Ubiquity of Discovery', Artificial Intelligence, 23 (1984)
Leytham, G. Managing Creativity. Peter Francis (The Old School House, Little Fransham, Dereham, Norfolk, NR19 2JP, UK), 1990
Michie, D. & Johnston, R. The Creative Computer. Viking, 1984
Milligan, S. The Goon Show Scripts. Woburn Press, 1972
Milton, J. Areopagitica & Milton's Poetical Works. Macmillan, 1929 edition
Minsky, M. The Society of Mind. Heinemann, 1987
Montagu, A. Growing Young. McGraw Hill, 1981
Muller, R. A Primer on Expert Systems. SD (Restricted circulation to European Space Agency Managers and their contractors), 1985
NEDC. The Innovation Management Toolkit. HMSO, 1990
Nelson, E. Literary Machines. The Distributors (702 South Michigan, South Bend, IN4668, USA), 1987
Ochse, R. Before the gates of excellence: the determinants of creative genius. Cambridge University Press, 1990
Olivier, L. (Director). Henry V (Film & video), 1944
Ovum. The Object Technology Sourcebook. Ovum, London, 1991

Ovum. Multimedia. Ovum, London, forthcoming
Peat, F.D. Superstrings and the Search for The Theory of Everything. Srcibners, 1991
Quantel. Paintbox: When Dreams Become Reality (Video). Quantel, Newbury, U.K., 1991
Raudsepp, E. Managing Creative Scientists and Engineers. Macmillan, 1963
Rosten, R. The Joys of Yiddish, Penguin, 1971
Rowe, J. & Partridge, D. 'Creativity: Learning Flexible Representations Through Emergent Memory', Computer Science Department, University of Exeter, UK (1991)
Ryder, S. Child of My Love.William Collins, 1986
Schumacher, E.F. A Guide for the Perplexed. Jonathon Cape, 1977
Shakespeare, W. The Complete Works of Shakespeare. Various Editions to date
Spielberg, S (Director). Raiders of the Lost Ark (Film & video), 1981
Sprott, W.J.H. Human Groups. Penguin Books, 1958
Sullivan, K (Direcor). Anne of Green Gables (Film & video), 1985
Taylor, G. Reinventing Shakespeare. Hogarth Press, 1990
Tyas, S. & Smith, M. More Book-Worm Droppings. Paul Watkins (18, Adelaide Street, Stamford UK), 1990
Welles, O. (Director) Citizen Kane (Film & video), 1941
Wilson, P. A. Computer Supported Cooperative Work: An Introduction. Intellect Books, 1991
Winnicott, D.W. Playing and Reality. Tavistock Publications, 1971
Winograd, T. & Flores, F. Understanding Computers and Cognition. Ablex, 1986
---. The Oxford Dictionary of Quotations. Oxford University Press, 1980
Musical creation eight: Beethoven's String Quartet opus 131 - the greatest music ever written.

Notes

* This paper is a modified version of the paper, Enhancing creativity, innovation and cooperation, which first appeared in *AI & Society*; 1193: 7.1